Monastic Visions

EDITED BY

ELIZABETH S. BOLMAN

PHOTOGRAPHY BY

PATRICK GODEAU

MONASTIC VISIONS

WALL PAINTINGS

IN THE

MONASTERY OF ST. ANTONY

AT THE RED SEA

AMERICAN RESEARCH CENTER IN EGYPT, INC.

YALE UNIVERSITY PRESS   NEW HAVEN AND LONDON

Frontispiece: Madonna and Christ Child, sanctuary apse
(S1; ADP/SA 6s 98)

Published by the American Research Center in Egypt,
Inc. (ARCE) / 2 Midan Kasr al-Dubara, Garden City, Cairo,
Egypt / and in the United States at Emory University
West Campus, 1256 Briarcliff Road NE / Building A,
Suite 423 West, Atlanta, GA 30306
and Yale University Press / 302 Temple Street, New Haven,
CT 06520-9040

This publication was made possible through
support provided by the Office of Environment and
Infrastructure/Environment and Engineering (EI/EE),
USAID/Egypt, United States Agency for International Development, under the terms of Grant No. 263-G-00-96-00016-
00. The opinions expressed herein are those of the authors
and do not necessarily reflect the views of the U.S. Agency
for International Development.

Designed by Leslie Thomas Fitch.
Set in Adobe Minion type by Leslie Thomas Fitch.
Printed and bound in Great Britain by Butler & Tanner Ltd,
Frome and London.

LIBRARY OF CONGRESS CATALOGING-IN-PUBLICATION DATA

Monastic visions: wall paintings in the Monastery of
St. Antony at the Red Sea / edited by Elizabeth S. Bolman;
photography by Patrick Godeau.

    p. cm.

Includes bibliographical references and indexes.
ISBN 0-300-09224-5 (cloth: alk. paper)

    1. Coptic mural painting and decoration—Egypt—
Red Sea Region. 2. Mural painting and decoration,
Medieval—Egypt—Red Sea Region. 3. Church of
St. Antony, of Egypt, Saint, ca. 250–355/6— 5. Christian
saints in art. I. Bolman, Elizabeth S., 1960–. II. Godeau,
Patrick.

ND2863.3 .M66 2002

751.7'3'09623—dc21   2001035760

A catalogue record for this book is available from the
British Library.

The paper in this book meets the guidelines for
permanence and durability of the Committee on Production
Guidelines for Book Longevity of the Council on Library
Resources.

10 9 8 7 6 5 4 3 2 1

Contents

PREFACE

Our small caravan wound its way toward the wall of mountains that emerged through the dust of the Red Sea deserts. For more than fifteen hundred years, countless pilgrims before us—the earliest Christians, Roman soldiers, Fayoumi bishops, Crusader warriors, Ethiopian clerics, Frankish travelers, Byzantine artists, and Egyptian Copts—had been making their way toward this remote location. In the distance, at the foot of the barren range, appeared a hint of green, miragelike and almost unidentifiable. Closer inspection revealed the unmistakable geometry of architecture (fig. 1). We were approaching the Monastery of St. Antony, widely believed to be the first and thus the oldest monastic establishment in the world.

Christmas 1997 was only a few days away. When we had first seen the Church of St. Antony, many months before, its interior was sooty and blackened. In the intervening months, conservation work had started on the wall paintings. Although earlier limited test cleanings had given us reason to believe that very fine paintings might lie hidden underneath, we had yet to see what a period of extended conservation could accomplish (fig. 2). Would there be a series of extraordinary works of art underneath centuries of grime and layers of overpainting, or would there be only disappointing obscurity? If it were the latter, our project would suffer the same fate. We could hardly contain our anticipation.

Once we passed through the low entrance door and out of the gusting wind, we adjusted our eyes to the refuge of the dark church. We were unprepared for the stunning scene that met our view. For gazing sternly yet serenely down on us from a height of four meters were four monastic saints of the Coptic Church who had not been seen

clearly in more than four hundred years. Their expressions, their demeanor, and their poses radiated dignity and holiness (fig. 3).

Stepping farther into the church, we looked up at the partially cleaned archway at the entrance to the khurus. There, soaring in brilliant colors, overwhelming our senses, was the archangel Michael (fig. 4). The quality of the paintings was literally breathtaking. With Western Christmas and its holy remembrance only a few days away,

1 OPPOSITE
Monastery of St. Antony

2
View into the khurus, with cleaning test areas visible
(ADP/SA 7s 27 96)

ix

3

Pishoi the Great, John the Little, and Sisoes (N7–N9; ADP/SA 1999)

4

The archangel Michael (K15; ADP/SA 10S 97)

we felt even more strongly than before the sense of the Christian tradition embodied in these figures. The Church of St. Antony is a masterpiece, and one that preserves the most complete iconographic program known from medieval Egypt.

A rare mix of individual dedication and joint collaboration across many areas of expertise propelled this special project through all its stages. The project concept should be seen in relation to the other conservation work in Egypt conducted by the American Research Center in Egypt (ARCE), in collaboration with the Egyptian Supreme Council of Antiquities (SCA). As a result of an initiative by the United States Congress, generous funding was made available through the United States Agency for International Development (USAID). Under this initial grant from USAID, a broad program of work was initiated encompassing the breadth of Egypt's history, including the prehistoric and pharaonic periods, as well as Greco-Roman, Coptic, Islamic, and Jewish contributions. Although more than forty projects in this first grant were balanced among these six cultures, at sites throughout Egypt, none centered on a specific Coptic monument, nor were any located in the Red Sea region. So when USAID offered additional funding for a second grant as an activity of Sub-committee

III for Sustainable Development and Environment of the U.S.-Egyptian Partnership for Economic Growth and Development, ARCE welcomed the opportunity to round out its conservation program, as well as to meet the objectives of the SCA and the Monastery of St. Antony.

The effects of this project are already widespread. It has opened a window of discovery for scholars, created a wonderful viewing experience for the public, and restored an important part of the Coptic heritage (fig. 5). With newly restored vigor, the church will continue its tradition of receiving pilgrims and visitors. And it of course remains the location of holy services for the monks who pray to their patron St. Antony, the great founder of the monastic tradition.

May you, too, become a visitor as you experience the church in the following pages. We hope this book will encourage you to visit the church yourself, or will serve as a meaningful record of a visit you have already made. Sales of the book will help the monastery by providing revenue to maintain the church. So in any case, you will have become a contributor to the sustainability of this wonderful, glorious representation of faith.

MARK EASTON AND ROBERT K. VINCENT, JR.

5

General view from the nave, after

cleaning (ADP/SA 1999)

Introduction

6 OPPOSITE
Church of the Holy Apostles seen
through street of monastic cells

7 ABOVE
Antony and Paul (N1–N2; ADP/SA
1999)

This book of essays is the record of two extraordinary and in many ways parallel stories. Both of them took place in the Monastery of St. Antony, in the eastern Egyptian desert, near the Red Sea (fig. 6). The subjects of the first story are the wall paintings that once again fill the Church of St. Antony with their vivid and powerful presence, but which until recently had for centuries been obscured by dense layers of soot and overpainting. These paintings are aesthetically compelling works of art, a delight to the eye (fig. 7). They are considerably more than that, however, and much of the subtle narrative in the individual paintings, and the sophisticated messages in their programs, will be missed by the viewer who is unaware of their history. It is the goal of this book to present the overall context for the paintings, including the life of St. Antony the Great, the Monastery of St. Antony, and the way of life of which he is the primary exemplar. The paintings in the Church of St. Antony were and are an essential part of this monastic life. They would not have come into existence without St. Antony (or Anthony), known in the East and the West as the father of monasticism (fig. 8).[1] Because of his prominence, and the desire of others to follow him, a community developed in this remote location. It has existed there almost without pause for more than eighteen hundred years and has experienced numerous periods of cultural importance and influence.

Even the briefest of investigations for evidence of St. Antony's status as it was expressed in art yields remarkable finds.[2] The oldest depictions of him date to the early Middle Ages, some from as far away as the British Isles.[3] He regularly appears in medieval and Byzantine art, in very dif-

ferent visual terms, as the painting from a Cypriot church
at Lagoudera (fig. 9) and a Western engraving by Martin
Schongauer (fig. 10) illustrate. In Eastern representations,
Antony appears as an isolated, iconic figure, often alone or
in the company of equally static monastic saints.[4] Not until
the fifteenth century do rare examples exist, from the eastern Mediterranean, that frame the still, imposing figure of
the saint with events from his life.[5] These narrative events
captured the imagination of Western artists beginning in
the early Middle Ages. In the West, numerous artists have
shown him fighting with devils, avoiding temptations, and
meeting St. Paul.[6]

One of the most significant moments in the history
of the Monastery of St. Antony was in the early thirteenth
century, when almost all of the paintings we now see in the
church were commissioned and made. They belong to a
Coptic artistic tradition that was then about eight hundred
years old. This tradition has often been characterized as
having atrophied after the Arab conquest of Egypt in the
seventh century.[7] This point of view has been tenable
because so much of the artistic heritage of Christian Egypt
has been lost or, as in the case of the painting in the

Church of St. Antony, was barely visible before cleaning
(fig. 11). The Coptic art historian who had worked most on
these paintings before their cleaning, Paul van Moorsel,
described the faces done by the master painter of the
Church of St. Antony as "mask-like," and of modest artistic merit.[8] The conservation of these paintings has shown
that his observations were correct in one sense, because
they were made when the most visible sections of the
images were those that had been overpainted, but such an
assertion would likely not be made today about the cleaned
thirteenth-century paintings. Van Moorsel's predecessor
Jules Leroy wrote that the highest-quality extant Coptic
wall paintings from the medieval period were those in the
Monastery of St. Macarius.[9] He said this even though the
paintings in the Monastery of St. Antony were well known
to him. A brief glance at the photographs of the paintings
in the Church of St. Antony before and after conservation
makes Leroy's and van Moorsel's assertions understandable, if mistaken (fig. 12). The medieval paintings in the
Church of St. Antony, together with other recent discoveries, attest to the continued richness and vitality of this
ancient Christian culture into the Middle Ages.[10] They

11
Interior of the Church, 1930–1931
(Whittemore Expedition. Courtesy
of Dumbarton Oaks, A80)

12

Virgin Mary (s1), during cleaning
(ADP/SA BW 131:8)

13 OPPOSITE

Sanctuary dome and apse, after
cleaning (ADP/SA 1999)

dramatically revise not only our ideas about the quality of
Coptic art well after the seventh century but also our
understanding of its links to the other cultures situated
around the Mediterranean.

The majority of the paintings in the Church of St.
Antony belong to a single program. We know from inscriptions that the date of this program is AM 949 *(anno
martyrorum),* according to the Coptic calendar, which
corresponds to AD 1232/1233.[11] It is the most complete
and extensive cycle preserved from this period in Egypt
(fig. 13). The paintings were commissioned during a time
of particular strength in the Monastery of St. Antony. A
group of more than thirty donors paid for their creation,
and a team of artists led by a master painter named
Theodore ("Gift of God") entered the church and commenced work there. His team consisted of at least four

individuals, and probably more. It certainly would have
included one or more assistants, there to do much of the
less-skilled work of preparing the plaster, mixing the
paints, and building the scaffolding. Something stopped
the work of this team just before it was finished. A second
group of painters was engaged to finish the work within a
few decades of this unknown interruption—a clear testament to the importance of images in the monastic life, and,
the prosperous state of the monastery in the thirteenth
century.

This slightly later group of artists may well have been
Copts, but their paintings belong to another artistic world.
They are part of a Mediterranean aesthetic that combines
elements from the Byzantine and Islamic traditions (fig.
14). These juxtapositions do not seem out of place in such
cosmopolitan centers as Cairo and Damascus, but their

14 LEFT
Khurus ceiling, after cleaning
(ADP/SA 1999)

15 RIGHT
Antony and Paul (N1–N2), before
cleaning (ADP/SA 12 S27 96)

appearance in this remote desert monastery surprises us. They show us that the community in the Monastery of St. Antony participated in the visual culture of a vastly larger region.

All these thirteenth-century secco wall paintings became part of the spiritual work and ritual performed in the church. As such, existing for centuries within a church filled with incense and lit solely by oil lamps and candles, the paintings acquired layer upon layer of soot. Dust, ever present in Egypt, added to their disfigurement. Periodic efforts to enliven the images resulted in the less-than-inspired overpainting of several of the most beloved: the Virgin Mary in the nave, St. Theodore the General, and, of course, St. Antony himself (fig. 15). In rare moments of abandonment, the monastery was inhabited by bedouin tribes, and the fires they lit within the church added to the increasing layers of obscuring blackness. Portions of the plaster on the walls fell off, and insects began burrowing behind the paintings. When the exteriors of several of the domes were repaired and replastered, windows were filled in, and less and less light entered the church. When I first visited the Monastery of St. Antony in 1994, I could barely make out the subjects of the paintings. The most visible of the figures were those who had been badly repainted over

the centuries. Their overall appearance was completely discouraging. Their story seemed near an ignoble end.

I didn't know at the time of my visit that the story that parallels the creation and first life of the paintings had already begun: the miraculous rescue of the wall paintings. As in the first story, there exists a pivotal figure without whom we would have no second story to tell. He is Father Maximous El-Anthony, a senior monk in the Monastery of St. Antony at the Red Sea. Having received training in conservation, Father Maximous was aware of the possibilities of this field.[12] Additional insights into the dangerously fragile condition of the paintings and the walls of the church came from a project, funded by the Royal Netherlands Embassy in Cairo and with the assistance of Zuzanna Skalova, to combat termite damage.[13] Father Maximous made the survival of the paintings in the Church of St. Antony his mission. The contributions of numerous other individuals also enter our story at this juncture, paralleling those made by the more than thirty donors of the early–thirteenth century Coptic wall paintings.[14] As in any narrative, aspects of lived experience are missing. I will surely fail to mention essential contributors, and I hope they will forgive my oversights.

Every major project requires assistance from many

sources. Funding for the Monastery of St. Antony at the Red Sea Wall Painting Restoration Project was forthcoming from the United States Agency for International Development (USAID), as part of the Subcommittee III for Sustainable Development and Environment of the U.S.-Egyptian Partnership for Economic Growth and Development. The Red Sea coast is undergoing intensive development for recreational tourism. One of the goals of the project was to balance this trend by actively preserving and promoting sites that are important for the cultural heritage of Egypt. The support of numerous people at USAID made this project possible, in particular the USAID Cairo Mission Directors John Westley and Richard Brown. All of us who have worked on the project are especially grateful to Thomas Dailey and Anne Patterson, USAID Project Officers, for their complete commitment to it.

The American Research Center in Egypt (ARCE) was funded by USAID to carry out this and the other cultural projects of the U.S.-Egyptian Partnership for Economic Growth and Development. The Antiquities Development Project (ADP) was formed at ARCE in January 1996 to manage several projects, among which was that at the Monastery of St. Antony. The dedication and constant encouragement, help, and support of Mark Easton (former director, ARCE), Robert Vincent (director, Egyptian Antiquities Project, / Antiquities Development Project, ARCE), Cynthia Shartzer (EAP grant administrator), and Madame Amira Khattab (deputy director, ARCE) have been invaluable for the success of this project. Although his tenure as director of ARCE began at the end of this project, Robert Springborg has nevertheless shown great and much appreciated support for it. Special commendation is also due Brian Martinson and Barbara Bruening, respectively grant administrator and associate grant administrator of the ADP. Perhaps the pivotal person for the success of this project, second only to Father Maximous, is Michael Jones, project manager of the ADP. From the beginning, Jones's vision for the church itself, and also for the supporting documentation—including this book—has been extraordinary. He is an inspiration to work with, and his creativity and patience are legendary.

Father Maximous contacted Paolo and Laura Mora, whose expertise has shaped generations of students at the Istituto Centrale di Restauro in Rome, and who have directed one of the most important conservation projects in Egypt at the Tomb of Nefertari in the Valley of the Queens. In 1996 the Moras inspected the Church of St. Antony and recommended the talented conservators Adriano Luzi and Luigi De Cesaris, both of whom had worked with the

Moras on the wall paintings in the Tomb of Nefertari, to take on the daunting task of conserving the paintings in the Church of St. Antony. Paolo Mora died on March 26, 1998, without ever having visited the monastery again. It is a great loss to all who worked on the project that he was not able to see its final results.

In consultation with Father Maximous, Luzi and De Cesaris determined a course of work that would include conservation and also restoration. Because the Church of St. Antony is part of an active monastery, it was decided that the conservators should present the original paintings as a coherent whole, as free as possible from the visual distractions of extant damage to the wall surface. A reversible reintegration was therefore made with paint in places that were missing their original plaster. All interventions on the walls were carefully documented in an extensive series of graphic and photographic records.[15] These materials are available for study at ARCE.[16]

The parallels to the creation of the wall paintings in the Monastery of St. Antony by Theodore, his workshop, and the second group of thirteenth-century painters, became particularly clear beginning in 1996. Just as the original painters worked in the church, so did Luzi, De Cesaris, and their team of conservators, Alberto Sucato, Gianluca Tancioni, Emiliano Albanese, Stefano Fulloni, and Massimiliano Gusmaroli (figs. 16, 17). They repeated most of the physical movements of the thirteenth-century artists, namely, traversing the walls and domes, standing and sitting precariously on scaffolding, standing on the floor, and leaning backward for hours at a time. They allotted work based on skills learned over years of training, and they also used the services of nonspecialist assistants provided by the monastery, who performed such essential tasks as mixing plaster and fetching supplies. Their efforts gave me insights into the often arduous physical aspects of the creation of such a large-scale artistic effort. My art historical work has been immeasurably enriched by the opportunity to watch them at work, and by their willingness to dispute various points with me and to explain their methods and ideas. Their humor and friendliness made them stimulating and delightful colleagues.

We have no idea what kinds of accommodations the medieval painters had while they were working in the monastery, or how good their food was, but we can assume that they were in no way as magnificently cared for and fed as were all the members of this project, thanks to the hospitality of the Monastery of St. Antony, as expressed through the services of Father Maximous, Father Isaac, Ramses, and others. Father Maximous and Father Isaac

16

Adriano Luzi working in the

sanctuary (s1; ADP/SA 18 s191 98)

17
Luigi De Cesaris, right, and
Gianluca Tancioni working in the
khurus (k16)

18

Whittemore Expedition with automobiles, 1930–1931 (Courtesy
Dumbarton Oaks, A198)

provided spiritual as well as material sustenance, assisted in this by the kindness and care of Bishop Yustus, Father Lazarus, Father Dioscorus, and other members of the community.

Both the scope and the length of this book are expansive, due in large part to Jones's understanding of the importance of interdisciplinary work in art history, history, archaeology, and related fields. Life happens to human beings before they have a chance to segment it into scholarly disciplines, and while this book depends on professionals in several of these areas of study, its goal is to surpass their individual efforts. The medieval wall paintings in the Church of St. Antony are significant works of art, whose raison d'être is the figure of St. Antony the Great, and the monastic life he inspired. In order to understand the paintings as fully as possible, it is necessary to know something about their setting. This book therefore provides the interested reader with focused information not only about the paintings but about their context and reception as well. This can only amplify our understanding of them. Differences of opinion and emphasis appear in this book. They enrich it significantly. Studies of the past often engender disputes, and properly so, for lived experience is filled with contradictions. Western scholars studying subjects that are outside of the Western tradition often interpret the past from a different perspective from that of those who belong to that tradition, and such has often been the case in Egypt. We do not have to look farther than previous scholarship on the Church of St. Antony to find an example of such a divergence of opinion. Western schol-

ars have long thought that the building dated to the thirteenth century, and its monastic residents have asserted a sixth-century date. Chapters 2 and 3 of this book present architectural and art historical evidence for the correctness of the earlier date. The collaborative efforts of the authors have created something much closer to the lived experience of history, as it relates to the paintings, than a straightforward, aesthetically oriented, art historical analysis would have done. In fact, the wealth of material considered as part of this project has inspired such a quantity of interesting work that much of it could not be included in *Monastic Visions*. Another volume is therefore planned, which will include significant additions to our understanding of the history of the monastery, its library, the lives of the fathers depicted in the paintings, and the graffiti written by visitors and residents alike.

Scholarly work at the Monastery of St. Antony first began with Thomas Whittemore's expeditions to the site, in a convoy of Ford automobiles, in 1930 and 1931 (fig. 18). Many of the best of the small community of scholars who have studied the art and architecture of Christian communities in the Middle East have turned their attention to the Church of St. Antony: Leroy, van Moorsel, Peter Grossmann, Pierre-Henry Lafferière, René-Georges Coquin, Alexander Piankoff, Karel Innemée, Marguerite Rassart-Debergh, Lucy-Ann Hunt, Gertrud J. M. van Loon, Jean Doresse, C. C. Walters, Pierre du Bourguet, and Otto Meinardus. Despite the obscuring effects of soot and overpainting, these scholars accomplished the major work of identifying the subjects of the paintings, deciphering inscriptions, and carefully documenting the program. Some specialized and thematic analysis was also available to the authors of *Monastic Visions*, most notably Innemée's studies of the ecclesiastical and monastic clothing in the paintings and van Loon's analyses of Old Testament themes and their connection with architectural symbolism.[17] All these fundamental efforts have made it possible for the authors of this volume to proceed with other aspects of art historical and historical interpretation.[18] Van Moorsel's pioneering work on the wall paintings was an especially valuable source of reference. He, along with Pierre-Henry Lafferière, paid a memorable visit to the monastery during October 1998. Sadly, he died in June 1999 and, like Paolo Mora, was not able to see the church fully restored.

This book is divided into four parts: historical context, art and architecture, reception and use of the paintings, and inscriptional evidence. The single chapter of part I is an analysis of the figure of St. Antony and the mon-

astery founded in imitation of his way of life. Tim Vivian gives us essential background information for our understanding of the Copts, monasticism, and Antony himself, impressively characterizing life at the monastery through 1232/1233.

Part II presents the architectural history of the Church of St. Antony, and the paintings in it. Using evidence from restricted archaeological work, careful study of architectural idiosyncrasies, and remnants of early Coptic paintings, Michael Jones presents us with a complete reevaluation of the architectural development of the church in chapter 2. I wrote the third chapter, an art historical analysis of the earliest paintings known in the church, which were recently found by the conservators as part of this project (fig. 19). My art historical evaluation complements Jones's reconstruction of the early phases of building at the site. The discovery of the paintings and of architectural evidence for pre–thirteenth century phases of construction is of exceptional importance because it enables scholarly analysis to bear out long-standing monastic tradition in dating the church to the sixth or seventh century.

Chapters 4–7 present and analyze the most extensive group of paintings in the church, those dated to 1232/1233. In chapter 4, I introduce the entire program painted by Theodore and his team. I analyze the larger programmatic messages and the individual narrative details in these expressive paintings. In chapter 5, I characterize the style of the paintings and also discuss the working practices of Theodore and his assistants. I explore the background of Theodore's paintings in the Christian art of Egypt and the eastern Mediterranean in chapter 6. In chapter 7 William Lyster focuses on a very important component of Theodore's program: the evidence in it for elements from the secular, predominantly Muslim world outside of Coptic monasticism. In this chapter, Lyster expands our understanding of Coptic culture as a part of Egypt in the thirteenth century, explaining, for example, why a Christian author would be painted wearing a turban.

In chapter 8 Lyster and I use art historical data and evidence provided by the conservation team to reconstruct the background of the artists who painted the remarkable ceiling zone of the khurus and to analyze their program. Although they may well have been Copts, they were certainly not painting in the long-standing Coptic tradition exemplified by Theodore's paintings. They belong to a different artistic world altogether, and they have left us surprising traces of it in this part of the church (fig. 20).

The most recent physical changes in the church have

Lower Zone, Old Church of St. Antony   Monastery of St. Antony at the Red Sea

Key to Numbered Plan

NAVE

N1 Antony the Great
N2 Paul the Hermit
N3 Anonymous
N4 Isaac the Presbyter
N5 Paul the Simple
N6 Samuel
N7 Pishoi the Great
N8 John the Little
N9 Sisoes
N10 Arsenius
N11 Barsuma
N12 Pachomius
N13 Arabic inscription on parchment
N14 Pakaou
N15 "Thouan" [Noua]
N16 Piroou and Athom
N17 Coptic arch inscription
N18 Theodore the Oriental
N19 Claudius
N20 Victor
N21 Menas
N22 Theodore Strateletes (the General)
N23 Sisinnius
N24 John of Heraclea (?)
N25 George
N26 Phoebammon
N27 Large heraldic graffito
N28 Shenoute
N29 Pisentius
N30 Moses the Black
N31 Coptic memorial inscription
N32 Maximus and Domitius
N33 Macarius the Great
N34 Macarius
N35 Macrobius (?)
N36 Virgin Mary and Christ Child
N37 Coptic arch inscription

KHURUS

K1 Unfinished painting, saint(s) with Christ
K2 Traces of paint
K3 Mercurius
K4 Coptic dedicatory inscription
K5 Abraham, Isaac, and Jacob in paradise
K6 The three Hebrews
K7 Nebuchadnezzar
K8 George
K9 Two scenes of the martyrdom of
    George, and Pasicrates
K10 Blank wall
K11 The empty tomb
K12 The three women at the tomb
K13 Coptic inscription
K14 Arabesque and Coptic inscription
K15 The archangel Michael
K16 The archangel Gabriel
K17 Coptic inscription
K18 Christ and the women in the garden
K19 Band of circular window panes set in
    stucco
K20 Decorative band, ceiling
K21 Arabic inscription, ceiling
K22–K30
    Decorative bands, ceiling
K31 Hexagonal window panes set in
    stucco, ceiling

K32–K34
    Decorative bands, ceiling
K35 Hexagonal window panes set in
    stucco, ceiling
K36–K44
    Decorative bands, ceiling
K45 Arabic inscription, ceiling
K46 Decorative band, ceiling
K47 Band of circular window panes set in
    stucco

SANCTUARY

S1 Christ in Majesty (upper zone) and
    the Virgin Mary and Child flanked
    by archangels (lower zone)
S2 Athanasius
S3 Severus
S4 Dioscorus
S5 Theophilus
S6 Peter
S7 Benjamin (?)

S8 Anonymous patriarch
S9 Anonymous patriarch
S10 Painted frame, unfinished composition
S11 Mark
S12 Christ Pantocrator
S13 Cherub
S14 Angel
S15 Cherub
S16 Angel
S17 Cherub
S18 Angel
S19 Cherub
S20 Angel
S21–S28
    Windows flanked by angels, octagonal
    drum of the dome
S29–S32
    Four decorated triangles (transitional
    elements below the dome)

S33–S36
    The twenty-four elders of the
    apocalypse
S37 Decorative motif
S38 The sacrifice of Isaac
S39 The sacrifice of Jephtha's daughter
S40 Angel
S41 Angel
S42 Isaiah and the burning coal
S43 Melchizedek and Abraham
S44 Decorative motif
S45 Jermiah
S46 Elijah
S47 Isaiah
S48 Moses
S49 David
S50 Daniel

DEESIS CHAPEL

C1 Niche of the precious cross
C2 Christ in Majesty

C3 Two living creatures (ox and eagle)
    and John the Baptist
C4 Fragmentary roundel with an
    unknown apostle
C5 Roundels with busts of Bartholomew
    and Thaddeus (?)
C6 Pair of roundels with busts of
    unknown apostles
C7 Christ in Majesty
C8 Roundels with the apostles Paul (?)
    and Peter
C9 Fragmentary roundel with an
    unknown apostle
C10 Two living creatures (man and lion)
    and the Virgin Mary

ANNEX

A1 The archangel Michael
A2–A8 Graffiti, wreathed crosses, graffito
    crosses, and traces of early paint
A9 The archangel Gabriel

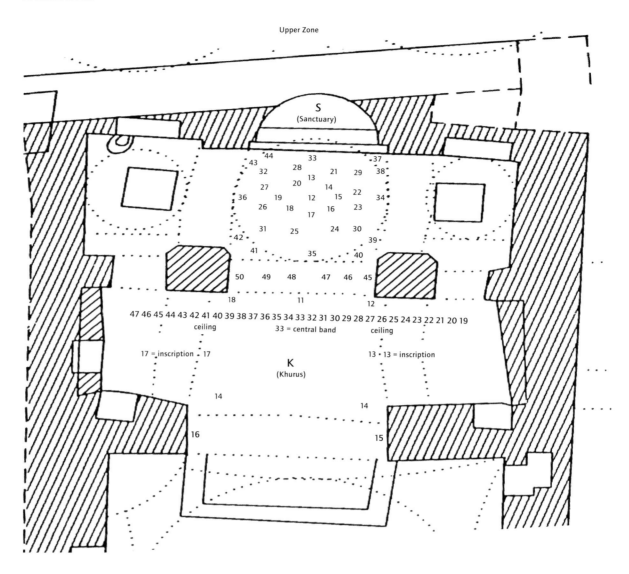

Upper Zone

S
(Sanctuary)

K
(Khurus)

47 46 45 44 43 42 41 40 39 38 37 36 35 34 33 32 31 30 29 28 27 26 25 24 23 22 21 20 19
ceiling   33 = central band   ceiling

17 = inscription • 17   13 • 13 = inscription

21

Plan of the Church of St. Antony,
with numbers keyed to the
paintings

been brought about by the conservation team. They have carefully stripped away the disfigurement of centuries to reveal the astonishing brilliance of the paintings from the thirteenth century. They have also discovered hidden paintings dating between the sixth and thirteenth centuries. Luzi and De Cesaris contribute to this book in two ways. Having cleaned the paintings, they enable all of us to appreciate—indeed, clearly see—them. They have also written an account of their remarkable work and findings, chapter 9.

Part III is entitled "The Viewer's Response: Past and Present." Gawdat Gabra, Father Maximous, Sidney Griffith, and Elizabeth Oram construct for us a complex picture of the many people who have come to the church since Theodore's paintings were completed and who are still coming today. The historical record commonly includes events tied to names of people of status in their own time. Gabra gives us an account in chapter 10 of these individuals, Copts and others, and their responses to the monastery and the paintings. He also identifies for us the smaller communities of Ethiopians, Armenians, and Syrians that have had close ties to the monastery. In chapter 11

Griffith presents the personal traces left by many individuals who are rarely included in historical accounts. His translation and analysis of selections from the graffiti in the church evoke for us the countless people, visitors and members of the monastic community, who have stood and prayed there.

In chapter 12, Father Maximous gives us a unique and penetrating look at the importance of images in Coptic monastic life today. As a monk in the Monastery of St. Antony, one with experience in and appreciation for the arts, he is singularly well placed to write on this subject. He illuminates for us the monastery's perspective on its medieval wall paintings, and on their icons. Father Maximous uses the word icon (literally, image) to refer to all sacred images, whatever their medium. Elizabeth Oram complements Father Maximous's chapter by presenting in chapter 13 yet another category of viewer: the Coptic pilgrim of today. The number of Coptic visitors to the site is expanding rapidly, attesting to a Coptic renaissance. Oram notes that Coptic pilgrims have a special appreciation for the antiquity of the Church of St. Antony, as a holy place where the Mass and prayers have been said almost continuously for centuries. The medieval paintings, which were made to be part of those sacred rituals, add to the sense of age in the church. Oram has also written about the importance of St. Antony himself to the Copts, and she includes a discussion of the people who have chosen him as their patron saint.

The final part of the book is devoted to the inscriptions. They embellish the thirteenth-century paintings, and most of them are written in the Bohairic dialect of Coptic (one addition is in Syriac, and one in Arabic). Birger Pearson translates them in chapter 14 and analyzes their language for information about the culture that produced them. Newly visible letters have enabled Pearson to resolve several of the mysteries of identification in the painted program. His painstaking work has been of exceptional help for the art historical analyses, providing as it does the basis for identification and interpretation of the paintings.

A numbering system will assist the reader in locating places, subjects, and inscriptions in the church (fig. 21). Each physical space or room in the church is given its own sequence (nave, khurus, sanctuary, annex, and chapel), which follows a clockwise order. Beginning with the nave, and starting as close to the center of the eastern wall as possible, the first painting is 1, with the capital letter N added as a prefix. Thus N1 is the number for the painting of St. Antony, which is the first painting to the right of the centrally positioned entrance between the nave and the khurus, on the eastern wall. N2 is to our right of St. Antony, a painting of Antony's friend and colleague in the ascetic life, St. Paul. When numerous inscriptions appear in one painting, as happens frequently, Pearson has given them an additional number, placed after the number for the painting. The first inscription in the sanctuary apse is numbered S1.1, the second is S1.2, and so on. All of the contributors to this book refer to the paintings and the inscriptions by these numbers.

Modern and late-antique personal and place names are used in this book, and are described and included with cross-references in the glossary. The earlier versions are usually, but not always, used for people. The saint known to scholars of late antiquity as Pishoi, for example, is known to Copts today as Bishoi, and the monastery named after him in the Wadi al-Natrun (the ancient Scetis) is called Deir Anba Bishoi. Nonspecialists may be helped to know that the Arabic word *deir* means monastery. English translations of monastery names have been used whenever possible, so, for example, instead of referring to Deir al-Shohada (sometimes spelled Chohada),

I have called this site the Monastery of the Martyrs, and I refer to Deir al-Baramus as the Monastery of the Romans. The context of discussion has usually determined the spelling chosen, so, for example, the names Father Maximous uses for saints and places have not been changed.

One other point of terminology should be mentioned here. The oldest building in the Monastery of St. Antony is the Church of St. Antony. It is often referred to as the Old Church of St. Antony, or just the Old Church. Although there is a new church at the monastery, St. Antony shares the dedication with St. Paul. In this book we have therefore dispensed with the identification of the early-medieval church of St. Antony as the Old Church.

All of the members of the project are indebted to the Supreme Council of Antiquities. The work was carried out under the auspices of the SCA, and we thank Minister of Culture Dr. Farouk Hosni and also Professor Dr. Abd el-Halim Nur el-Din, Dr. Ali Hassan, and Professor Dr. Gaballah Ali Gaballah, directors of the SCA. We are also indebted to Dr. Abdullah el-Attar, head of the Islamic and Coptic Sector of the SCA, for his assistance, and to Mahmud Ali and Abd el-Hamid Amin Ibrahim, inspectors of the SCA for the Red Sea region, for their helpfulness and support on site.

The project received the blessing of His Holiness, Pope Shenouda III, and His Grace, Bishop Yustus, head of the Monastery of St. Antony, and proceeded under the guidance of Father Maximous El-Anthony, who participated in the work as a member of the team. I acknowledge the efforts and generosity of numerous scholars, museum directors, librarians, administrators, and archivists, whose assistance I am grateful for, and also several institutions whose collections I have used: Alice-Mary Talbot; Natalia Teteriatnikov; Catherine Smith; Anne Gout; Annemarie Weyl Carr; Jaroslav Folda; Athanasios Papageorghiou; Renata Holod; Detlev Kraack; Getatchew Haile; Robert Nelson; John Williams; Charles T. Little; Johannes Den Heijer; Peter Grossmann; Bernard O'Kane; Christina Spanou; Michele Piccirillo; Father Martyrius of the Monastery of the Virgin Mary (Syrian Monastery); Father Benjamin of the Baramus Monastery; Cathryn Clyne; Terence Walz; Agnieszka Dobrowolska; Jarek Dobrowolski; Amir Hassan Abdel-Hamdi; Mary Sadek; Angela Jones; Derek Krueger; Gene Rogers; Georgia Frank; Darlene Brooks-Headstrom; Frances Vincent; Wlodzimierz Godlewski; Samir Morcos; Mandy McClure (for Arabic translation); Cynthia Hall (for a drawing); Dr. Mourad Tewfick, director of the Coptic Museum (Cairo); Madame Samiha A. El-Shaheed, general director for

Scientific Research at the Coptic Museum; Dr. Farouk Askar, director of the Islamic Museum (Cairo); Monica Blanchard; Dumbarton Oaks; Art Resource; the Institut Français d'Archéologie Orientale du Caire; the University of Pennsylvania Museum Library; the Kelsey Museum of the University of Michigan, Ann Arbor; the Princeton Art Library's Photographic Archive; the Deutsches Archäologisches Institut in Cairo; the library of the American Research Center in Egypt; and the libraries of the American University in Cairo. Vital funding and support for the final stages of this book project came from a National Endowment for the Humanities fellowship. USAID and NEH have made it possible for me to devote all of my energies to this project for a considerable length of time. Temple University generously assisted with some final unanticipated costs.

All of the contributors to this book have shared ideas and enthusiasm, resulting in a much more interesting and thoughtful work than I could possibly have imagined. They have exhibited patience and dedication through the editing process, for which I thank them. This book has also benefited from the extensive and excellent photographic record made by Patrick Godeau, and from the survey documents produced by Peter Sheehan and by Michael Malinson and his associates. The superior abilities and dedication of Judy Metro, Patricia Fidler, Dan Heaton, and Mary Mayer at Yale University Press have improved every aspect of this book. Allen Peacock, Karen Vellucci, William Lyster, and Eileen Markson provided excellent editorial assistance. In particular, Lyster sustained my flagging spirits on numerous occasions and had infinite patience for refinements to the manuscript. Anthony Cutler's thorough critique of this manuscript resulted in significant improvements to it. I am deeply grateful to all of these readers and editors for their encouragement and fortitude.

I am indebted to all of the people and institutions mentioned in this introduction, and also to a few who have not yet been named. These include Robert Harris and Dale Kinney, for their inspiring training in medieval and Byzantine art history; my parents, Katherine Bolman, William Bolman, and Victoria Asayama, for taking me to museums; and Patricia V. Pierce, for encouraging my study of art history and my decision to undertake this massive project.

My personal dedication of this volume is to the monks, past, present, and future, of the Monastery of St. Antony at the Red Sea (fig. 22). Without them and their tenacious commitment to an ancient and vital tradition, we would not have had the cultural richness of the paintings in the Church of St. Antony to share with a larger audience.

22

Monks from one of the Red Sea Monasteries, 1930–1931 (Whittemore Expedition. Courtesy of Dumbarton Oaks, A101)

PART I

ST. ANTONY THE GREAT

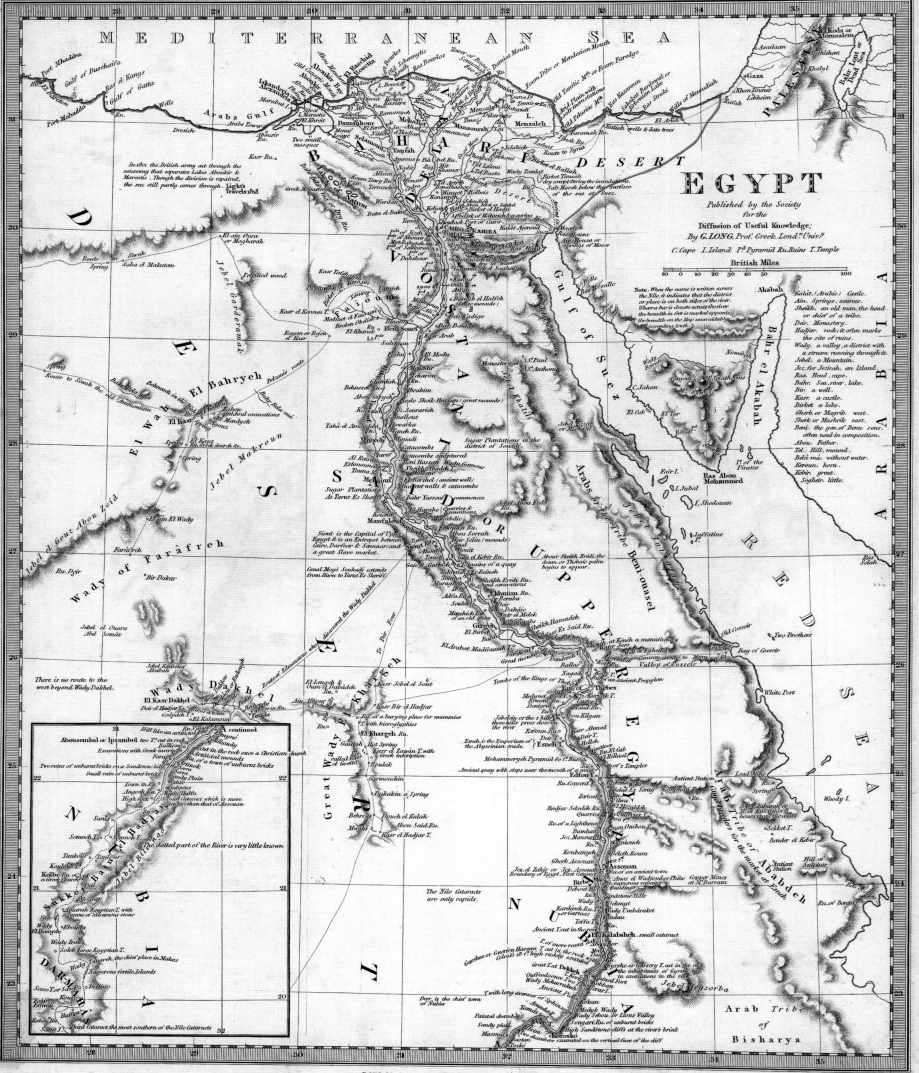

EGYPT

MEDITERRANEAN SEA

Published by the Society
for the
Diffusion of Useful Knowledge;
By G. LONG, Prof. Greek. Lond.ⁿ Univ.ˢ

C. Cape I. Island P.ᵈ Pyramid Ru. Ruins T. Temple

British Miles

Note. When the name is written across
the Nile, it indicates that the district
or place is on both sides of the river.
Where a bar is drawn across the river
the breadth in feet is marked opposite,
the breadth on the Map unavoidably
exceeding truth.

Kalát. (Arabic) Castle.
Ain. Springs, sources.
Sheikh, an old man, the head
  or chief of a tribe.
Deir. Monastery.
Hadjar, rock; it often marks
  the site of ruins.
Wady, a valley, a district with
  a stream running through it.
Jebel. a Mountain.
Jez. for Jezirah, an Island.
Ras. Head, cape.
Bahr. Sea, river, lake.
Bir, a well.
Kasr. a castle.
Birket, a lake.
Gherb or Magrib, west.
Sherk or Mashrik east.
Beni, the gen. of Benu sons,
  often used in composition.
Abou, Father.
Tel. Hill, mound.
Belá má. without water.
Kervoun. horn.
Kebir, great.
Sogheir, little.

BAHARI DESERT

In 1801 the British army cut through the
causeway that separates Lakes Aboukir &
Mareotis. Though the division is repaired,
the sea still partly comes through. Light's
Travels 1818.

VOSTANI

DESERT

El Wah El Bahryeh

Jebel Gardaramak

Jebel Makroun

Wady of Faràfreh

DESSORY

SSTANI

OR

UPPER

EGYPT

Siout is the Capital of Upper
Egypt & is an Entrepot between
Cairo, Darfoor & Sennaar; and
a great Slave market.

Sugar Plantations in the
district of Siouuit.

Arabs in the Jebel Tarabin Tribe Beni-ouasel

There is no route to the
west beyond Wady Dakhel.

Wady Dakhel

Great Wady El Kha geh

The Nile Cataracts
are only rapids.

NUBIA

Arab Tribe
of
Bisharya

GULF OF SUEZ

Gulf of Suez

Arabs in the Jebel Jarabin

Bahr el Akabah

ARABIA

RED SEA

Tribe of Ababdeh

Jebel Heyzorba

The dotted part of the River is very little known.

Abousembol or Ipsambol two T.ˢ cut in rock.

DARFUR

NUBIA

Published by Baldwin & Cradock 47 Paternoster Row Jan.ʸ 2.ᵈ 1831.

J. & C. Walker Sculp.ᵗ

CHAPTER 1

ST. ANTONY THE GREAT AND THE MONASTERY OF ST. ANTONY AT THE RED SEA, CA. A.D. 251 TO 1232/1233

At the end of the fourth century, less than fifty years after the death of St. Antony the Great, John Cassian journeyed from either Scythia or Gaul to Palestine and thence to Egypt on a spiritual and geographical odyssey to discover in the desert both the roots of Christian monasticism and the God-given springs that nourished those roots (fig. 1.1). Cassian had undoubtedly read one of the two Latin translations of the *Life of Antony*, written originally in Greek by St. Athanasius in 356/357; perhaps Cassian had even read the Greek *Life*.[1] For Cassian, Antony was Egypt's—and monasticism's—Abraham: just as Abraham was called to be the father of "a multitude of nations" (Gn 17:4), so Antony was called to be the father of monasticism (fig. 1.2).[2] Antony, modern scholarship has demonstrated, cannot claim sole paternity for Christian monasticism; Cassian himself was indebted more to Evagrius Ponticus and the monks of Lower Egypt (Nitria, Kellia, Scetis) than he was to Antony. But monasticism's shared paternity is not a modern discovery; in Cassian's Gaul in the middle of the fifth century, the monks of the Jura Mountains recognized a number of monastic forefathers: Martin of Tours, Basil of Caesarea, "the holy monks of Lérins," Pachomius, and "the venerable Cassian" himself.[3] Given the numerous references that the *Life of the Jura Fathers* makes to the *Life of Antony*, however, the *Life* of the Egyptian saint seems to have been primary. Thus Antony, a hundred years after his death, was already an "international" saint.

Antony of Egypt (251–356) is one of those larger than life figures who may well have been as large during his life as after his death, when he was immediately immortalized and canonized by Athanasius. His call to the ascetic life, thanks to Athanasius's telling, is one of the best known of

such experiences from late antiquity, second perhaps only to Augustine's account of his conversion in the *Confessions*. According to the *Life*, "Antony was an Egyptian by birth"; a later tradition gives his village as Koma, the modern Qiman al-Arias.[4] "His parents were well-born and possessed enough property to be self-sufficient. Because they were Christians, Antony was also brought up as a Christian" (*Life of Antony* 1.1).[5] Six months after his parents' death, when, according to the *Life*, he was around eighteen or twenty years of age,

> on his way to church he was . . . reflecting on . . . how the apostles gave up everything and followed the Savior, and how those in Acts sold their possessions and brought them and placed them at the feet of the apostles

for distribution to those in need. . . . Pondering these things, he went into the church; it happened that the Gospel was being read at that time and he heard the Lord saying to the rich man, "If you want to be perfect, go, sell all your possessions and give to the poor, and come follow me, and you will have treasure in heaven" [Mt 19:21]. When Antony . . . realized how that passage had been read for his sake, he immediately left the church, and the possessions that he had inherited from his ancestors (there were three hundred fertile and very prosperous acres), he freely gave away to people from his village so that they would not bother him or his sister about anything. He sold all his remaining possessions and, collecting a considerable amount of money, distributed it among the poor, keeping a few things for his sister. When Antony entered the church again and heard the Lord saying in the Gospel "Do not be concerned about tomorrow" [Mt 6:34], he could no longer bear to remain there so he left and distributed his remaining things among those less well off. His sister he entrusted to well-known and faithful virgins, giving her to them to be raised in virginity, while he devoted himself to ascetic practice in front of his home, watching over himself spiritually and practicing patient endurance. (*Life* 2.2–3.1)

According to the *Life*, Antony practiced asceticism first outside his village, then in a tomb, and next in a deserted fortress; around the year 285, after living ascetically for about fifteen years near home, Antony "set out for the mountain," Mount Pispir, east of the Nile (present-day Deir el-Maimun, just south of Koreimat), about 75 km. south of Memphis, halfway between present-day Itfih and Beni Suef.[6] Here he lived in a deserted fort, which was to become his "outer mountain" (*Life* 11.1).[7] After living as a solitary there for twenty years, Antony emerged around 305/306 to instruct the crowds that came to him in the ascetic life. Finally feeling hemmed in, around 313 Antony resolved to push further into the desert; while waiting on the banks of the Nile for a boat to take him south to the Thebaid, he had a vision instructing him to follow some Saracens into "the interior desert." According to Athanasius,

Antony traveled three days and three nights with them and came to a very high mountain, and at the foot of the mountain was very clear water, sweet and very cold. Away from the mountain there was a plain, and a few unattended date palms. Antony, as one moved by God, loved the place, for this was the place indicated by the

one who spoke to him on the riverbank. Then, after having first accepted some loaves of bread from those with whom he had traveled, he remained alone on the mountain, with no one else living with him. He was like someone who recognizes his own home: from that point on he considered the place his own. (*Life* 49.7–51.2)

This "mountain" was Mount Colzim (Qulzum), near the site of the present-day Monastery of St. Antony. In Egypt the Nile is the center of geography. Away from it is desert; beyond that is the "further" or "remoter" desert, where Antony now chose to live.[8] Therefore, although the Nile is in the center of the country, to move away from it is to journey not to the exterior, as we would think, but to the interior, to the desert. The early monks saw this interior wilderness as both a geographical and a spiritual reality, where they confronted the aridity of the earth and of the heart. But in this desert the monk, as a new Adam and Eve, also found paradise regained.[9] In this interior Antony found a water source and a cave, and he prepared a garden (*Life* 49–50; fig. 1.3). Fame, and disciples, followed him, however, and he journeyed back and forth between Colzim and Pispir. Antony was to spend the rest of his life at Colzim, dying in 356.[10]

While living on the inner mountain, Antony made frequent visits to Pispir to minister to the monks and crowds at the outer mountain. According to the *Life*, Antony was much sought after for counsel, healing, and even legal mediation. Athanasius portrays him as a wonder worker, healer, and seer. Monastic tradition independent of the *Life* reports that around 338 Antony, along with Amoun of Nitria, founded the monastic community of Kellia (Cells), between Nitria and Scetis (Wadi al-Natrun),

1.3
Entrance to the Cave of St. Antony

about halfway between modern Cairo and Alexandria; once when Antony visited, Amoun told him that because of his prayers the number of brothers at Nitria was increasing and some of them wanted cells where they could live in peace (that is, farther away from other monks). So Antony advised Amoun that after they ate at the ninth hour (around 3 P.M.), they should go out into the desert and look for a new location; they walked until sunset, prayed, and planted a cross to mark the new community.[11] They picked this spot so that the monks at Nitria could visit those at Kellia after the afternoon meal. "If they do this," Antony said, "they will be able to keep in touch with each other without distraction of mind."[12] Kellia, therefore, became a sort of "graduate school" for monks; after some time at Nitria, those who wished greater solitude, like Evagrius of Pontus, could then move to the Cells. Antony's rationale for the location, however, underlines the continued desire for community and concourse. The *Life of Antony* 60.3 says that the journey from Nitria to Antony's inner mountain was thirteen days and demonstrates that monks were already traveling between the northern monastic communities and Antony's. The *Apophthegmata*, or Sayings of the desert fathers and mothers, also reports visits to Antony by Amoun and Macarius the Great, the founder of monasticism in Scetis (Wadi al-Natrun).[13]

Thus Cassian's "Abrahamic" understanding of Antony is not wildly exaggerated. St. Shenoute is reported to have proclaimed, "If you gather together all the monks in the world, there would not be a single Antony among them," while Serapion, bishop of Thmuis and a disciple of Antony, wrote to Antony's followers after the great monk's death in 356 and told them that with Antony's departure Egypt was being torn apart and was in anguish.[14] Monasticism in the different parts of Egypt developed quite independently of Antony, with such leaders as Macarius, Apollo of Bawit, Pachomius, and Shenoute; nevertheless, the sources clearly show that Antony influenced the monastic communities of Scetis and Kellia.

Later tradition would remember Antony in even larger terms: when it was time for the founder of monasticism at Scetis, Macarius the Great, to go to his rest, Antony and Pachomius, the "cofounders" of monasticism, came to tell him the hour of his death.[15] Antoine Guillaumont accepts this ancient understanding: "The monastic life led in the deserts of Scetis, Nitria, and Kellia was along the lines of Antonian monasticism; its character was fundamentally anchoritic, distinguished from the monasticism, cenobitic in nature, that was led in the monasteries founded by St.

Pachomius in Upper Egypt. It was, to be more precise, semi-anchoritism, a type of life that assured a sort of equilibrium between the solitary and communal life."[16] The term *Antonian monasticism* needs to be carefully defined. Unlike Pachomius, Antony does not appear to have set out to "found" a type of monasticism, semianchoritism; thus "Pachomian" and "Antonian" monasticism should not simply be paired or juxtaposed as though all monasticism originates from these two founders. Furthermore, it is not known that Antony and his early disciples practiced the semianchoritic way of life followed at Kellia, although it seems likely that such a practice did develop at Mount Colzim in the fourth century.

Antony did indeed leave a legacy, both in Lower (northern) Egypt, at Kellia and Scetis, and in the south; in antiquity his feast day was a major celebration at St. Shenoute's White Monastery at Atripe (Panopolis/Akhmim).[17] "Antonian,"—that is, anchoritic and semianchoritic—monasticism was also influential in Sinai and Palestine.[18] Undoubtedly Antony left disciples. Shortly after his death, the monks who had gathered around him on Mount Colzim founded a monastery that to this day bears his name: Deir Anba Antunius.[19] The chronicler "Abu Salih" well represents Antony's considerable stature in tradition: "This great saint, Antony, was the first monk who clothed himself in wool, and exhibited the monastic habit, and left the world and dwelt in the deserts."[20] A great modern historian of Egyptian monasticism, Evelyn White, has nuanced Abu Salih's encomium and justly concluded: "It was Antony who first revealed the possibilities of the desert and thereby became the originator of monasticism."[21]

Antony and the monastery that bears his name are part of the amazing phenomenon of fourth-century Egyptian monasticism. Around 330, when Antony was living on the inner mountain, Amoun and Macarius founded monastic communities at Nitria and Scetis, respectively. By the end of the fourth century, a mere fifty years after Amoun and Macarius had gone out into the desert, Nitria may have had as many as three to five thousand monks.[22] Around 320 Pachomius founded the first community of his koinonia at Tabennesi in Upper (southern) Egypt; according to Jerome, around the year 400 "nearly fifty thousand monks took part in the annual meeting of Pachomian monks."[23] The *Historia Monachorum* reports that there were ten thousand monks at Oxyrhynchus in the fifth century; though the numbers may be exaggerated, Oxyrhynchus does seem to have been a monastic town. Shenoute may have led as many as four thousand male and female monastics.[24]

1.4

John the Baptist (C3)

Such numbers seem as astounding today as they were in the fourth and fifth centuries, though for different reasons. Why did so many people, both men and women, embrace the monastic life? It would be presumptuous to offer anything here other than a humble answer to such a vast and spiritually subtle subject. On this matter, perhaps it is best to quote someone who was a monk, a citizen of the fourth and fifth centuries, and a pilgrim to Egypt: Cassian. According to him, the monks "sought out the recesses of the desert not, indeed, because of faintheartedness or an unhealthy impatience but from a desire for higher progress and divine contemplation. . . . They desire to engage the demons in an open struggle and in out-and-out combat, and they are not afraid to penetrate the vast recesses of the desert in imitation of John the Baptist" (fig. 1.4).[25] Cassian here summarizes several main themes of monasticism: the desire for the contemplation of God, combat with the demons, and, in the figure of John the Baptist, the belief that monasticism is a biblical calling, even *the* biblical calling.[26]

Athanasius, in the *Life of Antony*, clearly understands Antony's call and life as a response to the commandments of Scripture; as Adalbert de Vogüé has concluded, "Athanasius sees in Antony's asceticism a discipline whose origins lie in Holy Scripture and in that alone."[27] Such a basic answer has been challenged recently by historians who emphasize political and sociological motives, but as Armand Veilleux has pointed out, "All the motivations that [the monks] themselves revealed to us in their writings came from Scripture. Do we have a right to pretend we know their secret motivations better than they did?"[28] Cassian's work as a whole demonstrates that the ultimate goal for the monk, biblically founded, is the Kingdom of God—that is, union with God in prayer. In one of the most eloquent summations of the monastic goal, Abba Isaac, a monk of the Egyptian desert, proclaims in the *Conferences* of Cassian that union occurs "when every love, every desire, every effort, every undertaking, every thought of ours, everything that we live, that we speak, that we breathe, will be God, . . . that whatever we breathe, whatever we understand, whatever we speak, may be God."[29]

The Letters of St. Antony

The Life of Antony presents the great ascetic as unlettered, defeating the pagan enemies of Christianity not with "empty syllogisms" but by deed and example (*Life* 1, 72–74), but this representation has more to do with Athanasius's purposes, it seems, than with the facts of Antony's life: Athanasius's goal is to show that a simple monk, living in accord with the Cross of Christ, is much closer to God than educated pagan philosophers (*Life* 72–80).[30] But Antony, it now appears certain, wrote a number of letters (seven are extant); not only that, the letters reveal someone well versed in popular Platonic philosophy and the Alexandrian theological tradition: Antony "was no 'ignorant monk' who had simply exchanged the garb of the peasant for the monastic habit," but was a teacher who knew the works of the great biblical exegete and Christian philosopher Origen of Alexandria (185–254) and who "wore a monk's garment as if it was the robe of a philosopher."[31] Such a conclusion is important with regard not only to our understanding of Antony but of early Egyptian monasticism in general: earlier scholars rejected the authenticity of Antony's letters because, they assumed, the early monks were uneducated and theologically naïve. Such, we now know, was not the case, either with Antony or with many other monks.

In his letters Antony emphasizes gnosis, "knowledge," and thus echoes the Greek philosophical tradition, "Know thyself." His use of "wisdom" also connects him with the biblical Wisdom tradition (Proverbs, Ecclesiastes, the Song of Songs). Antony does not stand alone in these emphases: both of these traditions manifest themselves in other early monastic writings.[32] The Antony of the *Life*, by contrast, uses gnosis only twice (*Life* 77.3–4), where it equals faith, and he does not make use of the Wisdom tradition. He does emphasize self-knowledge and discernment (*Life* 16–43), however, and other aspects of his thought in the *Life* mirror those found in the letters: the importance of understanding demons, the movements of the soul, polemic against the Arians, and Platonic ideas on divine immovability.[33] Thus, although much of the *Life of Antony* is dependent on Athanasius's own thought and theology, the Antony it presents cannot be divorced from the Antony of the letters, and thus from the ascetic and monk whose anachoresis (withdrawal) lies at the historical and spiritual foundation of the Monastery of St. Antony.

Abba Antony and the *Apophthegmata Patrum*

Athanasius's portrait of Antony was not the only one.[34] Other traditions about him circulated in desert circles, some of them recorded in a remarkable collection known as the *Apophthegmata Patrum,* or Sayings of the Fathers. Antony appears here not as a mythic hero unflinchingly battling the forces of evil. Instead, he speaks as a venerable abba (or "father"), one of the "old men" consulted by younger monks for advice on monastic living.

In the *Life*, Antony dramatically renounces his family holdings after hearing the story of Jesus' call to the rich young man. The *Apophthegmata*, likewise, portrays Antony as an advocate of radical renunciation. One day, he is approached by a monk who has supposedly "renounced the world" but has actually kept back a little money in safe-keeping, something to fall back on. The monk wants Antony's advice on the matter. Antony tells him that if he really wants to be a monk, he needs to go buy some meat and cover his naked body with it. An odd demand, but the monk does as he is told. Draped with meat, he finds himself nipped at by local dogs and pecked at by birds. It leaves him wounded all over. When he returns, Antony then answers him: "Those who renounce the world but want to keep something for themselves are torn in this way by the demons who make war on them."[35]

Athanasius's *Life* portrays Antony as a teacher of asceticism. The *Apophthegmata* stresses this as well. But here Antony delivers his ascetical message not in long orations but in terse epigrams:

> Abba Antony said: "Always have the fear of God before your eyes. Remember him who gives death and life. Hate the world and all that is in it. Hate all peace that comes from the flesh. Renounce this life, so that you may be alive to God. Remember what you have promised God, for it will be required of you on the day of judgement. Suffer hunger, thirst, nakedness, be watchful and sorrowful; weep and groan in your heart; test yourselves, to see if you are worthy of God; despise the flesh, so that you may preserve your souls."[36]

Here the accent is stern, austere. But other sayings offer balance. In one, Antony warns against excesses: monks who fast too much lack discernment and are "far from God."[37] According to the *Apophthegmata*, Antony sometimes practiced a measured laxity. Once a hunter was scandalized when he happened upon Antony enjoying himself with some of the brothers. To explain his behavior, Antony had the hunter shoot one arrow after another. After a while, the hunter grumbled that such overuse would break the bow. Antony then replied that it is the same with the brothers, that stretched too taut too often, they risk snapping.[38]

The *Life* emphasizes Antony's majestic calm and integrity. The *Apophthegmata*, too, mentions the power of his presence. One story recounts how three monks went out to visit him every year. Two poured out their inner thoughts and plied him with questions, but the third remained silent. One time Antony asked the silent one: "You come to see me, but ask nothing." The monk replied:

"Abba, it is enough just to see you."[39]

The *Life* portrays Antony as heroic, larger than life. The *Apophthegmata*, too, accords him great respect. When Abba Hilarion, a Palestinian monk, visited Antony, he called him a "pillar of light, giving light to the world."[40] And when Abba Sisoes, who took up residence on the Inner Mountain after Antony's death, was asked when he would reach his predecessor's stature, he replied: "If I had one of Abba Antony's thoughts, I would become all flame."[41] But such veneration is balanced by other statements. One saying notes, for instance, that Antony received a revelation that there was in Egypt a man of equal sanctity and that that man had achieved his sanctity not in the desert but amid the temptations of the city. The man, it turns out, was a doctor who gave the bulk of his earnings to the poor and each day sang the Trisagion ("Holy, Holy, Holy") with the angels.[42]

Although there are kindred themes between the *Life* and the *Apophthegmata*, even a few direct parallels, the differences are striking. The *Apophthegmata* makes no mention of the theological issues so central to the *Life*. The Antony of the *Apophthegmata* denounces neither Melitians nor Arians. He shows no knowledge of a theology of deification, nor does he make pronouncements on the generation of the Son from the Father. The Antony of the *Apophthegmata* teaches a simpler, blunter faith. When asked by a monk what he ought to do, Antony tells him: "Whoever you may be, always have God before your eyes; whatever you do, do it according to the testimony of the holy Scriptures; in whatever place you live, do not easily leave it. Keep these three precepts and you will be saved."[43]

There are other contrasts. When the Antony of the *Life* receives a letter from Emperor Constantine, he is reluctant to respond, saying that the emperor is a mere man; when the Antony of the *Apophthegmata* receives a letter from Emperor Constantius, summoning him to the imperial capital, he is tempted to go and asks the advice of his disciple, Abba Paul. Paul offers a shrewd warning: "If you go, you will be called Antony; but if you stay here, you will be called Abba Antony."[44] In the *Life*, Athanasius claims that after Antony's fierce early battle, he was ever after free from sexual temptation. The Antony of the *Apophthegmata* offers a very different perspective. He is remembered as saying that while most people face three conflicts—hearing, speech, and sight—the desert solitary is left with only one: fornication.[45]

But the contrast goes deeper. Whereas the Antony of the *Life* is fearless, unwavering in the face of ascetic hardships and demonic onslaughts, the Antony of the *Apoph-*

thegmata is more human and vulnerable. He anguishes about the justice of God—that some die young, that the wicked prosper, that human society is rent by fissures between rich and poor. He gets depressed, afflicted by the tedium of desert living. And when he is rescued from it by a vision, the vision itself is hardly spectacular. He sees a person—actually an angel in the appearance of a man—braiding rope, occasionally rising to pray and then returning to his work. "And the angel said to him, 'Do this and you will be saved.' At these words, Antony was filled with joy and courage. He did this, and he was saved."[46] finally, the Antony of the *Apophthegmata* reveals a person who has grown in his faith: "Abba Antony said, 'I no longer fear God, but love him. For love casts out fear.'"[47]

St. Antony and St. Paul the Simple

The *Life of Antony* speaks only of two (unnamed) disciples of the great monastic, although there were undoubtedly more. The most famous (along with Serapion of Thmuis) is Paul the Simple, who is known from a variety of sources: the *Apophthegmata*, the *Historia Monachorum in Aegypto*, the *Lausiac History* of Palladius, and the *Ecclesiastical History* of Sozomen. *Apophthegmata* Antony 31 identifies "Abba Paul" as a disciple of Antony (he is referred to as "the Simple" in the other sources, including *Apophthegmata* Paul the Simple 1). Sozomen vividly relates (*History* 1.13) that Paul lived in the country and was married to a beautiful woman, whom he surprised in flagrante delicto. He received this with equanimity, however, left her with her paramour, and went off immediately to join Antony in the desert. Because Paul was old and unaccustomed to ascetic rigor, Sozomen says, Antony tested him with various trials, found him evincing "perfect philosophy" (as monasticism is often called in the Greek sources), and sent him off to live as a hermit. Sozomen adds that Paul was known for his meekness and patience.

Palladius fleshes out this spare account in great detail (*Lausiac History* 22).[48] Paul, he says, was "a rustic herdsman" and his wife "a most beautiful woman of a debased character." When he caught her in adultery, he smiled and said to the man, "Go, have her and her children, too; I am going off to be a monk." He traveled for eight days and came to Antony and told him that he wished to become a monk. When Antony saw that Paul was sixty years old, he told him to return to his village: "You would never endure the trials and tribulations of the desert." When Paul insisted that he wanted to stay, Antony told him to go to a cenobitic community and closed the door on him. Three days later, Antony emerged to find Paul patiently waiting.

Antony then tried Paul with a series of ascetic tests, one of which, the *Historia Monachorum* reports, was to break a jar of honey, pour it out on the ground, then "gather up the honey again with a spoon without collecting any dirt with it."[49] After Paul passed these tests, Antony proclaimed, "Behold, you have become a monk." After Paul's "novitiate" of some months, Antony built a cell for him "three or four miles away" and told him, "Stay here by yourself in order that you may be tempted by demons." Paul, Palladius says, "stayed there a year and was deemed worthy of grace over demons and passions."

What is striking in the tradition is that Antony considered Paul to have a greater charisma over demons than he himself: "Indeed, those demons which Antony was unable to exorcise he sent to Paul, who drove them out instantly."[50] Palladius says that when a demoniac, "possessed as it were by the very Prince of Demons, one who cursed heaven itself," was brought to Antony, he confessed that he had "not yet been deemed worthy of power over the ruling order" of demons and sent the demoniac to Paul, whose "task" it was to heal the man. Paul at first was unsuccessful but finally went and "stood on the rock of the mountain and prayed" to Christ, "I will not come down from the rock, or eat, or drink, until death overtakes me, unless You cast out the spirit from the man and free him." Before Paul had finished speaking, the spirit came out of the man, changed into "a great serpent seventy cubits long and was swept into the Red Sea." This tradition, still remembered a hundred years ago, was told to Père Jullien, a Jesuit who visited St. Antony's in 1884. More than halfway up the trail to the Cave of St. Antony, Jullien's guide stopped him before a big rock within a small enclosure of dried brick and told him that these were the ruins of St. Paul's cell: "When the holy patriarch [Antony] found those who were ill or possessed whom he was unable to heal, he sent them to his disciple, convinced that Paul the Simple had received a more abundant grace in these matters. See this large rock weighing more than one hundred pounds: one day Paul placed it on his head, saying to God that he would not remove it until he had obtained healing for a possessed person who had been brought to him."[51] Those ruins are now a small barrel-vaulted chapel, of recent construction, that sits on a flat stretch of rock to the east, dedicated to Paul the Simple. According to Father Lazarus, a solitary who lives near the cave of St. Antony, each night a small party climbs the mountain to celebrate the Eucharist at midnight, either at St. Antony's Cave or, if the group is too large, in the Church of St. Paul the Simple. At a bend in the road visible to Lazarus in his hermitage, the party coming

1.5 LEFT

Raven and loaf (N1–N2; ADP/SA BW
122:6)

1.6 RIGHT

Icon of Antony and Paul (ADP/SA
4 S63 96)

up the hill signals to him which place they will meet;
Lazarus then turns and heads over the mountain to meet
them.[52]

St. Antony the Great and St. Paul of Thebes

Although Antony can justly be called the "father" or "originator" of monasticism, he was not the first ascetic or
monastic; the *Life* itself, dedicated to Antony's beatifica-
tion, reveals this fact (3.3); Antony's uniqueness, at least
initially, was his anachoresis, or withdrawal, into the desert
(11.1). *The Life of Paul, the First Hermit,* by the acerbic St.
Jerome, would deny even that honor to Antony.[53] Written
in Latin about 377, the *Life* purports to show that the two
disciples who buried Antony, Amathas, and Macarius (who
are anonymous in the *Life of Antony* 91.1, 92.2), "now also
swear that a certain man of Thebes named Paul was the
first hermit, although not recognized as such. This belief
we also follow."[54]

According to Jerome, Paul was sixteen at the time of
the Decian persecution in 250 (the year before Antony's
birth): "When the storm of persecution began to rage, he
withdrew to a remote and little-known estate"; then, be-
trayed by his brother-in-law, he "took refuge in an unin-
habited mountainous region."[55] There Paul lived as the
first hermit. When he was 113 and Antony 96 (in 347), "one
night a dream revealed to Antony that another and better
monk than he existed, one whom he ought to seek out."[56]
After much travel and encounters with beasts, centaurs,
and dwarfs, Antony found Paul in a cave. When the two sat
down to eat, a raven brought them a loaf of bread: "Truly,"
Paul said, "the Lord is gracious and compassionate. For

sixty years now, I have received half a loaf, but now that
you have come, Christ has doubled the ration for his soldiers" (fig. 1.5).[57] Paul then said that Antony had been sent
to bury him, and he asked his guest to bring "the cloak that
Bishop Athanasius gave you, to serve as a shroud for my
body."[58] When Antony returned, he found Paul kneeling
in prayer, dead. Two lions appeared and dug Paul's grave.
Antony buried Paul, then "claimed for himself Paul's
tunic" and returned to his own monastery. On Easter and
Pentecost "Antony always wore Paul's tunic" (fig. 1.6).[59]

Scholars, however, have been reluctant to follow
Amathas and Macarius, or Jerome.[60] Jerome, it must be
said, does not hide the tendentious nature of the *Life* he
has penned: *huius vitae auctor Paulus, inlustrator Antonius*
("the author of this [monastic way of] life was Paul,
Antony was its representative").[61] Six separate Greek translations of the *Life of Paul* show the popularity of Jerome's
revisionist efforts: Jerome was successful at asserting Paul's
priority, at least in the eastern Church, where Paul is remembered as the first monk.[62] The Coptic Church usually
remembers Antony and Paul in tandem: wall paintings at
the Monastery of St. Antony and the Monastery of St.
Macarius (Wadi al-Natrun) depict Paul and Antony together, while *The Commemoration of the Saints,* in the
modern Liturgy of St. Basil, invokes at the beginning of a
list of monastics "our righteous father the great Abba
Antony, [and] the righteous Abba Paul."[63]

Whatever the relationship between Antony and Paul,
the two monasteries that bear their names constitute "the
most venerable monuments of Coptic Egypt."[64] The fact
that the Gallic monk and chronicler Sulpicius Severus vis-

1.7
Monastery of St. Paul, 1930–1931
(Whittemore Expedition. Courtesy of Dumbarton Oaks, A126)

ited a monastery with Paul's name shows that it existed before 400.[65] Given Sulpicius's report, there is a strong possibility that Paul at least existed, regardless of Jerome's hagiographical improvements. It is possible that a community formed in the late fourth century around the site where Paul had lived and that a church was built for the monastic community in the fifth century.[66] "Abu Salih," who seems to have visited the monastery in the last quarter of the twelfth century, vaguely (but accurately) says that it "stands on the bank of the Salt Sea. . . . It stands in the Wadi al-'Arabah, near the pool of Miriam; and it is near Mount Sinai, but divided from it by the passage over the Salt Sea."[67] More specifically, St. Paul's (Deir Anba Bula) is located 244 meters above sea level in the Jabal al-Jalalah al-Qibliyyah or Southern Galala Plateau; St. Antony's and St. Paul's lie on opposite sides of this plateau, St. Antony's to the north and St. Paul's to the south (fig. 1.7). Situated 25 km. apart (86 km. by road), the monasteries of St. Antony and St. Paul, like their namesakes, have shared a common history.[68] As the Abba Antonius Doxology in the liturgy of St. Basil prays:

> Hail to our father Antony,
> The lamp of monasticism.
> Hail to our father Paul,
> The beloved of Christ.
>
> Ask the Lord on our behalf,
> our masters, the fathers who love their children,
> Antony and abba Paul,
> that He may forgive us our sin.[69]

The Monastery of St. Antony

GEOGRAPHY AND ORIGINS

According to the *Life of John the Little*, after the invasion of the monastic desert by marauders in 407, John "left Scetis with the rest of our God-bearing fathers, with Christ guiding him to the mountain of the great Antony in the interior of Klysma—a day's walk," while the Ethiopic Synaxary says that John "went to the monastery of St. Abba Antony in the desert of Kuelzem [Colzim]."[70] Klysma (al-Quzum) is at the top of the Gulf of Suez (it lies under the modern town of Suez), while Antony's monastery lies on the southern slope of the Wadi al-'Arabah, 350 m. above sea level, some 125 km. south of Klysma and 30 km. west of the Gulf—certainly more than one day's journey.[71] As mentioned earlier, Antony's first monastic site was at Pispir, modern-day Deir al-Maymun, where a village exists today, along with two churches. One ancient source describes Pispir as the "high mountain overhanging" the Nile, Antony's "outer mountain."[72] In his *Ecclesiastical History* 2.8, Rufinus says that he visited Pispir, "which was called 'Antony's mountain' [mons Antonii]."[73]

Antony's inner mountain, Colzim, is some 140 km. east of Pispir. According to the *Life,* "Antony traveled three days and three nights . . . and came to a very high mountain, and at the foot of the mountain was very clear water, sweet and very cold" (49.7).[74] An Arab tradition, mentioned by the historian Maqrizi, relates that the prophetess Miriam, the sister of Moses, bathed in this spring at the time of the Exodus.[75] It is not certain whether the present-day monastery of St. Antony is built on Antony's original site; it lies at the foot of mountains whose grottos, according to written tradition going back to the fifth century, were Antony's first retreat. "St. Antony's cave" lies two kilometers southwest of the monastery, 626 meters above the Red Sea, and 276 meters above the monastery.[76] As Jones has suggested, however, it is possible that Antony's first cave was the recess now found in the southeastern portion of the Church of St. Antony, off the western end of the nave, which may be the oldest part of the church; if so, this dwelling would have been only a minute's walk from the spring that to this day supplies the monastery with water. Thus the present monastery may indeed be built on the site of Antony's first occupation (fig. 1.8). The cave in the mountain, the site of the current shrine, may have been used by Antony as a "retreat." Whatever the case, Antony's cave is not mentioned in the *Life of Antony,* but references to it exist in other ancient sources: in 356, shortly after Antony's death, Sisoes, a monk at

1.8
Monastery of St. Antony

Scetis, found that monastic community too crowded and emigrated to Mount Colzim, where he may have lived in Antony's cave; the *Historia Monachorum* mentions Antony watching from his cave as his disciple Paul the Simple "roast[ed] in the sun."[77]

Very little is known about the monastic community that grew up in the second half of the fourth century around Antony's original site, but numerous monasteries were founded near a famous anchorite's dwelling.[78] According to local monastic tradition, the first construction of the monastery took place in 315, while "Abu Salih," the thirteenth-century chronicler, reports that the Monastery of St. Antony was built during the reign of Julian the Apostate (355–361). One reason that this site may have been chosen for a monastery was a nearby trade route that ran south from Clysma along the gulf, then turned inland where St. Paul's still stands in order to reach the Via Hadriana, which led to the Nile.[79] The Wadi al-'Arabah in antiquity was a well-known trade route from the Red Sea to the Fayoum.[80] Rufinus, the Latin monk and translator of many monastic works from Greek into Latin, apparently visited the area around 375.[81] Sulpicius Severus says that he visited "two monasteries of the blessed Antony, which are today occupied by his disciples," as well as the site of Paul the hermit.[82] Sulpicius's first Dialogue can be dated to the year 400, suggesting that a second Antonian community developed between Antony's death and the end of the fourth century; perhaps Sulpicius is referring to monastic com-

munities at Pispir and Colzim.[83] Rufinus and Sulpicius, in these earliest known reports concerning Antony's monasteries, demonstrate the renown that Antony (and Paul) already had in the Latin West during the fourth century. The pilgrims who today ride buses out to St. Antony's have spiritual ancestors dating back fifteen hundred years (see chapters 10 and 13).

Because the area around Deir Anba Antunius has not undergone systematic excavation, it is not possible to give a complete archeological history of the monastery, although parallel developments elsewhere suggest a plausible picture. The first community at the Monastery of St. Antony was probably a *laura*, consisting of scattered cells or *monastéria*, "small, low houses," where the monks lived separately, as did their brethren at Kellia and other fourth-century monastic communities.[84] The "monastery" also most likely included a well and a church, with a refectory being added later. This community was undoubtedly semianchoritic, like Kellia and Scetis in their early years, rather than cenobitic, like the communities of Pachomius and Shenoute: the monks lived in individual cells, separate from each other, and gathered together on Saturday and Sunday for a communal meal and worship, thus combining (in the felicitous phrasing of Antoine Guillaumont) "la vie solitaire et la vie solidaire" (solitary life and communal life).[85] The organization was minimal, with an abba or "father" as leader, without a formal rule.[86] As with other semianchoritic communities in Egypt, however, a "cen-

11

tripetal tendency," primarily for reasons of safety and security, gradually brought the monks together in more of a cenobitic community behind great walls, as one sees today in the monasteries of Egypt.[87]

This evolution usually had two stages: first, a keep (*qasr*) or tower of refuge was built, in which the monks could flee from marauders. The monasteries of Scetis (Wadi al-Natrun) were devastated many times in the fifth century, and it appears that keeps were built there in the mid–fifth century.[88] Later the central monastic area was fortified with a high wall; this took place in the ninth century at the monasteries of Scetis.[89] The Monastery of St. Antony, however, may have been fortified as early as the sixth century, possibly because of its remoteness and susceptibility to marauders.[90] Even with the "enclosing" of the monastery, however, it is probable that some monks continued their semianchoritic lives outside the walls.[91] The enclosing of the semianchoritic communities of Egypt "can thus be seen as a gradual process spread over the period between the fourth and ninth centuries, as the independence of the hermits was grudgingly surrendered. The first enclosures were the rudimentary walls around the cells of the more important anchorites. . . . Bitter experience then led to the rebuilding of the walls surrounding the nucleus in order to turn it into a defensible area."[92] Even after the enclosing of the central monastic area, many monks undoubtedly continued to live outside the walls in smaller compounds (Coptic: *ma n-shôpe;* Arabic *man-shobiyya*); these dwellings, or at least their sandy shadows, can still be seen at the abandoned (and as yet undated) Monastery of St. John the Little in the Wadi al-Natrun and at many other sites. By the fourteenth century, the monks throughout Egypt seem to have abandoned these buildings and moved behind central enclosures.

THE MONASTERY IN HISTORY

Any history of the Monastery of St. Antony will contain more silence than sound, and the historical traveler must learn to stand humbly before a desert expanse that has relatively few markers or landmarks.[93] This monastery apparently produced no histories, chronicles, or lives of the saints with which a historian might chart its course through the centuries. Its story, therefore, is known primarily through outside events or through individuals who found their way there—as monks, as spiritual tourists, or just as tourists—and whose lives were recorded in disparate sources (see chapter 8 for a discussion of many of these accounts). It is good to remember that before the construction of the Suez–Ras Gharib road in 1946, the

monastery was very isolated, and it took great desire and effort, and even courage, to venture there.[94] Nevertheless, numbers of people did find their way to the monastery by the Red Sea, and their stories shed light on both the history of the Monastery of St. Antony and the Coptic Church.

The story of Bishop Menas of Thmuis is representative: Menas, forced to marry against his will, left his wife and went to the Monastery of St. Antony. There he became the companion of Abba Michael. At some point the two left and went to "the mountain [monastery] of St. Macarius" in the Wadi al-Natrun. During the patriarchate of Simon I (689–701), Menas became bishop of Thmuis or Tmai, though "he wept, and afflicted himself, and lamented at quitting the desert." As bishop, he received the powers of healing and discernment.[95] This story shows the importance of both monasteries and demonstrates the central role of monasticism in the Coptic Church. After 451 the monasteries became increasingly important in the life of the church; by the late seventh century, bishops came largely from the monasteries and had a wide variety of civil and ecclesiastical duties, and numerous patriarchs came from monastic communities. But because the Monastery of St. Antony was so remote, it likely did not even lie within a typical diocese and thus did not contribute bishops to the local hierarchy. The first patriarch definitely known to have come from St. Antony's is quite late: Gabriel VI (1466–1475).[96]

Just as the Monastery of St. Antony must have had communication, though scarcely documented, with Alexandria, its monks probably also traveled on pilgrimage to the holy sites in Jerusalem and to the Monastery of St. Catherine on Mount Sinai, although unfortunately we have no record of it. We know more about connections between the Monastery of St. Antony and the church in Ethiopia. Early in the tenth century, two monks from the monastery went to Ethiopia, while during the patriarchate of Anba Yuannis VI (1189–1216), St. Antony's supplied the Ethiopian Church with leaders. Yûânnis consecrated a certain Kilus, bishop of Fuwah, for the Ethiopian Church. Four years later, accused of murder, Kilus had to flee, and Ishaq of the Monastery of St. Antony succeeded him.[97] An Ethiopian reference tells us that Ghabriâl ibn Turaik, seventieth patriarch of Alexandria (1131–1145), was banished to the Monastery of St. Paul for three years.[98] Links between the Monastery of St. Antony and Ethiopia continue to this day: a few years ago an Ethiopian monk, Moses (named after the famous Moses the Black of the fourth century, fig. 1.9), lived in a cave above St. Antony's for the fifty days of Lent.[99]

1.9

Moses the Black (N30; ADP/SA 18

S193 98)

AFTER CHALCEDON: THE SCHISM BETWEEN MELKITES AND COPTS

About one hundred years after Antony's death, in 451, the decisions of the Council of Chalcedon on the nature of Christ essentially severed the Church in Egypt from the sees of Constantinople and Rome.[100] The Egyptian Church became a national church, one that increasingly used Coptic as its liturgical, biblical, and theological language. Across this divide two groups confronted each other, often with hostility, sometimes with violence: the Melkites (those who supported Chalcedon, usually Greek-speakers), and the so-called Monophysites (those who opposed Chalcedon and who were usually Coptic-speaking).[101] This conflict, of course, came to bear on the monasteries of Egypt, including that of St. Antony. Because Copts have never appreciated the opprobrious term *Monophysite,* for the two sides in the dispute I will here use the terms *Melkites* or *Chalcedonians* on the one hand and *Coptic Orthodox* on the other.[102]

The monastic community of Kellia, west of the Nile delta, physically illustrates the schism between Melkites and Copts. Before 451, archeological evidence demonstrates, Kellia had one church; after the middle of the fifth century, it had two—one for each side of the Chalcedonian schism.[103] As Apa Phocas bluntly put it: "Kellia has two churches: the one belonging to the orthodox [Chalcedonians] . . . the other to the Monophysites."[104] (It is good to remember that each side called itself "orthodox.") Kellia came to be a community literally divided against itself.

After Chalcedon, Alexandria remained Melkite, while the monasteries and the countryside were Coptic Orthodox: "The loss of Alexandria to the Chalcedonians had the effect of polarising differences between an 'imperial' or 'Melkite' church in Alexandria and the 'Coptic' or 'Monophysite' church in the remainder of Egypt, whose center was now the Monastery of St. Macarius," southwest of the delta.[105] In 516 the people of Alexandria rioted against Emperor Anastasius's choice of patriarch.[106] The pro-Chalcedonian policies of Emperor Justinian I (527–565) caused havoc in the Pachomian monasteries and apparently precipitated the breakup and demise of the Pachomian koinonia. When Justinian attempted to force the Chalcedonian position on the monks, large numbers left the monasteries, including Abba Abraham, the abbot of the chief monastery at Pbow.[107]

St. Shenoute provided the Copts with a popular base that was never lost, though it was probably not until the early seventh century that the monks regarded themselves "consciously as both Egyptian and anti-imperial."[108] The

History of the Patriarchs asserts that during the reign of Peter IV (567–579), there were "six hundred flourishing monasteries, like beehives in their populousness, all inhabited by the orthodox, who were all monks and nuns, besides thirty-two farms called 'Sakatina,' where all the people held the true faith, and the father and patriarch Peter was the administrator of the affairs of all of them."[109] Late in the sixth century, John, bishop of Shmun and a monk, wrote an encomium on Antony in which he patriotically praises Antony as both the father of monasticism and the father of Egypt and extols Egypt's greatness.[110] In 631 Emperor Heraclius sent Cyrus (al-Makaukus) to Egypt, and Cyrus tried through force to unite the Melkites and Coptic Orthodox. Deir Metras, the monastery residence of the Coptic Orthodox patriarch, refused to accept Chalcedon, the monks "being Egyptians by race [that is, not Greeks] and all of them natives, without a stranger."[111] By the seventh century, before the Arab invasion in 641, "Egyptian monasticism was the heart and soul of Monophysitism."[112]

After the Chalcedonian schism, the monasteries of St. Antony and St. Paul, by contrast, seem to have remained in Melkite hands, under the influence of Mount Sinai, until at least the eighth or ninth century.[113] In 615 the Melkite patriarch, St. John the Almoner (609–620), gave Anastasius, *hêgoumenos* (abbot) of St. Antony's, a large amount of money to ransom those taken captive by the Persians.[114] Does that mean the monastery was Melkite? Probably, but John was known—indeed, canonized—for his generosity and for his support of the monasteries. In 790 or 799 Coptic Orthodox monks from the Wadi al-Natrun had to use subterfuge—and the help of bedouins or Arabs—to steal the body of St. John the Little from the Melkite Chalcedonians of St. Antony's.[115] Around 800 the monasteries of St. Antony and St. Paul may have temporarily come under Coptic control. According to Maqrizi, during the patriarchate of Anba Murqus II (799–819), the patriarch of the Melkites, trained in medicine, went to Baghdad to heal one of the caliph's concubines, a Christian. He cured her and, as a result, the caliph ordered the Copts to return to the Melkites monasteries formerly under their control. This order may have also affected St. Antony's.[116]

By the eleventh century or earlier, the monasteries of St. Antony and St. Paul were definitely in the hands of the Coptic Orthodox. The fascinating story of Mark ibn al-Kanbar, related by "Abu Salih," demonstrates this. It involves Chalcedonians and anti-Chalcedonians, the Monastery of St. Antony, and even the body of the blessed saint himself.[117] Al-Kanbar held a number of "unorthodox" beliefs, not the least of which was his adherence to the two natures and two wills of Christ, and thus he ran afoul of the Coptic patriarchs John V (1145–1167) and Mark III (1167–1189). He apparently attracted a large enough following that some bishops alerted the patriarch, who reprimanded him. In 1174 Mark was taken under guard "with deputies of the patriarch" to the Monastery of St. Antony, where he and his followers, their heads shaven, were interned. After entreaties to the patriarch by Mark's family, the pope ordered the superior of the monastery to lead "that Mark to the place in which the body of St. Antony lay, and require him to swear upon it and upon the Gospel of John" that he would mend his ways.[118] He did so and was released; however, he shortly "returned to his former ways and did even worse than before," and "God removed him from the ranks of the orthodox."[119]

The Monastery of St. Antony, as these stories illustrate, witnessed periods of turbulence and upheaval, not only between Chalcedonians and non-Chalcedonians but even within the latter group (which included both Coptic and Syrian Orthodox). After returning to the non-Chalcedonians, the Monastery of St. Antony seems for several centuries to have come under the control of the Syrian Monastery of the Wadi al-Natrun. The monastery appears to have come finally under Coptic control early in the thirteenth century—a fact vitally important for the history of the wall paintings at St. Antony's. According to a scribal note in a Syriac manuscript originally from the Syrian Monastery that can be dated to the thirteenth century, Abbot Constantine I, "fed up" with the insults of wicked monks, fled to St. Antony's and took "the book of Mar Isaac" with him, intending to return it; however, he fell sick at "the Monastery of the glorious Mar Antonius and died there." The note concludes: "Let the Syrian brethren who come after us to this monastery know that in the convent [monastery] of Abba Paulus, beside the Monastery of Mar Antonius, which belonged to the Syrians like this [one], there are many Syriac books still. But . . . the Syrians were driven thence: the Egyptians took it."[120] Another marginal note, "rather carelessly written," from another thirteenth-century Syriac manuscript, complains that the Syrians, legitimate owners of St. Paul's, have just been dispossessed by the Copts.[121] The troubles at the Syrian Monastery that led to Constantine's flight can be placed between 1222 and 1254.[122] We know that most of the wall paintings at St. Antony's date to 1232/1233.[123] Because their program is resolutely Coptic, and because we know that a Syrian scribe complained of the Syrians' losing St. Paul's in the thirteenth century, we can say that Constantine came to St. Antony's when it was still under Syrian control, sometime before 1232, but by that date the Copts had taken possession of the monastery. "Abu Salih," writing early in the thirteenth century, identifies seven churches in the vicinity of the Monastery of St. Antony, six Coptic and one Armenian, none Syrian.[124] Thus it seems that the wall paintings were commissioned as a sort of celebration of Coptic identity after the expulsion of the Syrians.[125]

The Plight of the Monasteries after 641

Muslim Arabs conquered Egypt in 641. Not long afterward, several important monastic communities went into decline: at the Monastery of St. Jeremiah at Saqqara, "first the sculptures representing living creatures had to be excised or hidden; then the monastery must have been sacked and the churches thoroughly destroyed."[126] The abandonment of the renowned monastic community of Kellia in the seventh to eighth centuries may have been due to changed economic conditions or to a combination of religious and economic pressures from the new rulers of Egypt.[127] Little is explicitly known of the Monastery of St. Antony in this period, so its history must be largely inferred from events taking place in Egypt as a whole.[128]

Initially—and contrary to what we might expect—the change from Byzantine to Arab rule after 641 does not seem to have been traumatic for the native Egyptian population. Maqrizi accurately, if understatedly, observes that at the conquest by the Arabs, "the land of Egypt . . . was full of Christians, but divided among themselves in two sects, both as to race and religion."[129] From the conquest until the reign of 'Umar ibn 'Abd al-Aziz (717–720), the Arabs were "broadly tolerant of the Christian Church and populace of Egypt" and supported the Copts over the Melkites. "Both Arabs and Copts regarded the Melkite Church as a Greek church, the tool of Constantinople and the representative of Byzantine interests in Egypt."[130] Soon, however, the monks came under increasing government scrutiny. During the patriarchate of Alexander I (701), the Arabs exacted six thousand dinars as tribute; 'Abd al-'Aziz Ben Merwan, emir of Egypt, ordered a census of the monks and levied a tax of one dinar on every monastic, the first tribute taken from the monks.[131] Late in the seventh century, monks had to wear badges; if one were found without his, his monastery could be sacked.[132] Early in the eighth century, 'Umar forbade public displays of Christian

symbols; during Alexander II's patriarchate (first quarter of the eighth century), 'Umar extended the *jizya*, or tax, to include monks because fugitive peasants often hid in the monasteries.[133] Apparently this was not strictly enforced, because later the poll tax was again applied to monastics.[134] By 725 the Coptic Church was no longer essential to the Arab rulers of Egypt, so the Caliphate allowed the first Melkite patriarch under Muslim rule and restored at least one church to the Greeks.[135]

Eight Coptic revolts took place from 725 to 832, mainly in the delta. After some initial success, however, the Copts were routed.[136] Maqrizi saw this as a turning point for the Copts: "From that time the Qibt [Copts] have been reduced throughout the land of Egypt."[137] Mass conversions seem to have followed shortly thereafter and Christians became a minority.[138] Maqrizi ends his *History* with the report that thousands of Copts had converted to Islam. "The greater portion of the population," he says, "are now descendants of the Muslims."[139]

Such events could not fail to affect the monks and monasteries of Egypt. Around 850 the Monastery of St. Jeremiah was abandoned; a tenth-century Arabic graffito at the now-deserted monastery gives a Muslim profession of faith.[140] The Arab geographer Yaqoubi describes Kellia as abandoned in the ninth century, and another geographer, Bakri, confirms that two centuries later.[141] According to Maqrizi and Sawirus, during the patriarchate of Mark II (799–819), the monasteries of the Wadi al-Natrun were attacked and burned, "and only a very small company of monks remained there."[142]

Due to their isolation, the monasteries of St. Paul and St. Antony may have been fortunate enough to escape some or even most of the events I have described.[143] These troubles were compounded in the eleventh century, especially during the patriarchate of Christodoulos (1047–1077), by rebellion by Kurds and Turks and by natural disasters: earthquake, pestilence, famine. The remnants of a defeated Turkic army invaded the Thebaide and pillaged the monasteries of St. Antony and St. Paul, killing many monks.[144] It is amazing that the monasteries survived at all, but survive they did. The Monastery of St. Antony endured, and even prospered.

An Oasis in the Desert

The Monastery of St. Antony reached its greatest heights from the thirteenth to the fifteenth centuries (Gabra, chapter 10). Numerous translations were done during this period at the monastery, from Coptic to Arabic to Ethiopic,

1.10

Monastery of St. Antony, distant
view of the Church of St. Antony
between the keep and the refectory

and its library played an important role in the Coptic-Arabic intellectual renaissance of the thirteenth century. The program of the wall paintings of 1232/1233 and the later paintings completed during the thirteenth century "constitute the best example we have of medieval Coptic art."[145] It is remarkable that, except for a brief period at the end of the fifteenth century, the Monastery of St. Antony has been continuously occupied since its founding in the fourth century—sixteen hundred years of nearly continuous monastic witness.[146] The longevity of the monastery bears living witness to Antony, the Egyptian monk who purposefully withdrew to the desert so long ago. To John Cassian, Antony was the church's Abraham, calling its people to follow God; in the *Life of Antony,* Athanasius prophesied that Antony would become the "father" of monasticism. When Antony emerges from the tomb in which he has sequestered himself in order to fight the Devil, an angel appears and tells him, "Antony, I was here, but I waited to see your struggle. And now, since you persevered and were not defeated, I will be a helper to you always and I will make you famous everywhere" (10.3). That fame was realized, and has endured, in both the Christian East and the West. And the Monastery of St. Antony has equally endured. More than eight hundred years ago, "Abu Salih" presented a picture of this community that is probably idealized but one that nevertheless strikingly resembles the monastery today (figs. 1.10, 1.11):

> This monastery possesses many endowments and possessions at Misr. It is surrounded by a fortified wall. It contains many monks. Within the wall there is a large garden, containing fruitful palm trees, and apple trees, and pear trees, and pomegranates, and other trees besides beds of vegetables, and three springs of perpetually flowing water, with which the garden is irrigated and which the monks drink. One feddan and a sixth in the garden form a vineyard, which supplies all that is needed, and it is said that the number of the palms which the garden contains amounts to a thousand trees, and there stands in it a large well-built qasr [keep]. . . . There is nothing like it among the other monasteries inhabited by Egyptian monks.[147]

ΟΑΓ℘ ΟΝΥΦΡΙ℘   ΟΑΓΙ℘ ΑΝΤΟΝΙ℘   ΟΑΓΙ℘ ΠΑΥΛ℘

1.11
Icon of Antony, flanked by
Onnophrius and Paul the Hermit,
ca. thirteenth century, Monastery
of St. Catherine, Mount Sinai
(Courtesy of the Michigan-
Princeton-Alexandria Expedition
to Mount Sinai)

PART II

THE CHURCH OF ST. ANTONY

Paintings and Architecture

CHAPTER 2

THE CHURCH OF ST. ANTONY

THE ARCHITECTURE

The first known settlement at the site of the Monastery of St. Antony the Great was some thirty-five kilometers inland from the Red Sea coast (fig. 2.1).[1] It sat on the natural ledges and terraces of the foothills, on the northern side of the South Galala Plateau, in the Wadi al-Araba. The current monastery occupies the same site, in this magnificent landscape, against the desert cliffs that rise steeply to more than a thousand meters above sea level. High in the cliffs is the cave in which St. Antony is believed to have spent the last years of his ascetic life in the desert. From here the view extends for many miles across the desert and the Red Sea to the Sinai Peninsula (fig. 2.2). This is the natural environment of the monastery.

The Church of St. Antony was built against the northern edge of one of the low desert terraces and was aligned along the natural topography on an axis roughly northeast to southwest.[2] It is at the heart of the historic and spiritual core of the monastery, where St. Antony himself is believed to lie buried (figs. 2.1–2.3). As one approaches the ancient church, it seems secluded behind the two defensive towers and the adjacent fifteenth-century Church of the Holy Apostles. It can be seen only from quite close, either across the gardens on the higher desert to the south, or glimpsed between the two towers from the open courtyard in front of the monastery guest rooms.

The church has undergone many alterations during its long history.[3] The most obvious changes took place in two stages during the thirteenth century, when the murals that constitute the main subject of this book were painted. At that time, the domed and vaulted roof was constructed, the connection between the side chapel and the main church was altered, the current entrance to the church was

either enlarged or created, and the current sanctuary may also have been added. In the western end of the nave the windows were blocked and the original access into the small chapel was closed. An outer stone facing was added to the west wall of the church, to support a new structure built on the side chapel and a corridor running along the southern side of the church. Sometime later, much of the upper-level building fell into decay and was removed. The interior, however, remained largely untouched after the thirteenth century until the restoration of the church in 1996–1999.

The Church of the Holy Apostles dates from the fifteenth century and abuts the eastern end of the Church of St. Antony. Today the two churches have become so integrated that from the outside they appear to be a single architectural unit. They are connected internally by a covered corridor running along the south side of the Church

2.1 OPPOSITE

View of the historic core of

the Monastery of St. Antony

(ADP/SA 18 s8 96)

2.2

Panoramic view of the monastery

(ADP/SA BW 46:31)

21

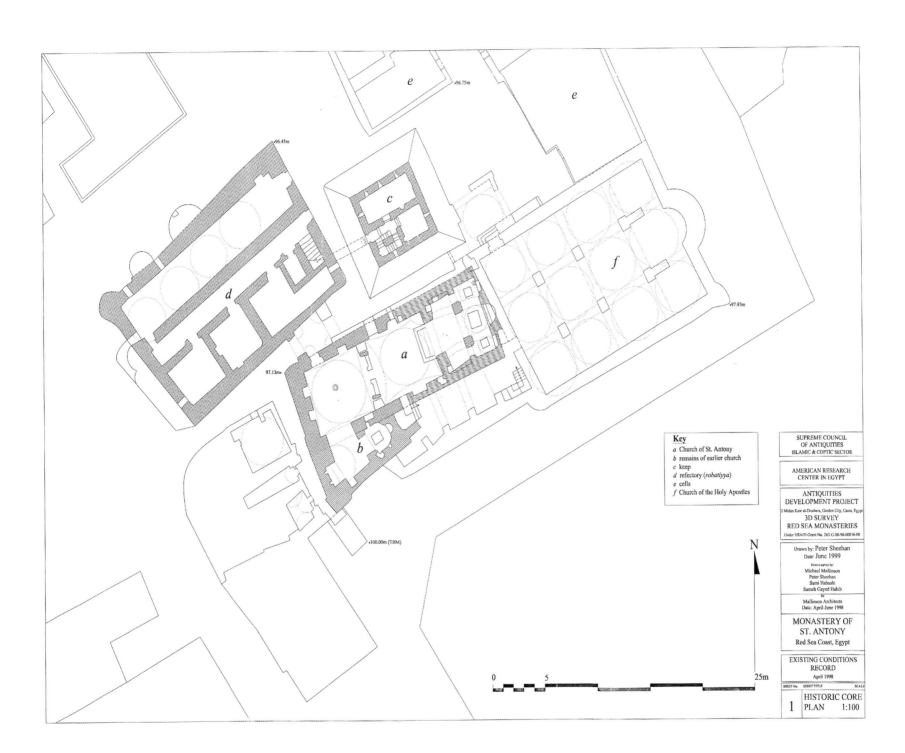

2.3

Plan of the Monastery of
St. Antony; shaded buildings
constitute the historic core

branches of acacia and olive trees obtained locally, and palm logs and timbers reused from dismantled rafters or screens. The walls are roughly 5 m. high, and rise to a rounded coping that forms a parapet of varying height around the north, south, and west sides of the roof. Access to the roof is by means of an outside staircase at the southwest corner of the building.

The roof of the church is dominated by two enormous domes that cover the two parts of the nave. Both were constructed in stages so that they rise in four uneven and unequal steps to a slightly rounded conical top. The stepped shape of the outside clearly reflects the method of building in layers, which is also visible on the inside of both domes. Although they are smoothly plastered, the inner surfaces are visibly contoured in horizontal rings that correspond to the external steps (fig. 2.5). It has been suggested that this unusual shape results from rebuilding following an early collapse of the domes soon after they were built, but this has yet to be ascertained.[4] The domes are pierced by windows of various sizes positioned irregularly. Some of the windows are set into niches and are framed externally with cawl-like hoods that are intended to protect them from rain.[5] As restoration work progressed, it was found that the smaller windows were covered with plain glass set in the plaster of the domes. Larger windows, however, were in various states of disrepair. Broken panes, in a variety of wooden and plaster frames, were set into the inner and outer surfaces of the domes. None were contemporary with the construction of the domes, although some were definitely "old." Most were too fragile to keep in place, so during the restoration of the roof, all the windows were replaced with new plaster and wooden frames and were fitted with ultraviolet screening glass.

of St. Antony, which is part of the early development of the site. To the north of the churches, separated from them by a narrow open corridor, are two great defensive towers. The towers were built at different times, as shown by their positions relative to nearby structures. Neither the original construction dates nor the various phases of rebuilding that are evident can be ascertained, however, because no serious archaeological work has yet been done at the monastery. This also applies to the original founding and to much of the early history of the church, and therefore the precisely dated thirteenth-century wall paintings play a key role, standing between the earlier and later phases of construction.

In its current form the Church of St. Antony is a simple, rectangular building surmounted by five domes and a barrel vaulted ceiling (fig. 2.4). It was constructed of limestone and mudbrick set in a tafl clay mortar, with internal and external coatings of lime and gypsum-based plasters, which have accumulated as the church was periodically resurfaced. Wood was used sparingly, as may be expected in the desert. Those pieces that were included comprised

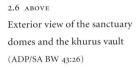

2.6 ABOVE
Exterior view of the sanctuary
domes and the khurus vault
(ADP/SA BW 43:26)

2.7 NEAR RIGHT
Exterior view, looking east
toward the current entrance portico (ADP/SA BW 43:31)

2.8 UPPER RIGHT
Exterior door, within the entrance
portico

2.9 FAR RIGHT
View of the annex from the
nave, after conservation (N14–N18;
ADP/SA 1999)

At the eastern end of the church three smooth-sided, conical domes cover the slightly raised roof level of the tripartite sanctuary. The central dome is the largest, having almost twice the diameter at the base and more than twice the height of those on either side. The khurus, in contrast, is covered at the sides with flat roofs, and in the center, lengthways, with a barrel vault (fig. 2.6). Before the restoration of the windows, the exterior of the vault was a plain plaster surface that merged into the flat roof beside it. Window restoration work required the plaster to be cut along the top and on both sides. In the process it was revealed that successive replasterings had caused the roof level to rise beside the vault by some 40 cm since its construction in the thirteenth century. Beyond the domes of the sanctuary a flight of steps leads to the higher roof of the Church of the Holy Apostles. The tall bell tower topped by

a cupola at the northeast corner of the Church of St. Antony seems to have been constructed with the later of the two churches, or at some time afterward.

The only doorway into the church from the outside is at the western end of the north wall. It leads directly into the nave (N23; figs. 2.7, 2.8). One's first impression on entering the church is of a spacious interior filled with light. This is thanks to the two large, white-plastered domes over the sections of the nave, and to the sunlight streaming through the windows in the domes. Immediately facing the entrance, on the southern side of the nave, is a wide archway leading to an annex and a side chapel (N17; fig. 2.9). The western end of the nave, which opens onto the eastern half, is divided from it by a wide archway. The arch rests on two columns positioned close to the nave walls. These columns are now completely plastered over and give

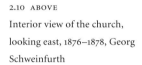

2.10 ABOVE
Interior view of the church,
looking east, 1876–1878, Georg
Schweinfurth

2.11 UPPER RIGHT
Interior view of the church, looking east, 1930–1931 (Whittemore
Expedition. Courtesy of Dumbarton Oaks, A1)

2.12 LOWER RIGHT
Interior view of the church, looking east, 1996 (ADP/SA BW 45:14)

the impression that double shafts may be concealed inside
them. The rudimentary capitals are shaped from mudbrick and plaster. At some time after Georg Schweinfurth's
visits to the church between 1876 and 1878, and before
Thomas Whittemore's expeditions of 1930– 1931, rectangular blocks of masonry were built up between the columns and the walls to add further support to the arch (N13,
N27; figs. 2.10, 2.11). Following this, no further significant
changes were made inside the church, as shown in a pre-
conservation view of 1996 (fig. 2.12). Low walls, about 1.05
m. in height, protrude into the nave from the columns,
leaving a gap 80 cm. wide in the center. In the south wall of
the eastern half of the nave, a low doorway (N8, N9) leads
to the corridor connecting this church with that of the
Church of the Holy Apostles. The corridor forms a covered space between the Church of St. Antony and the rock
escarpment beside it. Vital clues can be found here for
understanding the remains of the earliest traceable structures and their setting in the local topography. Opposite
this doorway, another in the north wall formerly led into
the church from the outside (N31). Until 1999 it had been
walled up, at least since December 1625, when the Franciscan Father Bernardus wrote a bold graffito across the
blocking.[6] Two windows in the north wall, one over the
formerly blocked doorway and the other beside it over a
niche (N32–N33), are the only windows in the church walls,
all the others being in the roof. They both belong to the
period before 1232/1233, as is shown by the way in which
the wall paintings have been designed around them.

At the eastern end of the nave there is another archway spanning the church (N37). It divides the nave from
the khurus and is preceded by three steps that effect the

2.13

Khurus ceiling from the nave, after conservation (ADP/SA 1999)

2.14 OPPOSITE

Khurus vault, detail looking east (ADP/SA 1999)

transition to the higher floor of the khurus. This archway is extraordinarily high and pointed. Its loftiness complements the high domes of the nave, and emphasizes the rising floor level and the transition from nave to khurus, and eventually to the sanctuary, by carrying the eye up into the central vault of the khurus roof. The khurus arch is supported by the lateral walls between the nave and khurus, which have been strengthened with an extra skin of brickwork on their east faces up to the springing of the arch, presumably to buttress the walls against the weight above. The presence of paintings dating to 1232/1233 on these walls (K5, K6) shows that this architectural work was completed before that time. On its northern side the khurus arch exhibits a curious twist that seems to be related to another unusual feature. In the northeast corner of the nave, above the painting of the Virgin Mary (N36), the dome does not rise straight from the wall as in the other three corners. Instead, it rests on a squinch made on an olive wood frame, and seems to have been a deliberate attempt to create a broader, more substantial support for the dome and the springing of this side of the khurus arch.

The two narrow rectangular spaces of the khurus and the sanctuary are each divided into three parts, dictated by

the three altars in the sanctuary (fig. 2.13). The central part of the khurus, which is also the largest, is a rectangular space created by four archways that rest on the walls between the nave and khurus, and on the two piers between the khurus and sanctuary. Both the northern and southern archways are crooked, and neither of them lines up with the sidewalls of the church. As we have seen, the khurus roof is in three parts. The side rooms have flat roofs resting on wooden rafters (four on the south and five on the north) laid north to south. Two of the rafters on the south are unfashioned natural timbers cut from the branch of a tree. All the others on both sides are reused pieces, including one with evenly spaced mortise and tenon joint slots that may have originally formed a beam of a wooden screen. Whether these side roofs predate the 1232/1233 murals is not certain, although it is possible that they were already in place when Theodore and his team painted the khurus walls. Wooden crossbeams were inserted into the walls at a lower level after they had been already painted, as is shown by the damage done to the murals.

The central roof is a barrel vault constructed of palm logs and wooden beams laid lengthwise between the two arches over the entrances to the khurus and the sanctuary. The whole interior surface was plastered and painted. Three sets of long, narrow gypsum window frames were built into the roof when it was constructed. All the glass had been broken, however, possibly in the period when the monastery was abandoned at the end of the fifteenth century. The roof had then been covered from the outside with palm logs, wooden planks, and matting, beneath an outer coat of plaster, which remained in place until 1998. Nevertheless, fragments of glass survived in almost all the window openings, so that it was possible to restore the entire roof to its original condition of ca. 1233–1283.[7] In the center at the top of the vault, there are two single frames set on either side of the central wooden beam, each comprising a row of seven identical hexagonal openings and six small circular openings (fig. 2.14). The hexagons contain panes of pinkish red, blue, pale blue, and clear glass. The round openings have dark red glass in the form of a cross, a modern design chosen in the absence of original glass. Along each side of the vault, resting on the sidewalls, is a single frame with a row of ten round openings containing plain glass. Small triangular openings between the circular panes are filled with green, amber, dark blue, and turquoise glass.

The sanctuary is a single transverse room divided into three open sections by interior archways, which span the spaces between the east wall of the church and the

2.15

Western exterior wall of the church, at left, showing stairs rising up the desert shelf to the south (ADP/SA BW 41:8)

pillars between the sanctuary and the khurus. The three entrances to the sanctuary are now closed by wooden doors on either side, and by an inlaid, eighteenth-century wooden screen across the widest space, between the two pillars in the middle. There are three solid altars with low arched compartments on the east sides at floor level. Behind the north and south altars are rectangular niches in the wall (s2, s11), while in the center there is a tall apse stepped into the wall to provide seats for clergy (s1). Each sanctuary is roofed with a dome. The central dome is the largest and is supported on an octagon containing eight rectangular windows. The square support for the octagon includes four windows that are now blocked. Three of them were closed and plastered over (s34–s36) before the paintings were created in 1232/1233. It is not clear whether the sanctuary was built well before 1232/1233 and later modified to accommodate the paintings, or whether a change in the painted program caused the newly built windows to be closed off. The eastern window (s33) has a painted frame. This window was probably open and functioning before the construction of the adjacent Church of the Holy Apostles.

Returning to the main entrance in the northwest corner of the nave, immediately opposite we see the wide

arch (N17; fig. 2.9) in the south wall leading to the annex and the side chapel. This arch occupies half the length of the wall and rises to the base of the dome. It was cut through the wall at a relatively late date, after the 1232/1233 paintings had been finished, and was apparently left unpainted for some time. The plaster on the eastern underside had cracked and accumulated dirt, and was then replastered before being painted (A1, A9).[8]

The plan (fig. 21, introduction; fig. 2.3) shows how the annex and side chapel are aligned at a strikingly oblique angle to the rest of the church. The point at which the south wall of the church abuts the north wall of the annex and chapel is visible: there is a marked change in direction in the wall on both sides beneath the arch. The annex is a high room with a pointed, vaulted ceiling aligned east to west. The south wall is built on the natural bedrock, the level of which is indicated by a bulge in the wall 2.85 m. above the current interior floor level. This difference in level indicates the face of a natural desert escarpment, against which the annex and side chapel were built either before or at the same time as the western end of the nave (fig. 2.15). To the east of the annex is the arched entrance of a chapel, which contains the earliest painting identified in the church (C4–C9; figs. 3.1, 3.3).[9] The chapel itself comprises a semidome with a small niche at the base of the east wall (C1). It is almost certain that this currently visible interior does not reflect the original appearance of the space. Precisely when remodeling occurred is not known.[10] Part of the original inner wall surface of the chapel was found during conservation work inside the small cupboard built into the north wall of the chapel. In addition, there are hollow cavities behind the semiapse, and features observable in the corridor to the east of the chapel suggest that the chapel was one end of what was a much longer room.

To the west of the annex is an archway, with a partially dismantled wooden screen, that leads to a shallow blind room. This room is now little more than a deep, square niche at the rear of the church (A5–A7; fig. 2.9). An examination of the interior shows that this was originally a much larger room extending farther to the west than the current back wall of the church. This is indicated by traces of a mudbrick dome that still survive in the two corners on the west side of the archway from the annex (A5, A7). The dome was removed and the room reduced to less than half its original size by the construction of a new west wall (A6). This wall continued northward along the outside of the west wall of the nave to form an additional outer skin of masonry against the exterior face of the west wall of the church, thereby also sealing the three original windows in the west wall of the nave. This new rear wall contrasts strikingly with the mudbrick walls of the room itself and the rest of the church. It was constructed of carefully fashioned limestone blocks laid in even courses. The stonework was built as high as the original western wall of the church and was then continued in mudbrick, again evenly laid in neat courses. The reduced room created by the new wall (A5–A7), in what is now a deep niche opening off of the west wall of the annex, is extraordinarily high, giving access to another space above. A skylight opens onto the roof of the church, next to the exterior stairs. A doorway is visible from the annex, in the wall above the western archway. It may once have been part of an upper story in the annex the floor of which is now lost.

The question of when the main church was built against the north side of the annex and chapel remains unanswered in absolute terms, but some relative chronological evaluation is possible.[11] Windows in the north and west walls of the nave were filled with mudbrick, blocked both inside and out, and covered by plaster shortly before Theodore's team painted the interior surface in 1232/1233. An examination of the windows showed clearly that they were built at the same time as the west wall; they therefore provide an important guide to the appearance of the earlier phase of the church.[12] The blocking of one window was dislodged when the current doorway of the church was either enlarged or inserted into the wall after 1232/1233 (N23, N24), probably when the arch between the nave and annex was made.[13] There are also two earlier layers of painted wall plaster visible on both the south and west walls of the nave, beneath the plaster layer painted in 1232/1233.[14] The clearest section is at the top of the south wall (N16, N17), where the later of the two earlier layers featured a series of standing figures. What remains is only a horizontal strip showing part of their clothing. All around the western end of the nave, the earlier layers of paintings have been cut off at the current upper edge of the wall, indicating clearly that before 1232/1233 this room, at least, had much higher walls than it has now. The contour of the cut indicates that it was made when the walls were trimmed off for the domes to be added, during reconstruction work before repainting by Theodore's artists.

The most plausible reconstruction of the architectural development of the complex is as follows: At an early stage, in the sixth or seventh century, or perhaps even before, the chapel, annex, and room west of the annex (now the niche A5–A7) formed a single structure built against the vertical face of a natural desert ledge. The group almost certainly included the corridor now connecting the two churches, east of the chapel today, as well as rooms farther to the west now disconnected by a passage leading around the west end of the church. The exact purpose and form of the chapel at this stage is unclear, except that by the end of the eighth century it already contained the painted arch (C4–C9). The height of this arch suggests that the original floor level must have been similar to the level of today. Somewhat later, the western end of the nave, and possibly the eastern end and khurus as well, were built in the space between the chapel and the western tower or keep. It is interesting to note here that the orientation of the keep is closely parallel with that of the annex and chapel, whereas the church respects the alignment of the eastern tower. The way that the church physically abuts the annex and chapel suggests that the two were always in some way connected, although this juxtaposition may have been dictated by requirements of space. Although the chapel certainly once had its own external entrance from the west, the church may have been built beside the annex with a small connecting doorway that was later enlarged into the current archway (N17).

The eastern part of the nave also has traces of murals underlying the 1232/1233 paintings, although they are obscure and fewer than in the western end. The positions of the formerly blocked doorway in the north wall and of the window over it (N31) are more helpful here. The window and doorway clearly go together and derive from the original design of the church. As we have seen, the two windows in the north wall are the only ones that remain in use from the period before the thirteenth-century modifications (N31, N33). From the exterior, this doorway is visible in the space between the two towers as one approaches the church from the north. It is thus on a significant axial route through the oldest part of the monastery. This alignment is maintained across the church nave, in the small doorway in the south side of the nave (N8, N9).

On passing through the south doorway (N8, N9) into the corridor (leading to the Church of the Holy Apostles), one is directed eastward up two steps onto a higher floor level. The floor rises again into a room at the western end of the corridor. This was at one time part of the larger room into which the apse of the chapel was later built. The floor level of this room is commensurate with the top of a natural rock shelf projecting into the church at the base of the south wall of the khurus, the inner face of which aligns on the oblique axis of the chapel and annex. According to the monastic tradition, an opening in this rock ledge leads to the grave of St. Antony. This opening was originally much taller than it is today, for it is now partly buried under the floor, which has risen in front of it. The matching levels on top of the rock shelf in the khurus and the floor of the room at the back of the chapel are only about 40 cm. higher than the floor of the corridor, which is itself some 60 cm. higher than the floor of the nave. There can be little doubt that all these surfaces correspond to the natural desert terracing against which the chapel and the church were built, and which can still be observed in the sloping surfaces both east and west of this group of churches.

During restoration work on the church floor, some of the sandstone slabs in the nave were removed. Below them, layers of building debris containing mudbrick, plaster, and roofing materials (including palm wood, fronds, and matting) were discovered, filling the floor to a depth of more than one meter. The material was deposited within the already standing building and had not been placed there as a platform for the construction of the church. There were also fragments of gypsum window moldings in the floor at the western end of the nave, which may have come from the blocked windows. The most significant detail to emerge was the fact that the current floor level is not original. At some stage, the level was raised approximately 50 cm. with this filling material and repaved with sandstone slabs to create its current surface. This work transformed the church. It created an internal space requiring new thresholds and higher doorways, and probably higher archways and a new roof. The original

windows would have been much higher in the walls than they seem now, and the original doorways may have been stepped down into the church. The new floor may also have brought the level up to the existing floor of the annex and closer to that of the chapel. No conclusive evidence was found for the material of the original church floor. A number of pieces of white, green, and black marble, however, shaped into lozenges, squares, and rectangles, and suggestive of opus sectile, were found in various parts of the church, either reused as filling between paving slabs or, in one instance, wedged into a hole in the south wall of the eastern part of the nave. Further evidence for the raised floor in the khurus was found in the form of a frieze of stylized plant motifs close to the current floor level. It had been covered by later layers of plain wall plaster and therefore belonged to a period before 1232/1233. It continues down the wall and disappears beneath the current floor level.

The only room of the church in which no traces were found of wall paintings earlier than 1232/1233 is the sanctuary. This room therefore may have been added as an extension to the earlier church, perhaps as late as the thirteenth century, during the rebuilding works described here. In this case the original sanctuary could have been where the khurus now is. This is an intriguing possibility in connection with the tradition that identifies this spot as the burial place of St. Antony, because the saint's body might be expected to lie beneath the altar of the church.

CHAPTER 3   THE EARLY PAINTINGS

Before 1998, when Adriano Luzi and Luigi De Cesaris discovered paintings under layers of blank plaster, the earliest known artistic works in the Church of St. Antony dated to 1232/1233. In fact, Western scholars believed that the church itself dated to the eleventh century at the earliest, and more likely the thirteenth century.[1] The oral tradition at the monastery, however, assigned the origins of the church to the sixth century.[2] Traces of pre–thirteenth century paintings exist in every part of the church except the sanctuary. There are probably remains of paintings from two pre–thirteenth century periods, but most of them are preserved too fragmentarily to be dated on the basis of style.

    Pre–thirteenth century paint remnants exist on a plaster layer that can be found under as many as three or four later layers of plaster. These paintings, in keeping with other Coptic wall paintings in Egypt, are done in a *secco* technique. Unlike the fresco technique of applying paint to wet plaster, common in Western wall paintings, Egyptian wall paintings consist of paint applied to dry plaster.[3] The clearest and best-preserved of the early secco remains in the Church of St. Antony are located on the underside of the arched entrance to the side chapel (c4–c9; fig. 3.1). The subject of this area is an enthroned Christ in Majesty with the Apostles. Small, flaking, colored remnants of red, blue, and yellow are visible in the annex (a5, a7), and traces of an inscription in Coptic are visible on an early plaster layer in the niche at n14. A dark red section has been discovered near the current entrance to the church, close to the floor level (n23), on the southern nave wall (n7, n8, n16), and also on the floor of the church. A decorative geometric or abstract plant motif, colored primarily in red and yellow, can be seen near the floor on the western wall of the khurus (k5). Based on the similarity of plaster consistency and color, these five areas seem to date from the same period. In numerous parts of the nave (n11, n15, 16, n20–22, n25, 26), and also in the chapel (c1, under the book of Christ) and upper zone of the khurus (k12, below the three women), the conservators have observed small sections of an even earlier layer or layers of painting. Particularly clear examples are located at n22, where one can see the remnants of a horse's tail (below the feet of the woman in blue, from a later period; fig. 3.2), and also bordering the top of the 1232/1233 paintings in the southwestern corner of the nave (n16, n20, 21). The pastel colors and loose brushstrokes of these paintings generally suggest a sixth- to eighth-century date, but these traces are too poorly pre-

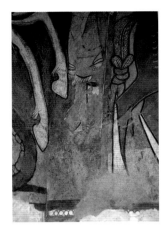

3.2

Traces of an early painting of a

horse (N22)

3.3

Christ in Majesty and the Apostles

(C4–C9), archway of the Deesis

Chapel (ADP/SA 1999)

served to make this more than a tentative suggestion. Finally, the edge of the large arch that bisects the nave along a north-to-south axis was originally painted with an edging of imitation brick. A segment of this work was found at N29, and it seems likely that this pattern appeared elsewhere. It is unusual in Coptic wall painting and is difficult to date, except to say that it must have preceded the 1232/1233 program that previously masked it.

The small band of paintings recently discovered on the underside of the arched entrance to the side chapel (C4–C9) are of exceptional importance to the history of the church (fig. 3.3). About 70 percent of the original composition has survived, enough to permit dating based on both iconography and style. The painting depicts a full-figure image of Christ in Majesty, enthroned, with his right hand raised in blessing, and his left balancing a book on his knee. He is oriented for the viewer entering the chapel and looking up, with his head to the west and his feet to the east. His head is framed by a cruciform halo, with a pearl border. He wears a dark red, long-sleeved tunic and a brown himation. Both are outlined in black. Only the red cushion of his throne has been preserved. The mandorla, or body halo, which completely encompasses the figure, would originally have been supported by the four incorporeal living beings of Revelation 4:1–8, with the heads of a man, an eagle, an ox, and a lion.[4] Only the head of the lion is clearly visible now, in the lower left corner of the mandorla. Christ is flanked by roundels on either side, in pairs, originally numbering twelve. They

contain bust-length portraits of the apostles, and seven remain in reasonably good condition. They are oriented perpendicularly to the figure of Christ, rising in pairs along the curving face of the archway, on either side of the viewer's head (fig. 3.4). Like the figure of Christ, they stare straight out at the viewer. They hold their hands open in front of their chests, palms facing outward in a gesture of prayer. Some have dark hair and others white, but all seven are bearded and bareheaded. They appear to have been identically dressed in dark red clothing. Centrally located in front of their chests but behind their hands are squares that may suggest books or decorated elements of their costume. One figure (C8) seems to hold a book in front of him and keys in his left hand, but early overpainting has rendered these areas difficult to read.[5] Only two roundels include enough of their original Coptic inscriptions to permit identification. One of these, the figure with the keys, is Peter, and the other, located across from him, in the second pair of roundels, is Bartholomew (C5). Yellow crosses with circles decorating the corners of each arm fill the spaces between these portrait busts.

The iconography of the enthroned Christ in Majesty is a standard type in early Byzantine art. This subject was rendered numerous times in wall paintings in the monasteries of Apa Jeremiah at Saqqara and Apa Apollo at Bawit, both large communities in Egypt with numerous paintings, generally dated between ca. 500 and 750.[6] It continued to be important in Coptic art after the Islamic conquest of Egypt in 641, and a similar composition from the thirteenth century can be seen in the sanctuary of the Church of St. Antony, in the eastern apse (S1).[7] The conjunction of Christ in Majesty with the apostles is typical of the sixth century. Sometimes the apostles stand below Christ, in the lower zone of a composition with two registers, or else they appear in roundels, as in a Coptic textile icon now in Cleveland (fig. 3.5).[8] The arrangement and even the choice of apostles vary in early medieval art, making it impossible, in the absence of inscriptions, to do more than guess at the identities of the seven individuals preserved in the archway.[9] We can be certain of the identity of Peter, thanks to the few letters remaining, and to his keys, which are among his standard attributes. Paul often appears next to Peter and is traditionally shown with a high forehead, dark hair, and a beard, as we see here in the figure to the left of Peter. A painting from cell 42 at Bawit shows Peter and Paul on either side of the enthroned Virgin Mary with Christ. Their hairstyles are identical with those seen in the Church of St. Antony, suggesting that the figure to Peter's left is indeed Paul.[10] Aside from Barthol-

3.4 LEFT

Apostles (C4–C6; ADP/SA 1999)

3.5 RIGHT

Textile icon of the Virgin Mary
and Christ Child. Egypt, Byzantine
Period, sixth century. Tapestry
weave, wool, 178 x 110 cm (© The
Cleveland Museum of Art, 2000,
Leonard C. Hanna Jr. Bequest,
1967.144)

omew, whom we know from his inscription, none of the
other figures has distinctive features or attributes to permit
identification.[11] The whole composition fits readily with a
group of sixth-century monuments in several media.

Owing to their subject matter, these early paintings
appear to belong to the sixth century. But because of the
enduring nature of the Christ in Majesty iconography,
style becomes a particularly important element in the attempt to date these paintings accurately. Having said that,
however, I must also acknowledge that style is a notori-
ously imprecise basis for establishing chronology. The traditional model for charting a chronology of style in Coptic
painting consists of a single trajectory in a state of progressive decline from Hellenistic naturalism to provincial
abstraction.[12] This model has numerous flaws, only one of
which is the possibility that several styles exist at one time.
Art historians studying Coptic material face an especially
difficult task constructing a new model based on datable
evidence, because early archaeologists, in their quest for
the pharaonic strata buried below later superimposed layers, did not properly excavate or in some cases even photograph or preserve early Christian and medieval layers.

Additionally, Coptic art has but rarely been considered a
serious field of study, and we are therefore only beginning
to understand it. This means that ideas about stylistic development and the dating of specific styles in Coptic art
rest not on a firm foundation but on what is at best loose
sand. The shortest span of years that we can posit for the
early painting in the Church of St. Antony is a 150-year period between ca. 550 and 700, based on close parallels with
other works of art dated by some of the best scholars in the
field. Many surprises still await us, however, and it may
one day prove necessary to revise these dates by as much as
a century in either direction.

The style of the paintings in the archway of the
chapel is characterized by an extensive use of outlines.
They are usually black or dark brown, and though they are
precise, their edges are nonetheless slightly blurred, giving
an impression of fluidity and softness. They are neither as
dark nor as sharply defined and hard-edged as the outlines
used in the 1232/1233 program in the Church of St. Antony.
The artist created schematic images that are not plausible
as three-dimensional figures. Despite this, they retain a
softness of line and here and there a suggestion of illusion-

3.6 LEFT
Christ in Majesty, detail (C7)

3.7 RIGHT
Icon of Bishop Abraham, ca. 600,
Luxor (?) (Staatliche Museen zu
Berlin—Prussischer Kulturbesitz,
Museum für Spätantike und
Byzantinische Kunst, inv. 6114)

ism that shows a connection to their Greco-Roman heritage. This is apparent in the depiction of the eye sockets, nose, and mouth of Bartholomew, which are not simply outlined but slightly modeled as well, conveying an impression of depth. The apostles' heads are long and rectangular, sometimes made narrower or broader by their beards. The rectangular shape of their heads is further accentuated in several cases by a squared-off beard. Christ's head, in contrast, is more rounded, and his head, hair, and beard combine to form an egg-shaped oval (fig. 3.6). Christ and several of the apostles have narrow mustaches and a small section of hair in the center of their chins, framed first by bare skin and then by dense beards. The lines marking the boundaries of their hair are black, even in those instances where the apostles are white-haired. The narrow band of hair at the top of the apostles' flat heads is marked by a distinctive line, which usually dips down in the center, above a high forehead. Christ alone is shown with long hair, extending down along both his shoulders. Eyebrows are also always painted black, though commonly enhanced by adding a parallel red line underneath that follows the same curved arch. Christ's eyes are somewhat more rounded than those of the apostles, most of whom have long and narrow eyes. In all cases, their pupils are pronounced, hardly distinguishable from the equally

large and dark brown irises, and all slightly covered by their upper eyelids. Their noses are long, their bridges delineated in red, and their tips marked by a distinctive looping brushstroke in black. Their mouths are straight lines, generally in black, with some touches in red. A restrained gesture toward shading is made in red, at the edges of their cheeks. While the apostles' hands are simply outlined, Christ's fingers are elongated, and his right hand includes three oddly placed fingernails. Christ's neck is partially visible, marked by a single curving line in red. The apostles' bodies are mere ciphers, suggested but truncated by the roundels framing them. Christ's body is short and stocky.

Close stylistic affinities exist between these paintings and a group of Coptic images on panels, plaster walls, and in textile, dated to the sixth or seventh century.[13] One noteworthy example, an icon of Bishop Abraham believed to be from the Monastery of Apa Phoebammon (Deir al-Bahri), on the West Bank at Luxor, has been very persuasively dated on the basis of historical and archaeological evidence to the decade or two ca. A.D. 600 (fig. 3.7).[14] The bishop's head, features, and clothing are shaped with dark outlines, similar to those used in the Monastery of St. Antony. He has a long and narrow face, and an expansive forehead. Although the shape of his head is rounded, unlike the flat-topped heads at the Church of St. Antony, the

3.8 LEFT

Apostle Paul (?) (C8)

3.9 RIGHT

Apa Apollo and other monks,

ca. sixth century, wall painting, cell

A, Monastery of Apa Jeremiah,

Saqqara

dip in the center of his hairline is similar to that shared by several of our apostles, Paul, for example (fig. 3.8). Another compelling point of comparison is the particular way the nose is shown: light red and gray lines descend from his eyebrows, marking the bridge, and a separate, pronounced black brushstroke outlines the tip. The lines on the icon are more subtle, but the device is identical to that used in the secco painting.

A wall painting of monks from cell A in the Monastery of Apa Jeremiah, and dated between ca. 550 and ca. 800, also includes several familiar features (fig. 3.9). The monks' heads are longish rectangles with flat tops and curving, high hairlines, all outlined in black. They have the very distinctive squared section of facial hair on their chins, framed first with bare skin, and then set in a circle made from their mustaches and beards. Their mouths are delineated principally with straight black lines, also very similar to the mouths of Christ and the apostles in the Church of St. Antony. Additionally, the crosses to either side of the figure of Apa Apollo from cell A are similar to those in our wall painting, though less elaborate. Small circles adorn the terminations of the arms and mark the crossing point in both.

An icon of Christ and Apa Mena from Bawit, generally dated to the sixth century (fig. 3.10), provides another

close stylistic parallel for our figures.[15] Not only are the soft dark outlines and two-color noses of both figures and the curving hairline of Mena familiar to us, but the oval face and head of Christ, framed by a wide band of hair falling over his shoulders, and including a mustache, short beard, and patch of hair on his chin, are all very close to the secco Christ. The wide-open eyes with large pupils and irises and the stocky proportions of both figures on the icon, as well as the squared neckline of Christ's robe, are also similar to the wall paintings. A faint line suggesting a crease around the necks of Mena and Christ on the icon is simply a more delicate example of the emphatic red line encircling the neck of Christ in the Church of St. Antony.

Fragmentary though they are, the pre-1232/1233 paintings in the church still furnish exceptionally important evidence for the dating, architecture, and decorative program of the Church of St. Antony. Enough is preserved of the painting of Christ in Majesty with roundels of the apostles to date it to the mid-sixth to seventh century on the stylistic and iconographic evidence. The similarity between the plaster below these paintings and plaster in the western wall of the room now functioning as the khurus shows that parts of the main body of the church, not simply sections of the annex and the side chapel, date to this early period. Peter Grossmann has established a seventh-

3.10

Icon of Christ and Apa Mena,

ca. sixth century, Bawit (Paris,

Musée du Louvre, 5718)

to eighth-century date for the introduction of the khurus as an architectural feature in Coptic churches, buffering the sanctuary from the nave.[16] The existence in the current khurus of plaster apparently dating to the sixth to seventh centuries, and its absence in the sanctuary, suggest that the sanctuary may have been added to the eastern end of the church sometime after 700, and that the room now used as the khurus was the original sanctuary. Probably of the same date, the dark red paint found on the floor and on the walls near floor-level in the nave, and the figural traces above it, attest to a standard early Christian treatment of the wall, and permits us to reconstruct the early appearance of the painted program in the Church of St. Antony. According to this system, derived from Roman painting, a band of geometric shapes often imitating colored stone encircles the lowest zone of the wall. Figural scenes usually surmount this lower zone. A fine first-century A.D. example of the lower zone, from Roman Egypt, still exists in the temple at Deir al-Haggar, in the Dakhla Oasis. A roughly 1.5 m.-high band of alternating squares of red and yellow imitation stone is painted on the inside of the enclosure

wall of this temple. An early Christian painting from Abu Girgeh and now in the Greco-Roman Museum in Alexandria includes a lower zone of imitation marble in alternating gray and reddish-orange, surmounted by a fragmentary figural composition showing the legs of St. Mena. The geometric pattern at floor level in the khurus is a more elaborate variation of what seems to have been a simpler lower zone in the nave. Since we know that the edge of the large arch separating the eastern and western halves of the nave was painted with an edging of imitation bricks at some point before 1232/1233, it seems likely that this motif was repeated elsewhere. Fragments of figural painting high up on the walls in the nave may belong to the same time span as the paintings in the chapel, that is, ca. 550–700, or they may be somewhat later. They certainly show that a developed scheme of painting in at least two zones, including geometric and figural subjects, existed in the church several centuries before the program that now predominates. This later program dates to 1232/1233 and is the subject of the following chapters.

CHAPTER 4

THEODORE, "THE WRITER OF LIFE," AND THE PROGRAM OF 1232/1233

4.1

Northwestern corner of the nave

(N21–N24; ADP/SA 1999)

The most extensive program of paintings in the Church of St. Antony was created in 1232/1233 by a team of Coptic artists (fig. 4.1). They were led by a master artist named Theodore. We know that they were Egyptians, from inscriptional information and also because of the subjects and style of the paintings, which belong to a long-standing tradition of Christian painting in Egypt stretching back at least to the fourth century. This chapter is concerned with the iconography of the paintings. Theodore's program extends throughout the church and will be analyzed following a description of the physical plan of the architecture. The various spaces in a church have specific functions, and different audiences, and the subjects and disposition of the paintings were designed with these factors in mind.

Memorial Inscriptions: Patrons and Artists

The paintings would not exist without patrons, people who paid for their creation. Imperial patronage results in the use of expensive materials, such as mosaic or marble, as we see in the decoration of the church in the Monastery of St. Catherine on Mount Sinai. A royal donor could also affect an artistic program, including in it messages of imperial power and status. The paintings at the Monastery of St. Antony had a very different background, which affected their content, medium, and style. As Tim Vivian explains in chapter 1, the Coptic Orthodox Church separated from the church of the Byzantine capital at Constantinople in the fifth century. The temporal rulers of Egypt from the middle of the seventh century were Muslims, and far from donating funds for churches and their embellishment, they actually taxed monks and forbade them from building churches without permission.[1] The high-quality paintings in the Church of St. Antony were painted on dry plaster, in a technique called secco.[2] Neither the pigments nor the plaster were of more than modest cost.

In the Church of St. Antony we are fortunate to have four inscriptions that give us precious detailed information about the patrons of these paintings. They are located at N31, K4.1, S1.14 and S33–36 (figs. 14.4, 14.5, 4.32). They tell us that at least thirty-three individuals helped pay for the paintings, and because some of the names are missing, and two or more patrons could have had the same name, the number may have been closer to forty. The longest of these inscriptions, at N31, characterizes the patrons as being lovers of God, Christ, charity, and offerings. Although many or all of the donors may have belonged to the community at the Monastery of St. Antony, the most senior among them certainly did. He is described as: "the archpriest Peter of this church" (N31). An important motivation for such donations is clearly articulated: "The Lord Jesus Christ give to them their [recompense] in (the) Jerusalem of heaven" (N31). They would have gained blessings in their efforts to attain salvation after death, by virtue of their sponsorship of the painters. It seems likely from the inscriptions, as Birger A. Pearson points out in chapter 14, that in addition to making a general contribution to the funding of the project, some of the patrons paid for individual paintings. The inscription at K4, to the right of Mercurius, mentions two brothers, the Priest Abba Michael and the Archdeacon Salib, sons of Abu Ghalib (fig. 14.5): "Lord, bless them, for they have provided for (the image of) the holy Mercurius. Lord, give them their recompense." These two, who are included in the long memorial inscription at N31, here gain special blessings through their support of the painting of Mercurius.

In addition to paying for the project, it is likely that one or more of these monastic patrons designed the program of the paintings. Although no definitive evidence on this subject is available, certain inferences can be made. As we shall see, the subjects of the paintings were carefully chosen to function in the various parts of the church, to express specific theological concepts, and also to tell stories. In the process of restoration, fluidly written words and names above the subjects of the nave were uncovered by Adriano Luzi. For example, the word *memorial* is located above the memorial inscription at N31 (fig. 14.4), and the name Maximus (directly to the right of *memorial*), is

positioned above the monastic father of that name (N32; fig. 12.1). These notations were covered with plaster, and are distinctly different in style than the formally written inscriptions which exist within the frame of each subject. The words above the paintings were written to mark out the subjects of the paintings for the artists, and are evidence of a carefully conceived plan.[3] The development of the plan would have required considerable knowledge of Christian symbolism, monastic history, and theology, subjects that are the province of educated monks and not very likely that of painters.

Two inscriptions memorialize the master painter of this extraordinary program. He is named Theodore, which means "Gift of God," and he calls himself by the Greek word for painter, *zographos*, literally, "writer of life" (S38.7; fig. 14.1). As is characteristic of medieval scribes and artists, he describes himself as "more sinful than anyone, unworthy of the name Theodore" (N35.3; fig. 4.2), and as an "apprentice painter" (S38.7), who asks God for forgiveness (N35.3).[4] Because his name is written not once but twice, alone of the many artists whose individual hands can be discerned, we know that he was the master in charge of the entire project. Like the patrons, he also would have gained blessings from such holy work, and no doubt presents himself in a formulaic, self-deprecating vein so as to appear modest and worthy of salvation.

The Functions of Paintings

One of the primary purposes of this book is the presentation and analysis of the wall paintings in the Church of St. Antony because they are compelling works of art. They are, however, considerably more than this. They were made in a cultural environment in which they were understood to do much more than passively depict or illustrate subjects. In pagan Egypt and the larger Mediterranean world, images could be objects of beauty, but they could also work magically—for example, to help heal the sick or revivify the dead. Christians believed that demons resided in pagan sculptures, and that saints could be reached by appealing to paintings of them.[5] In the contexts of pilgrimage and also Coptic monasticism, images have been shown to work as part of a process of imitation. In order to attain salvation, people strove to transform themselves into a higher spiritual state. Copying or imitating the acts of more elevated beings—for example monastic forefathers—was a crucial means by which transformation was achieved. Paintings of these exemplars worked in the same way that stories of them did: both served as models for

4.2

Northeastern corner of the nave
(N33–N36; ADP/SA 1999)

spiritual elevation.[6] The paintings in the Church of St. Antony thus performed several functions for their medieval audience.

The church has four spatial components: nave, khurus, sanctuary, and side chapel (fig. 21, introduction). The nave in the Church of St. Antony is divided into eastern and western halves by an archway and a low partition wall. The western end has sometimes been called a narthex but will here be referred to as part of the nave. Progressively more restricted access is permitted as one moves eastward, first into the khurus and then into the sanctuary. The building is oriented to the east, the direction from which Christians believe that Christ will come on the day of judgment. The eastern end is the location of the most sacred activities performed in the church, and therefore it is the most protected and exclusive part of the church interior. Symbolism is an essential component of church architecture, and two twelfth-century Coptic texts tell us that the church as a whole is the house of God.[7]

The history of public access to the nave is immediately apparent from the masses of graffiti in several languages which cover the lower sections of the walls, all the way around the nave (fig. 4.2). We know from an eighth-century account that at least one visitor, on pilgrimage to the Holy Land, stopped in Egypt and visited the Monastery of St. Antony. He was a monk, but likely some of the pilgrims who came to the monastery were lay Christians. Later reports show that the practice of including the monastery on pilgrimage itineraries continued, albeit irregularly, throughout the centuries.[8] Such outsiders would have participated in church services standing in the nave, the part of the church open to baptized Christians. Whether or not women ever joined in services in the monastery before this century is an open question.[9] We know that women went on pilgrimage and visited holy sites, and we also know that women sometimes entered the churches of men's monasteries, but we should certainly imagine that most if not all outsiders were men, in keeping with the exclusively male population of the monastery.[10]

The nave was not only a place for the congregation. A tenth- to thirteenth-century Coptic text describes the long-standing practice of reading the life story of each figure painted on the wall, on that saint's feast day. The congregants lit candles to the saint and prostrated themselves in front of the painting. The image was censed.[11] This largest of spaces would therefore have accommodated monks, visitors, and servants when no services were taking place; visitors, servants, and those monks who did not belong to the clergy during services (perhaps separated into two groups, visitors and servants at the western end, monks at the eastern end); and also processions of the clergy.

The khurus is a feature particular to Coptic church architecture. Although the word comes from the Greek *khoros*, or choir, its placement and character in Coptic architecture is distinct from the choir as it is known in the West.[12] It is an architectural element that first made its appearance ca. 700, most likely intended as an additional zone of protection setting off the nave from the sanctuary, where the holy mysteries were performed.[13] During the liturgy, members of the clergy (for example, priests and deacons) who were attending but not performing in the service may have stood in the khurus.

The sanctuary, also called the *haykal* in the Coptic tradition, is the site of the celebration of the Eucharist. The Church of St. Antony, in keeping with standard Coptic practice, includes three altars in the sanctuary. Domes mark their three separate spaces, which otherwise form a continuous long room. The central one is the largest and most important. The fourth architectural space in the

church is a side chapel, which is reached through a small annex off of the southwestern corner of the nave, called here the Deesis Chapel.[14] The general public may not have been permitted to enter this space, due to its diminutive size; the fact that it includes two short graffiti only, by a single author, is evidence that access was limited.[15] This paucity of graffiti is in striking contrast to the dense writing in the nave, some of it covering several successive layers of plaster.[16] An altar stands in the middle of this small chapel, making it clear that private and possibly solitary celebrations of the Eucharist could have taken place here. The space is not large enough to accommodate more than two or three people at a time.

THE NAVE: A GENEALOGY OF COPTIC MONASTICISM IN PAINT

Entering the nave from the door in the northeastern corner (N23, N24), one is immediately surrounded by a painted band of large figures on horseback (fig. 4.1). These are martyrs, individuals who died for their faith before the Roman Emperor Constantine's legalization of Christianity in A.D. 313. Looking across the nave and to the east, one sees that the circle begun by the equestrian martyrs is completed by standing figures of monastic saints, with the ad-

dition of an enthroned Virgin Mary and Child (fig. 4.3). The martyrs and saints were chosen to express a primary message about the importance of Egyptian monasticism. The figures shown here also performed other functions in the church, which will be addressed subsequently.

Martyrs have a special place in the Christian community. They were perfect witnesses to Christ, suffering the ultimate tests of faith, torture and death, and remaining steadfast in their beliefs. For this, they earned instantaneous salvation. Many of them, including most of those depicted on horseback in the nave, were originally soldiers in the Roman army. Because they refused to sacrifice to the emperor and pagan gods, they were condemned to death and became soldiers of Christ.[17] Martyr legends tell us that, through the grace of God, martyrs performed miracles and inspired conversions both while in the throes of torture and execution and also after death. The martyrs chosen for this painted program were the focus of particular veneration in Egypt, and some were Egyptians by birth.

Beginning with the equestrian figures and moving in a clockwise direction around the western half of the nave, we see Theodore the Anatolian (N18; the last figure on the southern wall, almost completely destroyed in the con-

4.5
North wall of the nave, western
end, showing the entrance to the
church (N22–N26; ADP/SA 1999)

struction of the archway), Claudius (N19), Victor (N20), Menas (N21), Theodore Stratelates (N22; Stratelates means "the general," and he is the last figure on the western wall), Sissinius (N23; largely destroyed due to the insertion or enlargement of the rectangular doorway), John of Heraclea (?; N24), George (N25), and Phoebammon of Ausim (N26; figs. 4.1, 4.4, 4.5). The most famous of the equestrian martyrs of Egyptian birth is Menas (4.6), a soldier in the Roman army who fled to the desert upon hearing an imperial order to worship the pagan gods:

> After a time the grace of God lighted upon him, and he saw heaven open, and the interior thereof was filled with angels of light who were carrying crowns of light, and laying them upon the heads of those who had consummated their martyrdom.... And Saint Mînâs longed to become a martyr for the Name of our Lord Jesus Christ . . . [and] a voice from heaven cried out . . . "Blessed art thou, Mînâs, for thou hast been called . . . and thou shall receive three crowns incorruptible, like [those of] the Holy Trinity: . . . one for thy virginity, and one for thy patient endurance, and one for thy martyrdom. And thy martyrdom shall be greater than the martyrdoms of a multitude of martyrs, and thy name

shall be honored, and multitudes of people shall come from every part of the world, and shall take refuge in thy church which shall be built in the land of Egypt, and works of power shall be manifest, and wonderful things, and signs, and healings shall take place through thy holy body."[18]

He subsequently left the desert to confront the pagan governor with his resolution, saying: "Because I wished to become a soldier of the Heavenly King I forsook the fleeting soldiery of this world."[19] He was whipped, had his flesh scraped off of his bones, was burned with torches, and finally decapitated. Fellow soldiers rescued his body from a pyre on which it had been cast to burn and carried it with them for protection.[20] From Alexandria, they took it to the region of Mareotis, a short distance to the west, where it assisted them in attaining victory in battle. "And when the governor wished to return to Phrygia he wanted to carry the body [of the saint] with him. And he placed it on a camel, but the camel was unable to move with it, and he placed it upon another camel, and the camel was unable to rise up; in this manner he placed it upon all the camels that were with him, and there was not one which was able to carry it away."[21] It was finally recognized that Menas was

refusing to leave that site, and his body was buried and its grave eventually forgotten. The saint's intransigence is illustrated below his equestrian figure on the western wall of the nave in the Church of St. Antony (N21; figs. 4.6, 4.7). Beneath the horse's feet, a man stands whipping a camel, which refuses to rise, its open-mouthed head reared back in what is almost an audible protest. A second camel behind this one suggests the series of camels in the story, with the charming addition of a baby camel tethered to its leg. The domed structure to the right of the scene, with a cross on the roof, an open door and hanging lamp, represent the shrine that was subsequently built to house the saint's body after a series of miracles ensured its rediscovery. One account describes the recognition coming about after the healing of a lame boy over the site of the grave. Such miracles continued for later visitors to Menas's shrine, earning him a reputation as a great healer.[22] In a characteristic example, Menas appears on his spiritual horse to save the life of a man being devoured by a crocodile.[23] We therefore see in the painting the saint himself on his spiritual horse, as countless of the faithful have seen him, with the three crowns of martyrdom described in the text above, one on his head and two, oddly duplicated in shafts of light, being held out to him from heaven. He sits on his horse, over the camels who refused to move him from his preferred place of rest and adjacent to the church built for him there. The site became the largest pilgrimage complex in the early Byzantine Mediterranean, drawing countless pilgrims.[24] The large hole that we see today in the middle of the painting is a window, which was part of the pre–thirteenth century building, later bricked up and painted over by Theodore's team. Photographs from the 1930s show that the painted plaster had already fallen off and the space had been filled in with plaster.

Menas's story is typical of martyrdom accounts in many respects. The saint was a soldier in the army who was called to his death as a soldier for Christ. He suffered almost unimaginable horrors with equanimity, and upon death achieved instantaneous salvation and crowns for his heroic qualities. His physical remains worked miracles. The saint would appear on horseback, responding to calls for help by the faithful, particularly those appeals made in the region of his body.

The painting to the right of Menas is particularly interesting for the history of art and also for its story. Although the origins of Theodore Stratelates (N22) are uncertain, we know that he was very popular in Egypt (fig. 4.8). Not only does the Coptic version of his life describe him as Egyptian, but many Coptic churches are dedicated to him, and he appears frequently in art.[25] The general is shown at a famous moment in his life before his martyrdom. A widow finds him passing by the town of Euchaites. She begs him to deliver her fatherless sons from the hideous fate of being sacrificed to a dragon that the townsfolk worship.[26] In the painting we see the two children bound and threatened. Pearson identified traces of inscriptions around their heads as names (fig. 4.9), which is fortunate, because the textual sources don't include this information.

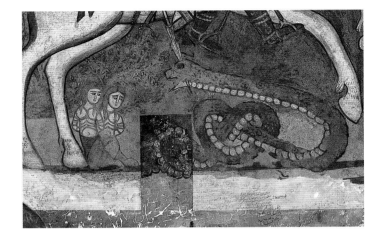

dragon from their location below the rear of the horse. Although the later painting includes elements missing in the earlier drawing—for example, the hand extending a second crown from heaven, the shield, and the wonderful knot formed by the coils of the beast—the similarities are close enough to make plausible two suppositions: first, that it repeats iconography from an earlier painting of Theodore Stratelates in the church, perhaps painted in this very spot, and second, that this manuscript almost certainly came from the Monastery of St. Antony.[30]

The painting of Claudius (N19; fig. 4.12) includes unusual subject matter. The fanciful coloring of the horse is startling, with its black and red cloverleaf designs and dots on ocher, as is the odd pointed shape of the horse's hooves. Additionally, the figure whom Claudius is piercing through his neck is a surprise (fig. 4.13). The inscription clearly identifies the crowned ruler as Diocletian, apparently the Roman emperor of that name (ruled A.D. 284–305), who was responsible for some of the worst persecutions of Christians. Scholars have been puzzled by his inclusion here, for Claudius is nowhere else credited with his death.[31] Some accounts say that George and the Archangel Michael performed the deed.[32]

One name is legible, Peter. With the help of the Archangel Michael, Theodore kills the dragon and saves the boys.[27]

Fragments of early paintings are visible to the right side of N22 and directly below the bare feet of the petitioning mother (fig. 3.2) Although we do not know whether the older paintings below the 1232/1233 layer depicted the same subjects as the ones we now see, the partially revealed layer shows a horse's hindquarters and tail. This suggests that the earlier program also included equestrian martyrs in this section of the church. On the western wall of an unidentified building from Tebtunis, in the Fayoum region of Egypt, a painting dating to the tenth century or later also shows Theodore Stratelates in a similar pose, spearing a giant snake (fig. 4.10).[28] In this painting, however, the snakelike dragon rises up to face Theodore. A depiction of the event that is virtually identical to that in the Church of St. Antony is a drawing made in the ninth or tenth century, two or three hundred years prior to the painting now visible on the wall, for a manuscript thought to have belonged to the Monastery of St. Antony (fig. 4.11).[29] The saint faces us from horseback, loosely holding the cross-headed spear that pierces the head of the dragon. The widow appeals to him with her right arm upraised, standing just in front of the horse. The children look at the

4.14
Victor (N20; ADP/SA 1999)

4.15 LEFT
Victor in the bathhouse furnace
(N20; ADP/SA 1999)

4.16 RIGHT
South wall of nave, looking east
(N2–N17; ADP/SA 1999)

Victor (N20; fig. 4.14) is shown next to Claudius (N19). The two were contemporaries and acquaintances. Victor is not dressed in armor because he refused to be a soldier, even though his father is described in the account of Victor's martyrdom as being one of the Emperor Diocletian's caesars, and a general in the Roman army.[33] Because of Victor's great popularity and his father's high rank, Diocletian sent him away to Alexandria to be tortured. There he was thrust into the furnace of a bathhouse, but the Archangel Michael rescued him from death.[34] We see a diminutive Victor in the bathhouse, located between the forelegs of the horse, with his hands raised in a gesture of prayer (fig. 4.15). Smoke pours from the chimney, suggesting the intense heat of the furnace. The domes of the bathhouse are painted with circles, depicting glass windows in keeping with medieval bath architecture. Although the extant Coptic text of Victor's martyrdom does not explain the scene in the lower left of the composition, a passage in the "Martyrdom of St. Theodore the Oriental" describes a stone slab on which Victor shed blood while being tortured, and fetters that bound his hands and feet. The chains are shown in this painting, and the stone is depicted here as a millstone of the kind visible in monasteries through-

out Egypt today. The text records that the stone and chains were kept in the martyrium church of the saint.[35]

The four standing figures on the southern wall, in the western end of the nave, seem at first glance to be out of place with the parade of equestrian martyrs (fig. 4.16). Visually, they appear to belong to the program in the eastern end of the nave. They stand calmly, facing forward, set within arcades, and wear monastic and priestly clothing more in keeping with the eastern group. The standing figure at the left is Pakaou, who holds the small devil Sofonesar by the hair (N14); to the right is Noua (misspelled as Thouan, N15), followed by Piroou and Athom together (N16; partially cut away by a later archway). Of the standing saints, Pakaou was an ascetic, Noua was a physician and possibly also a priest, and the pair Piroou and Athom were peasants.[36] The equestrian group, unlike the standing group, were all originally military men or nobility, or both. Several wear the tunic and cuirass of the Roman army, although other aspects of their costume and weaponry reflect post-Roman developments.[37] The standing saints are an integral part of the western group because they died as martyrs. All four were Egyptians. The figure closest to the east, Pakaou, provides a physical link between the two

4.17
Sofonesar the devil, held by
Pakaou (N14; ADP/SA 1999)

categories: he was a martyr and also belonged to the eastern group, which mainly comprises monks, the successors to the martyrs. Though soldiers of Christ, none of these four was a noble or a soldier in the Roman army; hence they are neither on horseback nor in military garb. It has been suggested that at least one additional standing figure was part of the original program of 1232/1233, although we cannot guess at his identity.[38] An archway cut into the wall at a later date obliterated most of the figures of Athom (N16) and Theodore the Anatolian (N18) and is wide enough to have destroyed one more painted figure.

At first sight, the paintings of the four standing figures appear to include considerably less narrative activity than those of their mounted companions. Pakaou (N14) holds the small black devil by the creature's startling ocher-yellow hair (fig. 4.17), and Noua (N15) swings a censer, but these depictions lack the elaborate scenes and buildings characteristic of the rectangular compositions with equestrians elsewhere in the western end of the nave. Despite the spareness of these paintings of standing martyrs, they do contain a subtle kind of narrative embedded in details of placement and even posture, and decipherable only to someone who knows the stories of the figures. Piroou and Athom (N16) are united by a single archway because they were brothers. They are juxtaposed to Noua (N15) because of an event linking them to him. They were peasants, and one day they encountered soldiers preparing to dispose of the body of a Christian man who had recently been martyred: Noua. The soldiers were going to throw Noua's body into the sea. Piroou and Athom bribed the soldiers to hand over the body, so that they could give it a reverent burial. After arranging for the continuing care of Noua's grave, they set forth to embrace their own martyrdom.[39] Never having met in life, the three stand together, companions in heaven.

In some cases, research has so far failed to uncover the full story suggested by these small narrative clues in the wall paintings. Pakaou, for example, is known to have been an ascetic who left his disciples upon being called to martyrdom by the archangel Gabriel.[40] We do not know, however, the story surrounding his encounter with the devil Sofonesar. Interestingly, this devil is credited with having been Eve's seducer in the Garden of Eden.[41]

In addition to martyrdom, another path to salvation was available to the devout Christian: it lay in attempting to live out one's life in a state of perfection. Roughly contemporary with the cessation of persecutions of Christians by the Roman state in 313, the institution called monasticism was developed, and aspects of it were patterned on

the act of martyrdom. According to tradition, Antony founded this new way of life. One of his most famous fellows was Pachomius, who is included in the gallery of saints in the nave (N12). Describing him and his brethren, Pachomius's biographer wrote: "Then they offered their souls and bodies to God in strict ascesis [ascetic practice] and with a befitting reverence, not only because they looked day and night to the holy Cross, but also because they saw the martyrs take up their struggles. They saw them and imitated them."[42]

Edward Malone, a historian of early monasticism, has the following to say on this subject: "Monastic life becomes a *militia spiritualis*, a spiritual warfare, or spiritual military service; the monk is now the soldier of Christ who goes forth to give battle for Christ against the evil spirits and the enemies of Christ in the world."[43]

Antony himself lived during the end of the period of persecution, and his biographer, Athanasius, makes it clear that Antony played a role that was as important as that performed by the martyrs: "He was praying that he, too, might be martyred, as I have said before, and he grieved because he had not yet been called to be a martyr, but the Lord was keeping him to help us and others that he might teach many the practice of asceticism that he had himself learned from the Scriptures. Many merely on seeing his way of life were eager to imitate [it]."[44]

One can thus see the program of paintings in the nave of the Church of St. Antony as a genealogy. It begins with the martyrs, both equestrian and standing, at the western end, and is completed to the east, with the rows of standing monastic saints (fig. 4.18). The subjects in the eastern half of the nave are all men who contributed sig-

4.18 ABOVE RIGHT
South wall of the nave (N8–N16),
with Pachomius (N12) at the center
(ADP/SA 1999)

4.19

Macarius and the Cherub

(N32–N34; ADP/SA 1999)

4.20

Cherub holding Macarius's wrist

(N33; ADP/SA 4 S193 98)

inspired is called eremetic, depending as it does on considerable solitude. The two figures depicted on the archway that divides the western from the eastern half of the nave were also instrumental in developing methods of monastic living. They are Pachomius (N12, on the south side; figs. 4.16, 4.18), and Shenoute (N28, on the north side). Pachomius (292–346) is famous for having been called by God to formulate a new system of monastic organization, one that emphasized community.[46] We know from his *Life* that he had a prophetic dream, on the night he was baptized: "He saw the dew of heaven descend on his head, then condense in his right hand and turn into a honeycomb; and while he was considering it, it dropped onto the earth and spread out over the face of all the earth."[47] He was later led to a deserted village, where a voice told him to build a monastery, in fulfillment of the dream.[48] Shenoute was born and lived in the region of Akhmim, between ca. 350 and ca. 450. He became abbot of the White Monastery around 385 and shaped the communal monastic life there along strict lines. He inspired strong feelings in his contemporaries, and although those feelings were not always positive, nevertheless a large following of petitioners from all walks of life came to him for blessings and advice. He is also known for having been tireless in fighting against pagans and heretics.[49]

One of the most vital centers of early monasticism in Egypt was Scetis, now known as the Wadi al-Natrun. In this region, monks seem to have followed a semianchoritic form of community.[50] Macarius the Great (N33), the legendary founder of monasticism in Scetis, was called to this task by a cherub while working in this region collecting natron salts (fig. 4.19): "One night when he was in the Natron Valley an angel showed him a vision of the inner valley and promised that it would be the heritage of his spiritual sons."[51] The cherub said to him,

"They are spiritual fruits, which are the commandments and virtues, and Christ our God will make you god over this land on which will live a multitude of people. Those who hear and keep and observe your commandments will be a wreath and royal diadem on your head in the presence of Christ the King." After the cherub had said these things to him, he crucified him on the land and said to him, "You will be crucified with Christ and you will join him on the cross with the virtues adorning you with their perfume, and your ascetic practices will spread to the four corners of the earth and will raise up a multitude sunk in the mire of sin and they will become warriors and soldiers in Christ's army."[52]

nificantly to the genesis and development of monasticism in Egypt, with one exception: the Virgin Mary and Child (N36). This painting is located on the eastern wall, to the north side of the entrance to the khurus. The eastern wall, closest to the altar, is a privileged position in the church. Balancing the painting of the Virgin Mary and Child, on the opposite side of the khurus entrance, are painted Antony (N1) and Paul (N2; fig. 7, introduction; fig. 4.3). As the father of monasticism and the figure who lived at and inspired the formation of a monastery at this site, Antony is depicted in a position of honor. The senior ascetic Paul's model brought into being the brother monastery to that of St. Antony's, located not far away (fig. 1.1, 1.7).[45] They both lived as hermits, and the form of monasticism which they

Macarius's place in the congregation of saints painted in the nave in the Church of St. Antony is assured for two reasons. According to the *Life* of Macarius, the saint visited Antony before the latter's death, and Antony is described as having "clothed Abba Macarius in the monastic habit and this is the reason he is called the disciple of Abba Antony."[56] Also, Macarius was known as the father of Scetis, and thus it is fitting that he should be included along with Antony, the father of monasticism.[57] In the painting of Macarius the Great, on the north nave wall (N33), this powerful leader is shown with his right wrist in the grasp of the cherub who showed him his destiny. The painting includes a stylized mountain, probably indicating Scetis, as a background for the cherub. The inscription within this painting is damaged and was illegible before it was cleaned, although previous identification of the saint as Macarius the Great was helped by the painter's inclusion of the cherub.[58] The discovery in cleaning of the first three letters of Macarius's name within the framing of the arcade is augmented by more freely written letters, discovered above the frame, under obscuring plaster, and reading: "the cherub . . . [unpreserved] the great"(N33; fig. 4.20).[59] These additional finds confirm the earlier identification of this figure as Macarius the Great.

Cherubim appear here and elsewhere in the church, and repay close examination. They are mentioned in the Old and New Testaments, and these sources are conflated in Coptic art.[60] They have four heads, those of a man, an ox, a lion, and an eagle. In N33 the head of the man is most prominent, but the small heads of eagle, lion, and ox peer out from the top and sides of the man's head. Wings extend above the cherub's head and at its sides, and also cover its body. A homily on Ezekiel's vision describes the cherub's wings being "completely covered with eyes." Two human-like arms extend outward from the body. The artist has painted eyes on the wings covering the cherub's body and above its head. The author of the homily associates these eyes—the "spiritual eyes of light"—with the light of the Holy Spirit as it shines through the eyes of the human soul.[61]

The renowned founders of four additional monasteries in Scetis are also shown in the nave. They are Maximus and Domitius (N32; fig. 12.1), Moses the Black (N30; fig. 4.21), Pishoi the Great (Bishoi, N7; figs. 4.22, 5.9), and John the Little (N8; fig. 4.22). The sources tell us that Moses was an Ethiopian, a former slave, who led a band of robbers. Upon encountering the monks of Scetis, he repented and became a particularly revered monastic father.[62] One account expresses the delightfully direct quality of so many of these early monks:

Shortly thereafter his wife and parents died, and he became a hermit, and was eventually visited a second time in a vision by the cherub.[53]

> Later, then, on an appointed day when he would receive the holy mysteries, as was his custom, alone in his cell, and when he would stand at the altar as was his custom, he looked toward his right and suddenly saw there a cherub with six wings and a large number of eyes. Abba Macarius began to observe him closely, saying, "Who are you?" Then because of the brightness and splendor of the cherub's glory, Saint Abba Macarius fell on his face and became like one dead. When he remained lying on the ground a short while, the cherub took hold of him and revived him and raised him to his feet.[54]

During this visitation, the cherub directed Macarius to leave for Scetis and begin his task of founding a monastic center there. The appearance to Macarius of the cherub, and especially the angel's act of taking Macarius by his right hand, shown in the painting, marked him as the chosen of God.[55] Scetis quickly came to be a major center of monasticism, and Macarius the Great's monastery there was, and is again today, famous.

4.22

Samuel, Pishoi the Great, John the
Little, Sisoes, Arsenius, Barsauma,
and Pachomius (N6–N12; ADP/SA
1999)

A brother at Scetis committed a fault. A council was called to which Abba Moses was invited, but he refused to go to it. Then the priest sent someone to say to him, "Come, for everyone is waiting for you." So he got up and went. He took a leaking jug, filled it with water and carried it with him. The others came out to meet him and said to him, "What is this, Father?" The old man said to them, "My sins run out behind me, and I do not see them, and today I am coming to judge the errors of another." When they heard that they said no more to the brother but forgave him.[63]

Pishoi the Great and John the Little are located next to each other on the south wall (fig. 4.22) and provide an interesting example of the subtle character of the narrative elements included in these paintings, similar to what we observed in our discussion of the martyrs. Pishoi and John lived in the fourth and early fifth centuries and were contemporaries of Macarius the Great. They were bound to each other in spiritual friendship, and so are shown side by side, and across the nave from the other monastic founders of Scetis.[64] Pishoi stands facing straight ahead, with his hands at chest level, palms facing outward, in the attitude of prayer. He is distinguished from the monks flanking him by a bust-length figure of Christ, who appears from between two arches at the top of the arcade, and points to Pishoi (fig. 6.22). This gesture immediately conveys the idea that Christ has singled Pishoi out for greatness, but it also refers to the fact that Christ appeared to Pishoi several times, even permitting the saint to wash his feet.[65]

Before the paintings in the nave were cleaned, the image now known to us as John the Little was unidentified (N8).[66] Pishoi and John stand within a four-part arcade with two other saints, Sisoes (Shishoi; N9) and Arsenius (N10; fig. 4.22). Their heads reach a roughly even height within the arches, Pishoi and Sisoes overlapping the arch above their heads slightly, and Arsenius intruding somewhat more over the curve. John's significantly shorter figure manages to reach the same general height of the other three because he is standing on a small hill. His short stature is an identifying element. Other features in this painting of John the Little are encoded with meaning. The small flowering tree adjacent to his left foot refers to the decisive moment when what may well be John's most famous miracle occurred. John's spiritual adviser, Father Amoi, tested him by placing a dry stick of wood about twelve miles from his cell and instructing John to water it daily. "Now the water was a long way from the place where

the tree was planted, but Abba John would leave with the water basin at night and he would return in the morning. He did this for three years, and the tree lived, blossomed, and brought forth fruit. The elder Abba Amoi took the fruit of the tree and brought it to the church and gave it to the elders, saying, 'Take, eat from the fruit of obedience.'"[67] John does not raise his hands in the common gesture signifying prayer. In his left hand he holds a staff topped with a cross, and his right hand appears to point, for his index finger is extended. This hand gesture refers to the high regard in which his fellows held him: "'What is the measure of Abba John the Little?' And the great elder, renowned both in monastic practice and deepest wisdom, stood in their midst and said to them, 'Abba John the Little is more exalted than us, especially because through his pure heart and true humility he has suspended all of Scetis from his finger.'"[68]

One of the monastic figures in the nave is not Egyptian, nor did he found a monastery in Egypt. He is Barsuma the Syrian (N11; figs. 4.22, 14.3), known as the father of the Syrian monks.[69] As such, it is fitting that he is painted on the narrow wall division that extends into the nave, so that he is facing Antony, the father of monasticism. Barsuma is famous for opposing the Council of Chalcedon of 451, and in this he was in agreement with the doctrinal position of the Coptic Church.[70] No doubt because of this he is described in the open scroll he holds as a combatant, in other words, one who fights against heresy. The pig and serpent at his feet surely refer to events in the saint's life, but their significance has yet to be explained.[71]

In summary, then, the painted program of the nave is a genealogy of Coptic monasticism. It begins with the first soldiers of Christ, the martyrs, who successfully forged a path to salvation. It continues with their successors, starting with Antony the Great, located in a place of honor on the eastern wall, because he is the father of monasticism. Like the martyrs, the monks shown here are known for developing a way of life that leads to salvation. They are also described as soldiers of Christ, and like the martyrs they perform miracles and defend the faith in the face of non-Christians and heretics. Although most of the martyrs are not Egyptians, they are all of special importance in Egypt. Their monastic successors inspired followers and founded monasteries in Egypt, and most were native Egyptians. In the case of Barsuma, the father of Syrian monks shared the position of the Copts in the doctrinal struggle against heresy, and he likely suggests the long-standing ties between Syrian and Coptic Christians.

In this painted program, the way in which the monks

imitate the martyrs is a clue in our effort to understand the full range of the meaning for these paintings. The essential goal of the Christian is to assimilate to Christ, and the challenge is figuring out how to do it. In the Gospel according to John, Christ says: "He who eats my flesh and drinks my blood abides in me and I in him" (Jn 6:56). This refers to the consumption of Christ in the bread and wine of the Eucharist, one important way to become Christ. The paintings in the sanctuary relate directly to this act. Imitation of Christ's sufferings is another method, as is expressed in passages from the recorded "Sayings" of the monks painted in the nave at the Monastery of St. Antony. "The definition of a Christian is the imitation of Christ."[72] The process of imitating Christ is a lengthy and difficult one, attained by degrees. An essential component of the process is patterning oneself on others who are more spiritually elevated than oneself, as in the monks' efforts to model themselves on the martyrs. Through death, martyrs imitate Christ. The monks imitate the martyrs, and Christ, without actually being killed. They nonetheless attempt to die to the world in advance of their physical death: "The brethren said, 'How is it possible for a monk to die every day for the love of Christ?' The old man said, 'A man [can do this] if he contemplate in silence at all seasons, and perform the other works of the body, I mean fasting, and vigil, and the recital of the books of the Psalms, and prayers, and genuflections, and pain, and weeping, and tears, and sighs, and the reading of the Holy Scriptures.'"[73]

Novice monks modeled themselves on senior monks and ascetics, as Athanasius wrote: "For simply by seeing . . . [Antony's] conduct, many aspired to become imitators of his way of life."[74] These acts of imitation were facilitated through spoken, written, and painted depictions of holy figures. Athanasius explained the rational for writing Antony's life as follows: "You have asked me about the career of the blessed Antony . . . so that you might lead yourselves in imitation of him."[75] And about the written collection of the "Sayings" of the fathers on the ascetic life, the compiler wrote: "This book is an account of the virtuous asceticism and admirable way of life and also of the words of the holy and blessed fathers. They are meant to inspire and instruct those who want to imitate their heavenly lives, so that they may make progress on the way that leads to the kingdom of heaven."[76] Like the written accounts of these exemplary figures, the images serve as models for imitation. An early indication that paintings themselves could participate in this process comes from Theodoret of Cyrrhus, writing in the fifth century, on the lives of Syrian

ascetics. Describing how these holy men were imitators of Biblical figures, Theodoret uses explicitly visual terms: they have taken on "the impress of all the virtue of" their models and become "living images [icons] and statues of them."[77] Two thirteenth-century Coptic authors address the role of images in churches. Abu al-Khayar ibn al-Tayyib describes the effect on the Christian viewer of seeing paintings of the martyrs. These models strengthen the viewers' faith and prepare them to hold fast to it, even to the point of death, should anyone attempt to persuade them to convert.[78] The issue of conversion was a sensitive one for both Muslims and Christians, and it is fascinating to read the views of Theodore's contemporaries, defending and explaining the very active role of images in churches. Al-Mu'taman Abu Ishaq al-'Assal devotes a whole chapter of his treatise to "the paintings of images in churches, models of those they represent, in order that one [the viewer] remembers them and asks them for their intercession with God."[79]

The marked Egyptian and monastic emphasis of the program is appropriate in this church, built in honor of the Egyptian father of monasticism, Antony the Great, in one of the most famous monasteries in Egypt. The paintings have a timeless relevance recording the historical importance of monasticism in Egypt. They also act as a visual focus for imitation, the path that leads to assimilation to Christ, and thereby salvation. The paintings have another specific message, which related to the events of the late twelfth and early thirteenth century, including the period when these paintings were made. As Vivian and Gabra explain in chapters 1 and 10, the Syrian and Coptic Churches were historically close, sharing a doctrinal view on the nature of Christ which was in opposition to the official position of the Byzantine empire. The decades preceding 1200 witnessed rising tensions between the Coptic and Syrian popes, over issues of authority. Marginal notations in two Syrian manuscripts from Egypt suggest that the monasteries of both St. Paul and St. Antony were in the hands of Syrian monks at this time. At some point before 1232/1233, they were taken over again by Coptic monks. Although the evidence for this is sparse and unclear, the painted program in the Church of St. Antony takes on an additional level of meaning if the monastery had recently been repossessed by the Copts. The Egyptian character of the monastic saints conveys a strong sense of pride. The inclusion of Barsuma suggests that matters between the two groups were not overtly hostile, but the emphasis is Coptic.[80]

PROTECTION, HEALING, AND INTERCESSION FOR FORGIVENESS

The martyrs announce the protection of the faith in the face of persecution and death, and also establish the role of soldiers of Christ, which the monks follow. In addition to expressing a genealogical relationship, the paintings of the martyrs also serve at least two other functions. Most of them are shown triumphing over evil, and they perform this task continuously, guarding the entrance to the church. The current door to the church, located in the northwest corner (N23, N24), may or may not be original (fig. 4.1).[81] The standard church plan includes one or more entrances in the western wall, and if doors existed there, they would also have been protected by paintings of martyrs. The two martyrs shown in the khurus also serve a protective function, guarding the sanctuary.

According to a modern Western approach, paintings are capable of expression and the illusion of life, but are lifeless in themselves. In the medieval world, the antithesis could be true, as a miracle performed by George demonstrates:

A group of Saracen soldiers insults Saint George by going into his church in order to drink, sleep, and even play dice. The Saracens have with them some Christian prisoners, one of whom warns them that the saint is able to repay such behavior. But the Saracens only laugh, and ask the prisoner to point out Saint George's portrait from among the holy images set above them in the church. The Christian indicates the mosaic of the martyr. . . . The fearsome character of this portrait . . . does not deter one of the Saracen soldiers from hurling a missile at it; whereupon the weapon is returned to the attacker in such a manner that it strikes him in the heart. The saint's active participation in this miracle is proved by the icon itself, which is seen by the other soldiers to stretch out its hand.[82]

Paradoxically, the western visual tradition prizes illusionism without believing in the life of the work of art, while in the Coptic tradition antinaturalistic images act as well as or better than living beings.

The graffiti below the martyrs suggest to us another use for these paintings. All the paintings in the nave were the focus of petitions to the individuals depicted in them, to intercede with God for healing and for the forgiveness of sins. We know this not only from the graffiti but also from miracle accounts.[83] Menas, for example, was known for his success in curing women and female animals of in-

fertility, and for revivifying the dead (fig. 4.6).[84] Piroou and Athom brought back to life the wife of the governor who had imprisoned them, converting her husband in the process (fig. 4.16).[85]

Paintings of monastic saints were vehicles through which these holy figures performed miracles. Several of the monastic saints depicted in the eastern half of the nave had reputations as healers. The saint always stresses that God has acted through him or her in performing the cure, or, as in the following passage from the *Life* of Antony, denies any role at all, even though the supplicant attained health while going to see Antony:

A young woman from Busiris in Tripoli also had a very terrible affliction and suffered terribly, for water fell from her nose and her ears and turned into worms. In addition, her body was paralyzed and her eyes were useless. . . . Her parents found out about some monks who were going to Antony . . . [and asked] if they could travel with them. . . . When the brothers went in to see Antony and started to tell him about the girl, he told them about her affliction and how she was traveling with them. . . . [And Antony refused to see her, and said:] "Go away and you will find her healed if she hasn't died. For this healing is not my doing, but the Savior's. . . . The Lord has given her healing when she prayed to him; as for my part, his goodness has told me that he will heal her." They left and found her parents rejoicing because their daughter had been healed.[86]

Barsuma the Syrian (N11; fig. 4.22) was reputed to have healed the broken heel of the son of aristocratic Frankish parents, who had petitioned him through an icon.[87] Paul the Simple (N5; fig. 5.12), a disciple of Antony's, was so good at exorcising demons that Antony sent the most difficult cases to him.[88] Across the nave from Paul the Simple, the two brothers Maximus and Domitius are shown together under a single arch (N32; fig. 12.1). They may also have been a focus for petitions for healing, for they were known to have cured a leper and "a man with an inverted face."[89] All of the martyrs and saints painted in the church could have been the specific focus of prayers and petitions, for healing and other needs as well.

The painting of the Virgin Mary in the nave may also have been used for protection and healing, and was certainly the focus of prayers for intercession, inscribed below in graffiti (figs. 4.2, 4.23).[90] An Ethiopian miracle story set in Cairo in the Monastery of St. Mercurius describes a blind monk, John of Bakansi, praying to an icon of the Virgin

4.23

Virgin Mary and Christ Child

(N34–N36; ADP/SA 1999)

Mary every night after the rest of the community had gone to bed. One night he saw her in a vision, taking milk from one of her breasts and anointing his eyes with it. This milk cured his blindness.[91] While currently known only in an Ethiopian version, this story was probably originally Egyptian.[92]

THE VIRGIN MARY

The Copts are well known for their particular devotion to the Virgin Mary.[93] It is therefore not surprising to find that the single painting in the nave program that depicts neither martyr nor monk is of the Virgin Mary and Child (N36; fig. 4.23). This painting provides a focus for prayers to the Virgin in the space with unrestricted access, the nave. As an obedient virgin, Mary was also a model for the ascetic life. Albeit in different ways, the Virgin Mary and monks share the experience of bearing Christ.[94] In this painting, the Virgin sits on a richly colored and decorated throne, expressive of her high status as *Theotokos*, or bearer of God. She holds an oval shape with pointed ends in front of her chest, within which is shown Christ as a child, in a seated position (although no throne or seat is visible). In his left hand he holds a book with a cross on it indicating at one and the same time that he is the *Logos*, or Word of God, and also that the book is the written word of God, the Gospels. His right hand is raised in a gesture of blessing.[95] The oval shape evokes the mandorla, or body halo, within which Christ is often shown. It is also suggestive of the *clipeus*, or shield, on which imperial Roman images and, later, images of Christ were depicted, as part of the visual symbols of imperial authority.[96] The position of the young Christ is identical to that of the two images of Christ enthroned that are located on the eastern walls of the sanctuary (S1) and the side chapel (C2), thereby emphasizing his divinity. These two paintings show the adult Christ as the ruler of heaven and earth. The iconographic type of the Virgin Mary holding a mandorla containing the Christ Child is sometimes called the *Nikopoios*, or "bringer of victory." In the medieval Coptic visual tradition Mary's hands support the disk from below, not from the middle.[97]

Two theories have been proposed to account for this iconographic type. In one, put forward by Hans Belting, the oval is a literal shield (clipeus) and therefore a physical object—a painted icon of Christ—which the Virgin holds. The primary meaning conveyed is the divinity of Christ, presented here as an image within an image, for worship. The scenario recalls the imperial Roman and Byzantine practices of worshiping the divine ruler's image.[98] In the second theory, expressed by Gustav Kühnel, the image depicts the Virgin Mary pregnant with Christ. "The clipeus before Mary's chest illustrates literally the verse in Psalms 46:6 'God is in the midst of her.' The unseen presence . . . inside her is alluded to by means of the picture of Emmanuel in the clipeus. The representation should be interpreted as the Logos before the Incarnation."[99] Kühnel's reading takes into account the resonance of the setting of this particular image of Christ, held as it is by the Virgin Mary, who is pronounced in the monogram framing her head as the Mother of God. The theories of Belting and Kühnel are complementary. The depiction of Mary as a mother also has a relevance within the larger setting of monastic leaders within a monastic church, because Mary was described by the prominent theologian and patriarch Cyril of Alexandria as "the mother of all the monks and all the nuns."[100] Mary belongs in the company of the monks painted in the eastern end of the nave as their mother, as a model of virginity and obedience, and as a focus of veneration.

THE KHURUS: SALVATION VISUALIZED

The khurus, which separates the nave from the sanctuary, is a feature unique to Coptic architecture. As we have seen, it was probably introduced in the seventh century to provide an additional buffer for the holiest part of the church, the eastern end. The shape of the khurus ceiling is distinctive and symbolic.[101] Two Coptic authors writing in the thirteenth and fourteenth centuries have explained that churches must include a vault, symbolic of Noah's ark, because both the church and the ark are ships of salvation.[102] The standard barrel vault in medieval Coptic churches is constructed of wood and built over the khurus.[103] In the Church of St. Antony, the vault is made of palm logs, and it has an irregular, almost undulating surface. The painted decoration now visible in the ceiling zone of the khurus postdates Theodore's program, but the essential shape of the ceiling and its symbolic meaning do not.[104] Salvation, the theme expressed in the arch of the ceiling, is carried out in the paintings from both periods in the khurus.

The two paintings on the inner face of the western khurus wall show the three Hebrews in the fiery furnace (K6; fig. 4.24, fig. 27, conclusion) and Abraham, Isaac, and Jacob in Paradise (K5; fig. 4.25). In the first image, the three young men are shown standing frontally in a gesture of prayer, with their hands held upraised, palms facing outward, amid the high flames of a furnace. The entire background is made of fire, the tops of the flames forking at head level. As we are told in the Book of Daniel, the three young Jews named Hananiah, Azariah, and Mishael, have

4.24
Three Hebrews (κ6–κ7; ADP/SA
1999)

4.25

Abraham, Isaac, and Jacob in
paradise (к5; ADP/SA 1999)

refused King Nebuchadnezzar's order to worship a golden idol.[105] In a rage, the king orders them burned alive in the furnace, but an angel of the Lord appears and protects them from the flames, causing the king to recognize the power of their God (Dn 3).

Three vignettes adjoin the right side of the painting, on the northern wall of the khurus (K7). Before the paintings were cleaned, the lowest scene was completely obscured, but even without being able to see this important section, van Moorsel correctly asserted that these scenes belonged to the narrative of the three Hebrews and not to the large framed subject to their right, George (K8; figs. 7.31–7.34; fig. 25, conclusion). The uppermost scene shows King Nebuchadnezzar, flanked by lance bearers. Similar guards or soldiers stand in the middle register, along with two identified as centurions (K7.3). A mass of soldiers holding whips fills the lowest zone, keeping the three young men inside the inferno. The extreme discrepancy in scale between the Hebrews and angel, on the one hand, and the king and soldiers, on the other, makes the narrative relation between these figures confusing for the modern viewer. The tie between them is made visually explicit, however, in the whip held by the soldier closest to the young men, which actually penetrates the interior of the furnace. Also, the brickwork under the feet of the Hebrews extends around the wall and into the space inhabited by Nebuchadnezzar's soldiers. The three young men were interpreted as an Old Testament type for the resurrection of Christ, and as such they work well in the khurus, along with the three patriarchs and the later paintings in the ceiling zone above.[106]

The scene on the other side of the western wall shows the faithful, saved in heaven. It is a scene of Abraham, Isaac, and Jacob in Paradise, holding in their arms the small, childlike figures of the saved (K5; fig. 4.25). The three patriarchs were the subjects of considerable veneration in Egypt and elsewhere, by Christians, Jews, and Muslims.[107] The site of their burial is believed to be in Hebron, which was a destination of Christian pilgrimage as early as 384.[108] Additional intensity was focused on this site in 1119, when a cave containing buried remains was discovered beneath the shrine.[109] The Gospel according to Matthew recounts: "I tell you, many will come from the east and the west and sit at table with Abraham, Isaac, and Jacob in the kingdom of heaven" (Mt 8:11). Elaborating on this, the Coptic liturgy to commemorate the dead includes a reference to them: all "who have fallen asleep and are gone to their rest in the faith of Christ, vouchsafe to grant rest to all their souls in the bosom of our holy fathers, Abraham and Isaac

and Jacob: nourish them in a place of pasturage beside the waters of comfort, in the paradise of joy, whence sorrow and sighing and weeping have fled away, in the light of thy saints."[110] Coptic tombstones regularly included reference to these three, and one example from Esna, dated to A.M. 699, A.D. 983, describes the setting in similar terms: "Lord Jesus Christ, give repose to his soul in the place of repose, and throw him in the breast of Abraham, Isaac, and of Jacob, in your paradise, in a green place, below a restful spring, the place where sadness flees, and also lamentation, in the light of your saints. Amen."[111]

In the compelling painting of 1232/1233, the three patriarchs are seated on a long, continuous throne, set against a green background filled with fruit-bearing trees and small, gamboling figures. From left to right, the three virtually identical elders are clearly named: Jacob, Isaac, Abraham. Inscriptions above and to the right of each halo and additional ones on the decorated bands of their sleeves make this clear. An interesting organizational pattern that does not conform to Western expectations is especially clear here.[112] The patriarchs are arranged according to their usual hierarchical order, but within a cultural context that has adopted the Arabic orientation of reading from right to left: the sequence has Abraham at the right, Isaac in the middle, and Jacob at the left. Each of the patriarchs holds a diminutive man or woman in his lap, or "bosom." We know that the now-destroyed figure in Abraham's lap was Lazarus, the poor man in the Gospel parable (Lk 16:19–31). Only his feet are still visible, extending from underneath Abraham's left hand. The area around the border of Paradise was covered with plaster at some point after 1232/1233.[113] The conservators removed this upainted layer to reveal a fascinating vignette. The small naked man enveloped in flames and standing in a brick structure of some kind, outside of the border surrounding paradise, provides the principal clue in identifying Lazarus. This unhappy figure is labeled "Nineve, the unmerciful," and below the brick enclosure is the word "hell." The rich man, nameless in the gospel, is called Nineve in the Coptic tradition.[114] In Luke he is described as looking up from hell, seeing Lazarus in the bosom of Abraham, and begging for a drop of water to put on his tongue.[115] We see him stretching out the finger of one hand in his desperate plea for water and touching his parched tongue with a finger from his other hand. The theme of salvation expressed in the khurus by the architectural reference to Noah's ark, and the painted depictions of the three Hebrews, and the vision of paradise are made more precious by the small visual reminder that not everyone succeeds in attaining this goal.

4.26

Mercurius (κ3–κ4; ADP/SA 1999)

The two equestrian figures on the northern and southern walls are not part of the message of salvation expressed in the rest of the khurus. They are the two most popular martyrs in Egypt, George (κ8, north wall; figs. 6.24, 7.31) and Mercurius (κ3, south wall; fig. 4.26). George is included here for the second time in the 1232/1233 program, and that is proof of his importance, especially when one considers that Antony is shown only once (N1; fig. 7, introduction).[116] These two soldiers of Christ are shown here in the same format as the equestrian martyrs in the nave, and they perform one of the same functions. They are here as guardians, protecting the sanctuary.

The story of the martyrdom of George includes several remarkable features. George was subjected to an exceptionally creative range of tortures, including having perforated iron boots put on his feet, into which nails were hammered; being lacerated with stakes and then boiled; and having his head beaten with nails until "his brains poured out through his mouth white as milk."[117] After experiencing these and other horrors, George died, and Christ caused the pieces of his dismembered body to join together again, and revivified him. George was tortured further and put in jail, where Jesus came to him and promised to bring him back from the dead two more times. Jesus said that after his fourth demise: "I will make thee lie down with Abraham, Isaac, and Jacob."[118] We can picture this vision of heaven, painted as it is in the opposite end of the khurus (κ5; fig. 4.25). The scene in between these two depicts a seated figure wearing a turban, twisting his head around to look up at the enormous figure of

George on horseback (fig. 7.5). This is Pasikrates, who earned salvation by recording George's sufferings and miracles. As his text tells us, George made the following request of Christ: "Do thou write in the Book of Life the name of every one who shall write down my martyrdom and the sufferings which I have endured."[119]

In the large scene of George on the north wall, the saint is shown spearing the evil general Euchius, who, according to the Coptic account of George's martyrdom, took three thousand soldiers with him and wreaked havoc on the churches of Egypt. After torturing and killing numerous Christians, Euchius went to Syria to overthrow a famous shrine of George.[120] When the general entered the church, a lamp exploded and he was covered with burning oil. His flesh became leprous and, as his followers abandoned him, he finally died. The fateful lamp is shown within the martyrium church of the saint, to the left of Euchius.

Across the khurus from George is another much-beloved martyr: Mercurius. He is commonly known as Abu Sefein, or the "father of two swords," perhaps because an angel of the Lord gave the saint a sword.[121] A monastery dedicated to him still exists today in Old Cairo, only one example of almost thirty churches and monasteries dedicated to him, according to the record written by Abu al-Makarim in the thirteenth century.[122] Mercurius is shown here in richly colored dress, on a black horse with magnificent trappings, and accompanied by two pages (fig. 4.26). The fabric of the horse blanket is virtually identical to the splendid painted cloth draped over the arms of the cross, in the side chapel (c1; figs. 4.40, 6.18).[123] One of his two swords is in its scabbard, behind his saddle, and he holds a second sword in his left hand. The angel touching the blade in the upper right corner indicates its miraculous origin (fig. 31, conclusion). Mercurius spells out the significance of his armor in the account of his martyrdom, when he addresses the Roman Emperor Decius: "I have upon me the whole armor of God, and the breast-plate of faith, by means of which things I shall overcome all thy designs and all thy crafty arts in respect of me."[124] We see a painting of physical armor standing in for spiritual armor.

Though possessed of two swords, the saint nevertheless pierces the small crowned figure directly below him with a spear. This man is the Roman Emperor Julian the Apostate, who was killed by Mercurius's spear in a posthumous appearance of the saint. Basil of Cesarea, shown to the right of the horse's head, saw this event in a vision and discovered that Mercurius's spear was no longer in his martyrium church—the saint had removed it to kill Julian.[125] A delightful thirteenth-century Coptic version of this event describes Basil in his prison cell with an icon of Mercurius. After expressing frustration that he could not help his brethren in the fight against Julian, he notices that the saint's image has disappeared from the icon. It reappears, and the painted spear is covered with blood. When asked whether he had killed Julian, the saint's image nods.[126]

The odd event shown to the right of the Julian illustrates the murder of Mercurius's grandfather by two *cynocephaloi*, or dog-headed cannibals (fig. 7.1). Before Mercurius's birth, his father- and grandfather-to-be went hunting. The elder man was attacked and killed by the monsters, but God stopped them from killing the younger man, who was needed to father Mercurius. The two beasts prostrated themselves in front of him. God rendered their nature sweet, and they converted to Christianity.[127]

THE SANCTUARY: THE PLACE WHERE HEAVEN AND EARTH MEET

The paintings in the sanctuary are closely linked to the ritual events that take place in this space (figs. 4.27, 4.28). Therefore, however ill-equipped the art historian is to explain the subtleties of the ritual, it is clear that such an effort must be attempted in order properly to understand the paintings. In essence, the celebration of the Eucharist commemorates Christ's sacrifice on the cross. Bread and wine are transformed in the ritual by the infusion of the Holy Spirit into the flesh and blood of Christ. Christ explained the purpose of this act during the Last Supper, and commanded his apostles to repeat it as a form of remembrance. The ritual is enacted by priests and other attendants, and the Christian faithful consume these substances and receive grace and the forgiveness of sins through the sacrament.[128] The participants in this act—priests, deacons, cantors, and so on—perform actions in imitation of Christ, the apostles, angels, and the prophets. When the ritual actions are properly followed, God in the form of the Holy Spirit changes the bread and wine into Christ's flesh and blood, and the space of the sanctuary becomes the Heavenly Jerusalem.[129] The paintings depict what few people are spiritually elevated enough to see but what they believe to be actually happening.

ARCHITECTURAL SYMBOLISM

The thirteenth-century "Order of Priesthood," by an unknown author, describes the sanctuary in terms of both Old and New Testaments, following a traditional Christian system of comparison, in which Old Testament events foreshadow or prefigure the people and happenings of the New Testament. The layers of meaning that it creates are apparent in both the architecture and the paintings of the sanctuary. In a groundbreaking study of the architectural symbolism of the Coptic sanctuary, Gertrude J. M. van Loon summarizes the anonymous author's text. The writer first describes the construction of the Tabernacle and the Temple of Solomon, in the earthly Jerusalem. He explains that the offerings of animal sacrifices prefigured the Christian ritual of the eucharistic sacrifice. He next describes the Heavenly Jerusalem, according to the Revelation of St. John, including the throne of God, the four living creatures, and the twenty-four elders of the apocalypse. The anonymous author credits John with deciding to build a sanctuary as a visible reminder of these two Jerusalems, "firstly as a type of the Tabernacle and the inner dome called the Holy of Holies, the place where one prays for forgiveness, and secondly in accordance with what was left in his mind by the divine revelation. This altar room, we see it with seeing eyes, was going to be a work based on these two examples, the earthly and sublime heavenly."[130] The theme of sacrifice and also John's vision of the Heavenly Jerusalem are carried out in the paintings.

THE PAINTINGS

"The Order of Priesthood" explains that a dome must be included in the sanctuary of a church.[131] A dome rises above each of the three altars in the sanctuary of the Church of St. Antony, but the largest, and the only one that is painted, is that over the central altar. Indeed, the density of painting is greatest above and around this section. The center of the dome is filled with a bust-length image of Christ Pantocrator set within a double-banded, circular frame (s12; fig. 13, introduction; figs. 4.27, 6.20). Christ faces the viewer below and is oriented with his head at the west, so that the priest celebrating the liturgy and facing east can see this image right side up. Christ holds a book in his left hand and raises his right hand in a gesture of blessing. The roundel is surrounded by four cherubim and four other angels (s13–20). The cherubim are also called the four incorporeal beings and are sometimes shown as four separate creatures, as in the sanctuary apse surrounding the mandorla of Christ (s1; figs. 4.28, 6.15) and in the side chapel, in pairs, flanking the same image (c3, c10; figs. 4.38, 12.7). The dome rests on an octagonal drum. Each of its eight sides includes a window, centrally positioned. The paintings in the drum are largely destroyed, but each panel originally consisted of two angels flanking

4.27
Apse and central dome of the
sanctuary (s1, s12–s44, s46–s49;
ADP/SA 1999)

4.28

Sanctuary apse (s1; ADP/SA 6s 98)

4.29
Detail of sanctuary apse and part
of the sacrifice of Isaac (s1, s38;
ADP/SA 4s 98)

each window (s21–s28; fig. 13, introduction; fig. 4.27). The drum is set on a square, and the square is supported below by four piers, which frame the central bay of the sanctuary. The four sides of the upper walls are divided horizontally into two registers. The uppermost depicts a continuous band of the twenty-four elders of the apocalypse, wearing crowns and holding chalices (s33–s36). Below them, on the western and eastern faces of the wall, are abstract designs and angels (s37, s40, s41, s44). The southern and northern walls show Old Testament scenes that are typologically related to the Eucharist. The underside of the central archway between the khurus and the sanctuary is painted with bust-length portraits of the prophets (s45–s50). The undersides of the archways to the other two bays of the sanctuary are unpainted.

The painting of the large eastern apse is divided into two levels (s1; fig. 4.28). At the top, a large and impressive Christ in Majesty sits enthroned, facing the viewer (the priest and celebrants of the liturgy). As in the image of Christ in the dome, his left hand holds a book and his right hand is raised in blessing. His feet rest on an arc, inscribed with the words "Behold, heaven is my throne and the earth is my footstool," from Isaiah 66:1 (s1.7). This tells us that we are seeing a vision of Christ in heaven. He is enclosed within an oval with pointed ends, a mandorla, or body halo, as we saw in the nave (n36; 4.23). Appearing as if

from behind the mandorla are the heads of an eagle, an ox, a lion, and a man, each set within layers of wings covered with eyes. To the left is a red sun, and to the right is a gray moon, both with faces. The archangels Michael and Gabriel gaze upward at the image of the Lord in reverence (figs. 4.29). The zone below this, in the bottom of the apse, is painted with an enthroned Virgin and Child with the archangels Michael and Gabriel. The Virgin sits looking directly out at the viewer, holding the Christ Child with her left hand and gesturing toward him with her right. In contrast to her static, frontal pose, Christ sits sideways, looking up at his mother and extending his right hand toward her, suggesting movement. This hand assumes the usual position signifying blessing. In his left hand he holds a scroll with crosses on it. The two archangels stand frontally, holding in their left hands large disks with letters signifying "Jesus Christ is victorious" (s1.11, s1.13). The upper edges of Michael's wings are shown as bands of flame.

Just as the architecture is symbolically expressive of sacrifice and of the earthly and heavenly Jerusalems, using elements and events from the Old Testament as prefigurations of those in the New Testament, so also are the paintings. Four kinds of written sources help the outsider to understand the paintings' meaning. The first is the Bible, and the second is the liturgy itself, the words recited as part of the celebration of the Eucharist. A third is the

4.30
Anonymous patriarch (s8; ADP/SA 1999)

ritual of monastic initiation. Descriptions of the miraculous events or visions that relate to the ritual and the paintings provide a fourth kind of textual source.[132]

Consider the paintings in the apse of Christ in Majesty (s1) and in the dome of Christ Pantocrator (s12), surrounded by cherubim and other angels, in light of the following texts (figs. 4.27, 4.28). Note also that images of priests are included in the sanctuary, on piers flanking the altar and in the southern end (s8, s9, s3–s7; figs. 4.30, 4.43, 7.14). In the late seventh century, the priest Theodore recounted the following: "I have heard in many places that at the time when the oblation is about to be offered up, the Son of God comes down with all His ranks and stands upon the altar until they have finished giving communion to all the people."[133] Similarly, another account tells us that "one day, Bishop Pisentius of Qift [painted in the nave, N29], . . . admonished a priest, who had behaved [in a] disorderly [manner] at the altar and reminded him: 'Dost thou not know that myriads of angels and Cherubim and Seraphim stand before thee upon the Sanctuary, singing with sweet voices in one chant?'"[134] The spiritual subjects that appear during the ritual event are painted directly above the altar. They are also referred to in the Coptic liturgy, when, during feasts of the Virgin and angels, the priest reads:

> Behold, Emmanuel our God, the Lamb of God, Who takes away the sins of all the world, is with us today on this table, Who sits on the throne of His glory, and before Whom stand all the heavenly orders, Whom the angels praise with the voices of blessing, and before Whom the archangels fall down and worship.
>
> The four Incorporeal Beasts sing the hymn of the Trisagion, and the twenty-four priests sitting on their seats, and twenty-four crowns of gold on their heads, and twenty-four golden vials in their hands, full of incense which is the prayers of the saints, and they worship before Him who is living unto the age of ages.[135]

The paintings also correspond to the description of the Heavenly Jerusalem, in the Book of Revelation. John describes the enthroned Christ (shown twice in the painted program of the sanctuary: in the dome, s12, and in the eastern apse, s1, fig. 4.27), the four incorporeal beings (also shown in both locations: s1 and s13, s15, s17, s19), and the twenty-four elders of the apocalypse (s33–s36; fig. 4.31). Describing paintings of this subject, the Coptic priest Abu al-Barakat ibn Kabar (d. 1324) wrote that "it shows Him as the word of God"—that is, the Logos.[136]

4.31 ABOVE RIGHT
One of the twenty-four elders of the apocalypse (s36; ADP/SA 20 s187 98)

Four events recounted in the Old Testament are pictured above the altar: the sacrifice of Jephtha's daughter (s39), the sacrifice of Isaac (s38), the meeting of Abraham and Melchizedek (s43), and Isaiah and the burning coal (s42). All of them foreshadow the sacrifice of Christ on the cross and its ritual commemoration on the altar below. In addition to this central meaning, some of the paintings also make references to the monastic life. The two images of sacrifice on the southern wall below the dome and over the altar are connected to each other as well as to the sacrifice of Christ and the ritual actions in the sanctuary (fig. 4.32). In the scene on the right (s39), King Jephtha is shown in the act of severing his daughter's neck. He had asked God for victory in battle and had vowed to sacrifice the first living thing he saw coming from his house upon his return home. Greeted by his much beloved daughter, he duly sacrificed her (Jgs 11:30–40). This subject is rare and may appear here because of a symbolic relationship with monastic initiation. According to this explanation, the novice presents himself as a sacrifice, paralleling the sacrifices of both Jephtha's daughter and Isaac. The novice offers his life to God and thereby becomes a monk.[137] In the much more commonly depicted image of the sacrifice of Isaac, Abraham prepares himself to commit the terrible

4.32

Sacrifices of Isaac and Jephtha's

daughter (s38–s39; ADP/SA 7s

170 98)

4.33

Isaiah and the burning coal (s42),
and Abraham and Melchizedek
(s43) (ADP/SA 8s 170 98)

deed at God's command but is stopped at the last moment
by an angel of the Lord (Gn 22:1–14). In these paintings,
the two children are shown almost identically: both are
naked to the waist, and bound, with their heads pulled
back by their fathers. The men firmly grasp their children's
hair and expose their necks to knives. In each case, a fire
burns on an altar in front of the victims. While the inscriptions around Jephtha are largely illegible, those in the
scene on the left are clear. Next to Abraham's head the text
reads: "He does not wish to kill Isaac" (s38.4). Indeed, nor
does Jephtha wish to kill his daughter, if the longing gaze
he directs to Abraham is any indication. The visual similarities in the two scenes underscore the painful difference:
Jephtha's daughter's eyes are closed, the knife her father
holds has severed her neck, and blood pours down her
chest. Abraham's gesture is stopped inches away from
Isaac's neck by the angel's voice, indicated by a hand extending into the picture from above. An inscription next
to the hand says: "the voice" (s38.1), and one next to the
sacrificial replacement reads "the ram bound" (s38.3).

The biblical account of Melchizedek and his meeting
with Abraham is brief (Gn 14:17–21; fig. 4.33). Melchizedek

is described as a priest and a king of Salem who offers the
victorious Abraham bread and wine. Considerable apocryphal literature elaborates on this short passage. Legends
about the parentage and significance of Melchizedek
abound from the first centuries of Christianity, based in
part on Jewish sources.[138] In early Christian and Byzantine
art, Melchizedek is a regal figure wearing a crown, dressed
as either a king or a priest.[139] In medieval Coptic art, however, Melchizedek is shown as an unkempt hermit.[140] One
primary source of influence for this unusual imagery is a
tradition that Melchizedek was a holy ascetic who lived in
a cave on Mount Tabor.[141] Pilgrimage texts indicate that
this notion developed after the Arab conquest of Egypt.[142]
A particularly compelling eyewitness account of this cave
and its significance comes from the Russian Abbot Daniel,
who traveled to the Holy Land between 1106 and 1108, a
century before Theodore worked in the Monastery of St.
Antony:

And on this same Mount Tabor, in a level place, there is
a very marvellous cave like a small cellar cut in the
rock. . . . In front of the doors of this cave grow small fig

4.34
David (S49)

trees and around it grow little trees of every kind. . . . In this small cave lived the holy Melchisedek, and Abraham came to him here and called him thrice, saying: "Man of God!" Melchisedek came out and brought bread and wine, and having made a sacrificial altar in the cave, offered up the bread and wine in sacrifice and this sacrifice was immediately taken up to God in heaven; and here Melchisedek blessed Abraham, and Abraham cut his hair and nails, for Melchisedek was hairy. This was the origin of the liturgy of bread and wine instead of unleavened bread. Of this the prophet says: "Thou art a priest for ever after the order of Melchisedek." (Ps 110:4)[143]

The wild hair and eyelashes of Melchizedek in the painting at the Monastery of St. Antony make sense in this context, which probably developed from an apocryphal story of Melchizedek that was widely available in the Mediterranean, in several languages, including Coptic and Arabic (fig. 6.12).[144] In this tale, Melchizedek realizes that there is only one God and flees his home when his father, in an anxious attempt to appease the gods, endeavors to offer Melchizedek up as a human sacrifice. When Melchizedek's father cannot find him, he offers up Melchizedek's brother instead, and Melchizedek asks God to make "Hades come and swallow them up." After seeing that God has heeded his prayer, Melchizedek goes to Mount Tabor "in great fear."

> And going into the brush of the forest, he remained there for seven years. He went about naked as from his mother's womb, and his fingernails became overgrown, and the hair on his head hung down to his loins, and his back became like the shell of a tortoise. . . . And after the seven years, a voice came to Abraham saying "Abraham, Abraham . . . saddle your beast and take costly garments and a razor and go up on Mt. Tabor and cry out three times 'Man of God!' And a wild man will appear; however, don't be afraid of him. Rather, shave him, and clip his nails, and clothe him, and be blessed by him."

And later, after this first meeting, Melchizedek met Abraham a second time, returning victorious from battle, and "gave him privately a cup of wine, putting down for him a piece of bread, and also for his people, being 318 men. . . . And thus he became the prototype of the bloodless sacrifice of the Savior, bringing an offering in holiness."[145] In the painting, the altar at the mouth of the cave is clearly visible. It parallels the actual three-dimensional altar below, as the offering of the chalice and bread to Abraham and his men parallels the priest's offering to the community of the faithful.

The cave and the hermitlike appearance of Melchizedek have been given a monastic interpretation, with good reason, by Paul van Moorsel.[146] Antony was only one of numerous ascetics and monks who lived in caves, a tradition that continues even today. Building on van Moorsel's association, it seems possible that the prominence of the scissors and knife or razor in the painting were intended to relate to the ritual tonsuring of the monk at his initiation. The following passages from the monastic rites of initiation in the Coptic Church equate hair with physical desires and the tonsured state with grace: "Bestow on him perfect submission, and may it be his purpose to turn himself away from the pleasures of nature, that, in the laying aside of the hair of his head, he may cast away from him unseemly acts and may receive unto himself the help of grace and the Holy Spirit. Take a pair of scissors, cut the hair of his head in the form of the Cross."[147]

The Coptic liturgy makes explicit the connection between the depiction of Isaiah and the burning coal on the north wall (S42; figs. 4.33, 5.8) and the consumption of the Eucharist. During the liturgy the priest says: "As thou didst cleanse the lips of thy servant Isaiah the prophet when one of the seraphim took a live coal in the tongs from off the altar and laid it on his mouth and said to him 'Lo, this hath touched thy lips: it shall take away thine iniquities and purge all thy sins': in like manner for us also humble sinners purge our souls and our bodies and our lips and our hearts, and grant us this true coal, quickening soul and body and spirit, which is the holy body and the precious blood of thy Christ."[148] In the painting, we see the seraph (depicted, like the cherub, with eyed wings and four heads) holding the burning coal to Isaiah's lips. This action is repeated by the priest when he offers the bread and wine to the communicants, whose sins are thereby forgiven.

The unusual inclusion of Jephtha's sacrifice and the extraordinary depiction of the meeting between Melchizedek and Abraham suggest that this program was thought out with care. While all four of the Old Testament

4.35 UPPER LEFT
Eulogia loaf from the Monastery of St. Antony, next to the painted disk held by the archangel Michael (s1)

4.36 LOWER RIGHT
Mark (s11; ADP/SA 7s 98)

narrative scenes depicted above the altar have a primary level of meaning that relates them to the Eucharist, three provide pointed visual models for the monk. Like Jephtha's daughter and Isaac, the monk sacrifices himself and is reborn in Christ. Like Melchizedek, he joins the ranks of Antony and other holy ascetics and cave dwellers, and also casts aside his earthly passions with the ritual tonsuring of his hair. The rare depiction of the meeting of Abraham and Melchizedek shows both that Coptic artists and theologians were sufficiently connected with the eastern Mediterranean world to be aware of the cave and traditions surrounding it, and that they adapted it for their own purposes.[149]

The archway between the khurus and the sanctuary is painted with portraits of six Old Testament prophets. Reading from south to north, they are Jeremiah, Elijah, Isaiah, Moses, David, and Daniel (s45–s50). These figures also relate to the service, to the prophetic relation between Old Testament and New Testament events, to the rest of the painted program, and to its monastic setting. It has already been pointed out that Isaiah (s47), for example, had a vision of the Lord on a throne supported by creatures with wings covered with eyes, and the heads of a man, an ox, a lion, and an eagle, and we see this vision painted in the upper zone of the apse (s1; fig. 4.28). Jerome described the prophets as "the monks of the Old Testament."[150] The image of the prophet David (s49; fig. 4.34) is a good example of the way these paintings could have multiple points of reference. As the author of the Psalms, which were read in the church and were also an important part of the monk's private spiritual work, he clearly belongs here.[151] David was also a model for the cantor, as a passage in the *Life* of Shenoute tells us, in which the monastic father says of the cantor: "Behold, there is a choir of angels around him responding to him. Look, there is the prophet David

standing at his side and giving him the words which need to be said."[152]

The largest single composition in the sanctuary is the painting in the apse (s1; fig. 4.28). It is divided into two zones, which can be understood to signify the two aspects of Christ: divine and human. In the upper zone, Christ in Majesty sits enthroned in a mandorla, supported by the four living creatures. These four guard the throne of the Lord and serve as models for ceaseless prayer. They are also important as intercessors.[153] This role is especially relevant in the paintings of the side chapel. In the upper zone of the sanctuary apse, Christ is shown in heaven, using the earth as his footstool, depicted as an arched support for his feet (s1.7). He holds a large book with a cross on it—literally a bible, but also a symbolic reference to Christ himself, who is the Word of God, the divine Logos. The archangels Gabriel and Michael face Christ and raise their hands in prayer (fig. 4.29). The simultaneous presence of the sun and moon suggests the timeless zone of eternity that Christ inhabits. Below, in the image of the Virgin and Child, the Word or Logos made flesh is shown, seated in his mother's arms and holding a scroll. Mary is presented as the Mother of God, seated on a throne that is equal in magnificence to that of Christ's above. The two

4.37

Unfinished decoration, north wall

of sanctuary (s10; ADP/SA 1999)

zones show Christ as eternal, in a timeless realm, and also as the divine and human child, incarnate, in following the human cycle of birth and growth within time. The pair is flanked by the archangels Michael and Gabriel. These two hold medallions embossed with letters signifying "Jesus Christ is victorious" (s1.11, s1.13; fig. 4.35). These disks are visually similar to Coptic Eucharistic loaves.[154]

The remaining paintings in the sanctuary all depict patriarchs (popes), the foremost rank of bishop. In a niche behind the northern altar sits the enthroned Mark the Evangelist, known as the founder of Christianity in Egypt and thereby also the founder of the Coptic Church (s11; fig. 4.36). The southern niche includes a painting of one of the most important figures in the early church. He is Athanasius, a patriarch of the Coptic Church and also author of the *Life* of Antony the Great (s2; fig. 6.8).[155] Two standing figures flank the main altar, on the piers that support the arched entrance to the khurus (s8, s9; fig. 4.30). We know that they are patriarchs from their dress and fragments of inscriptions, but too many letters are missing to permit additional identification. Before the conservation efforts of Luzi and De Cesaris, these two figures were covered with blank plaster and their existence was unknown. Five more patriarchs stand in an arcade, located high up on the wall in the southern bay of the sanctuary. From left to right they are Severus of Antioch (s3), Dioscorus (s4; fig. 7.14), Theophilus (s5), Peter (s6), and one anonymous patriarch, possibly Benjamin (s7; fig. 4.43). Severus, the only non-Coptic patriarch portrayed, is included here for his pivotal role as a defender of the faith.[156] Similar painted figures were planned for the wall directly across the sanctuary from these five, but they were never

completed. Additional patriarchs would likely have been shown here, almost definitely including Cyril of Alexandria, due to his prominence in the Coptic Church. This area (s10) also was covered under plaster before recent restoration.

One of Luzi and De Cesaris's most surprising discoveries took place in the sanctuary. Under blank, smooth plaster they found remnants of a painted frame (fig. 4.37). Its band of pearls edged with red and the vegetal decoration within a triangle are identical to decorative elements elsewhere in Theodore's program.[157] The artists never painted the planned figures in this frame. It is clear that their work was abruptly terminated. This explains why the painted program of the sanctuary is uneven, and also why another team of artists was brought in to work in the church so soon after Theodore left, as is shown in chapters 8 and 9. A buckled wall at the northern end of the eastern sanctuary wall, above the painting of Mark (s11; fig. 4.36), and evidence of plaster repairs within the unfinished painting on the north wall suggest that a physical collapse played a role in the cessation of Theodore's work. Perhaps Theodore was hurt and unable to finish. It seems likely that we shall never know.

The absence of all but one apostle in the entire sanctuary program is interesting. In earlier Coptic art, the apostles were a regular element in the apse program.[158] In the Coptic tradition, Mark is known as an apostle.[159] The fact that the single apostle included is Mark, who is known as the founder of Christianity in Egypt, is telling (fig. 4.36). The strongly Egyptian character of the nave paintings is continued here in the sanctuary, and the genealogical relationship is paralleled. The Coptic patriarchs are the successors to Mark, just as the monks are the spiritual descendants of the martyrs.

The enthroned Christ as shown in the dome and the apse, and indeed all the figures painted on the walls should be understood as being present during the celebration of the Eucharist. An account from a priest named Banub, which dates to the early thirteenth century—just when Theodore's paintings were created—makes this point clear:

> I celebrated the Divine Liturgy. . . . And when it was the time of the Aspasmos, which is the [Prayer] of Consolation, there appeared above on the dome of the altar a person seated on a throne, and . . . a person standing before him. . . . Then there appeared at the back of all the dome riders on horses like the pictures of the Saints which are in the churches, and they were turning about

4.38

Deesis Chapel (C1–C3, C10; ADP/SA

1999)

4.39

Ceiling window, Deesis Chapel

(ADP/SA 57 159 97)

the dome, and the tails of their horses were swishing, and all of them, namely the people, witnessed them. And when they reached the throne, they bowed in greeting, and they passed by, and they continued thus up to the time of the Communion, [and] they departed. And the like of this had appeared in the Church of Hanut, . . . the Church of Sabas, . . . the Church of the Mistress, . . . and in the Church of the Martyr Abba John, . . . and the Muslim inhabitants of the town testified to this.[160]

In conjunction with this vision, consider the final section of the liturgy, when the priest asks for blessings and intercession on behalf of the servants of God from many of the angels and saints depicted in both the sanctuary and the nave:

> By the intercession of the holy glorious ever Virgin Theotokos St. Mary and the prayers and the supplications of the holy archangels Michael and Gabriel, and St. John the forerunner and baptist and martyr, . . . and our holy fathers the apostles, and St. Mark the apostle and evangelist and martyr, and the holy patriarch Severus and our righteous father the great Abba Antony and our father Abba Paul and the three Abba Macarius and our father Abba John and our father Abba Pishoi and our Roman fathers [Maximus and Domitius] and our father Abba Moses and the forty-nine martyrs and the holy Abba John the Black and all the choirs of the saints, through whose prayers and supplications vouchsafe us, O our master, to attain unto a part and a lot with them in the kingdom of heaven.[161]

Almost all of the angels and saints included in the passages from Priest Banub and the liturgy are also depicted in Theodore's paintings throughout the church. This correlation demonstrates that the paintings were intended to show the spiritual reality that most humans are not able to see. In a sense, one can imagine the entire church as a stage set in the round, filled during services with human and sacred players, the latter visible through the paintings that cover its walls.

THE SIDE CHAPEL

Located through an annex (fig. 21, introduction; fig. 4.4), off of the southeastern corner of the nave, the side chapel may be the earliest site of devotion in the church and even the monastery. As Jones has observed, the eastern orientation is at a slight angle to that of the rest of the church, suggesting that the two spaces were not planned at the same time. Also, the chapel's floor is higher than that of the nave and annex, a feature determined by the gradual rising, in steplike levels, of the mountain at the foot of which the monastery is set. The chapel may have originally been a cave, perhaps even the first cave of St. Antony.[162] The space is an intimate one, accommodating at most two or three people with ease (fig. 4.38). The chapel is essen-

4.40
Niche of the precious cross (c1;
ADP/SA 10s 163 97)

tially a deep niche, with curving walls and a ceiling that arches overhead. An altar fills the center of the floor. Natural light enters from a small window above the entrance in the western wall (fig. 4.39). The painted program that we see today is not the earliest one. Remnants of sixth- to seventh-century paintings are visible on the underside of the arched entrance (fig. 19, introduction; figs. 3.1, 3.3, 4.39).[163] The conservators have noted the existence of paintings underneath those by Theodore and his team, so this chapel clearly predates the thirteenth century on the evidence of the paintings alone.

Paintings dating to 1232/1233 cover the entire upper half of the chapel, and a small, deep niche located in the lower part of the eastern wall (figs. 4.38, 4.40). The upper part of the program is an elaborate image of intercession and prayer, in which the Virgin Mary (c10), John the Bap-

tist (c3), and the four living creatures (c3, c10) face an image of the divine Christ in Majesty (c2). We see him here as we have before, seated on a magnificent throne, set within a mandorla, with his right hand raised in blessing and his left hand balancing a book on his left leg. What distinguishes this image from the almost identical one in the sanctuary apse (s1; fig. 4.28) is the fact that the four creatures stand apart from the mandorla, and angels take their places supporting this halo. This visual presentation of the four creatures underscores their importance in the painted program of the chapel.

The cherubim seen elsewhere in the church with their four heads have been separated into four single-headed creatures (fig. 12.7).[164] The standing Virgin Mary and John the Baptist (fig. 1.4) are shown with their hands raised toward Christ in a composition called the *Deesis*.[165]

4.41

Silk textile, Reliquary of St. Isidore, León, Real Colegiata de San Isidoro, León (Courtesy of C.T. Little)

This term refers to the act they are engaged in: petitioning Christ on behalf of humankind. The four creatures stand in the same pose, and because we know from textual sources that they intercede for all living things, we can read the entire group as a painted prayer for intercession. Theodore, taking advantage of his position as master painter, has included a small inscription that conforms with the intercessory character of the program: "Lord Jesus Christ, have pity on me" (c2.6). It is located at Christ's feet as if it were the petitioner himself.

The painting in the niche is of an elaborately patterned cross, draped with fabric and framed by two censing angels (fig. 4.40). The inscriptions convey the importance of this symbol, calling it "the precious Cross" (c1.3), "the tree of life" (c1.2), and "Jesus Christ" (c1.1). The angels framing it swing bowls containing incense, evoking a passage from the Coptic liturgy that fits the larger program as well: "We pray to thee, our master, accept our supplications and let our prayer be set forth in thy sight as the incense and the lifting up of our hands as an evening sacrifice: for thou art the true evening sacrifice, who was himself offered up for our sins on the precious cross after the will of thy good Father, who art blessed with him and the Holy Ghost the lifegiver and of one substance with thee, now and ever and world without end. Amen."[166]

The inclusion of a prominent painted cross in the program may also have a pro-Christian, anti-Muslim resonance. Prohibitions against crosses exist from the first years after the Islamic conquest of Egypt, prescribing in some cases the destruction of all crosses, and in others only of those displayed on the exteriors of buildings.[167] The seventh-century Syrian author Pseudo-Methodius uses the cross as the sign of a victorious Christianity in the face of Islam.[168] And although the intensity of the cult of the cross seems to have decreased in Byzantium after iconoclasm, the major role it played in Coptic church paintings, at the Monastery of St. Antony and elsewhere, suggests that the cult did not decline in Egypt.[69]

The fabric shown hanging over the arms of the cross suggests an additional layer of meaning for this image. The textile is of high quality, and cloth with a similar pattern is shown elsewhere in the Church of St. Antony, and also throughout the Mediterranean in contemporary or earlier paintings, dressing emperors and prophets, and covering the bier of the Virgin Mary.[170] A reliquary of St. Isidore made in León in the middle of the eleventh century (fig. 4.41), is lined with pieces of silk that bear a close resemblance to the painted cloth hanging on the cross in the Deesis Chapel. The León textile is related to cloth from a North African Ummayad workshop, and the patterns are Near Eastern in origin.[171] The painted textile suggests great luxury in all of its settings. Here it competes for lavish pattern and color with the cross itself, the tree of life.

The combination of a niche setting, the elaborate decoration, expensive fabric, inscriptions, and censing angels all draw the viewer's attention to the cross and suggest that it plays an important part in the larger iconographic composition of the Deesis Chapel. Although research on this subject has so far failed to yield a medieval text to support the following interpretation, modern practice at the Monastery of St. Antony consists of the placement of fabric on a large processional cross, kept in the main sanctuary by the altar. It represents the shroud of Christ, which he has cast off (fig. 4.42). A black cloth is used during Passion Week, a white cloth is draped on the cross for Easter and Christmas, and a patterned fabric is otherwise used. If this tradition is ancient, as seems likely, considering the cult of the cross in Egypt and the generally conservative nature of the Coptic Church, then we see an image of the cross that signifies the resurrected Christ.[172] Petitions for intercession with Christ have as their ultimate goal salvation—in other

4.42 ABOVE RIGHT

Draped processional cross, modern, Church of the Holy Apostles, Monastery of St. Antony

4.43
Patriarchs Dioscorus, Theophilus,
Peter, and Benjamin (?) (s4–s7;
ADP/SA 9s 166 98)

words, everlasting life in Christ. The inclusion of fabric on the cross in the Deesis Chapel makes a visual reference to the divine Christ, whose resurrection and ascension Christians hope to emulate.[173]

Analysis of the program of the paintings dated to 1232/1233 in the Church of St. Antony shows it to be carefully constructed. Each section of the church has its own principal theme, although paintings can and do have more than one level of meaning, and relations with paintings throughout the church. The paintings in the nave demonstrate the vitality of Christianity in Egypt, with specific reference to the martyrs and their successors, monks. This theme is historically appropriate, coming as it does shortly after the possible repossession of the Monastery of St. Antony by Copts, from Syrians. It is also particularly fitting at this site, because Antony the Great is the father of monasticism. The paintings in the khurus are about faith, salvation, and, in a small visual aside, the consequences

of sin. The paintings in the sanctuary are intimately connected to the ritual mysteries enacted in this space and depict spiritual realities. We see the Egyptian theme of the nave repeated in the lateral rooms of the sanctuary, with their emphasis on the Coptic tradition (fig. 4.43). The paintings everywhere in the church exemplify the use of imitation as a method of spiritual ascent. They also repeatedly underscore the significance of the Old Testament prophets and events as precursors to the New Testament, particularly the paintings in the khurus and sanctuary. Such unusual visual elements as the hairy, naked Melchizedek show that the Copts were participants in the world of Christian pilgrimage and culture outside of Egypt, and adapted it for their own uses. Altogether, the program is a masterful demonstration of theology and Coptic monastic identity, compellingly expressed in visual terms, in the early thirteenth century.

CHAPTER 5 THEODORE'S STYLE, THE ART OF CHRISTIAN EGYPT, AND BEYOND

The newly visible early thirteenth-century paintings in the Church of St. Antony are so greatly at odds with art historical expectations that they mandate a near total reevaluation of Coptic art after the Arab conquest of Egypt. Until recently, it has been possible to dismiss post–seventh or eighth century Coptic art as being cut off from interaction with artistic currents outside of Egypt, and also as lacking a strong, internal artistic force.[1] The dating of Coptic art of any period is often still based on guesswork, for some of the most significant finds of Coptic paintings were excavated without serious analysis of the material evidence, and we lack contextual data for many more.[2] New discoveries of important Coptic wall paintings, covered for centuries by layers of plaster, add impressively to the corpus of Coptic art between about 1000 and 1300. The most significant of these, from the Syrian and Naqlun Monasteries and the Monastery of the Romans, show the richness of Coptic art in this period. But even the most remarkable of the new discoveries are only fragmentary remains from much larger programs. Add to this the fact that inscriptions with dates are rare, and the confusion that surrounds the character and chronology of Coptic art becomes understandable.[3]

Although art historians have known the paintings in the Monastery of St. Antony at least since the early twentieth century, these images have been virtually invisible under their covering of soot and later overpainting. Paul van Moorsel, quite understandably, described them as being of modest artistic quality.[4] The pioneering Coptic art historian Jules Leroy wrote as recently as 1982 that the most important Coptic paintings, after the preconquest examples from Bawit, belonged to the Monastery of St.

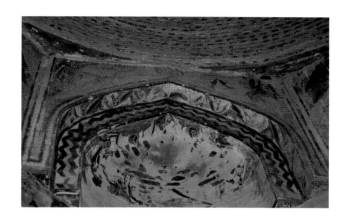

Macarius, in the Wadi al-Natrun (figs. 5.1, 5.18, 5.19, 6.11).[5] Although these are certainly impressive, they in no way surpass those which we can now see clearly at the Monastery of St. Antony, and are both far fewer in number and significantly less well preserved.

The paintings in the Church of St. Antony were obscured to such an extent that in their cleaned state they should be considered as a new discovery in the history of Coptic art. One example will make this point unequivocally. A comparison of the precleaning image of Theodore Stratelates (N22) with the same image after conservation (figs. 5.2, 5.3) reveals striking differences. In the overpainted version, the saint's face was painted with shaky and uneven lines, the skirt of his tunic was an unappealing green, his shield was unadorned, and the sword hilt was roughly drawn. In the cleaned painting, now stripped of its later "refreshment," one can immediately see that the lines and colors have been applied with confidence. The artist has rendered Theodore's face with skill, conveying an im-

5.1
Annunciation to the shepherds, ca. 1200, wall painting, Haikal of St. Mark, Monastery of St. Macarius, Wadi al-Natrun

pression of alertness. The skirt of his tunic is now blue. His
shield is elaborated with an elegant decoration, including
an Arabic inscription around its edge. Not only is the hilt
of his sword cleanly defined, but a composite bow is also
visible next to it.[6] The combination of soot and overpainting masked the artistic force and even elements of the
dress and weaponry in the original painting. The cleaned
painting shows a well-conceived composition, dominated
by the figure of St. Theodore astride his horse. Without
confusion or disharmony, the Coptic artist has filled the
field of the painting completely. The motionless, frontal
head and torso of the saint stabilize the forward movement of the horse. The woman and the horse's head on the
right are balanced by the saint's cloak and right arm, seen
on the left. Theodore stabs the serpentlike dragon through
the head with his cross-topped spear, but he looks out at
us as if the act was effortless. Receiving the crown of martyrdom from heaven, the saint is above temporal concerns.
In a smaller scale, the petitioning mother, below the
horse's head, and her two sons, under the horse, express
the drama of the narrative moment and the anxieties of
everyday people. The artist has used devices such as scale,
facial expression, and composition to convey the different
states of being of the figures (holy vs. secular), and the elements in the story. All the figures, including the horse, express personality.

The condition of the paintings in the Monastery of
St. Antony is significantly better than that of other recent
Coptic finds. It is also by far the most complete program

from this period, and it includes inscriptions with a precise date: 1232/1233.[7] Because only small sections of these
paintings were covered with plaster, most of the images
lack the destructive traces of later plaster applications,
marked by gouges in the earlier plaster. Before their cleaning, it was not possible to identify with confidence the en-
tirety of the program that we have here attributed to
Theodore and his workshop.[8] The clarity with which the
viewer can now see and comprehend the full program
makes these paintings a great resource for identifying the
characteristics of a major Coptic workshop, operating in
the first half of the thirteenth century, and also helps with
the establishment of a chronology of Coptic painting.

Theodore's Style

The style of Theodore's paintings is characterized by a confident and vigorous use of line, color, and pattern. The
subject matter is representational—that is to say, it consists largely of persons, incorporeal beings, and identifiable objects. However, these subjects are rendered with a
two-dimensional approach to space. Thirteenth-century
Coptic art uses visual tools that are unfamiliar to many
Westerners. Modern Western viewers commonly use Italian Renaissance art as a standard against which to evaluate
other artistic systems. Renaissance art strives to convince
us that paint on a two-dimensional surface is actually an
opening into space. Its tools are perspective and model-
ing—in other words, the use of light and shadow to suggest mass. What we see here, in the paintings by Theodore

5.4 LEFT

From right, Abraham, Isaac, and Jacob in paradise (K5; ADP/SA 1999)

5.5 RIGHT

Virgin Mary and Christ Child (S1; ADP/SA 6s 98)

and his workshop, is something very different: a representational art that is expressed through conventions, almost diagrams, built on linear schemata, and filled with patterns and saturated colors.

The picture is conceived first and foremost as a colored pattern. Large, almost life-size figures fill the pictorial field and gaze out at the viewer. They are delineated with heavy black lines, both around the outsides and within their fields of dense color. The lines often segment parts of the body and clothing, almost as if the artist were working in a medium that required this technique, like stained glass or enamel. We see this feature in the hair and right forearm of the patriarch Jacob, and in the arms, torso, and legs of the small person who sits on his lap (K5; fig. 5.4). Smaller figures, sometimes in movement, occupy the periphery of the framed space, and less often its center, but do not unbalance the fixity and frontality of the principal, large personages. These diminutive beings are often engaged in actions that tell stories about the saints, but these events exist within time, while the major figures, with their grand scale and iconic presentation, seem to reside in an eternal, timeless reality.

Faces are most often shown frontally, as is the case with the three patriarchs. Eyes gaze directly out at the viewer. Black lines divide major parts of the face and facial hair, and they are filled in with other colors—beige, pink, red, white, and brown. Only the slightest traces of light and shadow are visible on the faces, to suggest depth and corporeality. A second common mode of presentation

shows the face from a three-quarters view. This view includes a reduced, angular depiction of the eyes, eyebrows, and nose, which conveys alertness and movement quite effectively. It is almost always used for figures that are shown in a smaller scale, such as the saved in paradise (K5; fig. 5.4) or the face of the Christ Child in the apse (S1; fig. 5.5).

Clothing is defined with black lines and is also suggested with lines and patterns made up of darker shades of the fabric's color. We see darker yellow-ocher lines on Isaac's yellow himation, or mantle, and darker pink lines on his rose-colored tunic. Certain details in the rendering of drapery, characteristic of Theodore and his workshop, act as a kind of signature. One of these is the delineation of rounded, three-dimensional elements such as knees, shoulders, and buttocks, with circles bisected by a zigzagging line.[9] Another feature is the small, opposed curls that enliven a solid, continuous edge. These curls are black or colored, as we see in the detail of Christ, from the apse. The dense black lines are often, but not always, overlaid by thin, calligraphic lines that meander delightfully along the course of the outlines. Some of these can be seen in the drapery of Abraham. Consider as well the very distinctive fold that is characterized by a capital T shape in the center. We see it here, in the figures of Abraham and Isaac, at the far right end of their tunics' hems. It is also particularly clear in the hem of the angel from the apse, on the left side of the figure of Christ in Majesty (fig. 5.16).

Another treatment of drapery is seen infrequently in these paintings. It consists of delicate, swirling lines set

5.6 LEFT
Christ in Majesty (s1; ADP/SA
8s 98)

5.7 RIGHT
Christ in Majesty (c2; ADP/SA
1999)

within the larger segments made of the standard heavy black lines. One example is the rendering of the himation wrapped around the Christ Child's tunic in the apse (s1; fig. 5.5). In this case, the lines are pale yellow, reminiscent of gold. Both the tunic and himation of the Christ Pantocrator (s12; fig. 6.20) in the dome are done in this technique, but in this painting the lines are awkward, in contrast with the sophisticated elegance of the same feature elsewhere.[10]

The field of the painting is often edged with a row of pearls set within a red border, but frames can also be defined with simple red bands. Figures regularly transgress the frame, or exist outside of the framed group altogether. In the sacrifice of Isaac (s38; fig. 4.32), Abraham's feet overlap the border below him. The pages behind Mercurius (κ3; fig. 4.26) are left outside of the picture field, as if the frame were moving with Mercurius and they had somehow escaped its confines. These transgressions surprise modern viewers, who expect framed segments of wall or canvas to present the illusion of being windows into the three-dimensional world around us, at least when they depict figural subjects.

The high white walls and domes of the nave are the backdrop for a brightly colored horizontal band of paintings. The paintings begin about five feet from the current floor level (figs. 4.1–4.5).[11] The paintings in the khurus are positioned at a slightly lower level, and those in the sanctuary at varying levels. The sanctuary also includes paintings in two low niches, the large, tall apse, and the entire

region of the dome over the central altar (fig. 4.27). Evidence exists in the nave for a lower band of dark red, below the extant paintings. These may or may not belong to the 1232/1233 program. The painted areas of the wall are segmented into framed squares, rectangles, and occasionally less regular geometric shapes. The settings for the equestrian martyrs, in the western end of the nave and also the two ends of the khurus, include banded backgrounds, suggesting the concept of a ground line and a horizon without conveying a sense of space (figs. 4.1, 7.22). The standing figures, martyrs and monks, are usually set within arcades (figs. 4.2, 5.12). Rarely, abstract hills stand in as ciphers for landscapes (figs. 4.19, 8.19). The two scales used for figures, roughly life-size and about a quarter-life-size or smaller, as well as the numerous miniature buildings, contribute to the viewer's awareness that the artist is not attempting to depict the world as we see it.[12]

The field within the frame is built up of competing systems of pattern, made up of figures (for example, Abraham or Mary), elaborately carved and colored furniture, and ornamented columns, all of which contribute to the visual richness of these images. Several decorative motifs are often used within the same piece of furniture or architectural framework, indicating that varieties of pattern were an essential part of this stylistic language. The device of filling the frame with two-dimensional colored designs results in the almost complete absence of anything that could be construed as atmosphere, distance, or three-

5.8
Isaiah and the angel (s42)

dimensional space. Even the seated figures—for example, the three patriarchs (K5, fig. 5.4) or the Virgin Mary (N36, S1; fig. 5.5)—seem to have been conceived of as decorative shapes in front of their thrones rather than as concrete masses seated on top of them. The pillows on which they sit are completely undisturbed by any weight.

Despite the abstract characteristics of this style, the figures represented here convey a strong sense of life and personality. One feels the calm presence of the Virgin Mary gazing out at us in the painting in the apse (S1). The eyes and outstretched arm of the Christ Child express an intimacy with Mary. The solid weight and intense gaze of Mark (S11; fig. 4.36) convey a strength of character and conviction suitable to the apostle who brought Christianity to Egypt. The monastic saints in the nave stand in virtually identical poses but suggest individuality, not sameness.

Theodore and His Workshop

Careful stylistic analysis has made it possible to identify several individual painters who contributed to the pictorial program in the Church of St. Antony. This information enables us to construct an idea of the working practice of Theodore and his workshop. I shall begin with Theodore, who wrote his name twice in the church, demonstrating his status as master painter. How can it be determined that more than one artist was at work in the program and, that established, which parts of the painting are by Theodore's

hand? The application of a technique from the branch of art history that is called connoisseurship has yielded impressive results.

Analysis of ears and other features—for example, eyebrows, hands, and drapery—combined with such factors as confidence of line and color use, has resulted in the identification of several distinct hands. A brief consideration of ear types supports this discrimination. The artist who painted the two single most important works in the church, the Christ in Majesty in the sanctuary apse (S1; fig. 5.6) and the Christ in Majesty in the side chapel (C2; fig. 5.7), used a distinctive hook shape for his ears. The ears and several other features are so similar in these two faces of Christ that we can safely assume that they were painted by the same hand. Given the significance of the subject matter and location of these two paintings, it is most probable that Theodore, the master painter, created them himself.[13]

A second, distinctive type of ear is used in the program. It is oval and is either thin with a dark vertical line marking the center, or fat with a thin or a broad vertical pink line suggesting its interior. Several artists, with varying degrees of competence, were painting oval ears. The most accomplished seems to have been the equal of Theodore, in skill if not in status, and I am calling him the Second St. Antony Master. His work can be seen in the spare oval ears, with a vertical line in the center, of the prophet Isaiah (s42; fig. 5.8). The upper edges of the ears

5.9

Samuel, Pishoi the Great, and John
the Little (N6–N8; ADP/SA 1999)

are positioned just about at the figure's eye level. They are
virtually identical with the shape and position of the ears
on Abraham, Isaac, and Jacob in Paradise (K5; fig. 5.4), although the patriarchs' ears lack the characteristic lines in
the center. Nonetheless, similarities in the structure of the
eyes, the growth pattern of the beards, and the mouths
suggest that the Second Master is responsible for both of
these paintings and several more besides.

Variations suggest yet more hands at work. The fat
ovals framing the face of Sisoes (N9; fig. 5.10) are positioned significantly lower down on the sides of his face
than are those of the Second Master. The ears of Athanasius (s2; fig. 6.8), which are filled with a wide pink line, are
located very high up on the sides of his face. The identification of two major and several minor ear types reveals
that at least two masters, and as many as four or five less
skilled artists, were at work.

Further stylistic analysis tells us a great deal about the
working practices of Theodore's team and shows that more
than one artist usually painted each figure. An example
from the southern nave wall illustrates this point. The four
monks standing within an arcade show two closely related
facial types and appear to be by the same hand (N7–N10;
figs. 5.9, 5.10). All four have identically shaped broad oval
ears, and other features of their faces and beards are similar. The pair on the left, Pishoi the Great and John the Little, have gently arched eyebrows. The pair on the right,
Sisoes and Arsenius, have angular eyebrows and wrinkled
foreheads. It seems plausible that one artist painted all four
faces, using eyebrows, foreheads, and other details to indi-
vidualize them. When we consider the style of the monastic cloak that these four monks are wearing, it becomes
immediately evident that the garment on the far right is
out of place. Arsenius (N10) is shown here with much

5.10
Sisoes and Arsenius (N9–N10;
ADP/SA 1999)

more bulk than the others, most of which is conveyed through the folds of his apparel. His silhouette is uneven, especially on the left side. In contrast to this, the torsos of the three other figures are virtually dematerialized by their cloaks, which are filled with a grid of almost mathematically precise lines. The controlled linearity of the entire figure of Sisoes (N9) forms a consistent whole. Arsenius's face (N10) matches this linearity, but the treatment of his body does not. These differences lead me to conclude that one artist painted the three figures at the left, and also the face at the far right (N10), but that another artist painted the body of Arsenius. Extending our consideration to the figure painted to the far right of the group of four, in the curved space of the nave division (N11), we see that the bulky form of Barsum the Syrian was also shaped by the artist who painted Arsenius's body (fig. 4.22).

This absence of complete stylistic unity suggests that a somewhat flexible working process was used in the church. The rows of saints in the eastern half of the nave demonstrate this again. At first glance, we see uniform rows of saints standing within arcades. All are facing us, and all are roughly the same size. A closer look shows that although most of them are framed by arcades, not all are. Also, the row of saints is segmented into separate squares or rectangles. These boxes have different widths, and each one follows its own internal laws with respect to the type of column used, if any, the height of the frame, the relation of the arch to the frame, and the contour of the wall. On the northern nave wall, the columns are set on stepped bases, and the tops of the pointed arches pierce the upper frame (N34, N35; fig. 5.11). A continuous narrow, horizontal band of Arabic inscription extends between the columns and behind the saints. This feature may be intended to represent a decorated tie beam or a carved frieze that wraps

83

around the back of a series of niches.[14] On the southern nave wall we see different methods for segmenting the space (fig. 5.12). Columns are noticeably absent in the eastern end of this wall, and framing rectangles are narrower in width (N1–N6). The attenuated columns to the west form an elegant, continuous arcade not found elsewhere in the church program (N7–N10).

What can these irregularities tell us about the working practice of Theodore and his team of artists? An interesting discovery made by Adriano Luzi in the course of his conservation work in the nave helps us reconstruct the actions of the painters. An unpainted plaster layer was added to the domes at some point after Theodore's paintings were finished. It terminated along the upper level of the paintings on the nave wall. Luzi discovered that this layer covered some words, which were painted just above the upper frames of the wall paintings. He found one of them above the lengthy inscription on the nave wall (N31; fig. 14.4), and it is Coptic for "memorial." In the body of the inscription, this text is called a memorial because it commemorates the donors, asking blessings on them for their offering. Luzi found "cherubim," written above the cherub at N33 (fig. 4.20). A distinct stylistic difference exists between the letters within the painted fields and those above them. The higher letters seem to have been written casually, in a more cursive style. These words state the subjects of the paintings below them. They must have been written

at the direction of the person, perhaps a priest from the monastery, who designed the program.[15]

After the program for the paintings was mapped out, sections of wall were divided as well (fig. 5.12). One can almost see Theodore marking out a baseline for the paintings, for it is continuous, except around the corners. After this, he would have assigned single artists or small groups to paint areas of the wall, and perhaps would have given them general instructions to present the figures standing and facing the viewer. He does not seem to have directed their framing of the monastic leaders, as an examination of the southern nave wall suggests. SS. Antony and Paul are enclosed as a pair in an arcade (N1, N2). The heads of the next three saints to their right are set in much simpler arcs, which lack columnar support altogether (N3–N5). Samuel is shown in a simple rectangle, with a plain red frame (N6). In a slightly larger scale, and with a considerably greater height, the next four saints are framed in a finely proportioned arcade (N7–N10). So different is its conception that it is evident that this section was not painted by the same person or people who made the frames for the saints to the left. And, as we have seen, two artists contributed unequally to these four figures. Either of these two, or perhaps even a third, could have painted the colonnade.

The evidence considered so far suggests that the subjects of the paintings were dictated to the painters and sections of wall were marked out. While general directions

5.13 LEFT
One of the saved in paradise
(K5; ADP/SA 9 S172 97)

5.14 CENTER
Presentation in the temple,
detail, ca. 1200–1250, wall painting,
Northwestern Gallery Chapel,
Monastery of St. Mercurius,
Old Cairo

5.15 RIGHT
Transfiguration, detail, ca.
1200–1250, wall painting, North-
western Gallery Chapel,
Monastery of St. Mercurius,
Old Cairo

were given, the variety in the framing of the saints shows us that individual artists or small teams had a certain autonomy. The variations in style that are often apparent within a single figure show us that artists worked closely together. One person may have blocked out the figure and painted the face of a saint, while another artist painted his clothing and possibly a third worked on the enframing columns and background.

Theodore's Style and Coptic Art

We have seen how much new work is possible now that the paintings at the Church of St. Antony have been cleaned. Although stylistic similarities exist between them and murals in other Coptic churches, these ties are not close enough to warrant a definite attribution to Theodore and his workshop. However, stylistic analysis can also help us advance the state of Coptic art history. As I have mentioned, we lack precise dates for most medieval Coptic wall paintings. In fact, a range of as much as two or three centuries is often suggested for many paintings. Two examples will indicate the potential of the newly cleaned work in the Monastery of St. Antony to improve the chronology for medieval Coptic painting. Images in the northwestern gallery chapel, dedicated to the Virgin, in the Church of St. Mercurius at the monastery of the same name in Old Cairo, have been given dates ranging between the eleventh and fourteenth centuries.[16] Some close stylistic similarities

between these murals and those by Theodore and his workshop make it possible to assign to them a much more precise date.

A comparison of the seated patriarch Jacob, holding one of the saved on his lap (K5; fig. 5.13), with the Christ Child in the Presentation in the Temple, from the Monastery of St. Mercurius (fig. 5.14) is revealing. A similar use of heavy black outlines to segment parts of the figures is evident in both cases. Particularly noteworthy is a comparison between the face of the diminutive saved person and that of the Christ Child. The two faces are almost identical, with their three-quarter presentation, forceful eyebrows made of single, straight black lines, and angular eyes, looking off to the right. Also from the same chapel in Cairo is a painting of the Transfiguration (figs. 5.15, 5.20). The face and pose of the figure at the bottom are similar to those of the saved, particularly in the way that both figures twist while reaching to the right. The directional emphasis of the upper halves of their bodies is to the right, while that of their lower bodies is to the left. This torsion is rare in Coptic art, and as will be explored below, it may show the painter's interest in Western art. The essential factor here is the existence of this unusual feature in both programs.

Another compelling point of similarity is the capital T-shaped fold that we see in the hem of an angel's skirt from the apse in the Monastery of St. Antony (S1; fig. 5.16) and in the hem of one of the figures from the Transfig-

5.16 LEFT

The archangel Michael adoring
Christ (s1; ADP/SA 1999)

5.17 RIGHT

Lower zone of the apse (s1), before
cleaning (ADP/SA 11 s35 96)

uration in Cairo (fig. 5.15). These parallels show that the gap in dates between the work by Theodore at the Monastery of St. Antony and the work at the Monastery of St. Mercurius by unknown painters is not great. Rather than electing to date the paintings in the Church of St. Mercurius loosely, on stylistic grounds, as has usually been done, we can compare them to the precisely dated works from the Monastery of St. Antony and assign them more confidently to a fifty-year span around 1232/1233. Before cleaning, dirt obscured the details of the angel's hem in the Church of St. Antony (fig. 5.17), so this feature could not be seen and associated with the T-fold detail in Cairo.

Other paintings in the Monastery of St. Mercurius include parallels to those in the Monastery of St. Antony. Their dating is significantly less problematic now than it has been, due to impressive new work by Gertrud van Loon, but it is not absolutely conclusive. Based on somewhat uncertain inscriptional evidence, and on stylistic analysis, she argues persuasively for a date of ca. 1168–1175 for all the paintings on the gallery level, including those in the Chapel of the Virgin.[17] Similarities of style between the paintings in Old Cairo and those in the Church of St. Antony make it possible to build on van Loon's carefully mapped out conclusions about the temporal unity of the Cairene images and suggest a possible, minor difference in dating. A diamond grid filled with plant motifs is employed behind the figures of two archangels, one on the north wall of the north gallery and the other in the Chapel

of St. George.[18] Precisely this diamond-and-plant pattern is used by Theodore's team behind the archangel Michael (s1; fig. 4.28), and also on the mountain next to Samuel the Archimandrite (N6; fig. 5.9). Additionally, although slight differences exist, the three-quarter face, eyes, and beard of the head of Abraham in the Chapel of St. George in Cairo are strikingly similar to those of the same personage in the painting of Abraham with Melchizedek (s43; fig. 6.12) in the Church of St. Antony.[19] Van Loon has noted an emphasis on the lower eyelid in the Chapel of St. George, which gives the suggestion of a pouch.[20] Though not ubiquitous, this feature is common at the Church of St. Antony, most notably in the figures of Athanasius (s2; fig. 6.8), Mark (s11; fig. 4.36), John the Baptist (very pronounced, C3; fig. 1.4), the Christ Child (s1; fig. 5.5); Piroou and Athom (N16; fig. 4.4); and Sisinnius (N23; fig. 4.8). Similarities in the rendering of drapery can be ascertained, most notably the distinctive T-fold described earlier is visible in the hem of the tunic worn by Christ in the apse of the Chapel of St. George.[21] Although some of the best parallels to the paintings by Theodore can be found in the Monastery of St. Mercurius in Cairo, they are not close enough to assert the same hand. But they certainly suggest a significant relationship and might lead one to date the paintings in Cairo somewhat later than van Loon has, or within a roughly fifty-year span beginning with the latest date she proposes, 1175, and ending with the date of the paintings in the Monastery of St. Antony, namely 1232/1233.

5.18

Deesis, ca. 1200, wall painting,
Haikal of St. Mark, Monastery of
St. Macarius, Wadi al-Natrun

One other group of wall paintings with salient visual links to Theodore's work has been preserved in the Sanctuary of St. Mark at the Monastery of St. Macarius the Great, in the Wadi al-Natrun (fig. 5.18). Leroy has dated them very generally to the eleventh or twelfth century, with a preference for the beginning of that period; van Loon has shown that the architecture of this sanctuary dates to the years immediately before 1133, and suggests the period between 1133 and 1150 for the paintings.[22] Because this is the first study of the paintings in the Church of St. Antony since their cleaning, it is now possible to observe that numerous features of style and decoration connect the paintings by Theodore to those in the Sanctuary of St. Mark. The two basic eye types used in both programs are similar, though not identical. Both are characterized by the use of bold, heavy strokes to shape the outlines of the face itself and the features. The most prevalent eye type is even and almond-shaped, commonly seen in the frontal figures. In Theodore's paintings, the lines of the eyebrow and the nose are usually regular. Occasionally, the eyebrows are angular and calligraphic, with varying widths— for example, in the faces of SS. Sisoes and Arsenius (N9, N10; fig. 5.10). It is this expressive eyebrow that is more commonly seen in the paintings in the Sanctuary of St. Mark. Even when they are gently arched, their width varies. The depiction of Isaiah's eyebrows, with their sharp corners and sophisticated variation of line thickness, is typical of the paintings in the Monastery of St. Macarius,

and the even eyebrows shown in the painting of St. Antony in the Wadi al-Natrun exemplify an alternate version of the first eye type (fig. 6.11).[23] The second method for representing eyes, found in both programs—and, as we have seen, in the Monastery of St. Mercurius in Cairo—is characterized by a right angle in the inner corner of the eye, which marks the upper line of the open eye and the straight line of the nose.[24] In Theodore's work, the eye is surmounted by the short straight line of the eyebrow. In the paintings in the Wadi al-Natrun, this straight upper line is included, but it is used to define the upper lid. A longer, curving, and more articulated eyebrow arches over the eye. In both programs, the angular eye type appears commonly when the face is shown in a three-quarters view.[25]

The rendering of drapery in the Monasteries of St. Antony and St. Macarius is different in conception but shares a few features. The abstract and linear monastic cloak, which is common in Theodore's work, is painted in a similarly two-dimensional manner in the murals in the Monastery of St. Macarius. An example of this is the figure of Macarius the Great with the cherub (fig. 5.19).[26] The drapery here is usually shown as more fluid and naturalistic than we see in the Monastery of St. Antony (fig. 4.19). Although the artist or artists working in the Wadi al-Natrun have not segmented the clothing into two-dimensional patterns to the same degree, they have nevertheless used black outlines and have also occasionally painted

5.19

St. Macarius and the cherub, ca. 1200, wall painting, Haikal of St. Mark, Monastery of St. Macarius, Wadi al-Natrun

over them in a thin, mobile white line, as we saw in Theodore's paintings.[27] The T-shape for the hems of drapery that is found in Theodore's work and that of the painter or painters from the Monastery of St. Mercurius is not precisely replicated here, but a related, more loosely conceived relative of it can be seen in the Sanctuary of St. Mark.[28]

Several distinctive features of decoration are identical in both programs. The red-framed pearl border is the most obvious of these (fig. 5.18), but the background of meringuelike mountains behind the cherub (fig. 5.19) and the diamond-patterned grid filled with plant fronds, also used as a background pattern, are the same at both sites. An accordion-like folded-ribbon design is an exact parallel, from its green central stripe on a red ground to the decorative yellow triangles that fill the interstices between the ribbon and the red bands of the border. The ribbon design in the Monastery of St. Antony defines the curve of the arch over the niche with the cross in the Deesis Chapel (C1; fig. 4.40), and in the Monastery of St. Macarius it plays the same role, but with a keel-shaped arch, in a much larger scale, underneath the scene of the Annunciation.[29] Although decorative motifs can be an untrustworthy basis for dating, the use of several of the same ornamental elements in both painted programs is likely significant.[30] Numerous other points of similarity and difference require close analysis before the precise relation between the two programs can be ascertained, but this evidence suggests that Leroy's and perhaps even van Loon's dates for the paintings in the Sanctuary of St. Mark are too early. The fixed date from the Monastery of St. Antony enables us to suggest that the paintings under consideration in the Monastery of St. Macarius are not earlier than the twelfth century in date, and may even belong to the thirteenth century.

Stylistic Ties Beyond Egypt

The style of the paintings by Theodore and his team of artists is thoroughly Coptic. Its frontality and linear, schematic qualities build on those found in Egyptian art from late antiquity. But for art to be Coptic in character in the thirteenth century meant something different from its meaning in the first centuries of Christian art in Egypt. The thirteenth-century Copts participated in the secular culture of the ruling Muslim society, and their involvement is apparent in the 1232/1233 paintings in the Monastery of St. Antony, so to characterize these paintings as Coptic is to incorporate, rather than to exclude, their secular elements. Lyster analyzes this aspect of Theodore's paintings in depth in chapter 7. Although iconographic elements from posticonoclastic Byzantine art are easy to chart in Theodore's program, as we shall see in chapter 6, the same is not true for style. Theodore seems only very rarely to have drawn on artistic traditions beyond Egypt. A trace of Byzantine art can be identified, and, with less certainty, an echo of Romanesque art as well. The Romanesque device may have made its way into Coptic art through the agency of the Crusades.

Theodore has employed one readily apparent detail from the Byzantine stylistic repertoire. It is the use of very thin, swirling lines, which appear only rarely in these paintings, in the rendering of drapery. An impressive example can be seen in the clothing of the Christ Child from the apse (s1; fig. 5.5). The thin lines here are pale yellow, evocative of the curving lines made of gold wire in Middle Byzantine enamel work. Elegant gold lines are also common in Byzantine icon painting of the period, examples of which could have been seen in the Monastery of St. Catherine, and very possibly within the collection of the Monastery of St. Antony itself.[31]

Finally, a suggestion of Romanesque art can be discerned in both Theodore's paintings and those in the Church of St. Mercurius (figs. 5.13, 5.20). The torsion described above, in both programs, is not characteristic of Coptic art. Although similarly extended figural rotation can be found in Byzantine art of this period, there it is used with attenuation and conveys an ethereal impression. The short proportions and torsion that we see in the Coptic paintings finds its closest parallel in Romanesque art—for example, in the drawing of a child from a Romanesque missal (fig. 5.21).[32]

Theodore and his workshop produced visually engaging paintings that show an impressive command of composition, color, pattern, and line. Rendered with an emphasis on two-dimensionality, their figural subject matter

5.20 LEFT

Transfiguration, detail, ca.
1200–1250, wall painting, Northwestern Gallery Chapel, Monastery
of St. Mercurius, Old Cairo

5.21 RIGHT

Child, detail from the arrest
of Christ, after a drawing in a
Romanesque missal, treasury of
the Cathedral of St. Étienne,
Auxerre

nevertheless expresses personality and intensity. This thir-teenth-century Coptic art continues the tradition of early Coptic painting, though with distinctive variations, and el-ements unknown to the earlier artists. Some of the most salient features from early Coptic art that are still in use in Theodore's program are a preference for frontality and shallow or nonexistent pictorial fields inhabited by large figures; the segmentation of pictorial subjects by black or colored lines; and the tendency to restrict movement. Close analysis of the style of the 1232/1233 paintings in the Monastery of St. Antony shows them to have been the work of several hands, at least two of whom were artists of great skill. A group of four or more painters worked together in a process that followed specific guidelines for subject matter and general presentation, but which other-wise seems to have left them considerable freedom.

The style of these paintings has close parallels in other Christian monuments within Egypt, specifically the Monasteries of St. Mercurius (Old Cairo) and St. Macar-ius (Sanctuary of Mark, Wadi al-Natrun).[33] Lyster demon-strates their intimate ties to the shared secular realm of art in Egypt, dominated by Muslim rule.[34] Hunt has iden-tified a workshop of artists active in Egypt between 1200 and 1250, likely based in Cairo, which created wall paint-ings at the Syrian Monastery and illuminated manuscripts and icons.[35] The cleaned paintings in the Monastery of St. Antony make it clear that a separate school of painting, with recognizable stylistic characteristics, was working in Egypt at the same time, and probably beginning somewhat earlier. Although similarities abound, I do not see pre-cisely the same hand at work in the three monuments I have grouped together, and it therefore seems most plausi-ble to me that their artists came from a single, large work-shop or school that was active over an extended period. No doubt more than two schools existed in this culturally stimulating period, as I suggest in the conclusion of this book. Stylistic parallels with Christian art outside of Egypt are difficult though not impossible to locate. With the un-derstanding that areas of overlap existed between Coptic and Muslim visual culture, we can conclude by charac-terizing the style of these paintings as a vivid, thirteenth-century expression of the longstanding Coptic tradition.

Elizabeth S. Bolman

CHAPTER 6

THEODORE'S PROGRAM IN CONTEXT

EGYPT AND THE MEDITERRANEAN REGION

In 726 the Byzantine emperor Leo III began a fateful movement called iconoclasm. It not only condemned the depiction of Christ and the saints but also called for the destruction of existing representations of these subjects, in any medium. The effect of iconoclasm on the course of Byzantine art can hardly be overstated. It lasted for roughly a century, and the art of the Byzantine empire after Christian images were once again legalized was markedly different in character.[1] During its formative years, the art of Christian Egypt participated first in Roman and then in Byzantine visual culture. But by 726 Egypt was no longer part of the Byzantine empire. In 641 it had been taken over by the armies of Islam. The Copts were thus not obliged either to destroy their images or to cease making new ones during the iconoclastic period. In medieval Coptic art, then, we have a vital continuation of the earliest Christian artistic traditions, uninterrupted by iconoclasm.

The paintings dating to 1232/1233 in the Church of St. Antony are the outgrowth of early Christian art in the Mediterranean region. The Copts sustained their commitment to religious images in the face of Byzantine iconoclasm, as well as Islamic prohibitions against religious images.[2] The major subjects in Theodore's program have a long pedigree, visible in early monastic art and continuing in Egypt after the political separation of that country from Byzantium. Because so much new Coptic art from the period after the Islamic conquest has come to light in recent years, consideration of this neglected topic is now possible to an unprecedented degree.[3] The scope of this chapter permits only a brief discussion of it, but one that I hope will engender future studies. Much less clear in this evaluation of the place of Theodore's program in Mediterranean art is the relation between Coptic and Crusader art.[4] The question of the ties between the paintings in the Church of St. Antony and the Muslim tradition is also essential to any discussion of postconquest Coptic art, and William Lyster treats it in depth in the next chapter.

Early Byzantine Egypt

By far the most numerous and important examples of early Byzantine monastic painting come from Egypt. This preponderance has to do both with the strength and vitality of early monasticism in Egypt, and also with its dry climate, ideally suited for preservation.[5] The Kellia (cells) provide us with the largest number of early Coptic monastic paintings. Excavations revealed only a few depictions of Christ, saints, martyrs, and apostles, but a rich array of decorated crosses.[6] Two sites with an exceptional range of figural paintings are the Monastery of Apa Apollo at Bawit and the Monastery of Apa Jeremiah at Saqqara. Few precise dates exist for early Christian art in Egypt, but the paintings in both monasteries are roughly dated between the sixth and eighth centuries.[7] Almost all the paintings from these three locations were found not in churches but in monastic oratories, or rooms for prayer.[8] Some of the functions of the oratory are the same as those of a church. Prayer was the central activity in both spaces. Certain basic architectural and artistic similarities exist as well, particularly the significance of the eastern wall. We know that this wall was the focal point of the room because prayer was undertaken facing east, the direction from which it is believed that Christ will appear at the Last Judgment. Also, the apse is located in the center of the eastern church wall,

6.1
George (partial view) and Phoebammon (N25, N26; ADP/SA 1999)

6.2 UPPER LEFT

Phoebammon, ca. sixth century,
wall painting, chapel 17, Bawit

6.3 RIGHT

Sisinnius, ca. sixth century, wall
painting, chapel 17, Bawit

6.4 BOTTOM

Christ in Majesty above the Virgin
and Christ Child with the apostles,
ca. sixth century, wall painting,
room 6, Bawit

6.5 UPPER RIGHT

Virgin and Christ Child, ca. sixth
century, wall painting, chapel 28,
Bawit

and the niche—in a sense a miniature apse—exists in the eastern oratory wall. The subjects of the paintings in the apse and niche are similar: Christ in Majesty predominates, sometimes combined with other figures or groupings.[9] Technically, the paintings in both venues are made of inexpensive secco painting on plaster, which is not surprising, given the monastic environment. None of these monasteries and churches had the benefit of imperial patronage. Although we should not overlook the difference between the monastic oratory and the church, in the virtual absence of extant painted churches from roughly the first millennium in Egypt, we have no choice but to consider oratories in their stead. It is interesting that significant iconographic parallels exist between these early paintings from oratories and the 1232/1233 paintings in the Church of St. Antony.[10]

A few examples from Bawit illustrate the three most common iconographic themes found in the Monastery of St. Antony: equestrian martyrs, standing monastic saints, and Christ in Majesty surrounded by the four incorporeal beings. Oratory 17 includes equestrian martyrs, among them renderings of Phoibammon and Sisinnius, who are both depicted in the Church of St. Antony (N26, figs. 6.1, 6.2; N23, figs. 4.8, 6.3). Standing saints and patriarchs appear in oratory 56, among them the earliest known image of St. Antony (fig. 8, introduction). The enthroned Christ in Majesty, surrounded by the four incorporeal beings, is likely the most popular image from oratories at Bawit and Saqqara and is often shown by itself in a niche.[11] The best-preserved example is from Bawit, room 6 (atypically, it was not located in an oratory), and is now in the Coptic Museum, Cairo (fig. 6.4).[12] It contains all of the essential ele-

6.6 LEFT

Virgin and Christ Child (N36),
with view east into the sanctuary
(ADP/SA 1999)

6.7 RIGHT

Antony, Athanasius, and
Pachomius, ca. tenth century, wall
painting, Tebtunis, Fayoum (The
Griffith Institute, Ashmolean
Museum, Oxford)

ments we see in the Church of St. Antony (s1, fig. 4.28, and
with variations, c2, fig. 4.38): the two-zoned composition,
with Christ in Majesty above and other figures below. As in
room 6, these are usually the enthroned Virgin Mary and
Christ Child.

Some less common themes from Theodore's program were also chosen for these early monastic environ-
ments. The Virgin Mary holding a *clipeus,* or shield, with
the image of the Christ Child was found at Bawit, where
the Virgin grasps the clipeus from the sides and positions
it slightly off center (fig. 6.5). The composition is similar to
that in the church (N36), but there the Virgin's hands are at
the base of the mandorla, and she holds the image centrally (fig. 6.6).[13] The jeweled cross that we see in the Deesis
Chapel in the Church of St. Antony (c1; fig. 4.40) also has
numerous antecedents in the oratories of both the Kellia
and Saqqara.[14] The three Hebrews (K6; fig. 4.24) were popular in earlier centuries, as their appearance at Saqqara and
another monastic site, Wadi Sarga, suggests.[15] Some scenes
from the Old Testament, prefiguring the sacrifice of Christ
on the cross, were also included in the monastic oratories
of early Byzantine Egypt. One well known to us from
Saqqara and beyond Egypt in the same time period, and
also in the thirteenth-century paintings at the Monastery
of St. Antony, is the sacrifice of Isaac (s38; fig. 4.32).[16]

Postconquest Egypt: The Tenth and Eleventh Centuries
Tenth- and eleventh-century paintings in churches have
been preserved in Egypt and also include many of the ele-
ments we see in the paintings of 1232/1233 in the Church of
St. Antony. Some of the paintings found at Tebtunis in the
Fayoum, which were photographed but not preserved, are

dated by an inscription to 953 (A.M. 669).[17] Leroy has
pointed out that the paintings in the South Church at the
Monastery of the Martyrs (Deir al-Shohada) were painted
some time before the year 1000; he suggests a date of ca.
950.[18] Another striking monastic church program from
this period has been recently uncovered at the Naqlun
Monastery in the Fayoum. The paintings on the northern
nave wall and in the apse date between 1022–1032.[19]

Equestrian martyrs figure among the standard subjects at Tebtunis and Naqlun. These include an imposing
painting of Theodore Stratelates photographed at Tebtunis
(fig. 4.10), which is similar in iconography to the painting
of this saint in the Monastery of St. Antony (N22; fig. 5.3).[20]
In both paintings the saint is much larger than the other
figures. From below the horse's head, the widow implores
the saint to rescue her two sons, who are positioned below
the horse, along with the snakelike dragon. The most significant difference is that at Tebtunis the dragon rears its
head up above the widow and is therefore not speared at
the same angle as in the Church of St. Antony. A close predecessor to the painting of St. Mercurius (K3; fig. 4.26) is at
Naqlun, on the northern nave wall.[21] The saint's black
horse and elaborate weaponry, as well as the unseated emperor Julian the Apostate, appear in both compositions.

Standing and seated monastic saints and patriarchs
figure prominently in church painting during the tenth
and eleventh centuries. The same few personages are singled out repeatedly, and placed with care, to express the
stature of Egyptian monasticism and the Coptic Church.
As in the Church of St. Antony, standing monastic saints
lined the walls at Tebtunis. The status of Antony as the
father of monasticism is underscored in both programs. In

6.8

Athanasius (s2; ADP/SA 6 s165 98)

4.18). When moving from one half of the nave to the other, one walks below and between the two figures of Pachomius and Shenoute, which formally mark the transition from the painted theme of martyrs to that of their monastic successors.

A compositional predecessor to the two figures of Mark the Apostle (s11; fig. 4.36) and Athanasius (s2; fig. 6.8) in the Church of St. Antony can be found in the early–eleventh century paintings in the sanctuary at Naqlun (fig. 6.9).[24] The two enthroned figures are set within niches, as we see them in the Monastery of St. Antony, but at Naqlun these niches are within the central sanctuary apse. The identity of Mark is definite in the earlier program, but not that of Athanasius.[25] In the Church of St. Antony, the niches act as small, miniature apses placed directly to the east of each of the two lateral altars in the sanctuary. Athanasius is also singled out for prominence in the apse painting of the South Church at Esna, where he stands to one side of the enthroned Christ.[26] This theme of patriarchs of the Coptic Church is expanded at the Monastery of St. Antony. Mark, the first patriarch, and Athanasius, Antony's biographer, are given the greatest prominence (s11, s2). Excluding the Virgin Mary and Christ Child flanked by the archangels Gabriel and Michael, all of the standing figures in the lower zone of the sanctuary are patriarchs. Only one patriarch is Syrian, Severus (s3), included for his close ties to the Coptic Church and his doctrinal position.[27] The monastic forefathers Antony (n1) and Pachomius (n28) also fill key positions in the nave program, but here as in the sanctuary they are joined by a host of other monastic exemplars. Based on the extant evidence, the Egyptian character expressed in abbreviated form at Tebtunis seems to have been enlarged in later programs, particularly in the Church of St. Antony but also in the Monastery of the Romans in the Wadi al-Natrun.

The subject of Abraham, Isaac, and Jacob in the Monastery of St. Antony (k5; fig. 4.25) finds its only known Egyptian parallel in the Syrian Monastery.[28] Its date has still not been fixed, but it was covered by a layer of plaster dating to the thirteenth century.[29] Its basic iconographic format, showing the three patriarchs seated on a continuous throne and holding the diminutive figures of the saved, is the same in both paintings. At the Syrian Monastery, the saved are naked and numerous, while they are fewer and clothed in the Church of St. Antony. Both of these compositions depict the saved freely disposed in the laps of the patriarchs and behind them. This presentation is not found in Syrian or Crusader depictions of the same motif, which most often show the heads of the saved or

the earlier program, instead of the usual inclusion of the Virgin Mary in the zone beneath the enthroned Christ in Majesty, we see the enthroned Patriarch Athanasius, flanked by the standing figures of Antony and Pachomius (fig. 6.7).[22] Athanasius represents the Coptic Church, Antony the origin of monasticism, and Pachomius the organization of the ascetic movement into a cenobitic form.[23] In the Church of St. Antony, the painted figure of Antony stands on the eastern nave wall, on one side of the entrance to the khurus (n1; fig. 7, introduction). Athanasius is also shown enthroned in the church (s2; fig. 6.8), but he is located in a niche, behind the southern altar in the sanctuary. Pachomius's important contribution to Egyptian monasticism is expressed in his pairing with Antony at Tebtunis, and it is signaled in the Red Sea church by his placement on the underside of the archway separating the western and eastern ends of the nave (n28; fig.

6.9 LEFT

Athanasius (?), 1022–1032, wall
painting, Naqlun (Courtesy
W. Godlewski)

6.10 CENTER

Claudius, twelfth century,
wall painting, Monastery of
the Martyrs, Esna

6.11 RIGHT

Paul and Antony, ca. 1200, wall
painting, Haikal of St. Mark,
Monastery of St. Macarius, Wadi
al-Natrun

their entire bodies held within pieces of cloth, stretched
between the patriarchs' hands.[30] In Byzantine art, the scene
is commonly reduced to show only Abraham of the patriarchs, but also includes the Virgin Mary.[31] Its presence in
Egypt could be either a result of its continuation from
early Christian art or a feature that Coptic artists borrowed
from Byzantine and Crusader art. A fourth-century reference to a painting of the patriarchs, by Epiphanius of Salamis, shows that it existed in art well before iconoclasm.[32]

Finally, we turn to the major composition of Christ
in Majesty, so prevalent in all periods of Coptic art. In the
upper zone of the apse at Tebtunis, above Antony, Athanasius, and Pachomius, part of a painting of Christ in Majesty was visible at the time of excavation (fig. 6.7).[33] Christ
is framed by a star-studded mandorla, supported by the
four incorporeal beings and flanked by the sun and moon.
All these details can be seen in Theodore's rendition (s1;
fig. 4.28) as well. The inclusion of stars on the wide band of
the mandorla seems to be a new element in the tenth and
eleventh centuries.

The Twelfth and Thirteenth Centuries

Several major painted church programs exist from the
twelfth and thirteenth centuries, most notably in the Monastery of the Martyrs in Esna and the Monasteries of St.
Macarius and of the Romans (Baramus) in the Wadi al-
Natrun. The popularity of the subjects chosen for earlier
monastic oratories and churches continues in this later
period: equestrian martyrs, standing saints, events from
the Old Testament, the Virgin Mary, and Christ in Majesty.

The equestrian martyr Theodore Stratelates from the
North Church at the Monastery of the Martyrs near Esna

is dated by an inscription to either 1129/1130 or 1179/1180.[34]
Claudius and one anonymous equestrian saint, likely of
the same date, also join Theodore in protecting the sanctuary at Esna (fig. 6.10). Their placement echoes a similar
arrangement in the Monastery of St. Antony, where
George and Mercurius perform this apotropaic function
(K3, K8; figs. 6.24, 4.26). In the Monastery of St. Antony,
the saints Theodore and Claudius are located on the western nave wall (N19, N22; figs. 5.3, 4.12), where they are part
of the group that is guarding the door.

Standing saints are included in the paintings in the
Monasteries of St. Macarius and of the Romans, although
in neither case are these saints located in the nave. The
paintings in the sanctuary of Mark, in the former, are most
likely dated to the late twelfth or early thirteenth century.[35]
In the Monastery of St. Macarius, several standing saints
bear a close iconographic similarity to those in the Church
of St. Antony, including a paired Paul and Antony (fig.
6.11). Most notable is Macarius the Great, with a cherub,
standing in front of a mountainous background (fig. 5.19),
that is very close to the one seen in Theodore's program
(N33; fig. 4.19). In what are probably late–thirteenth
century paintings in the Monastery of the Romans, we
encounter several saints familiar to us from the Church of
St. Antony, including Antony the Great, Paul the Hermit,
Macarius the Great, Pachomius, Barsum the Syrian, possibly also Moses the Black, and finally the two Romans
after whom the monastery was named, Maximus and
Domitius.[36]

Old Testament scenes of sacrifice are included in the
Monasteries of St. Macarius and of the Romans, as they
are in the Monastery of St. Antony. All three depict the ex-

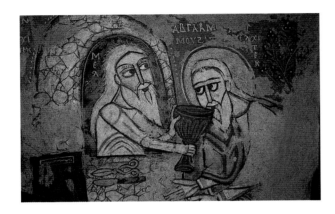

ceptionally rare iconographic representation of Melchizedek as a naked (or barely clothed) hermit with long hair, presenting a cup to Abraham (s38; figs. 6.12, 6.13).[37] Melchizedek is usually shown dressed as a priest or a king, in both the Western and Byzantine traditions (fig. 6.14). The much more common sacrifice of Isaac (s39) and Isaiah and the burning coal (s42) are similarly represented in the Monasteries of St. Macarius and of St. Antony.

The representational type of Christ in Majesty shown at Esna and also in the Chapel of the Virgin (the northwestern gallery chapel) in the Monastery of St. Mercurius in Old Cairo is close to that seen in the Monastery of St. Antony (s1). From the perspective of iconography, this subject is probably the most stable and consistent of any throughout the history of Coptic art. In the paintings at Esna, Cairo, and the Church of St. Antony, the four incorporeal beings have three sets of layered wings with eyes, each set of which is painted with a solid color. In the Monastery of St. Antony the innermost wings are ocher, the intermediate layer is blue-gray, and the outermost layer is red (fig. 6.15). This stylization, together with the stars in the mandorla of Christ, are the most notable iconographic changes we see in paintings of Christ in Majesty from its early appearance in the monasteries at Bawit (fig. 6.4) and Saqqara.

The single closest parallel to the two-zoned composition of the Christ in Majesty above the Virgin Mary and Child flanked by archangels (s1; fig. 4.28) in the Church of St. Antony belongs to the twelfth century and can be found in the Monastery of the Martyrs at Esna. In addition to the similarities of frontality, location under a Christ in Majesty scene, and the archangels' pose, the position of the

6.16 LEFT

Angel, detail from Virgin and
Christ Child with archangels,
twelfth century, wall painting,
Monastery of the Martyrs, Esna

6.17 RIGHT

The archangel Gabriel (s1; ADP/SA
12 s191 98)

6.18 BELOW

Niche of the precious cross (c1;
ADP/SA BW 144:23)

Virgin's arms makes this comparison particularly close. The archangels stand looking straight ahead, guardians for the pair between them, with their wings held out stiffly at their sides (s1; figs. 6.16, 6.17). The upper sections of the wings are patterned and framed with a border. The tapering of the wings is rendered with simple vertical bands. All the angels hold discs in their left hands, wear rectangular crowns, and have mantles fastened on their right shoulders.

Another subject that requires a brief note here is the composition called the Deesis, or petition for forgiveness of sins. It consists of a central figure of Christ, flanked by the Virgin Mary and John the Baptist, each of whom turns slightly toward Christ with hands raised in supplication. The Deesis is included in the programs in the Monastery of St. Macarius (fig. 5.18) and in the Monastery of St. Antony (c2, c3, c10; fig. 4.38). In the Monastery of St. Macarius, it is set between windows. The figure of Christ is standing, and, uncharacteristically, is positioned below the Virgin and John. These two are bust-length portraits in medallions. In the painting in the Monastery of St. Antony, Christ is enthroned, and the Virgin and John are shown full-length. Theodore has included two unusual elements: the four creatures, in what is best described as a standing position; and the juxtaposition of the Deesis with an elaborately painted cross in the lower niche (fig. 6.18).

A late–eleventh or twelfth-century Coptic example that has often been associated with Theodore's paintings is found in the White Monastery near Sohag.[58] In the south semidome in the White Monastery church, the figures of Mary and John the Baptist flank a central mandorla (fig. 6.19). This field is not, however, filled with the figure of Christ in Majesty, as it is in the Monastery of St. Antony. In

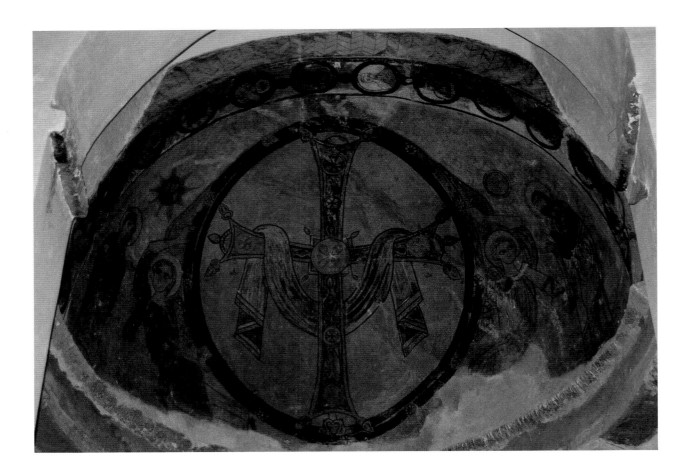

6.19

Deesis, with the Cross, late
eleventh or twelfth century, wall
painting, White Monastery, Sohag

the White Monastery the depiction of a cross draped with
cloth fills the space, the same motif that we see in the
Deesis Chapel in the Church of St. Antony, but in the
composition in the Monastery of St. Antony both Christ in
Majesty and the draped cross are included (C1). In both
paintings, angels support the mandorla, two at the White
Monastery and four in the Deesis Chapel. The fabric
draped cross is not rare in Coptic art, but only in the Monastery of St. Antony and the White Monastery is it associated with the Deesis. Several examples have survived in the
Monastery of Apa Fana, near Minya, and in the Red
Monastery near Sohag.[39]

This iconographic review from early monastic oratories and from churches shows that many of the subjects in
the program at the Monastery of St. Antony have been
used continuously in Coptic church decoration from the
sixth or seventh century through the thirteenth century.
Foremost among these are equestrian martyrs, standing
saints, the enthroned Christ in Majesty and the enthroned
Virgin and Child.[40] As we have seen in chapter 4, their
choice and disposition was meaningful. It would be mis-
leading, however, to focus solely on the perpetuation of
traditional representations in Theodore's program. Omis-
sions are also part of the construction of meaning in this
monastic art, and repay scrutiny.

It is telling to consider which paintings, common
elsewhere in Coptic art, are missing from the Church of St.
Antony. The most salient absence is of the apostles, excepting only Mark (s11; fig. 4.36). Standing rows of apostles are common in the early Byzantine period, as well as in
postconquest Coptic painting. We find them in the ca. 950
paintings in the sanctuary of Benjamin (Monastery of St.
Macarius), in the eleventh-century paintings in the sanctuary at Naqlun, in the paintings of ca. 1200 in the Chapel
of the Virgin in the Church of St. Mercurius (Old Cairo),
and in the late–thirteenth century paintings in the sanctuary at the Monastery of the Romans. The absence from
Theodore's program of all of the apostles but Mark is
meaningful. Tradition has it that Mark brought Christianity to Egypt. His successors are the Coptic patriarchs, and
many of the most famous of these are included in the sanctuary at the Monastery of St. Antony (fig. 4.43). One is
Severus, patriarch of Antioch in Syria (s3; fig. 7.14). He is
important to the Copts for his objection to the Council of
Chalcedon, a position which the Copts also held.[41] Es-
teemed Coptic patriarchs, such as Cyril of Alexandria,
were likely intended to be depicted on the northern sanctuary wall, where a framework for them was begun, but
were never completed.[42] The selection of Mark and the
Coptic patriarchs was surely not intended to minimize the

6.20

Christ Pantocrator in central

sanctuary dome (s12; ADP/SA 1999)

programs, as they are in Coptic church programs.[43] Neither drew on the other, but both grew out of the common cultural environment in late antiquity. Furthermore, some subjects that were commonly featured in the early period, such as equestrian martyrs, stopped being a standard part of the Byzantine program after iconoclasm. They were resumed within that tradition—for example, in Greece—but not as a continuation of their own past. Their reappearance is the result of interaction with the Crusaders.[44] In Coptic art, paintings of equestrian martyrs exist from all periods and were clearly part of a continuous tradition. What we must identify, for our analysis of Theodore's use of Byzantine art, are aspects of his program that were not part of the shared heritage but were newly developed in posticonoclastic Byzantine art.

The first of these is the image of the Christ Pantocrator, or ruler of the universe, shown bust-length, in a medallion (s12). In the Church of St. Antony this painting is located in the center of the dome, over the altar (fig. 6.20). In Byzantine art, it is closely tied to dome architecture. The existence of the dome itself, in the Church of St. Antony, is not indicative of Coptic architects' borrowing from Byzantine practice. Domed architecture in Egypt became common in the Fatimid period (eleventh and twelfth centuries), and by the thirteenth century it was a standard part of church architecture.[45] In Coptic churches, such as the Church of St. Antony, the Church of St. Sergius in Old Cairo (rebuilt in the Fatimid period), and many others, domes were built over the sanctuary. They are attached to a traditional basilican structure—that is, to a church with a rectangular nave and a dominant focus on the eastern end. The middle Byzantine dome with the image of the Christ Pantocrator is part of a completely different architectural system, one that places the major dome over the naos, or nave.[46] The image of Christ is therefore centered over a space that is accessible to the congregation, and not over the celebrants around the altar.[47] The domes in the Church of St. Antony derive from architectural developments in Egypt and the Islamic world. But the inclusion of the bust-length image of Christ in the center of that dome is not common in Egypt. The medallion of Christ Pantocrator in the dome of the Church of St. Antony, with its encircling band of angels, is borrowed from Byzantine art and placed in a different position in this Coptic program.

A second clear example of a detail taken from middle Byzantine art is the inclusion of the Deesis in the side chapel (c2, c3, c10; fig. 4.38). As we have seen, the Deesis is a compositional type that shows a frontal, enthroned

status of the other apostles but simply to stress, once again, the richness of Egyptian Christianity. In this way, the program of the sanctuary in the church continued the genealogical theme of the nave: as Coptic monks carried on the work of the martyrs, Coptic patriarchs carried on the work of the apostle Mark.

Beyond Egypt: Byzantine and Crusader Art

Clear evidence exists in Theodore's paintings of elements drawn from posticonoclastic Byzantine art. The relation between the Coptic paintings in the Monastery of St. Antony and both Byzantine and Crusader art, however, is a complex topic, which will require much future work. At this point, it is possible only to show a few of the ways in which the art of Byzantium, and possibly also that of the Crusaders, was used by Theodore in the Church of St. Antony. Another issue that can only be touched on here is the possible use by Byzantine and Crusader artists of Coptic iconography, perhaps from the Monastery of St. Antony itself.

An analysis of Theodore's interest in Byzantine art must begin with a recognition of the fact that many of the shared features in these two traditions come from their past. Standing saints, for example, are a regular component of middle and late Byzantine (posticonoclastic) church

6.21 LEFT

Deesis, 1183, wall painting,
Hermitage of St. Neophytus,
Cyprus (Courtesy of Dumbarton
Oaks, neg. H63.2)

6.22 RIGHT

Detail of Christ addressing Pishoi
(N7; ADP/SA 2 S153 97)

Christ flanked by the standing figures of the Virgin Mary and John the Baptist.[48] A representative Byzantine example can be found in the Hermitage of St. Neophytus on Cyprus (fig. 6.21). It is an image of entreaty or petition, directed to Christ and presented on behalf of the faithful by the two people who were closest to Christ on earth.[49] It is standard in the Byzantine sphere and seems to have been considered particularly appropriate for small chapels in the twelfth and thirteenth centuries.[50] We find it in just such a small chapel in the Monastery of St. Antony. In this instance, the inclusion of the subject and also its presentation in a side chapel may be an indication of borrowing from middle Byzantine practice.

Another example of an iconographic detail brought into Coptic art at a late date is the diminutive image of Christ, leaning out from heaven to address or point at saints and martyrs below him. We see him in several places in Theodore's program—for example, above Pishoi the Great (N7) and the brothers Piroou and Athom (N16). In the first of these, Christ leans from our right, above Pishoi, and points down to him (fig. 6.22). In the second painting,

Christ is positioned between the brothers and extends a hand to each figure. This device for showing Christ appearing from heaven is commonplace in Byzantine and Crusader art by the thirteenth century. It appears in what may be a tenth-century icon of the Virgin Mary from Cyprus, and also in the mosaics from before 1143, in the Church of St. Mary's of the Admiral in Palermo (fig. 6.23). In both these examples the figure of Christ emerges from the upper corner of the field. In a twelfth-century illumination in the Homilies of Gregory of Nazianzos, Christ is shown in a half-circle, emerging from the center of the upper border.[51] Crusader manuscripts that are contemporary with Theodore's paintings also include this image.[52] Although the Crusader artists no doubt took this feature from Byzantine art, we cannot know whether Theodore learned of it from that source or through an intermediary. Clear and demonstrable evidence that Theodore and his team drew on Crusader art has yet to be identified.

Byzantine vita icons of saints furnish us with a final example of Theodore's familiarity with posticonoclastic art. Numerous large-scale icons of standing saints survive

6.23 LEFT

Virgin Mary and George of
Antioch, with Christ, before 1148,
mosaic, St. Mary's of the Admiral,
Palermo

6.24 RIGHT

George and scenes of his martyrdom (K7–K9), during conservation
(ADP/SA 7S 97)

from the thirteenth century.[53] They are framed with small
scenes showing events from their lives. The painting of
George in the khurus (K7–K9) shows a similar combination of iconic and narrative art in a single composition
(fig. 6.24). In the painting in the Church of St. Antony,
George is on horseback, and a narrative event is shown in
the lower zone of the central field. In these respects, the
painting is unlike Byzantine biographical icons. But the
essential effect of this painting of George is iconic, and the
central image is framed to the right and left with small narrative scenes. Those to our right (K9) relate directly to the
life of George. Those to our left (K7) do so only indirectly,
their major connection being to the painting of the three
Hebrews (K6; fig. 4.24).[54] The principal device of framing a
large iconic image with scenes from the life of the saint is
the same, however. A discussion of this subject is not complete without noting that we do not see narrative images
around the figure of the most important saint in the
church: Antony. The single image of Antony in the Church
of St. Antony (N1) includes only the subtlest details of narrative: his placement next to Paul, and the crow between

the two ascetics. Vita icons of Antony could have existed in
this period, but we have no evidence of them until the
fifteenth century, and they seem to have been rare until the
seventeenth century.[55]

Representations linked to the major feasts of the
church, such as the Nativity and the Baptism, are characteristic of middle Byzantine art. They are conspicuously
absent from Theodore's program. We see partial feast cycles
in the thirteenth-century paintings in the Monasteries of
the Syrians and the Romans, however. It is difficult to
evaluate the significance, if any, of their absence from the
Church of St. Antony. Certainly, the unpainted higher
zones of the nave walls and domes could have accommodated them.

As even this brief study shows, the iconography of
the Christ Pantocrator in the dome, the Deesis, the small
pointing figure of Christ, and biographical scenes derive
from the middle Byzantine world, not from the common
heritage of the Coptic and Byzantine traditions.[56] Theodore and other Coptic artists were familiar with Byzantine
art, at least to some extent. In the 1232/1233 paintings, the

6.25

Icon of St. Macarius and the
cherub, ca. thirteenth century,
Monastery of St. Catherine, Mount
Sinai (Courtesy of the Michigan-
Princeton-Alexandria Expedition
to Mount Sinai)

Byzantine elements are incorporated effectively and do
not stand out as interpolations from another realm. The
degree to which Christian artists outside of Egypt were
drawing on Coptic painting is more difficult to address at
this point. But a previously unpublished icon from the
Monastery of St. Catherine on Mount Sinai (fig. 6.25) suggests that this subject is worthy of closer study. It shows
St. Macarius the Great standing in a frontal position, with
his hand in the grasp of a cherub, as we see him in the
paintings in the Monasteries of St. Macarius (fig. 5.19) and
of the Romans in the Wadi al-Natrun and in the Monastery of St. Antony at the Red Sea (fig. 4.19). Because
Macarius the Great lived in Egypt and founded his famous
monastery there, and because this iconographic type is
uncommon elsewhere, it seems most plausible to imagine
that Egypt was its source.[57] Connections between the
Monastery of St. Antony and that of St. Catherine can be
assumed, providing a regular passage for artistic cross-
fertilization. Not only did a chapel dedicated to St. Antony
exist in the vicinity of the Monastery of St. Catherine, but
the Sinai foundation owned lands along the Red Sea coast,
and so pilgrims and itinerant artists are likely only two of
the categories of travelers who would have been in both
monasteries.[58]

The iconographic program in the Church of St.
Antony is in many respects representative of Coptic monastic art, from its beginnings. Such traditional figures as
martyrs, saints, and patriarchs are arranged to accentuate
the monastic life, as exemplified by the father of monasticism, Antony the Great. Elements from the posticonoclastic Byzantine world also play a role, but not a dominant
one. Theodore and his team of artists were active participants in the complicated visual culture of the Mediterranean region in the thirteenth century.

CHAPTER 7

REFLECTIONS OF THE TEMPORAL WORLD

SECULAR ELEMENTS IN THEODORE'S PROGRAM

Theodore painted a vision of eternity in the Church of St. Antony, but within that vision are reflections of the temporal world in which he lived. His program of 1232/1233 contains elements that correspond to Egyptian society in the thirteenth century, when Muslims, Christians, and Jews all partook of the same artistic and cultural milieu.[1] Because these elements derived from a shared tradition, which transcended religious differences, they are described here as being secular. Of course, each religious community of medieval Egypt also maintained a separate sphere in which its own unique customs and beliefs were preserved. The Monastery of St. Antony is an example of such exclusivity, but it is instructive to note that Theodore nevertheless integrated details from contemporary society into the paintings he produced for the monastic church. The secular elements in the 1232/1233 program have received little attention, yet without an understanding of the predominately Islamic culture of Egypt, and of the ways that Christians participated in it, a fascinating aspect of these paintings is ignored.

When Theodore painted the Church of St. Antony, Egypt had been under Islamic rule for nearly six hundred years. Throughout that time, Christians and Muslims had lived as neighbors in the Nile Valley during periods of both intense friction and relative calm. The Copts were a close-knit community but participated as administrators, merchants, craftsmen, and peasants in the broader society within which they lived. They were classified by the Arabs as *ahl al-dhimma*, a "protected people," whose faith was to be respected. Christians and Jews were "People of the Book," the recipients of scriptures from the same divine source that inspired the Qur'an. As protected subjects, the

Copts were granted personal security, freedom of religion, and a degree of autonomy in the conduct of their communal affairs. They were also obliged to pay additional taxes and accept certain legal and social restrictions. Theory and practice did not always coincide, however. Discriminatory measures were frequently not enforced, while in some periods the physical safety of the Copts was at risk.[2]

After the Arab conquest, the Byzantine system of taxation was adopted largely unchanged and left in the hands of the Copts, who were to staff the Egyptian fiscal administration for centuries. Official records were first kept in Greek, as they had been under the Byzantines, but in 705 the Umayyad governor 'Abd Allah ibn 'Abd al-Malik issued an edict imposing Arabic as the language of government. Thereafter, Coptic officials had to speak the language of the Qur'an if they wished to keep their administrative posts. It was an important step in the spread of Arabic among the Christians of Egypt. In time, Arabic completely replaced Coptic as the mother tongue of the Nile Valley.[3]

The adoption of spoken Arabic by the Copts paved the way for their use of it as a literary language as well. By the tenth century, Christian writers in Egypt were producing both translations of Coptic texts and original compositions in Arabic. Under the Fatimid caliphs (969–1171) and the Ayyubid sultans (1171–1250), Christian Arabic literature flourished to such an extent that it completely eclipsed the writing of Coptic. Efforts were taken to preserve the language through the compilation of Copto-Arabic dictionaries, but the last substantial Coptic literary work dates from the fourteenth century.[4]

The gradual Arabization of the Copts involved not just a linguistic transformation but also the adoption of

7.1

Grandfather of Mercurius being attacked by *cynocephaloi* (K3; ADP/SA 1 S172 97)

Arab manners, customs, and dress. The sumptuary laws that were promulgated throughout the medieval period indicate that the religious communities of Egypt all wore similar clothing (fig. 7.1). These regulations were aimed at segregating and humbling non-Muslims. One law compelled Christians and Jews to wear colored turbans (blue and yellow, respectively) in order to distinguish them from Muslims, who wore white. The frequency with which these laws were decreed suggests that, until at least the fourteenth century, they were rarely enforced for long.[5] In 1138, for example, Ridwan ibn al-Walakhshi, the Sunni Muslim wazir of Caliph al-Hafiz, removed Coptic officials and renewed the usual sumptuary laws. Ridwan had come to power by overthrowing his predecessor, a Christian Armenian. His persecution of non-Muslims was used to consolidate his position and win popular support. It quickly subsided once the wazir had achieved his objectives.[6]

In spite of such periodic setbacks, the Christians of Egypt enjoyed a long period of relative peace and prosperity between the tenth and fourteenth centuries. They were part of a sophisticated and wealthy society. Egypt was a major international power, and Cairo was one of the great-est centers of trade in the world. The Copts held key positions within the government of Egypt. Their main area of competence was as tax collectors and scribes in the civil service, but particularly capable individuals could achieve even greater authority. During the reign of the Fatimid caliphs, the Copts were particularly favored.[7] The church enjoyed an increase in its revenues, resulting in the construction or restoration of numerous churches, including most of those of Old Cairo.[8] This same medieval era of prosperity also witnessed what seems to have been a resurgence of the production of wall paintings in the churches of Egypt.[9] The work of Theodore in the Church of St. Antony is the best-preserved example from this era of Coptic painting.

It is evident from Theodore's work in the remote Monastery of St. Antony that he and his workshop were professional painters who were prepared to travel long distances in order to accept commissions. Not only were they trained in the Coptic iconographic tradition, Theodore and his men probably had ample opportunity to observe earlier examples of wall paintings throughout Egypt. The images in Theodore's program are rendered according to

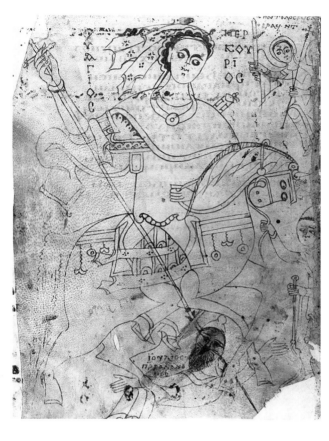

7.2 LEFT

Head of Mercurius's horse (K3; ADP/SA 1 S172 97)

7.3 RIGHT

Mercurius, ninth or tenth century, manuscript illumination, Egypt (Vatican City, Codex Vatican Copto 66, fol. 287v)

the Coptic tradition of painting, in which iconographic subjects often remained unchanged for centuries. This dependence on a pictorial tradition, rather than on observation from life, can be seen in Theodore's handling of the horses of the equestrian saints. The upper portion of their heads is turned toward the viewer, showing both pairs of eyes and ears, but the mouth is presented in profile (fig. 7.2). This distinctive manner of drawing a horse's head may have its origin in Byzantine imperial portraits, such as a gold medallion (electrotype) of Justinian (ca. 527–538) in the British Museum, where the head of the emperor's horse turns slightly to reveal both eyes (fig. 7.18). Although this positioning of the horse's head is only occasionally found in classical or Byzantine art, it was evidently popular among the Copts, especially in the more exaggerated form that we see in Theodore's work. It was employed in the sixth- or seventh-century wall paintings of equestrian saints in Chapel XVII at the Monastery of Apa Apollo at Bawit (figs. 6.2, 6.3) and in textile designs of the same period.[10] Somewhat later, the three-quarter profile is found in wall paintings of horses at Naqlun and Esna (fig. 6.10). It also appears in a number of manuscript illuminations

of equestrian saints produced before the eleventh century (figs. 4.11, 7.3).[11]

A particularly telling indication of Theodore's reliance on traditional forms is the way in which he positions the legs of his horses. Most of the horses are shown raising two legs, both on the same side. This pose could not have been observed from life, for a horse attempting it would topple over. The painting of Sisinnius in Chapel XVII at Bawit also shows his horse in this position (fig. 6.3). The other horses in the same chapel are depicted more accurately, with only one leg raised. The particular stance of Sisinnius's mount may have been a misreading of this more traditional form, but whatever the origin, the pose seems to have entered the tradition of Coptic painting at an early date. It was adopted at Naqlun for the horse of St. Pijosh and was eventually used by Theodore as his principal method of depicting the horses of equestrian saints.[12]

Only two of the horses in the Church of St. Antony are shown in a different pose. Theodore Stratelates (N22) and Sisinnius (N23) are both dragon slayers guarding the entrance of the church (figs. 7.15, 7.25). Their horses rear up on their hind legs above serpents, which are being

speared by the saints. Although this pose is anatomically more correct than the more commonly depicted one, it is unlikely to have been drawn from life. It too has a precedent in Coptic art—witness a traditional equestrian image often found on sixth-century Coptic textile panels.[13] Given the conservative character of these paintings, it comes as no surprise that this rearing pose from late antiquity was part of Theodore's artistic repertoire.

Despite the traditional nature of Coptic painting, there are details within Theodore's program that are drawn from contemporary life. They are incorporated into the timeless realm of Coptic religious art but reflect the enormous changes that had taken place in Egypt since the Arab conquest. These elements are minor details that do not affect the Christian iconography of Theodore's program, but they do enrich it and distinguish it from early Coptic painting. Examples include the style of arches painted to frame saints, the use of Arabic calligraphy, and some of the costumes and elements of dress worn by figures in the paintings. Although they show the influences of the predominantly Muslim culture of the time, these details are essentially secular in nature. In the thirteenth century, the Muslim, Christian, and Jewish communities of Egypt were part of the same society. They all spoke Arabic, wore the same style of clothing, and used the same construction techniques in their religious and secular buildings. Each religious community employed and contributed to the diverse cultural heritage of medieval Egypt. Scattered throughout Theodore's program are details that offer us a glimpse of this pluralistic society.

Turbans are perhaps the most obvious example of medieval secular elements in the program of Theodore. This distinctively Arab style of headdress is worn by four of the minor figures associated with the equestrian saints. Their turbans give us no indication of their religious affiliation, however. One of the figures is identified as a pagan soldier (N26; fig. 7.4), one as a Jew (N25; fig. 7.22), two others as Christians (K3, K9; figs. 7.1, 7.5). In the thirteenth century, this form of headdress was particularly associated with civilian administrators, who were known as "men of the turban."[14] As such, it indicated a position of social status in medieval Egypt, not religious affiliation.[15] Theodore employs turbans in his program to convey this same contemporary usage. The turbans worn by his figures indicate their membership in the civilian or military elite, and thus enhance their authority, whether as enemies of the church or as influential Christians. The turban worn by Pasicrates (K9; fig. 7.5) identifies the biographer of St. George as a member of the influential scribal class.

One of the means by which contemporary elements

7.6 LEFT
Sisoes (N9), detail with arch,
capitals and impost blocks
(ADP/SA 8S 97)

7.7 RIGHT
Capital, Mosque of Salih Tala'i',
1160, Cairo (EAP/ARCE EG 5 BW
12/95)

may have entered the Coptic tradition is suggested by Theodore's attention to detail, apparent in such diverse elements as arcades, furniture, and horse trappings. His paintings of the arcades framing the monastic saints in the nave include small, rectangular impost blocks between the capitals and the springing of the arches (fig. 7.6). It is a detail without any iconographic significance, but it indicates an awareness of contemporary architectural practice in Egypt. The *riwaqs* (arcades) of the Fatimid mosques of Cairo often employed wooden *tabliyas* (impost blocks) as a structural feature that increased the stability of the arcade by providing a cushion between each capital and arch.[16] At the Mosque of Salih Tala'i' (1160), the tabliyas comprise three layers of wood, all carved with five-pointed leaves (fig. 7.7). Theodore seems to be suggesting a similar type of carved, wooden impost block, except that in the Church of St. Antony the examples are also gilded and painted. The thrones in Theodore's program follow established Copto-Byzantine prototypes, but they are shown with such care that every inlaid panel, balustrade, and carpenter's joint is precisely indicated. Theodore may have been working with traditional painted models, but his details suggest a familiarity with actual thrones of this type. His spiritual father, Bishop Gabriel of Petpeh, mentioned in the two "signature" inscriptions (N35, S38), may have

possessed a similar episcopal throne.[17] Theodore's paintings of the mounts of the equestrian saints depict their harnesses, from bit to filet-string, with an accuracy that implies a practical knowledge of horses. The saddle of Theodore Stratelates (N22; fig. 7.15), for example, is held in place by a double girth, a precautionary measure to prevent the rider from losing his seat in the heat of battle.[18]

Perhaps a similar attention to detail on the part of earlier Coptic artists caused them to gradually incorporate secular elements into their work. A concern for accuracy when painting an arcade could lead a painter to adopt the pointed arched he knew from current churches. A desire to render horse equipment correctly might have encouraged another artist to add a large saddle blanket of the kind worn by the mounts of contemporary notables. Once a new element was used, other painters would copy it in their own work. It would then be passed on to their followers. Some of the secular details in Theodore's program may have been regarded as traditional by 1232, having been employed by Coptic artists for more than a century. The use of turbans is one such example. The early–eleventh century wall painting of Athanasius at Naqlun shows the great Alexandrian patriarch wearing a turban (fig. 6.9).[19] The headdress is perhaps intended to indicate his episcopal authority, in which case it is used to convey social sta-

7.8 LEFT

Arcade, Mosque of Salih Talaʾiʿ, 1160, Cairo (EAP/ARCE EG 5 BW 14/95)

7.9 RIGHT

Moses the Black (N30), detail showing arch and capitals (ADP/SA May 98)

tus in a manner similar to that found in Theodore's program two hundred years later.

Other secular details could have entered the Coptic tradition closer to Theodore's own time. Unfortunately, the scarcity of surviving medieval Coptic wall paintings makes it impossible to distinguish to what extent Theodore was an innovator, when it came to including contemporary elements in his program. What seems clear from his work is that the adoption of such elements into Coptic painting was a slow process. Many of the secular details in his program can be dated on stylistic grounds to the era of the Fatimid caliphs, who were overthrown sixty-two years before Theodore was active in the Church of St. Antony.

The painted arcades surrounding the saints in the nave will serve as an example. Although the use of an arch or a niche to frame a sacred image is a feature of Copto-Byzantine art that predates Christianity, the arcades in Theodore's program are rendered in a style reminiscent of the architecture of the Fatimid period. Before the Arab conquest, the Roman round arch was standard in both Coptic architecture and Coptic paintings of arcades. In Theodore's program, only two examples of the round arch

are found in the nave (N4, N5; fig. 5.12). They are painted in such a simplified form that they seem to have been added as an afterthought. Instead, most of Theodore's arches have profiles with a pronounced point (fig. 7.6).[20] This form of arch had been employed in the Islamic architecture of Egypt since the ninth century (fig. 7.8).[21] Marble columns of different hues support the arcades. Many have stylized Corinthian capitals (fig. 7.9), but some have clock-formed (bell-shaped) capitals and bases (fig. 7.6).[22] Egyptian artisans produced columns with clock-formed capitals throughout the medieval period.[23] Muslim builders generally preferred to reuse marble columns and capitals from pre-Islamic buildings. The Corinthian order was particularly popular, or at least easily obtainable, but a delight in variety seems plausible as a motivation for its regular inclusion.[24] In the Mosque of Salih Talaʾiʿ in Cairo (1160) no two capitals are the same (figs. 7.7, 7.8).

Were it not for the images of the saints, the painted arcades in the nave of the Church of St. Antony could easily be a depiction of a riwaq in a Fatimid mosque. The pointed arches, the ornamented impost blocks, and the lack of homogeneity of column and capital types in Theodore's program all closely resemble similar features in the twelfth-century mosques of Cairo. It is unlikely, however, that the arcades painted by Theodore were directly influenced by Fatimid architecture. The forms were probably drawn from Coptic churches that were erected at the same time. Among the most celebrated from this period are those of Abu Sarga, Sitt Barbara, and al-Mu'allaqa in Old Cairo. These three medieval churches retained the traditional basilican plan used by the Copts since the fourth century, but with the addition of more current architectural forms, such as the pointed arch.[25]

The spandrels between most of the arches in Theodore's program are decorated with a vine-and-leaf design, a ubiquitous feature in classical and medieval art and architectural decoration. In the examples found in the Church of St. Antony, the central element is usually a large leaf framed by a heart-shaped vine (fig. 7.6).[26] Often the leaf is broken open, providing another frame for a smaller offshoot. Other vines grow from the center, producing leaves shaped to fill the corners. This playful use of vine-and-leaf designs has close parallels in Fatimid luster-painted ceramics (fig. 7.10), but it continued to be popular during the Ayyubid period of Theodore. In the thirteenth century, similar vine-and-leaf designs were used as architectural decoration in miniatures and wall paintings produced by both Christians and Muslim painters in Egypt, Syria, and Iraq.[27]

Theodore's adoption of contemporary motifs is limited. His use of pointed arches indicates an awareness of contemporary architectural forms, but these same forms

had been constructed in Egypt for centuries. The vegetal decoration on the spandrels had a wide popularity in Theodore's day but also represented a time-honored style. In contrast, Theodore seems to be unfamiliar with more recent artistic trends, such as the complex geometric designs and elaborate arabesques developed by the Fatimids and their eastern Muslim neighbors. Coptic painters eventually adopted these newer styles, but they are not part of Theodore's artistic vocabulary.

Another indication of the conservatism of Theodore's program is that all of the important inscriptions are in Coptic. There is nothing surprising about this in a medieval Coptic church, but in 1232 many Copts spoke Arabic as their first language. The thirteenth century was also a great era of Christian-Arabic literature.[28] The limited use of Arabic by Theodore is therefore significant. The extent to which the Coptic community had been Arabized by his time is suggested by the names of the donors recorded in the memorial inscriptions (N31, K4).[29] Most of the individuals are named after Christian saints, including Peter, Michael, Mark, and John; some have what may be Coptic names, such as Setakleh (?) and Fmon (?); but about a quarter of those mentioned have names conforming to Arabic usage. Archdeacon Salib, who is mentioned in both inscriptions, has a name that means "cross" in Arabic. His name would immediately identify him as a Christian in Arabic-speaking company. The same is not true of al-Razi, however. The name is probably a variant of al-Radi (the Satisfied), which could be used by either Christians or Muslims. A number of the other donors have *kunyas* (Arabic formal names), whereby the individual is identified by the name of his son, such as Abu al-Faraj (Father of Relief), Abu Ghalib (Father of [the] Victor), and Abu 'Uz (Father of Affluence). It is not always clear whether these names indicate actual parentage or were used metaphorically. They also give no indication of religious affiliation.

The only Arabic used in Theodore's program is the single phrase *al-Fadi* (الفادي; the Redeemer). It is employed primarily as a decorative motif, albeit one that contains an encrypted prayer. The phrase is found on architectural elements, on thrones and footstools, and on various textiles depicted throughout the church (fig. 7.11). It is always repeated, forming a continuous line of text. The inscription is written in kufic, the style of Arabic calligraphy favored by the Fatimids. The form used in Theodore's program combines elements from naskhi, a cursive script, which under the Ayyubids replaced kufic as the predominate style of calligraphy in Egypt. This blend of kufic

7.10
Luster painted bowl, eleventh or twelfth century, Egypt. Stattliche Museen zu Berlin—Preussischer Kulturbesitz (Museum für Islamische Kunst, inf. J. 35/64)

7.11 ABOVE

Niche of the precious cross (C1),
detail of draped textile featuring
the Arabic phrase *al-Fadi* (ADP/SA
10S 163 97)

7.12 RIGHT

Luster painted plate, eleventh
century, Egypt (Benaki Museum,
Athens, inv. 216)

and naskhi was widely employed in inscriptions on Fatimid textiles of the twelfth century.[30]

Luster-painted ceramics from the same period are often decorated with similar repeated words or phrases written in kufic, such as *al-surur* (joy) or *al-yumn* (good fortune). The inscriptions are apotropaic, warding off malign influences and bringing good luck to the owner. The use of *al-Fadi* in the church is an interesting Christian adaptation of this style of calligraphy. The obscure manner in which the phrase is written is also characteristic of inscriptions on Fatimid lusterware. Arabic phrases are sometimes written in such a decorative manner that the meaning of the words is not immediately clear. A luster-painted plate in the Benaki Museum, for example, is decorated with the repetition of two words: one undeciphered, the other *al-yumn* (fig. 7.12).[31]

The method of writing *al-Fadi* in the Church of St. Antony is an example of such a cryptic style. The alif (ا), lam (ل), fa (ف), and alif follow each other in the expected manner, but the dal (د) grows out of the top of the second alif. The last letter, ya (ي), is written as an alif, which also serves as the first letter of the next repetition. This blending of the first and last letter of the phrase is a reference to the traditional Christian concept that Jesus is the alpha and the omega, the first and last letters of the Greek alphabet. The biblical source is Revelation 22:13, "I am the Alpha and the Omega, the First and the Last, the Beginning and the End," which in the Arabic translation reads, "I am the Alif and the Ya."[32]

Perhaps the most interesting usage of *al-Fadi* in Theodore's program is its appearance on tiraz bands worn on the robes of angels, patriarchs, bishops, and figures from the Old Testament. Tiraz (from the Persian *tarazian*, to embroider) was an official, honorific textile denoting high rank or royal favor; it usually featured inscriptions praising the ruling dynasty.[33] Ibn Khaldun (d. 1406), the Arab historian and philosopher, observed: "It is part of royal and government pomp and dynastic custom to have the names of rulers . . . put on the silk, brocade, or pure silk garments that are prepared for their wearing. . . . Royal fabrics are embellished with such a tiraz, in order to increase the prestige of . . . those whom the ruler distinguishes by bestowing on them his garment when he wants to honor them or appoint them to one of the offices of the dynasty."[34]

The simplest form of tiraz used by the Fatimids was a band of embroidered silk, backstitched on earlier fabrics, which was attached to a court robe. In the Ayyubid period, this form of armband was a standard element in popular

7.13

Miniature by Yahya al-Wasiti in
the Maqamat of al-Hariri, 1237 Iraq
(Bibliothèque National, Paris, MS
Arabe 5847 fol. 59r)

dress throughout the Islamic world. They are shown on
the robes of men and women of all ranks and occupations
in Arab miniatures of the thirteenth century (fig. 7.13).
These "public" (*'amma*) tiraz bands came in three styles:
plain, with inscriptions, or with floral motifs. They continued to be popular under the early Mamluk sultans but
appear less frequently on noncourt robes after the mid-
fourteenth century.[35]

In Theodore's program, tiraz bands follow the earlier
khassa (private) model designating positions of authority.
Twelve of the saints depicted in the church wear bands of
this kind just below their shoulders (fig. 7.14).[36] Those who
are identifiable by inscriptions are all bishops and patriarchs, and it seems safe to assume that the three anonymous saints in this group also held episcopal rank. Under
the Fatimids, the leaders of the religious communities of
Egypt were always present in attendance at court. They
protected the interests of their community while serving
as guarantors of their people's loyalty. In about 1070 the
sixty-sixth Coptic Patriarch Christodulos relocated the pa-
pal seat from Alexandria to Cairo to be closer to the center
of power.[37] In the Church of St. Antony, the bishops' tiraz
bands suggest that these men are court officials as well as
the pastors of the Coptic community.

The word *tiraz* also referred to the royal production
of all textiles used by Muslim courts. Besides robes of various types, the tiraz workshops produced numerous other
woven goods, including turbans, curtains, banners, sad-

dlecloths, cushions, and tents. Nasir-i Khusraw, an Iranian
traveler visiting Egypt in the reign of al-Mustansir (1036–
1094), described a Fatimid procession featuring "ten thousand horses with gold saddles and bridles and jewel stud-
ded reins . . . all of them with saddlecloths of Byzantine
brocade . . . woven seamless to order. In the borders of the
cloth are woven inscriptions bearing the name of the sultan of Egypt."[38] In the Church of St. Antony, three of the
equestrian saints have saddlecloths with similar epigraphic
decoration (figs. 7.19, 7.22, 7.23).[39] The tiraz inscriptions of
the bishops and military martyrs, however, do not name a
secular monarch but declare allegiance to the Lord Jesus
Christ, "the Redeemer."

Apart from the occasional tiraz band, the celestial
beings, standing saints, and biblical figures in Theodore's
program are shown wearing approximations of late antique dress. This conservatism in the depiction of fashion
does not apply equally to the equestrian martyrs. Previous
scholars studying these paintings have identified the military vestments of the soldier saints as being from the Hellenistic and Roman periods.[40] In fact, most of the military
costumes found in Theodore's paintings suggest a later
date. Much of the equipment is Byzantine, but some of it
derives from the more current Turkish style that was introduced into Egypt by the Ayyubids. Theodore draws
upon both of these military traditions in his paintings of
equestrian saints in the Church of St. Antony. The Byzantine style is best represented by Theodore Stratelates (N22),
while Mercurius (K3) most closely resembles the Turkish
model.

Theodore Stratelates (fig. 7.15) is dressed in a manner
almost identical to that of Basil II (d. 1025), as shown in a
miniature painting celebrating the emperor's victory over
the Bulgars (fig. 7.16). Both the saint and the emperor wear
knee-length tunics, high boots, and military cloaks. Each is
armed with a lance and a sword. Over the tunic, each one
wears a lamellar cuirass comprising small, rectangular
plates laced together by leather thongs. This form of armor
was called a klibanion in Byzantium, a name derived from
the Latin *clibanarius* (a heavily equipped cavalryman).[41] In
a Byzantine ivory icon from the second half of the tenth
century, St. Demetrius wears a klibanion over a second
suit of lamellar armor that covers his upper arms and extends to his thighs (fig. 7.17). Apart from this extra protection, his costume is nearly the same as that worn by
Theodore in the Church of St. Antony.

The horse equipment used by Theodore Stratelates is
also recognizably Byzantine. Similar trappings are shown
on equestrian portraits of the Emperor Justinian (d. 565),

7.14

Severus and Dioscorus (s3–s4;

ADP/SA 11s 98)

7.15 LEFT

Theodore Stratelates (N22; ADP/SA 1999)

7.16 CENTER

Miniature of Basil II, Psalter of Basil II, ca. 976–1025, Constantinople (Biblioteca Marciana, Venice)

7.17 RIGHT

Ivory icon of St. Demetrius, ca. 950–1000, Byzantium (The Cloisters, The Metropolitan Museum of Art, New York, 1970.324.3)

7.18

Justinian on Horseback, ca. 527–538, gold medallion (electrotype), Byzantium (© The British Museum, London, 071962)

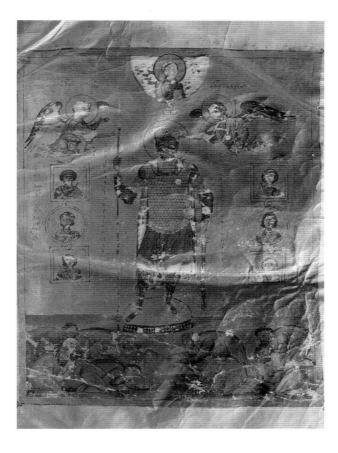

such as the Barberini Ivory in the Louvre and the gold medallion in the British Museum (fig. 7.18).[42] The saint's embroidered saddlecloth is small; a tethering rope is wrapped three times around the neck of his horse; and rows of medallions are suspended from the harness.[43] This last feature is one of a number of ways in which the martyr adopts imperial attributes.[44] Another example is the sash worn by Theodore. It is tied with the knot used by Hercules to secure the paws of a lion's skin around his chest. The Herculean knot was thought capable of providing protection from danger in battle, and so Roman emperors and generals wore it as a talisman and an indicator of rank.[45] A sculptural group from Aphrodisias in Turkey depicts Nero (d. 68) wearing such a knotted sash. The Christian Emperor Honorius (d. 423) is shown on a carved ivory in the Aosta Cathedral Treasury with a sash tied in the same manner.[46] Basil II, however, does not wear a knotted sash in the miniature from his Psalter (fig. 7.16), which suggests that the Herculean knot may have fallen out of use in the Byzantine army by the early eleventh century. Nevertheless, it continued to be depicted on icons of military saints during the Middle Byzantine period (fig. 7.17).

Mercurius (fig. 7.19), on the other hand, is dressed in the manner of a thirteenth-century Ayyubid amir. He wears a quilted coat known as a kazaghand. It fastened down the front and had a slit at the back from hem to crotch, so that it could be worn on horseback. An outer shell of silk brocade concealed various layers of mail and padding.[47] Usamah ibn Munqidh (d. 1188), the Arab lord of Shayzar in Syria, described a kazaghand in his memoirs. It "enclosed a Frankish coat of mail extending to the bottom of it, with another coat of mail on top of it reaching as far as the middle. Both were equipped with the proper linings, felt pads, rough silk and rabbits' hair."[48] The saint wears a lamellar cuirass over his kazaghand. This form of armor was known as a jawshan in Arabic and was identical to the Byzantine klibanion. The lamellae could be made of iron, horn, or hardened leather.[49] Christian and Muslim cavalry troops of the period also both wore cloaks, leggings, and boots. Mercurius's leggings are quilted, and patches of the same material cover his elbows. His headgear seems to be a kalawta, the small woolen cap worn by Egypt's military aristocracy.[50] Sisinnius (N23; figs. 7.25, 7.28) is the only other equestrian saint in Theodore's program with a similar cap. Unfortunately, this painting is severely damaged, making it impossible to determine whether he also wore a quilted coat.

In accordance with Coptic iconography, Mercurius is armed with two swords and a lance, but he also carries a composite bow, the Turkish weapon par excellence. Nine pieces of wood, reinforced by horn, formed the body. The

7.19

Mercurius (κ3; ADP/SA 5 s147 97)

7.20 LEFT

Detail of Blacas Ewer, 1232, Iraq (© The British Museum, London, OA 1866.12–29.61)

7.21 RIGHT

Inlaid bronze ewer, 1246/1247, Iraq or Syria (The Walters Art Gallery, Baltimore, inv. 54.456)

alternating stiff and flexible elements used in the bow's construction added considerably to its power. The composite bow was the most effective weapon developed before the invention of firearms. It had a range of five hundred meters and could penetrate body armor at shorter distances.[51] Mercurius carries his bow in Turkish fashion in a case hanging behind his saddle. The tail of the saint's horse is also knotted in a distinctively Turkish manner. Knotted horsetails were common throughout the eastern lands of Islam in the thirteenth century. They are often shown on Islamic ceramics and metalwork of the period (fig. 7.20). Muslim cavalry troops of the same time also used large saddlecloths for display and to shield their horses from the sun (fig. 7.21).[52] Mercurius's saddlecloth reflects this tradition. It is ornately decorated and completely covers the back of the horse. St. Phoebammon (N26; fig. 7.23), another example of this Turkish type of equestrian, has an equally elaborate saddlecloth. The diamond-shaped studs may suggest that an under layer of leather was secured to the blanket in order to protect the horse from arrows.

Earlier Coptic paintings provide prototypes for the use of both the Byzantine and the Turkish military equipment in the 1232/1233 program. Coptic equestrian saints

had been painted in the Romano-Byzantine manner for centuries, and most of the iconographic details employed in the Church of St. Antony derive from this ancient tradition. Many of the Turkish elements are also found in earlier Coptic paintings. The three equestrian saints in the Monastery of the Martyrs at Esna all sit on large saddlecloths (fig. 6.10). Two of them, Theodore and an anonymous saint, wear quilted armor similar to that of Mercurius in the Church of St. Antony.[53] A photograph taken at the end of the nineteenth century of a monastic church at Tebtunis shows one of the horses of the equestrian saints with a knotted tail.[54] The dates of these wall paintings are not certain, but they seem to have been made before the thirteenth century.[55]

The military costumes represented in the paintings of Theodore Stratelates and Mercurius derive from two distinct traditions, but the elements from each one are combined in both saints. Mercurius wears the Roman knotted sash with his otherwise Turkish costume. Theodore Stratelates resembles a Byzantine emperor, but he also has a composite bow, a shield inscribed in Arabic, and a horse with a knotted tail. None of the dress of the equestrian saints in Theodore's program belongs exclusively to

one style. For example, St. George (N25; fig. 7.22) is dressed as a Byzantine soldier, but his horse is equipped in Turkish fashion.[56]

The overlapping of elements from the two military traditions depicted in the church is by no means unique to Theodore's program. Muslim and Christian warriors in the age of the Crusades sometimes adopted the arms and armor of their opponents. Usamah ibn Munqidh's padded kazaghand contained a Frankish (Crusader) coat of mail. By the second half of the twelfth century, some Crusader knights had adopted a similar Muslim style of padded armor, which they referred to as a jazerant.[57] This borrowing of military equipment is also seen in the art of the period. A Byzantine soldier saint in a twelfth-century mosaic in Cefalù Cathedral is dressed in the same manner as is Theodore Stratelates, with a tunic, cuirass, and knotted sash, but he also holds a circular shield with a pseudo-Arabic inscription around the rim, similar to those carried by some of the equestrian saints in the Church of St. Antony.[58] The composite bow was not widely used by the knights of western Europe, but after the Crusaders encountered armies of mounted Turkish archers, the bow

began to appear in their paintings of military saints. An icon at the Monastery of St. Catherine portrays SS. Sergius and Bacchus as Byzantine horsemen armed with Turkish bows (fig. 7.24).[59] They resemble turcopoles, the light cavalry troops of Byzantine and Crusader armies that used Muslim equipment.[60] The icon appears to have been one of a group produced by Syrian Orthodox painters for Crusader patrons in the thirteenth century. It has been suggested that Latin settlers in Syria adopted Eastern equestrian saints because of their local reputations as effective spiritual protectors against the threat posed by Islam.[61] The saints' role as spiritual defenders of the Latin Kingdom is emphasized in the icon from the Monastery of St. Catherine, which arms Sergius and Bacchus with composite bows, the chief weapon of the Muslim opponents of the Crusaders.

The serpents under Theodore Stratelates (N22) and Sisinnius (N23) may be another example of the cultural fusion of the period (figs. 7.15, 7.25). Both saints are renowned in the Coptic tradition as dragon slayers.[62] They are the only equestrians in the church shown spearing serpents. Their placement above and adjacent to the entrance

Icon of Sergius and Bacchus, thirteenth century, Monastery of St. Catherine, Mount Sinai (Courtesy of the Michigan-Princeton-Alexandria Expedition to Mount Sinai)

Theodore Stratelates (partial view) and Sisinnius (N22–N23; ADP/SA 1999)

of the church at the northwest corner of the nave suggests they had a prophylactic role, protecting the church from evil. This entrance was enlarged sometime after 1233, resulting in the destruction of more than half of the painting of Sisinnius. When the painter Theodore worked in the church, there may have been a much lower entrance at the same site. If so, the dragon-slaying equestrians would have been the first saints a visitor encountered after entering the door. An anecdote about the Fatimid Caliph al-Amir (d. 1130) supports the notion that the thirteenth-century entrance of the church could have been very low. The caliph is said to have stayed in Coptic monasteries while out hunting. He was once invited to visit a monastic church, "but he found the doorway, which was closed by an iron door, too low for him, and as he would not consent to enter with a bowed head, he turned his face to the outside, and his back to the door, and crouched down, until he had entered."[63]

The Hellenistic and Roman image of a horseman killing a serpentine adversary was probably first employed as imperial iconography by Constantine (d. 337) to symbolize his victory over Licinius. This Constantinian composi-

tion was known throughout the late Empire by a coin type depicting an equestrian emperor rearing in triumph over a serpent.[64] The dragon-slaying saints in the Church of St. Antony illustrate the tenacity of this image in Coptic art. Theodore, however, makes one very significant modification to this traditional form. In his paintings, the serpents are knotted. In Islamic astrology of the same time, the knotted dragon represented invisible planets associated with the nodes of the moon's orbit.[65] It was a symbol of eclipse and evil fortune. Muslim rulers often employed the motif in the thirteenth century as a talisman protecting entrances. The knotted dragons above the main gate of the Ayyubid Citadel of Aleppo (1209) are the most celebrated example (fig. 7.26).[66] Theodore may have adapted this contemporary symbol of eclipse to the traditional image of the dragon slayer in order to emphasize the powers of the equestrians, painted to frame the entrance to the nave.[67]

Neither of the two equestrian saints, Victor (N20; fig. 7.27) or Menas (N21), carries arms or wears armor. Each holds a cross in his right hand instead of a lance. Although both paintings are damaged, it appears that the saints are dressed as princes rather than as soldiers. Victor was a

7.26 ABOVE
Knotted Dragons over the
entrance of the Ayyubid Citadel
of Aleppo, 1209, Syria

7.27 BELOW
Victor (N20; ADP/SA 1999)

7.28 ABOVE RIGHT
Sisinnius (N23)

Roman officer martyred for renouncing his rank in favor of devoting his life to Christ. Menas is usually depicted as a military saint in Coptic iconography, but one version of his legend states, "He withdrew from his regiment to a solitary retreat where he remained in tranquillity, worshipping God with his whole heart."[68] The two martyrs are clearly linked in Theodore's program. Their horses face each other, while a single groom stands between them holding the reins. Whatever the hagiographic significance of this pairing, the nonmartial character of the saints is suggested by the manner of their dress. Victor, the better preserved of the two, wears Arab-style trousers, known as sirwal, under his robe. They were woven with an extremely wide crotch, which made them ideal for horseback riding. Muslim soldiers tucked the sirwal into their boots or covered them with leggings. Victor, however, wears slipper-shoes of a kind favored by the civilian population of the thirteenth century.[69] The legs of his sirwal hang free.

The equestrian saints in the Church of St. Antony are supplied with some Muslim equipment, but they remain essentially Copto-Byzantine horsemen in their pose and iconographic detail. Theodore seems to have been less tied to tradition, however, when painting the small narrative

figures usually found beneath the equestrians. These figures are used to depict scenes from the life of each saint. Although drawn from Coptic literary sources that describe events dating to late Antiquity or earlier, many of the figures are dressed in the fashion of Theodore's own time. This is particularly true of the Roman and Babylonian soldiers, who are painted in the military costume of the contemporary army of Egypt (N26, K7–K9).

The Ayyubid sultans redefined the visual appearance of the Muslim ruling elite of Egypt by wearing clothing that followed Turkish fashion. The dress of this military aristocracy was thereby distinguished from that of the civilian population, who continued to wear long robes and turbans in the Arab style (fig. 7.13).[70] The traditional costume of the Turk was designed for horseback riding. It consisted of a tight tunic with a wide skirt reaching to the knees. The tunic buttoned diagonally across the chest and was worn over trousers. High boots or leather leggings were common, but sometimes the legs of the trousers were secured with cross-garters. Turkish headgear was also distinctive. Unlike the turbans worn by their subjects, the ruling elite favored a variety of caps. Military commanders (amirs) wore the sharbush, which the Mamluk historian al-Maqrizi (d. 1441) describes as "a thing resembling the crown, as if of triangular shape, put on the head without a kerchief (being wound around it)."[71] It was often trimmed with fur and included a metal plaque positioned above the forehead. All ranks wore the kalawta, a lighter wool cap, usually yellow or red, which featured a broad-banded border. Just as the turban was associated with civilian officials, so the kalawta became the symbol of the military aristocracy, who occasionally were called, as a class, mukalwatun (people of the kalawta).[72] Turkish soldiers could also be

7.29 RIGHT

Miniature in the Maqamat of al-Hariri, ca. 1220–1230, Iraq (Bibliothèque National, Paris, MS Arabe 3929, fol. 7v)

7.30 BELOW

Pages of Mercurius (к3; ADP/SA 14 S171 97)

identified by their long hair, which they often wore in braids. Male Muslim civilians shaved their heads.[73]

In Theodore's program, the figures dressed in this Turkish fashion are identified by Coptic inscriptions as soldiers. They are described as centurions, *quaestionarii*, and lance bearers.[74] The terminology reflects Roman military rank and function, but their costumes are portrayed in the style of the thirteenth century. The centurion beneath Phoebammon (N26) wears a Turkish tunic with tiraz bands on the sleeves (fig 7.23). He is the only soldier in the church with a turban, a detail suggesting he is an Arab rather than a Turk or Kurd. The other military men wear triangular caps, which are probably kalawtas (к7, к8, and к9; fig. 7.31). The equestrian martyrs Sisinnius (N23; fig. 7.28) and Mercurius (к3; fig. 7.19) wear similar caps. All the soldiers have long hair, and most have beards. The few beardless soldiers (к7, к9) in the program may be *ghilman* (pages). In Ayyubid military society, the bodyguard of the sultan was usually composed of Turkish *mamluks* (military slaves), brought from the steppes as boys and trained as soldiers. Those of particular ability or beauty staffed the palace, serving the sultan as cupbearers, sword carriers, and poison tasters. On completing their period of training, the young mamluks were manumitted and given permission to grow beards. They were the sultan's most loyal followers and were commonly promoted to high rank. Arab miniature paintings often show ghilman standing in attendance around their lord. Two examples from separate thirteenth-century editions of the *Maqamat* of al-Hariri feature clean-shaven pages with their hair plaited in long braids, wearing garments in the Turkish style. In the first painting, undated, a single page stands behind the throne of his master (fig. 7.29). He wears a pointed kalawta cap. The second painting, from 1237, features a seated amir with six armed attendants, all of whom wear fur-lined sharbushes (fig. 7.13).

The two figures standing behind Mercurius (к3) are dressed in the same fashion as the soldiers depicted in the rest of the church (figs. 7.19, 7.30). They can be safely identified as the pages of the equestrian saint. They are the only soldiers among the nonsacred narrative figures who are depicted as Christians. Both have crosses on their caps and banners. The other military men are all enemies of the faith. Euchius (к8, fig. 7.31), who is shown being speared by St. George while in the act of burning a church, is identified as a "wicked soldier." The swallow-tailed banners held by the pages of Mercurius are a recognizable military flag of Theodore's time. Battling horsemen depicted on a thirteenth-century pilgrimage canteen, in the Freer

7.31
Palace of Nebuchadnezzar (κ7),
between the three Hebrews (κ6)
and George (κ8; ADP/SA 1999)

7.32 RIGHT

Palace of Nebuchadnezzar (κ7), detail of upper level (ADP/SA 7 s146 97)

7.33 BELOW CENTER

Palace of Nebuchadnezzar (κ7), detail of middle level (ADP/SA 8 s146 97)

7.34 BOTTOM

Palace of Nebuchadnezzar (κ7), detail of bottom level

Gallery, carry much larger standards of the same shape.[75] This canteen, made of brass inlaid with silver, is one of a group of metal objects produced in Ayyubid Syria that combines Islamic courtly themes with images taken from Christian iconography.[76] The Crusader icon of Sergius and Bacchus from the Monastery of St. Catherine shows a similar lance standard, except that it has three extending pendants (fig. 7.24). An anonymous French chronicler of the Crusaders' struggle against Salah ad-Din, the founder of the Ayyubid dynasty, remarked circa 1191 that "the Amir Taqadin, a close relative of Saladin, displayed in a most curious manner, a pair of drawers upon his banner."[77] The Crusader historian may have been referring to a double-windsock banner. The shape would have been much the same as those held by the pages of Mercurius.

In most of Theodore's program, narrative figures and elements are used to convey details from the lives of the saints. Menas, for example, is identified by his camels, Victor by the manner of his death, Mercurius by the wicked king he killed. The Palace of Nebuchadnezzar (κ7; figs. 7.31–7.34) is one of the most elaborate examples of this style of painting in the Church of St. Antony. Although the palace is part of the narrative of the three Hebrews (κ6), it occupies its own distinct panel on the north wall of the khurus. The painting is unique in Theodore's program in that it contains no sacred images. The palace is populated only by figures representing the forces of iniquity. The domed monastery of the Anatolian Fathers on the opposite wall of the khurus (κ3, κ4; fig. 7.19) serves as a holy counterpoint to this domed palace of Babylon.

Nebuchadnezzar's palace is part of a larger composition derived from the Book of Daniel, in which the painting of the three Hebrews (κ6) is the most important component. This latter image, on the west wall of the northern side of the khurus, shows the three young men standing with an angel in the fiery furnace. The palace is placed on the adjacent north wall, sandwiched between the three holy youths and the equestrian portrait of St. George (κ8; fig. 7.31). The two parts of the composition are shown in different scales. The Hebrews fill the entire pictorial panel, while the palace and its inhabitants are shown in the much smaller size used for narrative figures. Despite this discrepancy, the two sections are linked in both time and space. In the pictorial logic of the composition, the furnace is part of the palace, and Nebuchadnezzar and his soldiers are shown reacting to the miracle occurring within it. Schematic architectural elements are used to divide the composition at κ7 into three registers, where different events occur simultaneously. The lowest level is a vaulted

7.35
Manuscript illumination in the
Gospel of Matthew (approach to
Jerusalem, entry to Jerusalem, wise
and foolish virgins, blessing at
Bethany, washing of the feet, and
Last Supper), New Testament,
1249/1250, Cairo (© Institut
Catholique, Bibliothèque de Fels,
Paris, MS copte-arabe 1, fol. 19r)

dungeon that contains the furnace depicted at K6 on the adjacent wall (fig. 7.34); an arcade outlines the middle level (fig. 7.33); and the upper floor of the palace consists of a domed throne room, where the Babylonian king sits in state (fig. 7.32).

This composition has the largest number of narrative figures in a single image in the church. They are also the most animated. Babylonian soldiers are shown crowded around the mouth of the furnace in the vaulted dungeon. They are depicted in ranks, with the heads of those behind appearing above the figures in the front row. The soldiers look at each other, expressing astonishment that the Hebrews remain unharmed. One of them extends his hand toward the flames as if to test the heat. The passions of the Coptic martyrs often contain anecdotes of soldiers severely injured in this manner. Saints Cyriacus and Julitta were thrown into a cauldron of molten copper, but thanks to divine protection, it felt as refreshing as dew from heaven. When a few drops splashed on the watching governor, however, he was burned to the bone.[78] We see that news of the miracle in the furnace has spread through the palace. Soldiers on the middle level whisper about it among themselves. Members of the royal guard inform the king. He places his finger to his mouth in amazement.

The Palace of Nebuchadnezzar shares a number of features with Arab miniature paintings of the thirteenth century. The artist, whether Theodore or a member of his team, seems to have been familiar with contemporary book illustrations. Byzantine illuminated manuscripts produced between the ninth and twelfth centuries exerted a profound influence on the development of miniature painting in Armenia, Georgia, Russia, the Crusader states, and the Arab world.[79] The production of Arab illustrated manuscripts seems to date from the second half of the twelfth century. Copies of medical and scientific works based on Greek originals were popular among the literate middle class. Illustrated editions of secular literary works, however, best represent the Arab style of miniature painting. A favorite illuminated book of the period was the *Maqamat* (assemblies) of al-Hariri (d. 1122).[80] It consists of fifty tales about an eloquent rogue named Abu Zayd (Father of Anyone), who uses his astonishing persuasive abilities to extract money from gullible listeners in different parts of the Islamic world. The painters of the *Maqamat* were less concerned with the linguistic fireworks of the text than with depictions of daily life. Their miniatures are set in mosques, palaces, taverns, libraries, slave markets, and rural hamlets, providing what Richard Etting-

7.36

Miniature by Yahya al-Wasiti in
the Maqamat of al-Hariri, 1237,
Iraq (Bibliothèque National, Paris,
MS Arabe 5847, fol. 122v)

part of the same artistic milieu.[86] The *Maqamat* copied and illustrated by al-Wasiti (1237) and the Cairo New Testament (1249/1250) were produced by men of different faiths, living in separate parts of the Arab world, but the paintings have stylistic features in common that transcend religious and geographical boundaries. Some of the artistic devices employed in these two manuscripts are also found in the painting of the Palace of Nebuchadnezzar in the Church of St. Antony.

Many of the miniatures of al-Wasiti are set within buildings, which are symbolized by schematic arches and domes. In a few examples, the figures inhabit more than one level of the building. One of Wasiti's most ambitious architectural paintings is of a palace of an Indian potentate (fig. 7.36). The wife of the king is shown giving birth in a chamber on the ground floor. Female attendants wait in side rooms. Her husband sits enthroned upstairs. Abu Zayd and a companion calculate the child's horoscope in domed rooms flanking the throne hall. Red bands indicate the separate rooms on each level, which are ornamented with simplified architectural elements. The parable of the wise and foolish virgins in the Cairo New Testament is set in a similar two-story building (fig. 7.35). The foolish virgins wait below, outside a closed door, while the bridegroom and wise virgins celebrate in an arcaded upper chamber. The painter of Nebuchadnezzar's palace uses the same two-dimensional architectural frame. Another close parallel is visible on the south side of the khurus, where Basil and Gregory stand underneath a domed building surmounted by a cross (K3, K4; fig. 7.19). The visual analogy to the illumination from the *Maqamat* is particularly clear in the tall narrow shape of the domed side rooms on the upper level of the Indian palace.

A number of al-Wasiti's miniatures feature crowds of people. They are depicted in the same manner as the mob of Babylonian soldiers outside of the fiery furnace. The double-paged painting of the "twenty-first session," for example, shows a huge crowd standing at the door of a mosque listening to a sermon (fig. 7.13). The individuals are shown in five rows rising one above the other. We see the full bodies of the figures in the bottom row but only the heads of the men behind them. The painter of the Cairo New Testament uses this same device when depicting the apostles around Jesus (fig. 7.35). This figural grouping can be found in manuscript illuminations from the late antique and medieval worlds, both Western and Eastern, but is not a feature of Coptic wall painting of any period.[87] It therefore seems probable that Theodore and his team of

hausen and Oleg Grabar refer to as a unique mirror of contemporary society.[81] The best-known manuscript of the *Maqamat*, now in the Bibliothèque Nationale in Paris, was copied and illustrated in 1237 by Yahya al-Wasiti of Iraq.[82]

Illustrated manuscripts produced by Christians living under Muslim rule were another source of inspiration for Arab painters.[83] The earliest known Egyptian manuscripts with miniatures from this period are Coptic, including a lavishly illuminated gospel book written in the Bohairic dialect in 1179/1180 at Damietta.[84] Eastern Christian painters may have served as intermediaries between Byzantine and Islamic art, but the traffic of cross-cultural exchange went both ways. They also borrowed freely from contemporary secular illuminations found in works of Arabic literature. A Copto-Arabic New Testament produced in Cairo in 1249/1250 contains miniatures that are a fascinating blend of Christian and Muslim styles of painting (fig. 7.35).[85] Jesus and his disciples wear biblical costumes and are placed against a golden background, evocative of Byzantine icons and mosaics. But other elements are drawn from contemporary Muslim society. Figures are depicted wearing turbans and seated cross-legged in the Arab manner. Soldiers are shown in the military garb of the period. Arabesques and geometric patterns, derived from Islamic art, are used as borders and decorative details. The thirteenth-century miniatures of Iraq, Syria, and Egypt are so closely related in theme and style that the painters, whether Christian or Muslim, must have been

artists would have been familiar with this convention
either from seeing, or more likely from actually producing, illustrated books.

Two other features seen in the paintings in the khurus show a familiarity with contemporary illuminated
manuscripts. The first, Nebuchadnezzar's gesture of placing his finger to his mouth, is recognizable as a convention
expressing amazement.[88] It is employed by al-Wasiti in
fourteen separate illustrations of the *Maqamat*.[89] His figures use it to convey their wonder at the eloquence of Abu
Zayd (fig. 7.37). The gesture later became commonplace in
Persian miniatures.[90] The second element is the king's
throne, which is unlike any other in the church (fig. 7.32).
It is a *sella curulis* (curule seat), the folding stool used by
Roman emperors on state occasions.[91] This type of throne
became less common in the later Empire but seems to have
enjoyed a revival among Muslim dignitaries.[92] It is featured in a number of miniature paintings from the twelfth
and thirteenth centuries. The ʿAbbasid caliph is shown on
one in a Byzantine chronicle copied in Palermo circa 1175.
In contrast, the same painting depicts the emperor on a
large wooden throne.[93] Badr al-Din Luʾluʾ, the lord of
Mosul, sits on a sella curulis in two frontispieces from a
multivolume edition of *The Book of Songs* of al-Isfahani,
dated 1218/1219.[94] An illustrated copy of the *Materia Medica*
of Dioskorides, produced in Iraq in 1224, has a medical
attendant seated on the same type of folding stool while
stirring a poultice in a large basin.[95] This type of seat was
clearly in common use in the Muslim world and was also a

standard feature in manuscript illuminations, so it could
have been familiar to the painter of Nebuchadnezzar from
both life and art. The Monastery of St. Antony possesses
an actual example of a sella curulis (fig. 7.38). It is perhaps
too small ever to have served as a functioning stool, but it
may have been used as a *kursi* (throne) for the Bible.

What do these elements from thirteenth-century
Arab illuminated manuscripts tell us about the team that
painted the Church of St. Antony? Hunt has identified a
workshop of Christian painters based in Cairo and active
circa 1220–1250.[96] She believes that this group produced
wall paintings in monastic churches, icons, and illuminated Bibles, including the Cairo New Testament. Apart
from these religious commissions, the painters also appear
to have made illustrated editions of Arabic secular literature, such as a copy of the *Maqamat*, dated 1222/1223,
which is now in Paris.[97] The painting of Nebuchadnezzar's
palace suggests that at least one member of Theodore's
team was also creating similar secular manuscripts.

The paintings of the Church of St. Antony are unique
in that they constitute an almost complete program of
Coptic painting from the medieval period. The absence of
comparable material makes it is difficult to determine to
what extent Theodore's employment of secular elements is
typical of Egyptian Christian art in the thirteenth century.
Earlier surviving paintings suggest that the adoption of
contemporary motifs into the Coptic tradition was well established by the time Theodore was active, while later
works indicate that the practice was to continue into the

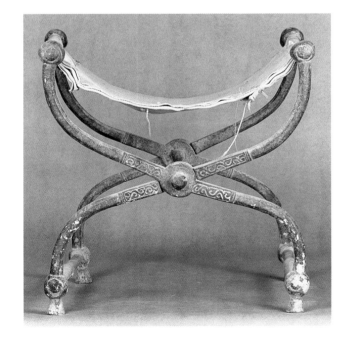

fourteenth century.[98] It seems likely that there was nothing particularly unusual in Theodore's use of current elements in his religious paintings. The fact that his program is securely dated, however, allows us to examine these secular details in the light of the predominately Islamic Egyptian culture of the same time.

One of the most characteristic features of Theodore's work is his conservatism in the use of contemporary motifs. Some of the secular elements in his program can be dated on stylistic grounds to the previous century, when Egypt was ruled by the Fatimid caliphs. Examples include the pointed arches and the vegetal decoration of the painted arcades of the nave, as well as the turbans and tiraz bands worn by certain figures to indicate positions of authority. It is important to remember that these architectural forms, decorative motifs, and details of dress would not have been regarded as novelties in Theodore's day. In 1233, they had been used in Egypt for centuries and would continue to be employed throughout the medieval and early modern periods. We should therefore see these secular elements as being in current use when Theodore painted the Church of St. Antony.

In some aspects of his program, however, Theodore seems almost consciously retardataire. This is especially true of the single Arabic inscription, al-Fadi. The use of the kufic script and the cryptic manner in which the phrase is written recalls Arabic calligraphy of the eleventh or twelfth century. In contrast, Theodore shows no awareness of the more contemporary cursive Arabic scripts, even though earlier Coptic artists had employed them. The frontispiece of the illuminated Coptic gospel book produced in 1179/1180 at Damietta, for example, shows the enthroned Christ framed by an inscription in the cursive naskhi script.[99] Theodore's use of an earlier form of Arabic calligraphy highlights the difficulty of dating Coptic paintings solely on stylistic analyses of secular elements. Walters suggests that the paintings at Tebtunis of Theodore Stratelates and an anonymous equestrian were produced circa 950–1050, based on the kufic script found on both saints.[100] Although such a date is consistent with similar Fatimid tiraz inscriptions, Theodore's work indicates that the same

style of Arabic script could still have been in use in Coptic painting more than a hundred years later.

It is nevertheless apparent that secular elements continued to enter Coptic religious art under the rule of the Ayyubid sultans. The military equipment of the equestrian saints in the Church of St. Antony is the best example of these more recent additions. The quilted armor, large saddlecloths, and knotted horsetails are all features that reflect the introduction of Turkish-style cavalry troops into Egypt after 1171 by Salah ad-Din and his successors. The change in military equipment that occurred during the Ayyubid period is important for determining when medieval Coptic depictions of equestrian saints were produced. The painting of Theodore Stratelates in the Monastery of the Martyrs at Esna, for example, has a date that can be read either as A.M. 846 (1129/1130) or as A.M. 896 (1179/1180).[101] Based on the saint's quilted armor and large saddlecloth, the later date, which corresponds to the early Ayyubid period, seems more likely.[102]

Still other secular elements may have entered Coptic art in Theodore's time, such as the details derived from Arab miniature paintings found in the palace of Nebuchadnezzar. In particular, the king's gesture of amazement, his folding throne, and the manner in which his soldiers are shown crowded around the mouth of the furnace are not part of the Coptic tradition. Instead, they represent current secular painting, which was being practiced throughout the Arab world in the first half of the thirteenth century. Theodore's suggested link with the production of miniatures, therefore, may have been a means by which new secular elements were introduced into Coptic religious painting.

The integration of secular elements into the Coptic tradition certainly did not end with Theodore. An especially conservative feature of his program is that it does not contain any arabesque or geometric patterns of the kind that represented the most advanced style of Islamic art of his day. Yet as Bolman and I demonstrate in the next chapter, within less than fifty years, another Christian painter in the Church of St. Antony used these very motifs to decorate the vault of the khurus.

CHAPTER 8   THE KHURUS VAULT

AN EASTERN MEDITERRANEAN SYNTHESIS

8.1

Upper zone of the khurus

(ADP/SA 1999)

On the basis of style and ornament, the paintings in the ceiling zone of the khurus do not belong to the Coptic tradition as exemplified by Theodore (fig. 8.1). The work of two principal artists can be identified in this small space, with distinct artistic genealogies. An Ornamental Master specialized in abstract designs popular in the Islamic world, and a Figural Master worked in what may generally be described as a Byzantine manner. The works of both also include features belonging to additional cultures and regions. It is unlikely that one artist completed the entire area, simply because none of the decorative elements in the Ornamental Master's work appears in any of the sections with figural paintings. Based on the technical observations of Luzi and De Cesaris, it is apparent that the whole area was painted at one time.[1] The painters were responsible for discrete sections of the khurus. Each one worked in a style that was current in the thirteenth century and that was as distinct from the other as both were from Theodore's earlier program.

The khurus is the transitional space in Coptic churches between the nave and the sanctuary (fig. 21, introduction). In the Church of St. Antony, the khurus is entered through a large archway containing a wooden partition. Beyond the partition is a rectangular room. Its center is covered by a high, vaulted roof, supported by four arches. The two largest arches direct one's view from the nave to the central sanctuary. The side arches frame the viewer's entrance to the northern and southern ends of the khurus, each of which gives access to the lateral sanctuaries. The weight of the vault rests on the two largest arches that separate the nave from the sanctuary. Each one supports a curved tympanum of plastered brick. Seven rectan-

gular palm trunks have been placed on top of the tympana in an east-west orientation. These beams form the frame of the vaulted roof. The interstices between the beams are filled with wooden planks, and the entire ceiling is covered with plaster. The vault has an irregular profile. The basic shape of the khurus vault was already present when Theodore was active in the church. The current ensemble of palm trunks, wooden panels, and plaster may belong to the new campaign, but could also predate it. Rows of round windows separate it from the side walls of the khurus, and these regular, simple windows certainly predate the painted phase now visible.[2]

Before the work of the anonymous masters, the archway leading from the nave to the khurus was heightened. Its new profile allowed the khurus vault to be seen easily from the nave. The painters then covered the vault in plaster that is distinguished from earlier layers in the church by a faint pinkish cast. This plaster was also applied on the domes and around the frames of Theodore's paintings. Figures from the earlier program that transgressed the frame were covered over. This is most evident in the lower zone of the khurus, where the pages of Mercurius (κ3; fig. 7.19) and the figure of the rich man in hell next to Abraham, Isaac, and Jacob in Paradise (κ5; fig. 4.25) were completely obscured. Luzi and De Cesaris have hypothesized that this was motivated by a desire to make the appearance of the church interior neater, including regularizing the borders and frames of the earlier paintings.

The conservators have suggested that only a relatively short span of time separated the work of Theodore and that of the later painters. They observed that the accumulation of soot and dirt was slight on the sections of Theo-

8.2 ABOVE

The archangel Gabriel

(K16; ADP/SA 1999)

8.3 BELOW

The archangel Michael

(K15; ADP/SA 8 s164 97)

dore's 1232/1233 paintings that were covered over with the new plaster. The plaster was, in effect, clean. We know that the monastery was inhabited and that the Church of St. Antony was in use at this time. How long would the plaster of Theodore's level retain this pristine condition if exposed to the smoke of incense and lamps and the dust of the Egyptian desert? Certainly not more than fifty years separated the two campaigns, but it is possible that they were painted only a decade apart.

At perhaps the same time that the khurus ceiling was being prepared, an archway was cut between the southwestern corner of the nave and the annex. We do not know whether a door originally existed here, but because this archway destroyed at least two figures from Theodore's program (between N16 and N18; fig. 4.4), its later date is apparent. Stylistic and material evidence makes it clear that the paintings in this archway were made somewhat later than those in the upper regions of the khurus.[3]

The Figural Paintings

Paintings of human, angelic, and divine beings cover two areas in the khurus ceiling: the underside of the arch be-

tween the nave and the khurus (K15, K16) and the western-facing wall above the archway between the khurus and the sanctuary (K11, K12, K18). The first of these areas is filled with two enormous archangels, Gabriel (on the left, or northern side; fig. 8.2) and Michael (on the right, or southern side; fig. 8.3). They exemplify many of the characteristic features of style seen in this program and serve as representatives of the larger group of figural paintings. They stand in a static, frontal position against an intensely saturated orange-red background. In their left hands, each holds a white disk painted with a red cross and letters signifying the phrase "Jesus Christ is victorious." In their right hands they hold tall, golden-colored staffs surmounted with crosses. Their wings arch elegantly above their shoulders and sweep down almost to their feet. Like their pose, their curved faces are virtually identical: broad through the eyes and forehead and tapering gracefully to the chin, so that each visage is longer than it is wide (fig. 8.3). Their expressions convey an intensity and otherworldliness through the calligraphic sweep of their dark eyebrows, slightly furrowed brows, and their eyes, which are almost completely dominated by large, dark pupils. The planes of the face are built up with numerous thin brushstrokes that are visible from several feet away but are not apparent from floor level. The artist has shaped the forehead, cheeks, chin, and neck with a combination of white and pink shades. Dark outlines delineate the eyes, nose, and Adam's apple, which are given depth and definition with narrow areas of shadow (for example, below the brows), and dark pink lines (shaping the pouches below the eyes). Their ears are shown as downward sloping loops. Their hair is composed of thick strands of dark brown outlined in black and enlivened with lighter strands, appearing at the top to be loosely braided, and terminating in rounded curls along the neck and shoulders. Their long

8.4

Eastern wall of the khurus
(K11–K12, K18), with the sanctuary
apse in the background (ADP/SA
1999)

hands may be the most refined features in these paintings. The attenuated index finger of each angel's right hand is particularly effective as a device leading the viewer's eye to the face.

When caught by the camera from a position directly in front of each figure, their bodies appear to be of normal height, but a bit stocky in the waist and hips. This effect is not apparent from the floor of the nave, where the prominent arch and indirect point of view elongate the figures. Their faces, too, appear considerably longer and more narrow from the nave floor than they do from a raised, head-on view obtainable only with the aid of scaffolding. The location from the floor of the church is the principal one from which these figures were meant to be seen.

The imposing angels cast no shadows on the intense red background. They have considerable presence without conveying real physical substance. Their rigidly frontal poses, and the completely two-dimensional patterning of such areas as the decoration at the bottom of their long tunics, or the band around their wrists, contradict any sense of mass conveyed by the folds of clothing and faint

shadows on their faces. They do not stand on any ground, but hover above us in the archway.

The western-facing wall at the back of the khurus is oddly shaped (fig. 8.4). The pointed arch leading to the sanctuary cuts into it, making the center considerably more narrow than the sides. The upper edge describes a curve that is less sharp than the archway itself but is complicated by the beams that support this roughly barrel vaulted space. The artist has depicted two scenes in this awkward space. The scene at the right shows the three women at the tomb (K12), as they confront an angel and realize that Christ has risen from the dead. The tomb of Christ (K11) divides this event from the meeting of Christ and the women in the garden (K18). The rendering of the faces and hands of the women and angel in these two scenes is by the same hand as that of the archangels Michael and Gabriel (K15, K16). Variations also exist between the painting of the archangels and the rest of the figures, particularly in the face of Christ, which is built up of very prominent lines. Although the basic delineation of the eyebrows, eyes, nose, mouth, and ears is similar, their

8.5 LEFT
Angel of the stone (K12)

8.6 RIGHT
Icon of the archangel Gabriel,
ca. 1200, Cyprus (Courtesy of
A. Papageorghiou)

effect in the face of Christ is somewhat harsh. Also distinct from the archangels are the proportions and poses of the figures on this wall. Their bodies are short. They are not shown frontally, and their varied positions express interaction. Some of them stand, albeit uneasily, on the mountainous ground under their feet. The alternating intensity in the colors of their draperies and the occasional use of thin black lines give these figures a greater sense of mass than the archangels have. No abstract, completely two-dimensional pattern on their clothing disturbs this sense of volume, although the stability of the two standing figures in the meeting of Christ and the women in the garden is undermined by the fact that each one extends a foot into the red border of the painting.

The scene of the women at the tomb is a masterpiece of compositional ingenuity. The uneven, cramped space is filled with a cascade of figures, gracefully disposed along the descending archway. The angel sits with his feet on top of the stone that had sealed the tomb, thus fitting easily into the reduced space at the center of the wall. He gestures toward the tomb with his left hand, formed by a long curving line that leads the eye toward the sepulcher. Sunlight damage suffered over the centuries has badly eroded the beige paint of this hand. With his right hand, the angel points to the letters written in Coptic in front of him: "an angel of the Lord." He and the first of the women look at each other, while the second of the women turns her face toward the third. The raised hands and furrowed brows of the women express surprise and distress at this apparition, and at the empty sepulcher.

The tomb presents us with a problem. It is impossible to know whether the painted lower zone and the

opening above it combined to show the tomb. The lower section clearly shows the tomb and the two pieces of fabric left inside it by Christ. The actual opening above the tomb was at one time a window into the sanctuary, on which side it was bricked up, plastered over, and painted in 1232/1233. The question is why the opening onto the khurus was left open. Luzi and De Cesaris have pointed out that no light would have come through it from above, because an earlier, low wooden ceiling blocks it off. They also note that the opening is framed with a solid red band, identical to that which borders the entire double composition. Expressing the opinion that it would have been easier for the artists to close this space up and plaster it over, they conjecture that it was important in some way. One suggestion is that it held an icon that was framed by the painted wall.[4]

The meeting of Christ and the women in the garden is somewhat less successful as a composition than its counterpart. The standing Christ has a large head and a comparatively short body, and even so he doesn't fit the space: his left foot rests on the border, outside of the scene. He holds the book of the Gospels with his left hand in an implausible grip. With his right, he gestures to the two Marys. The position of his ring finger is rendered as if it were bent sideways instead of forward. As with many of the hands in these paintings, the palm is displayed; fingernails should not be visible, but they are. The poses of the two women are not as graceful as the group of three on the right. The standing Mary presents an ungainly silhouette, as does the crouching woman at Christ's feet. An awkward empty space fills the center of the scene. In several places, corrections made to the composition are visible. A line of preparatory drawing, tracing a larger curve for Mary's head, is apparent through the yellow of her halo. Additional lines, showing earlier efforts at drawing Christ's halo and right hand, are seen through the background color. Sunlight and the passage of time have damaged this composition considerably. The red of the Virgin's dress has flaked off, showing part of the kneeling woman that would have originally been covered. The base of a palm tree rises behind Christ, but its upper green fronds have been destroyed. Altogether, this composition does not give as fluid and unified an impression as does that on the right. Certainly, some of this effect is due to the loss of compositional elements, perhaps in the center of the painting, and the appearance of underpainting and corrections, which would not have been visible originally.

Again, we know from the layer of plaster on which these scenes were painted that they must have been made after the 1232/1233 program. Their style and technique are markedly different from the work of Theodore. In color, also, they stand apart. The bright orange-red of the later paintings is in contrast to the darker red of 1232/1233. The bright blue used for the clothing of four of the nine figures in the paintings of the upper khurus is nowhere present in the earlier program, where a less intense blue is used sparingly.[5] Both palettes include strong yellow and ocher tones, but their greens differ considerably. Theodore's are either olive or, used sparingly, an intense, bright green.[6] The hue found in the upper section of the khurus is either a dark blue-green (in the background), or a light mint green (in the abstract ceiling patterns).

In style, painting technique, color, and even subject matter, these paintings do not belong to the long-standing tradition of Coptic painting in Egypt, exemplified so magnificently in the paintings of Theodore and his workshop. Several questions arise from this observation. To what tradition or traditions do the figural paintings belong? Who painted them, and when? How do they come to be here, in this remote site in the Egyptian desert?

THE FIGURAL MASTER

The works of the Figural Master belong to the larger sphere of the Byzantine world. This environment extended beyond the territories held at any given time by the empire itself, interacting with art produced at places remote from Constantinople, like the Monastery of St. Catherine on Mount Sinai and the Crusader kingdoms of the East. One such region, no longer part of Byzantium politically by the thirteenth century, but still creating art in the Byzantine tradition, was Cyprus. From the tenth century to 1191, Cyprus was an important territory for Byzantium. After 1099 the imperial fleet was stationed at the island, which was a commercial center and also a common resting point for pilgrims on their journey to the Holy Land. In 1191 it was conquered by Richard the Lion Heart, who sold it first to the Knights Templar, then, when they gave it back, to Guy de Lusignan, a Frankish knight. Guy's brother established the Kingdom of Cyprus in 1197.[7] The development of art on Cyprus in the ensuing centuries is complicated. Before the Crusader takeover, artistic production was related to current trends in Constantinople. After 1191 this source was cut off, and in the thirteenth century Cypriot artists continued to elaborate on earlier Byzantine sources, of the Comnenian period in the twelfth century.[8] Other elements—for example, from Latin patrons, and Syrian monastic art—have also been identified.[9]

On the basis of style and painting technique, the closest analogies to the work of the Figural Master come from the island of Cyprus and the Monastery of St. Catherine on Mount Sinai in the late twelfth and the thirteenth century. Parallels are revealed when we compare an icon of the archangel Michael from the Katholikon of the Monastery of Hagios Chrysostomos at Koutsovendis of ca. 1200 with the paintings in the upper zone of the khurus (figs. 8.5, 8.6).[10] Although the archangel of the icon has small pupils and red cheeks, in contrast to the large pupils and white cheeks of the Figural Master's work, almost every other feature of comparison is identical: the forehead, furrowed with two principal lines (the upper line tracing a minor, downward curve, and the lower, longer line a high curve arching over the eyebrows, dipping as it meets at the bridge of the nose); the shape of the eyes, rendered with a thin red line near the crease of the upper lid; the pouch below the eyes, which follows the same line as well; the thin, long nose; the small mouth; the downward loop of the ears and the Adam's apple. Thin lines build up the planes of the face on the icon and the faces of women and archangels in the wall paintings. The hair of the angels is identical as well: loosely braided, with two small tufts of hair that extend from the center of the forehead and curve toward the viewer's left; strands of brown hair, outlined in black and marked with highlights. The long hands and narrow fingers are also very similar, as is shown by a comparison of the right hand of the archangel Michael from the icon, with the right hand of the Virgin Mary, who stands to the left of Christ in the painting in the Church of St. Antony. The outlines, proportions, and form are the same. Altogether, the style is characterized by a curvilinear approach to the shapes of the various parts of the body, which is always interesting, and never completely regular. The similarities between the Cypriot icon and the figural painting in the khurus are striking, especially when we consider that one is a painting on a wooden panel, meant to be seen from nearby, and the others are wall paintings, in a completely different scale and medium, and intended to be viewed from a considerable distance.

The thin, simply arching eyebrows of the icon at Koutsovendis are repeated in the same feature of the angel on the stone, by the Figural Master. The other painted subjects in the khurus have expressive, angular eyebrows, and these also we can find in Cypriot paintings. The depiction of the impression left by Christ's face on the mandylion, from the Church of the Archangel Michael, at Kato Lefkara, exemplifies the more dramatic type (fig. 8.7). Note the

deep U shape formed between the two eyebrows, and compare it to the same shape formed on the face of the woman
at the extreme right, in the three women at the tomb (fig.
8.8). A feature that is characteristic of Cypriot painting is
the wide space at the inner corner of the eyes, showing the
tear ducts.[11] The face of Christ in Kato Lefkara illustrates
this peculiarity.

The Virgin Mary at the far left of the khurus wall exhibits some ties to an icon now in the Monastery of St.
Catherine (figs. 8.9, 8.10), which may also have been
painted by a Cypriot master. The pose of the two figures is
similar, as both figures assume a position directly facing
neither the viewer nor Christ, but midway between the
two, with hands outstretched. Their heads are inclined at
the same angle. The icon forms part of a Deesis composition, in which the gesture is a request for intercession. Because the wall painting depicts a different subject, the pose
may be understood here to suggest greeting. The faces of
the two are similar in shape, particularly their definition:
slightly angular at the top, undulating along the right side,
and curving around a smooth, fleshy chin and up along
the wide expanse of the cheek to the viewer's left. The main
points of difference between the two faces are the mouth
and the sides of the nose. In the wall painting, the Virgin's
top lip is rendered with a simple, thin line, which is in contrast to the slightly protruding upper lip seen in the icon.
The icon remains unstudied, but likely dates to the thirteenth century.[12] Its existence in the collection at Sinai does
not mean that it was made there, but the wide tear ducts
may point to a Cypriot origin.

As we have seen, the face of Christ in the Church of
St. Antony is rendered in a more linear manner than the
other faces in the khurus (fig. 8.11). The painter has used
thicker, more prominent lines. The cheeks are outlined in
a brown and pink oval, which curves down from the
pouches under the eyes and is filled with mostly straight
lines set at an angle to the rest of the lines of the face. Kurt
Weitzmann identified this feature on several icons in the

Monastery of St. Catherine. He explained it as a device
brought either by a Venetian painter, working at Sinai, or
by way of a panel painting from the Veneto.[13] Equally compelling parallels, or perhaps even more compelling ones,
exist in the Byzantine art historical record. This type of
rendering appears as early as 1060, in a mosaic icon of
the Virgin and Child in the Greek Orthodox Patriarchate
at Istanbul and in the face of the Virgin Mary from the
late–twelfth century Byzantine mosaics at Torcello (fig.
8.12).[14] Other details of Christ's face are readily found in
the Byzantine tradition, in icons at the Monastery of St.
Catherine, and also on Cyprus. The narrow face, long
strands of twisted hair, with two shorter tufts descending
into the center of the forehead, the short beard and mustache are all common traits seen in numerous images belonging to the late twelfth and the thirteenth century.[15] The
flaring ends of the cross in Christ's halo in the khurus
image are a more exaggerated version of what we see in
several of these paintings as well.[16]

Three other stylistic features remain to be discussed.
One is the appearance of short bodies and comparatively
large heads on all of the figures in these paintings except
the two archangels. Thirteenth-century Cypriot painting
gives us examples of these somewhat ungainly proportions. The wall paintings in the Church of the Panagia at
Moutoullas, dated to 1280, provide a host of examples.[17]
The same paintings include another distinctly Cypriot element, the use of red backgrounds, which also set off the
mandylion in Kato Lefkara (fig. 8.7). Not only is the background of the paintings of the archangels Michael and
Gabriel bright red, but so is the inner face of that same
wall, with an elaborate arabesque (K14).[18] The third feature
has thus far proven impossible to place, and that is the rendering of drapery. It is characterized by the juxtaposition
of dark areas with either light shades of the same color, or
perhaps a semitransparent white which alters the darker
shade. Most of the folds are long and vertical and parallel
each other. Occasionally, angular folds are rendered with V

8.9

Meeting of Christ and the women
in the garden (κ18), detail of Mary
(ADP/SA 12 s161 97)

8.10

Icon of the Virgin, ca. thirteenth
century, Monastery of St. Catherine, Mount Sinai (Courtesy of the
Michigan-Princeton-Alexandria
Expedition to Mount Sinai)

8.11
Face of Christ (κ18)

8.12 RIGHT
Face of the Virgin Mary, late
twelfth century, mosaic, Torcello
(Courtesy of Dumbarton Oaks)

shapes. The fall of the maphorion around two of the five female faces is jagged and angular, as was standard in Byzantine art in this period. The three other faces lack this distinctive feature and appear with lines on the fabric about their heads, as if their head coverings were folded but nonetheless circumscribed an unbroken, curving line. This treatment of the maphorion is less common, but can be seen in Byzantine or Byzantine-inspired art—for example, in an icon of the Crucifixion of ca. 1270, in the Monastery of St. Catherine.[19]

The style of the paintings by the Figural Master in the Church of St. Antony belongs to the artistic sphere of Byzantium. We know that these works of art were painted sometime after 1233, the date of the earlier program by Theodore and his workshop. Yet they relate not to developments in Byzantium proper in the thirteenth century but to an earlier Byzantine style that was still a primary source of influence in Cyprus in the thirteenth century. Numerous details in the rendering of the Figural Master's faces and hands make this assertion possible, as do the short proportions and large heads (excepting the archangels in the khurus archway). The Cypriot image that is closest to the khurus paintings, however, the icon of the archangel Gabriel, is not completely characteristic of the art of that island.[20] The definition of the khurus figures' drapery is not closely tied to any identifiable tradition, and perhaps we should conclude that the artist studied Cypriot paintings but was not shaped in that environment alone. Another possible network of contact that seems to have operated in this period existed between monasteries and was not mapped out along the territorial lines of secular powers. The ties to Cyprus and Sinai may be accounted for within this model.[21] When we expand our view of the khurus paintings from the figural subjects to include the work of the Ornamental Master, it is apparent that an even broader context for these paintings must be considered. We know, from the conservation work, that the period of time that elapsed between the work of Theodore and that of the Figural Master was not great. This observation accords well with the stylistic comparisons we have made, so we can conclude on both counts that the paintings in the upper section of the khurus were created in the thirteenth century.

ICONOGRAPHY

The two archangels rising inside the archway between the nave and the khurus forcefully announce the Byzantine character of the post-1233 paintings, wearing as

8.13 LEFT

The archangel Michael, late twelfth century, marble, Constantinople (Staatliche Museen zu Berlin–Prussischer Kulturbesitz, Museum für Spätantike und Byzantinische Kunst, inv. 2429A)

8.14 ABOVE RIGHT

Disk held by the archangel Gabriel (к16)

8.15 BELOW RIGHT

Greek Orthodox Eulogia loaf

they do the ceremonial dress of Byzantine archangels and emperors (fig. 8.13), and carrying disks.[22] These roundels are also held by the angels in the 1232/1233 paintings (s1, lower zone; figs. 4.35, 6.17), where they look much like Coptic eucharistic loaves, with their impressed center and upraised circular edge. In the case of the later paintings in the khurus archway, the rendering of the image recalls loaves from the Byzantine Orthodox tradition, particularly the design and the smoother surface (figs. 8.14, 8.15).

Two events from the life of Christ are told by the paintings on the eastern wall of the khurus vault (к11, к12, к18; fig. 8.4). Both are recounted in the Gospel of Matthew (Mt 28:1–9) and have been shown in Christian art since its earliest centuries. The three women at the tomb (к11, к12) are depicted on the right, and the meeting of Christ and the women in the garden (к18), which happened shortly after the first encounter, appears on the left. These are paintings of events that proved that Christ was the son of God. He rose from the dead (witness the empty tomb) and

met and spoke with two women who knew him. In this painting, as is often the case in artistic representations of this subject, a monogram identifies one of these women as the Virgin Mary (fig. 8.9), although the Gospel account describes her as Mary, mother of James.[23] Her inclusion makes the recognition of the risen Christ even more certain, for who would know him better than his own mother, who had seen him crucified? These visual proofs of Christ's resurrection combine with the scenes of the three Hebrews in the furnace (к6; fig. 4.24) and Abraham, Isaac, and Jacob in Paradise (к5; fig. 4.25), in the lower portion of the khurus, to make a coherent statement about salvation. The three young men function as a typological prefiguration of the resurrection of Christ, proving the reality of salvation for the Christian faithful.[24] The vehicle is Jesus Christ, who is shown above, and the goal is the paradise of the patriarchs included across the khurus from the three young men. The pictorial programs of both zones, though painted at different points in time and in distinct

8.16 TOP

The women at the tomb and the
meeting of Christ and the women
in the garden, 586, manuscript
illumination, Rabbula Gospels,
Syria

8.17 BOTTOM

Crucifixion, detail, 1183, wall paint-
ing, Hermitage of St. Neophytus,
Cyprus (Courtesy of Dumbarton
Oaks, H63.83)

artistic traditions, are unified by this theme, combining events from both the Old and the New Testaments.

Reading from right to left, the two scenes follow the narrative sequence of events in the Gospels. This ordering recalls the right-to-left placement of the three patriarchs below, and for the same reason.[25] The person who planned the choice and disposition of the scenes was a native speaker of Arabic and was accustomed to reading from right to left. Not only is the standard organization in Christian art of these two events left to right, but the figures within these scenes also usually face in the opposite direction from the depiction here. A detail from the Rabbula Gospels of A.D. 586 of the women at the tomb and the meeting of Christ and the women in the garden shows the typical organization of the two events and also of the iconographic elements in them (fig. 8.16). The women approach the angel from the far left. He sits facing left, with his back to the tomb. The open door of the tomb sends out rays of divine light, which immobilize the soldiers. Christ,

facing right, strides toward the two women who kneel at his feet. Small details, such as the inclusion of the soldiers, and the scroll in Christ's hand in place of the bound codex, differentiate these subjects in the Rabbula Gospels from those by the Figural Master of the Monastery of St. Antony. But despite the passage of roughly seven hundred years, the iconography of the two is astonishingly similar—only reversed.

The poses of the three women standing before the angel express anxiety and agitation, with their upraised hands and creased brows. This emotional group would also have reminded the sophisticated medieval viewer of Christ's death, through a visual analogy with paintings of three women at the Cross. The tight grouping, the alternating directions of the women's heads, and even some of their upraised hands are paralleled in numerous paintings of the Crucifixion. One slightly earlier example can be found in the Hermitage of St. Neophytus, on Cyprus (fig. 8.17), and in both compositions the three women form a single mass.[26] They all express consternation, with their furrowed brows and upraised hands. Particularly striking are the alternating directions of their faces—the first and third look at the angel or Christ, and the middle woman looks back at the third. Henry Maguire has studied the use of comparison in the literature and art of Byzantium and has observed that "comparison was an essential part of the mental equipment of any educated Byzantine. This habit of comparison is very important for an understanding of Byzantine art, because it was especially applicable to visual media."[27] The visual similarity between these scenes would have emphasized both the plan inherent in all of the events of Christ's life, and the miraculous fact of his resurrection.

A second source for the Figural Master's work is tied to only two details in these paintings, but it suggests something very important for our understanding of the artistic milieu of Christian Egypt. The first detail is the pose of the angel on the stone. In Byzantine and Western medieval painting, the angel in this scene always sits with his legs hanging down over the side of the stone. In the two roughly contemporary Coptic wall paintings of this subject, the angel also sits with his legs over the side of the stone.[28] In only one example is the angel sitting knees up, with his feet resting just below the top of the tomb, a bit lower than we see in the khurus, where the angel's feet are actually on top of the stone. This image is from a gospel manuscript that was made in Cairo in 1249/1250.[29] The manuscript is unusual and fascinating because it is clearly a Christian book, but it is painted in a style which owes a

8.18

Heading of the Gospel of Luke
(annunciation to Zacharias,
annunciation, and visitation),
manuscript illumination, New
Testament, 1249/1250, Cairo
(© Institut Catholique, Bibliothèque de Fels, Paris, Ms. copte-
arabe 1, fol. 106r)

great deal to the Islamic artistic tradition. People of importance, such as Pilate, are shown seated in an Eastern manner with their legs up on the seat of a throne or chair.[30]
The precise position of the angel in the khurus painting
appears in illumination in this manuscript from Cairo depicting the Virgin of the Annunciation (fig. 8.18).[31] One
knee is raised, with the sole of the foot flat on the ground
(or stone), and the second knee is lower, with the sole
of the foot facing outward, and placed adjacent to the
first foot.

The second detail that connects the Figural Master's
work with Christian painting in Cairo ca. 1250 is the rendering of the mountainous ground on which the Byzantine-inspired figures in the Church of St. Antony stand.
This terrain is shown as an assemblage of discrete, essentially flat elements with undulating tops. They give the
appearance of being stacked up on top of each other. They
can also be found in the illuminations of the Cairo New
Testament of 1249/1250 (fig. 7.35), and their origins lie in
the Islamic and ancient Near Eastern worlds. One well-
known example comes from a wall painting at Samarra
dating to 836–839.[32] We have also seen this motif in the earlier paintings in the church by Theodore (fig. 8.19).

The Figural Master's work shows his participation in
the Byzantine cultural sphere in the thirteenth century.
Details of style and iconography tie him to Cyprus and
also to works of art now in the Monastery of St. Catherine

on Mount Sinai. The closest Cypriot example is not representative of art from Cyprus, however, and his rendering
of drapery is unusual. His inclusion of iconographic features from the art of the Islamic world shows his familiarity with it. Therefore he cannot be identified completely
with any one place. His paintings were definitely made for
an Eastern Christian audience that was accustomed, by
centuries of Arab rule, to reading texts and images from
right to left. This organizational strategy may have been
the Figural Master's own choice or may have been determined by the monastic patrons of the paintings.

THE ANNEX ARCHWAY: A LATER ADDITION

At first sight, the paintings of two archangels in the
underside of the archway between the nave and the annex
(A1, A9; fig. 8.20) look almost identical to the two that precede the khurus ceiling (K15, K16; fig. 8.1).[33] All four are
frontally positioned in static poses and hold disks or orbs,
and crosses on tall staffs. They are dressed identically. Each
pair depicts Michael and Gabriel. One clear variation is the
painting of the young Christ as Emmanuel, in the disk held
by Gabriel, in the annex archway. The corresponding disk
held by Michael (A1) has the same inscription as the two
shown in the khurus.

Despite these similarities of pose and iconography,
the annex archway was not painted by the same artists
whose images and patterns float above our heads in the

8.19

Samuel (N6; ADP/SA 4 S152 97)

8.20

Annex archangels (A1, A9; ADP/SA
6 S160 97)

8.21

Detail of the archangel Michael

(K15; ADP/SA 10 S164 97)

khurus. Differences in style are great. One nonstylistic feature that makes the different authorship of the two compositions obvious is the arrangement of the inscriptions framing the angels' heads. In the archway preceding the khurus, the inscriptions are organized in vertical sections that are read from left to right (fig. 8.21). The identifying words "the Archangel Michael," for example, are divided up into four parts: *the archa* (at the farthest left), *ngel* (to the right of this, but still on the left side of Michael's head), *Micha* (directly to the right of the angel's head), and *el* (to the far right). The same phrase is divided into three sections in the annex archway, and though the two segments of the word *archangel* are read from left to right, they are on the right side of Michael's head (fig. 8.22). His name is written out in a long vertical band at the far left. Arabic inscriptions and narrative scenes in the khurus paintings run from right to left, and Coptic inscriptions run from left to right. The annex archangel inscriptions do neither consistently, but combine both systems in a confusing mixture. Also, although the formation of many of the letters is similar in the khurus and annex arch paintings, their spacing in the annex composition is too close, and the overall effect is not as elegant.

The outlines of the angels' faces in the annex archway are of an unrelieved regularity. Their eyes, noses, and mouths are similarly precise and even in formation, giving these figures a wooden effect that is sharply at odds with the archangels in the khurus. These two lack the graceful, stylized swooping lines of the forehead, and also of the ribbons which appear behind the khurus angels' heads and flare to the sides. The proportions of such elements as the hands, the crosses on the tops of the tall staffs, the wide bodies, and the fussy shaping of the drapery folds into overcomplicated patterns make it absolutely clear that the same hand did not paint all four archangels.

The artist of the later pair did not have access to scaffolding for his work of studying the khurus angels, as is revealed by the yellow triangles of the angels' loros, within which are set smaller triangles of blue.[34] In the khurus loros, the red design on the yellow was painted as a continuous pattern, and the blue triangle was added afterward, obscuring the central section of the motif. In the annex paintings, the yellow triangles were divided into four separate triangles first. The central one was painted in blue, and the three surrounding shapes were individually decorated with red lines, and each was furnished with a border around all three sides. This is obviously the work of someone who was observing the khurus archangels from the floor of the nave and copying them after the scaffolding in the khurus area had been taken down.

138

8.22

Detail of the archangel Michael

(A1; ADP/SA 1 S160 97)

Analysis of the composition of the pigments in both groups, undertaken by Luzi and De Cesaris, shows them to be identical. Because pigments were not purchased ready made but were mixed and prepared by each team or individual artist, the conservators assert that it is impossible that centuries or even decades passed between the painting of the two archways. Additional observation by their keen eyes provides evidence for a likely scenario. Underneath the paint of the angel Gabriel's feet in the annex appear traces of one of the many paintings of crosses framed by a circle of leaves and pomegranates, which are found throughout the church. These crosses are otherwise positioned below the paintings (figs. 4.2–4.4, 4.16). In this case the cross was painted before the archangel. Also, an angular, jagged line of damaged and lost paint cuts across the archangel Michael. It was caused by its insecure adherence to a poor-quality plaster repair job.

Based on combined evidence from conservation and stylistic analysis, we can propose the following chronology for this archway. At some point after 1233 it was cut into the south nave wall, destroying some of the paintings of Theodore. Most likely, the work was carried out at the same time as the enlargement of the khurus arch, but the one leading to the annex was not painted. The artists, who worked on the Byzantine-inspired paintings in the khurus,

finished and left the monastery. The annex archway settled, and small cracks appeared. At some point before or after this damage, the cross was painted on the inner surface of the archway at the west. The cracks in the wall were filled in with inferior-quality mortar. One member of the previous team, perhaps the least skilled, returned within a few years to paint the second archway, using leftover pigments. Alternatively, a visiting artist or a resident monk undertook the task, using the pigments made by the earlier artists. It seems unlikely that the time difference between the creation of the two pairs of archangels was large, because the same pigments were employed in both sections. Despite this, the variations of style and rendering between the two groups of paintings are so great that we consider it possible that the annex pair were painted decades or centuries after the khurus archangels.

One important iconographic feature distinguishes the later pair of archangels from their model. Instead of depicting both of them holding the white globe or disk inscribed in red with a cross and the abbreviation for "Jesus Christ is victorious," the later artist has painted a pale green, monochrome portrait of the young Christ (fig. 8.23). This bust-length portrait includes the same hand gesture of blessing that we see in the Christ of the Figural Master. The flaring cross of the halo is similar as well, but

8.23 BELOW

The archangel Gabriel (A9), detail
of hand with medallion, partially
cleaned (ADP/SA 97)

8.24 RIGHT

Icon of the archangel Michael,
ca. 1474, Church of Archangelos
Pedoulas, Cyprus (Courtesy of
A. Papageorghiou)

this young Christ holds a scroll and not a codex. This is an
image of Christ as Emmanuel, the "preexistent logos," or, in
other words, Christ of the incarnation.[35] The iconographic
combination of the archangel Gabriel, or Michael, or both
together holding a medallion with a bust-length image of
Christ is called the Synaxis of the Archangels. The earliest
surviving example of it dates to the eleventh century, although it has been suggested that the type was first formulated in the ninth century.[36] It was clearly created in the
Byzantine realm sometime after Egypt was lost to the empire.[37] Numerous icons of the Synaxis of the Archangels
exist from Cyprus and elsewhere, from the thirteenth century on, and the subject was included in wall paintings
in the thirteenth and fourteenth centuries.[38] The closest
visual parallel is a much later icon of the subject from the

Church of the Archangelos Pedoulas, on Cyprus, which is
dated to ca. 1474 (fig. 8.24). The color and pose of the
figure of Christ are virtually identical in the icon and the
wall painting in the Church of St. Antony.

The Ornamental Paintings

The Ornamental Master painted two areas in the upper
khurus: the vault (K13, K17, K19–K47; fig. 8.25) and its eastern-facing wall (K14; figs. 8.26, 8.27). The ceiling of the
vault is divided into rows of windows or long painted panels. Seven rectangular palm trunks project down from the
ceiling, each one providing three additional surfaces for
decoration. The khurus vault is thus divided into thirty-
one decorative bands, including the Coptic inscriptions
(K13, K17) painted on the lateral walls beneath the vault.
The sequence of bands is arranged symmetrically, so that
the north and south sides mirror each other.

The eight areas of ceiling between the palm trunks
are the widest bands in the khurus vault. Windows occupy
half of them. At the lowest point in the arc of the vault, just
above the Coptic inscriptions, are a series of round windows (K19, K47). Rows of hexagonal windows flank the
beam at the top of the vault (K31, K35). The remaining four
areas of ceiling repeat a uniform design consisting of a
frame of interlacing lobed medallions and a network of
arabesques (K23, K27, K39, K43).

Next in size are the bottom surfaces of the seven
palm trunks, painted with four types of bands. The lowest
two beams are decorated with an Arabic inscription that is
interrupted at regular intervals by circular medallions
containing crosses (K21, K45). The second set of palm
trunks has a floral pattern with alternating red, blue, and
pale green blossoms, interspersed with crosses in round

8.25

General view of the khurus ceiling

(ADP/SA 1999)

8.26
Spiral arabesque (κ14), western wall
of the khurus (ADP/SA 1999)

8.27
Detail of spiral arabesque (κ14)

medallions (κ25, κ41). The third pair of beams features a black and white geometric design edged with red, with more medallions displaying crosses (κ29, κ37). Another geometric pattern composed of shapes resembling arrowheads embellished with arabesques is painted on the central beam (κ33). This motif occupies the apex of the vault, and because the sides mirror each other, it is not repeated.

The sides of the palm trunks offer the smallest surface area for decoration. These fourteen painted bands are the simplest in the vault. The most prominent are decorated with three interlacing scrolls (κ26, κ40). Half of the bands of this group are a simple undulating vine-and-leaf pattern (κ24, κ28, κ30, κ32, κ34, κ36, κ38). The bands least visible from the ground have been painted a monochrome red or white (κ20, κ22, κ42, κ44, κ46).

The finest work of the Ornamental Master is a spiral arabesque on the western wall of the vault (κ14; fig. 8.26). It is painted above the arch separating the khurus from the nave and is visible only to a viewer standing in the khurus or sanctuary looking west. The raising of the archway left considerably less space here than on the opposite wall, where the Figural Master painted the three women at the tomb (κ12) and Christ and the two women (κ18). A Coptic inscription frames the edge of the arch (κ14), leaving a crescent-shaped area beneath the vault for the arabesque.[39] Two levels of vine scrolls are placed on a red field. Tightly

coiled white vines with small leaves form the background. The upper level has looser yellow scrolls and large stylized leaves of various shapes. The painter shows real mastery at fitting the rhythmic curls of the yellow vines to the irregular space of the wall. He does miscalculate once, however, in the middle of the southern side of the composition, where the circle is distorted (fig. 8.27).

THE ORNAMENTAL MASTER

Based on the observations of Luzi and De Cesaris, the Ornamental Master worked in the Church of St. Antony within fifty years of Theodore. He was therefore active sometime between ca. 1233 and 1283, a period of great artistic vitality throughout the Islamic world. During this time, local artisans were sponsored by both royal patrons and a prosperous urban middle class. They excelled in the production of ceramics, inlaid metalwork, carved wood, and enameled glass. In spite of the traditional suspicion of figurative art in Islam, an explosion of such imagery was produced in Egypt, Syria, Iraq, and Anatolia between the twelfth and fourteenth centuries. Artisans delighted in the representation of astrological subjects, real or mythical animals, and scenes of princely entertainment. Figures even adorn the coins and public monuments of the Ayyubids and other neighboring Muslim dynasties.[40]

8.28

D'Arenberg Basin, ca. 1240–1249,

Syria (Courtesy of the Freer

Gallery, Smithsonian Institution,

Washington, D.C., inv. F 1995.10)

The same period saw an enormous growth in international trade. Merchants enjoyed an extraordinary degree of freedom of movement. Goods were transported across political and religious boundaries, often regardless of the hostilities between governments. The Mediterranean linked western Europe to the Levant. The Red Sea gave Egypt access to the spice markets of the Indies. Camel caravans, following the pilgrimage routes to Mecca, carried goods between North Africa and Iran. Embargoes on exports or imports were rare. Christian and Muslim governments were much more likely to exercise their rights as first buyer than to ban merchandise.[41]

A characteristic feature of the age was the remarkable degree to which Muslims, Christians, and Jews shared the same secular culture. The artistic by-products of this pluralism are surprising to anyone conditioned to view the arts of Islam and Christendom as separate and mutually exclusive categories. The d'Arenberg Basin (fig. 8.28), in the Freer Gallery, for example, was made in Syria for the Ayyubid Sultan al-Salih Ayyub (d. 1249), who is referred to in the inscriptions as "the defender [of the faith], the warrior [of the frontiers], the supporter [of Islam] . . . the beloved of the Commander of the Faithful [the 'Abbasid caliph]."[42] Yet the basin is decorated with five scenes from the life of Christ and an arcade of standing saints. It also

features more traditional Islamic subjects, including inscriptions in different Arabic calligraphic scripts, bands of arabesque, depictions of polo matches (a favorite sport of the sultan), and processions of rabbits, griffins, and other lucky animals.

The paintings of the Ornamental Master in the khurus vault are another example of the way in which Christians and Muslims were part of the same cultural milieu. Although most likely a Copt, the Ornamental Master worked in a contemporary decorative style originating in the Islamic world. His repertoire of arabesque and geometric paintings and epigraphy was currently popular in Egypt, Syria, and Iraq. The painted designs of the Ornamental Master are decorative motifs without any religious significance. In the thirteenth century, they were employed on religious and secular objects and buildings. Most of them were developed for Muslim patrons and are thus identified as part of Islamic art. The designs, however, pertain not to the religion of Islam but to the predominantly Muslim culture that produced them. They are essentially secular in nature and were employed by Christians as well as Muslims. The same is also true of Arabic calligraphy, which originated as a means of writing the Qur'an in a script beautiful enough to do justice to the words of God but was also used for secular inscriptions.[43] The d'Aren-

bid Sultan al-Kamil in 1211.[44] A similar arabesque was employed on two astrolabes produced in 1228 and 1236 by ʿAbd al-Karim al-Misri (the Egyptian).[45] A miniature from the Paris Maqamat of 1237, painted by Yahya al-Wasiti probably in Baghdad, depicts a veiled woman wearing a red cloak decorated with a white spiral arabesque.[46] The continuing popularity of this design in Egypt among both Muslims and Christians at the end of the thirteenth century is demonstrated by the *minbar* (pulpit) presented to the Mosque of Ibn Tulun in Cairo by the Mamluk Sultan Lagin (1296) (fig. 8.29) and the carved wooden door panels from the Muʿallaqa Church (ca. 1300), now in the British Museum.[47] In the Coptic example, spiral arabesques are used as a background for crosses (fig. 8.30) and for scenes from the Gospels.

The painter's other arabesque design is used four times on the khurus ceiling (K23, K27, K43, K39). Its central

8.29 ABOVE

Wooden inlay on Minbar of Mamluk Sultan Lagin, 1296, Mosque of Ibn Tulun, Cairo

8.30 BELOW

Wooden panel from doors in the Muʿallaqa Church, ca. 1300, Old Cairo (The British Museum, Department of Medieval and Later Antiquities, London, inv. 1878, 12)

berg Basin and the façade of the funerary complex of the Mamluk Sultan Qalawun (1285) in Cairo both have inscriptions praising their royal patrons. The Ornamental Master uses a similar cursive Arabic script for writing the Psalms in the khurus vault of the Church of St. Antony.

The Ornamental Master was obviously trained in a different tradition from that of Theodore, but the styles of the two painters were contemporary. Theodore worked in a conservative Coptic tradition of figural, religious painting. The Ornamental Master practiced a style of ornamental art current in Egypt, Syria, and Iraq. Documented examples of most of his patterns were in use in 1233. He could have painted the khurus vault immediately after Theodore's departure. On the other hand, his decorative vocabulary was to remain popular in Egypt well into the fourteenth century. The motifs employed by the Ornamental Master therefore do not provide us with a precise framework for dating the paintings in the khurus.

DECORATIVE MOTIFS

The arabesque on the western wall of the khurus (K14) is the Ornamental Master's largest and most striking composition. His spiraling vines and prominent leaves resemble those carved on the wooden cenotaph presented to the Mausoleum of Imam al-Shafiʿi in Cairo by the Ayyu-

8.31
Detail of decorative bands on the
khurus ceiling (κ21–κ29; ADP/SA 8s
149 97)

The Ornamental Master employed the interlacing medallions as a frame for his arabesque. Contemporary metalworkers, however, usually filled medallions with motifs different from those of the rest of the decorative band. The upper register on the exterior of the d'Arenberg Basin has an Arabic inscription in a plaited kufic script that is interspersed with lobed medallions containing scenes from the life of Christ. The Blacas Ewer exhibits medallions filled with geometric designs that punctuate inscriptions and figurative scenes (fig. 8.32). The Ornamental Master uses medallions filled with crosses in the same way on six of the decorative bands of the khurus (к21, к25, к29, к37, к41, к45). In the Bahri Mamluk period (1250–1382), leading amirs possessed heraldic blazons denoting elevated rank that were often displayed on inlaid metal work, ceramics, and enameled glass. The base of a brass candlestick made ca. 1290 for Amir Kitbugha, now in Baltimore, has a bold cursive inscription interrupted by rounded blazons containing a bar placed over a stemmed cup, indicating that the owner had been a *saqi* (cup-bearer) of the sultan. The Ornamental Master's use of similarly shaped medallions filled with crosses was likely a Christian adaptation of this Mamluk decorative practice.[49]

The geometric designs on the medallions of the Blacas Ewer are variations on the one painted on bands к29 and к37 in the khurus (fig. 8.31). They are based on the hexagon and what has been termed the root three system of proportion.[50] These hexagonal repeat patterns were evidently popular in the thirteenth century.[51] The example in the khurus is more complex than those found on most metalwork of the period. A diagram of the expanded design, derived from a later Cairene architectural source, parallels the form seen in the khurus ceiling (fig. 8.33).[52] It is also found on a painted wooden ceiling from the early fourteenth century in the *Qaʿa* of Ahmad Kuhya (fig. 8.41). This ceiling shares a number of decorative motifs in common with the khurus vault.

8.32 ABOVE
Blacas Ewer, 1232, Iraq (The British Museum, London, inv. OA 1866.12-29.61)

8.33 BELOW
Hexagonal pattern (drawing after Prisse d'Avennes 1877, pl. 58)

element is a chain of lobed medallions formed by blue interlacing bands. Weaving between the medallions is an arabesque composed of two leaf-sprouting vines, one painted white and the other ocher (fig. 8.31). Both of these ornamental elements were popular in the Near East in the thirteenth century. Variations of the arabesque network are found in illustrated Syriac manuscripts, such as a gospel book produced in Mosul in 1220, which has a miniature of the entry into Jerusalem that is framed by the motif.[48] The d'Arenberg Basin is decorated with a more elaborate version of the design around its base (fig. 8.28). The exterior of the basin is divided into four horizontal registers by thin bands of silver. The bands interlace at regular intervals, forming lobed medallions similar to the central element of the khurus chain. Metalworkers of Iraq and Syria often shaped interlacing borders in this manner. The Blacas Ewer in the British Museum, made at Mosul in 1232, features an interlocking chain of quatro-lobed medallions on its neck that is identical to the one found in the khurus (fig. 8.32).

8.34 LEFT

Arrowhead motif (κ33)

8.35 RIGHT

Madrasa of Mamluk Sultan al-Zahir Baybars, 1262/1263, Cairo

8.36

Interlacing vine scrolls (κ26)

8.37

Interlacing vine scrolls, 1300, Minbar of Mamluk Amir Baktimur, Mosque of Salah Tala'i', Cairo (Drawing by Agnieshka Dobrowolska)

Another geometric design used by the Ornamental Master is painted on the central palm trunk at the highest point of the vault (κ33; fig. 8.34). Red arrowheads, outlined in yellow, point in alternating directions on a blue field. Each one is filled with an arabesque. A variation of this design is found on the surviving portion of the Madrasa of the Mamluk Sultan al-Zahir Baybars in Cairo (1262/1263; fig. 8.35). It is carved in stone above the lintels of the recessed windows. The stone lintels are decorated with hexagonal repeat patterns.

The interlacing vine scrolls on bands κ26 and κ40 (fig. 8.36) are found on an inlaid censer made in Damascus in the early thirteenth century, which is now in the Aron Collection.[53] Alternate versions of the motif composed of two undulating scrolls are employed as decorative borders in the Sircali Madrasa (1243) and the Karatay Madrasa (1253) of Konya in Turkey.[54] The minbar donated to the Mosque of Salih Tala'i' in Cairo by the Mamluk Amir Baktimur in 1300 features the same three-scroll interlace as the one used by the Ornamental Master (fig. 8.37).

Most of the designs used by the Ornamental Master seem to have been drawn from the Islamic world. The alternating red, blue, and pale green blossoms on bands κ25 and κ41, however, may have originated in the Armenian kingdom of Cilicia. The earliest example can be found in a gospel book in the Walters Art Gallery. It dates to 1262 and thus fits within the time period we are suggesting for the khurus ceiling program.[55] The motif is frequently used in Armenian books to decorate columns and other architectural elements framing the canon tables, as can be seen in an example from the Glajor Gospels (ca. 1300–1307; fig. 8.38).[56] With slight changes, this floral motif is found on the ceiling of the Qaʿa of Ahmad Kuhya (ca. 1310), indicating that it was employed in Egyptian art at about the same time (fig. 8.41). It is interesting to note that the floral motif was used in both real and imaginary architectural decoration.

INSCRIPTIONS

The use of inscriptions in the program of the Ornamental Master is another departure from the tradition exemplified by the 1232/1233 paintings. Inscriptions do not have much of a decorative function in Theodore's program. Their purpose is to convey information. Most identify the figures in the paintings and are not part of the pictorial composition but are written wherever space allows. At times, they resemble graffiti. Theodore's memorial and dedicatory panels are given more prominence but are equally lacking in decorative embellishments (N31, κ4).

8.38 ABOVE RIGHT
Canon table, Eusebian prologue, with portrait of Carpanios, Armenian manuscript illumination, 1300–1307, Cilicia (Glajor Gospels, Armenian MS 1, UCLA, p. 5)

The two most visually impressive inscriptions from the 1232/1233 program each form a single line of text painted in white on a long blue band. Both are located in the central sanctuary in positions of obscurity. A dedicatory inscription (s1.14) is placed at the base of the apse hidden behind the altar. A continuous memorial (s33–s36) is painted beneath the Twenty-four elders in the upper zone of the sanctuary.[57] Theodore's sole use of Arabic is the encrypted prayer al-Fadi (الفادي, the Redeemer).[58]

The Ornamental Master placed greater emphasis on inscriptions in his decorative program. Two of the wooden beams in the khurus vault are devoted to an Arabic inscription (κ21, κ45). The letters are white, outlined in red, on a blue band (fig. 8.31). They are written in naskhi, one of the six styles (al-aqlam al-sittah) of cursive calligraphy developed in Iraq in the tenth century. The inscriptions are severely damaged, making it difficult to decipher the complete text, but the southern one has been identified as verses from Psalm 121 (122).[59] Three red medallions containing yellow crosses interrupt the inscription on each beam. The medallions do not correspond to breaks in the text. Rather, they serve a decorative function, having been painted at regular intervals along the band, to which the inscription was then added. Both the text and the medallions proclaim a Christian message, but the prominence given to the inscription, and the use of a contemporary Arabic script, show participation in the same tradition that inspired most of the decorative motifs in the program of the Ornamental Master.

8.39
D'Arenberg Basin, ca. 1240–1249,
Syria, interior view (Courtesy of
the Freer Gallery, Smithsonian
Institution, Washington, D.C.,
inv. F 1995.10)

vegetal motifs resembling those used by the Ornamental Master.[63] These two Muslim inscriptions were produced about forty-five years apart. It was during the same time span that the Ornamental Master was active in the Church of St. Antony.

The Arabic inscriptions of the khurus are part of the decorative scheme of the ceiling zone. They are employed as one of many types of ornamental bands. This new decorative emphasis is also seen in the three Coptic inscriptions of the upper khurus (K13, K14, K17). They resemble the two inscription bands painted by Theodore in the central sanctuary. White letters forming a single line of text are placed on a blue band. The Ornamental Master, however, took this traditional form of inscription and modernized it. The Coptic inscriptions of the khurus are large and prominently placed. The letters were carefully formed in a more calligraphic style than that used by Theodore. The Ornamental Master also painted a background of decorative vegetal elements.

The northern and southern inscriptions are painted along the top of the walls and thus become the lowest register of bands decorating the ceiling zone (K13, K17). They are set on a background of spiraling yellow vines. On the west wall, beneath the arabesque, the inscription follows the contours of the archway leading to the nave (K14). It is interrupted at the apex by a medallion bearing a cross. The letters are painted closer together than on the side inscriptions, leaving less room for vegetal decoration. The three bands are a continuous inscription from Psalm 86 (87).[64] The sequence is noteworthy. The psalm begins on the northern wall (K17). It is read from left to right toward the sanctuary. The second part begins on the opposite wall (K13) and reads from the sanctuary to the nave. The third installment is above the arch that leads back to the nave (K14). To read the complete inscription requires turning in a full circle.

The five inscriptions in the ceiling zone of the khurus are an intrinsic part of the Ornamental Master's program. He appears to have been equally capable of using both Coptic and Arabic calligraphy as part of his decorative scheme. There may have been a third painter specializing in inscriptions, but if so he was working with the Ornament Master. It is less clear who painted the inscription of Psalm 83 (84) on the opposite side of the archway overlooking the nave (N37). Its red background and braided border are not used for the inscriptions in the khurus. The letters of the archway inscription are distinguished by unique decorative flourishes—the O's contain crosses, for example, and the A's end in bird heads—that are not seen

The Fatimids (969–1171) established the Cairene tradition of placing inscriptions on public buildings as decoration and as a means of conveying religious and political messages.[60] Their public texts are written in kufic, an early Arabic script developed in the Iraqi town of Kufa. Theodore wrote his single Arabic phrase in a form of kufic. The Ayyubids (1171–1250) continued the practice of using architectural inscriptions but favored the more recently developed cursive scripts. Their first public inscription, recording the foundation of the Citadel of Cairo in 1183, is written in naskhi, the Arabic script used by the Ornamental Master.[61] Thereafter, the cursive scripts replaced kufic as the predominate form of Arabic calligraphy in Egypt. Under the Mamluks (1250–1517), continuous inscription bands became a standard decorative feature in the Islamic architecture of Cairo. The funerary complex of Sultan Qalawun (1285) has a foundation inscription, which runs the length of the façade, a distance of more than seventy-five meters. The interior of the tomb chamber has an equally monumental inscription giving the names and titles of the sultan.[62]

The Ornamental Master painted the first substantial Arabic inscriptions in the Church of St. Antony. Although they are Arabic translations of psalms, their calligraphy and decorative form derive from contemporary Muslim models. The d'Arenberg Basin has a similar naskhi inscription that is also interrupted by medallions (fig. 8.39). On the façade inscription of the Qalawun complex, the spaces between the upright letters are filled with knots and simple

8.40
Frontispiece of the Epistles and
Acts, showing standing saints,
manuscript illumination, New
Testament, 1249/1250, Cairo
(Cairo, Coptic Museum, Ms. Bib.
94, fol. 131v)

elsewhere in the upper zone of the khurus.[65] The decorative use of the inscription, however, is in keeping with the aesthetic of the khurus program. The red band is set against the white plaster of the upper level of the nave. It draws the viewer's attention upward into the khurus vault. Beneath the inscription, on the underside of the arch, are the archangels painted by the Figural Master. Beyond the archway can be seen the ornamented ceiling and the paintings of the three women at the tomb and the meeting of Christ and the women in the garden.

THE KHURUS VAULT

The barrel vault covering the khurus was probably present in the Church of St. Antony when Theodore was active in 1232/1233. It was no doubt originally intended to symbolize Noah's ark, and thus emphasizes the church's role as the ship of salvation.[66] The Ornamental Master, however, took this traditional Coptic architectural form and transformed it by painting the khurus vault in a manner suggesting the ceiling of a palace. The spiral arabesque above the archway leading to the nave (K14) is often employed in miniature paintings of the period to embellish the façades of schematically represented palaces. The khurus arabesque is thus an actual example of architectural decoration known from contemporary art. A copy of the Maqamat of al-Hariri produced in Baghdad (ca. 1225–1235) has a number of miniatures showing palaces with archways decorated with spiral arabesques.[67] An illustrated Copto-Arabic New Testament produced in Cairo in 1249/1250

uses nearly identical architectural elements decorated with spiral arabesques as frames for portraits of the evangelists (fig. 8.40).[68] The Armenian Glajor Gospel in the collection of the University of California employs a similar architectural setting for its canon tables. On several folios, the spandrels of the arches are painted with the same type of spiral design (fig. 8.38).[69] The placement of this style of arabesque above archways seems to have been widely associated with palace architecture in the thirteenth century.

Mamluk literary sources describe the palaces in the Citadel of Cairo as being elaborately decorated. The historian al-ʿUmari visited the Striped Palace of Sultan an-Nasir Muhammad soon after it was completed in 1315 and wrote that the façade is "built of black and yellow stone, and within are dadoes of marble and gold and floriated mosaics, heightened with mother of pearl and colored paste and various colors. The ceilings are all gilded and paved with lapis lazuli. The light comes through windows filled with colored glass from Cyprus resembling necklaces of precious stone. All the floors are paved with marble of incomparable quality transported from all the countries of the world."[70]

The construction and the decoration of the khurus vault are consistent with contemporary palace architecture. A large reception hall known as a qaʿa was the central architectural unit of medieval Egyptian palaces. It consists of two or more raised, covered chambers (*iwans*) that open on to a lofty, central court (*durqaʿa*). The ceilings of the durqaʿa and the flanking iwans are made of carved and painted wood. Two types of wooden ceilings seem to have been favored by Mamluk builders.[71] In the Qaʿa of Muhib ad-Din al-Muwaqqiʿ (ca. 1350) wooden beams project down from flat wooden ceilings.[72] The method of construction closely resembles the one used in the khurus. In Mamluk examples, the beams are often palm trunks dressed with panels of imported wood.[73] The khurus, therefore, can be seen as an inexpensive version of these palatial ceilings. The Qaʿa of the Palace of Amir Bashtak (ca. 1339) has wooden ceilings of a different type. The iwans are covered with rows of painted, hexagonal coffers that form miniature domes.[74] The Palace of Amir Taz (ca. 1352) contains both of these styles of ceilings.[75] It also has an interesting blending of the two. The painted, wooden ceiling of the *maqʿad* (raised reception room), which overlooks an inner courtyard of the palace, consists of projecting rectangular beams alternating with rows of recessed, square coffers.[76] This same combination of beams and coffers is also found in the Qaʿa of Ahmad Kuhya (ca. 1310).[77]

Both of these architectural types are incorporated in the construction of the khurus vault. The alternation of palm trunks with recessed wooden panels is in the style of the Qaʿa of al-Muwaqqiʿ. The rows of hexagonal windows flanking the central beam of the khurus are deeply recessed, suggesting the coffered ceilings of the Bashtak Palace. These windows show such contemporary taste that it is likely that the Ornamental Master suggested their addition to the khurus vault.

The closest surviving example of the Ornamental Master's style of decorative painting in the khurus is found in the Qaʿa of Ahmad Kuhya (fig. 8.41). The ceiling of the chamber, located between the current street entrance and the southern iwan, is made of projecting beams separated by rows of recessed wooden panels. It is larger and more elaborately ornamented than the khurus vault, but both share a remarkable number of decorative motifs, including the black and white hexagonal pattern, the alternating arrowheads, the "Armenian" floral design, an arabesque network, and two varieties of undulating vine and leaf. These striking similarities suggest that the two painted ceilings might even have been produced by the same workshop, which could have been active between ca. 1283, our latest date for the Ornamental Master, and ca. 1310, the date suggested for the ceiling of Ahmad Kuhya.[78]

The inscriptions in the program of the Ornamental Master also emphasize the palatial nature of the khurus. The archway overlooking the nave is framed by a Coptic inscription (N37) reading, "How worthily beloved are your dwellings, [O] Lord, God of Powers. My soul . . . " There was not room for the complete second verse of Psalm 83 (84), " . . . yearns and pines for your courts." The three Coptic inscriptions at the base of the khurus vault are from the first verses of Psalm 86 (87). "His foundations are on the holy mountain. The Lord loves the gates of Zion more than the dwellings of Jacob. Things have been spoken about you, [city of God]" (K17, K13, K14).[79] The legible portion of the two Arabic inscriptions (K21, K45) is Psalm 121 (122):3–6.[80] The first verse of the same psalm begins, "I was glad when they said unto me, Let us go to the house of the Lord." All of these inscriptions are appropriate for the khurus, because they draw attention to its role as the entrance chamber of the sanctuary in the house of God. The ornamental vault serves as a visual expression of the same role. It is decorated in a style appropriate for the entrance corridor of a palace.[81]

It seems certain that the Ornamental Master was a professional painter of ceilings. His knowledge of contemporary motifs suggests he catered to cosmopolitan tastes. He probably worked in Cairo, the only major city in medieval Egypt. The Ornamental Master was most likely a Copt, but he could have had Muslim as well as Christian clients. Houses of the wealthy were decorated in the same manner regardless of the religious affiliations of the owners.[82] His work at the Monastery of St. Antony may have been sponsored by a satisfied Coptic patron.

The paintings in the ceiling zone of the khurus belong to an eastern Mediterranean artistic world that encompassed varied religious and secular territories. They have close stylistic and iconographic ties to two cultures. One is a Byzantine artistic realm, particularly as found on Cyprus and in the Monastery of St. Catherine. The second is a more avant-garde Islamic art being made in Egypt, Syria, Iraq, and Turkey. The work of the two khurus painters is paralleled in illuminated manuscripts of the period. The pose of the Figural Master's seated angel (K12) is employed in the Cairo New Testament of 1249/1250, while the spiral arabesque of the Ornamental Master is found in that Christian manuscript, and also in Arab miniatures from the first half of the thirteenth century. Another Coptic Gospel book, dated to 1205 and originally in the Monastery of St. Antony, includes illuminations in a Byzantine mode.[83] We have suggested that the floral motif found in the khurus ceiling derived ultimately from Armenian illuminations made in the Kingdom of Cilicia. Manuscript painting, however, is only one of the numerous media in which the artistic vocabulary of the thirteenth century is expressed, as the range of comparanda in this chapter shows.

In this context, it is interesting to note that Hunt has also identified ties between painters active in Egypt, Cyprus, and Armenia.[84] She compiles evidence for the assertion that the same men worked on large-scale wall paintings (specifically those in the Monastery of the Syrians, Wadi al-Natrun) as well as on icons and manuscript illuminations.[85] Hunt characterizes these painters as belonging to "a workshop of Christian artists from different backgrounds, who had previously worked at different centers. The relationship is proposed here with a wide spectrum of art in the Eastern Mediterranean of the twelfth to early thirteenth centuries. Such a mélange is explicable at Deir es-Suriani, where the various Christian communities coexisted and maintained contacts outside of Egypt."[86] The same might be said of the khurus ceiling painters, of a slightly later date. This characterization of Christian art in Egypt would not be complete without reference to

Robert Nelson's evaluation of manuscript illumination in the thirteenth and fourteenth centuries, because although we have sometimes identified artistic synthesis in the khurus paintings (for example, the angel of the stone, K12), more often we have found artistic coexistence. Nelson presented a model for Coptic book illumination that can usefully be adapted for art in other media in this period. The progression of Coptic illuminations "cannot be seen as a continuous evolutionary development, but rather is characterized by a series of discrete accommodations to the artistically more powerful cultures of Byzantium and Islam."[87] We would suggest one modification to Nelson's description. Instead of seeing the khurus paintings in the Monastery of St. Antony as "accommodations to" Byzantine and Islamic art, we should rather view them all as partaking in a shared visual culture, in this period. In fact, even the discrete characters of Byzantine and Islamic art have recently come under scrutiny. Anthony Cutler has revealed significantly blurred boundaries between the art of these two civilizations.[88]

The inability to categorize the khurus ceiling paintings neatly into one region or tradition is characteristic of twelfth- and thirteenth-century Mediterranean art. It fits completely into an artistic world that had permeable boundaries. One example of this is the Cappella Palatina at Palermo from the mid-twelfth century. Its mosaics are Byzantine, its ceiling paintings are Muslim, and its patron is the Norman King Roger II. Crusader-period icons made in a Byzantine style, but with Latin rather than Greek inscriptions, are another instance of this fascinating and polyglot visual culture. We cannot say anything about the ethnicity of the two masters who painted the upper zone of the khurus in the Church of St. Antony. They may have been Copts, but if so, the Figural Master probably underwent training in Cyprus or Sinai, while the Ornamental Master seems linked to Cairo. As has been demonstrated in the chapters on the 1232/1233 program, the master painter Theodore was aware of artistic developments in the Byzantine, Crusader, and Islamic worlds. His style was nevertheless emphatically Egyptian Christian. The paintings in the khurus ceiling, on the contrary, could have been found as easily in Jerusalem or Damascus as here in the eastern desert of Egypt (fig. 8.42).

CHAPTER 9 CONSERVATION OF THE WALL PAINTINGS IN THE MONASTERY OF ST. ANTONY AT THE RED SEA

9.1
Virgin Mary (N36), before cleaning

The conservation of the paintings in the Monastery of St. Antony required a stay of more than twelve months, extending over a period of three years between 1996 and 1999.[1] The project was planned and directed by the authors of this chapter, who were assisted by Alberto Sucato (all missions from 1996), Gianluca Tancioni (all missions from 1997), Emiliano Albanese (third and fourth missions), Stefano Fulloni (fifth mission), and Massimilano Gusmaroli (first mission).

In 1992 we were requested by the Coptic authorities in charge of the monastery to prepare a preliminary study on the paintings in the church and the conditions of the entire architectural complex.[2] Our in-depth investigation was conducted during the group's first period at the monastery in December of that year. The main focus of the study was the state of the paintings and the techniques required to conserve them. After examining preliminary photographic documentation, we executed cleaning tests on areas that represented various states of repair in the church. This procedure enabled us to identify the methods of intervention we would use. Our study of the paintings was also an excellent opportunity to obtain an initial understanding of the materials used by the artists in the thirteenth century. As an essential prelude to our work on the pictorial surfaces, an architectural study was carried out in 1994 under the direction of Michael J. Kujawski.[3] It was aimed at verifying

the static equilibrium of the walls and structures supporting the paintings. With that study, the preliminary phase of the project was concluded, and the way was open for restoration work.

During our examination of the Church of St. Antony in 1992, it was immediately evident that the whole complex, and in particular the cycle of thirteenth-century paintings, was in serious need of conservation. Photographs taken over the previous twenty years reveal a progressive and rapid deterioration in the paintings themselves.[4] Apparently, a desire to rediscover obscured textual and iconographic elements in the cycle, and also to photograph and document them, had led to several previous attempts to clean the painted surfaces, attempts that, sadly, only caused further damage. These degenerative factors seem to have had an especially negative effect on the inscriptions found in the paintings, many of which have been compromised or partially lost.

Other circumstances that have accelerated the deterioration of the paintings can be blamed on the unavoidable daily use of the environment for religious purposes, including repairs and renovation; shifts in temperature and humidity, which would have fluctuated depending on the number of people in the church; and the presence of carbon deposits from the smoke of incense and candles. The church's paintings and numerous inscriptions were often inexpertly touched up, or even over-painted (fig. 9.1). Some of these maintenance operations were carried out with inappropriate materials, which in specific instances have completely changed the nature of the surfaces of the walls. A decisive element affecting the state of conservation is the seepage of rainwater on the painted surfaces. This

9.2

Conservation record, Mercurius

(κ3), 3.6.1

CONDITION OF PREPARATORY LAYERS

 Wear of the intonaco
(top layer of fine plaster)

Deep lacuna showing the arriccio
(base layer of course plaster)

Deep lacuna showing the masonry

Pick holes on the intonaco

damage is marked in the central part of the khurus, where the water has penetrated windows and openings.

After careful study, we identified certain fundamental problems threatening the paintings and the environment as a whole. A major concern centered on the fragmentary surfaces of the pictorial layer, originating from structural modifications made to the building. Closely related to this was the problem of falling plaster, and the presence of some extensive areas of earlier repair of the resulting gaps. A thick layer of carbon black and incoherent deposits covered the interior walls and vaults of the church, rendering the surface illegible. The paintings were further obscured by the presence of superimposed substances used to brighten the images and by the numerous inscriptions and graffiti, up to a height of approximately two meters above ground level.[5] Finally, in certain areas, such as the Deesis chapel, damage to the plaster caused by insects had resulted in further loss of the pictorial layer. The condition of the painted wall surfaces was carefully documented before and during conservation, as is shown here for St. Mercurius (κ3; figs. 9.2–9.7, 9.10, 9.11).

Preparatory Survey

ARCHITECTURAL STRUCTURE

The mural support of the church consists of raw bricks, made up of local soil and gravel combined with plant materials added as reinforcement. The mortar used to join these bricks is made of materials similar to those in the raw bricks themselves, but with a much lower percentage of plant fibers. As far as it has been possible to see, irregular lithic elements, such as sedimentary limestone from the surrounding area, are also present in certain points of the wall, as well as a number of ligneous elements, which occasionally serve as architraves over doors, windows, and frames for niches but which are also used as strengthening elements for the structure. The walls have generally been coated with a rough layer of sienna-colored plaster, of variable consistency, to render the surface more even.

The mural structure of the cupolas covering the nave and sanctuary is also raw brick covered by plaster. The central vault of the khurus is made up of seven palmwood beams set longitudinally to the axis of the church, and inserted into the brickwork (figs. 8.1, 8.25). The beams in the lateral areas of the khurus, which are made from different types of wood, are salvage materials that were inserted into the vertical walls transversally to the axis of the church. A framework of woven palm leaves is fixed to these beams to support a covering of plaster.

A considerable number of stucco fragments were found in the window embrasures of the nave, khurus, and sanctuary.[6] The shapes of these pieces suggest that the window frames were made before being set in place. This observation is particularly noteworthy in the upper zone of the khurus, where the two rows of round windows at the base of the vault (κ19, κ47) were certainly coeval with the wall structure and were probably made in a countermould to provide the precise thickness of the frame. Various pieces of colored glass, in round and angular shapes, were then added while the plaster was still fresh from the mould. The visible part of the frame was then worked in gesso, using a spatula. Each row of windows was made from two separate moldings that were connected at the center by wooden hinge pins. The completed window frames were finally placed in the khurus vault, and their upper and lower edges were hidden by a layer of plaster. The two rows of coffered windows at the apex of the vault (κ31, κ35), made of stucco obtained from a mixture of soil and plaster, were presumably also made on site, using hexagonal countermoulds with pairs of cylindrical holes set at intervals between them.

9.3
Conservation record, Mercurius
(κ3), 3.6.2

CONDITION OF PREPARATORY LAYERS

 Lack of adhesion between layers

PLASTER LAYERS

The surface of the entire architectural complex comprises overlapping layers of plaster, similar in appearance but with varying percentages of component elements. The mixture, made up of gesso, calcite, and organic fibers, is white with a light amber shade given by the vegetable content.[7] It is possible to identify four separate layers of plaster that were applied between the sixth and late-thirteenth centuries. The two most extensive phases of intervention both date to the end of this period. For the sake of convenience, these two major layers are categorized as the Coptic phase (dated 1232/1233) and the Byzantine phase.

It is important to keep in mind, however, that the layering of plaster can be quite complex. Because of this, it is necessary to describe the succession of painting phases in greater detail. The oldest extant painted plaster in the Church of St. Antony has been assigned to the sixth or seventh century.[8] It shows Christ with the apostles framed by roundels on the underside of the archway leading into the Deesis chapel (c4–c9). The plaster supporting the image was made using an ochre-colored mortar, to a thickness of

3–4 mm, containing few organic fibers and characterized by a low level of gesso. A second layer of plaster, subsequently painted, was added to the church at an unknown date. Traces of this pictorial program have been identified in the nave and in the Deesis chapel. These two early phases precede the paintings dated to 1232/1233 and the somewhat later, Byzantine-inspired paintings, which are visible today. The multiple layers of painted plaster created a palimpsest that we were able to correlate in many parts of the building. For example, we were able to determine from the three plaster sequences covering the archway of the Deesis chapel that the current thirteenth-century painting within the chapel was executed on a plaster layer superimposed on a previous pictorial phase, even though only traces of the underlying work could be seen through the numerous small gaps in 1232/1233 painting.

The plaster of the Coptic phase—on which is found the pictorial decoration of the whole nave, the lower area of the khurus, the sanctuary, and the chapel—has an overall thickness and composition that is more or less uniform in all the areas. The layer found in the bowl-shaped vault of the Deesis chapel is thin, with a depth of 2 to 5 mm, laid over older paintings, which were first chiseled off. It has an extremely imprecise surface, no doubt due to underlying irregularities and hollows that may have created difficulty in applying the mortar to the concave wall. When the conditions of the older plaster were considered good, the normal layer of plaster was replaced by one made up of gesso and calcite with a thickness of 1 to 3 mm laid directly over the underlying plaster. On closer inspection it appears rough and slightly lacking in homogeneity. This method was used extensively in the nave.[9] When gaps appeared in this thirteenth-century layer, earlier painting frequently emerged.

The Coptic plaster layer of 1232/1233 was applied after a campaign of architectural modifications had been carried out in the church, including the filling of several windows with raw bricks, which were plastered over. The Byzantine phase of intervention, likewise dating from the thirteenth century, also involved structural changes to the church, most notably the opening of a new arch between the southwestern corner of the nave and the annex leading to the Deesis chapel (A1, A9).[10] A new layer of plaster was then introduced on the underside of the archway between the nave and the annex (A1, A9); the archway between the nave and the khurus (κ15, κ16); and the entire upper section of the khurus. It thus forms the foundation for the work of the artists identified as the Figural and Ornamental Masters by Bolman and Lyster in chapter 8. Compared with that of the earlier phases, the Byzantine plaster is

9.4

Conservation record, Mercurius

(κ3), 3.6.3

CONDITION OF THE PAINT LAYERS

 Wear

 Lacuna

Lack of cohesion

more refined in composition, more compressed, with a finer granulation and a higher percentage of plant fibers. The unpainted sections of the church, including the cupolas and the lower sections of the walls, were also covered with this plaster. It was at this time that the final arrangement of the unitary program currently visible throughout the complex was achieved.[11]

During the conservation work it was also noted that the Byzantine plaster covered the top and bottom margins of the Coptic paintings in the nave, the lower area of the khurus, and the sanctuary in a fairly regular manner. During work on the upper portions of the paintings on the north wall of the nave, a number of inscriptions came to light beneath the plaster. They named the figures illustrated in the paintings below and must originally have served as captions on the unpainted Coptic plaster above the pictorial band (fig. 4.19). In the khurus, the paintings of the rich man in hell, to the right of the three patriarchs (κ5), and the two pages of Mercurius (κ3; fig. 9.2), though in a perfect state of conservation, were completely obscured by the Byzantine layer. These figures were painted

outside the frames of the larger pictorial compositions. We can conjecture that both the captions in the nave and figures in the khurus were covered over in an attempt to bring greater order and uniformity to the painted program of the church.[12]

We know that the Byzantine layer of plaster was done within a relatively short period of time after the completion of the Coptic phase. When we uncovered paintings from 1232/1233 that had been plastered over, they were revealed to be almost completely free of smoke and dirt. This remarkable state of cleanliness suggests a passage of time of less than half a century between the two phases.

Pictorial Layer

For the sake of convenience, the pictorial layer of the successive phases will be dealt with using the following distinction, which is similar to the one previously used for the plaster: the early paintings (ca. 550–700); the Coptic paintings (1232/1233); and the Byzantine paintings (ca. 1235–1285). All of the paintings in the church are done in the *secco* technique. We will examine the distinctive features and painting techniques of each phase, paying particular attention to both preparatory drawings and the final execution of the paintings.

Early Paintings

The early painting on the underside of the arched entrance of the Deesis chapel shows Christ and the apostles framed in roundels (c4–c9; figs. 3.3, 3.4).[13] Irregular areas of color were used to define faces, clothing, and background, which then received brushstrokes of thicker, denser color. The mantle of Christ, for example, was first painted yellow, before a reddish-brown color was superimposed.[14] Tiny decorative elements were then added, using black and white pigment. Flesh tones were created, using a background of pale ochre, on which foreheads and lips were defined in red and eyes in white. Finally, all the figurative elements were finished with a black outline.[15]

The slight differences in diameter of the roundels, their irregularities in outline, and the lack of symmetry in the frames lead us to think that there was no planned division of the space before painting commenced. Traces of a preparatory drawing in red, executed using a brush, can, however, be identified along the outline of the red cloaks of the apostles.

Coptic Paintings

Analysis of the binding agent of the paint has yielded the presence of animal proteins and traces of polysaccha-

9.5

Conservation record, Mercurius (K3), 3.6.4

CONDITION OF THE PAINT LAYERS

 Continuous organic deposit

rides. At the moment, the only binding agent that differs from the homogeneous one used generally is beeswax, employed for a particular type of green that is very bright and semitransparent. This color, which is used for finishing touches, was probably applied hot. In fact, the thickness and irregular appearance suggest rapid application using a not particularly fine brush, in order to prevent the binding agent from cooling down too quickly.

The pictorial layer is generally applied in flat fields of color of a certain thickness, which in some cases overlap by several centimeters. Each area of color defines some aspect of the larger painting, including faces and clothes, architectural details, and background. On these homogeneous fields, all the other decorative elements were gradually added in more detail, with increasing care. A characteristic of the technique of these painters is an almost transparent brushstroke that adds shading to draperies and architectural elements. In the final stages of work, the paintings were defined even more. Not only were edges outlined precisely in black, but fine white lines were added as a finishing touch that further enhances the pictorial

image. This white pigment was also used to highlight many of the decorative elements and inscriptions in the program.[16]

It is interesting to observe the method used to paint flesh. The face and hands were first outlined in yellow. This preparatory painting was then filled in with an ochre color, and the lines were carefully painted over in the same pigment to give more precise definition to the eyebrows, eyes (shaded on upper lids), mouth, and fingers. At this point, using an even thinner and more precise black line, the painters drew in the eyes (generally a single arc from the eyebrows to the tip of the nose), the irises, and the profile. Finally, white was added to the beard, earlobes, and eyes.

We did not identify a systematic method of dividing the space on the wall before the painting of the 1232/1233 program. Rather, the lack of uniformity in frames and architectural elements leads to the supposition that the layout for the paintings was developed as the work progressed. The extensive gaps in the pictorial layer revealed that the preparatory paintings were applied by fast but decisive brushstrokes of yellow. In almost all the cases we could determine, this preparatory stage was followed faithfully in the execution of the final painting.[17] In a few cases, such as the twenty-four elders of the apocalypse (S33–S36), we found holes where nails were used to anchor string that guided the formation of the red frames surrounding the paintings. We assume that the frame containing Christ Pantocrator (S12) was made with a compass, although the central hole has not been found.

While working on the equestrian martyrs in the western half of the nave, we found traces of earlier paintings beneath Theodore Stratelates (N22) and the horse of George (N25), which suggests that there may be a connection between the iconographic layout of the underlying paintings and that of the 1232/1233 program.[18] A red inscription identifying Claudius (N19) on either side of the saint's head may be another indication of this relation. The words AGIOC KLAYTIOC can be perceived because of the thinness of the overlying paint.[19] They were probably written as a temporary mark identifying the subject.

Byzantine Paintings

In the areas painted with figurative scenes—the western-facing wall of the upper zone of the khurus (K11, K12, K18), the underside of the archway between the nave and the khurus (K15, K16), and that between the nave and the annex (A1, A9)—systematic means of transposition of the drawing do not appear. The only exception is the use of a compass for the roundels decorating the garments of the archangels, and perhaps also for the two globes they hold. It is probable that the geometrical irregularity of the surface and the execution of a complex series of figures in such a confined space resulted in the immediate elaboration of the pictorial elements. Numerous changes in the program, both after the preparatory drawing (halo of Christ, K18; fig. 8.11), and following the application of paint (overlapping of Mary Magdalene's mantle and the Virgin's dress, K18; fig. 8.4), suggest that the composition was fully defined only during painting.

Analysis shows the presence of animal proteins in the Byzantine binding agent. The technical methods employed during painting, which can easily be compared with those used on icons from the same period, make it possible to identify this binding agent as egg yolk. The pigments are more finely ground than the ones used during the Coptic phase, resulting in a transparency that allows plant fibers in the underlying plaster, as well as preparatory drawings, to show through on occasion. These delicate layers of pigment were applied a number of times to obtain more intense shades of color. This characteristic layering is not seen in more compact and thicker areas of color, such as the blue of Mary's dress. In those instances, a lighter shade of the color, obtained by mixing the pigment with white, is used to define drapery or light falling on rocks.[20]

A series of steps was required to produce flesh tones on faces and hands. After the application of the preparatory drawing, which was traced in brown and is still visible in areas, the background color was added in a solid field of transparent ochre. Once this initial phase was completed, the shaded areas of the face and hands were added by applying additional transparent layers of color on top of one another. Next, the outlines were redrawn and underlined with decisive black lines. The application of the paler areas of flesh then followed, with the painters maintaining the transparent ochre background in many areas while elsewhere painting over it with thin strokes in a variety of shades of pink mixed with white. This application takes the characteristic form of thin parallel lines, almost like a network of brushstrokes, which at times leave the underlying drawing visible and at other times cover it. This procedure was used to delineate forms in all the areas that tend to catch the light, such as the brows, the cheekbones, and the eyes themselves (fig. 8.3). The calligraphic and geometric appearance of this technique when viewed close at hand is transformed, when viewed from a distance, into an extremely effective sense of volume and contrast between areas of light and shade. Certain facial features were then retraced, using a dark pigment to define anatomical details. At times a naturalistic effect emerges—for example, in the Virgin's eyebrows, where the use of alternating parallel dark and light lines is effective in depicting the brows themselves. A similar effect is used to strengthen the dark tones in the iris of her eyes.[21]

Similarities in the composition of the two pairs of archangels caused us to wonder whether they had been traced using a template.[22] Although certain correspondences exist between the outlines of the faces and haloes of the archangels between the nave and khurus (K15, K16; fig. 8.1), substantial differences are also evident. Somewhat closer analogies were found between the profiles of the other two Byzantine archangels on the archway between the nave and the annex (A1, A9; fig. 8.20). Their overall outlines are very similar, especially in the faces, lower bodies, and wings. If models were used in either case, they must have been adapted to the irregularities in the architectural structure and modified during painting. This is noticeable both in the use of different decorative details and in the presence of adaptations and resizing, which understandably would have occurred at the time of painting.

Finally, a special wax treatment used on the archangels between the nave and annex (A1, A9) requires discussion. This wax was applied hot, with a brush, in a rapid manner that at times left various areas of paint uncovered. We found no trace of dirt between the wax and the pictorial layer, which means that the fixing-encaustic operation was carried out very shortly after painting. It must be specified that the paintings on the arch were applied to a surface that had been plastered for some time. Under the pictorial layer, a cross that was painted when the archway was still otherwise undecorated can be seen near the right hand of one of the archangels (A9). At the time of the final pictorial phase, the wall had cracked and been repaired, with heterogeneous materials different from those used for the plaster on which the archangels were painted. There is thus an interesting palimpsest, not of layers of plaster, but of pictorial layers: the cross painted in red with a wax-application of green; a protective layer of wax; the pictorial layer with the archangels; and a wax coating.[23]

A very different working method is found on the decorative bands of the khurus vault (K19–K47; fig. 8.25). The geometric, arabesque, and vegetal patterns were transposed using a compass and guidelines of fine cord impregnated with red. In the large arabesque on the eastern-facing wall of the upper khurus (K14; fig. 8.26), however, preparatory methods are less evident. The geometrical ir-

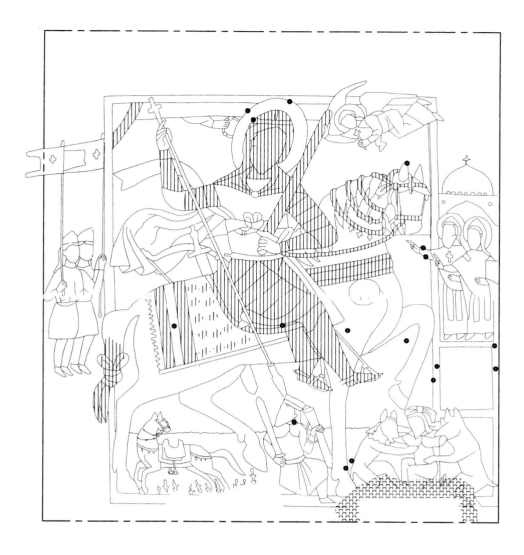

9.6

Conservation record, Mercurius

(к3), 3.6.5

PREVIOUS TREATMENTS

 Nail hole

 Overpainting

Gypsum-based fills

regularity of the surface made the use of systematic instruments (thread and compass) difficult when laying out the composition. In all probability the compass was simply used as a measuring device to fix the reference points required to trace the spirals, and perhaps to draw the circle at the center of the inscription. The gaps in the pictorial layer have allowed us to observe that the preparatory drawing was painted in yellow.

State of Preservation

Our analysis of the conditions includes assessment of architectural structure, plaster layers, pictorial layers, and previous interventions (figs. 9.2–9.7, 9.10, 9.11)[24]

ARCHITECTURAL STRUCTURE

Modifications made to the external structure of the vaults resulted in an increase in weight that caused compression of the original mud bricks and the cracking of some of the walls. Alterations in the static equilibrium are especially evident in the khurus vault, where there is frac-

turing and deformation of the painted wooden beams above the longitudinal window on the north side. The wide gap at the bottom of the scene showing the three women at the tomb (к12; fig. 8.24) was certainly caused by compression of the central area of the wall. A large central crack in the eastern wall (к11, к12, к18) is also apparent. Equally evident is the longitudinal cracking found throughout the archway between the nave and the khurus (к15, к16; fig. 17, introduction). A similar situation can be found in the sanctuary on the two side walls supporting the central cupola, and again on the northeastern wall, where the compression has caused three extensive gaps at approximately 1.5 m above floor level. Severe areas of plaster detachment in the nave were caused by compression of the walls. The damage is particularly apparent in the paintings of Shenouda, Pachomius, and Barsauma (N28, N12, N11; fig. 4.22) on the archway. The entrance of the Deesis chapel has been reduced by approximately 30 cm of its original height due to structural modifications.

Stability of the walls has been further compromised by changes to the interior of the church, especially the creation of niches below the painted zone in the nave at the center of the west wall (N20, N21), the northeastern corner (N34), and under the dedicatory inscription (N31). The introduction of such wooden elements as iconostasis, beams, and doorways also damaged the surface of the walls. Examples can be seen in the nave between N23 and N24 (architrave of the entrance door); at N31 (where the door was transformed into a cupboard); and at N7 and N32 (the insertion of the first of the two wooden screens). Further examples were found in the khurus on the walls at к5 and к6 (beams inserted above the paintings, and long shelves added at their base); below к4 (insertion of a metal chest); at к7 (introduction of a cupboard); at к9 (a new architrave above the paintings); and at к1 and к10, where the wooden entrance to the sanctuary and the overlying beam in the arch abut. In many cases later insertions have been removed, and the plaster repaired (for example, к7).

PLASTER LAYERS

A widespread loss of adhesion between the various layers of plaster, as well as from the supporting wall, could be seen in the proximity of these architectural modifications.[25] Particularly extensive and deep were the detachments of the plaster on the wall bearing the Easter cycle in the khurus (к11, к12, к18). The two side walls that support the vault and bear the Coptic inscriptions also revealed serious detachment, in this case caused by rain.[26] At the lower level of the khurus, the plaster on the walls

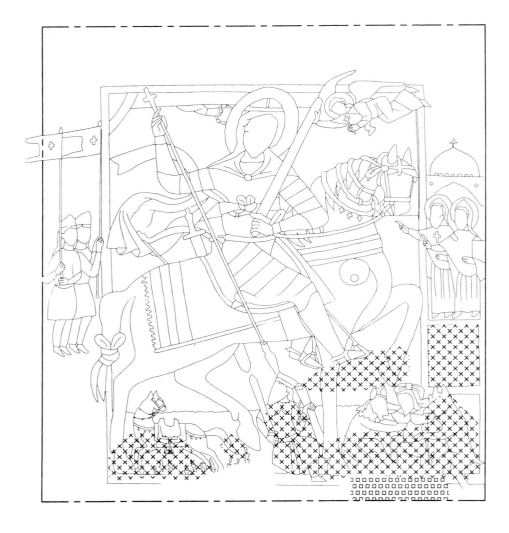

9.7
Conservation record, Mercurius
(κ3), 3.6.6

PREVIOUS TREATMENTS

 Fixative and wax

Cement-based fills

depicting George (κ8) and Mercurius (κ3) also suffered from loss of adhesion, which in all probability is due to the presence of sealed-off windows (fig. 9.3).[27] In the sanctuary, detachment was evident in the semidome of the central apse and along the central and lower area of the north and east walls. In the nave a particular type of detachment between plaster and wall could be found where the windows have been sealed off (an operation that took place during the thirteenth century).

In the Deesis chapel, the paintings on the archway showed an alarming degree of detachment, caused by structural modifications to the walls. The loss of adhesion here depended on the particular characteristics of the application techniques used and the presence of earlier layers of plaster. In this case, the thirteenth-century level was laid over two previous plaster levels that in all probability already presented a delicate state of balance. A number of holes made by insects were also found in the chapel. Feeding on the organic fibers in the wall, they tunneled through the unbaked bricks of the structure, exacerbating plaster detachment.

Partial or total loss of the layers of plaster also occurred in the form of deep gaps (fig. 9.2).[28] This damage resulted from a number of causes, including the opening of niches close to paintings, the insertion of wooden elements, and the sealing off of windows before the paintings were applied. In the latter case, the loss of plaster is to be attributed to the more fragile conditions of unbaked bricks used as fill.

In some areas of the church, loss of cohesion of the plaster caused the subsequent crumbling of the inert materials between the organic fibers. This phenomenon is mainly evident in the areas on the side walls of the upper portion of the khurus, and in the Deesis chapel. When the compression of the wall structure is particularly severe, the plaster debris has been deposited inside the deeper cracks.

We also discovered fragments of plaster that bore traces of paintings and had been detached accidentally, or as a result of human intervention, in the window embrasures of the drum of the cupola in the central sanctuary. Another painted fragment, from κ7 and κ8, was found during the removal of the cupboard.

PICTORIAL LAYER

Total or partial absence of the pictorial layer is evident throughout the paintings. The damage is generally very extensive, and is due to a number of factors:

1 Infiltration of rainwater from the windows in the khurus, in the drum of the sanctuary, and in the nave at N3, N19, N21, and N33;

2 Humidity in the upper part of the sanctuary, where the hermetic sealing of windows interacted with the particular thermohydrometric conditions of the site, in particular, the great differences in temperature typical of the desert environment;

3 New layers of plaster superimposed on earlier levels could also accentuate the gaps. A representative case can be found in the arch band of the chapel (C4–C9), where the already precarious state of preservation of the original painting may have been compromised further by the two subsequent applications of undecorated plaster, one irregular, and the other particularly fine.

Other damage to the pictorial layer includes:
1 Raised flaking of the paintings, which is especially present close to the perimeters of the gaps in the pictorial layer, and where the pigments were applied in particularly thick layers;

2 Poor adhesion of the pigment to the support, caused by a lesser amount of gypsum in the components making up the original plaster (c4–c9);

3 The use of wax in the application method, resulting in widespread damage. In the painting of the archway at the entrance to the annex (A1, A9), tears and flaking of the pictorial layer have occurred at points where the wax covering is thickest.

4 Spider webs and butterfly nests, generally present in the upper areas of the church, and in the Deesis chapel.

5 Small corrugations in the surface of the pictorial layer resulting from a white coating of soluble salts, such as sulfates and chlorides, located along the edges of the plaster fillings, and in the areas most affected by abundant and persistent infiltration of rainwater. These localized phenomena are found in the sanctuary, the khurus, and parts of the nave walls.

6 The sliding of the pictorial layer, another type of damage always associated with the presence of water. It was less widespread, but was found in the upper area of the khurus, by the longitudinal windows, and on the east wall of the nave.

7 Mud deposits caused by rainwater, found in the vicinity of windows or in relation to faults in the roof.

Chromatic alteration of the paintings has also occurred over time. Colors obtained by adding white lead oxidize when exposed to heat, resulting in a more extensive browning.[29] This phenomenon can be seen on the whites used in the upper zone of the khurus (K11, K12, K14, K18; fig. 8.5), and to a lesser extent in the Coptic inscription and depiction of the archangel Gabriel (K16). The color change appears in correspondence with the areas that would have been exposed to the direct light of the sun when the windows were in use.[30] A similar discoloration occurred at the lower areas of the paintings, where the heat of candle flames caused the oxidation of the yellow ochre pigment.[31] The alterations to this pigment, however, are limited.[32]

A more widespread phenomenon is atmospheric particulate and carbon residue deposited on the surface of the paintings. These particles form because the church is situated in a desert environment, where almost-constant winds carry extremely fine sand and organic dust. The car-

bon residue is likewise due to the ritual use of incense, candles, and oil lamps during liturgical practices. The buildup is more accentuated in those areas where the walls are not perpendicular but lean outwards—for example, in the area depicting the Coptic patriarchs in the sanctuary (s5–s7) and the paintings of Mercurius (K3; fig. 9.5) and George in the khurus (K8).

PREVIOUS INTERVENTIONS

Another aspect of the general darkening of the surfaces is caused by the presence of residual material (including oils, waxes, and resins) from inadequate previous restoration works, presumably applied to brighten or consolidate the paintings. These substances are widely located along the whole lower strip of paintings in the church and are particularly thick on the wall of the apse in the sanctuary (s1).

The use of water and popular solvents during attempts to clean the paintings is particularly significant in the depictions of St. Paul and St. Antony (N1, N2) in the nave. A related problem is the lack of cohesion of the pictorial layer resulting from the pulverization of pigments. This phenomenon mainly arose from incautious sponging and other exposure of the surface to water during periodic attempts to improve legibility of the figurative and written elements.

Repairs made during various stages of maintenance caused abrasion and wear. The damage is particularly evident on the lower levels of the paintings, because they are more accessible. In some cases, traces from the tools used to lay on the new mortar can be identified. Repair of cracks using materials unsuitable because of their hardness and components altered the original physical equilibrium of the plaster layer. Various types of plaster have been identified, but they cannot be related precisely to the phases of intervention. It is possible, however, to identify three types of gypsum-based plaster (two grayish-white, the third pinkish in color), as well as a cement-based type. These all overlap extensively onto the pictorial layer, coating it with drips and splashes of mortar; only a few areas were later reintegrated with rough paintings. For the exact location, reference should be made to the graphic documentation (figs. 9.2–9.7, 9.10, 9.11). The lack of care that characterizes all these repairs leads us to suppose that these were limited and unplanned maintenance operations.

The possible presence of earlier consolidation work is indicated by large bulges in the khurus (K3–K5, K8) and the Deesis chapel, and by drippings from a gypsum-based mortar in proximity to several holes in areas where exten-

sive detachment of the preparatory layers from the sup-port has occurred. Evidence of occasional anchoring has been identified in the khurus along the entire edge of the vast gap in the plaster, in the scene showing the three women at the tomb (K11, K12). Small anchoring points were made using bridges of cotton and what is presumably vinylic resin.

After the completion of the 1232/1233 program, there were successive repainting operations that resulted in rad-ical changes to the appearance of Theodore's work. These later interventions were particularly obvious in the figures of Theodore (N22; figs. 5.2, 5.3), George (N25), Antony and Paul (N1, N2; fig. 15, introduction), the Virgin Mary in the nave (N36; figs. 9.1, 9.8, 9.9), and Mercurius in the khurus (K3; fig. 9.6). Portions of the original paintings were com-pletely hidden, such as the bow of Theodore, the decora-tive motifs on George's saddle, and the marble-inspired

decoration on the column beside the Virgin. Some details were modified; for example, the mantles of Theodore and George were lowered by several centimeters. Others were completely changed: the tip of George's sword was turned into drapery, and the white mane and tail of his horse were changed to red. Emblematic of these over-paintings is the transformation of the faces of Theodore's figures. In the case of George, the Virgin (fig. 9.8), and Paul, the facial features have been moved by a few centimeters. The only pictorial repairs made by painting on fresh, white gyp-sum–based plaster were found on the wall depicting Antony and Paul and in the lower area of paintings on the southern nave wall. It should be noted that both the upper and the lower area of the sanctuary have been exempted from any repainting, possibly because they were reserved for the celebrants.

The oldest paintings in the Church of St. Antony

9.9
Virgin Mary (N36), with all of the
overpainting removed

9.10
Conservation record, Mercurius
(κ3), 3.6.7

PRESENT TREATMENT

 Re-establishment

Stabilization B

were discovered on the underside of the archway leading into the Deesis chapel (c4–c9; figs. 3.1, 3.3, 3.4). On this surface a number of pictorial interventions successive to the original painting have been identified. These at times almost amount to revisions and are extremely interesting because they date from a very antique period. A consistent layer of dirt can be seen between the original pigment and the later pictorial revisions, clearly indicating that the earliest painting on the arch band had been exposed for a long period before being refreshed.

During the course of the early restoration of the painting, the red borders of the roundels surrounding the apostles were emphasized, as were almost all the black outlines. In the top portion of the roundels, the original background of light blue was painted over with a darker shade in which a slightly green color prevails. This intervention is more evident on the west side. The face and hand of Christ and the face of James show a reworking of the flesh tones that changes the original ochre tints to a slightly pink

color. It is particularly interesting to observe how the lower part of Peter has been covered by a layer of grayish-white, on which the confused lines of the hands, bible, and keys have then been summarily outlined. Within the roundels of Peter and James, various traces of black lettering, contemporary to the repainting operation, have been identified. It is important to underline that during restoration it was decided to preserve the preceding interventions because of their particular antiquity.

Operations Performed

Considering the delicate state of preservation and the poor legibility of the entire pictorial cycle, we thought it was advisable to proceed with all the phases of conservation in limited areas at one time. This process facilitated recovery of every fragment, even in places where there was significant damage to pictorial layers, such as in the upper part of the sanctuary or in the episodes relating to the life of George (κ9). Our intervention usually consisted of the fol-

REMOVAL OF OLD OVERLAPPING PLASTER AND SPLASHES OF MORTAR

The plaster was removed mechanically using a scalpel and mechanical precision devices. This operation required particular attention in order to ensure that even the smallest fragments were recovered from where the plastering overlapped the painted surface (fig. 9.13).

9.11 ABOVE

Conservation record, Mercurius (κ3), 3.6.8

PRESENT TREATMENT

▨ Stabilization A

◩ Micro fills

▦ Stabilization of the paint layers

▥ Tratteggio reintegration

9.12 ABOVE RIGHT

Adriano Luzi at work (ADP/SA 16 s192 98)

9.13 BELOW RIGHT

Alberto Sucato at work (ADP/SA 3 s 194 98)

lowing phases: (1) preliminary cleaning of the surface, (2) removal of the old overlapping plaster and splashes of mortar, (3) preconsolidation of the pictorial layer, (4) readhesion of flaking areas of pictorial layer, (5) consolidation of areas of plaster at risk and readhesion of fallen areas of plaster bearing traces of pictorial layer, (6) cleaning, (7) consolidation of deep and surface detachments of plaster, (8) repair of plaster, (9) consolidation of the pictorial layer, and (10) pictorial reintegration of gaps (figs 9.10–9.13).

PRELIMINARY CLEANING OF THE SURFACE

Before commencing conservation operations it was necessary to perform mechanical removal, using soft sable brushes, of the incoherent deposits on the whole surface, in particular on the nonperpendicular walls (fig. 9.12). The strips used for provisional anchoring of areas at risk during the emergency interventions in 1992 were also removed, using an organic solvent (nitre thinner).

9.14
Emiliano Albanese at work
(ADP/SA 2 s 194 98)

PRECONSOLIDATION OF THE PICTORIAL LAYER

In certain restricted areas it was necessary to carry out preconsolidation using an acrylic resin solution (2 percent Paraloid B72 in a nitre thinner). More specifically, this was used to treat the black identification inscriptions written in Coptic and some of the black outlines around the figures. In some cases, it was considered advisable to extend preconsolidation operations to the whole surrounding area—for example, in the vicinity around the inscription at the base of the cupola in the central sanctuary, and of over-painted images. The preconsolidation was particularly necessary for the paintings on the archway of the Deesis chapel (C4–C9), where the desire to preserve the old pictorial repairs made it necessary to repeat the operation.

READHESION OF FLAKING AREAS
OF PICTORIAL LAYER

Flaking areas of the pictorial layer were made to readhere by infiltration of an emulsion of acrylic resin (15 percent Primal AC33 in water) and the gentle pressure of the spatula. At times, in more delicate areas, a sheet of silicon paper or of polyethylene was interposed to facilitate adhesion.

CONSOLIDATION AND READHESION

During the first stage of operations it was preferred to limit consolidation only to areas of plaster that were at risk, using injections of an emulsion of acrylic resin (20 percent Primal AC 33 in water) and a limited amount of plastering (fig. 9.14). The mortar used was similar in both appearance and composition to the original one, based on gypsum and sieved soil in a ratio of 1:2.

The areas of painted plaster that had fallen due to human causes connected with normal use of the site were replaced using a layer of mortar made of sieved soil and gypsum in a ratio of 1:1. This operation was also guaranteed by the use of adhesion points, formed by limited infiltration of an emulsion of acrylic resin (20 percent Primal AC33 in water). The backs of the fragments were treated with a solution of acrylic resin (3 percent Paraloid B72 in nitre thinner) before being replaced.

CLEANING

The method used during this phase of the operation was determined according to the substances to be removed and the resistance of the pigments, the latter being determined by the state of the pictorial layer and by the technical characteristics of the painting. The layer of coherent deposits and carbon black was rich with greasy substances. It was also characterized by a composite but almost homogeneous nature. A method was developed that simultaneously used solutions and solvents with different polarities, in a variety of concentrations and combinations. Of fundamental importance was the use of acetone to speed up the time of evaporation of the partially polar solutions. The organic solvent was added to the solution in proportions of from 20 to 60 percent. In some cases the operations were performed by immersing the swab first in the polar solution and then in the organic solvent. When confronted by a more coherent layer of dirt, the surface was treated using a brush or tissue with organic solvents (nitre thinner or a mixture of nitre thinner, amyl acetate, and dimethylformamide in a ratio of 1:½:½) (figs. 9.15, 9.16).[33] Then the polar solution was applied on a swab before evaporation of the solvent itself. In areas where the pictorial layer showed a relatively good state of preservation (K11, K12, K15, K16, K18), the polar solution (which always included acetone) was simultaneously buffered with white spirit.

When confronted with over-painting, and oily or resinous substances, mixtures of organic solvents were used (Didax, that is to say, dimethylfomamide, nitre thinner, acetone, and xylol in the amounts of 35 cc, 15 cc, 10 cc, 10 cc; and nitre thinner, dimethylfomamide, and water in a ratio of 11:3:1). Greasy substances and wax were removed using chlorinated solvents, in some cases warmed in a double boiler to a temperature of approximately 45° C. Where the wax was of considerable thickness (due to splashing from candles), cleaning was facilitated by warming the surface using thermocautery before removing the wax mechanically or with solvents.

168

9.15 LEFT
Luzi at work in the sanctuary, removing thick deposits from the archangel Gabriel (s1; ADP/SA 2 s192 98)

9.16 RIGHT
The archangel Gabriel (s1) with one remaining uncleaned strip (ADP/SA 6 s192 98)

CONSOLIDATION OF DEEP AND SURFACE DETACHMENT OF THE PLASTER

After cleaning, all the areas of discontinuity between layers of plaster were identified by lightly tapping the surface, and then drawing a map to indicate hollows. Deep cracks and bulges were treated using injections of mortar based on gypsum and sieved soil, with the ratio of charge to binding agent determined according to each individual situation. Where necessary, adhesion was first guaranteed by means of localized injections of an emulsion of acrylic resin (20 percent Primal AC33 in water), in some cases charged with inert substances (calcium carbonate).

REPAIR OF PLASTER LAYERS

Gaps in the plaster and pictorial layers were first treated with a solution of acrylic resin (3 percent Paraloid B72 in nitre thinner). They were then filled with a mortar as similar as possible in both appearance and consistency to the original. The composition was adjusted according to the size of the gap. Deep gaps were repaired using unbaked bricks, covered by a mortar made up of sieved soil

and gypsum in a ratio of 2½:1, whereas small amounts of plaster based on gypsum and cellulose derivatives (in the same composition ratio) were used for surface gaps as a binding agent.

Surface plastering was performed to level, with the aid of a scalpel and abrasives. The plastered surface was treated to give an effect similar to that of the original, but distinguishable by its greater regularity and homogeneity. For the coffered ceiling of the khurus, the gaps were repaired using a mortar made from sieved soil and gypsum in a ratio of 5:2, laid on in successive layers, using shaped or cylindrical acetate countermolds in the damaged areas to re-create the static continuity of the original structure. In the deep cracks local stone material was used as filling, to reduce the humidity content. In this case, surface treatment of the plastered areas was performed during the period of drying, using spatulas of different sizes.

CONSOLIDATION OF THE PICTORIAL LAYER

The pictorial layer, where necessary, was consolidated using a solution of acrylic resin (3 percent Paraloid

169

9.17
Luigi De Cesaris at work
(ADP/SA 10 s102 96)

B72 in nitre thinner) applied slowly with a brush at least twenty-four hours after the cleaning operations had been completed.

PICTORIAL REINTEGRATION OF GAPS

Pictorial reintegration was carried out using water-colors, and in the waxed areas, gloss paints, varying the type of intervention according to the size and position of the plastered gaps (fig. 9.17). Large areas of missing pictorial layer were treated in lower tones, a method which is designed to reach chromatic values similar to those of the general state of conservation of the damaged surface by application of a succession of thin layers of color, thus minimizing the visual impact of the gaps in the painting. Restoration of all gaps has not been dealt with in the same way, but all can be recognized by the uniformity and homogeneity of the repaired surface. In some cases, repairable gaps have been drawn in, using vertical dashes, according to the technique called tratteggio (fig. 9.11).

PART III

THE VIEWER'S RESPONSE

Past and Present

CHAPTER 10 PERSPECTIVES ON THE MONASTERY OF ST. ANTONY

MEDIEVAL AND LATER INHABITANTS AND VISITORS

The roughly eight hundred–year span between the early thirteenth century and the present is a fascinating one in the history of the Monastery of St. Antony, with periods of great influence and others of hardship and even abandonment (fig. 10.1). During this time, most of the paintings we see in the Church of St. Antony were first created and cherished, then damaged, and finally restored once again for our enrichment. Most of the buildings that we see today in the monastery were also constructed in this era. Many individuals who separately and collectively sustained monastic life in the Monastery of St. Antony are responsible for the preservation of this site, and for the extraordinary fact that a nearly complete program of medieval wall paintings has survived to the twenty-first century.

A Brief History of the Monastery of St. Antony

In the thirteenth century, the Monastery of St. Antony was one of the most important ascetic communities in Egypt. Abu al-Makarim, writing ca. 1200, wrote that it was inhabited by "many monks" and that there was nothing like it elsewhere in the country.[1] Although its significance undoubtedly derived from its foundation by Antony the Great, the "father of monasticism," it was sustained and amplified by a series of spiritual leaders who came from its community. Some of these led the Coptic Church, and others were sent to Ethiopia. The first Coptic patriarch elected from among the monks of the Monastery of St. Antony had been Khail I (744–767), and after an interval of five centuries another monk of St. Antony, Gabriel III (1268–1271), was chosen as patriarch. The thirteenth and fourteenth centuries can be considered a golden age of art

in the monastery. Not only were the majority of paintings now visible created then, but the manuscripts from this period bear witness to the literary activities of the monastery's monks.[2]

The following centuries were significantly harder for the monastic community. Ogier VIII, Seigneur d'Anglure, noted in 1395/1396 that more than a hundred monks lived in the monastery, but by 1422 Ghillebert de Lannoy counted only fifty.[3] Despite the rapid decline in the number of monks, the monastery was still inhabited by important figures. One was its abbot, Andrew, whom Patriarch John XI chose to represent him and the Copts in the Council of Florence in 1440.[4]

The patriarch Gabriel VI (1466–1475) came from the Monastery of St. Antony, where he had been a monk and then later the abbot of the monastery. This demonstrates that the monastery was still controlled by the monks in

the late fifteenth century, before being occupied by bedouins. The drastic deterioration of the monastery at the
end of this century is illustrated in a colophon written by
Patriarch John XIII (1484–1524) in the manuscript Vatican
Coptic 9 in the year A.M. 1222 (A.D. 1506). The following
passage reveals the situation clearly: "Whereas the monastery of our holy father Antonius, known as the monastery
of Al ʿArabah in the desert of Al Kulzum inhabited by
monks, was vacant without residents, ravaged by the
Arabs, and this book was [then] taken from the hand of
the Arabs, who ravaged the place utterly."[5]

We do not know exactly when or how this happened.
The majority of scholars conjecture that the bedouins
massacred the monks in 1484. The year 1484 was mentioned first by Rufailah, and was then followed by many
scholars, although others prefer 1493.[6] No contemporary
source has yet come to light to support either of these two
dates.[7] There can be no doubt, however, that bedouins pillaged the monastery and that it remained in ruins for
many years. It is unlikely that this occurred during the
pontificate of Gabriel VI.[8] The colophon written by John
XIII documents that at first the monastery was emptied of
its monks, then plundered by the Arabs, and after that the
manuscript was taken from their hands. The sequence of
events shows that there was neither a sudden attack on the
monastery nor a massacre of its monks by the bedouins.
Rather, conditions declined rapidly in the monastery, and
the bedouins controlled it after its total abandonment.
The reclamation of the manuscript from the bedouins in
1506 indicates that they were not the main barrier in the
way of repopulation of the monastery.

It was Patriarch Gabriel VII (1525–1568) who improved the fortunes of the monastery: "This father spared
no effort in the reconstruction of the monasteries and the
churches, restoring and fortifying them, one of them is
this holy community, known as Dayr al-ʿAraba, the abode
of our great father Antonius; for it was he who reopened it
in his Patriarchate—may God protect it [the monastery],
inhabited, forever and grant the abundance of its monks—
after a long period of time, in which it had remained in
ruins and no one was able to reopen and repopulate it except this father."[9]

The text shows the significance of the "abundance"
of monks for the monastery's security. Because Patriarch
Gabriel needed only twenty monks to reinhabit the Monastery of St. Antony, it is clear that the number of bedouins
was not fearsomely large.[10] Gabriel VII must have known
of the situation of the monastery during the patriarchate
of his immediate predecessor John XIII. Certainly, Gabriel

read John XIII's colophon, for he acquired the manuscript
in November 1525, just two months after his consecration.[11] One of the Arabic graffiti was inscribed in the
Church of St. Antony on the twenty-second of Baramhat,
A.M. 1260, which corresponds to March 18, A.D. 1544. Because the graffito documents the visit of a group of pilgrims, the monastery must have been restored before that
date.[12] Additional help identifying the date of the monastery's repopulation by monks comes from the gift of an
icon by King Lebna of Ethiopia. He died in 1540, so the
monastery must have been reopened before that year.[13]
Since its reestablishment by Gabriel VII, the monastery has
been continuously inhabited.

The monks of the Monastery of St. Antony were a
powerful force in determining the history of the Coptic
Church for about two centuries following its repopulation.
Eight Antonian monks in unbroken succession became
patriarchs, from John XVI (1676–1718) to Cyril IV (1854–
1861).[14] During these centuries the monasteries of the
Wadi al-Natrun, which had provided numerous patriarchs
in the past, were in a dilapidated state, and new spiritual
leadership was drawn instead from the Monastery of St.
Antony, where the conditions were comparatively better.[15]

Many scholars consider the advent of Muhammed
ʿAli in 1805 as the beginning of modern Egyptian history.
The short interval of time that preceded his ascension to
the throne of Egypt was among the most difficult periods
in Egyptian history. The inhabitants of Egypt suffered an-
archy, plunder, and hunger, and the regular progress of
caravans from the Nile Valley to the Monastery of St.
Antony ceased. Colophons in manuscripts from the
monastery's library document this situation.

> In the same year [that is, A.M. 1521, or A.D. 1805] there
> were twenty-five monks at the monastery, for it was an
> end of time. They were in great hardship because of the
> Bedouins. The caravans to the monastery were inter-
> rupted, and even the news. And all the inhabitants suf-
> fered severe trouble. The entire land of Egypt was
> devastated and it was without control. This happened
> during the pontificate of Anba Mark, the hundred and
> eighth patriarch of the fathers, the patriarchs. One [of
> the bedouins] tried to make a hole in the enclosure wall
> at night but did not succeed. They [the bedouins] re-
> opened the eastern spring. It was in every respect a bad
> year for the monks, who were dwelling at the
> monastery, especially because of the interruption of the
> caravans.[16]

This challenging time was the last during which the

10.2

Portrait of Pope Cyril IV (ADP/SA 2
s73 96)

mission in Ethiopia. If this really happened, it would be the first time that a Muslim ruler financed the construction of part of a Coptic religious complex.[21]

A Diverse Christian Community

One of the most interesting features of the Monastery of St. Antony is the multicultural and multiethnic character of its Christian community. Copts, Syrians, Ethiopians, Franciscans, and perhaps also Armenians visited and lived there at one time or another in the medieval and later periods. Except for the Franciscans, all these Christians shared the doctrinal position of the Coptic Church. Such was its fame and significance within and outside of Egypt that it was a regular destination for study and pilgrimage.

THE SYRIANS

The Syrian Church is important in the history of the Coptic Church because of two factors. First, there were long-standing good relations between the two monophysite sister churches of Alexandria and Antioch, relations accentuated by their isolation from much of the rest of the Christian world after the Arab occupation of Syria and Egypt in the seventh century.[22] Second, the Syrians' purchase of one of the monasteries of the Wadi al-Natrun from the Copts and its conversion into a Syrian monastery in the eighth century gave them a permanent base in Egypt. Although they no longer inhabit it, this site still bears the name Deir al-Surian, "the Monastery of the Syrians."[23]

A curious marginal note in a Syrian manuscript raises the possibility of the occupation of the Monastery of St. Antony by Syrians, sometime before 1232. It says of Constantine I, the abbot of the Syrian monastery at the Wadi al-Natrun (ca. 1235–1245):

monks had to defend themselves against serious threats by the bedouins.

The long patriarchate of Peter VII (1809–1852) coincided with the relatively liberal reign of Muhammed 'Ali, making it possible for the pope to improve the conditions of the Copts and the Coptic Church.[17] Peter's patriarchate paved the way for his successor, Cyril IV (1854–1861), one of the most important reformers and greatest figures in the history of the Coptic Church (fig. 10.2). Cyril is still known as the Father of Reform for his work. Education was the main focus of Cyril's activities, for clergy and lay adults and also, remarkably, both boys and girls.[18] In September 1856 he was entrusted with undertaking an official political mission to Ethiopia on behalf of Sa'id Pasha, the ruler of Egypt.[19] Cyril was enthusiastic about restoring Coptic monasteries and churches.[20]

The dilapidated condition of the monastery described in the colophon was consistent with the troubled state of Egypt in 1805. The enclosure wall had proven to be the decisive factor for the protection of the monks and probably influenced Patriarch Cyril IV to rebuild and extend the area of the walls in the middle of the nineteenth century. As part of this effort, the southern wall was extended, so as to incorporate the springs directly into the monastery as a protection against future attacks. It is said that Sa'id Pasha ordered at his own expense the completion of work on the renewal and enlargement of the enclosure wall of the Monastery of St. Antony during Cyril's

> [When he] was fed up (sic) with the abbacy, that is, the dangers and insults from the monks who were of an evil spirit [he] departed, that is, fled, to the Monastery of Abba Antonius and took the book of Mar Isaac with him to read and delight in it and then return it to this monastery. It chanced that he fell sick in the monastery of the glorious Mar Antonius and died there; and the book, the pair of this, remains there to our day. . . . Let the Syrian brethren who come after us to this monastery know that in the Convent of Abba Paulus, beside the Monastery of Mar Antonius, which belonged to the Syrians like this, there are many Syriac books still. But because of what was to come [?] the Syrians were driven thence: the Egyptians took it, but . . . there is none to examine them and release it from their hands.[24]

We do not know whether the Syrians controlled the Monastery of St. Antony. Even if we were to take the implications of the note at face value, three observations should be made. Ibn al-Qunbar, who died in 1208, was exiled to the Monastery of St. Antony by the order of the Coptic patriarch Mark III (1167–1189) in A.M. 890 (A.D. 1174).[25] In 1210 a monk of the Monastery of St. Antony was made *abun* of the Ethiopian Church.[26] These two events would not have occurred without the Coptic patriarch's control of the monastery. Although the marginal note suggests that tension existed between the Coptic and Syriac communities, evidence of peaceful coexistence between the two also exists. In the second half of the thirteenth century, a monk of the Monastery of St. Antony became patriarch of the Coptic Church as Gabriel III (1268–1271).[27] He was known as the Syrian, likely because of his origins, and his case is not an exceptional one.[28] Also, two Syrians are included in the painted program of 1232/1233: Severus of Antioch (s3; fig. 7.14) and Barsum (N11; figs. 4.22, 14.3), whose scroll includes an inscription in both Coptic and Syriac. Epigraphic evidence for the presence of Syrians at the Monastery of St. Antony exists in Garshuni, which is Arabic written in Syriac characters.[29] In 1393 a Syrian monk at the monastery copied a manuscript in Garshuni, so Syrians were clearly at the very least long-term visitors to the Monastery of St. Antony.[30]

THE ETHIOPIANS

The tradition of consecrating a Coptic monk to be abun of Ethiopia originated in the middle of the fourth century, when Patriarch Athanasius (328–373) consecrated Frumentius as that country's first metropolitan.[31] This practice continued until an agreement was reached in July 1948, giving the Ethiopian Church autonomy.[32] Good relations between the two churches have often been affected by the distance separating them and by the Muslim rulers of Egypt, without whose approval the new metropolitan could not go to Ethiopia. It was in the early thirteenth century that we hear for the first time of a monk from the Monastery of St. Antony being consecrated as abun of the Ethiopian Church. The consecration of this monk, named Isaac, as metropolitan of Ethiopia took place on the seventh of March 1210, during the pontificate of Patriarch John VI.[33] At the same time, John also sent Joseph to be a priest for the Ethiopian Church.[34] The fact that both Isaac and John were monks from the Monastery of St. Antony suggests its high status.[35] Another monk from the Monastery of St. Antony of importance to the Ethiopian Church was the Coptic Patriarch Gabriel III (1268–1271).

He was held in special reverence by the Ethiopians, whose Synaxarion commemorates him.[36]

Evidence exists for a significant and sustained Ethiopian presence in the Monastery of St. Antony itself. Around 1400 a certain Sem'on translated the Arabic Synaxarion of the Copts into the ancient Ethiopian language Ge'ez there.[37] At one time or another in the medieval period, Syrian and Ethiopian monks lived together at the Monastery of St. Antony. In particular, the community seems to have included a considerable number of Ethiopians in the middle of the sixteenth century. The numerous graffiti in Ge'ez are a testament to their place as part of the community. About 1520 the monastery served as a stopping point for Ethiopian royalty on a pilgrimage to Jerusalem. The Ethiopian king, Lebna Dengel (1508–1540), provided the monastery with an icon (fig. 10.3). Moreover, an Ethiopian monk wrote a treatise on penance at the monastery in 1561.[38] Johann Michael Wansleben, who visited the monastery in October 1672, mentions Ethiopians there.[39] In 1841 Patriarch Peter VII (1809–1852) consecrated Andarawus, a young Coptic monk at the Monastery of St. Antony, as a metropolitan (Salama III) for the Ethiopian Church.[40] When Cardinal Gugliemo Massaia was in the monastery in 1851, he saw the cell of Anba Andarawus, whose name was written in English as well as in Italian on its door.[41] These translations may reflect the conflict of the different Christian missionaries and foreign political influences in Ethiopia.[42] At the same time, Daoud, the abbot of the Monastery of St. Antony, was sent by Patriarch Peter VII to Ethiopia on a mission with ecclesiastical and political aims.[43] Having spent eighteen months in his mission, he returned to Cairo on July 17, 1852, and found that Patriarch Petrus VII had died. Abbot Daoud became the patriarch of the Coptic Church in 1854 and was sent again in 1856 by Sa'id Pasha, the ruler of Egypt, on a political mission to Ethiopia.[44] These sources show that, beginning in the thirteenth and continuing at least through the nineteenth century, the Monastery of St. Antony played a significant and ongoing role in the close relationship between the Copts and the Ethiopians.

THE ARMENIANS

Armenian Christians began living in the Nile Valley in late antiquity. The monastic center of Nitria received Armenian monks during the fourth and the fifth centuries, and there was an Armenian monastery near the Monastery of John the Little in the Wadi al-Natrun, which may have been established as early as the eleventh century. It was already in ruins sometime before 1441.[45] Armenian inscrip-

10.3
Icon given to the Monastery of
St. Antony by King Lebna Dengel
of Ethiopia, ca. 1520 (ADP/SA 1
s64 96)

tions belong to wall paintings of the Monastery of Anba Shenuda (the White Monastery) near Sohag and bear witness to the Armenian influence in Egypt during the Fatimid period.[46] The Armenian presence receded into insignificance during the reign of Saladin (1171–1193).[47]

Assessing the presence of Armenians within the Monastery of St. Antony is problematic. Two Armenian graffiti in the Deesis Chapel, also known as the Chapel of the Four Living Creatures, read: "Holy, holy, holy, Lord." As the paleography of the inscription is characteristic of the thirteenth century and thus contemporary with the paintings, Coquin and Laferrière suggested an Armenian painter for the chapel, but van Moorsel and Bolman have refuted this attribution.[48] Close examination shows that the words are not part of the formal inscriptions of the paintings, which are in Coptic. It is now apparent that these two phrases were written after the paintings were completed. They join several examples of newly found Armenian graffiti in the nave of the Church of St. Antony, all of which attest to an Armenian presence there.[49]

THE FRANCISCANS

The history of the Franciscans in Egypt can be traced back to the thirteenth century. In 1219 Francis of Assisi was present at the Crusaders' siege and capture of Damietta and met the Ayyubid Sultan al-Kamil.[50] During the Mamluk period (1250–1517), the Franciscans continued their activities, providing spiritual care and assistance for Catholic foreigners in Egypt and for pilgrims on their way to and from the Holy Land. Some of the friars suffered martyrdom during this period.[51]

By the seventeenth century, the Monastery of St. Antony had become the destination of many pilgrims. In that century, a number of Franciscans decided to enter the monasteries of St. Antony and St. Macarius to learn Arabic. The Monastery of St. Antony was used by the Franciscans as a language school for the preparation of their missionaries to the Orient, and in particular to those to Ethiopia. In 1625/1626 Father Bernardus left his mark in different places at the Church of St. Antony, as well as at the Church of St. Mark.[52] More graffiti by him have been uncovered as part of the conservation work in the Church of St. Antony.[53] Documents dating to 1639 record that the expenses for two or three Franciscans at the Monastery of St. Antony were forty scudi, which were to be paid to the Coptic monks annually.[54] But the Franciscan missions to Ethiopia were not successful, and most of the friars were killed by Ethiopians, were taken captive by the Turks, or died of disease.[55] Jean Coppin states that in 1638 the French

priest Agathange visited the Monastery of St. Antony, where he stayed four months, with the goal of converting the monks to Catholicism.[56] His efforts were unsuccessful.[57] He and the priest Cassien then left for Ethiopia, where they obtained the crown of martyrdom. Mark III, a monk of the Monastery of St. Antony who later became the metropolitan of Ethiopia, knew them well in Egypt, but he was unable to help them.[58] The priest Antonius Gonzales, who visited the monastery in 1665, reports that a Franciscan priest had been studying Arabic at the monastery for some years.[59] When the Franciscans stayed at the monastery in the seventeenth century, they were authorized to celebrate the mass in the Church of St. Mark.[60]

European Travelers and Western Scholars

St. Antony was well known in Europe, thanks principally to the biography written by the Patriarch Athanasius (326–373), as Vivian discussed in chapter 1. Therefore it should come as no surprise that many European travelers visited the Monastery of St. Antony during the Middle Ages and afterward (fig. 10.4).[61] The monastery was a goal of religious pilgrimage before the Arab conquest of Egypt in 641, and by the fourteenth century it had become one again.[62] European travelers, among others, visited the monastery on their pilgrimage to the Holy Land and to the Monastery of St. Catherine. Travelers who called at the monastery on Sinai but did not visit the Monastery of St. Antony were nevertheless aware of its location in the eastern desert.[63] Moreover, because of St. Antony's fame, some travelers, such as Ludolph von Suchem and Niccoldi Poggibons in the fourteenth century, referred to and even described the monastery, although it seems that they did not actually visit it.[64]

One of the earliest descriptions of the monastery is attributed to Ogier III, Seigneur d'Anglure. He also visited the Holy Land and the Monastery of St. Catherine, and his pilgrimage lasted from June 15, 1395, to July 22, 1396. Ogier was impressed by the monastery, which he found more beautiful than the Monastery of St. Catherine in every respect, except for its church. In particular, he admired its garden. He noted that more than one hundred monks belonged to the community, and he described them as being holy and conducting a good life. They did not drink wine and were generous to the pilgrims, they performed the service with chants, and they seemed devoted to their language.[65]

Ghillebert de Lannoy visited the monastery in 1422, and its beautiful garden full of palms and fruit trees pleased him as well. He mentioned a building that resembled a

10.4

General view from the
monastery walls, looking southwest, 1876–1878

castle and was constructed around a spring.[66] De Lannoy noted that there were only fifty monks in the monastery, half of its late-fourteenth-century figure. By that time some of the monasteries of Wadi al-Natrun were completely abandoned, and there were only a few monks in the famous Monastery of St. Macarius.[67]

Two European travelers, Jean Coppin and Johann Wansleben, separately provide a considerable amount of information about the monastery during the seventeenth century. In 1638 Coppin remarked that all of the buildings and the gardens were surrounded by a wall about five hundred paces long and between twenty-six and twenty-seven feet high, and that visitors were drawn up over the enclosure by a pulley.[68] Visiting the Church of St. Antony, he reported that it was not very large and that a wall separated the church from its choir, probably referring to the wooden iconostasis screen that separates the nave from the khurus. He noticed that the altar area was appropriately decorated with several images of the saints, in which he saw a Greek influence. The belfry was but a simple wall pierced with windows, where the bells were hung. Coppin admired a long vaulted passage, sixty paces in length, for

conducting water from the spring, which was then located outside the enclosure of the monastery.[69] He noted the presence of forty brothers, among them twenty-two monks, and stated that at one time there had been three hundred residents in the monastery, each with his own cell.[70]

In autumn 1672 Johann Wansleben spent two weeks in the monastery. His observations provide us with the most significant information about its state in the seventeenth century.[71]

There is no gate to the monastery, one enters in by a pulley, men and beasts are all drawn up over the wall. In the middle is a Dungeon, and round about many houses where the monks live.... Here are three churches, the chief is that of S. Antony; it is little, but very ancient; and as the monks told me, it is the same that S. Antony built, and the only thing of the monastery that hath escaped the rage of the Arabians. Within are pictures of many saints, painted in an antick and simple fashion: The smoke of the frankincense that is burnt there at Divine Service, hath made them appear as black as a chimney [fig. 10.5]. Near this church is an-

179

other dedicated to S. Peter and S. Paul, within [which] a little tower, and one bell, about a foot and a half in diameter, serves to call the monks to the Service of God, and to their other imployments. There is no other bell in all Egypt. The third church is in the garden, dedicated to a lay monk, called Mark, who died with a reputation of holiness; his body is kept there. In the middle of the monastery there is a square tower, with stone walls, very strong; in this tower the monks keep all their provisions, and their best moveables; and they fly to it when the roguish Arabians threaten them: They then draw the bridge, and beat them off with stones from the platform.

Claude Sicard, a French Jesuit, pursued missionary activities in Egypt between 1712 and 1726. In 1716 he had the first known plan of the monastery prepared, probably by an Armenian icon painter. It is roughly drawn and imprecise, but most of the details are accurate.[72] Richard Pococke published a version of Sicard's plan in *A Description of the East* (1743). Although professionally redrawn, it exaggerates the errors of the original (fig. 10.6).[73] Sicard noticed that there was a chapel in the garden dedicated to St. Mark, "the hermit and disciple of St. Antony." He saw thirty cells, a refectory, a bakehouse, a mill, and offices that were arranged in little streets. In their midst stood two churches, one dedicated to Sts. Peter and Paul, the other to St. Antony. The two churches were connected by a covered passage. Sicard also noticed that the walls of the churches were covered with paintings that were obscured by the smoke from the incense used during the divine offices.[74]

Most information for the history of the Monastery of St. Antony during the nineteenth century comes from European travelers, including Count de Forbins (1817), Abraham Norov (1834), Henry Tattam (1839), Sir Gardner Wilkinson (1843), Porphyrius Uspensky (1845), Cardinal Gugliemo Massaia (1851), Greville J. Chester (1870), Georg Schweinfurth (1876, 1877, 1878), and Michel Jullien (1883).[75] Several of these visitors had scholarly interests, anticipating the intense periods of study in the monastery beginning in the twentieth century. Sir Wilkinson pointed out that the Monastery of St. Antony was the principal monastery in Egypt, especially because the election of the patriarchs was made from among its monks.[76] Porphyrius

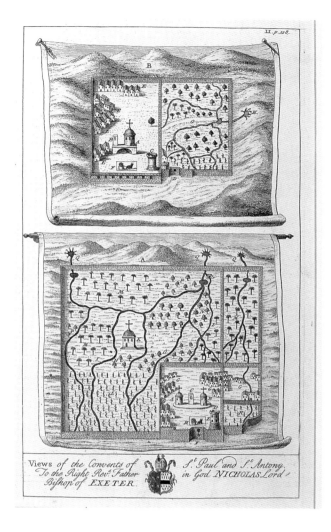

10.6

Map of the monasteries of
St. Antony (below) and St. Paul,
1743 (Courtesy of Adriano Luzi)

house three floors high, a little house for the patriarch, an isolated church dedicated to St. Mark in the North-East corner of the garden, and the well. . . . The Church of St. Antony is entered from the North. It is subdivided, according to the Coptic custom, into three parts by little stone walls not higher than two Arshins. In the first part of the church on the Western wall is seen a Latin inscription of Bernardus Ferulensis, from Sicily, who visited the monastery in 1626, and on the left wall is represented an iron helmet with decorations on it like four green serpents. . . . In the second part of the Church, under the three steps which lead into the passage before the altar is the grave of St. Antony. But they are not sure themselves, whether this grave contains the relics of the Saint of God or not. The third part of Church, just before the altar, is intended for the readers and singers, and is very dark. Its ceiling is made of palm boards and has the shape of a barrel vault. Here, on both sides of the high arch is a Coptic inscription. The letters are very large and are like our Slavonic script. I have copied only one part of it, as it was very difficult to stand on a ladder and to write in darkness. The sanctuary itself is small and dark, it is subdivided into three parts by stone walls with communicating doors. It is badly lit through little, dim windows which open in the little cupola. Almost all of the church has been painted over at different periods. On the walls and under the arches one sees darkened faces of prophets and apostles, those of saints and martyrs on horseback. The painting is very bad. In places are Coptic inscriptions. The monks told me that the church was consecrated in old times to the Panagia [the all holy Virgin Mary]. . . . To the South-Western part of this church adjoins a little chapel, quite dark, in the name of the four beasts which in Jeremiah represent symbolically the four Evangelists. . . . Very wonderful is the architecture of the Church of St. Antony. The first two parts of it and the sanctuary are covered up by three cupolas, quite similar to overturned funnels [figs. 2.4, 2.5]. On the roof of the church, they have a sharp outline and are only two Arshins high. When seen from the inside each of them is resting on a stone circle with windows and window-frames composed of little circles of glass. The cupola above the altar is smaller than the rest. It was the first time in my life that I saw funnel-shaped cupolas.[78]

The Jesuit Michel Jullien visited the Church of St. Antony in 1883 and remarked that "the walls of it are covered with paintings in the old Byzantine style, where one

Uspensky, a Russian archimandrite and ecclesiastical writer, came to Egypt to acquire manuscripts. Uspensky believed that a union between the Russian Orthodox Church and the Coptic Church was possible. He visited the monastery in 1850. Daoud, the abbot of the monastery and the future patriarch Cyril IV (fig. 10.2), accompanied him. In 1865 Uspensky published his account of the journey in Russian.[77] In his unpublished manuscript on the history of the monasteries of St. Antony and St. Paul, Alexander Piankoff, also a Russian, translated some passages from Uspensky's book into English, which "although full of naïvetés, are nevertheless valuable." The following selections contain interesting details about the monastery and shed light on the state of research on it in the nineteenth century:

All the buildings in it as in all the Egyptian Monasteries are grouped together in a North-West corner. The rest of the space is taken by the garden. Besides the narrow, gloomy and untidy cells of the monks scattered without order, the main buildings are: the cathedral church with the adjoining Church of St. Antony, the vestry and the library in the crenellated tower, the dining hall, a store-

Jabatian magali
(glockenthurm)

qasr
(See Burg)

Eingang zur neuen Kirche
und el-Qasr im Kloster St. Antonius
1876

10.7

Entrance to the Church of the
Holy Apostles and the keep,
1876–1878

recognizes, in spite of the ravages of time, warriors, angels, apostles, and the Infant Jesus borne on the arms of His Holy Mother. . . . The paintings appear to us to belong to the first centuries of Byzantine art. They merit study by some scholarly archaeologist."[79]

According to Georg Schweinfurth, who visited the monastery three times, in 1876, 1877, and 1878, there were forty monks in the monastery. He lamented the fact that visitors, even Greek patriarchs and Russian archimandrites, had scratched their names on the painted walls of the Old Church. Schweinfurth also incorrectly attributed the wall paintings from the church to the first centuries of Christian art.[80] His drawings of the monastery show architectural features that have since been changed, and also show monks wearing turbans (figs. 2.10, 10.4, 10.7).[81]

It was not until the twentieth century that scholarly studies began to appear about the monastery, especially on the wall paintings of the Church of St. Antony and on some of the manuscripts belonging to the library.[82] Josef Strzygowski was the first scholar to visit the monastery after 1900. He described some of the equestrian saints, and published a description and an illustration of the sixteenth-century Ethiopian icon given by King Lebna Dengel (fig. 10.3).[83] The first detailed description of the Monastery of St. Antony in Arabic was published by Labib Habachi and Zaki Tawudros, who visited the monastery in 1927.[84] Johann Georg, Duke of Saxony, visited the monastery in 1928 and published a short description of it, including

many photographs (figs. 10.8, 12.4). The duke counted eighteen monks and four novices at the monastery. The figure of eighteen monks that he mentioned might be wrong, for Simaika, who visited the monastery in 1929, mentions seventy monks.[85] According to Johann Georg, their knowledge of theology was meager. Their food consisted mainly of lentils and olives, grown in the monastery, and the monthly caravan provided them with their remaining needs. The bedouins lived on food from the monastery.[86] The duke stated that the Monastery of St. Antony was the most valuable monastery he had seen in the Orient.[87] He reported inspecting the keep, where he admired a precious medieval icon of the Virgin Mary. The hegumenos of the monastery gave it to him as a present.[88]

In 1930–1931 an expedition of the Byzantine Institute of America under the leadership of Thomas Whittemore made a trip to the monastery in Ford automobiles. They carried out a survey of the monastery, including all of its buildings, took photographs, made a short silent film, and copied some of the inscriptions and paintings (figs. 11, 18, and 22, introduction, 10.5). The scholarly credentials of the expedition were impressive. It counted among its members the architect Oliver Barker, the artist Netchetailov, the photographer Kazazian, and the epigraphist Alexandre Piankoff. Unfortunately, the results of the expedition, which were to have been printed in Oxford, remained not only unpublished but largely unavailable to scholars until their removal to Dumbarton Oaks and the University of Michigan.[89] The exception to this were three articles published by Piankoff, who identified with clarity for the first time the themes of the wall paintings and provided a plan locating them in the Church of St. Antony. Piankoff also noted the dating of one of the paintings to 1232/1233.[90] The contributions of Piankoff attracted the attention of two great specialists, Jules Leroy and R.-G. Coquin, who then studied the wall paintings and inscriptions intensively and published their results in 1976 and 1978.[91] H. Romilly Fedden went to the Monastery of St. Antony in 1936 and published a plan of it, which was drawn by the architect Hassan Fathy in 1937.[92] Fedden found ten priests and fifteen lay brothers in the monastery.[93] He commented that the paintings "are in a very bad state. They are neither as aesthetically interesting, nor as well preserved, as those at St. Paul's Monastery. Talbot Rice [a Byzantine art historian] places them in the late Byzantine period, that is between the thirteenth and fifteenth century."[94] Remarking on Fedden's evaluation of the paintings, the historian Otto Meinardus wrote: "To consider the wall-paintings of the Church of St. Antony aesthetically inferior to those in the Cave Church of St. Paul is to betray an almost unpardonable igno-

10.8

General view of the monastery from the guest quarters to the mountain, 1928

rance."[95] Fedden's study of the monastery's churches, the keep, the refectory, the springs, and the enclosure wall includes a list of the architectural activities at the monastery during the second half of the eighteenth century: Hassaballa al-Bayadi rebuilt the church of St. Mark in 1766; Lutfalla Shakir rebuilt the Church of the Apostles and the eastern wall by 1772; Ibrahim al-Gawhari renovated the monastery walls in 1783.[96] According to Grossmann, only the Church of St. Antony has any historical significance, and only the smaller keep "lays claim to a somewhat advanced age."[97] The contribution of Meinardus to the monastery's history is useful, especially for the descriptions by travelers.[98] An exhaustive bibliography is to be found in the thorough account of Stefan Timm.[99] The Coptic art historian Bourguet also visited the site, and apparently planned but never published a complete study of the paintings in the Church of St. Antony.[100] Recent work on the wall paintings depends on the first book devoted to them by van Moorsel, with contributions by Innemée and Grossmann, which is sure to remain indispensable for many years to come.[101]

The disparate sources drawn on here combine to provide us with impressions of the ascending and declining fortunes of the Monastery of St. Antony over the past eight hundred years. Despite its remote location and dependence on caravans for foodstuffs, its inhabitants often played a major role in Egypt and Ethiopia. At the beginning of the period, ca. 1200, Abu al-Makarim wrote that it was unparalleled among the monasteries of Egypt. The thirteenth and fourteenth centuries witnessed the creation of the major artistic and scribal work that still captivates our attention today. Members of the Christian communities that shared the doctrinal views of the Coptic Church (monophysites) were a regular part of the monastery.

Christians outside of the group formed by the Copts, Syrians, Ethiopians, and Armenians also lived for periods at the monastery and were regular visitors, causing Belon du Mans to write in 1547 that the Red Sea monastery was inhabited by Christian monks of different denominations.[102] Many of these inhabitants, and also visitors, wrote prayers and petitions on the walls in the Church of St. Antony, and Sidney Griffith has studied these graffiti (chapter 11).

Conditions at the monastery entered their worst period in the late fifteenth century, when it was abandoned and then sacked by bedouins. Sometime before 1540 Patriarch Gabriel VII reopened it, and since that time it has been a continuously functioning monastic community. Even during times of local and regional trouble, the Monastery of St. Antony has retained its high status, as witnessed by the fact that monks were selected from there to lead the Coptic and Ethiopian Churches.

Western visitors provide us with the most specific information about the site and physical condition of the monastery, and also occasionally mention the paintings. They note the verdant garden, three churches, a library, and significant additions to the enclosure wall. Their evaluations of the paintings vary, likely influenced to a certain extent by the significant accretions of soot and dirt. These were notable as early as 1627, when Wansleben described the paintings as being "black as a chimney."

The twentieth century marked the beginnings of serious scholarly interest in the monastery and its paintings, an interest that has resulted in numerous studies, including this book. Visitors have not been exclusively foreign, as a subsequent chapter by Oram describes. Since the paving of the Suez to Zafarana road in 1946, and subsequent establishment of a highway between Cairo and the Red Sea Coast, Coptic pilgrims regularly visit the monastery, drawn by the sanctity of the place and the spiritual advice they receive from the monks. The advent of the automobile has brought the modern world to the Monastery of St. Antony. The number of monks and the size of the monastery enclosure increased exponentially in the last decades of the twentieth century. New guest houses and gardens have been built, and a museum is being prepared to exhibit the monastery's remarkable collection of icons, textiles, and metalwork. A second and much larger wall and monumental entrance gateway enclose many of the new structures, gardens, and a parking area. The large-scale project to clean and restore the paintings in the Church of St. Antony is only one of many indications that the monastery is enjoying another period of fruitfulness and renown.

بسم الله الرحمن الرحيم وافتح لنا يا الله القدير بالله الصمد

لما كان بتاريخ يوم الثلثا المبارك تاسع عشرين شهر ... المبارك ... جماعة ... وأين ملة هذه الاطراف ...

... السيد ... البطرك ... الحاضرين والمدعوين في عدة الاطراف الذكرى من ... ناحية في ... معان

... ماروني ... على الوجه ... وانقطاع ... السلطان الرب ...

... يرضى ... ويانحه ... الدين خرج لحد يا ياض ...

... يجمعهم شاء ... على هذا لجميع المذكورين ... العيون ... الدين ...

... وعلى ... دالي وجميع ... على عمر ...

... ويوم عاشر ... الاداء الرحما ...

CHAPTER 11 THE HANDWRITING ON THE WALL

GRAFFITI IN THE CHURCH OF ST. ANTONY

The following anecdote is recorded of the Caliph al-Ma'-mūn (813–833) when he was on a journey from Baghdad to the Byzantine frontier in the year 830. His traveling companion left this account:

> He and I entered an old church in Syria which had marvelous paintings and in which he walked around at length. When it was time to leave he said to me, "When strangers on journeys and people far removed from their friends and companions enter a well-known place and famous site, it is their habit to leave behind a record of their presence in order to seek blessing in the prayers of (other) strangers, travelers, and people bereft of their kith and kind (on their behalf). I want to join in, so get me a pot of ink." He then wrote the following verses midway on the altar gate:

> O strangers! May God grant you safe return
> and may you soon meet your loved ones.
> My heart has been afflicted with pity and fear for you;
> may God heal it by bringing you to safety.
> I wrote in order to support you;
> so when you read it, know that it was I who wrote it.[1]

Few of the hands that wrote on the walls of the Old Church of St. Antony belonged to so famous or so exalted a personage as the Muslim caliph, nor do their names now claim any immediate recognition in the wider world. But it is immediately clear to the modern visitor that earlier travelers shared al-Ma'mūn's habit of leaving behind "a record of their presence in order to seek blessing." Even in its present state of restoration and spotlessness,

the church's walls carry hundreds of graffiti in Arabic, Garshuni, Syriac, Ethiopic, Armenian, Greek, Latin, Russian, and a scattering of modern languages (fig. 11.1). Although it is impossible to catalogue all of them here, a task that will be carried out in other scholarly publications, a survey will give the impression of the rich testimony these texts provide to the devotion of visitors over the centuries, and the popularity of pilgrimage to the church from the thirteenth century to the twentieth.

To begin with, one must say a word about the graffiti in general. They are to be distinguished from the formal inscriptions, almost entirely in Coptic, that are included in the decorative programs on the upper walls and the ceilings of all the parts of the church. Unlike the inscriptions, the graffiti, none of which are in Coptic, are occasional texts, written in the everyday languages of the pilgrims, as the opportunity presented itself, on the lower walls, mostly in the nave, but with some appearing in the khurus and in the sanctuary as well. People wrote them quickly, wherever they could find a suitable space, sometimes in close proximity to the icon of a favorite saint or patron. Most of them were written with pen and ink; some are in charcoal or pencil; a few have been incised into the plaster.[2] One assumes that over the centuries many graffiti have been washed away when the walls were cleaned, and many more were covered over by successive layers of plaster and whitewash. Nevertheless, enough of them remain to provide a fascinating record of the passage of numerous visitors come to ask the forgiveness of the Lord for their sins, and the blessing of St. Antony. The most expeditious way to review them here is by language groupings.

11.1
Graffiti under Antony and Paul
(N1–N2; ADP/SA BW, May 1999, 6)

Arabic Graffiti

By far the largest number of graffiti in the Church of St. Antony are in Arabic. Although a few of the most important of them, longer, more detailed, and more sophisticated than the others, have already been published and analyzed, they will be repeated here because of their historical importance, due to the names and dates they contain.[3] But the vast majority of the Arabic graffiti are only a line or two: they are formulaic, as the reader will see, scarcely varying in the choice of words from one to another, save for the names and places of origin of the pilgrims, and other particulars. Yet these are the graffiti that give the best sense of the frame of mind of the typical petitioner. In the ensemble they record a mood of compunction for sin and a confidence in the intercessory power of prayer for oneself and for others—mostly family members living and dead—made in the church or to St. Antony personally. Although some of the these graffiti have been written by monks, the vast majority of them seem to be by lay people.

One group of Arabic graffiti serve a practical purpose for the visitor. On the lower registers of the walls of the nave, under the portraits of several of the saints painted high aloft, in a small, neat hand, someone has inscribed at eye level the names of the saints portrayed above. At one time, such names may have appeared under all of the portraits. Four of them were recorded by earlier researchers.[4] After the recent cleaning, seven such labels are now legible:

ابو بساى (Apa Bishoi; N7); اكلوديوس (Claudius; N19); بقطر ابن رومانوس (Victor, son of Romanos; N20; fig. 11.2); مينا (Menas; N21; fig. 11.3); تادرس ابن يوحنا (Theodore, the son of John—that is, Theodore the General; N22); اقلوديوس (Claudius, written under the portrait of Sisinnius; N23); اباينا الروم (our two fathers, the Romans—that is, Maximus and Domitius; N32).[5]

One of the most important Arabic graffiti in the church is surely the long notice written on the wall under the portraits of St. Antony and of St. Paul, the Hermit (N1, N2; fig. 11.1). It is almost more than a graffito, having the character of an official notice of the death and burial of Patriarch Gabriel VII (1525–1568), who was responsible for the restoration of the monastery in the sixteenth century.[6] The importance of the text is indicated by the fact that in the seventeenth century (A.D. 1663/1664) a monk copied it into the manuscript of a Coptic lectionary in the monastery's library, and thereafter, information from it appeared in other manuscripts.[7] The text says:

In the name of the Father, and of the Son, and of the Holy Spirit, the one God.

On Tuesday the blest, the 29th of the month of Bābah the blest, in the year 1285 of the righteous martyrs,[8] (May the Lord bestow on us their blessings. Amen), the master, the father, the great patriarch among the patriarchs, Anba Gabriel, the 95th of the fathers, the patriarchs on the Markan throne, died. Due to his righteous resolve, his demise was in the company of the monks of this holy convent, at the lower monastery, on the seashore. His pure body was transported to Miṣr [Cairo], the well-guarded, on the 25th of the month of Hathor,[9] of the year, the date of which is above. We conducted the funeral service in the church of the great martyr, Mercurius, in Miṣr, in which he was buried, in a new grave under the body of Mercurius.[10] As for the number of priests and bishops who attended his funeral, there were 285.[11] As for the people, their number was unlimited. This father occupied the Markan throne for forty-three years.[12] He shepherded God's people with the best of shepherding, and he exerted a successful effort in the rebuilding of monasteries and churches and restoring them; he would even make them stronger—most of all, this holy convent, known as the monastery of the ʿArabah (Dayr al-ʿArabah), the home of our father Antony. He was the one who in his days opened it (May the Lord give him perpetual life and bring about prosperity and abundance), and he was fortunate enough to

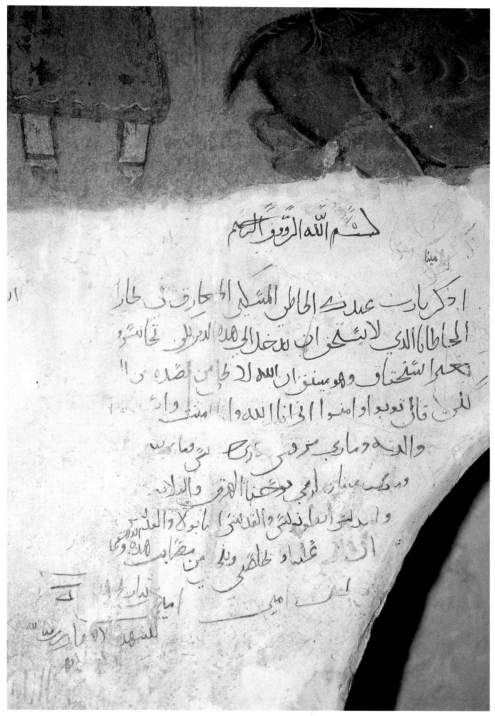

11.3

Graffito under Menas's camel

(N21)

make it house monks again after an extended period of ruin. No one was able to open it and rebuild it except [this father, whom the enemy of the good opposed] a number of times during its ruin, but the Lord, praised be He, did not let the enemy's purpose be achieved in this matter. He lived with the monks and was in this monastery most days. By means of his prayers, may the Lord God, praised be He, populate this holy monastery to the last soul; may He give his soul rest in the paradise of happiness. May He have mercy on His scribe by means of his prayers. Amen. Praise be to God everlastingly.[13]

Three other dated Arabic graffiti to be found in the church, all of them written on the wall in the year 1260 of the martyrs—that is, A.D. 1544—call for special attention.[14] First of all, the mention of the year 1260 of the martyrs in all three of them possibly indicates the date by which Patriarch Gabriel's restoration of the monastery was complete. And all of them begin with a formulaic phrase that is to be found in scores of other, humbler graffiti on the walls, "Remember, O Lord, your poor servant, drowning in the sea of sin," اذكر يا رب عبدك المسكين الغارق في بحار الخطايا This formula well expresses the penitent attitude with which the pilgrims who wrote graffiti customarily came to visit the church. Typically, they go on to mention their own names and the names of other members of their families. Sometimes they mention as well the names of the saints whose intercession they seek. For example, the first of these three graffiti dated to A.D. 1544 is inscribed under the portrait of St. Menas (N21; fig. 11.3), on the back wall of the nave, and in the text the writer mentions the names of St. Mark, St. George, St. Menas, St. John of Heraclea, St. Antony, St. Paul the Hermit, and others whose names are now effaced.[15] It is noticeable that all the names still legible are of saints represented in the paintings on the upper walls. Clearly the inscriber was attentive to the program of portraits in the restored church. In the second of the three graffiti, written under the portrait of St. Victor (N20) on the back wall, the petitioner prays that God will protect Patriarch Gabriel, indicating his awareness of the debt of gratitude owed to the church's restorer.[16]

The third of these graffiti, written on the north side of the archway into the khurus, under the portrait of the archangel at K16, is dated specifically to "the 22nd of Baramhāt in 1260 of the holy martyrs"—that is, 18 March 1544.[17] An interesting feature of this graffito is the note written just above it, in which the inscriber says he has "written this at the hands of the master, the patriarch (على ايدى السيد الاب البطرير ك)," as if to exculpate himself for the responsibility for writing on the wall, and suggesting Patriarch Gabriel's presence at the time of the writing.[18] In the body of the text, he mentions his own name, Sergius (سركيس), and goes on to name many of the people in his family. A line written on the wall just above the seemingly exculpatory note at the beginning of the graffito, in much smaller characters, which Coquin and Laferrière seem not to have noticed, says, "the wretched Sergius wrote it (كتبه الحقير سركيس)," as if to answer any doubt about whether or not the same person was responsible for both the introductory note and the body of the graffito.[19] Finally, at the end of this interesting text, in an apparent reference to monks on pilgrimage, the writer penned the prayer that "God might bless brethren (اخو ة) for visiting St. Antony."[20]

There are literally hundreds of Arabic graffiti on the walls of the church, particularly in the nave. The heaviest concentration of them are on the back, western wall, to the right of the door as one now enters the church, and in the northeastern corner, with a dense concentration under the icon of the Virgin Mary (N36). Here, on several layers of plaster, are graffiti in Arabic, Ethiopic, and Syriac characters, many of them no longer fully legible, but all of them testifying to the penitent sincerity of the pilgrims who came to ask pardon for their sins.

The following graffito is inscribed under the portrait of Patriarch Theophilus in the sanctuary of the church (s5):

اذكر يا رب عبدك مقارى
واذكر يا رب عبدك اسحا ق
واذكر يا رب عبدك ابراهيم
واذكر يا رب ابونا سليمان
واذكر يا رب امنا ست البيت
نيح يا رب نفو سنا في فردوس
اليوم امين امين امين

Remember, O Lord, your servant, Makarius,
and remember, O Lord, your servant, Isaac,
and remember, O Lord, your servant, Abraham,
and remember, O Lord, our father, Solomon,
and remember, O Lord, our mother, the lady of the house.
Give our souls rest, O Lord, in paradise
today. Amen. Amen. Amen.

Evidently the brothers Makarius, Isaac, and Abraham came on pilgrimage to the church and inscribed the names of their family members on the sanctuary wall, per-

haps in the hope that an officiating priest would remember them in the course of the divine liturgy. It is noticeable that the mother's name is not given in public. This usage is in accord with the practice of the Copts from the time of the Islamic conquest up until the beginning of the twentieth century.[21]

Very typical of many of the Arabic graffiti in its language and motivation is the following text, inscribed under the portrait of St. George (N25) on the northern wall of the nave:

اذكر يا رب عبدك الخا طي المسكين الغارق
في بحر
الخطايه والذنوب اغفر له جميع خطاييه
برحمتك
انت القادر علي كل شي اغفر لعبدك
انطون الخاطي انت
الله اغفر له وتجييه من جميع ال...

Remember, O Lord, your servant, the poor sinner, drowning
in the ocean of his sins and crimes. Forgive him all of his
sins, in your mercy. You are powerful over everything.
Forgive your servant, the sinner Anton. You, O God, forgive
him and save him from all . . .

One of the numerous, short Arabic graffiti from under the portrait of the Virgin Mary at N36, written in the upper left quadrant of the upper left cross, says simply:

اذكر يا رب
عبدك جرجس ووالده
منصور

Remember, O Lord,
your servant, George, and his father,
Manṣūr

Under the portrait of St. Menas (N21; fig. 11.3) on the west wall of the nave, a church deacon penned the following prayer for forgiveness:

اذكر يا رب عبدك الخاطي
المسكين الغارق في
بحار الخاطايا الذى
لايستحق ان يدعا
شماسا من اجل كثرة خطاياه...

Remember, O Lord, your poor sinful servant, drowning in the sea
of sins, who is not worthy to be called a deacon because of the
multitude of his sins. . . .

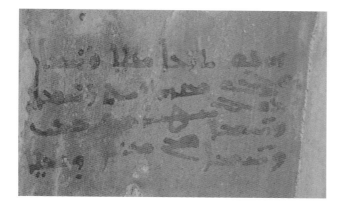

This is the door full of love,
and within it is love.
Enter, sinner; pray [much]
for love from your Lord, full
of love.

Other graffiti in Syriac characters inside the church are actually in the Arabic language; Christians with a Syriac liturgical and patristic heritage often employed this script from the sixteenth century onward. Three such graffiti are still legible on the wall under the portraits of Antony and Paul (N1, N2; fig. 11.1), on the east end of the nave, written to the side of and under the long Arabic graffito that gives notice of the death and burial of Patriarch Gabriel VII. One of them, inscribed vertically, on the lower right-hand side of the much longer Arabic graffito, directly under the portrait of St. Paul the Hermit, says:

Have mercy on your servants, the sinners, by the prayer of Anbā Paul, the greatest of the anchorites, your servants Matthew and Muqaddasi . . . East Syrian priests, from [Methed] of Persia, in the year . . . [23]

The same names, Matthew and Muqaddasi, also appear in another brief Garshūnī graffito, written at a slant under the longer graffito about Patriarch Gabriel, just under the portrait of St. Antony (N1). The invocation asks Abūnā (our father) Antony (صور) to have mercy on the petitioners. A third Garshūnī graffito in the same location, with different petitioner names, asks both "the great ones," St. Paul and St. Antony, to have mercy on them. All three of these texts were presumably penned by the same group of pilgrims. There are traces of other Garshūnī graffiti at other locations in the church—for example, on the wall under the portrait of the Virgin Mary in the northeastern corner of the nave (N36)—but not enough of it remains to decipher the message. In the ensemble, these few texts testify to the wide popularity of the shrine church among eastern Christians, even beyond the bounds of the denomination of the Copts.

Ethiopic Graffiti

The significance of the Ethiopic graffiti in the Church of St. Antony is in their age.[24] Most of them are written, most

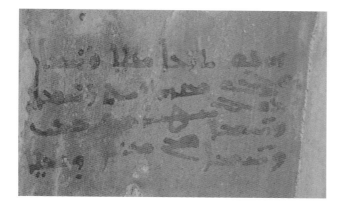
11.4
Syriac graffito at the entrance of the church

Finally, under the portrait of Sts. Maximus and Domitius (N32), on the northern wall of the nave, is the following graffito, in which the petitioner, Sergius, invokes the intercession of the fathers, the prophets, the apostles, and the martyrs, all the saints pictured on the walls. He wrote:

Remember, O Lord, your servant, Sergius. Snatch him from the snares of Satan and forgive him disobedience and procrastination by the prayers of the fathers, the prophets, the apostles, the martyrs, and the saints . . .

There are literally hundreds of prayers like these, longer and shorter, on the walls of the church. Many of them contain names, dates, and places from which the petitioners came. Only a full catalog of them will reveal all the information they contain about the devotees who in all ages came as pilgrims to the monastery. Perhaps these few examples will suffice to give some sense of the religious fervor that motivated the petitioners to inscribe their prayers on the walls. No doubt they hoped that later pilgrims would join their prayers with those of the earlier ones, to create a community of intercession, over time, to pray for the forgiveness of their sins from the Lord, through the intercession of the prayers of the saints whose portraits are on the walls.

Graffiti in Syriac Script

There is only one surely Syriac graffito at the church, but there are several of them in Arabic in Syriac characters—that is to say, in Garshūnī writing.[22] As for the Syriac text (fig. 11.4), it is a brief exhortation to the visitor, penned in fading brown ink, on the wall at eye level, by the upper right lintel of the door by which one enters the church today, at the northwest corner of the nave. It says:

189

11.5

Geʿez graffito under Maximus

(N32)

under the portrait of Maximus and Domitius (N32). It is notable for its invocation of the blessing of Sts. Antony and Paul, as well as for its allusions to important figures in Ethiopian monastic history:

> In the name of the Holy Trinity.
> I, Gälawdəyos, and Gäbrä Qirqos,
> Näbiyud, and Giyorgis came to the Monastery of
> [Abba] Antony
> on the 12th of the month of Säne [June 6 or 16].
> May the blessing of Our Father Antony and the
> blessing
> of our Father Pauli [Paul] be with us. Amen. And may
> the blessing of Our Fathers
> Abba Täklä Haymanot of abundant good deeds
> and Abba Samuʾel, an angel on earth,
> be with us, for ever and ever.[28] Amen and amen.
> Let [it be
> so; let it be so.]

The sixteenth-century Ethiopic texts that appear under the portrait of the Blessed Virgin Mary (N36), one of the most attractive spots for graffiti writers of all languages in the whole church, implore the intercession of Mary, of St. Antony, and of Gabriel, probably the angel Gabriel, whose namesake was Patriarch Gabriel VII, the church's restorer in the very century when the pilgrim who wrote these texts made his visit:

> (A)
> O, my Lady.
> O, my Lady.
> May you not drive me away from your shadow.

> (B)
> [ ] Christ. Abba [Antony]
> [and] who is clothed in flesh. O [who is] born [ ]
> I take refuge in My Lady Mary.
> I take refuge in your holy body [so that you may
> save]
> me from my enemies; and preserve [me]
>
>   [Amen]
> and Amen. [Let it be so;] let it be so;
> I take refuge with Gabriel, [I pray that]
>   Mary [may save]
>   me [ ].
>   what.

probably, in hands of the sixteenth or seventeenth century. Perhaps they are evidence that Ethiopian monks lived in the monastery. Tradition has it that the Monastery of St. Antony was the one from which Coptic monks were chosen for the Ethiopian metropolitanate. So far, seven Ethiopic graffiti have been found in the church. It is interesting to note that five of them are on the northern wall of the nave, in the general area under the portrait of St. Moses the Black (N30), but they are actually written under the memorial inscription (N31), the portrait of Sts. Maximus and Domitius (N32), the portrait of St. Macarius the Great (N33), and the portrait of the Virgin Mary (N36).

A particularly interesting Ethiopic graffito was written on the eastern face of the niche (blocked-off doorway), under the memorial inscription (N31). It was written in A.D. 1542, just a few years after Patriarch Gabriel VII's restoration of the church. The text reads as follows:

> In the name of the Holy Trinity.
> I, [Arkä] Mikaʾel,[25] came to this Monastery of
> Antony. He [the Lord] has shown me that which many
> righteous people and
> monks—nəburanə əd[26] and officials
> —have not seen. Praise is fitting for
> the giver of grace. You who
> read my [ ], pray for me to
> God [his good
> things]. May God preserve
> you [in your cells] and
> strengthen [your cells] for you like the house
> founded upon a rock. May he [the Lord] [multiply
> you very much in it], like the mustard seed
> sowed in the field of the Gospel and which then
> rose so high that it sheltered the birds of the sky.
> Forever and ever. Amen [and]
> amen. Let it be so; let [it be so.]
> In the year 202.[27]

Another text (fig. 11.5), rich in personal names, which was inscribed sometime in the sixteenth century, appears

Armenian Graffiti

Armenian graffiti are to be found in some half-dozen locations in the church.[29] The most widely known of them is the liturgical exclamation "Holy, Holy, Holy, Lord," written on both sides of the depictions of the angels carrying the mandorla of Christ in the small chapel (C2).[30] Unfortunately, the Armenian graffiti at the other locations are very difficult to decipher, due to the peculiarities of the script and the colloquial character of the language. They are still under study. But already it is clear that those who inscribed them have recorded their pleas for the forgiveness of their sins, and that they have sought the intercession of the saints who are venerated in the church. For example, the Armenian graffito written under the portrait of Phoebammon at N26, on the northern wall of the nave, clearly seeks the intercession of all the saints.

11.6
Heraldic drawings (A2–A3; ADP/SA
BW medium format, Nov. 99, 1:3)

Medieval Western Graffiti

Texts and designs inscribed on the walls of the Church of St. Antony by medieval noblemen from the west have a strikingly different character from the graffiti left behind by the pilgrims who wrote in oriental languages.[31] Visitors who wrote in Arabic, Syriac, Armenian, and Ethiopic wrote votive graffiti; that is to say, they inscribed on the wall their prayers for forgiveness of sin and to seek the blessings of God and his saints. Western noblemen, and even clerics, by way of contrast, were more inclined to leave behind a record of their own passage. They themselves, rather than the saints, are the focus of attention. A startling example of this practice, still to be seen in several locations in the church, is the name of the Franciscan Frater Bernardus Ferulensis Siculus, who came to visit in 1625 and 1626, and wrote his name and the date several times in the church, in gigantic Latin characters, with no word of prayer or intercession, or any other expression of religious sentiment.[32]

A fascinating class of graffiti left behind by western nobles on their visits to the church of St. Antony from the fourteenth to the sixteenth centuries is to be seen in the heraldic displays, carved, scratched, painted, or drawn on the walls at various locations (fig. 11.6). They are typical of the practice of itinerant western noblemen of the period—whether they were on Crusade, making a pilgrimage, or just making the grand tour—of leaving behind their names, coats of arms, crested helmets, and the symbols of the chivalric orders to which they belonged. Travelers' accounts from the period make it clear that local stonemasons and emblazoners were often employed for fashioning and installing these designs. The painted helmet with plumes on the north side of the nave (N27) is an especially noticeable instance of this phenomenon in the Old Church of St. Antony. It displays the heraldry of a German family of counts, von Looz, a member of which could have visited the church as early as the fourteenth century.[33] On the western wall of the nave, under the portrait of St. Menas (N21), there is the heraldic design of the Schinkel family, together with the inscribed name of Detlev Schinkel, who gave the year of his visit in Roman numerals as 1436.[34] What is more, it is clear that Schinkel had been to the Monastery of St. Catherine at Sinai, and to Cyprus, before coming to the Monastery of St. Antony, as indicated by the symbols of the chivalric orders connected to these places. Other heraldic graffiti in the church can be recognized as belonging to members of the medieval Voserie and Croy families. All in all, from these and other heraldic designs still waiting for identification, it is clear that the Monastery of St. Antony must have been frequently visited by European nobles during the fourteenth and fifteenth centuries. What is more, in terms of the number of the heraldic graffiti to be found here, the church is comparable to other popular sites for the noble, western visitors of the Middle Ages, such as the "old refectory" at the Monastery of St. Catherine, or the Church of the Nativity in Bethlehem.

Nineteenth- and Twentieth-Century Graffiti

In modern times, foreign visitors to the monastery continued to write their names on the church wall. Many of them, however, were content to leave only their names behind, and sometimes the date of their visit, in marked contrast to the practice of the Coptic pilgrims in every era who, in addition to their names, inscribed their prayers in Arabic under the portraits of the saints whose intercession they sought for the forgiveness of their sins.

An almost official-looking notice in Greek appears on the wall under the portrait of St. Shenoute (N28), recording the visit of the Greek Orthodox patriarch of Alexandria, Kallinikos (1858–1861):

Τῷ 1859 Μαιου

Καλλινικος Πατριαρχη

Αλεξανδρειας

μετα της Συνοδιας αυτου

Γρηγοριου και Γαβριηλ των ιεροδιακον

και Θεοδωρου Ραβδουχου[35]

In May 1859 this patriarch visited the monastery, together with the members of his synod, Gregory, Gabriel, and Theodore. In all likelihood, the visit was in connection with Patriarch Cyril IV's known interest in fostering ecumenical relations between the several Orthodox churches present in Egypt, particularly the Armenian and the Greek.[36]

A well-known figure in the travel accounts of the nineteenth century is the Russian Archimandrite Porphyrius Uspensky, who visited the Monastery of St. Antony in 1850 in the company of the future Coptic Orthodox Patriarch, Cyril IV (1854–1861).[37] He wrote his name on the western wall of the nave, where it is still to be seen, under the portrait of St. Menas (N21). Archimandrite Porphyrius was an avid ecumenist, who fostered hopes of restoring ecclesiastical communion between the Coptic Orthodox Church and the Russian Orthodox Church.[38] Another Russian visitor, presumably in the entourage of Archimandrite Porphyrius, wrote his name, P. Soloviev, and the

year, 1850, under the portrait of Phoebammon (N26) on the northern wall of the nave.

Some modern visitors left their names in both Arabic and Latin scripts. A case in point can be seen under the portrait of St. Menas (N21), where the name Georges Hayati/جورج حياتى appears. On the wall to the right of the modern entrance to the church of St. Antony, a number of modern visitors have left their names. The most prominent of these persons are King Farouk (1935–1952) and his wife, Queen Faridah. Their names, though faintly written, can still be clearly read high on the wall: فاروق الاول ملك مصر وصودان "Farouk I, King of Egypt and Sudan," and just above this notice the additional phrase: الملكة فريدة, "Queen Faridah." There is no indication of the date on which the royal couple came to the monastery.

Hundreds of other less famous names have been written on the walls. A number of them were put there by visiting servicemen from abroad. For example, on the wall to the right of the modern entrance, one can still read: L. G. Philpott, RAOC, 25/7/40. And even modern monks have not shied away from recording their presence in the monastery by inscribing a graffito on the wall. On the same space as the serviceman's name there is the following inscription: Abdel Masih El Antoni, 1934.

Reading the Graffiti

The hand that wrote on the plaster of the wall of the king's palace in the biblical narrative of the book of Daniel (5:5) was a disembodied specter, and the words it inscribed were mysterious and threatening; only a prophet could decipher them. The graffiti on the wall of the Church of St. Antony, by contrast, represent a rare connection people of our day have with the hundreds of pilgrims and visitors who came to the church over the centuries. All who wrote on the wall must have done so with the knowledge that those who would come after them would be able to read the record of their passage. In this way the handwriting on the wall offers the modern visitor a living connection with his or her predecessors. It is evident that some came in a spirit of prayer and devotion, and some came with a sense of personal fulfillment, bent only on leaving behind a memorial of their sojourn. All of them enable the modern pilgrim or visitor to enter a network of fellow travelers who have come to a holy spot from many countries and language communities, over a long period of time.

The most immediately striking impression one receives from the graffiti in the ensemble is of the variety of languages in which they are inscribed, testifying to the wide appeal of the holy place. The large number of them is also immediately evident, and the significance of this realization is enhanced when one recalls that the successive plaster layers must hide many more hundreds of graffiti than can currently be read in the church. The fact that the preponderant majority of them are in Arabic, and that in formulaic fashion they implore the intercession of the saints for the forgiveness of sins, testifies to the lively faith of the Coptic Orthodox Church, whose members over the centuries have been the largest single group of pilgrims to come to the church. The graffiti in Syriac, Ethiopic, and Armenian go together with other historical records to tes-

tify to the presence in the monastery of monks and visitors from the other churches with whom the Copts have historically been in ecclesiastical communion, for whom the Monastery of St. Antony has had a more than ordinary importance. In short, the presence of the graffiti helps to bring the site alive in a way that enables one to learn something of the thousands of people who since the thirteenth century at least have entered the church to pray, and to view with awe the paintings of the martyrs, patriarchs, and monks, whose portraits high on the walls still command the attention of visitors, whether to give a focus to their religious devotion or to excite their admiration.

CHAPTER 12 WINDOWS INTO HEAVEN

ICONS IN MONASTIC LIFE TODAY

The monastic life in Egypt is experiencing a period of renaissance. This is a result of the general ecclesiastical rebirth taking place among the Copts in Egypt and abroad, which is itself a result of the ecclesiastical, spiritual, educational, and administrative awakening effected by the pastoral care of Pope Shenuda III (Patriarch of the Sea of St. Mark).

The monastic life in Egypt is Christianity transformed into living practice. It was established by St. Antony, the father of all monks, and has endured from that time down to the present day. The monasteries are still filled with monks and nuns from all areas of Egypt, living according to original monastic custom and the traditions and teachings received from the first monastic fathers (fig. 12.1). In the monasteries, continued daily use is made of the Coptic language, in liturgy, prayers, and sacraments. The monks still live according to traditional monastic laws in matters of daily work, prayers, and spiritual exercises. Modern monasticism keeps to original monastic practice in matters of *metanoia* (praying mindfully with penitence), prostration, work, and spiritual exercises. The Coptic Church believes that monasteries and the monastic life are like a fortress that preserves the entire ecclesiastical tradition. They are the spring from which the whole church drinks. The spiritual atmosphere special to the monasteries is distributed to all areas of the country by the priests, who begin their priestly lives in a monastery. They draw as much as possible from this deep source of living tradition, and with this experience behind them they begin their mission and service.

In years gone by, the monasteries were not charged with the care of the regular believers, as they were tradi-tionally cut off completely from the world and received few visitors. Long distances separated monasteries from cities, and traveling was difficult. Monastic teachings also advocated withdrawal from the world and all that is in it. There are many stories from the history of monasticism and also from the lives of the saints that reveal how complete was this separation between the monasteries and the people. Many monks fled from people, and it was a lucky visitor who actually managed to arrive at a monastery for a visit.

In the modern era, alongside ecclesiastical and monastic renaissance, however, the economic, psychological, and social pressures on people have increased significantly. It has thus become inevitable that monasteries must open their doors to all, because individuals have found that the monasteries with their saints offer a unique opportunity for them to partake of spiritual blessings. When Coptic Christians visit monasteries and the shrines of saints with an avowedly spiritual aim, they are able to wash themselves from the inside, and find solutions to their problems, relief from their worries, and cures for their sicknesses. The monasteries and monks have brought salvation to many, and they have lit the paths of many more by becoming an example for them on their spiritual journeys, and even on their way through the world.

The Coptic Church is very proud that its monks have stood behind the church and strengthened, supported, nourished, and protected it, and have participated in the service of its wide-ranging activities. The successful service that contemporary monks have established reflects the entry of more educated people into the monasteries and their development of a philosophy combining the past

12.1
Maximus and Domitius (N32; ADP/SA 1999)

195

with the present, supported by the Holy Spirit and the prayers of the saints.

A crucial aspect of life in the monasteries of Egypt is the liturgical life. The monks live this life believing in what they are practicing with love and strength and piety, knowing that the goal of their faith is their own salvation. Collective and individual prayers, and the service of Mass with all its rituals, constitute the basis upon which the monk builds his monastic life. Hence the monasteries are keenly interested in collective prayers, such as the midnight hymns sung in the Coptic language and accompanied by traditional Coptic melodic compositions. The monks pray in two choral groups and express a deep and profound spiritual harmony. The Mass, too, is among those ritual liturgical services that still represent the basic part, indeed the greatest part, of the monastic life in all of the monasteries. The monks live it, devoting much attention to its rituals, melodies, and language. This is all in addition to the artistic and educational aspects of the monks' lives, in which they produce and express those spiritual feelings inside themselves and translate them in the form of numerous artistic products.

Icons and Icon Making in the Life of the Monk

The monk is an icon, pulsating with life, and wherever a monk is found, icons, too, are found in all their different forms (panel painting, mosaic, wall painting, manuscript illumination, and so on; fig. 12.2). If it is true that one cannot find a Coptic Church without icons, it is also true that one cannot find a Coptic monk without icons. Indeed, the monk is at one with his icons, and this is attributable to the clear relation between the monk and Heaven. In both their limited exterior form and their unlimited interior perspective icons resemble windows: indeed icons are the windows through which the monk gazes at Heaven.

The cell is the place in which the monk lives, by himself, all of his life. Inside this cell, which normally has few windows, the monk strives to see the heavenly world through the windows of icons. Inside the cell, the monk sees nothing of the world, for he has entered this enclosed space and shut the door. Rather, he gazes beyond the physical realm to see the entire heavenly world. Hence in that special place in his cell where the monk offers his private prayers, we find various icons hung in random ways. Through these icons, and during his prayers, the monk strives to see Heaven. It is the icons which open his mind, his sight, and his eyes so that he may gaze with devotion on an icon of Christ as a young child carried by his mother, of His face only or Him among his students, His trans-

figuration, His entry into Jerusalem upon an ass, His pain wearing the crown of thorns, of Christ crucified or rising from the dead or ascending into the heavens, sitting as a judge on the Day of Judgment, or any of the other numerous depictions of Christ.

The monk also offers his prayers to the Mother of God, the Holy Virgin Mary, for she is the mother of the Savior and one may always seek her intercession. She occupies a central position in the lives of Coptic monks, and no cell is without an icon of the Holy Virgin Mary. The monk has a special love for her in his heart, for she is the intercessor for all of humankind, and the monk presents many prayers to her. The monk also dedicates his prayers before icons of the angels, martyrs, and saints. The monk's cell is filled with many icons, though we should remember that each monk has his own intimate and beloved angels and martyrs and saints. We find that he is particularly devoted to their icons, and he keeps them in front of him at all times, raising prayers and pleas for intercession to them always.

Nor does the monk interact with the icon only through prayers. There are several ways of expressing devotion, such as lighting a candle in front of the icon. We find that many monks light candles in front of icons in their cells, particularly icons of the Holy Virgin, the

196

12.3

Monks of the Monastery of
St. Paul at the terrace near the
basket lift, 1930–1931 (Whittemore
Expedition. Courtesy of Dumbarton Oaks, F35)

monastery's founding saint, the monk's namesake, or his patron saint.

There are other manifestations as well of monks' devotion and tribute to icons (fig. 12.3). We find that on those holy days special to Christ, the Holy Virgin, the martyrs, and those saints who hold a special place with the individual monk, each monk lights candles for the whole period of their feast days. This takes place not only inside the cell but also outside of it, in one of the cell's windows, in front of it, or at its entrance. Monks also carry icons in their pockets, inserted within their Bible, their prayer book of the canonical hours (*horologion*), their book for the midnight praises, and any other books they may possess.

For the monk, the meaning of the icon is not located in its material or manufacturing techniques but rather in the person whom the icon represents. For the monk and the purposes of his interaction with the icon, it does not matter whether the icon is made of certain materials, manufactured in a particular way, and drawn with the quill of an artist, or whether it is printed on paper or any other material. The size, too, is not important; the monk interacts with the small, printed icon as he does with a large icon made according to artistic specifications. Coptic monks believe intensely that the icon is not the material itself, but the thing which is seen—a depiction of a living person embodied in a visible form.

Monks believe in the miraculous power of icons. They believe that icons protect them from all kinds of danger and that the presence of an icon blesses their cells. They believe that an icon sanctifies their lives and helps them in their search for holiness. The monk fears the icon as he would a person standing before him; hence he strives not to err in the presence of the icon, neither in thought nor in deed. The monk takes refuge in the icon and seeks its aid in his spiritual life. The monk also seeks intercession with the person depicted on the icon, believing in the working of miracles, whether it be in the healing of illness, or in dispelling anguish or any other needed aid.

The monk speaks with the person of the icon, face to face and in an audible voice (praying, seeking intercession, requesting help, rebuking, thanking), believing that the presence of the person is a palpable, visible, audible truth. Thus the monk interacts with the icon not only in prayer before it but in mutual contact. He often kisses the icon, puts his hands on it, kneels before it, or embraces it.

The Coptic monk also uses the icon to adorn his cell, placing it on furniture or above his bed or next to his books. The monk can find no better gift to give than an

12.4

Procession of monks, Monastery
of St. Antony, 1928

icon. By giving it to others, he conveys his faith in it and his relationship with it, making others cherish it and want to own it. Monks throng around beautiful icons and they want to purchase them, particularly if they are made according to traditional specifications.

Because of their love for icons, monks devoted themselves to the art of icon making in the first centuries of monasticism. They painted the churches in their monasteries and their manuscripts with icons. The monasteries avidly produced a great variety of icons and preserved and passed on the art of making them. Throughout our history, many monks and bishops were skilled artists who made icons of all forms and types. In continuation with this tradition, some monks and nuns have begun to devote their attention to reviving the production of icons, combining the painting of icons with their prayers and asceticism. In the past few years, we have witnessed a great number of monks and nuns in all the monasteries taking up icon drawing, whether for their own monasteries or for sale to churches and individuals. This renewed effort has encouraged the spread of icons everywhere.

The production of icons is part of the original work

of monks, for it requires time, patience, deliberateness of spirit, and contemplation, all monastic virtues. This is why the production of icons is referred to as "monks' work." It is one of the important facets of the monastic life, for it is not merely material work but spiritual as well. The monk is able to imbue the icon with the breath of life, something a lay person cannot do because the art of icon making is one of the works of the Holy Spirit. The Holy Spirit guides the painter of the icon to fill it with the mark of the Spirit. The icon is the work not of the monk but of the Holy Spirit, as is much spiritual writing; the monk is a tool in the hand of the Holy Spirit. This the monk achieves through his spiritual life, led by the Holy Spirit.

Hence the painting of icons is one of the manual labors of monks that help to consecrate the spiritual life and lead the monk to live in holiness. The majority of icon making takes place on days of fasting, which are considered the most holy and spiritual days.

Icons in the Liturgical Life of the Monk
An icon is an icon in any place and in any form in the life of a monk. It occupies an important position not only in

his personal life and in his cell but in his ritual and liturgical life as well. The liturgical life of the monk begins as soon as he sets foot inside the monastery. When he enters the church, he performs the liturgy of veneration and respect and offers up his prayers. When he stands before the door of the temple (the sanctuary), he performs his prayers of humility, accompanied by prostrations and prayers. He then stands and prays, after which he begins greeting those in the church. He greets those in heaven and then those on earth. He begins by greeting the Lord Jesus and the Holy Virgin, the angels, the martyrs, and the saints through their icons. The monk passes by them, greeting each in turn and taking from them peace and blessings. He either kisses the icon directly, if its location permits this, or, more often, places his hand on the icon and then kisses his hand. He then begins greeting those in the church—the relics of the saints, the ranks of the clergy, and his brother monks. Nor is the monk's greeting to the icon limited to a kiss, but there are also icons in the church before which the monk can light a candle, praying for himself and others. The lighting of the candle before an icon is an act of faith in the power and efficacy of its saintly subject and an expression of the belief that the candle is the oblation the monk can offer to the person of the icon every day and every moment in which he sees the icon.

The monk strives to place in a prominent position the appropriate icon for each particular feast the church celebrates, or the icon of a saint or martyr on his day, if it is available. This is so that the monk can live with the person of the icon in his remembrance, recalling his faith, his struggle, and his prayers, making of him a living example to be followed in the monk's own life. The monk breathes in his pungent fragrance. It is as if the icons are roses, and the monk smells each day a different flower with its own distinguishing fragrance. Icons particular to special occasions are placed next to the door of the temple in front of all, and are among the first icons to be greeted by the monk. The monastic priest performs a special ceremony with the icons during the liturgical prayers, called the "incense procession." This is a procession undertaken by the monks during the liturgical prayers, whether it is offering up incense during the morning or evening prayers or during the Mass. In it the priest-monk passes by with an incense burner, giving and presenting incense before the icons in a prescribed ritual form. He presents them with incense, offering his prayers to the person of the icon, seeking succor in all his needs and the needs of those who asked him to pray for them. This is an example of another interaction between the monks and icons found in the church as a whole. Just as the scent of the lives of those in icons was fragrant, so also does the scent of incense presented to them represent their perfumed lives.

In the monasteries, the monks pay close attention to the festivals of the saints, because these remind them of their own struggles. The monks perform a ritual parade of the icon on these special occasions (fig. 12.4). During the celebration of a festival of a martyr, saint, prophet, or angel, the monks carry the appropriate icon and circle the inside of the church with it, having decorated it with flowers and candles, chanting joyous songs. Each also carries a candle, illuminating himself as the person of the icon illuminates others with his life. If the occasion is a celebration for the founder of the monastery, the monks, radiant and joyous, carry his icon and circumambulate both inside the church and outside on the paths of the monastery, letting everyone touch the icon and take its blessing with strong yearning and faith. At the end of this procession, whether it is during the evening prayers or the special mass held for the person of the icon, one of the monks carries the icon and stands with it at the door of the temple. Then, one by one, the bishops and priests begin offering incense to the icon while the monks chant the appropriate melodies. After the presentation of incense, the icon is placed in its spot next to the door of the temple, and a candle is lit in front of it for the duration of the celebration.

When one of the saints or martyrs or the Holy Virgin is honored, the monks stand before the icon, glorifying it with the appropriate chants while some of them read about the honoree's life. They conclude the exaltation by receiving a blessing from the icon.

During the Mass an icon of the Lord Jesus sitting on the throne is placed in the eastern part of the temple, because it is by lifting our eyes to him in prayer that our hearts are also raised to Heaven. The Lord Jesus is always placed in the eastern part of the temple, from which he will come, and also on the altar, where he is imminent.

On the altar is the "pedestal of the chalice," a box in which the chalice is placed during the Mass. The box is adorned on all four sides with icons. On the western side, in front of the priest, appears an icon of the Last Supper, and on the eastern side an icon of the Resurrection. On the north side there is an icon of the Holy Virgin, and on the south, the church's intercessor.

When the monks want to pay tribute to one of the saints and perform an exaltation, they put the icon before them and present it with exaltations and the appropriate chants. In this case, the icon represents the presence of the person in the midst of the monks.

12.5 ABOVE
Icon of the baptism of Christ
(ADP/SA 8 s64 96)

12.6 BELOW
Censer (ADP/SA BW 74:19)

Occasions and Celebrations

THE FEAST OF THE EPIPHANY

During the prayers for celebration of the Feast of the Epiphany, we perform what is called the Mass of the Baptismal Font, or the Water Mass. In this mass, the monks wear their sacerdotal vestments and go to the baptismal font. They stand before an icon of the Epiphany in which John the Baptist is shown baptizing the Lord Jesus in the River Jordan (fig. 12.5). Then the monks begin their prayers to consecrate the water of the font.

PALM SUNDAY

We practice the rite of Palm Sunday by raising incense early in the morning (fig. 12.6). This magnificent ritual involves the participation of other icons, which join with us in celebrating Christ's entrance into Jerusalem, just as when Christ entered Jerusalem and everyone celebrated with him, even children. It is an open invitation to all the inhabitants of heaven and the saints and martyrs to participate (fig. 12.7). The rite begins with a series of twelve stops or stations. The monks carry the festal icon of Christ entering Jerusalem to the praises of the people. They begin before the sanctuary and proceed around the remaining eleven prescribed icons. At each stop the monks chant the doxology of Palm Sunday, read from the Holy Bible and offer up incense. They carry the icon of the triumphal entry, and the cross and palm branches. Finally they return to the altar where the rite ends.

PASSION WEEK

During the week preceding Easter the monks place an icon of Christ in pain, or an icon of Christ crucified, in the middle of the church, and they light candles and oil lamps before it. When the monks enter the church, they kneel before this icon and kiss it. This icon holds a special place, for through it the monks are able to contemplate the torments of Christ during His Week of Suffering. Accompanied by mournful chants, the icon helps to create an atmosphere of living with Christ in his pain. Traditionally worshipers do not kiss either each other in greeting or the icons after Tuesday evening in memory of Judas's kiss of betrayal. Monks also follow this practice and refrain from kissing the icon.

GOOD FRIDAY

On Good Friday, the icon of the Crucifixion is adorned with all types of decoration. The monks are extremely devoted to this ritual, staying up late Thursday night preparing this and all the other icons special to this occasion.

They prepare the place in which the Crucifixion icon will
be put, paying close attention to all the details. They offer
any flowers, perfumes, and oils that they possess. On this
day the monastic priest presents the icon with incense, and
through it the monks live with the crucified Messiah above
Golgotha Hill. At the end of the day Friday, the monks
carry the icon in all its adornment and circumambulate
the church three times, alternating between sorrow and
joy. They are mournful for the crucifixion of Christ and his
sufferings, but they are overcome with the joy of redemp-
tion. (In some Egyptian villages, we find special conditions
governing who may carry this icon during its tour in the
church, and many compete for the privilege.)

THE ICON OF THE ENTOMBMENT

The icon of the Entombment is used in the Coptic
rite to represent the burial and the resurrection of Christ.
It is a small icon, with a painting of the entombment of
Christ on one side and, on the other side, one of Christ

rising from the grave. When the liturgy of the entombment is performed, the priest takes the icon and adorns it
with fragrances and flowers and wraps it as Christ was
wrapped in his shroud. It is then placed on the altar and
remains there Friday and Saturday, not being removed
until dawn Sunday morning.

THE ENACTMENT OF THE RESURRECTION

In the ritual of the enactment of the resurrection, the
icon of the Entombment is unwrapped from the shroud to
symbolize Christ's rising from the dead. Afterward, the
monks celebrate the resurrection by circling the church
with the icon, chanting joyful songs of the resurrection.
During this tour, everyone kisses the icon, breathing in the
fragrance of resurrection through the smell of perfumes
and flowers. Once the parade is completed, the priest offers incense to the icon before the door of the temple, and
it is placed there, to remain for the duration of the celebration of Eastertide.

Key

a Church of St. Antony
b remains of earlier church
c keep
d refectory (rabatiyya)
e cells
f Church of the Holy Apostles
g Church of St. Mark
h winch

i gardens
j library
k old guest house
l new guest house
m museum
n new church of St. Antony
o ossuary
p workshops
q water tower
r new cells
s animal pen
t spring of St. Antony
u new guest dormitories

SUPREME COUNCIL
OF ANTIQUITIES
ISLAMIC & COPTIC SECTOR

AMERICAN RESEARCH
CENTER IN EGYPT

ANTIQUITIES
DEVELOPMENT PROJECT
2 Midan Kasr el Doubara, Garden City, Cairo, Egypt
3D SURVEY
RED SEA MONASTERIES
Under USAID Grant No. 263-G-00-96-00016-00

Drawn by: Peter Sheehan
Date: June 1999

Plan survey by:
Michael Mallinson
Peter Sheehan
Sami Habachi
Saundi Gayed Habib

Mallinson Architects
Date: April–June 1998

MONASTERY OF
ST. ANTONY
Red Sea Coast, Egypt

EXISTING CONDITIONS
RECORD
April 1998

SHEET No. SHEET TITLE   SCALE
   5   Main Monastery
           Plan   1:500

0   50m

CHAPTER 13 IN THE FOOTSTEPS OF THE SAINTS

THE MONASTERY OF ST. ANTONY, PILGRIMAGE, AND MODERN COPTIC IDENTITY

At two o'clock in the morning, I climbed onto a bus along with forty or more young men and women and a few small families to begin our two-day *riḥla* (pl. riḥlāt), or short pilgrimage trip, to the Monasteries of St. Antony (fig. 13.1) and St. Paul. We would be staying in the special guest dormitories each monastery had constructed outside its walls for visitors. Most riḥla pilgrimages do not include an overnight stay, but those to the Red Sea monasteries often do, because the journey takes at least four hours, and there are usually enough beds to accommodate all the visitors. Participants also want to feel that they have enough time to perform all of the religious activities, informal and formal, that are available to them at the Monastery of St. Antony, especially the optional climb to the hermit's cave, which can take several hours.

People piled onto the bus, squeezing by each other, juggling thermoses of tea and bags full of crackers, tangerines, falafels, bean sandwiches, and other vegetarian food. Although we were not in one of the liturgically prescribed periods of fasting, many people had decided as a spiritual gesture to abstain from eating animal products during the trip.[1] As people chose their seats and settled into them, a young man in his twenties named Maher made his way to the front of the bus and took up a microphone, introducing himself as the trip leader. He began by leading us in the Lord's Prayer, starting out in a loud voice, "Abāna alethi fi as-samawāt . . . " The entire bus quieted down instantly, people turning their faces and hands upward in a posture of prayer. Each finished the prayer silently, then came a collective "Amīn" out loud, accompanied by genuflection. Maher welcomed us again and began to explain the schedule of our activities. We would arrive at the Monastery of

St. Antony by 6 A.M., in time to attend the mass conducted by the monks. The rest of the day would be free time, during which we might climb the mountain that runs up the back of the complex to St. Antony's cave, or simply walk around the places inside the monastery that are open to the public. Every monastery has areas where the pilgrims may move about freely, but there are also zones reserved only for the monks' use, and pilgrims are expected to respect these boundaries.

People would also be able to use their free time during the day to make arrangements to meet with individual monks. Some pilgrims had come to see particular monks, either because they were kin or because they sought their advice and counsel on specific personal matters. The majority simply wanted to interact with any monks they might see as they walked the grounds, asking for their blessing and hoping to receive their grace *(baraka)*. Maher finished outlining our schedule by reminding us that lights-out was at 10 P.M., when the monastery shut down its generators. Those who so wished could attend the liturgy the next morning from its very start, the matins prayers *(tasbiḥa)* that would begin at 3 A.M. We would leave after the mass ended at 9 A.M. for our next stop, the Monastery of St. Paul, only a short distance away.

For the duration of the bus ride we sang contemporary spirituals *(taranīm)*, played biblical knowledge games for small prizes, and bought raffle tickets from two girls moving up and down the aisle for the most valuable prize, a Virgin Mary clock embellished with shells. As we neared the monastery, Maher stood up again, this time with a stack of photocopies. While passing them out, he explained that this was the *tamgīd*, or text of praise to St. Antony,

13.1
Monastery site plan, existing conditions, 1999

that we would be singing as a group in the church.[2] Maher read the text out loud once through, and then two young men accompanied us with the traditional cymbals *(daff)* and triangle *(muthalath)* as we practiced:

In the Church of the first Born	In the congregation of the Saints
He stands with great respect	Peniot[3] Ava Antonious
He stands with great esteem	Among those who wear the eskeem[4]
At the rank of the cherubim	Peniot Ava Antonious
With spirit-filled prayers	With godly life story
You consecrated the wilderness	Peniot Ava Antonious
Striving in prayers	Tens and tens of years
With tears and prostrations	Peniot Ava Antonious
Monastic in your fasts	For days and days on end
Your soul seeks no rest	Peniot Ava Antonious . . .
You are the power and the symbol	For those who seek an example
The dweller of high mountains	Peniot Ava Antonious
Example of purity,	The power of spirituality
And the peace of the wilderness	Peniot Ava Antonious
Like the odor of sweet incense	Like the beautiful sound of psalms
Your life story is a light	Peniot Ava Antonious
You are great in tribulations	You are wise in counsel
Intercede on our behalf	Peniot Ava Antonious
Can we follow your example?	Can we trace your every step?
Pray on our behalf	Peniot Ava Antonious . . .[5]

We were still chanting as the sun began to rise and the monastery appeared in the distance. At least ten other tour buses were already parked outside the walls, and groups of people were streaming through the main gate on their way to Mass. We pulled up, disembarked, and joined them on this first step of our pilgrimage (fig. 13.2).

A Modern Form of Pilgrimage

This type of pilgrimage, what I will henceforth refer to as riḥla pilgrimage, is a modern phenomenon. Although it can be traced only to the mid-1970s, it has become immensely popular, especially among young, urban, working-class men and women. Riḥla pilgrimage differs from the other most popular form of Coptic pilgrimage, which is much older and revolves around local saint festivals called mūlids or ʿaiyād.[6] The ʿaiyād take place annually at a variety of ancient holy sites, including historic churches and monasteries that hold the remains of well-known saints, as well as grottos where it is believed the Holy Family stayed during their sojourn in Egypt.[7] These cele-

brations draw thousands of participants, some of whom arrive as much as a month in advance with their families to camp out around the site. Most can attend only one of these festivals a year and wait to perform certain rites or prayers, for it is believed that they will be more effective during the mūlid. Among such rites are the baptism of children and the making of religious vows called nadr.[8] The festival typically reaches its climax on the evening before the saint's feast day, called al-layla al-kabira, which is marked by processions, the slaughtering of sacrificial animals, and the consumption of meat to break the fast. ʿAiyād resonate with the lifeways of rural populations and are tied to the agricultural seasons of planting and harvest, often symbolized by bringing first fruits to be distributed in the name of the saint.[9] They embody a rich mix of sacred and cultural activities that function to reaffirm both spiritual ties with God and the social bonds of the group. This type of traditional religious festival has been documented among Muslim, Christian, and Jewish communities throughout the Middle East, and most authors agree that it plays a critical role in maintaining the cultural fabric of traditional societies.[10]

Riḥla pilgrimage, by contrast, is a peculiarly modern Coptic practice. It attracts primarily the young working-class Copts of the cities, the children of immigrants from rural Egypt who flocked to urban centers in the 1950s and 1960s, when decreasing land yields and increasing population pressures forced tens of thousands of Copts and Muslims to abandon agriculture and become wage laborers. Riḥla pilgrimage differs from ʿaiyād in that it occurs throughout the year (usually on Fridays and Sundays), and attendance does not require great planning. Many riḥlāt are organized only days before they occur, either by church youth groups or individuals who rent an independent tour bus and invite friends. The target destinations of riḥla are working Coptic monasteries, most of which had not previously been associated with ʿaiyād and thus were unused to welcoming large numbers of visitors. The activities associated with riḥla are different as well: pilgrims come not only to be in contact with a holy place, as they do during the ʿaiyād, but also to interact with living monks and to learn about Coptic history by taking tours of the monasteries. And whereas ʿaiyād reaffirm ties between extended families, riḥla pilgrimage forges new ties between Copts who are increasingly mobile and separated from one another, as the exodus from villages continues. In short, riḥla pilgrimage is part of a process that is creating new communal ties and promoting a connection between contemporary Copts and their history.

13.2

View of the monastery showing
the historic core, modern parking
area, and guest houses, 1996
(ADP/SA BW 47:1)

The growth of this new form of pilgrimage has transformed many monasteries, including that of St. Antony, from isolated outposts to modernized centers of mass pilgrimage. Most have had to construct new buildings and introduce electricity and modern plumbing. The presence of so many pilgrims has further affected the understanding of the monastic vocation. No longer limited to a personal struggle with temptation carried out in isolation, monasticism now entails new roles for the monk as a tour guide, teacher, and spiritual mentor. As a result, increasingly the philosophy of *khidma,* or service to the church and its community, is highlighted in modern Coptic monasticism, rather than that of *tawaḥḥud,* or the anchoretic life.

Riḥla pilgrimage has also changed the meaning and experience of monasteries for the Coptic laity. For the older generation, these were important sacred sites within the Coptic religious imagination but not places to be visited. In upper Egypt, for instance, a family whose son chose to enter a monastery would give him a symbolic funeral after his departure, expressive of his absolute separation from "the world" and his family. Now roads, mass transport, and the frequency of pilgrimage trips have made the once-real barrier of the desert into a metaphoric one.

The 'Coptic Renaissance'

When the current pope, Shenouda III, ascended to the papapacy in 1971, he inherited a troubled generation. The Egyptian defeat at the hands of Israel in 1967 and the death of President Gamal Abdel Nasser in 1970 had left the nation depressed. Accelerated population growth, rapid urbanization, and unemployment were exacerbating the challenge of revitalizing the country. The sense of fragmentation and anomie, especially among urban populations, was leading not only to a sense of dislocation but at times to incidents of social unrest.[11] And although Copts had always been patriotic citizens, the growth of radical Islamicist movements that called for a religiously based state made Christians increasingly unsure of their identity as part of the nation.[12]

In an attempt to strengthen the Coptic community, Pope Shenouda initiated a wide range of reforms and new programs that greatly expanded the role of the church. The success of these programs in drawing Copts to the church and promoting a renewed interest in Coptic history and identity is often called the Coptic Renaissance, or *al-naḥda al-gibṭiya.* The administrative, educational, and social reforms wrought by Pope Shenouda were (and continue to be) the most expansive the Coptic Church has ever known. But he built upon a spirit of change that had begun under the previous pope, Kyrollious VI (1956–1971). Kyrollious had encouraged the expansion of social outreach programs like the rural *diakonia,* and educational initiatives such as Sunday schools. There had also been a renewal of interest in the monastic life, and a new cadre of educated and socially concerned young men had joined monasteries.[13]

Pope Shenouda continued to modernize and centralize the structure of the church. He created new dioceses and bishophrics, reorganized church lands, and instituted a centralized salary system for priests. He also began new social programs that distributed financial aid to the poor and set up infirmaries next to churches to provide free health care.[14] But his most extensive initiatives were directed at the youth, the "new generation," or *al-gīl al-gadīd.* It was this segment of the Coptic population that was hit hardest by such social pressures as unemployment and who were most vulnerable to feelings of dislocation, particularly in urban centers like Cairo. For them he instituted youth groups and service programs organized into units called *ʿāʾila* (pl. *ʿāʾilāt*), or families. These "families," often named for a saint (for example, the family of St. Abraam), became involved in a range of activities that included visiting the sick and poor, putting on religious plays, organizing outings, and inviting outside speakers. As participation in the *ʿāʾilāt* grew and their structure became more regularized, they provided youth with an opportunity to travel throughout Egypt, meeting other *ʿāʾilāt* on exchange programs and spiritual retreats and through Bible competitions. The activities sponsored by the *ʿāʾilāt* provided a new place for Coptic youth to meet each other and form a sense of community.

Pope Shenouda's new programs also encouraged the use of modern technology and secular academic research to promote a sense of community. He established a printing press on the grounds of the patriarchate in downtown Cairo and encouraged the publication of a variety of simply written works on Coptic spirituality, history, and language for mass distribution. An audio library and later a video library were established to circulate tapes of lectures and sermons, as well as religious movies. Originally, movies were imported, but during the 1980s an indigenous Coptic film industry grew up and began producing its own videos, most often on the lives of Egyptian saints.

Finally, there was a renewed focus on the development of departments of academic research on what is called collectively *turāth,* or Coptic heritage. The Coptic language began to be taught to children in Sunday school. The Institute for Coptic Studies, which had been established decades earlier but had fallen into a state of disrepair, began to attract new students. Master's degrees were offered in subjects such as Coptic language, history, architecture, and art. The Department of Coptic Art, headed by the renowned artist Isaac Fanous, was particularly successful in turning out a new cadre of icon and mosaic artists trained in the tenets of traditional Coptic art. Throughout the nineteenth and early twentieth century, Coptic Church art had been dominated by an imported Italianate style. Churches began to remove this artwork and order icons from the institute to replace it.

These new initiatives not only modernized the church, they shaped a new generation of Copts. For al-gīl al-gadīd, the church became a social and educational center. Linked through service activities, retreats, and outings, and more aware of their historical identity than previous generations, al-gīl al-gadīd responded enthusiastically to the new spiritual and social opportunities offered by riḥla pilgrimage.

Opening the Monasteries to Modernity

Until the 1970s Egyptian monasteries were for the most part difficult to reach, and they attracted few lay Copts as visitors. Those who did come were mostly Western travelers, frequently in search of texts and manuscripts to take with them to the growing collections in Europe. Although colonial travelers marveled at the desert settings, the architecture, and the libraries, they were often disappointed with the monks themselves. Baron Von Tischendorf, for instance, who traveled to the Monastery of the Romans (Baramous) at the end of the nineteenth century, made this typical observation:

> Here the cells were the blackest of all. The superior here had a peculiar custom; he sat beside me in the cell, and as often as a pause was made in the conversation, he interposed the formula of welcome, Salam, Salam, and repeated the pantomime of his hands. What I inquired for, and everywhere in vain, was manuscript accounts of the history of the monastery. But not a line of such a record was known. Thus they live carelessly from day to day. To such an existence, what is the past and what is the future?[15]

Such remarks are rooted in a larger colonial discourse about Copts as "Sons of the Pharaohs," or living representatives of Egypt's past, and thus imaginary repositories of key elements of history. In colonial narratives, when Copts are perceived to fall short in this role, either by not conducting themselves "authentically"—the way ancient texts might indicate they did—or by not placing an emphasis on the preservation of material things such as texts, their actions evoke disappointment in westerners. This is the case in this reported interaction, in which the monk's actions, intended to make the visitor feel honored and welcomed, do not have the desired effect, but instead provoke anger and the judgment that the monk cannot distinguish between the trivial (human interaction) and the important (texts).

As the colonial presence in Egypt dwindled throughout the first half of the twentieth century, Coptic monasteries faded from the Western imagination as storehouses of texts and icons for the taking, and the journeys through the deserts to see them were much reduced. Until the 1970s most monasteries remained isolated and sparsely populated. The Coptic laity had no tradition of visiting monasteries, and monasticism was understood to be a solitary spiritual pursuit. But as al-gīl al-gadīd took shape outside the monasteries and the new cadre of monks grew into positions of authority within them, possibilities of opening these places to the public began to be imagined. Particularly appealing was the idea of bringing Copts directly into contact with their history. As the scholar Dina El-Khawaga has pointed out regarding the Coptic Renaissance, the very idea of a renaissance "implies by definition an effort of rupture, of a selection of foundational origins and a reformulation between the present and a specific past."[16] The opening of the monasteries and their subsequent modernization could be said to form part of this process, for in them the laity experienced a new blending of modern technology, ancient spirituality, and communal identity.

The process of making monasteries accessible to the public had of course been made easier by the general improvement of Egypt's road system. However, the service road built out from the monastery to the main road remains a powerful symbol of a new era for its residents. Guide books produced by monasteries often begin with the story of how their road was built as a type of founding tale and go on to detail the ensuing physical growth of the site which happened as a result. The guidebook to the Monastery of the Romans, for instance, describes the construction of their road as the beginnings of a "revolution":

> For any "revolution" to succeed, whether it be . . . economic, social or ideological, there must be easily accessible roads to lead to those places where it is hoped the revolution will spread. Thus the beginning of the "revolution" in the Monastery of Baramous (and what can be said pertaining to the Monastery of Baramous might be said about all the working Egyptian monasteries) in the

13.3
Printing press of the Monastery of
St. Mena, Marriout

era of Pope Shenouda III is rooted in this development; the construction of a road making exchange possible between the world and the monastery. Thus the world now drinks deeply from the spirituality of the monastery and the monastery itself benefits from the numerous scientific inventions which come to it from the world.[17]

This "exchange . . . between the world and the monastery" initiated by the building of roads turned out, however, to be a complex interaction with far-reaching consequences. First, pressure to accommodate the waves of pilgrims who began to arrive and the new availability of "scientific inventions . . . from the world" began a process of renovation and modernization in all the monasteries. Some made only modest architectural additions, whereas in others, the older structures all but disappeared behind the new construction. At the very least, electricity and plumbing were introduced, new kitchen facilities installed, rest houses erected for pilgrims' overnight stays, and, in some instances, new churches built next to the ancient ones, which could no longer hold the numbers of pilgrims who came to attend the masses. A portion of this physical growth has also been due to the construction of accommodations for the growing numbers of new monks. Despite the strict standards and long evaluation periods, most monasteries have waiting lists for admission. The population of St. Antony's has grown, for example, from twenty-four in 1960 to sixty-nine in 1986. By the time of my fieldwork in 1996, the monastery was reported to have approximately ninety monks. Similar increases have occurred in almost every monastery in Egypt.[18]

Pilgrims have become a new source of income that can be used to finance further projects within the monasteries. For centuries monks depended exclusively on charity for support. Donations of money and also of goods were collected by the *maqarr,* the monastery's outpost in a nearby town, to sustain the monks. They also lived on the proceeds from lands that had been bequeathed to them by

individuals *(awqāf).* Charity, and especially the awqāf, are still important forms of support, but now in addition monasteries produce a wide variety of goods for sale to pilgrims and for export. Several monasteries have also acquired computers and printing presses and have become active in producing pamphlets and guidebooks detailing their institutional histories (fig. 13.3).

Other kinds of income-generating projects have been made possible through the importation of new technologies for desert agriculture and animal husbandry. These activities, which used to be limited to supporting the alimentary needs of the monks, have been expanded into small industries. The monasteries of the Wadi al-Natrun in particular have been leaders in this field, importing new varieties of plants in order to increase the production of fruits and vegetables. The Monastery of St. Bishoi has even started a fishery project and has constructed a high technology lake in the middle of the desert.

The financial and architectural changes to the monasteries have been accompanied by a deeper philosophical change in the understanding of the role of the individual monk. On the one hand, he participates in new kinds of collective work within the monastery, like large-scale farming, technical projects, or service to pilgrims. On the other hand, he may be called beyond the monastery to serve the larger Coptic community, where he might act as a priest to a congregation that does not have one, or in a more elevated stage, as bishop to a diocese. The need for new priests and bishops has grown dramatically in the recent past, as a result of the multiplication of diocese under Pope Shenouda's organizational reforms and of the enormous growth of the Coptic community outside of Egypt.

Certainly, the boundaries between the world and the monastery have become more porous. It is important to note here, however, that although openness to contact with the laity and the concept of khidma have reshaped modern monasticism, the ideal model of monastic life is still a subject of discussion in many monasteries. There continue to be monks who favor the anchoretic life, living outside the monasteries in caves or man-made *qalāyāt* (cells), and important religious figures who support this philosophy of isolation or *tawaḥḥud.*[19] I also occasionally encountered pilgrims during riḥlāt who questioned whether monks had enough time for prayer, given the extent of their involvement in all the new projects in the monastery. But these reactions were rare, and most often the modernization of the monasteries was seen as an indication of the spiritual health of the Coptic community as a whole.

Past and Present

To the Western gaze, which values "authenticity" and seeks to differentiate between the "ancient" and the "modern," the developments that have taken place in contemporary Coptic monasteries may seem like additions, or overlays, both physically discontinuous with the "real" monastery and contradictory to the philosophy of isolation and meditation upon which monasticism was initially built. But the many monks and pilgrims I spoke with during the course of my research did not make these sharp distinctions between "tradition" and "modernity," nor did they describe feelings of contradiction connected to the site of the monastery. One monk from the Wadi al-Natrun responded to my general questions about the "changes" in his monastery in this way:

> I prefer to call them *taṭwwarāt* [developments] and not *taghayyarāt* [changes], for just as the world has advanced, so has the monastery. In order to understand life in the monastery today, you must understand what life was like in the fourth-century world. If you look at the technology and the pace of life in the fourth-century world, the move to the monastery was not that big. In fact, in the fourth century, the technology and architecture in use in the monasteries was "state of the art." The leap one has to make today, the things he leaves behind, is much greater.

The younger monks who joined the monasteries recently even felt that their ability to pursue their vocation was made possible only because modern technology made life in the monastery more efficient. One noted, "Instead of spending four hours washing my clothes, for example, I can spend the time praying. And if you think about the number of visitors who come here, how would we deal with them all if we couldn't cook with electricity and so on? About one hundred tour buses show up every Friday and Sunday, carrying fifty visitors apiece. Think about it, that makes about five thousand visitors a week!"

These indigenous reactions to the introduction of technology into the monasteries point to a more fundamental difference in the way that history itself is imagined in relation to these sacred sites. Although they may run technologically sophisticated machinery, monks are also understood to be "closer" to the past. They are viewed as guardians of important sites that hold the memories of meaningful events and the bodies of saints and martyrs. They are thought to be responsible for sustaining these places particularly through conducting daily masses. Externally, they continue to be linked with things ancient,

13.4

Burial place of St. Antony, with a modern image of the saint and written prayers left by pilgrims, before conservation

(K3, K4 ADP/SA 9 s2 96)

through their traditional vestments and by giving up their own names to adopt the names of saints or martyrs whose qualities they hope to bring alive in themselves.[20] In short, even as he participates in modern activities, the monk's body and the rhythm of his life are understood to be mimetic of saintly bodies and lives from the past.

What we need to pay attention to here is not the existence of the epistemological categories of past and present but rather the relation between them in the Coptic religious imagination. This brings us back to the interaction between Baron von Tischendorf and the abbot of Al-Baramous. The Baron represents a peculiarly Western set of beliefs about what history is, how it can be known, and what one does with that knowledge. Here history settles in objects and artifacts that can be scrutinized and whose details can be woven into a master narrative. This Western scientific method revolves around the establishment of criteria for distinguishing, as I have said, the "authentic" from the "inauthentic" based largely on chronology: often it is the older that is considered more authentic. Yet however it is evaluated, the past remains distinctly in the past, carried objectively into the present by artifacts, from which it can be examined and cataloged by scholars who can "read" their meanings. Within the Coptic religious imagination, by contrast, it is precisely the fact that the past can break through into the present, in objects, people, and places, that makes these things "true." For instance, anyone who has entered a Coptic Church in Egypt has seen new posters of the Virgin Mary, Christ, and saints displayed alongside historic icons (fig. 13.4). This visitor will have seen the Copts inside the church walking by, touching and praying in front of the new ones with the same frequency as (if not sometimes more than) the old ones. I have been with people who have remarked that this was an indication that Copts were not generally educated about art and history and thus couldn't tell the difference between a poster and a "real" icon. But when I asked people how they felt when they prayed in front of posters or icons, they always said that it made no difference because they felt that the holy figure was there, and that his or her eyes were looking at the petitioner, whose prayers were thus being heard. And so it is with modern technology in the monasteries. It is not understood to challenge the authenticity of monasticism as much as it is seen to enable the powerful spirituality of the saints to be made available to the Coptic community in the present.

Ritual Practices at the Monastery of St. Antony

The Monastery of St. Antony provides an excellent example of the ways in which riḥla pilgrimage has transformed a once-isolated site into an important social and spiritual center for the modern Coptic laity. Western travelers who were drawn by its ancient buildings and tales about its well-stocked manuscript library had long visited this monastery. Yet perhaps because of its location, removed from the population centers of the Nile Valley, it never developed a well-attended ʾaid festival, and Copts themselves had little contact with it. Today, the Monastery of St. Antony is one of the most popular riḥla destinations. In the past the monastery had to be approached from the Nile side, where tracks led from the towns of Boush and Kuraimāt through the desert to the site. The Suez-Ras Gharib road was constructed in 1946 by the Shell Corporation and has been constantly improved, giving access from the Red Sea coast and cutting the journey from several days to several hours. There have been improvements in the kitchen facilities, and the construction of a large bookstore and male and female dormitories outside the old walls. Another addition common to most monasteries is a new retaining wall that juts far out from the monastery and encloses all the lands that it owns. In other monasteries this land has been used for large-scale farming projects, but at St. Antony's it is almost empty. When I asked the

monks what, then, the external retaining walls were for, they answered that they had been built to ensure that peace, tranquility, and the desert would always surround the monastery (fig. 13.2).

Unlike some other Christian pilgrimage traditions that prescribe a correct way of moving through a holy site and a sequence of activities to be completed, the pilgrimage to the Monastery of St. Antony is not made up of a set series of ritual actions that must be performed in order for it to be considered successful. There is little regulation of pilgrims once they arrive in the monastery, and large groups quickly break down into smaller ones, made up of friends and family, who move through the monastery at their own pace. People spend different amounts of time engaged in activities, moving off alone and then coming back together into groups, all of which gives pilgrimage a fluid and sometimes disorganized appearance.

PRAYER

Prayer is a complex ritual action that can take many forms, from the deeply personal to the highly formalized. Pilgrims carry out both during their stay at the monastery. Most trips include at least one mass conducted by the monks, which almost everyone attends. The liturgy itself is considered to be a powerful collective ritual in which prayer and praise are sent to heaven in the same way that incense floats upward toward God.[21] Masses take place more than once a day, but there are two constraints on the number that may occur. First, a priest must conduct a mass, and only a small number of monks are ordained as priests. Second, masses cannot be held consecutively on the same altar because ritually the altar must "rest" or "fast" (yiṣūm) for at least six hours after the completion of the service. Thus the number of consecrated altars in the monastery and the number of available priests limit the schedule of masses during the day. But the morning liturgy of praise, which begins at 3 A.M. and usually ends around 6:30 in the morning, is a constant feature at the Monastery of St. Antony. The consistency of this particular mass is quite important to pilgrims, whether or not they attend the service, because it affects the way they imagine the holiness of the site. Many mentioned to me that they thought one of the most important duties of the monks was to continue to say this daily mass, and that part of the miracle of the place is that the mass has been said in the same place for hundreds of years.

Whether or not pilgrims attend the formal mass, they always enter the church to say a personal prayer in front of the altar (haykal). Ritually, this requires removing one's shoes and either standing with face and hands turned upward or, alternatively, bowing to touch the forehead to the ground at the steps leading to the altar screen. Usually one begins with the recitation of the Lord's Prayer and ends with a personal supplication. This prayer can be performed in any of the churches, but pilgrims seem to express some preference for the Church of St. Antony as the "most ancient church." This echoes a more general feeling that the "layering" of prayer upon prayer and mass upon mass through the centuries not only reconfirms the holiness of the monastery's original inhabitant, St. Antony, but also magnifies each individual prayer.

Prayer around the bodies of the saints interred in the monastery is also an essential part of the pilgrimage. Here, too, there are two types of prayer: individual supplication and a more ritualized group prayer. Next to the haykal, the bodies of saints provide the most powerful locus of baraka in the monastery. Whereas entrance to the haykal itself is not permitted, the remains of saints are openly displayed in wood and glass cases, called *maqsurāt*. At any given moment one can find many people crowding around the maqsurāt, touching them, leaning over them, kissing them and making personal supplications. A few pilgrims spend almost the entire time in front of these reliquaries, setting up blankets and food on the floor in the corners of the room, simply to be near them and to absorb, in a sense, the blessing emanating from the holy remains. From time to time a group gathers to chant a tamgīd to St. Antony or the Virgin Mary. The chanting of the tamgīd is an important moment during the course of the pilgrimage: attributes of the saint and events of his or her life are recalled, reminding people of the figure's historicity as well as the continued relevance of the saint's spirituality for the contemporary believer.

CONSUMPTION

Part of every pilgrimage involves the acquisition of blessed items that can be taken home and retained for personal use or given away to friends and family. These mementos may be purchased at the bookstore or received as a gift from the monks. One of the most popular items for women are the St. Antony headscarves, to be worn during the Mass and communion. I remember being struck by these headscarves the first few times I attended masses in Cairo. Looking out over the women from the back they provided me with a sort of visual map of the monasteries they had visited, or an honor roll of saints they felt especially close to. Such a "patron saint" or personal intercessor, is called one's shafiʿ in Arabic. Not all Copts have

a shafiʿ, but many adopt one either because they are attracted by the power of the saint's life story or because they feel a certain saint has performed miracles for them. Several people I spoke with on rihla to the Monastery of St. Antony had come because Antony was their shafiʿ and they wanted to strengthen their relationship with him by visiting his "home."[22] These people in particular seek to acquire things bearing the image of the saint to wear, carry, and place around their homes as a sign of their continuing devotion.

Small vials of holy oil and cards with bits of *ḥanūt* (spices used to perfume the remains of the saints) are also popular items to acquire on pilgrimage. They cannot be bought but are given out by monks. Holy oil, or simply *zayt*, has been specially blessed in the monastery and is considered to be particularly efficacious for those suffering from certain sorts of illnesses.[23] Ḥanūt cards are made by taping small pinches of the fragrant embalming spices onto the reverse of cards that picture the saint. There is usually plenty of ḥanūt available to make these cards for visitors, because the remains of the saints are ceremonially rewrapped every year with new spices on the saint's festival day. Monks give zayt and ḥanūt to pilgrims at the close of a conversation, along with a final blessing.

CONTACT

An important part of the rihla to the Monastery of St. Antony is the feeling of being quite literally in touch with the holiness of the place. This holiness or blessing is loosely translated by the Arabic term *baraka*. Baraka is an indigenous concept found throughout Middle Eastern cultures. It bears a family resemblance to the Western category of blessing, but also overflows that category, making a simple translation difficult.[24] For Copts, one of the characteristics of baraka is that it is gained by saints and martyrs through their virtuous acts, both during their lives and also after death, when it continues to reside in their remains. Baraka is considered to be so powerful that it exudes from these holy remains and imbues everything around them with holiness as well. As the bodies of pilgrims come in contact with this baraka-filled place, they hope to incorporate a small part of this holiness into themselves by sitting next to it, by leaning on it, by touching and breathing it. This is not to imply that the experience of pilgrimage does not encourage use of the mind; it certainly does. As we have seen, the vast majority of pilgrims emphasized that prayer is the most important ritual action in which they participate. However, the desire to obtain baraka reminds us that the pilgrimage experience

13.5
Group of pilgrims setting off for
the Cave of St. Antony

for Copts encompasses not only the mind and heart but all the senses. One person said to me, "It's like when someone has been to Mass and they come home and you smell the incense on them. The holiness of the saints is like that, it can go into you like that."

Pilgrims also seek contact with the monks. Like a priest, a monk is understood by the laity to be two things at once: an individual and an instrument of God. Sometimes, for instance, my informants complained about some aspect of their local priest, but this never in any way diminished their respect for him during Mass. "A priest is a man," said one person, "but when he is at the haykal, God works through him during the communion." Most pilgrims hope to greet any monk and obtain his blessing, not for his individuality but because of his generic status as an exemplary servant of God. In some cases pilgrims do seek to meet with particular monks because they have developed a counseling relationship with them over time. In my experience, it was particularly young unmarried men and women who sought counsel on matters in their lives, often because they felt monks would be more impartial than their own family members, or even their local priests. But on the whole, visitors will approach any monk they see in order to greet him, kiss his hand, and obtain baraka.

MIMESIS

The kinds of activities we have observed so far occur in almost every Coptic monastery during riḥla trips. But the specificity of the pilgrimage to the Monastery of St. Antony is to be found in the informal ritual of climbing the steep path up Mount Clysma to visit the cave of the hermit himself (fig. 13.5). There are no activities on other pilgrimages to Coptic monasteries that require the level of exertion that this practice does.[25] It involves three stages: climbing the path, entering the cave to receive the baraka of the place, and leaving a small wooden cross planted near the cave. The effort of the climb is considered ritually incidental to the goal of reaching the cave, for Copts have no tradition of self-mortification as part of pilgrimage.[26] But on the occasions I climbed with other pilgrims, I found that it was a critical period of time during which people thought about the saint's great faith as well as their own lives, as they followed his trail up the mountain. One group I accompanied had grown weary about midway up the mountain, when they began to marvel at the great faith St. Antony must have had to come all the way down from his cave to get water, and then climb all the way back up. As we continued to walk, people began to tell the stories they knew about St. Antony and his life and then stories about how the saint had touched their own lives. Physical exhaustion merged with collective storytelling, and through it, the saint's history and faith came alive.

Once at the top, pilgrims enter St. Antony's cave to receive the baraka of the place (fig. 1.3). They must make their way down a narrow natural corridor in the rock about ten meters long in order to reach the inner chamber and the altar set up inside it. Several people told me that they felt particularly close to St. Antony in this place, especially because his actual body, believed to be buried in the monastery (fig. 13.4), is not accessible to pilgrims in the same way that the remains in the maqsurāt are.

After visiting the cave, many people scavenge for bits of wood and craft them into a cross, which they plant on the hillside near the cave entrance. Looking out over the rock-strewn cliff face one can see dozens of such crosses thrust between the boulders and into cracks, many of them falling apart only to be recovered by future pilgrims and lashed into new crosses (fig. 13.6). Placing these crosses recalls other practices, such as writing messages to the saints in wax on the protective glass of their icons or stuffing small handwritten messages into the maqsurāt so that they fall near the holy remains. They indicate a desire on the part of the pilgrim not only to remember the life of the saint but also to be remembered. Further, they demonstrate the constant tension between the effacement of self through the promotion of a sense of *communitas* on the one hand, and the desire to mark one's individuality and personal petitions on the other.

The modern phenomenon of riḥla has brought many ancient monasteries out of the Coptic religious imagination and transformed them into important new sites of spiritual and communal renewal. As the laity has come into closer contact with the living history of the monasteries, the monastic vocation itself has been reimagined to include an unprecedented component of social contact and service to the wider Coptic community. Although riḥla could be called a new or "invented" tradition, its age

is of little consequence to its practitioners. It has become a powerful means for an urban generation to "drink deeply from the spirituality" of its collective religious past and use it as a resource to face the pressures of contemporary Egyptian life.

On our way back to Cairo, I asked one of my fellow pilgrims if she felt sad now that our trip was coming to an end. She said that while she did wish she could spend more time at the monastery, she felt peaceful going home. "I do not know what I would do if I could not go on riḥlāt from time to time," she said. "The pressures we face in society are great, but the peace and baraka I gain from spending time with the saints and learning about how they dealt with difficulties, it helps me in my own life so much." Riḥla pilgrimage acts as a bridge, bringing the ancient Coptic past and contemporary parishioners together so that each might sustain the other.

13.6

Crosses at top of the mountain,

near the Cave of St. Antony

CHAPTER 14 THE COPTIC INSCRIPTIONS IN THE CHURCH
OF ST. ANTONY

Although most of the Coptic inscriptions published here have been published before, this study presents significant new material. Alexandre Piankoff published some of the inscriptions between 1954 and 1958.[1] Then in 1978 René-Georges Coquin and Pierre-Henry Laferrière published all of the Coptic and Arabic inscriptions that they could see, based on whatever limited cleaning of the paintings could be done for that purpose.[2] Paul van Moorsel was able to provide additional epigraphic information in his detailed study of the paintings in the church. His work was completed in 1986 but published only in 1998.[3] The recent restoration work done in the church has made it possible to see much more of the inscriptions previously published, as well as newly revealed inscriptions hitherto unpublished.

The Coptic inscriptions are of several kinds: inscriptions accompanying and identifying the figures portrayed in the paintings; inscriptions describing or commenting on aspects of narratives portrayed in the paintings or aspects of the figures' stories; inscriptions with biblical and/or liturgical texts; donor inscriptions; and "signature" inscriptions (fig. 14.1). In each of these five groups of inscriptions interesting variations occur.

Biblical figures are usually identified by name, with occasional reference to a function (for example, the prophets in s45–s50, or the priest Melchizedek, s43). Other features of a painting are also often labeled—for example, "the tree of Mamre" and the divine "voice" in s38. Monastic and ecclesiastical figures are identified by name, preceded by the honorific "Abba" (father). Monastic figures so designated are concentrated in the eastern section of the nave, ecclesiastical figures (patriarchs) in the sanctuary. Additional identifying features also occur—for example,

s1.1, where Antony is identified as "father of the monks," or s2.1, where Athanasius is identified as "the apostolic patriarch of the city of Alexandria." Martyrs, concentrated in the western section of the nave (sometimes called the narthex), are identified by name, each preceded by the predication "holy is," usually followed by "the martyr of Jesus Christ" and sometimes by the place where the subject came from or was martyred. Some of the saints also have invocations addressed to them—for example, Arsenius (N10.2), Barsuma (N11.2), and Theodore Stratelates ("the General," N22.3).

Narrative action, reflecting stories associated with the various figures, is indicated in the inscriptions with the use of a form of the Coptic verb. The first of many examples is N2.2: "the raven brought the food to Abba Paul."

Biblical and liturgical inscriptions are placed at strategic locations in the church. Psalm 26:1 (LXX Ps 27:1: "The Lord is my light and my salvation, whom shall I fear?" [RSV]) is prominently inscribed above the arch leading from the nave into the annex and chapel (N17).[4] The verse represents the faith of the martyrs portrayed in that section of the nave. It might also be noted that Psalm 26 (27) is one of several used in the service for the consecration of a church.[5] The other arch inscription in the nave (N37), above the arch leading into the *khurus* (choir, Greek χορός), is Psalm 83 (84): 1–2. That psalm originally described the joy of the ancient worshipper in the Jerusalem Temple, which is here represented as the church. Similar use is made of Psalm 86 (87), a song celebrating Zion (Jerusalem). Verse 1 is inscribed on the north wall of the khurus, at the base of the vaulted roof (K17); part of verse 2 is inscribed on the south wall of the khurus (K13); and the rest of verse 2 plus part of verse 3 is inscribed on the west wall, above the arch leading into the nave (K14). Psalm 86 is one of several used in the daily offices (prayer services) of the Coptic Church.[6] The inscription encircling the base of the central dome in the sanctuary may be another passage from the Psalms, but there is too little of it left to identify it. Other biblical texts occur within some of the panels containing paintings of biblical figures.

As might be expected, inscriptions consisting of liturgical phrases are concentrated in the sanctuary and in the chapel, the foci of liturgical action in the various services held in the church. The apse in the sanctuary and the niche in the chapel are dominated by the figure of Christ in majesty. On either side of the enthroned Christ is "Emmanuel, our God" (S1.2; C1.4), a phrase found in one of the prayers ("King of Peace") of the eucharistic liturgy (anaphora), and also in the formula said at the distribution of the sacrament.[7] Christ's feet rest upon a footstool on which is inscribed Isaiah 66:1 ("Heaven is my throne and the earth is my footstool," S1.7; C2.5). The Trisagion ("Holy, holy, holy," Is 6:3), used in a number of places in the Coptic liturgy, appears several times in various forms (S13, 15, 17, 19; C3.2; C3; C10.2–3). The opening verses of the Gloria in Excelsis, or "Hymn of the Angels," also occur in

the sanctuary and chapel (S14, 16, 18, 20; C3.1; C10.1). This hymn is sung in the morning and evening prayers of the Coptic church.[8] The opening passage of the Magnificat (Mary's song, Lk 1:46–55) appears with the Virgin in the chapel (C10.9). The Magnificat is sung in a number of settings in the Coptic liturgy, including the services for Holy Saturday, and the Theotokia (hymns to the Virgin, "Mother of God") are sung daily in the monasteries during the month preceding Christmas.[9] The Agnus Dei ("Lamb of God," Jn 1:29) appears with John the Baptist in the chapel (C3.10). The Agnus Dei is not part of the ordinary (invariable parts) of the eucharistic liturgy of the Coptic Church (as it is in Western churches), but it is reflected in the use of the term *Amnos* (Greek ἀμνός, lamb) for the loaf used in the service of Holy Communion (anaphora).[10] It is, of course, incorporated within the "Hymn of the Angels" as part of an invocation of Christ, and occurs in some of the variable prayers offered at the fraction (breaking of the loaf).[11]

There are four dedicatory or donor inscriptions in the church, inscriptions commemorating the persons who contributed to the cost of the paintings (N31.2; K4.1; S1.14; S33–S36.2). These inscriptions follow, in some respects, a formulaic pattern found elsewhere in donor inscriptions associated with church wall paintings. This pattern is best illustrated by five inscriptions found at Dayr al Fakhury near Esna, published by René-Georges Coquin: (1) "the Lord bless" (either as a wish or a prayer) the (2) "God-loving" donors who have (3) "provided for" (ϥι ⲡⲣⲟⲟⲩϣ) the painting(s), and (4) give them their "recompense" in heaven.[12] At the Monastery of St. Antony the first item of the formula ("The Lord bless") is found in K4.1 and S36, repeated in K4.1. Item 2 ("God-loving") is found in N31.2, item 3 ("provided for") in K4.1, and item 4 ("recompense" in heaven) in N31.2 and K4.1. Another feature found at the Monastery of St. Antony is the use of the term *memorial* (ϣⲉⲛⲉⲣⲫⲙⲉⲟⲩⲓ) for the inscription and the donations, expressed in the following way: "This memorial happened through (the beneficence of) . . ."(N31.2; S1.14; S33–S36.2).[13] Two of the donor inscriptions begin with an invocation of the Holy Trinity (N31.2; S1.14).

Something of the social background of the donors can be seen from their names and titles. They include monks, priests, and other clerics, all presumably associated in some way with the Monastery of St. Antony. A number of them have Arabic names, an indication that Arabic was the dominant language among them, as it was by that time among Egyptians in general.

Especially interesting are the "signature" inscriptions

in the church, inscriptions in which the painter, Theodore, identifies himself. In these inscriptions Theodore is clearly following a well-established tradition, attested not only in Egypt but in virtually the entire Byzantine world of the twelfth and thirteenth centuries.[14] These signature inscriptions often begin with "the hand of," and the painter then expresses his sense of unworthiness ("the sinful," "pitiful," and the like) as a "servant" of God. His humility extends even to his own craft ("hardly a painter"). Painters typically pray for God to "remember" them and extend to them his "mercy" and "forgiveness" on the day of judgment.[15] Our painter, Theodore, adheres perfectly to this tradition in his two signature inscriptions. In N35.3 he identifies his "hand" as one of a "poor" and "sinful" person, who cries out for God's "forgiveness." In s38.7 he asks God to "remember" him, a "poor...servant." When he refers to himself as an "apprentice painter" (s38.7), he is clearly expressing his humility, for his paintings show him to be a master. An inscription in the chapel might be understood in this context as well: "Lord Jesus Christ, have pity on me" (c2.6). This "Jesus prayer" is commonly found inscribed on monastery walls, and is indicative of Theodore's piety.

From Theodore's signatures we also learn something of his own background: In both he identifies himself as "son" (disciple) "of Abba Gabriel, the bishop of the city of Etpeh." It is possible that Theodore was not his original name, for that name appears to be quite common among painters of the period.[16] The name of his home town is more correctly rendered as Petpeh in Coptic, the name of the ancient town of Aphroditopolis on the east bank of the Nile, not far from the Fayum. The Arabic name for the town is Atfih or Itfih. Theodore's faulty rendition of the name of his home town is likely an indication that his first language was Arabic, a deduction that can be made as well from the language of the inscriptions.[17]

The language of the inscriptions is nonstandard Bohairic Coptic. That is to say, the inscriber clearly intended to write Bohairic, the official language of the Coptic Church since the eleventh century, but he was not completely successful in his attempt. There are two indications of this. First, there are a number of "Sahidicisms" in the language of the inscriptions.[18] This probably indicates that the painter wrote under the influence of the Sahidic dialect of Coptic, the dominant language of his native Nile Valley for many centuries. Second, there are numerous errors in orthography and grammar, indicating that the painter-inscriber had a deficient knowledge of Coptic. His command of Greek was even less, as we can see not only from

numerous errors in the spelling of Greek words but also from the idiosyncratic rendition of Greek case-endings.[19] But Theodore's deficiencies in the knowledge of Coptic and Greek should come as no surprise. By the thirteenth century Arabic was the dominant language of Egypt, even among Christians, and the knowledge of Coptic was in steep decline, except among a few scholars.[20] By the seventeenth century the Egyptian people's loss of their native tongue was virtually complete, at least as a spoken language. Its continued limited use in the liturgy of the church, along with Arabic, can be compared to that of Latin in the Roman Catholic Church in the years just after the Second Vatican Council.

Texts, Translations, Commentary

Before we examine the inscriptions themselves, some preliminary remarks are in order on the conventions used by the painter-inscriber, and on the editorial principles that govern my presentation. First, it should be noted that the inscriber has followed well-established Byzantine-Coptic traditions in the inscriptions that accompany the paintings. Second, it should also be remembered that his command of the Coptic and Greek languages was limited. Thus numerous errors of grammar and orthography occur in the inscriptions.

As to the first observation, we note first the inscriber's use of traditional *nomina sacra* and other abbreviations, based on centuries-old traditions established in the copying of Greek and then Coptic manuscripts. Nomina sacra (sacred names) are traditional abbreviations, marked with a supralinear stroke (as was done with letters used as numerals) of divine names and other religiously charged words. The oldest of these, attested in manuscripts going back to the second century, are the following four: $\overline{\text{ΘC}}$ for θεoς, God; $\overline{\text{KC}}$ for κύριoς, Lord; $\overline{\text{IC}}$, $\overline{\text{IH}}$, $\overline{\text{IHC}}$ for Ἰησoῦς, Jesus; and $\overline{\text{XC}}$ for Χριστóς, Christ.[21] Case endings in Greek are also indicated in the nomina sacra, for example, $\overline{\text{Θ}\text{Υ}}$ (genitive), "of God." These four nomina sacra occur among our inscriptions in the following forms (citing the first occurrence of each):

$\overline{\text{Θ}}$ (N10.2); $\overline{\text{Θ}\text{Υ}}$ (N36.1).

$\overline{\text{KC}}$ (N19.1?, K3.2); $\overline{\text{KE}}$ (S40.1).

$\overline{\text{IC}}$ (N13.1); $\overline{\text{IHC}}$ (N31.2).

$\overline{\text{XC}}$ (N13.1); $\overline{\text{XPC}}$ (N31.2); $\text{Π}\overline{\text{XC}}$ (with Coptic definite article, K4.1).

There are also specifically Coptic forms of "God" and "Lord":

ϢϮ for ⲪⲚⲞⲨϮ, God (N35.3).

ⲡⲟⲥ (N17.1 for ⲡⲟⲥ); ⲡⲟⲥ (N31.2) for ⲡϭⲟⲓⲥ, the Lord.

Other common nomina sacra used from ancient times include the following:

ⲡⲛⲁ for πνεῦμα, Spirit (N31.2, there with ⲉⲟⲓ for ⲉⲟⲩ = ⲉⲑⲟⲩⲁⲃ, Holy).

ⲙⲏⲣ for μητήρ, Mother (N36.1), written as a ligature, the as a cross-bar joining ⲙ and ⲡ.

ⲓⲗⲏⲙ for Ἰερουσαλήμ, Jerusalem (N31.2).

ⲩⲥ for υἱός, Son (K15.2).

ⲥⲱⲣ for σωτήρ, Savior (C10.9, variant of ⲥⲏⲣ).

Analogous use is made of the name John (the Baptist): ⲓⲱ (C3.8). Note also ⲁ and ⲱ (Alpha and Omega, N10.2).

Traditional monograms are also found among our inscriptions: the "Christ monogram" ⲣ (N10.2); ⲡⲟⲓ for πόλις, city (N13.1), ⲙ̄ for μάρτυρος, martyr(s) (N13.1); and ⳨ for χρόνος, literally time but here era (N31.2). The last two are traditionally used to designate the "Era of the Martyrs," which begins in the year of Diocletian's accession as emperor (A.D. 284). Also traditional is the use of the rebus ⲟϥ for amen (N31.2). Other abbreviations include ⲡⲡ for πάπας, papa or father, here translated priest (N31.2); ⲕⲣⲣⲓ for κύριος, Sir (N19.1); ⲕⲉ for καί (N31.2; ⲕ at S11.1); and ⲁ for amen.

Other features of orthography include frequent (but not exclusive) use of the ligature ⲩ for the letter combination ⲟⲩ. In my transcription I render the full form rather than the ligature. Letters added above the line are not marked in my transcription. A curved stroke at the end of a line indicating a final ⲛ is transcribed as ⲛ. Use by our inscriber of supralinear dots (djinkim) and supralinear and sublinear strokes is quite irregular; I try to indicate these in my transcription as they appear in the inscriptions. I have introduced word division to facilitate reading, following the editorial conventions used by Walter Till in *Grammatik*.

Because the irregularities of grammar and orthography are so numerous, I have elected to render the inscriptions as they appear, usually without comment, or without any attempt to correct them. One exception to this is the occasional use of parentheses to indicate missing letters

erroneously omitted by the inscriber. Specialists will immediately notice the mistakes, and to the nonspecialist reader they will be of no consequence.

Finally, I have elected to render each inscription with a normal horizontal line. Many of the inscriptions are vertical, and many are rendered vertically with clusters of horizontal letters. Rendering these according to their actual orientation would require far too much space. The actual disposition of the letters in the inscriptions is evident in the plates in which the paintings appear. I do indicate the color of paint used in each inscription.

The numbering of the inscriptions follows the numbering assigned to the paintings and/or panels, with each inscription within a given panel indicated with a number. To be sure, thanks to the work of the restorers, many more of the inscriptions can now be seen than was the case before, and I have included all of them here. On the other hand, there is evidence of some loss of material since the work of Coquin, Laferrière, and van Moorsel.[22] Because of space limitations, I have usually refrained from noting the numerous instances in which my rendering of the inscriptions differs from that of Coquin and Laferrière.

The following sigla are used in my transcriptions and translations:

. A dot placed under a letter in the transcription indicates that the letter is visually uncertain, even if the context makes the reading certain. Dots on the line outside of brackets in the transcription indicate missing letters that cannot be restored but of which vestiges of paint remain. Three dots on the line in the translation indicate the presence of substantial untranslatable material.

[ ] Square brackets indicate a lacuna where it is believed writing once existed. When the text cannot be restored with reasonable probability, the number of estimated letters, up to five, is indicated in the transcription by dots; six or more letters are indicated with a number, preceded by a plus-or-minus sign (±). A question mark within brackets indicates that the number of letters missing cannot be determined. In the translation a bracket is usually not allowed to divide a word (except in the case of some proper names); a word is placed either entirely inside brackets or entirely outside, depending on the relative certainty of the Coptic word it translates.

( ) Parentheses in the transcription indicate letters erroneously omitted by the inscriber. Parentheses in the translation indicate material supplied for the sake of clarity, or translations of words or morphemes erroneously omitted by the inscriber.[23]

Inscriptions in the Nave

N1. ANTONY THE GREAT[24]

1 To left and right (from the viewer's point of view) of Antony, in white paint:

ⲁⲃⲃ(ⲁ) ⲁⲛⲁ[ⲱⲛ]ⲓⲟⲥ   Abba Antony,
ⲫⲓⲱⲧ ⲛⲛⲓⲙⲟⲩⲛⲁⲭⲟⲥ   father of the monks.

The final *a* of *Abba* is elided. *Abba,* spelled variously, means father in Aramaic; it is a traditional term in Coptic Christianity, which is why I use it here and elsewhere.

N2. PAUL THE HERMIT[25]

1 To left and right of Paul, in white:

ⲁⲃⲁⲃ ⲡⲁ[ⲩⲁ]ⲉ ⲁⲅⲣⲁⲩⲗⲱⲥ   Abba Paul, (the) rustic,
ⲡⲓⲛⲓⲱϯ [ⲛ]ⲁⲛ[ⲁ]ⲭ[ⲱ]ⲣ[ⲓ]ⲧ[ⲏⲥ]   the great [anchorite].

The inscriber, who is probably also the painter, has inverted the letters *ba* in *Abba.* The reading *rustic* (Gr. ἄγραυλος) is uncertain.

2 Above and between Paul and Antony, in white:

ⲡⲓⲁⲃⲟⲕ ⲁϥⲛ ϯⲑⲣⲟⲫⲏ ⲛ̄ⲛⲁⲛⲃⲁⲁ ⲡⲁⲩⲗⲱ
The raven brought the food to Abba Paul.

The inscriber has put in an extra *a* in *Abba.* One would expect a circumstantial or present II form of the verb. The prefix ⲁ- is used for both the perfect form and present II, but present II ⲁϥⲛ with a definite object would be a violation of the "Jernstedt Rule."[26] The position of the inscription, and the fact that the bird has a whole loaf instead of Paul's usual portion, a half-loaf, indicates that the food is for both Paul and Antony at their famous meeting. The raven incident is reported by St. Jerome.[27] Food brought by ravens is a biblical motif, associated with the prophet Elijah (1 Kgs 16:6).

N3. ANONYMOUS

1 To left and right of the saint, in white:

ⲁ[ⲃⲃⲁ ?]ⲡ.[?]   [Abba] . . .
[?] ⲛ [?] ⲡ[?]   . . .

Whoever this is, he probably has a *p* or *b* toward the end of his name. One could conceivably restore the name as [ⲥⲁⲣⲁ]ⲡⲓ[ⲱⲛ], Sarapion. Sarapion, a monk and bishop of Thmoui, was a friend of Antony's.[28]

N4. ISAAC THE PRESBYTER[29]

1 To left and right of Isaac, in white:

ⲁⲃⲃⲁ ⲓⲥⲁⲕ   Abba Isaac,
ⲡⲓⲱ[ⲓⲍ] ⲡⲓⲡⲣⲉϫⲃⲓⲧⲉⲣⲟⲥ   the [wrestler],[30] the presbyter.

N5. PAUL THE SIMPLE[31]

1 To left and right of Paul, in white:

[ⲁⲃⲃ]ⲁ ⲡⲁⲩⲁⲏ ⲡⲓⲁⲡ   [Abba] Paul, the
ⲁⲟⲩⲥ ⲙ̄ⲙⲏⲓ   truly simple.

N6. SAMUEL[32]

1 To left and right of Samuel, in white:

ⲁⲃⲃⲁ ⲥⲁⲙⲟⲩⲏⲁ   Abba Samuel,
ⲡⲓⲭ[ⲁⲣⲙⲁⲧ]ⲣⲓⲧⲏⲥ   the archimandrite.

The same strange spelling of *archimandrite* (Gr. ἀρχιμανδρίτης) occurs in N28.1. An archimandrite is a monastery head; Samuel (7th c.) was founder of the Laura of Qalamun in the Fayum.

2 Above the angel, in white:

ⲡⲓⲁⲅⲅⲉⲗⲟⲩ ⲕ̄ⲥ̄   The angel of the Lord.

N7. PISHOI THE GREAT[33]

1 To left and right of Pishoi, in white:

ⲁⲃⲃⲁ   Abba
ⲡⲓϣⲱⲓ   Pishoi.

This Pishoi (Bishoi, Bishai, 4th c.) is undoubtedly the monk at Scetis who was a friend of John the Little and founder of the monastery in the Wadi al-Natrun that bears his name.[34]

N8. JOHN THE LITTLE[35]

1 To left and right of John, in white:

ⲁⲃⲃⲁ ⲓⲱⲁⲛ[ⲏ]ⲥ   Abba John
ⲡⲓ[ⲕⲟⲗⲟ]ⲃ[ⲟⲥ]   the [Little]

The word translated *little* (Gr. κολοβός, *undersized* or *short*) is a regular epithet of John; so the conjectured reading is reasonably safe. (An alternative spelling in Coptic sources is ⲕⲱⲗⲟⲃⲟⲥ.)

2 At John's feet, in black:

ⲡ[. . .] ⲉⲧⲁ.ⲣⲣⲉ.ⲉ. . . .   The [. . .] which . . .

This inscription is probably a comment on John's famous "tree of obedience," here shown.

14.2

Arsenius's scroll (N10; ADP/SA BW medium format 123:2)

14.3

Barsuma's scroll (N11; ADP/SA BW medium format 122:1)

N9. SISOES[36]

1 To left and right of Sisoes, in white:

ⲁⲃⲃⲁ	Abba
ϣⲓϣⲱⲓ	Sisoes.

N10. ARSENIUS[37]

1 To left and right of Arsenius (fig. 14.2), in white:

ⲁⲃⲃⲁ ⲁⲣⲥⲏⲛⲓⲟⲥ	Abba Arsenius,
ⲡⲓⲥⲁϧ ⲛⲧⲉ ⲛⲓⲟⲩⲣⲱⲟⲩ	the teacher of the emperors.

2 In the scroll in Arsenius's hand, in black:

ⲁ̄ ⲱ̄	Alpha, Omega.
ⲑ ⲥⲩⲛ	With God.
ⲉ ⲇ̄ⲅⲟⲛ	O combatant,
ⲇⲁ ⲱ̄ ⲁⲣ	O Ar-
ⲥⲏⲛⲏ ⲫⲟⲧ	senius, the pure (?)
ⲃⲟ ⲱ̄ ϧⲓⲃⲟ	O lamb (?),
ⲭⲁⲣⲟⲕ ⲉⲕ	be silent as you
ⲛⲁⲛⲟ	will be
ϧⲟⲙ	saved.

"Alpha and Omega," the first and last letters of the Greek alphabet, refer to the Lord God, "the first and the Last," in Revelation 1:8, and to Christ in Revelation 22:13. To left and right of "with God" is the "Christ monogram" and a square cross (*crux quadrata*). The Christ monogram here and elsewhere is originally a sign of the cross (staurogram ⲣ) but frequently replaces the Christogram (chi+rho, ⳩) in Coptic manuscripts, paintings, and inscriptions.[38] The phrase "with God" (Gr. σὺν θεῷ) ap-

pears frequently at the beginning of Coptic manuscripts and inscriptions. The words here translated "pure" and "lamb" are taken as hitherto unattested forms of ⲧⲃⲃⲟ, purity, and ϧⲓⲉⲓⲃ (Boh. ϧⲓⲃⲉ), lamb. Arsenius's silence and concern for salvation are features of his story.

N11. BARSUMA[39]

1 To left and right of Barsuma (fig. 14.3), in black:

ⲁⲃⲃⲁ	Abba
[ⲡⲁⲣ]ⲥⲱⲙⲁ	[Bar]suma.

2 In the scroll in Barsuma's hand, in black:

ⲁ̄ ⲱ̄	Alpha, Omega
(FIVE LINES OF SYRIAC)	
ⲁⲅⲟⲛⲁ[ⲁ] ⲉⲑ[ⲓ]	Holy combatant,
ⲱ ⲡⲁⲣⲥⲱⲙⲁ [ⲧϩ]	O Barsuma, [accompany]
ⲃⲟ ⲛⲛⲓⲉⲑⲛⲟⲥ	all the
ⲧⲏⲣⲟⲩ ⲉⲕⲛⲁ	nations as you will
ⲟⲩⲛⲟϧ .ⲛ[.].	appear . . .

The abbreviation ⲉⲑⲓ (ⲉⲑⲟⲩⲁⲃ, holy) also occurs at N31.2, line 1. The word here restored and translated as "accompany" (or "bring back") is taken as a variant form of ⲧϩϥⲟ. The reading "appear" (or "reveal") is uncertain. A tentative reading of the Syriac has been offered by V. Gold and M. Guinan: "In the name of God / . . . holy life / [Bar]suma / . . . accompany . . . / . . . nations . . ."

3 To right of the pig's head at Barsuma's feet, and to left of the serpent's coiled body, in black:

ⲡⲓ(ⲉ)ϣⲱ   The pig.

ⲡⲓϩⲟϥ   The serpent.

These inscriptions are no longer visible.[40]

N12. PACHOMIUS[41]

1 To left and right of Pachomius, in black:

[ⲁⲃⲃ]ⲁ ⲡⲁϭⲱ[ⲙ]ⲓⲟⲥ   Abba Pachomius,

[ⲫⲓⲱⲧ] ⲛ[ⲧⲉ] †[ⲕ]ⲱ[ⲛⲟ]ⲛ[ⲓ]ⲁ   [father] of the [Koinonia].

Pachomius (4th c.) is the reputed father of coenobitic monasticism—that is, monastic life in a community (Gr. κοινωνία), in contrast to the eremitic type of monasticism associated with St. Antony (cf. N1).

N14. PAKAOU[42]

1 To left and right of Pakaou, in white:

ⲁⲡⲁ ⲡⲁⲕⲁⲟⲩ ⲡⲓⲙⲟⲛⲁⲭⲟⲥ
ⲁⲟⲛ ⲙ̄ ⲛⲧⲉ ⲓ̄ⲥ̄ ⲭ̄ⲥ̄ ⲡⲓⲙⲁⲣⲧⲣⲟⲥ ⲙⲡⲱⲙⲙⲏ / ⲡⲓⲱⲙ
ⲁⲣⲥⲱⲛⲟⲃⲏ ⲙ̄

Abba Pakaou, the monk,

the martyr of Jesus Christ, the martyr of Pomme, Fayum, the town (of) Arsinoe.

2 The name of the little demon held in Pakaou's hand is given below it, in white:

ⲟϛⲟϥⲟⲛⲏⲥⲁⲣ   Sofonesar.

This demon is said in the saint's life to be the instigator of the fall of Eve.[43]

N15. "THOUAN" [NOUA][44]

1 To left and right of "Thouan," in white:

ⲟⲩⲁⲅⲓⲟⲥ
ⲡⲓⲟⲩⲏⲃ ⲁⲡⲁ ⲑⲟⲩⲁⲛ ⲛⲧⲉ ⲛⲥⲙⲙⲟⲩ ⲁ[ⲟⲛ] ⲙ̄ ⲓ̄ⲥ̄ ⲭ̄ⲥ̄

Holy is

the priest, Abba Thouan of Nsmmou, [the] martyr (of) Jesus Christ.

The translation "Holy is" is based on the assumption that ⲟⲩ is the indefinite article, here used to indicate a predicate. Alternatively, it could be taken as a rendering of the Greek definite article ὁ, but that is less likely. The Coptic name of "Thouan's" hometown is unfortunately not clear. This saint's real name was probably Noua, a saint martyred at Pelusium; so the place name ⲛⲥⲙⲙⲟⲩ may be a corruption of ⲡⲉⲣⲉⲙⲟⲩⲛ, Peremoun, the Coptic name for Pelusium (al-Farama). The name Thouan is the result of a misreading of the name Noua in Arabic, in which the letters *n* and *t* look very much alike.[45]

N16. PIROOU AND ATHOM[46]

1 Jesus Christ is portrayed above and between the two saints in a mandorla, with the name inscribed both inside and out, to left and right, in black and white, respectively:

ⲓ̄ⲥ̄ ⲭ̄ⲥ̄   Jesus Christ.

2 Below the mandorla and between the two saints, in white:

ⲛⲓⲙⲁⲣⲧⲩⲣⲟⲥ   The martyrs

ⲛⲧⲉ ⲥⲟⲙⲡⲓⲧ   of Sanbat

ⲡⲉⲙϩⲓⲧ   North.

Sanbat "North," in the delta (modern Sumbat), is here distinguished from another Sanbat in the Fayum.[47] ⲥⲟⲙⲡⲓⲧ (Sompit) is a corrupted form of the Coptic name for the place, Tasempoti.

3 To left of Piroou, in white:

ⲟⲩⲁⲅⲓⲟⲥ ⲡⲓⲣⲟⲟⲩ ⲁⲟⲛ ⲙ̄ ⲓ̄ⲥ̄ ⲭ̄ⲥ̄

Holy is Piroou, the martyr (of) Jesus Christ.

A similar inscription undoubtedly existed to the right of Athom, but the construction of the present doorway leading into the annex destroyed it.[48]

N17. COPTIC ARCH INSCRIPTION[49]

1 On the south wall, above the arch leading into the annex, in white paint within a red band, with decorations:

ⲡ̄ⲟ̄ⲥ̄ ⲡⲉ ⲡⲁⲟⲩⲱⲓⲛⲓ ⲛⲉⲙ [ⲡⲁⲛ]ⲟϩⲉⲙ ⲁⲓⲛⲁⲉⲣϩⲟ†
ϧⲁⲧϩ ⲛⲛⲓⲙ ⲡ̄ⲟ̄ⲥ̄ ⲡⲉⲧ† ⲉϧⲣⲏⲓ ⲉⲍⲉⲛ ⲡⲁⲟⲩ(ⳉⲁⲓ)

The Lord is my light and my safety. Whom shall I fear? The Lord is the one who fights for my salvation.

This ornate inscription is the first verse of Psalm 26 (27 in Hebrew and English versions). The inscriber ran out of space at the end and could not finish the word *salvation*. The ending has been supplied as a graffito by an unknown visitor.

N18. THEODORE THE ORIENTAL[50]

1 To right of Theodore, in white:

ⲡⲓⳉⲟ[ⲣⲓ ⲛⲁ]ⲛⲁⲧⲱⲗⲉ[ⲟⲥ] [ⲁⲟⲛ] ⲙ̄ ⲓ̄ⲥ̄ ⲭ̄ⲥ̄

The [mighty] Oriental, [the] martyr (of) Jesus Christ.

The saint himself and part of the inscription have been obliterated by the construction of the doorway leading into the annex.[51] Theodore the Oriental (or "Easterner") is called ⲡⲓⳓⲱⲣⲓ ("the strong or mighty") in the superscript introduction to his martyrdom; hence the conjectured reading here.[52] To left of the saint was, no doubt, "Holy is Theodore."[53]

2 Above the mounted saint's horse's head, Jesus Christ in a mandorla, with the following to left and right of Christ's head, in black:

ⲓ̅ⲥ̅ ⲭ̅ⲥ̅   Jesus Christ.

A vision of Christ is part of Theodore's story.[54]

N19. CLAUDIUS[55]

1 To left and right of Claudius's raised arm, in white:

ⲟⲩⲁⲅⲓⲟⲥ   Holy
ⲛ̅ⲕ̅ⲥ̅ . .   to the Lord (?) . . .

Visible in red beneath ⲛ̅ⲕ̅ⲥ̅ . . is ⲟⲩⲁⲅⲓⲟⲥ, which originally was penciled in. The present inscription in white represents a correction to what was initially planned. In the expanded version ⲟⲩⲁⲅⲓⲟⲥ is moved to the left of Claudius's arm.

2 To right of Claudius, in white:

ⲕ̅ⲣ̅ⲣⲓ ⲕⲗⲁⲩⲧⲟⲥ ⲇⲟⲛ ⲏ̅ ⲛ̅ⲓ̅ⲥ̅ ⲭ̅ⲥ̅
Sir Claudius, the martyr of Jesus Christ.

In red beneath ⲕ̅ⲣ̅ⲣⲓ is ⲕⲗⲁⲩⲧⲟⲥ, originally planned.

3 Under the horse's forelegs, on the façade of the building, in white:

ⲛⲓϣⲏⲟⲩⲓ ⲛ̅ⲛⲓⲁⲟⲗⲟⲛ   The altars of the idols.

ⲓⲁⲟⲗⲟⲛ is taken here as the Greek word εἴδωλον. Coquin and Laferrière translate ⲛ̅ⲛⲓⲁⲟⲗⲟ [sic] as "the gifts" (Greek δῶρον).[56]

4 Within the open door, in white:

ⲫⲣⲟ   The door.

5 To right of the crowned figure under the horse's hind legs, in black:

ⲡⲟ(ⲩ)ⲣ[ⲱ] ⲇⲓⲱⲭⲁⲏⲇⲓⲁⲛⲟⲥ   The emperor Diocletian.

Here Claudius is credited with the death of Diocletian, something not otherwise attested in Coptic sources.[57]

6 In the scroll in Diocletian's left hand, to left and right of his hand, in black:

ⲡ. . .ⲟⲩⲱ   . . .
. . .ⲡⲥ. . .   . . .

The scroll presumably represents Diocletian's letter demanding Claudius's submission.

N20. VICTOR[58]

1 To left and right of the mounted saint, in white:

ⲟⲩⲁⲅⲓⲟⲥ
ⲁⲡⲁ ⲃⲓⲕⲧⲟⲣ ⲇⲟⲛ ⲏ̅ ⲛⲧⲉ ⲓ̅ⲥ̅ ⲭ̅ⲥ̅
Holy is
Abba Victor, the martyr of Jesus Christ.

2 Within light rays coming down on the saint's right and left shoulders (to left and right), in red:

ⲡⲓ(ⲕ)ⲗⲟⲙ   The crown.
ⲡⲓ(ⲕ)ⲗⲟⲙ   The crown.

The crown is the "crown of life" promised to the martyrs in Revelation 2:10.

3 Under Victor's horse, in red:

ⲧⲥⲓⲱⲟ(ⲩ)ⲛⲛ   The bathhouse.

In Victor's story, one of the attempts to kill him involved throwing him into the furnace used to heat the baths in Alexandria.

N21. MENAS[59]

1 To left and right of the mounted saint, in white:

ⲟⲩⲁⲅⲓⲟⲥ
ⲁⲡⲁ ⲙⲏⲛⲁ ⲇⲟⲛ ⲏ̅ ⲛⲧⲉ ⲓ̅ⲥ̅ ⲭ̅ⲥ̅
Holy is
Abba Menas, the martyr of Jesus Christ.

2 Within light rays coming down on the saint's right and left shoulders (to left and right), letter traces in red:

ⲡⲓ(ⲕ)ⲗ[ⲟ]ⲙ   The crown.
[ⲡ]ⲓ(ⲕ)[ⲗⲟ]ⲙ   [The crown]

The restorations are based on N20.2; Victor and Menas are presented in similar fashion. The crowns, seen in Menas's vision of the martyrs, are also part of his story.

3 Above the camel beside the shrine, letter traces in black:

[ⲡⲓⳓ]ⲁ[ⲙ]ⲟⲩⲗ   [The camel].

The reconstruction, admittedly tentative, is based on the prominence of the camel in the story of Menas's burial.

N22. THEODORE THE GENERAL[60]

1 To left and right of the mounted saint, in white:

ⲞⲨⲀⲄⲒⲞⲤ ⲐⲈⲰⲆ[Ⲟ]ⲣⲟ[Ⲥ]
ⲠⲒⲤⲦⲣⲁϯⲗⲁⲦⲎⲤ ⲆⲟⲚ ⲓⲋ ⲚⲒⲤ ⲬⲤ

Holy is Theodore
the General, the martyr of Jesus Christ.

2 To right of Theodore's head, within the shield, in red:

ⲒⲤ ⲬⲤ   Jesus Christ

3 At upper right hand corner, within a half-circle from which a hand extends, in black:

ⲱ ⲐⲈⲰⲆⲞ	O Theodore,
ⲣⲟ[Ⲥ] ⲫⲎ Ⲉ	the one
ⲦⲈⲔ[. .].ⲱϥ	whose [. . .]
ⲈϥⲈ[	. . .[
.Ⲗⲓ[	.[

The inscription is presumably a divine address to Theodore, a voice from heaven, symbolized by the extended hand. An appearance of Jesus Christ promising him victory is part of Theodore's story.[61]

4 Above the praying woman, in white:

[?]ⲣⲚ[?]Ⲛ[?]   . . .

This is presumably the name, otherwise unattested, of the widow whose two sons were saved from the dragon by St. Theodore.[62]

5 Below the dragon's head, in white:

.[. . .].Ⲛ
[?]. .[. .]. . .

This inscription relates to the dragon slain by Theodore. If the inscription began to the left of the point of Theodore's lance, one could restore on the first line: [ⲠⲒⲆ]ⲣ[ⲀⲔ]ⲱⲚ, "the dragon."

6 To left of the boy on the left:

ⲠⲈⲦⲣⲟⲤ   Peter

7 To right of the boy on the right:

.Ⲛⲁ[?]   . . .

Not enough is left to provide this boy's name. The boys are not given names in the extant versions of Theodore's story.

N23. SISINNIUS[63]

1 To left and right of Sisinnius, in white:

ⲞⲨⲀⲄⲒⲞⲤ   Holy is

ⲤⲞⲨⲤⲒ[ⲚⲒⲞⲤ] ⲆⲞⲚ [ⲓⲋ ?]ⲃⲟ⌉ ?] Sisi[nnius], the [martyr] . . . .

"Of Jesus Christ" would be expected after the conjectured *martyr*. Construction of the new door has destroyed most of the painting and other inscriptional evidence that might have existed.

N24. JOHN OF HERACLEA (?)[64]

1 To right of the mounted saint's missing head, in white:

ⲒⲰⲀ ⲠⲀⲗϥⲎⲱ Ⲛ.[.] ⲚⲚⲈⲤⲀⲚ ⲙ̄ ϦⲚⲈϚ [ⲆⲞ]Ⲛ ⲓⲋ Ⲛ[ⲦⲈ] ⲒⲤ ⲬⲤ

John (?), the . . . of the brothers (?) of the city of Hnes, [the martyr] of Jesus Christ.

John's name is given in abbreviated (suspended) form. On the problem of the identity of this saint see Coquin and Laferrière, who hesitatingly entertain the possibility that this is John of Heraclea, originally from Heraclea in the Pontus region of Asia Minor but martyred in Antinoe in Egypt.[65] In that case, John's home town of Heraclea has been confused with Heracleopolis in Egypt, Coptic Hnes, as given in the inscription (modern Ihnasya al-Madina). The identity of Eutychius in N24.2–3 remains a mystery, and this is one factor in Coquin and Laferrière's hesitation to identify this particular saint as John of Heraclea. Nevertheless, such an identification is made all the more likely by a mention of him in the Arabic inscription associated with St. Menas.[66] There "Mari Mina" is named in association with "Mari Yuhana al-Harqly" (John of Heraclea), which may indicate that the inscriber of the Arabic inscription understood the saint of N24 to be John of Heraclea. (Menas appears at N21). This John is not included in the Coptic (Arabic) Synaxary, but is in the Ethiopic.[67] The word ⲠⲀⲗϥⲎⲱ ("the *alfesh*"), after John's name is another problem, for there is no such word in Coptic or Greek. But perhaps it is a deformation of Arabic ʾ*al harqly* ("of Heraclea"). Confusion of *q* and *f* is, in any case, easily understandable, for *q* and *f* in Arabic are very similar (identical except that *f* has one dot, *q* two). If this conjecture is accepted, we have confirmation of this saint's identity, John of Heraclea.

2 To right of the figure under the saint's horse, in white:

ⲈⲨⲦⲈⲬⲒⲞⲤ   Eutychius.

3 Below the same figure, in black:

ⲈⲨⲦⲈⲬⲒⲞⲤ ⲠⲒⲦⲞⲨⲝ   Eutychius the duke.

Presumably this Eutychius would have been involved in the saint's martyrdom, but no such person is mentioned in the extant story concerning John. There is a count named Eutychianus in the story of St. Victor's martyrdom.[68]

N25. GEORGE[69]

1 To left and right of George's raised arm, in white:

[OⲨⲀ]ⲤⲒⲞⲤ   Holy is
ⲄⲈⲰⲢ[Ⲅ]ⲒⲞⲤ   George.

2 To right of George, in white:

.[?]Ⲅ.[.]Ⲙ[. . .]Ⲙ[. . .]Ⲉ[?]† Ⲭ[?] ⲚⲈ[?] Ⲙ[?

. . .

There is nothing translatable in what is left of this inscription. Coquin and Laferrière read: Ⲅⲣⲟ Ⲙ[ⲘⲞⲔ] Ⲉ†Ⲭ [. . .] ⲚⲈ[, "Strengthen [yourself] to give . . . "

3 To left of the person between the hind legs of George's horse, in white:

ⲠⲒⲒⲞⲨⲆⲀⲒ [Ⲉ]ⲦⲀϤⲄⲒⲞⲨⲒ ⲚⲒ[Ⲥ]Ⲕ[ⲈⲨ]ⲞⲤ [Ⲛ]ⲦⲈ
†.ⲀⲚⲀⲀ[?   The Jew who stole the [vessels] of the . . . .

This refers to the third posthumous miracle of St. George.[70]

4 Above the church portrayed under the horse's forelegs, in white:

†ⲈⲔⲔⲀ̅Ⲏ[ⲤⲒⲀ] Ⲙ[?   The church of. . . .

Perhaps read Ⲙ[ⲠⲒⲀⲄⲒⲞⲤ ⲄⲈⲰⲢⲄⲒⲞⲤ], "of St. George."[71]

5 Inside the church's open door, in red:

†ⲈⲔⲀ̅ⲎⲤⲒⲀ   . .[?   The church . . . .

N26. PHOEBAMMON[72]

1 To left and right of the mounted saint's raised arm, in white:

[OⲨ]ⲀⲄⲒⲞⲤ   Holy is
[Ⲫ]Ⲓ̅ⲂⲀⲘⲞ[Ⲛ]   Phoebammon.

2 To right of the saint, in white:

Ⲛ̅ⲦⲈ ⲦⲈⲚ[?] ⲚⲞⲨ [?] Ⲡ̅Ⲓ.ⲣⲉ Ⲛ† Ⲙⲁⲓ̅
ⲞⲨⲰ[ⲤⲒⲘ] ⲆⲞⲚ Ⲙ̅ ⲚⲦⲈ Ⲓ̅Ⲥ̅ [Ⲭ̅Ⲥ̅]
of . . . of the city (of) Au[sim], the martyr of Jesus [Christ].

Phoebammon (Bifam, Bafam) of Ausim, a martyred Christian nobleman, is here (as frequently) identified with a soldier martyr of the same name, Phoebammon of Preht.[73] Ausim, also called Wasim or Boushem, ancient Latopolis, is the modern Ashum.

3 Above the woman between the two horses' heads, in white:

ⲦⲈϤⲘⲀⲨ   His mother.

The lament of Phoebammon's mother over his impending martyrdom is part of his story.

4 Below, above the child held by its mother, in white:

ⲠⲒⲔⲞⲨⲀⲒ ⲈϤ[†] ϦⲞ   The little boy beseeching.

The compound verb here translated "beseech" can also be translated "encourage." The boy is probably the fellow student healed by Phoebammon while he was still a school boy.

5 To left of the boy's mother, in white:

ⲐⲘⲀⲨ Ⲙ̅ⲠⲒⲔⲞⲨⲀⲒ ⲈⲦ† ϦⲞ ⲈⲠ[?
The mother of the little boy who is beseeching [. . .].

Perhaps read ⲈⲠ[ⲒⲘ̅ⲙ̅Ⲏⲓ], "the martyr."

6 Above the church under the horse, in white:

ⲈⲔ[ⲔⲀ̅]ⲎⲤⲒⲀ [Ⲛ̅Ⲫ̅Ⲓ̅Ⲃ̅]ⲀⲘⲞⲚ   (The) church of [Phoeb]ammon.

The construction of a church in his honor after the martyr's death is part of his story.

7 To right of the figure receiving the saint's lance, in white and black, respectively:

ⲠⲒⲔⲀⲦⲀⲚⲦⲀⲢⲬⲰⲤ   The centurion.
ⲠⲒⲔⲀⲚⲦⲀⲢⲬⲰⲤ   The centurion.

This is presumably the commander of the soldiers who beheaded Phoebammon.

N28. SHENOUTE[74]

1 To left and right of Shenoute, in white:

ⲀⲂⲂⲀ ϢⲒⲚⲞⲨ†   Abba Shenoute.
[ⲠⲒⲬ]ⲀⲢⲘⲀⲦⲢⲒⲦⲎⲤ   [The] archimandrite.

N29. PISENTIUS[75]

1 To left and right of Pisentius, in white:

ⲀⲂⲂⲀ ⲠⲒⲤⲎⲚⲐⲒⲞⲤ   Abba Pisentius,
ⲠⲒⲈⲠⲒⲤⲔ[Ⲟ]ⲠⲞⲤ Ⲛ̅Ⲁ̅ ⲔⲈⲂⲦ   (of) the town (of) Qift.

N30. MOSES THE BLACK[76]

1 To left and right of Moses, in white:

ⲀⲂⲂⲀ   Abba
ⲘⲞⲨⲤⲎ[Ⲥ]   Moses.

2 Above and to right of the border, in the plaster, in black paint:

ⲘⲞⲨ[ⲤⲎⲤ] Ⲡ̅ⲒⲘⲀ.[?] ⲚⲀ[Moses, the [. . .

14.4

Memorial inscription (N31; ADP/SA
BW medium format 149:9)

Perhaps read ⲡⲓⲙⲁⲣ[ⲧⲩⲣⲟⲥ], "the martyr." Elsewhere martyr is usually rendered with the monogram ⲙ̅, but see N13.1, where both forms occur. The inscriptions in the plaster outside of the painted panels were presumably put there to indicate where the respective paintings should go, according to a preset plan. They would then have intentionally been covered over, only to be exposed as part of the latest restoration work.

N31. COPTIC MEMORIAL INSCRIPTION[77]

1 In the plaster above the panel, in black (fig. 14.4):

ⲡⲓϣⲉⲛⲏⲣⲉϥⲙⲉⲟⲩⲓ   The memorial.

2 "Memorial" inscription, within red borders, in black paint:

ⲣ ⲥⲧⲛ ϧⲉⲛ ⲫⲣⲁⲛ ⲛⲙ̅ ⲫⲓⲱⲧ ⲛⲉⲙ ⲡⲓϣⲏⲣⲓ ⲛⲉⲙ
ⲡⲓⲡⲛ̅ⲁ̅ ⲉⲑ̅ⲟ̅ ⲟ̅ϥ̅ / ⲁϥϣⲱⲡⲓ ⲛ̅ϫⲉ ⲡⲁⲓϣⲓⲛⲉⲣⲉⲟⲙⲓⲟⲩⲓ
ⲉ[ⲧ]ⲧⲛⲉⲩⲧ ⲛⲧⲉ ⲛⲓ/ ⳓⲱⲅⲣⲁⲫⲓⲁ ⲛⲧⲉ ⲧⲁⲓⲉⲕⲗⲁⲥⲓⲁ
ⲉⲑⲟ ⲛ̅ⲧⲡⲓⲛⲓϣϯ ⲁⲛⲧⲱⲛⲓⲟⲥ / ⲉⲃⲟⲗ ϩⲓ[ⲧ]ⲱⲧⲟⲩ
ⲛⲛⲉⲛⲓⲟϯ ⲉⲑⲟ ⲙ̅ⲙⲁⲓⲛⲟⲩϯ ⲟⲩⲟϩ ⲙ̅ⲙⲁⲓⲁⲅⲁⲡⲏ /
⁵ⲟⲩⲟϩ ⲙ̅ⲙⲁⲓⲡⲣⲟⲥⲫⲟⲣⲁ ⲙ̅ⲙⲁⲓⲭ̅ⲣ̅ⲥ̅ ⲛⲓⲙⲟⲛⲁⲭⲟⲥ
ⲟⲩⲟϩ ⲙⲡⲛⲁ̅ⲧⲟ / ⲫⲟⲣⲟⲥ ⲉⲧ[ⲉ] ⲛⲁⲓ ⲛⲉ ⲁⲣⲭⲏⲡ̅ⲡ̅

ⲡⲉⲧⲣⲟⲥ ⲛ̅ⲧⲉ ⲧⲁⲓⲉⲕⲗⲏⲥⲓⲁ ⲛⲉⲙ ⲡ̅ⲡ̅ / ⲙⲓⲭⲁⲏⲗ ⲛⲉⲙ
ⲡ̅ⲡ̅ ⲥⲏⲧⲁⲕⲗⲉϩ ⲛⲉⲙ ⲡ̅ⲡ̅ ⲡⲉⲧ[ⲣ]ⲟⲥ ⲛⲉⲙ ⲡ̅ⲡ̅ ϫⲁⲙⲟⲩⲗ
ⲛⲉⲙ / ⲡ̅ⲡ̅ ⲙⲁⲣⲕⲟⲥ ⲛⲉⲙ ⲡ̅ⲡ̅ ⲙⲁⲣⲕⲟⲥ ⲛⲉⲙ ⲡ̅ⲡ̅
ⲡⲟⲩⲗ ⲙⲁ[ⲟⲩ]ⲛⲉ ⲛⲉⲙ ⲡⲓⲁⲣⲭⲏⲇⲓⲁⲕⲟⲥ / ⲥⲁⲗⲓⲡ
ⲛⲉⲙ ⲓⲱⲁⲛⲛⲏⲥ ⲛⲉⲙ ⲡⲟⲩⲗ ϥⲁⲣⲁϫ ⲛ[ⲉ]ⲙ ⲡⲉⲧⲣⲟⲥ
ⲛⲉⲙ ϫⲁⲕⲁ/ ¹⁰ⲣⲓⲁⲥ ⲛⲉⲙ ϥⲙⲱⲛ ⲛⲉⲙ ⲱⲩⲗⲕⲟⲓⲛⲉ
ⲛⲉⲙ ⲕ[.] . . [ⲛⲉⲙ] ⲡⲟⲩⲛⲉ ⲛⲉⲙ /
ⲙⲁⲣⲕⲟⲩⲣⲓ ⲛⲉ[ⲙ] ⲡⲟⲩ ϩⲁⲗⲉⲡ ⲛⲉⲙ ⲓⲱⲁⲛⲛ[ⲏ]ⲥ
ⲉⲧϫⲏⲕ ⲁⲗⲟⲓ ⲛⲉⲙ / ⲡⲉⲧⲣⲟⲥ ⲛⲉⲙ ⲉⲡⲟⲩⲗ ⲟⲩ̅
ⲛⲉⲙ ⲓⲁⲕⲱⲛ[.] ⲛⲉⲙ ⲓⲱⲁⲛⲛⲉ ⲛⲓϣⲏⲣⲓ / ⲙ̅ⲡ̅ⲡ̅ ⲡⲟⲩⲗ
ⲙⲁⲟⲩⲛⲓ ⲛⲉⲙ ⲉⲗⲣⲁϫⲓ ⲛ[ⲉ]ⲙ ⲡⲉϥⲥⲟⲛ ⲡⲁⲗⲁ/ⲗⲉⲙ
ⲛ[ⲓϣ]ⲏⲣⲓ ⲙ̅ⲡⲁⲗⲉⲥⲁⲧ ⲁⲙⲉⲛ [ⲕ]ⲉ ⲁ̅ vacat /¹⁵ⲛⲉⲧⲉ
ⲉ̅ⲧ[ⲁⲛⲧⲁⲟⲩ]ⲟ ⲛⲛⲟⲩⲣⲁⲛ ⲛ[ⲉ]ⲙ ⲛⲉ ⲉⲧⲉ
ⲙ̅ⲡⲟⲛⲧⲁⲟⲩ/ ⲱ̅ ⲛ̅ⲟⲩⲣⲁⲛ ⲛⲉⲙ [ⲛ]ⲏ ⲉⲧⲁⲛϣⲉⲡ
ϩⲙ[ⲟⲧ ⲛⲧⲟⲧⲟⲩ ⲉⲧ]ⲃⲉ ⲧ[ⲁ]ⲓⲉ[ⲕ]ⲕ̅/ⲗⲏⲥⲓⲁ
ⲡ̅ⲟ̅ⲥ̅ [ⲓ]ⲏ̅ⲥ̅ ⲭ̅ⲥ̅ ⲉϥⲉϯ ⲛⲱⲟⲩ ⲡⲉⲧϣ[ⲓⲃϯ] ϧⲉⲛ ⲓ̅ⲗ̅ⲏ̅ⲙ̅ /
ⲛⲧⲉ ⲧⲫⲉ [ⲡ]ⲓⲙⲁ ⲉⲧⲁϥⲫⲱⲧ ⲉⲃⲟⲗ [ⲛ]ϩⲏⲧϥ ⲛϫⲉ
ⲡⲓⲉⲙ / ⲕⲉⲛϩⲏ[ⲧ] ⲛⲉⲙ ϯⲗⲩⲡⲏ ⲛⲉⲙ ⲡⲓ[ϥⲓⲁϩⲟ]ⲙ
ⲁⲙⲏⲛ ⲕ̅ⲉ̅ ⲁ̅

(decoration)

✝ ⳨ ⲙ̅ⲓ̅ [ⲣ]ⲙⲑ
]ⲁⲙⲟ[..]ⲡⲓϣ. ⲛ/ .[?]/[?]/ . ⲓⲥ

With Christ. In the name of the Father and the Son and the Holy Spirit. Amen (99). / This dedicated memorial of the / paintings of the holy church of the great Antony happened / through (the beneficence of) our holy fathers, (who are) lovers of God and lovers of charity / 5 and lovers of offerings (and) lovers of Christ, the monks and Spirit- / bearers, who are the archpriest Peter of this church, and the priest / Michael, and the priest Setakleh (?), and the priest Peter, and the Priest Jamoul, and / the priest Mark, and the priest Mark, and the priest (A)bu l-Maʿani, and the archdeacon / Salib, and John, and (A)bu l-Faraj, and Peter, and Zachary / 10 and Fmon (?), and Oulkoine (?) and K . . . , [and] Poune, and / Mercurius, and (A)bu Ghalib, and John who is truly perfect (?), and / Peter, and Abū l-Uz, and Jakon[.], and John, the sons / of the priest (A)bu l-Maʿani, and al Razi, and his brother Palalem (?), / the sons of Palesat. Amen [and] amen. / 15 Those whose names [we have mentioned] as well as those whose names we have not mentioned, / together with (all) [those to whom] we have given [thanks] for this / church—the Lord Jesus Christ give them their [recompense] in (the) Jerusalem / of heaven, the place from which has fled away / (all) pain and sorrow and [sighing]. Amen and amen.

(decoration)

The Era of the Martyrs [9]49.

. . .

This is a dedicatory inscription commemorating the donors who contributed financially to the cost of the paintings in the church. There are three others, one in the khurus (K4.1), and two in the sanctuary of the church (S1.14, S33–S36.2). The word here translated "memorial," which occurs four times with various spellings (inscription above, and line 2 here [misspelled: ⲑ for ⲫ]; cf. s1.14, s33.2), is a form of ⲱⲉ ⲛⲉⲣ ⲫⲙⲉⲧⲓ in standard Bohairic, remembrance. ⲱⲉⲛⲉⲣⲫⲙⲉⲧⲓ is a term that can be applied to any dedicated object, such as a painting or a set of paintings.[78] In line 1 "Christ" is rendered with the Christ monogram; cf. ɴ10.2 and note. The numeral 99, translated as "amen," is an isopsephism (rebus) that occurs frequently in Greek and Coptic Christian manuscripts and inscriptions ($\alpha=1$, $\mu=40$, $\eta=8$, and $\nu=50$, adding up to ϙθ=99). The names given here with a question mark are uncertain. In line 8 the repetition of the name Mark may be a dittography (scribal error). In line 11 the word translated "truly" is taken as an erroneous adverbial use of the Greek word for truth, $\dot\alpha\lambda\acute\eta\theta\epsilon\iota\alpha$. If this is correct, it is probably an indication that this John has recently died ("been perfected"); that death means being perfected is a common notion in Coptic Christianity. ⲛⲉⲧⲉ at the beginning of line 15 is presumably a mistake; ⲛⲏ is expected. Lines 15–19 reflect the language of intercessory prayer in the Coptic liturgy. The formulaic conclusion in lines 18–19 ("from which has fled") referring to the Heavenly Jerusalem, based on Isaiah 51:11, is taken from one of the intercessions for the souls of the saints in the service for "the raising of incense for the evening and the morning."[79] The same phrase occurs in the "Diptych" of the Anaphora of St. Basil.[80] The year given here at the end, A.M. 949 = A.D. 1232/1233, is completely extant in another inscription (ᴋ4.2); so the restoration is virtually certain. The material represented by additional letter traces in the lower right corner of the panel may have added specific information on the date of the inscription (month, day, and so on), although such details usually precede the year in Coptic inscriptions. Alternatively, this may have been a pious prayer added by the painter on his own behalf; cf. ᴄ2.6. Construction of the window under the inscription has contributed to the damage.

N32. MAXIMUS AND DOMITIUS[81]

1 To left and right of Christ in the mandorla, in red:

ⲓ̄ⲥ̄ ⲭ̄ⲥ̄   Jesus Christ.

2 Outside the mandorla, on either side, in white:

ⲙ̇ⲙⲁ / ⲛ̣ⲟⲩⲏⲗ   Emmanuel.

See s1.2 and note.

3 To left and right of Maximus, in white:

ⲁⲃⲃⲁ   Abba
ⲙⲁⲝⲓⲙ[ⲟ]ⲥ̣   Maximus.

4 To left and right of Domitius, in white:

ⲁⲃⲃⲁ   Abba
ⲇⲱⲙⲏⲇⲓⲟⲥ   Domitius.

5 Between the two, in white:

ⲛⲓⲱⲏⲣⲓ ⲙⲡⲟⲩⲣⲱ[ⲟⲩ]   The sons of the Emperor.[82]

6 In the plaster above the painting, in black:

ⲙⲁⲝⲓⲙⲟⲥ ⲓ̄ⲥ̄ ⲭ̄ⲥ̄ ⲇⲱⲙⲏⲇⲓⲟⲥ   Maximus, Jesus Christ, Domitius.

N33. MACARIUS THE GREAT[83]

1 To left and right of Macarius, in white:

ⲁⲃⲃⲁ   Abba
ⲙⲁⲕ[ⲁⲣⲓⲟⲥ]   Macarius.

2 In the plaster above the painting, to left of cherub and right of Macarius, in black:

ⲡⲓⲭⲉⲣⲟⲩⲃⲓⲙ   The cherub.
[ⲙⲁⲕⲁⲣⲓⲟⲥ ⲡ]ⲓⲛⲓⲱ†   [Macarius the] Great.

In Coptic the Hebrew plural ending -im is not recognized as such. Macarius's vision of a cherub is part of his life story. The cherub leads Macarius to the site where the monastery is to be located.

N34. MACARIUS[84]

1 To left and right of Macarius, in white:

ⲁ[ⲃⲃⲁ]   Abba
ⲙⲁⲕ[ⲁⲣⲓⲟⲥ]   Mac[arius.]

2 In the plaster above the painting, to right of Macarius, in black:

[ⲁ]ⲃⲃⲁ ⲙⲁⲕⲁⲣ[ⲓⲟⲥ]   Abba Macar[ius.]

N35. MACROBIUS (?)[85]

1 To left and right of the saint. in white:

[ⲁ]ⲃⲃⲁ ⲙ[ⲁⲕⲣⲱⲡⲓⲟⲥ]   M[acrobius].

2 In the plaster above the painting, to right of the saint, in black:

[ⲙⲁⲕⲣⲱ]ⲡ[ⲓⲟⲥ]   [Macro]b[ius]

Because this saint's name begins with M and probably includes a p (=b), I conclude tentatively that this is one of the saints named Macrobius. Two of these are mentioned by O'Leary, one a monk and the other a martyr.[86]

Because all the other saints in this part of the nave are monastic figures, the monk Macrobius is more likely. He was a disciple of Moses of Abydos and founder of a monastery south of Asyut (Lycopolis).[87]

3 In the corner, to right of one of the two pillars flanking the saint, in white:

[ⲑ] / ⲥⲩⲛ / ⲧ̣ϫⲓϫ / ⲛⲁⲧⲁ / ⲕⲟⲡⲉⲥ / ϩⲁ[. .]ⲁ / ⲙⲟⲩ̣ⲛ ⲉ/ [ⲃ]ⲟⲗ ⲡ̣[ⲓ]/ [ⲉϥⲓⲏⲛ]/ ⲙⲣⲉϥⲉⲣ / ⲛⲟⲃⲉ ⲙ/ ⲡⲁⲣⲁ ⲟⲩ/ ⲟⲛ ⲛⲓⲙ/ ⲙ̣ⲡ̣ⲁⲧⲙ/ [ϣⲁ] ⲛ̣ⲣ̣ⲁⲛ / ϫⲉ ⲑⲉⲱ/ ⲇⲟⲣⲟⲥ / ⲡϣⲏⲣⲉ/ ⲛⲁⲃⲃⲁ / ⲅⲁⲃⲣⲓⲏⲗ / ⲡⲓⲉⲡⲓⲥ/ ⲕⲟⲡⲟⲥ / $\overset{\text{ⲗ}}{\text{ⲡⲓ}}$ ⲉⲧⲡⲉϩ ⲡⲉⲧⲛⲁ / ⲱϣ ⲙⲙ/ [ⲟⲥ] ⲉϥϫⲟ/ ϫⲉ ⲫϯ/ ⲕⲟ ⲛⲁ/ [ⲓ] ⲉ/ⲃⲟⲗ /ⲑ̣̅ϥ̅

With God. The hand of (one) not free from toil (?) under continual (?) . . . , the [poor], more sinful than anyone, unworthy of the name Theodore, the son of Abba Gabriel, the bishop (of the) city (of) (P)etpeh, who will cry out, saying, "God, forgive me. Amen (99)."

This is a "signature" inscription, made by the painter in charge of the wall paintings in the church, Theodore, the spiritual "son" of a bishop named Gabriel. The word translated "not free from toil" is here taken as a combination of the Coptic negative prefix ⲁⲧ- plus Greek ἄκοπος, free from trouble. For the restoration [poor] cf. the other signature inscription, s38.7. Theodore is apparently aware that his Greek name means "Gift of God." The town of Petpeh (Coptic ⲡⲉⲧⲡⲉϩ, Arabic Atfih or Itfih) was ancient Aphroditopolis, and in the thirteenth century it had numerous churches.[88]

N36. VIRGIN MARY AND CHRIST CHILD

1 To left and right of the Virgin, in white:

ⲙ̅ⲏ̅ⲣ̅	Mother
ⲑ̅ⲩ̅	of God.

2 In the plaster above the painting, in black:

ϩⲁⲅⲓⲁ ⲙⲁⲣⲓⲁ	Saint Mary.

N37. COPTIC ARCH INSCRIPTION[89]

1 On east wall, above the arch leading into the khurus, in white paint within a red band, with decorations:

ϩⲱⲥ ϩⲁⲛϣⲟⲩⲙⲉⲛⲣⲓⲧⲟⲩ ⲛⲉ ⲛⲉⲕⲙⲁⲛϣⲱⲡⲓ ⲡ̅ⲟ̅ⲥ̅ ⲫϯ ⲛⲧⲉ ⲛⲓϫⲟⲙ ⲧⲁⲯⲩⲭⲏ

How worthily beloved are your dwellings (O) Lord, God of the Powers. My soul . . . .

This is the first verse and part of the second of Psalm 83 (84). There was not room for the entire second verse, but it was probably assumed that the worshiper who could read could also supply the rest of the verse from memory.

Inscriptions in the Khurus

K3. MERCURIUS[90]

1 To left and right of Mercurius's head, in white:

ⲟⲩⲁⲅⲓⲟⲥ ⲙⲉⲣⲕⲟⲩⲣⲓⲟⲥ	Holy is Mercurius,
ⲇⲟⲛ ⲙ͞ⲣ ⲛⲓ̅ⲥ̅ ⲭ̅ⲥ̅	the martyr of Jesus Christ.

2 Below the angel at top right, in white:

ⲁⲅⲅⲉⲗⲟⲩ ⲕ̅ⲥ̅	Angel (of) the Lord.

The visit of an angel to Mercurius is part of his story.

3 Under Mercurius's horse, in white:

ⲡⲟⲩⲣⲟ ⲓⲟⲩⲗⲓⲁⲛⲟⲥ	The emperor Julian.

The death of Julian "the Apostate" is attributed to the miraculous intervention of St. Mercurius, many years after his martyrdom.

4 To left, above the small horse, in white:

ⲡⲓϩⲧⲟⲣ ⲛⲓⲟⲩⲗⲓⲁⲛⲟⲥ	Julian's horse.

5 Under Mercurius's horse's raised hoof a man, above whose head is, in white:

ϥⲉⲓⲣⲟ	. . .

The person in question is presumably Mercurius's grandfather, eaten by the two dog-faced cannibals. This inscription differs from the others in the shape and size of the letters, and the extant letters do not render anything intelligible in Coptic.

6 To left of the left dog-faced creature, in black:

ϩⲣⲟⲛϥⲟⲥ ⲡⲓϩⲟ ⲛⲟⲩϩⲟⲣ	Rufus, the dog-faced.

7 To right of the right dog-faced creature, in black:

ⲥⲱⲣⲕⲁⲛⲉ ⲡⲓϩⲟ ⲛⲟⲩϩⲟⲣ	Sorkane, the dog-faced.[91]

8 To the right, under the dome and above the two saints' heads, in white:

ⲡⲁⲥⲓⲗⲉⲟⲥ ⲅⲉⲣⲕⲟⲣⲓⲟⲥ	Basil (and) Gregory.

St. Basil (here with his brother Gregory) is associated with Mercurius in that he is reported to have had a vision crediting Mercurius with the death of Julian.[92]

κ4. COPTIC DEDICATORY INSCRIPTION[93]

1 In a separate panel, in white (fig. 14.5):

ⲠⳞⲤ ⲒⲤ ⲠⲬⲤ ⲤⲘⲞⲨ Ⲉ	Lord Jesus Christ, bless
ⲠⲈⲔⲂⲞⲔ ⲠⲠ ⲀⲠⲠⲀ	your servant, the priest
ⲘⲒⲆⲀⲎⲀ ⲚⲈⲘ ⲠⲈⳡ	Abba Michael, and his
ⲤⲞⲚ ⲠⲒⲀⲢⲬⲆⲒⲀⲔ ⲤⲀ	brother, the archdeacon
⁵ⲀⲓⲠ ⲚⲒϢⲎⲢⲒ ⲚⲠⲞⲨ	Salib, the sons of (A)bu
ⲄⲀⲖⲈⲠ ⲠⳞⲤ ⲤⲘⲞⲨ Ⲉ	Ghalib. Lord, bless them,
ⲢⲰⲞⲨ ⳫⲈ ⲚⲐⲰⲞⲨ ⲀⲨ	for they have
ⳡⲒ ⲪⲢⲰⲞⲨϢ ⲘⲠⲀ	provided for (the image of)
ⲄⲒⲞⲤ ⲘⲈⲢⲔⲞⲨⲢⲒⲞⲤ	the holy Mercurius.
¹⁰ⲠⳞⲤ † ⲚⲞⲞⲨ ⲚⲦⲞⲨϢⲈⲂⲒ	Lord, give them their recompense.
ⲀⲘⲎⲚ	Amen.

This is another dedicatory inscription, this one to honor the two donors of the Mercurius painting. They and their father, Abū Ghalib, are mentioned in the large dedicatory inscription in the nave (N31.2).

2 Under the panel, in white:

ϯ ⲢⳠⲐ   (The Era of the) Martyrs 949.

The date here given (= A.D. 1232/1233) supplies the missing numeral in that of N31.2.

κ5. ABRAHAM, ISAAC, AND JACOB IN PARADISE[94]

1 Above and to right of each of the patriarchs, left to right, in white:

ⲒⲀⲔⲞⲂ ⲒⲤⲀⲔ ⲀⲂ[ⲢⲀⲆⲀⲘ]   Jacob, Isaac, Ab[raham].

2 Their names are also inscribed on the sleeves of their raised hands, in white:

ⲒⲀⲔⲰⲂ ⲒⲤⲀⲔ ⲀⲂⲢⲀⲆⲀⲘ   Jacob, Isaac, Abraham.

3 The rich man in Hades appears to Abraham's right. Above his head, in black:

ⲚⲒⲚⲈⲞⲨⲈ   Nineve,
ⲠⲒⲀⲐⲚⲀⲒ   the unmerciful.

The rich man of Jesus' parable in Luke 16:19–31 is uniformly called Nineve in the Coptic tradition, beginning with the Coptic translations of the New Testament.[95]

4 Below him, in black:

ⲀⲘⲎⲚϯ   Amente.

Amente, an old Egyptian word for the underworld, is regularly used in Coptic literature for Hell or Hades.

5 To left of Nineve's upraised arm, in black:

ⲠⲒⲚⲞⲨⲚ   The abyss.

This is probably the "chasm" referred to in Luke 16:26.

κ6. THE THREE HEBREWS

There are no inscriptions preserved in this badly damaged painting. But part of κ7 belongs to this painting.

κ7. NEBUCHADNEZZAR[96]

1 To left and right of Nebuchadnezzar on his covered throne, in black:

ⲠⲞⲨⲢⲞ   The king
(Ⲛ)ⲀⲂⲞⲬⲞⲦⲞⲚⲈⲤⲤⲞⲢ   Nebuchadnezzar.

2 Above the lance bearers on either side, in black:

ⲠⲒⳡⲀⲒⲖⲞⲚⳬⲈ ⲠⲒⳡⲀⲒⲖⲞⲚⳬⲈ   The lance bearer. The lance bearer.

3 In panel below, left to right, in black:

ⲠⲒⳡⲀⲒⲖⲞⲚⳬⲈ   The lance bearer.
ⲚⲒⲔⲈⲚⲦⲈⲢⲒⲞⲤ   The centurions.
ⲠⲒⳡⲀⲒⲖⲞⲚⳬⲈ   The lance bearer.

The lower panel has no extant inscriptions. The entire scene is related to κ6, the story of the three Hebrew youths in the fiery furnace, in Daniel 3. But its position here next to St. George (κ8) may be because King Nebuchadnezzar is mentioned in connection with the miracles performed by George after his martyrdom in Tyre. In the encomium attributed to St. Theodosius of Jerusalem, Tyre is said to be the city of King Nebuchadnezzar.[97]

K8. ST. GEORGE[98]

1 To left and right of George, in white:

ⲟⲩⲁⲅⲓⲟⲥ ⲅⲉⲱⲣⲅⲓⲟⲥ   Holy is George,

ⲇⲟⲛ ⲫⲓ ⲛⲧⲉ ⲓ̄ⲥ̄ ⲭ̄ⲥ̄   the martyr of Jesus Christ.

Cf. N25.

2 To left and right of Euchius, in black:

ⲉⲩⲭⲓⲟⲥ   Euchius,

ⲡⲓⲙⲁⲧⲟⲓ ⲉ[ⲧ]ϩⲱⲟⲩ   the wicked soldier.

Euchius, the "wicked soldier" of Diocletian, is featured as a destroyer of churches in the story of the ninth posthumous miracle of St. George.[99]

3 On the roof of the church, in black:

. . . ⲉⲗⲁⲏⲛⲁ   . . . Helen.

Queen Helen, together with the emperor Constantine, her son, is featured in the encomium of Abba Theodotus as worshiping in the martyrium of St. George in Diospolis, here portrayed.[100] Before Helen we would expect ⲧⲉⲣⲱ, "the queen," but that does not match what is visible there in the inscription.

K9. MARTYRDOM OF GEORGE, AND PASICRATES[101]

1 In top panel, to left of George, in black:

ⲅⲉⲟⲣⲅⲓⲟⲥ   George

2 Above the figure to left of George, in black:

ⲡⲓϩⲏ[ⲡⲉⲣⲓⲧⲏⲥ]   The [servant].

3 Above the figure to right of George, in black:

ⲡⲓϩⲏⲡⲉⲣⲓⲧⲏⲥ   The servant.

4 In middle panel, to left of Pasicrates, in white:

ⲡⲁⲥⲓⲕⲣⲁⲧⲏⲥ [ⲉϥⲥ]ϩⲁⲓ   Pasicrates writing.

Pasicrates, George's servant, is credited with writing down the story of the martyrdom.

5 In bottom panel, between the two torturers, in black:

ⲛⲓⲕⲉⲥⲧⲉⲛⲛⲁⲣⲓⲟⲥ ⲉⲩϩⲓⲟⲩⲓ ⲉⲅⲉⲱⲣⲅⲓⲟⲥ   The torturers beating George.

The word translated "torturer" is a Copticized form of Latin *quaestionarius*, a Roman military officer whose duty is to extract information from an accused with the aid of torture. The Latin term occurs in a number of Latin martyrologies. In the Coptic form it is used several times in the Coptic martyrologies, including the *Martyrdom of George*.[102]

6 Above George, in black:

ⲅⲉⲱⲣⲅⲓ[ⲟⲥ]   George.

K12. THE THREE WOMEN AT THE TOMB[103]

1 Between the angel and the women:

ⲟⲩⲁⲅⲅⲉⲗⲟⲥ ⲛⲧⲉ ⲡⲟ̄ⲥ̄   An angel of the Lord.

The angel is that of Matthew 28:2.

K13. COPTIC INSCRIPTION[104]

1 On the south wall, at the base of the vaulted roof, in white paint outlined in red, within a blue band, with decorations:

ⲡⲟ̄ⲥ̄ ⲙⲉⲓ ⲛⲛⲓⲡⲩⲗ[ⲏ ⲛⲧⲉ ⲥ]ⲓⲱⲛ ⲉϩⲟⲧⲉ

The Lord loves the gates [of] Zion more than

This is the first part of the second verse of Psalm 86 (87).

K14. COPTIC INSCRIPTION[105]

1 On the west wall, above the arch leading into the nave, in white paint outlined in red, within a blue band, with decorations:

ⲛⲓⲙⲁⲛϣⲱⲡⲓ ⲛⲧⲉ ⲓⲁⲕⲱⲃ ⲁⲩⲥⲁϫⲓ ⲉⲑⲃⲏϯ ⲛϩⲁⲛϩⲃⲏⲟⲩⲓ

The dwellings of Jacob. Things have been spoken about you.

This is the continuation of Psalm 86 (87):2 plus the first part of verse 3. Cf. K13 and 17.

K15. ARCHANGEL MICHAEL[106]

1 Within the arch, south, to left and right of Michael, in white:

ⲟⲩⲁⲣⲭⲏⲁⲅⲅⲉⲗⲟⲥ   (The) archangel

ⲙⲏⲭⲁⲏⲗ   Michael.

2 Within the medallion in Michael's hand, in red:

ⲓ̄ⲥ̄ ⲟ̄ⲥ̄ ⲛ̄ⲓ ⲕ̄ⲁ̄   Jesus the Son (of God) is victorious.

This traditional sentence is completely in Greek: Ἰησοῦς υἱὸς νικᾷ. More frequently ⲭ̄ⲥ̄ "Christ" (Χριστός) appears instead of ⲟ̄ⲥ̄. Cf. s1.11, c3.12, a1.2.

K16. ARCHANGEL GABRIEL[107]

1 Within the arch, north, to left and right of Gabriel, in white:

ⲞⲨⲀⲢⲬⲎⲀⲄⲄⲈⲖⲞⲤ   (The) archangel
ⲄⲀⲂⲢⲓⲎⲖ   Gabriel.

2 Within the medallion in Gabriel's hand, in red:

ⲒⲤ ⲟ̄ⲥ ⲛ̄ⲓ ⲕ̄ⲁ   Jesus the Son (of God) is victorious.

Cf. K15.2 and note.

K17. COPTIC INSCRIPTION[108]

On the north wall, at the base of the vaulted roof, in white paint outlined in red, within a blue band, with decorations:

ⲚⲈⲩⲤⲉⲚ[ϯ ⲆⲉⲚ ⲚⲓⲦ]ⲱⲟ[ⲩ] ⲉⲑⲟⲩⲁⲃ ⲑⲉ
His foundations are [on the] holy [mountains].

This is the first verse of Psalm 86 (87).[109]

K18. CHRIST AND THE WOMEN IN THE GARDEN[110]

1 Above Mary, in white:

ⲙ̄ⲏⲣ ⲟ̄ⲩ   Mother of God.

2 To left of Christ, in white:

ⲓ̄ⲥ   Jesus.

Presumably, to the right of Jesus was X̄C̄, Christ. The appearance of the risen Christ to his mother is part of an ancient tradition in Eastern Christendom, based on an identification of "the other Mary" of Matthew 28:1 with the Virgin Mary.[111]

K21. ARABIC INSCRIPTION[112]

On the south wall of the ceiling, in white paint outlined in red, within a blue band, with decorations:

متفقه * لان هناك صعدت القبايل *
قبايلالرب شاهدا لاسرايل
تشكر *اسم الرب لانه [استوت (؟)]*
كراسي [كراسي] داود اسلوا السلامه

... agreeing. Because there risen the tribes, the tribes of the Lord, witnessing to Israel, to give thanks unto the name of the Lord. [For there are set (?)] thrones [of judgment, the thrones (?)] of David. Pray for the peace [of Jerusalem . . .]

The line starts with the last word of Psalm 121 (122) verse three. From the second word onward, this inscription renders verses four and five and the first half of verse six. This awkward situation seems to suggest that the inscription was executed by an artist who was unaware of its contents.

K45. ARABIC INSCRIPTION[113]

The colors and format of this inscription are the same as those on the south side (K21), except that the letters on this side are so poorly preserved as to make identification of the text impossible. Because in the southern inscriptions the Coptic and Arabic do not correspond (K17, K21), there seems to be no reason to presume that such would be the case in the northern inscription. At any rate, none of the words appearing in the accompanying Coptic version of Psalm 86 (87) can be identified in Arabic.

Inscriptions in the Sanctuary

S1. CHRIST IN MAJESTY AND THE VIRGIN MARY AND CHILD[114]

1 To left and right of Christ's head, in white:

ⲓ̄ⲏⲥ   Jesus
ⲭ̄ⲣⲥ   Christ

2 To left and right of his throne, in white:

ⲙⲙⲀⲚⲟⲩⲏⲖ   Emmanuel,
ⲡⲉⲚⲚⲟⲩϯ   our God

Emmanuel (Hebrew ʿimmanuʾel, "God is with us") is the name of the royal son prophesied by Isaiah (Is 7:14). In Christian tradition this name is applied to Jesus Christ.

3 Above Michael, to left of Christ, in white:

ⲀⲄⲄⲈⲖⲟⲤ ⲙⲓⲭⲀ[ⲏⲖ]   (The) angel Micha[el].

4 Above Gabriel, to right of Christ, in white:

ⲀⲄⲄⲈⲖⲟⲤ ⲄⲀⲂⲢⲓⲎⲖ   (The) angel Gabriel.

5 Above the sun and the moon, left and right of Christ, in white:

[ⲡⲓⲣⲏ]   [The sun.]
ⲡⲓⲟⲏ   The moon.

6 Beside the four living creatures, top left, top right, bottom left, bottom right, in white:

ⲡⲓⲚⲟ ⲚⲢⲱⲙⲓ   The human-faced.
[ⲡⲓⲚⲱ] ⲚⲀ[Ⲛⲱⲙ]   [The eagle-faced.]
ⲡⲓⲚⲱ [Ⲛ]ⲙⲟⲩⲓ   The lion-faced.
ⲡⲓⲚⲱ ⲚⲙⲀⲤⲓ   The ox-faced.

The four living creatures are those of John's vision in Revelation 4:6–7. Cf. Ezekiel 1:10. They play an important role in Coptic tradition.[115]

7 On the footstool under Christ's feet, within a red band in white:

ϩΙΠΠΕ ΤϤΕ ΠΕ ΠΑΘΡΟΝΟC ΠΚΑϨΙ ΠΕ ΠΙΜ[Α ΝC]ΕΜΕ

Behold, heaven is my throne, (and) the earth is the (foot-)stool.

Isaiah 66:1. There was not room for ΝΤΕ ΝΑϬΑΛⲍ ("of my feet") at the end, which would complete the phrase translated as "my foot-stool." Cf. C2.5.

8 To left and right of the Virgin's head, in red:

ΜΗ̅Ρ̅   Mother
Θ̅Υ̅   of God.

9 To left and right of the Virgin's throne, in red:

ϯΠΑΡΘΗΝΟC   The Virgin
Μ[Α]Ρ[ΙΑ]   M[a]r[y].

10 Above Michael, to the Virgin's left, in white:

[ΟΥΑΡ]ΧΗΑΓΓΕΛΟC ΜΙΧΑΗΛ   [(The)] archangel Michael.

11 Within the medallion in Michael's hand, in white:

Ι̅C̅ Χ̅C̅ Ν̅Ι̅ Κ̅Α̅   Jesus Christ is victorious.
Cf. K15.2 and note.

12 Above Gabriel, to the Virgin's right, in white:

ΟΥΑΡΧΗΑΓΓΕ[ΛΟC ΓΑΒΡΙΗΛ]   (The) archangel [Gabriel].

13 Within the medallion in Gabriel's hand, in red:

Ι̅[C̅] [Χ̅C̅] Ν̅Ι̅ Κ̅Α̅   Jesus Christ is victorious.

14 At the base of the apse, beneath the Virgin, within a blue-gray band, in white:

ϨΕΝ ϤΡΑΝ ΝΙΘΡΙΑC Ε[ΘΟΥ]ΑΒ ΑΜΗΝ ΑϤϢⲰΠΙ
ΝϪΕ ΠΑΙϢΙΝΗΡϤΜΕΟΥΙ ΕΒΟΛ ϨΙΤΟΤϤ ΜΙΑΡΧ . . . Ε
[. . .] . . . ΠΟⲖ ϤΑϨΡΙ Α . . . . ΝΙ . . . . ΙϨ

In the name of the [Holy] Trinity, amen. This memorial happened through (the beneficence of) . . . (A)bu l-Fakhry . . . .

This is another dedicatory inscription, commemorating the donors who contributed to the paintings in the apse of the sanctuary. There was not room for the full invocation; so "Holy Trinity" is used instead. Literally, the text reads "Holy Trinities" (with the plural definite article), but the inscriber intended to invoke the three persons of the Trinity. Cf. N31.2 and commentary.

S2. ATHANASIUS[116]

1 To left and right of Athanasius, in white:

ⲀΒΒⲀ ⲀΘⲀΝⲀCΙΟC ΠΙⲀΠΟCΤΟ
ⲖΙΚΟC ΠⲀΤΡΙⲀΡΧ(ΗC) Ν̅ ⲀⲖΗΚCⲀΜΘΡΙⲀ

Abba Athanasius, the apostolic patriarch (of the) city (of) Alexandria.

S3. SEVERUS[117]

1 To left and right of Severus, in white:

ⲀΒΒⲀ CΥΟΥΙΡΟC   Abba Severus,
ΠΙΝΙϢϯ ΜΠⲀΤΡΙⲀΡΧΗC   the great patriarch.

S4. DIOSCORUS[118]

1 To left and right of Dioscorus, in white:

ⲀΒΒ(Ⲁ) ϯⲰCΚΟΡΟC ΠⲀΤΡΙⲀΡΧΗC
ΝΤΕ ϯ Ν̅ ΡⲀΚΟϯ

Abba Dioscorus, patriarch of the city (of) Alexandria.

Rakote (Bohairic Rakoti, as here) is the usual name in Coptic sources for Alexandria. It is the name of a village on the site of the new city of Alexandria founded by Alexander the Great (fourth century B.C.), and also the name given to the native Egyptian district of the new city.

S5. THEOPHILUS[119]

1 To left and right of Theophilus, in white:

ⲀΒΒⲀ ΘΕⲰΦΙⲀΛΟC   Abba Theophilus,
ΠΙ[Π]Ⲁ[ΤΡΙⲀΡΧΗC] ΝΤ[Ε   the [patriarch] of [Alexandria].

Very faint letter traces appear where one would expect the name of the city, Alexandria.

2 In red band, above and to left of Theophilus, in white:

[ΘΕⲰΦΙ]ⲖⲀ[ΟC]   [Theophilus.]

S6. PETER[120]

1 To left of Peter, in white:

[ⲀΒΒⲀ] Π[ΕΤ]Ρ[Ο]C [?]ⲍ[?   [Abba Peter] . . . .

There is nothing left of the inscription on Peter's right, except a red tracing of the monogram for "city." That inscription identifies him as a patriarch of Alexandria. Coquin and Laferrière were able to see the last three letters of "Alexandria." This saint is probably Peter I, "the seal of the martyrs" (d. 311) and seventeenth patriarch.

2 In red band, above and to left of Peter, in white:

ΠΕΤΡΟC   Peter

S7. BENJAMIN (?)[121]

1 To left and right of the saint, in white:

ⲁⲃⲃⲁ ⲃ.[Abba B.[?],

[ⲡⲓ]ⲡⲁⲧⲣⲓⲭⲁⲣ ⲡⲁⲗⲏⲕⲥⲁⲛⲑⲣ[ⲓ]ⲁ

patriarch of Alexandria.

Coquin and Laferrière read ⲁⲃⲃⲁ ⲃ[ ]ⲣⲱⲁ, and suggest St. Cyril as a possibility.[122] Van Moorsel read: ⲃⲁ::ⲏⲁⲥ, and argued against Cyril, leaving the identity open.[123] There is now nothing visible after the initial ⲃ of the name, except something that looks like a ⲫ. The only Alexandrian patriarch through the seventh century whose name starts with a ⲃ is Benjamin, thirty-eighth patriarch (seventh century). The only other patriarch from that period whose name has a *b* in it at all is Abilius, a shadowy figure from the first century, third in succession after Mark and Anianus. The identity of this saint is truly a puzzle, in view of the conflicting epigraphic evidence.

2 In red band, above and to left of the saint, in white:

..[.....]ⲛ   ...

If, indeed, the saint's name begins with *B* and ends with *n*, he could only be Benjamin.[124]

S9. ANONYMOUS PATRIARCH

1 To right of the saint's head, in white:

[?]ⲕⲁⲧ.[?]ⲙ[?] ⲟ̄ⲓ [?]ⲑⲟⲛ[?]   ... city (of) ...

This saint's name would have appeared to his left. No trace remains of that inscription. Whoever this is, he is probably a patriarch.

S11. MARK[125]

1 To left and right of Mark, in white:

ⲟⲩⲁⲅⲓⲟⲥ ⲙⲁⲣⲕⲟⲥ

ⲁⲡⲟⲥⲧⲟⲗⲟⲩ ⲕ̄ ⲟⲩⲁⲅⲅⲉⲗⲓⲥⲧⲟⲩ ⳾

Holy is Mark, apostle and evangelist, martyr.

S12. CHRIST PANTOCRATOR[126]

1 To left and right of the Pantocrator (universal ruler) at the top of the dome, in red:

ⲓ̄ⲏ̄ⲥ̄ ⲭ̄ⲣ̄ⲥ̄   Jesus Christ.

2 At the base of the dome, below the angels and cherubim, an inscription of 360 degrees, presumably beginning and ending at the easternmost point, within a blue band in white.

[±6] ⲕ. .[. . .].[. . .]ⲱ[. . . .].[. .]ⲛ⳾. . . . . ⲛⲧⲉ ⲥⲟⲙⲑⲉ[. . .] ⲧ̇. .ⲛⲱ̇ⲟⲓ̇ⲏ [.].ⲟⲩ ⲛⲧⲉⲡ[. . . . .]. . .ⲛⲟ̣ⲛ̣. ⲁⲓⲱⲉⲑⲃⲉ[.]ⲱ⳾ⲁⲛ ⲛⲧⲉ ⲡⲉⲛⲛⲟⲩ⳾ ⲍⲉ ⲛⲑⲟ ⲡⲉⲧⲉⲣⲉ ⲡ̇ⲛ.[. . . .].[. .]ⲛⲏⲧⲛ ⲟⲩⲟⲧⲩⲛⲟⲩ ⲛϩⲏⲧ⳾ ⲁⲁⲁ̣ⲏ.[. . . .] ⲁⲙ[ⲏⲛ . . . . .]

[. . .] . . . of . . . of our God, for you (fem. sg.) are the one whom . . . to you (pl.) joy in you (fem. sg.) . . . amen (?) [. . .]

This is presumably a biblical or liturgical verse, so far unidentified.

S13, S15, S17, S19. CHERUBIM[127]

1–4 Attributed to each of the four cherubim, in white:

ⲁⲅⲓⲟⲥ ⲁⲅⲓⲟⲥ ⲁⲅⲓⲟⲥ   Holy, holy, holy.

This is the Trisagion, the song of the Seraphim in Isaiah's vision, Isaiah 6:1–3.

S14, S16, S18, S20. ANGELS

1–4 Attributed to each of the four angels, in white:

ⲟⲩⲱⲟⲩ ⲫ⳾ ϧⲉⲛ ⲛⲏ ⲉⲧϭⲱⲥⲓ

Glory (to) God in the highest.

This is the song of the angels celebrating the birth of Jesus, Luke 2:14. It is also the opening passage of a more extended hymn used in Christian liturgy, "the Hymn of the Angels." Cf. C3.1, C10.1.

S25. ANGEL

1 To right of the angel, in black:

ⲁⲅⲅⲉⲗⲟⲥ   Angel.

2 At the angel's feet, in black:

.[. . .]. . ⲛⲧⲉ ⲟⲩ. . . .ⲱ. . .ⲙⲡⲟ̄ⲥ̄.   .. of ... of the Lord.

There were presumably other inscriptions accompanying the other angels (s21–s24, s26–s28), but they are lost.

S33–S36. THE TWENTY-FOUR ELDERS OF THE APOCALYPSE

1 To left of each of the elders, in white:

s33 (east wall):	ⲁ̄ ⲃ̄ ⲅ̄ ⲇ̄
s34 (south wall):	ⲉ̄ ⲍ̄ ⲏ̄ ⲑ̄ ⲕ̄ ⲗ̄
s35 (west wall):	ⲙ̄ ⲛ̄ ⲝ̄ ⲟ̄ ⲡ̄ ⲣ̄
s36 (north wall):	ⲥ̄ ⲧ̄ ⲩ̄ ⲫ̄ ⲭ̄ ⲯ̄ ⲱ̄

These are the twenty-four letters of the Greek alphabet, here marked as numerals. The twenty-four elders, seated on twenty-four thrones, are part of John's vision in Revelation 4:4. In Coptic tradition these elders are given names, each beginning with one of the letters of the Greek alphabet, from ⲁⲍⲁⲏⲁ to ⲱⲇⲓⲑⲓⲏⲁ.[128]

S33–S36. COPTIC INSCRIPTION[129]

2 In a continuous band, separating the twenty-four elders from the lower part of the four walls of the sanctuary, the remains of a single inscription beginning with the east wall, and continuing on the south, west, and north walls, within a blue band in white:

[33].[. .].ⲟ ⲁϥϣⲱⲡⲓ ⲛⲋ̅[ⲉ ⲡⲁⲓ]ϣⲉⲛⲉ[ⲣⲫⲙⲉⲟⲩⲓ . . . .
.]ⲏ ⲉⲃⲟⲗ ϧⲓⲧⲟ[ⲧϥ±13] / [34]ⲧⲁⲓⲥⲩⲧⲙⲟⲩⲛⲁⲭⲟⲥ ⲡⲓⲇⲓ-
ⲁⲕⲟⲛ ⲅⲁⲃⲣⲓⲏⲗ ⲡⲟϥ ⲏⲣⲏϥ[. .].[.]. .[±22] / [35]ⲑⲣ[. .
.].ⲉⲗⲓⲧⲏ[. .]ⲇ ⲛⲧⲁⲃ[ⲣⲓⲏⲗ].[.]. ϥⲁⲧⲗⲉⲁ ⲛ̅[ⲉⲙ
ⲓ]ⲱϧⲁⲛⲛⲏ ⲛⲉⲙ ⲛⲉϥ. .[. . . .]. ⲛⲉϥⲥⲛⲏⲟⲩ ⲡⲟⲩⲥⲁ /
[36]ⲓⲇ ⲛⲉⲙ ⲡⲟⲩⲋ̅. .]ⲣⲉⲩ[. .]ⲉⲙ ⲡ̅ⲟ̅ⲥ̅ ⲥⲙⲟⲩ ⲉⲣⲱⲟⲟ[ⲩ]
.[. . .]ⲉⲧⲣⲟⲓⲥⲧⲟⲥ ⲛⲋ̅ⲉ ⲡ̅ⲡ̅ ⲡⲉⲧⲣⲟⲥ ⲛⲉⲙ ⲙⲓⲭⲁⲏⲗ
ⲛⲉⲙ ⲡ̅ⲡ̅ ⲉ.ⲃ. . .

[33] . . . [This memorial] happened [. . .] through (the beneficence of) [. . . of] / [34] this monastery (?), the deacon Gabriel (A)bu I- . . . [. . .] / [35] . . . Gab[riel] . . . Fadlel [and] John and his . . . his brothers (A)bu Sa / [36] id and (A)bu . . . . Lord, bless them . . . . , that is, the priest Peter and Michael and the priest . . . .

This is another dedicatory inscription. John and the priests Peter and Michael are probably those persons mentioned in the dedicatory inscription in the nave (N31.2). After "Lord, bless them," the extant material looks like the top of a decorative stop. The puzzling prefix ⲥⲩⲧ in the word here translated "monastery" is possibly to be construed as a contraction of something like Greek συντυχία, association, here an "association of monks," hence a monastery.

S38. THE SACRIFICE OF ISAAC[130]

1 Above left, between the finger and Abraham's head, in white:

ⲧ̅ⲥⲙⲏ   The voice.

The voice is that of God ("the angel of the lord") intervening in the intended sacrifice. See Genesis 22:1–14, esp. 11–12.

2 To left and right of the tree, in white:

ⲡⲓϣⲏⲛ ⲛⲧⲉ ⲙⲁⲙ[ⲣⲉ]   The tree of Mamre.
ⲡⲓϣⲏⲛ ⲛⲧⲉ ⲙⲁⲙⲣⲉ   The tree of Mamre.

3 To left of the ram, in white:

ⲡⲓⲱⲓⲗⲓ ⲉϥⲥⲟⲛϧ   The ram bound.

4 To right of Abraham's head, in white:

ⲙⲉϥⲟⲩⲱϣ ⲉϧⲱϧⲅ[ⲉ]ⲗ ⲛ[ⲓ]ⲥⲁⲕ [±6].
He does not wish to kill Isaac [. . .]

5 Between Isaac and the knife, in white:

ⲓⲥⲁⲕ   Isaac.

6 To right of Isaac, in white:

[?]ⲥⲛⲁⲉⲓⲁⲑⲙⲟⲛ   . . .

7 Below the ram:

ⲑ / ⲥⲩⲛ / ⲁⲣⲓ ⲡⲙⲉⲩⲉ ⲡ̅ⲟ̅ⲥ̅ ⲙ̅ⲡⲉⲕϧⲉⲙ / ϧⲁⲗ
ⲡⲓⲥⲃⲟⲩⲓ ⲛϧⲟⲅⲣⲁⲫⲟⲥ / [5]ⲡⲓⲉϥⲓⲏⲛ ⲡⲓⲁⲧⲉⲙϣⲁ
ⲙ̅ⲡⲓⲣⲁⲛ / ⲋ̅ⲉ ⲑⲉⲱ / ⲇⲟⲣⲟⲥ ⲡϣⲏⲣⲓ ⲛ̅ / ⲁⲃⲃⲁ ⲅⲁⲃⲣ
ⲓ / ⲏⲗ ⲡⲉⲡⲓⲥ [10]ⲕⲟⲡⲟⲥ ⲛ̅/ ⲙ̅ⲧ̅ / ⲉⲧ / ⲡⲉϧ

With God. Remember, O Lord, your servant, the apprentice painter, the poor, unworthy of the name Theodore, the son of Abba Gabriel, the bishop of the city (of) (P)etpeh.

This is another signature provided by the painter, Theodore. Cf. N35.3 and note. The Christ monogram appears at the left.

S39. THE SACRIFICE OF JEPHTHAH'S DAUGHTER

1 To left of Jephthah, in white:

[?]ⲧ.ⲁ[. . . .].[?]   . . .
ϣⲉⲣⲓ [ⲛⲧⲉ ⲓⲁ]ⲫⲑⲉ[ⲁ ?]   daughter [of Jephthah
[±8]ⲥⲓⲁ   . . .
[. . . . .].[. . .]ⲡ[?]   . . .

Perhaps read in the third line ⲟⲩ]ⲥⲓⲁ, "sacrifice." On Jephthah's vow and the sacrifice of his daughter see Judges 11:29–40.

2 At top right, in white:

]ⲋ̅ⲣⲟ[   ] victorious (?) [

Jephthah's victory over the Ammonites is recorded in Judges 11:32–33.

3 To right of Jephthah's daughter, in white:

ⲧϣⲉ[ⲣⲓ] ⲛ[ⲓ]ⲁⲫ]ⲑⲁ   The daughter of Jephthah.

4 To right of altar, faint letter traces, illegible.

S40. ANGEL

1 To right of the angel, in white:

ⲁⲅⲅⲉⲗⲟⲩ ⲕ̅ⲉ̅   (An) angel (of) the Lord.

S41. ANGEL

1 To right of the angel, in white:

ⲀⲄⲄⲉⲗⲟⲩ ⲕⲥ̄   (An) angel (of) the Lord.

S42. ISAIAH AND THE BURNING COAL[131]

1 To left of Isaiah, in white:

ⲎⲤⲀⲒⲀⲤ ⲠⲒⲠⲢⲟⲫⲎⲦⲎⲤ   Isaiah the prophet.

2 Between Isaiah and the seraph, in white:

[? ⳓⲙ]ⲟⲙ ⲁϥϯ ⲛ̄ϫⲉⲃⲥ ⲛ̄ⲎⲤⲀⲒⲀⲤ
He is giving the [burning?] coal to Isaiah.

This refers to the action of one of the winged seraphim in the account of the call of Isaiah, Isaiah 6:6–7.

3 To right of seraph, in white:

[?] ⲀⲎ.ⲁ[?]ⲧⲉ[?]ⲛ [?] . .   . . .

4 On the altar in the middle of the wall, in white:

ⲠⲘⲀⲚⲉⲢϢⲱⲧⲩϢ[Ⲓ]   The altar.

The word translated "altar" means literally "place of sacrifice." The altar is presumably the one referred to in Isaiah 6:6. Farther down on the altar is a cross.

S43. MELCHIZEDEK[132]

1 Between the altar and Melchizedek, in white:

ⲠⲒⲞⲨⲎⲂ ⲚⲦⲉ ⲘⲉⲀⲬⲒ[Ⲥ]ⲎⲦⲉⲕ ⲠⲞⲨ[Ⲣ]Ⲟ [ⲚⲦⲉ Ⲥ]ⲁ[ⲗ]ⲉⲙ
The priest Melchizedek, the king [of Salem].

The first ⲚⲦⲉ ("of") was written in error, unless the inscriber meant to add "God Most High." The story of Abraham's encounter with Melchizedek is found in Genesis 14:17–20. There Melchizedek is called "priest of God Most High" and "king of Salem" (Gn 14:18).

2 To left of Melchizedek's head, in white:

ⲘⲉⲀⲬ[ⲒⲤ]ⲉ[Ⲧⲉⲕ]   Melchizedek.

3 Above Abraham's head, in white:

ⲀⲂⲢⲀⲀⲘ [ⲁ]ϥϫⲓ ⲤⲘⲞⲨ ϩⲓⲦ[Ⲟ]Ⲧϥ ⲘⲉⲀⲬⲒⳓⲉⲦⲉⲕ
Abraham is receiving (a) blessing from Melchizedek.

One can also restore [ⲉ]ϥϫⲓ, "receiving" (without "is," a circumstantial form of the verb). The blessing is recorded in Genesis 14:19–20. Here it is associated with the wine (Gn 14:18) in the chalice from which Abraham is drinking.

S45. JEREMIAH[133]

1 To left and right of Jeremiah, in white:

ⲒⲉⲢⲉⲘⲒⲀⲤ   Jeremiah
ⲠⲢⲞⲫⲎⲦⲎⲤ   (the) prophet.

2 In the scroll in Jeremiah's hand, in black:

ϯⲠⲢⲞⲫⲎⲦ[ⲁ] ⲚⲒⲉ[Ⲣ]ⲉⲘ[Ⲓ]ⲁ[Ⲥ]
The prophecy of Jeremiah.

S46. ELIJAH[134]

1 To left and right of Elijah, in white:

[Ⲏⲗⲓⲁⲥ]   [Elijah]
ⲠⲢⲞⲫⲎⲦⲎⲤ   (the) prophet.

2 In the scroll in Elijah's hand, in black:

ⲠⲢⲞⲫⲎⲦⲁ ⲚⲎⲗⲓⲀⲤ ⲠⲢⲞⲫⲎⲦⲎⲤ
(The) prophecy of Elijah (the) prophet.

Elijah (1 Kgs 17:1–2 Kgs 2:12) was one of Israel's non-literary prophets (9th c. B.C.).

S47. ISAIAH[135]

1 To left and right of Isaiah, in white:

ⲠⲢⲞⲫⲎⲦⲎⲤ   (The) prophet
ⲎⲤⲀⲒⲀⲤ   Isaiah.

2 In the scroll in Isaiah's hand, in black:

ⲠⲢⲞⲫⲎⲦⲁ ⲎⲤⲀⲒⲀⲤ   (The) prophecy (of) Isaiah.

S48. MOSES[136]

1 To left and right of Moses, in white:

ⲘⲰⲨⲤⲎⲤ   Moses
ⲠⲢⲞⲫⲎⲦⲎⲤ   (the) prophet.

2 In the scroll in Moses' hand, in black:

ϯⲠⲢⲞⲫⲎⲆⲒⲀ ⲘⲰⲨⲤⲎⲤ   The prophecy (of) Moses.

The five books of Torah, traditionally ascribed to Moses, are here taken as a single scroll of "prophecy." Moses is called a prophet in Deuteronomy 34:10.

S49. DAVID[137]

1 To left and right of David, in white:

ⲆⲀⲨⲒⲆ   David
ⲠⲒⲉⲢⲞⲨ̄ⲯⲁⲗⲦⲎⲤ   the singer of psalms.

2 In the scroll in David's hand, in black:

ⲡⲣⲟⲫⲏⲧⲁ ⲇⲁⲩⲓⲇ ⲡⲓⲉⲣⲟⲩⲯⲁⲗⲧⲏⲥ

(The) prophecy of David the singer of psalms.

David is called a prophet in Acts 2:30.

S50. DANIEL[138]

1 To left and right of Daniel, in white:

ⲇⲁⲛⲓⲏⲗ   Daniel
ⲡⲣⲟⲫⲏⲧⲏⲥ   (the) prophet.

2 In the scroll in Daniel's hand, in black:

†ⲡⲣⲟⲫⲏⲧⲁ ⲛⲇⲁⲛⲓⲏⲗ   The prophecy of Daniel.

Inscriptions in the Deesis Chapel

C1. NICHE OF THE PRECIOUS CROSS[139]

1 To left and right of the top of the cross, in black:

ⲓⲏⲥ   Jesus

ⲡⲭⲥ   the Christ.

2 Just below, to left and right of the cross, in white:

ϩⲩⲗⲱⲛ   Tree

ϫⲱⲏⲥ   of life.

3 To far left and far right, written vertically in white:

†ⲙⲓⲟⲩ   (The) precious

ⲥⲧⲁⲩⲣⲟⲩ   cross.

4, 5 To right of the censing angel on the left, and to left of the censing angel on the right (twice), in white:

ⲁⲅⲅⲉⲗⲟⲩ ⲕⲉ   (An) angel (of) the Lord.

C2. CHRIST IN MAJESTY[140]

1, 2 Above each of the two upper angels holding the mandorla in which Christ is seated, in white:

ⲁⲅⲅⲉⲗⲟⲩ ⲕⲉ   (An) angel (of) the Lord.

3 To left and right of Christ's head, in white:

ⲓⲥ   Jesus

ⲭⲥ   Christ

4 To left and right of Christ's throne, in white:

ⲙ̇ⲙⲁⲛⲟⲩⲏⲗ   Emmanuel

ⲡⲉⲛⲛⲟⲩ†   our God.

Cf. s1.2 and note.

5 Within and below the red band at Christ's feet, in white:

ⲓⲥ ϩⲓⲡⲡⲉ ⲧⲫⲉ ⲡⲉ ⲡⲁⲑⲣⲟⲛⲟⲥ ⲡⲕⲁϩⲓ ⲡⲉ ⲡⲙⲁ /
ⲙⲭⲏⲙⲛⲓ ⲛⲧⲉ ⲛⲁϭⲁⲗⲍ

Behold, the heaven is my throne, the earth is my foot-stool.

Isaiah 66:1. Cf. s1.7.

6 Below that, in white:

ⲡ̄ⲟ̄ⲥ̄ ⲓⲥ ⲡⲭⲥ ⲛⲁⲓ ⲛⲏⲓ   Lord Jesus Christ, have pity on me.

This is undoubtedly a prayer by the painter on his own behalf. Cf. Theodore's signature inscriptions, N35.3 and s38.7.

7 Below the mandorla framing Christ, in black:

ⲡ̄ⲟ̄ⲥ̄ ⲓⲥ ⲡⲛⲟⲩⲧⲉ ⲙⲡⲓⲛⲁⲉ ⲛⲁⲛⲉ ⲙⲧⲉⲯⲩⲭⲏ
ⲛⲛⲉⲕϩⲉⲙϩⲉⲗ

Lord Jesus, God of mercy, (you are) good to the soul(s) of your servants.

8 Faintly visible to left of the lower left angel holding the mandorla, in white:

ⲁⲅ[ⲅ]ⲉⲗⲟⲩ ⲕ[ⲉ]   (An) angel (of) the Lord.

There was probably a similar inscription accompanying the lower angel on the right, but no trace of it remains.

C3. TWO LIVING CREATURES (EAGLE AND OX) AND JOHN THE BAPTIST[141]

1 Under the lower right-hand angel holding the mandorla, in black:

ⲛⲉⲙ ⲟⲩⲇⲓⲙⲁ† ϧⲉⲛ ⲛⲓⲣⲱⲙⲓ ⲧⲉⲛϩⲟⲥ ⲉ̇ⲣⲟⲕ
ⲧⲉⲛⲥⲙⲟⲩ ⲉ̇ⲣⲟⲕ

and good will among people. We sing to you, we praise you.

This is a continuation of the opening part of the "Hymn of the Angels," sung in the Coptic liturgy. Cf. c10.1.

2 To lower left of the ox-headed creature, in black:

ⲭⲟⲩⲁⲃ ⲭⲟⲩⲁⲃ ⲭⲟⲩⲁⲃ ⲡ̄ⲟ̄ⲥ̄ ⲡⲛⲟⲩⲧⲉ ϣⲁ̇ⲓ ⲉ̇ⲛⲉϩ
ⲛⲓⲛⲉϩ ⲁ̇ⲙⲏⲛ

Holy, holy, holy are you, O Lord God, for ever and ever, amen.

Cf. Isaiah 6:3.

3 Between the two creatures, below, in black:

ⲁ̇ⲅⲓⲟⲥ ⲁ̇ⲅⲓⲟⲥ ⲁ̇ⲅⲓⲟⲥ   Holy, holy, holy.

The Trisagion (Is 6:3) in Greek. This hymn is attributed to the four living creatures in Revelation 4:8.

4 Above the moon, on either side, in white:

ⲡⲓⲟ︤ϩ The moon.

5 Below the moon, between the two living creatures, in white:

ⲡⲓⲇ̄ ⲛ̄ⲍⲱⲟⲛ ⲉⲛⲁⲥⲱⲙⲁⲧⲟⲥ The 4 bodiless living creatures.

See s1.6 and note.

6 Below that, accompanying the eagle-headed creature, in white:

ⲡⲓⲍⲱⲟⲛ ⲛ̄ϩⲟ ⲛⲁⲓⲉⲧⲟⲥ The eagle-headed creature.

7 To left of the ox-headed creature, in white:

ⲡⲓⲍⲱⲟⲛ ⲛ̄ϩⲟ ⲙⲁⲥⲓ The ox-headed creature.

8 To left of John, in white:

ⲁⲅⲓⲟⲥ ⲓ̄ⲱ̄ Saint John.

The ⲁ is contained within a circle.

9 To right of John, in white:

ⲃⲁⲡⲧⲏⲥⲧⲟⲩ ϩⲟ[ⲛ] ⲫⲓ ⲇⲟⲛ ⲡⲣⲟ[ⲇⲣ]ⲟ̣[ⲙⲟⲩ ⲡⲣⲟⲫ]ⲏⲧⲟⲩ

(The) Baptist, the martyr, the [forerunner (and) prophet].

John is regularly referred to as "prophet and forerunner, Baptist and martyr" in litanies of the Coptic liturgy.[142]

10 To lower left of John, in black:

ⲓⲥ ⲡⲓϩⲓⲉⲃ ⲛ̄ⲧⲉ ⲫϯ ⲫⲏ ⲉⲧⲟⲗⲓ ⲛ̄ⲛⲉⲛⲟⲃⲓ ⲛ̄ⲙ̄ⲡⲓⲕⲟⲥⲙⲟⲥ
Behold the lamb of God who takes away the sins of the world.

This is John the Baptist's reference to Jesus in John 1:29, the source of the Agnus Dei in Christian liturgy.

11 Below the painting, to left and right of the wreathed cross, in black:

ϯⲙⲓⲟⲩ ⲥⲧⲁⲩⲣⲟⲩ (The) precious cross.

12 Within the wreathed cross, in black:

ⲓ̄ⲥ̄ ⲭ̄ⲥ̄ ⲛ̄ⲓ̄ ⲭ̄ⲁ̄ Jesus Christ is victorious.

Cf. k15.2 and note.

C5. BARTHOLOMEW AND THADDEUS (?)

1 To left and right of the figure in the left roundel, in black:

ⲃⲁⲣ[ⲑⲟⲗ]ⲟ[ⲙ]ⲉ̣ⲟ̣[ⲥ] Bar[thol]omew.

2 To left (and right) of the figure in the right roundel, letter traces in black

ⲑⲁⲇ[ⲉⲟⲥ] Thadd[eus.]

3 In the plaster to left of the border, letter traces in black:

?]. .[. . .

ⲑⲁⲇⲉⲟⲥ Thaddeus (?)

The upper inscription can possibly be restored to read [ⲃⲁⲣⲑⲟⲗⲟ]ⲙⲉ̣[ⲟⲥ], "Bartholomew." On the function of inscriptions in the plaster outside of the panels see note to n30.2.

C7. CHRIST IN MAJESTY

1 To left and right of Christ's head, in white:

[ⲓⲥ] [Jesus]

ⲭⲥ Christ.

C8. THE APOSTLES PAUL (?) AND PETER

1 To right of the figure in the left roundel, in black, unreadable letter traces.
This figure is probably Paul.[143]

2 To left of the figure in the right roundel, in black:

ⲡⲉ[ⲧ]ⲣⲟ[ⲥ] Pe[ter.]

C10. TWO LIVING CREATURES (MAN AND LION) AND THE VIRGIN MARY[144]

1 Under the lower left-hand angel holding the mandorla, in black:

ϫⲉ ⲟⲩⲱⲟⲩ ⲫϯ ϧⲉⲛ ⲛⲓⲉⲧϭⲟⲥⲓ ⲛⲉⲙ ⲟⲩϩⲓⲣⲏⲛⲓ ϩⲓϫⲉⲛ ⲡⲓⲕⲁϩⲓ

Saying, "Glory (to) God in the heights and peace upon the earth."

This is the opening part of the "Hymn of the Angels," continued on the other side. Cf. c3.1 and note.

2 To left of the angel, in black:

ⲭⲟⲩⲁⲃ ⲭⲟⲩⲁⲃ ⲭⲟⲩⲁⲃ ⲡ︤ⲟ︥ⲥ︦ ⲡⲛⲟⲩⲧⲉ ⲧⲫⲉ ⲛⲉⲙ ⲡⲕⲁϩⲓ ⲙⲉϩ ⲉⲃⲟⲗ ϧⲉⲛ ⲡⲉⲕⲱⲟⲩ ⲉⲑ︦ⲟ︦ ⲁⲙⲏⲛ

Holy, holy, holy are you, O Lord God. Heaven and earth are full of your holy glory, amen.

Isaiah 6:3. Cf. c3.2 and note.

3 Between the two creatures, below, in black:

ⲀⲄⲒⲟⲤ ⲀⲄⲒⲟⲤ ⲀⲄⲒⲟⲤ   Holy, holy, holy.

Cf. c3.3 and note.

4 Above the sun, on either side, in white:

ⲠⲒⲢⲎ   The sun.

5 Below the sun, between the two living creatures, in white:

ⲠⲒⲆ ⲚⲌⲱⲟⲚ ⲈⲚⲀⲤⲱⲘⲀⲦⲟⲤ   The 4 bodiless living creatures.

6 Below that, accompanying the human-faced creature, in white:

ⲠⲒⲌⲱⲟⲚ ⲚⲠⲟ ⲚⲢⲱⲘⲒ   The human-faced creature.

7 To right of the lion-faced creature, in white:

ⲠⲒⲌⲱⲟⲚ ⲚⲠⲟ ⲘⲘⲟ[ⲩ]Ⲓ   The lion-faced creature.

8 To left and right of the Virgin's head, in white:

ⲘⲎⲢ ⲐⲨ   Mother of God.

9 To lower left of the Virgin, in white:

ⲀⲦⲀⲯⲨⲬⲎ ⲞⲒⲤⲒ ⲘⲠⳞⲤ ⲞⲨⲟⲈ ⲚⲦⲈ ⲠⲀⲠⲚⲀ
ⲐⲎ[ⲖⲎⲖ] ⲈⲌⲈⲚ ⲪⲦ ⲠⲀ[Ⲥ]ⲱⲢ

My soul has magnified the Lord, and my spirit has [rejoiced] in God my Savior.

This is the opening verse of the Magnificat, Mary's song in the birth story of Jesus, Luke 1:46.

10 Below the painting, to left and right of what remains of the wreathed cross, in black:

[ⲌⲨⲖⲱⲚ]   [Tree]
ⲌⱁⲎ[Ⲥ]   of life.

Inside the wreathed cross would undoubtedly have been:

ⲒⲤ ⲬⲤ ⲚⲒ ⲔⲀ,   Jesus Christ is victorious.

Cf. c3.12.

Inscriptions in the Annex

A1. ARCHANGEL MICHAEL
1 To left and right of Michael's head, in white:

ⲘⲎⲬⲀⲎⲖ   Michael
ⲠⲒⲀⲢⲬⲎⲀⲄⲄⲈⲖⲟⲤ   the archangel.

2 Inside the medallion held in Michael's left hand, in red:

ⲒⲤ ⲬⲤ Ⲛ[Ⲓ] ⲔⲀ   Jesus Christ is victorious.

Cf. k15.2 and note.

A9. ARCHANGEL GABRIEL
1 To left and right of Gabriel's head, in white:

ⲄⲀⲂⲢⲒⲎⲖ   Gabriel
[ⲠⲒ]ⲀⲢⲬⲎⲀⲄⲄⲈⲖⲟⲤ   the archangel.

The medallion in Gabriel's left hand bears an image of Christ instead of the expected inscription. Cf. A1.2.

CONCLUSION

Monastic Visions began with two stories: one of the creation, and the other of the conservation, of the thirteenth-century wall paintings in the Church of St. Antony. Both narratives have been greatly amplified and enlarged by the contributions to this book. The authors have given us a multifaceted history of the beliefs that first inspired habitation, and then campaigns of building and painting, in this remote desert location (fig. 23). Their account spans more than sixteen hundred years. The rocky and austere locale of the Monastery of St. Antony had only rarely been seen by human beings before the third century A.D. Through the agency of St. Antony the Great, and the power of Coptic monasticism, it came to be filled with them. The greatest influx has been in the past decade, and it is certain to increase, including both those who come for the saint and those who come for the paintings.

The authors have produced insightful and thought-provoking chapters from their diverse perspectives, and thus each one contributes to our understanding of life and art at the Monastery of St. Antony (fig. 24). The pieces of lived historical experience they present often mesh as well with other pieces of data, and with other interpretations, to bring to life new aspects of the paintings and their monastic environment, past and present. In this respect, all of the book's authors have become like Theodore, the Coptic artist who used the Greek word *zographos* (ζωγραφος) to describe his profession. Zographos means painter, but literally translated it is "writer of life."[1]

The first and most important result of the past several years of intensive work on the paintings in the Church of St. Antony is their preservation. When ARCE began this USAID-funded project, the paintings were in a precarious

state indeed. If they had been left unattended, the combination of surface damage and structural weakness of the walls, together with the significant deterioration of the water-soluble pigments by rainwater and sponging (in earlier attempts to see the paintings and inscriptions), not to mention simple degradation over time, would almost certainly have resulted in their destruction before another century had passed. The walls are now stable again, and

23 OPPOSITE

Monastery garden, looking toward new church (EAP 2 S127 97)

24

Adriano Luzi, Father Maximous El-Anthony, Luigi De Cesaris, Gianluca Tancioni, Stefano Fulloni, Patrick Godeau, Alberto Sucato, and Emiliano Albanese in the sanctuary, in 1999. Courtesy of Patrick Godeau

the paintings are cleaned and protected. Extensive graphic documentation of the work of conservation and a comprehensive photographic record are available for study.[2] The St. Antony Project has engendered significantly more than this, however, adding to the base provided by van Moorsel's publication on the paintings, and, we hope, inspiring further studies.

The discovery by Luzi and De Cesaris of previously unknown paintings in the small side chapel off of the nave has given Jones and me ample evidence for a major revision of the age of the Church of St. Antony. Dating the paintings of Christ in Majesty and the Apostles (c4–c9) to ca. 550–700 is consistent with the monastic tradition that the church was built in the sixth century. Jones's careful reading of the material elements of stone, brick, and plaster has resulted in a chronology for the architectural development of the church and the monastery. He has proposed that the Deesis Chapel was the earliest component of the extant architectural complex, and has shown that it was also the sanctuary of an independent small church. The conservators found other areas of pre–thirteenth century paintings, sometimes more than one layer, everywhere except in the current sanctuary. The implication is that the eastern end of the Church of St. Antony was located at or around the easternmost wall of what is now the khurus. Because we know that windows below the central dome (s34–s36) were filled in and covered over before Theodore's team began work, we can deduce that the current sanctuary was constructed before the 1232/1233 campaign.[3]

Conservation has shown that paintings from six distinct periods exist in the Church of St. Antony.[4] The first, in the arched entrance to the Deesis Chapel, belongs to ca. 550–700. Two layers of pre–thirteenth century paintings were discerned, but in such a fragmentary state that most of them cannot be dated. The lowest of these may correspond to ca. 550–700, but their age is uncertain. The third clearly established period is that of Theodore's paintings (fig. 25), dated by two inscriptions to 1232/1233. The fourth group is located in the upper section of the khurus, and was most likely created between 1233 and ca. 1283. The slightly later rendition of the two archangels in the archway leading into the annex and Deesis Chapel (a1, a9) belongs to the fifth period. On technical (although not art historical) grounds, they appear to have been made within a decade of the fourth group, therefore ca. 1243–1293. Finally, the overpainting of areas of the paintings, as part of their "refreshment," belongs to the final period of painting (figs. 5.2, 9.8).[5] These last can no longer be seen

on the walls, but they have been thoroughly documented.

In addition to preserving the known wall paintings, the conservators found significant areas of figural painting that had been covered over with undecorated plaster for centuries.[6] Cleaning also revealed additional letters and entire inscriptions that had never been studied before. Pearson has established the identity of three figures previously unidentified (John the Little, n8; Sisoes, n9; and Phoebammon, n26), confirmed the identity of one (Sisinnius, n23), and suggested names for three more (John of Heraclea, n24; Macrobius, n35; and Benjamin, s7). Father Maximous first proposed that the figure designated as n9 was Sisoes (Shishoi), and Pearson has followed his lead. Pearson has translated many of the previously unpublished inscriptions, has filled in lacunae in partially known sections, and has retranslated the remainder. Altogether, his contributions have added considerably to our knowledge of the inscriptions and the paintings.

The painstaking work on this project, carried out in so many disciplines, has particular significance for the history of Coptic art. Western scholars have long considered Coptic art to be a marginal field. Archaeologists have excavated through postpharaonic layers in their search for ancient Egyptian artifacts, almost never preserving and rarely even recording Coptic finds. Earlier generations of Western art historians branded Egyptian Christian art as inferior and even pornographic, seeing it as low culture and falsely attributing to it pagan subjects, such as Leda and the Swan.[7] Although some Egyptian Christian works have been included in the corpus of important art from the late Roman and Byzantine worlds, art historians all too often still ignore Coptic art, or describe it as having entered a terminal decline following the Islamic conquest of Egypt in 641.[8] Writing in 1974, Leroy went so far as to summarize scholarly opinion about Christian Egyptian art after about 1000 as being no longer "Coptic art" but rather "the art of the Copts." Under the "influence" of Islam, its own character had been effaced.[9] The paintings created by Theodore and his workshop in the Church of St. Antony emphatically disprove all such notions. In their newly cleaned state they can be seen and appreciated for the first time in centuries. They provide us with a stunning array of new images with which to revise our understanding of the value and nature of Coptic art in the thirteenth century. The interdisciplinary character of this book is designed to show that the paintings relate to much more than a narrowly defined history of art. They belong to a functional context tied to the beginnings of Christianity in Egypt, to the visual culture of the eastern Mediterranean in the

25

Palace of Nebuchadnezzar and George

(κ7–κ8; ADP/SA 1999)

26

Monk from one of the Red Sea
monasteries, 1930–1931
(Whittemore Expedition.
Courtesy of Dumbarton Oaks,
A179)

twelfth and thirteenth centuries, and also to the living
Coptic culture of today, lay and monastic.

The historical chapters by Vivian and Gabra illumi-
nate the inspiring and also tenacious character of Coptic
monasticism, beginning with St. Antony the Great, and
continuing through periods of growth and influence, but
also of severe trial and adversity. The Monastery of St.
Antony is shown to have been a center of authority and
learning from which leaders of the Coptic and Ethiopian
Churches were drawn (fig. 26). The expansive picture
shaped by Vivian and Gabra is given yet more detail by
Griffith in his study of the graffiti in the Church of St.
Antony. The monastery not only offered leaders to the
larger Christian community outside of its confines, it also
drew monks and pilgrims from the churches of Syria,
Ethiopia, Armenia, and Russia, as well as from the West.
Griffith has made their presence in the church almost audible. Gabra has charted both the religious visitors to the
site and the scholars, showing how diverse the compul-
sions are that cause people to travel there.

The chapters by Father Maximous and Oram com-
plement the information presented by Gabra, in their focus
on the present state of the monastery. Father Maximous
has given us a rare view of the role of icons in the monastic
life of this ancient community. His explanation of images
as "windows into heaven" meshes with the perspective on
the historical meaning of the images that I presented and
suggests that there is a functional continuity in the role of

art in Coptic monasticism. He describes the monk as
"an icon, pulsating with life," and Oram relates that "the
monk's body and the rhythm of his life [are understood by
the Copts] to be mimetic of saintly bodies and lives from
the past." These comments have a direct bearing on the
wall paintings. When we see a monk, we see a living example of the figures depicted in the church, and this link
between the monk and history is keenly felt by Coptic pilgrims, and by the monks themselves. Oram's vivid portrayal of the monastery from the perspective of the Coptic
lay population gives us an understanding of its vitality
today, during this phenomenal modern phase of expansion. Her analysis of pilgrimage has a dimension of detail
possible only to an eyewitness, and her portrayal amplifies
our understanding of the pilgrims of the past, the fragmentary traces of which have been so carefully pieced together by Vivian, Gabra, and Griffith. To Coptic pilgrims,
the past is accessible and palpable. Oram reports that they
appreciate the antiquity of the Church of St. Antony and
sense in it a "layering of prayer upon prayer, and mass
upon mass through the centuries." Within this tradition,
monks forge and sustain this dense sanctity.

The historical, inscriptional, and functional perspectives on the Monastery of St. Antony provide a setting in
which the paintings become comprehensible, as links with
the past and the present; as windows into heaven, and also
to the spiritual realm around us. The complex painted
program was designed to suit the various activities undertaken in each part of the church. It also relates to the larger
context of this particular monastic site, which Vivian has
evoked so well. At this place, founded by the Father of
Monasticism, the paintings illustrate a genealogy of Coptic monasticism and of the Coptic Church.

They also repay analysis as great works of art. Theodore and his team of artists painted with skill and confidence. Stripped of the disfiguring "refreshment" and
dirt, their paintings emerge full of visual complexity and
sophistication. They stand within a long tradition of Christian painting, which began in late antiquity. It was unbroken by iconoclasm, the prohibition against religious
images that disrupted the course of Christian art in Byzantium for roughly one hundred years in the eighth and
ninth centuries. Theodore's paintings include subjects and
iconography familiar from monastic art of about the fifth
century onward (fig. 27), but also from posticonoclastic
Byzantine art. More pervasive by far than the occasional
element of Byzantine style or iconography are the numerous features from the secular world. As Lyster has shown,
Coptic art underwent a kind of Arabization in the cen-

27
Three Hebrews, detail (K6; ADP/SA 9 S169 97)

turies after the conquest. The inclusion of tiraz bands and the decorative script repeating the phrase "al-Fadi" show an adaptation from the Islamic court, and a transformation of meaning that is specifically religious. "In the Church of St. Antony, the bishops' tiraz bands suggest that these men are court officials as well as the pastors of the Coptic community. . . . The tiraz inscriptions of the . . . [patriarchs] and military martyrs, however, do not name a secular monarch but declare allegiance to the Lord Jesus Christ, 'the Redeemer.'"

As Lyster and I show, far from being cut off from developments in Islam and Byzantium, the thirteenth-century artists at the Monastery of St. Antony incorporated elements of decoration and subject matter that were developed in the eastern Mediterranean well after the Islamic conquest, revealing the Copts' participation in the visual culture of the region. These sources are married seamlessly to the ancient Coptic tradition, resulting in a coherent and engaging whole. The contributions of Gabra and Lyster describe a monastic world that was part of a larger cultural renaissance. The paintings are a visual record of this stimulating time. The stylistic competence of these paintings makes it clear that the tradition of high quality Coptic painting begun in late antiquity had continued up until this time. We may have few remnants of it left, but in terms of iconography and style, these paintings are an outgrowth of the preceding centuries of Coptic art.

The survival, in excellent condition, of this near-complete and dated program of paintings opens up vistas of possibility for the art historical analysis of medieval Coptic art. In this field, firm dates are exceptionally rare, and were it not for the inscriptions, which include the date A.M. 949 (A.D. 1232/1233), it would likely have been necessary to suggest a two-century span for Theodore's paintings—perhaps between 1100 and 1300. The program in the Church of St. Antony therefore gives us a fixed point for comparison with other, undated, Coptic paintings (fig. 28). The potential that the newly visible paintings by Theodore and his team have to contribute to our understanding of the twelfth and thirteenth centuries has only been suggested in this book—for example, with the observation of close stylistic ties between the paintings in the Church of St. Antony and those at two other sites: the Sanctuary of St. Mark in the Monastery of St. Macarius (Wadi al-Natrun), and the gallery chapel dedicated to the Virgin in the Monastery of St. Mercurius (Old Cairo).

Luzi, De Cesaris, Lyster, and I have studied the khurus ceiling paintings from different points of view: conservation and technique, Islamic art, and Byzantine art. Our conclusions are complementary. We can therefore assert with unusual confidence that the paintings in the upper zone of the khurus were made within at most fifty years of Theodore's original 1232/1233 program—so not after ca. 1283, and likely well before that date. The figural paintings belong to the Byzantine tradition, but they are not a homogeneous extension of it (fig. 29). They have their closest ties to the Byzantine art of Cyprus and icons in the Monastery of St. Catherine on Mount Sinai, but belong to neither. Also, the Ornamental Master's sources are part of artistic developments in cosmopolitan centers in the Arab world (fig. 30). He quotes palatial architectural decoration, remnants of which still exist in Cairo, to make a fitting house for God.

By themselves, the paintings of Theodore and his workshop are of exceptional importance for the study of thirteenth-century Coptic art. The unexpected masterpieces of the Figural and Ornamental Masters are also of great relevance. The interesting juxtaposition of the two distinct programs, between 1232 and 1283, raises questions about the character of artistic production in Egypt in this period. Theodore painted his program in a confident Coptic style, repeating traditional iconographic conventions and methods of representation. He drew on the venerable Coptic tradition of art and brought in to it elements from posticonoclastic Byzantine art and Fatimid and Ayyubid visual culture. In his work, these traditions are fully syn-

28
Severus of Antioch (s3), detail of
book with portrait of Christ
(ADP/SA 7 s180 97)

29 ABOVE
Detail of women at the tomb (K12)

30 BELOW RIGHT
Detail of spiral arabesque
(K14; ADP/SA 18 s162 97)

thesized; they permeate but do not dominate it. Also, a temporal lag existed between the moment that many of these external features were current, and the time that Theodore quoted them. A second, utterly different artistic world exists in the khurus ceiling. Two dominant spheres are apparent in these later paintings: that of the Byzantine cultural world, on the one hand, and of Muslim art from the Ayyubid and Bahri Mamluk dynasties, on the other. The program of this vault could have been painted almost anywhere in the Muslim-controlled Near East. It belongs to a polyglot Mediterranean visual culture in which subjects and visual elements from a variety of sources are juxtaposed and rarely synthesized.[10] The essential feature in this program that ties it to Arabic-speaking Christians, as opposed to those who spoke Greek or Latin, is the organization of the narrative scenes from right to left. It differs from one of its famous predecessors, the mid–twelfth century Cappella Palatina at Palermo, in that elements from Islamic art can be clearly discerned *within* the figural paintings of Christian subjects, and vice versa. At the Cappella Palatina, the ceiling was painted in an Islamic mode, while the mosaics of the walls are manifestly Byzantine.[11] About a hundred years later, at the Monastery of St. Antony, the new ornamental styles of the ruling Muslim dynasty were used, with an addition from Armenian Cilicia—a Christian kingdom. The figural paintings, in a provincial Byzantine mode, include two salient Muslim features: the mountains and the seated pose of the angel. The fashion of combining visual elements from the varied cultures then coexisting in the Mediterranean has moved from one of the juxtaposition of defined pictorial fields to one of the juxtaposition of elements within pictorial fields, and even,

in the case of the angel, of synthesis.[12] Also, unlike many products of the Mediterranean in the period of the Crusades, the painters of the khurus ceiling did not make use of Latin styles or iconography. And finally, the Ornamental Master worked with current secular motifs, not those of an earlier period.

Despite their distinctly different characters, both groups of painting in the Church of St. Antony are representative of thirteenth-century Coptic art. These styles are three of what were perhaps four modes that were employed in Christian art in Egypt during this period. One, exemplified by Theodore's program, grew out of the regionally specific and identifiable Coptic style (fig. 31). It continued in Egypt into the fourteenth century. A general chronological sequence for this mode from ca. 1180 to ca. 1350 includes paintings in the Monastery of St. Macarius (Sanctuary of St. Mark), the Monastery of St. Mercurius (Chapel of the Virgin); the 1232/1233 paintings in the Church of St. Antony; the Monastery of St. Paul (Sanctuary of St. Antony); the Monastery of the Romans (sanctuaries in the Church of the Virgin); the Chapel of the Martyrs at the Syrian Monastery; and finally two paintings in the White Monastery at Sohag.[13] More than one school or workshop was working in this Coptic manner. A second stylistic group or mode looks Islamic to Western eyes, but, as Lyster has shown, it was a current artistic fashion in the eastern Mediterranean. Muslims and Christians used it for secular and religious art and architecture in numerous media.[14] We see one variation of this in the khurus ceiling program, chiefly in the work of the Ornamental Master, and more in the Cairo New Testament of 1249/1250 (figs. 7.35, 8.18, 8.40).[15] A third mode was inspired by Byzantium. In the Figural Master's work, the regional characteristics of art in Cyprus and Sinai are apparent. A manuscript originally in the Monastery of St. Antony, dated to 1205, shows the existence of a Byzantine mode in another

31

Angel touching the sword of
Mercurius (κ3; ADP/SA 20 s171 97)

medium, and it seems probable that some Coptic icons also belong to it.[16] Architectural examples of this are documented as well, witness the church at the Monastery of Arsenius at Turah, which belonged to the middle Byzantine octagon-domed church type.[17] Finally, paintings in the Syrian Monastery, with Syriac inscriptions and dating to ca. 1225, seem to constitute a fourth stylistic mode.[18] This one may be indigenous to Egypt, and it may also have been imported from Syria. Our knowledge of Eastern Christian art is still too rudimentary for more definite conclusions.[19]

A characteristic of many of these modes or schools is that they include work from several media, most commonly wall painting, manuscript illumination, and panel painting, but also metalwork, stucco, and woodcarving.[20]

The khurus ceiling paintings show that more than one mode can be found in a single work. The Byzantine mode is sometimes tied to a Melkite community, as at Turah, and sometimes is not, as in the Monastery of St. Antony. In this it is generally consistent with the Arabized mode: style does not necessarily convey meaning. These comments about the range of modes of Christian painting in Egypt are tentative, first because the field of Coptic art history is barely mapped out, and second because so much material evidence has been lost. However, numerous new discoveries, and conservation work now under way in Egypt make these hypotheses and open questions exciting challenges.[21] In this fruitful period, the authors of *Monastic Visions* look forward to future analysis of and debates about the material presented in this book.

Abbreviations

AB   *Art Bulletin.*

ABD   *Anchor Bible Dictionary.* Editor in chief David Noel Freedman. New York: Doubleday, 1992.

Acta   *Acta ad Archaeologiam et Artium Historiam Pertinentia. Institutum Romanum Norvegiae.* Vol. 9, *Miscellanea Coptica.* Rome: Giorgio Bretschneider, 1981.

Acts 3   *Coptic Studies: Acts of the Third International Congress of Coptic Studies.* Edited by Wlodzimierz Godlewski. Warsaw, August 20–25, 1984. Warsaw: PWN—Éditions Scientifique de Pologne, 1990.

Acts 4   *Actes du IVème Congrès Copte.* Edited by M. Rassart-Debergh and J. Ries. Louvain-la-Neuve, September 5–10, 1988. 2 vols. Louvain-la-Neuve: Université Catholique de Louvain, Institut Orientaliste, 1992.

Acts 5   *Acts of the Fifth International Congress of Coptic Studies.* Washington, D.C., August 12–15, 1992. Edited by David W. Johnson. 2 vols. Rome: C.I.M., 1993.

Acts 6   *Ägypten und Nubien in spätantike und christlicher Zeit: Akten des 6. Internationalen Koptologenkongresses.* Münster, July 20–26, 1996. Edited by Stephen Emmel, Martin Krause, Siegfried G. Richter, Sofia Schaten. 2 vols. Wiesbaden: Reichert Verlag, 1999.

Antonius Magnus   *Antonius Magnus Eremita 356–1956: Studia ad Antiquum monachismum spectantia.* Edited by B. Steidle. Studia Anselmiana, fasc. 38. Rome: Herder, 1956.

BAR   *British Archaeological Reports.*

BIFAO   *Bulletin de l'Institut Français d'Archéologie Orientale du Caire.*

BMGS   *Byzantine and Modern Greek Studies.*

BSAC   *Bulletin de la Société d'Archéologie Copte.*

CE   *The Coptic Encyclopedia.* Edited by Aziz S. Atiya. 8 vols. New York: Macmillan, 1991.

C-L   Coquin, R.-G., and P.-H. Laferrière. "Les inscriptions pariétales de l'ancienne église du monastère de S. Antoine, dans le désert oriental." *BIFAO* 78 (1978): 267–321, plates 87–92.

CSCO   *Corpus Scriptorum Christianorum Orientalium.*

DOP   *Dumbarton Oaks Papers.*

EI1   *Encyclopaedia of Islam.* 4 vols. Leiden: Brill, 1913–1934.

EI2   *Encyclopaedia of Islam.* Leiden: Brill, 1960—.

Graf, GCAL   Georg Graf, *Geschichte der christlichen arabischen Literatur,* vols. 1–5 (Studi e Testi, 118, 133, 146, 147, 172). Vatican City, 1944, 1947, 1949, 1951, 1953.

Grammatik   W. C. Till. *Koptische Grammatik.* 2d ed. Leipzig: VEB Verlag, 1961.

IFAO   Institut Français d'Archéologie Orientale du Caire.

JARCE   *Journal of the American Research Center in Egypt.*

Liturgy   *The Coptic Liturgy.* Trans. Athanasius and Iris H. El Masry. Los Angeles: St. Mark Orthodox Church, 1974.

LSJ   Liddell, H. G., R. Scott, H. S. Jones, and R. A. McKenzie. *Greek-English Lexicon.* Oxford: Clarendon, 1940.

MIFAO   *Mémoires de l'Institut Français d'Archéologie Orientale du Caire.*

OCP   *Orientalia Christiana Periodica.*

ODB   *Oxford Dictionary of Byzantium.* Ed. in chief A. Kazhdan. Oxford: Oxford University Press, 1991.

PL   *Patrologia Cursus Completus. Series Latina.* Ed. J. P. Migne. Paris, 1844–1864.

Themelia   *Themelia: Spätantike und koptologische Studien Peter Grossmann zum 65. Geburtstag.* Edited by Martin Krause and Sofia Schaten. Sprachen und Kulturen des Christlichen Orients, v. 3. Wiesbaden: Reichert Verlag, 1998.

Notes

Introduction

I am grateful to Michael Jones for his additions to the acknowledgments.

1 The two oldest known Coptic representations of St. Antony both come from Bawit. One was photographed but not preserved, and is illustrated here. Another was listed in the archaeological report, but was neither photographed nor preserved. It was in Chapel 28. Clédat 1904, 155, 160–161.

2 Trebbin 1994. The popularity of St. Antony is sometimes expressed in church dedications, as in the Church of St. Antony at a site on Cyprus called Kellia (perhaps after the famous site of the same name in Egypt). Stylianou and Stylianou 1997, 433–437. Another church in Nicosia is dedicated to him as well.

3 The best-known early examples from the West are on the Irish high crosses: Harbison 1992, esp. 1: 302–309.

4 A few of the numerous examples from the Byzantine tradition are as follows: Hermitage of St. Neophytus, Cyprus; Mavriotissa Monastery, Kastoria; San Pantalemon, Nerezi; Cathedral of the Assumption, Vladimir; Nea Moni, Chios; Hosios Loukas; Asinou; and Monreale. The Crusader paintings in the Church of the Nativity at Bethlehem include one of St. Antony on a nave column. St. Antony was chosen as the subject of the frontispiece illustration for an Armenian MS of the *Apophthegmata Patrum*. Jerusalem MS 285. Museum Bochum and the Stiftung für Armenische Studien 1995, 204–205.

5 Ministry of Culture 1985, 158–159, 162, 164.

6 In addition to those mentioned above, in Harbison 1992, and the famous depiction by Martin Schongauer illustrated here, a few other Western examples can be found in the Chapter House of the Brauweiler Abbey; Cologne Cathedral; Church of St. Francis (Lower), Assisi; La Madeleine, Vézelay (twice); and Chartres Cathedral, in glass and stone. Ferrari 1956 lists numerous depictions of St. Antony.

7 "Other artistic traditions of the Christian East, such as the Coptic or Syrian, falter with the rise of Islam." Mathews and Sanjian 1991, 1. Although there have always been a few art historians who have treated early medieval Coptic art seriously, postconquest art is usually ignored. This attitude is beginning to shift, if the entries in the *Glory of Byzantium* catalog are any indication. Evans and Wixom 1997.

8 Van Moorsel 1983, 28; 1992, 176–177; 1995b, 184.

9 Leroy 1982, 19.

10 Paintings have been found under later layers of plaster in recent years in several monastic churches: the Monastery of the Archangel Gabriel at Naqlun, and the Monasteries of the Syrians, the Romans, and also of St. Bishoi, in the Wadi al-Natrun. Godlewski 1997; 1999; Innemée 1998b; 1999b; van Moorsel 1992; 1995a; van Loon 1999b, 75–82.

11 Alexander Piankoff was the first scholar to decipher and publish the dated inscription. Piankoff 1954, 22. Van Moorsel was the first to assert that the artist named in the inscriptions (Theodore) was most likely responsible for the entire program, alone or with assistants, barring only the paintings in the Byzantine style. Van Moorsel 1995b, 179–183.

12 Mention must be made here of Zuzanna Skalova, whose tireless efforts over the past decade to conserve the icons of Egypt have inspired so many. Her teaching and high standards have done a great deal to raise awareness of the importance of Coptic icons and also of the science of conservation.

13 Royal Netherlands Embassy project number KAP 3494 was undertaken between 1991 and 1994.

14 For more on the donors, see Pearson, chapter 14, and Bolman, chapter 4.

15 The graphical documentation for conservation work on the painting of Mercurius (K3) is fully illustrated in chapter 9.

16 In the painting of St. Antony (N1), the right hand of the saint was destroyed when the wooden khurus screen was installed, sometime before 1626. The graffito of Father Bernardus, written in 1626, provides a *terminus ante quem*. At the request of the monastery, this hand was reconstructed during the conservation work, in *tratteggio*, and is the only case of such a reconstruction.

17 Innemée 1990, 161–163; 1992; 1998a, 446–449. Van Loon 1992; 1993; 1999a; 1999b. Unfortunately, van Loon 1999b appeared too late for me to give it thorough consideration.

18 Van Moorsel 1978; 1983; 1991b; 1995b; 1998; Leroy 1976; Grossmann 1982; 1991d; C-L; Doresse 1951; 1952; Piankoff 1942; 1943; 1946–1947; 1950–1957; 1954; 1956a; 1956b; Rassart-Debergh 1981, 249–251; Walters 1974, 302–309; Hunt 1985; Meinardus 1961, 1–31; 1964; 1966; 1972; Fedden 1937; du Bourguet 1951.

1. St. Antony the Great

I wish to thank Elizabeth S. Bolman, Gawdat Gabra, Michael Jones, and Maged S. Mikhail for their suggestions.

1 Vogüé 1991, 17–22.

2 Ramsey 1997, 121.

3 *Vita Patrum Iurensium* 11 and 174; see Vivian, Vivian, and Russell 1999.

4 See Sozomen, *Ecclesiastical History* 1.13.2; Athanasius 1994b, 131, n. 1.

5 The numbering of the *Life* is that of Athanasius 1994b, 123–377, while the translations are from Athanasius 2001.

6 For a map, *CE*:8, 7.

7 All dates for events in Antony's life are conjectural and rely on Athanasius. Athanasius 2001.

8 See Festugière 1971, 1:44–45; Russell 1981, 59.

9 See Vivian 1996, 166–187.

10 According to Athanasius (2001), 91.7, 92.2, Antony ordered his two disciples to bury him and tell no one of the site.

11 For good illustrated introductions to Kellia, see Kasser 1989 and Rassert-Debergh 1989.

12 *Apophthegmata* Antony 34; Ward 1984, 8.

13 *Apophthegmata* Amoun 1 and Macarius the Great 4 and 26; Ward 1984, 31, 127, 133.

14 Bell 1983, 69. Serapion of Thmuis, *Epistola ad discipulos Antonii* 5; Draguet 1951, 1–25.

15 This passage is found in the Coptic version of the *Lausiac History* of Palladius; Bunge and Vogüé 1994, 123.

16 Guillaumont 1988, 7.

17 See MacCoull 1998, 408.

18 See Patrich 1995, 47.

19 For more on the monastery, see Meinardus 1992, supplemented by Vivian 1999, 277–310.

20 Evetts 1895, 161. It seems probable now that the *History of the Churches and Monasteries of Egypt*, traditionally assigned to Abū Salih, should be attributed in the main to Abū al-Makarim, who was writing around 1170.

21 Evelyn-White 1973, 12. Antony figures prominently in both the *Apophthegmata* and the *Lausiac History* of Palladius. For the *Apophthegmata* see Ward 1984, 1–9, 265; for the *History*, Meyer 1964, 234.

22 Rufinus of Aquileia, *Historia ecclesiastica* (*PL* 21.461–540: 2.3), reports three thousand around the year 373, while Palladius (Meyer 1964, 40), about twenty years later, speaks of five thousand at Nitria and six hundred at Kellia.

23 Jerome, *Regulae Sancti Pachomii*, Praefatio 7 *PL* 23.64.

24 Leipoldt 1903, 93.

25 Ramsey 1997, 639.

26 In the Deesis chapel in the Church of St. Antony, John the Baptist, along with Mary, adores Christ in Majesty.

27 Vogüé 1991, 32.

28 Veilleux 1986, 306.

29 Ramsey 1997, 375–376.

30 Much of this section is drawn from Rubenson 1995.

31 Rubenson 1995, 11; for his translation of the letters, see 197–231.

32 See Orlandi 1988 and Vivian 1997b, 105–116, and Vivian and Pearson 1998, 86–107.

33 On demons: Athanasius 1980, 21–41; Rubenson 1995, 199 (Letter 1), 215 (Letter 5), and 218–219 (Letter 6). On movements of the soul: Athanasius 1980, 55.7; Rubenson 1995, 179 (Letter 1.35–41). On the Arians: Athanasius 1980, 69; Rubenson 1995, 211 (Letter 4.17). On divine immovability: Athanasius 1980, 74.5–6: Rubenson 1995, 66–67.

34 Much of the material in this section is drawn, with kind permission of the author, from Harmless forthcoming.

35 *Apophthegmata* Antony 20; Ward 1984, 5.

36 *Apophthegmata* Antony 33; Ward 1984, 8.

37 *Apophthegmata* Antony 8; Ward 1984, 3.

38 *Apophthegmata* Antony 13; Ward 1984, 3–4.

39 *Apophthegmata* Antony 27; Ward 1984, 7.

40 *Apophthegmata* Hilarion 1; Ward 1984, 111.

41 *Apophthegmata* Sisoes 9; Ward 1984, 214. A painting of Sisoes is at N9.

42 *Apophthegmata* Antony 24; Ward 1984, 6.

43 *Apophthegmata* Antony 3; Ward 1984, 2.

44 *Apophthegmata* Antony 31; Ward 1984, 8.

45 *Apophthegmata* Antony 11; Ward 1984, 3. A better reading for "fornication" is "his heart."

46 *Apophthegmata* Antony 1; Ward 1984, 1–2.

47 *Apophthegmata* Antony 32; Ward 1984, 8.

48 Meyer 1964, 76–81.

49 *Historia Monachorum in Aegypto* 24 (= 31 in Rufinus's Latin version); Russell 1981, 114.

50 *Historia Monachorum* 24; Russell 1981, 115.

51 Jullien 1884, 237.

52 For the story of Father Lazarus, see Vivian 1999.

53 For an English translation, see Harvey 1990, 357–369.

54 *Life of Paul* 1; Harvey 1990, 360. This Macarius came to be later identified with Macarius the Great.

55 *Life of Paul* 4; Harvey 1990, 362.

56 *Life of Paul* 7; Harvey 1990, 363.

57 *Life of Paul* 10; Harvey 1990, 366. See 1 Kgs 17:1–6. For Coptic iconographic representations of Antony and Paul, see Bolman, introduction, and chapters 4 and 6.

58 *Life of Paul* 11; Harvey 1990, 366–367; on the cloak see *Life of Antony* 91.8, 92.3.

59 *Life of Paul* 15–16; Harvey 1990, 368–369.

60 See Harvey 1990, 357, and Doresse 1952, 3–14. For contrary views see Evelyn-White 1973, 12, and Ramsey 1997, 657.

61 Jerome, Epistle 22.36 (to Eustochium); Wright 1980, 142.

62 *Synaxarium Ecclesiae Constantinopolitanae* (29 October); cited by Wortley 1992, 383–404, 395. An icon at the Monastery of Saint Paul identifies Paul as "the first anchorite," an epithet common to many icons of Saint Paul.

63 N1–N2. For the painting at Saint Macarius's, see Leroy 1982, pls. 75–76. In Ramsey 1997, 18.5.4, Cassian pairs Antony and Paul as the cofounders of anchoritism. Committee Formed by His Holiness Pope Shenouda III 1993, 253. Ramsey 1997, 639, yokes together "the holy Paul and Antony" as "the leaders of this profession."

64 "Les monuments les plus vénérables de l'Égypte copte." Doresse 1952, 4.

65 Sulpicius, Dialogue 1.17; Peebles 1949, 184.

66 Butler 1967, 1.231–32; Evelyn-White 1973, 12 n. 4; Walters 1974, 33, 239.

67 Evetts 1895, 166–167.

68 Meinardus 1992, 33–47.

69 Committee Formed by His Holiness Pope Shenouda III 1993, 59.

70 *Life of John the Little* 77; Mikhail and Vivian 1997, 51. For accounts of numerous later visitors to the monastery, see Gabra chapter 10; for an account of a recent visit, see Vivian 1999.

71 Amélineau 1893, 228–229.

72 Festugière 1971, 15.1.

73 Amélineau 1893, 353.

74 Abu Salih concurs that Saint Antony's "is a distance of three days' journey" to the Nile. Evetts 1895, 159–160.

75 Cited by Chester 1873, 105–116, 113.

76 A booklet published by the monastery puts the elevation at 300 m. (1,050 ft.).

77 Regnault 1990, 23, 55. See *Apophthegmata* Sisoes, 7, 8, 9, 15, 18; Ward 1984, 213–216; and Festugière 1971, 24.2. Russell 1981, 114.

78 For examples, see Walters 1974, 7.

79 Littman 1953, 1–28, 27. According to the *Life of Antony* 49.5–7, Antony traveled with Saracens for three days to reach his retreat in the desert; if this report is accurate, they would undoubtedly have followed some trade or caravan route.

80 The coastal route passes the important Roman fort at Bir Abu Darag, which was later occupied and adapted by Christian anchorites. There were also hillside dwellings about 6 km. north of Bir Abu Darag, almost certainly occupied by Christian anchorites, that have revealed ceramics from the fifth to seventh centuries. Thanks to Michael Jones for this information.

81 Butler 1967, 223.

82 See Sulpicius, *Dialogue* 1.17; Peebles 1949, 184.

83 See Butler 1967, 231–232 and 232 n. 2.

84 Grossmann 1991d. Grossmann reports that the monastery retained its original anchoritic structure as late as the visit by Vansleb in 1672.

85 Guillaumont 1977, 194.

86 See Evelyn-White 1973, 16.

87 Walters 1974, 7.

88 See Walters 1974, 11–12, 86, and Jones 1995, 40 n. 23. Care is needed in dating the keeps because the towers have been reinforced and rebuilt numerous times.

89 Around 870 Patriarch Shenouda had the Monastery of St. Macarius surrounded by a high wall; see Evelyn-White 1973, 9.

90 See Walters 1974, 11–12. The dating, he says, is "somewhat conjectural." The booklet published at the monastery dates the keep to 537.

91 The excavators at Kellia have dated the abandonment of the outer cells and the concomitant retreat inside protective walls to the second half of the fifth century; at the end of the fifth century or beginning of the sixth, however, some monks remained in their isolated cells, fleeing inside the walls in case of danger; see Guillaumont 1977, 200, 202.

92 Walters 1974, 11.

93 To cite just two examples: According to Sawirus al-Sawirus, Patriarch James (819–830) went to Upper Egypt "to make a visitation of the people and the monasteries," but St. Antony's is not mentioned. Evetts 1904–1914, 10.5, 454. Wüstenfeld 1979, 85–117, lists eighty-six monasteries, including the four monasteries of the Wadi al-Natrun, but not the Monastery of St. Antony (though he does include the Monastery of St. Paul).

94 In 1884 the journey to the Monastery of St. Antony began with three hours by railroad from Cairo to Beni Suef, then took four to ten days by camel to the monastery. Jullien 1884, 189. Before the arrival of Jullien's group, monks at the monastery had not seen a stranger in more than four years (224).

95 Synaxarium Hatûr 7 (Nov. 3); Bassett 1904, 182–183. See Evelyn-White 1973, 284.

96 Atiya 1991b; 1918. See also Gabra, chapter 10.

97 Eusebius Renaudotius, cited by Meinardus 1992, 8–9.

98 Meinardus 1977, 504.

99 Father Lazarus the solitary told me his story. See also Gabra, chapter 10, for Ethiopians at the Monastery of St. Antony in later centuries.

100 For this period, see Müller 1964, 271–308.

101 See Frend 1972.

102 See Johnson 1986, 218–222.

103 Descoeudres 1989, 48, and Guillaumont 1977, 193. Each church had its own baptistery, possibly for baptizing "converts" from the other side.

104 *Apophthegmata* Phocas 1. Ward 1975, 240.

105 Frend 1972, 326.

106 Frend 1972, 73.

107 See Goehring 1999, 139, 155, and esp. 241–261.

108 Frend 1972, 73.

109 Evetts 1904–1914, 1.472.

110 See Garitte 1943, 100–134, 330–365; for the date, see Garitte 1943, 101. For an English translation, see Athanasius 2001.

111 Evetts 1895, 1.498.

112 Frend 1972, 139.

113 Meinardus 1965, 350, believes that Melkite occupation lasted until the eighth century; he bases this assessment on the story about the theft of the body of John the Little.

114 *The Life of John the Almsgiver* 9; Delehaye 1927, 24–25, and Dawes and Baynes 1977, 203–204. As Cauwenburgh succinctly notes, "This is the only mention that we have found of this monastery [of St. Antony] during the period that we are studying." Cauwenburgh 1914, 74 n. 1.

115 See Doresse 1952, 4–5, who says that John was buried in the church, and Regnault 1991c, 1361. *The Ethiopian Synaxary* says that this event took place during the reign of Anbâ Yûânnis IV (777–799). John is depicted at n8 in the Church of St. Antony.

116 Maqrizi in Wüstenfeld 1979, 59.

117 See Evetts 1895, 20–43, and his notes.

118 Tradition has St. Antony's body reposing in the southeastern end of the khurus, below the painting of St. Mercurius (k3), in the Church of St. Antony. Abu Salih says that "the pure body" of Saint Antony is "buried in his cave, in which he used to pray" and is "walled up within." Evetts 1895, 160.

119 For an account of al-Kanbar's beliefs, see Evetts 1895, 33–43; Malan 1873, 94.

120 Evelyn-White 1973, 389–390, who gives incorrect manuscript and page numbers for Wright 1870–1872, no. 696, 580.

121 Doresse 1952, 6; Evelyn-White 1973, 317 n. 4 (again with confused reference to Wright 1870–1872); Wright 1870–1872 (correctly), no. 695, 579–580. Doresse 1952 says that the note was written "shortly after 1235," but he does not cite his evidence for this, and I have not been able to corroborate it.

122 Evelyn-White 1973, 389 n. 2, suggests 1235–1245.

123 A.M. 949. The date may be found in an inscription to the right of the painting of St. Mercurius in the khurus. See Pearson, chapter 14.

124 Evetts 1895, 162–163.

125 See Bolman, chapter 4.

126 Quibell 1912, 4: vi; 3: iii. See also Grossmann 1991e, 774.

127 Economic reasons: Kasser 1989, 6; religious and economic pressures: Descoeudres 1989, 45. The communities of Kellia were not pillaged or destroyed; they were abandoned.

128 For details on this period see Maqrizi; Malan 1873, 72–83; Butler 1902, xix.

129 Maqrizi; Malan 1873, 72. For Maqrizi's fascinating chronicle of the period, see Malan 1873, 58–71.

130 Lapidus 1972, 249.

131 Maqrizi; Malan 1873, 76.

132 Lane-Pool 1914, 38.

133 Lapidus 1972, 250; Partrick 1996, 58; Evetts 1904–1914, 5.51.

134 Lapidus 1972, 252.

135 Lapidus 1972, 253.

136 Dunn 1975, 164–168. See also Lane-Poole 1914, 38.

137 Malan 1873, 82. I wish to thank Maged S. Mikhail for Mikhail, n.d.

138 For more details see Lapidus 1972, 257, 260; Malek 1993, 2:2, 291–311.

139 Maqrizi; Malan 1873, 109. See also Lane-Poole 1914, 39; Lapidus 1972, 258.

140 Quibell 1908, 4.vii; 3.iii; 3.7, plate L, 4.

141 Guillaumont 1977, 200.

142 Malan 1873, 81; Sawirus, *History of the Patri-archs,* 1.19; Evetts 1895, 10.5, 440–441.

143 Lapidus 1972, 259. For details concerning this period, see Maqrizi; Malan 1873, 86, 89, 91; Lapidus 1972, 259–260; Meinardus 1992, 8.

144 Meinardus 1992, 8.

145 Doresse 1952, 9. See also Piankoff 1950–1957, 163.

146 For the fifteenth-century hiatus, see Meinardus 1992, 12–13.

147 Evetts 1895, 160. *Misr* can mean either Cairo or, more broadly, Egypt (which designated the area around Cairo).

2. The Church of St. Antony

1 Meinardus 1961, 77–78, 29 (with aerial view of 1960), gives a brief description. Grossmann 1995, 1–19, with figs. 2–6, is the only serious study previously published.

2 A conventional east-west axis is used to describe the church.

3 Michael Mallinson and Peter Sheehan surveyed the monastery in 1998, and Peter Sheehan and Michael Dunn completed the detailed survey of the church. The drawings in this chapter were prepared by Peter Sheehan.

4 Personal communication from Father Maximous El-Anthony, who draws attention to other evidence of structural failure in the church: the north wall of the haikal, apparent buttressing of the northeast corner of the nave beneath the khurus arch, and cracking in the archway between the nave and the side chapel.

5 Water leaked from the dome windows during heavy rains in 1971 due to ponding on the roof.

6 This is one of five bold graffiti in different parts of the church that record Father Bernardus's visit during the winter of 1625–1626. It was removed to the monastery museum when the doorway was unblocked in December 1999.

7 Giorgio Funaro and Rita Rivelli (FORME), Rome, specialists in the restoration of stained glass windows, restored the khurus vault windows in May 1998, using German handmade glass.

8 Observed by Adriano Luzi during conservation.

9 See Bolman, chapter 3.

10 Traces of paintings were reported by the conservators under the thirteenth-century plaster layer in the area of the gospel held by Christ and beside St. John the Baptist.

11 For other examples of chapels adjoining churches in Egyptian monasteries, see van Loon 1999b, 79–81.

12 The plaster surface covering all the blocked windows had detached from the interior walls long ago, causing the large lacunae in the paintings. The cavities were filled with mortar and rubble, which was replaced with plaster during conservation in 1998. One window (N21) has been left open as far as the external blocking as an example. Those fragments of the original blocking that survived bore no traces of paintings earlier than the thirteenth century, whereas fragments of two earlier layers are visible elsewhere on the same wall.

13 Lyster has pointed out the strong possibility that the current doorway was created by enlarging an already existing earlier entrance; see chapter 7.

14 See Bolman, chapter 3.

3. The Early Paintings

1 Grossmann 1995, 14–15. Grossmann notes that the side chapel is earlier, Grossmann 1995, 2.

2 The oral tradition is recounted by Father Maximous.

3 Luzi and De Cesaris, chapter 9. See also Rutschowskaya 1992, 24–25.

4 Old Testament sources are also drawn on; Is 6:1–6; Ez 1:4–11; Dn 7:9.

5 De Cesaris has identified traces of early over-painting in some areas of these paintings, most markedly over the figure of St. Peter, and also on the face of Christ.

6 Rutschowskaya 1992, 72–77; Severin 1991, 364; Krause and Wessel 1966, 570–573.

7 The Christ in Majesty in the chapel is different in that angels, not the four creatures, support Christ's mandorla. Examples from Bawit: cells 17, 26, and others, in Clédat 1904, pls. 42, 40. From Saqqara, cell 709, in Quibell 1909, pl. 8. A fifth- or sixth-century Byzantine example in mosaic is in Hosios David, Thessaloniki.

8 Apostles below Christ: Bawit, room 6. This painting may be earlier or later than the sixth century. Apostles in roundels: Shepherd 1969, 101–105. The textile icon also includes a Christ in Majesty (without the four living creatures), and roundels of the apostles. Other examples are the sixth-century mosaics in the Monastery of St. Catherine (Mount Sinai), the Panagia Kanakaria (Cyprus), and San Vitale (Ravenna).

9 Shepherd 1969, 101–103.

10 An unpublished photograph showing a detail of this painting (which was not preserved by its excavators) clearly identifies both figures. Photograph: École des Hautes Études, in Paris, C-2208; a copy is in the Dumbarton Oaks Photograph Collection. An icon dated to the seventh or eighth century also shows Peter and Paul with these hairstyles. Weitzmann 1976, 58–59, cat. B33, pl. 85.

11 In the group of mosaic roundels in the Monastery of St. Catherine, only the evangelists carry codices (Shepherd 1969, 104). The square designs in the painting in the Church of St. Antony may suggest books, but because there are more than four, this element does not help with identification. In our case, the books correspond more closely to the painting from room 6 at Bawit, where all of the apostles hold them. The position of open hands in front of a book, but not supporting it, is peculiar, and suggests that a design in cloth, rather than a codex, is shown here.

12 "The style [of early Coptic art], still reminiscent of the Hellenistic alertness and supple lines in the earlier examples (Karmuz, Bagawat, Abu Hennis), soon presents an unswaying frontality and rigidity of design (Bawit) gradually increasing (Saqqara) into schematic effects." Badawy 1978, 227.

13 Painting of monks, cell A, Monastery of Apa Jeremiah at Saqqara, now in the Coptic Museum, Cairo; icon of Christ and Apa Mena, Musée du Louvre, inv. E 11565; icon of Bishop Abraham, Berlin, Staatliche Museen, inv. 6114; icons of St. Mark the Evangelist, Fr. 1129a, and an angel, Fr. 1129, Paris, Bibliothèque Nationale, Cabinet de Médailles; tondo of the Virgin Mary, Cairo, Coptic Museum, inv. 9104; textile icon of the Virgin Mary with Christ, Cleveland, Cleveland Museum of Art, inv. 67.144; two icons of monks from Bawit, painted on sycamore wood, Auch, Musée des Jacobins, inv. 985.228 and 985.229, and illustrated in Institut du Monde Arabe 2000, catalog numbers 73–74, p. 110.

14 Berlin, Staatliche Museen, inv. 6114; Krause 1971, 106–111; Godlewski 1986, 60; Rassart-Debergh 1990, 61–62.

15 Musée du Louvre, inv. E 11565; Weitzmann 1979, 589–590, cat. 529.

16 Grossmann 1982, 112; Grossmann 1995, 6.

4. Theodore, "The Writer of Life"

1 See Vivian, chapter 1.

2 See Luzi and De Cesaris, chapter 9.

3 For more discussion of the directions to the painter and their implication for our understanding of Theodore's working process, see Bolman, chapter 5.

4 See Pearson, chapter 14.

5 Vikan 1984, 65–86.

6 Vikan 1982; Vikan 1998, 229–266; Bolman 1998, 65–77, plates 1–7.

7 Anonymous, (The Order of Priesthood), ca. 1200–1250; and Yuhanna ibn Abi Zakariyya ibn Sabba ʿ, *Kitab al-gauhara al-nafisa* (The Book

of the Precious Pearl), chapter 27, ca. 1350; in van Loon 1993, 2:497–508.

8 In the seventh or eighth century, the monk Epiphanius traveled from Scetis and Babylon in Egypt (the modern Wadi al-Natrun and Cairo) to the Monastery of St. Antony, and thence up and around the Red Sea to the Monastery of St. Catherine on Mount Sinai. Wilkinson 1977, 11, 119, map 35. A late, nonmonastic example is the Baron d'Anglure, who in 1395 went to the Monastery of St. Antony and then the Monastery of St. Catherine. Labib 1961, 43. See chapters 1, 10, and 11 for more discussion of visitors.

9 One graffito includes the name of a nun, in addition to that of monks (s6). Because it was written in the sanctuary, where women are not permitted, it seems most likely that one of the monks wrote it to commemorate all of the monastics listed, and that it does not provide proof that a woman was in the church. Due to limitations of space, Sidney Griffith does not discuss this graffito in chapter 11. My thanks to Michael Jones for its translation.

10 Walters notes that in the fifth century, Shenoute occasionally invited people from the surrounding community to participate in services within the monastic church. His source is the *Life* of Shenoute, Amélineau 1894, 392–393. Walters 1974, 36.

11 Anonymous, *Kitab tartib al-kahanut* (The Order of Priesthood). Paraphrased in Zanetti 1991, 78. Ritual processions, extending into the nave, are known to have taken place in the Coptic church in the twelfth century. Hunt 1995, 194.

12 Van Loon 1999b, 117, 206–207.

13 Grossmann 1982, 112–113; Grossmann 1990, 9.

14 The side chapel has been known as the Chapel of the Four Animals, but this designation seems to stem from an unusual rendering of the Four Creatures. The appellation after the Four Creatures may have originated with P. Uspensky, who visited the site in 1850 and reported that the chapel was dedicated to the *zoa*. Werner 1989–1990, 15, n. 47. Though of great interest to art historians, an iconographic peculiarity does not seem to be an appropriate basis for naming the entire chapel. The program is best characterized by its intercessory function, thus the term *Deesis*.

15 These consist of the Armenian word for "holy" repeated three times, in each graffito. Griffith, chapter 11.

16 Griffith, chapter 11.

17 For a discussion of the concept of martyrdom see Malone 1956, 201–210.

18 "The Martyrdom of Saint Mînâs: From Ethiopic," British Museum Oriental 689, fols.

74b1–74b2, probably a fifteenth-century text that accords in most respects to earlier versions. Budge 1909, 27, 46–47.

19 BMO 689, fol. 75a1; Budge 1909, 48.

20 Variations of this story exist, as is the case with any popular martyrdom account. Compare BMO689 fol.77a2–77b1, in Budge 1909, 54–55, and Budge's summary of the major events in Menas's life, which is drawn from a wide array of sources. Budge 1909, 23–25.

21 BMO689, fol.75a1; Budge 1909, 48.

22 BMO689, fols.78a1–78a2; Budge 1909, 56–57.

23 Coptic Miracle number 17, Ethiopian Miracle number 19; Devos 1959, 456–457.

24 For the archaeological site, see Grossmann's numerous publications, some of which are included in Grossmann 1991a, 24–29.

25 O'Leary 1937, 262–263; Walters 1989, 193–194; Orlandi 1991b, 2237–2238.

26 O'Leary 1937, 264; Winstedt 1979, 123–132.

27 Winstedt 1979, 129–131.

28 Walters 1989, 193–194, and pl. XVIII. Theodore Stratelates is also shown at Esna, but without the same narrative details.

29 This MS is now in the Vatican Library: MS Copto 66, f. 210v: Leroy 1974, 105. Leroy notes that the MS must predate A.D. 1067 because of a notation in it that was probably made by a reader (A.M. 783), but that it is most likely of a ninth- or tenth-century date. Leroy 1974, 184–186. Two folio numbers are given for this subject, which seems to have been reproduced twice in the MS: fol. 194 and fol. 210v.

30 See Lyster, chapter 7, for a discussion of the saint's dress and weapons.

31 C-L 292–293; van Moorsel 1995b, 164.

32 C-L 293. Tenth-century and later icons from outside of Egypt show George spearing Diocletian.

33 BMO7022, fol. 1b, dated to A.D. 951. Budge 1914, xviii, 255.

34 BMO7022, fols. 8a, 14a; Budge 1914, 266–267, 276.

35 BMO7030, fol. 3b2; Budge 1915, 580.

36 O'Leary 1937, 176–177, 233–234.

37 See Lyster, chapter 7.

38 Van Moorsel 1995b, 119, fig. 33, and 125–127.

39 O'Leary 1937, 233–234.

40 O'Leary 1937, 176.

41 C-L 271; van Moorsel 1995b, 127.

42 The Bohairic *Life* of Pachomius, chapter 1, Veilleux 1980, 24.

43 Malone 1956, 211.

44 Athanasius, *Vita S. Antonii* 46, in Malone 1950, 214.

45 For the history of Antony and Paul, see Vivian, chapter 1.

46 Veilleux 1991, 1859–1860.

47 The Bohairic *Life* of Pachomius, chapter 8, in Veilleux, 1980, 1: 28–29.

48 *Life*, chapter 17; Veilleux 1980, 1: 39–40.

49 Kuhn 1991, 2131–2133.

50 Cody 1991, 2102.

51 O'Leary 1937, 182.

52 Vivian forthcoming.

53 O'Leary 1937, 183.

54 Vivian forthcoming.

55 A precedent from the Old Testament Apocrypha is 1 Enoch 71:3, describing movement from earth to heaven: "And the angel Michael, one of the archangels, took hold of me by my right hand, and raised me, and led me out." On the right hand see also Psalm 73:23–24 and the Manichaean Apocalypse of Sethel. Reeves 1996, 122–124, 193. Thanks to William Lyster for this reference.

56 Vivian forthcoming, chapter 19.

57 Macarius as father of Scetis: Cody 1991, 2103.

58 C-L 280; van Moorsel 1995b, 145.

59 See Pearson, chapter 14, N33.

60 Ezekiel 1:4–24; Isaiah 6:1–9. Isaiah describes similar creatures but calls them seraphim, Rv 4:6–9. Werner, 1989–1990, 2–4.

61 Homily 1, 1–2; Maloney 1992, 37. Thanks to Georgia Frank for this reference.

62 O'Leary 1937, 206–207.

63 Ward 1975, 138–139.

64 For their bond see Coquin 1991c, 2029.

65 Coquin 1991c, 2029–2030; Budge 1928, 1084.

66 C-L ignore him altogether. According to his position in the nave, he should be discussed on 273–274. Van Moorsel describes him as anonymous. Van Moorsel 1995b, 133–134.

67 Zacharias of Sakha, *Life* of John the Little, Mikhail and Vivian 1997, chapters 25, 31.

68 Mikhail and Vivian 1997, chapters 16, 28. I am grateful to Father Maximous, who first explained the meaning of this gesture to me.

69 O'Leary 1937, 99.

70 For more on this subject, see Vivian, chapter 1.

71 C-L 272–273.

72 Guy 1993, 122–123.

73 Budge 1907, 327.

74 Athanasius 1980, 66.

75 Athanasius 1980, 29.

76 Ward 1975, xviii.

77 Theodoret of Cyrrhus, prol. 2, in Krueger 1997, 418.

78 Abu al-Khayar ibn al-Tayyib, "Le remède de l'intelligence," in Zanetti 1991, 78–79.

79 Al-Mu'taman abu Ishaq al-'Assal, "Somme des aspects de la religion," ca. 1250–1300; in Zanetti 1991, 79–80.

80 Monica Blanchard suggests that outright polarization between the Syrians and the Copts had not occurred, but that each group may be characterized as having a strong sense of pride in its own heritage. Blanchard, in conversation, 1999. See also the single addition of a Syrian in the sanctuary, Severus of Antioch, s3.

81 See Jones, chapter 2, and Lyster, chapter 7. A door also existed at N31. See Jones, chapter 2.

82 Maguire 1993, 78.

83 See Griffith, chapter 11.

84 Drescher 1946, miracles 2 and 4, 107, 113, 116–118.

85 O'Leary 1937, 234.

86 Athanasius 1994a, 40.

87 Hunt 1991, 116.

88 Guillaumont 1991d, 1923.

89 Van Esbroeck, 1991a, 1576.

90 See Griffith, chapter 11.

91 Miracle 14. Budge 1923, 47–48.

92 Many of the miracles of the Virgin Mary preserved in Ethiopian manuscripts have been shown to originate in the West. Baraz 1994, 69–71. The miracles involving the use of the Virgin's breast milk to cure eye diseases are a continuation of ancient Egyptian and Coptic medical practice. Breast milk was used in Egypt for diseases of the eye, but not in the Greco-Roman medical tradition. Bolman 1997, 120–124, 142–148.

93 The Theotokia, Coptic hymns dedicated to the Virgin Mary, are one indication of this devotion. In the Middle Ages, they seem to have been sung throughout the year, although now they are sung only in the month of Khiak (December). O'Leary 1950, 417, 419; Kabès 1952, 7.

94 I thank Derek Krueger, Georgia Frank, Gene Rogers, and Sidney Griffith for their assistance with this interpretation. Ladner 1958, 88–94. Augustine, "On Virginity," 3, Oden and Hall 1998, 48–49.

95 It is very difficult to determine the meaning of hand gestures in these paintings. Writing in the early fourteenth century, the Coptic theologian Abu al-Barakat ibn Kabar described the confusion over the meaning of Christ's hand gesture even at that time. "La lampe des ténèbres," Zanetti 1991, 84.

96 Belting 1994, 102–109.

97 For a description of the type, see Buckton 1994, 232. The iconographic type is also called the *Platytera,* and an eighth-century example from Santa Maria Antiqua in Rome shows the Virgin Mary holding the aureole from below and flanked by Elizabeth with John the Baptist as a child and the Virgin's mother, Ann, holding Mary as a child.

98 Belting 1994, 102–114.

99 Kühnel 1988, 190. Belting and Kühnel are, of course, only two of the many authors who have interpreted this iconographic type.

100 Cyril of Alexandria, "Discourse on the Virgin Mary," BMO6782, fols.32b1–32b2; Budge 1915, 720.

101 Unfortunately, van Loon's exceptionally fine book appeared too late for its contributions to be thoroughly integrated into this book. It is by far the most interdisciplinary and thorough treatment yet written of the Coptic khurus and sanctuary, their function, meaning, and relation to the paintings found in them. Van Loon 1999b, esp. 109–124.

102 Anonymous, *Kitab tartib al-kahanut* (The Order of Priesthood), ca. 1200–1250; Yuhanna ibn Abi Zakariyya ibn Sabba', *Kitab al-gauhara al-nafisa* (The Book of the Precious Pearl), ca. 1350, chapter 27. Translated and analyzed in the extremely useful article by van Loon 1993, 497–498.

103 Van Loon 1993, 497–498.

104 Luzi and De Cesaris have noted that the two rows of glass circles along the sides of the vault are earlier than the paintings currently visible, so the basic shape of the ceiling dates at least to 1232/1233, if not earlier. See Bolman and Lyster, chapter 8, for a discussion of the khurus vault paintings.

105 The more common version of their names is the Babylonian: Shadrach, Abednego, and Mesech. For their names in the Coptic tradition, see Mikhail and Vivian 1997, 48 and n. 196.

106 "Constitutions of the Holy Apostles" 5.1, Oden and Hall 1998, 244; Schiller 1972:2, 4.

107 Pringle 1993:1, 224–229. Folda 1995, 82. For the Christian cult see Teteriatnikov 1992, 109.

108 Pringle 1993:1, 224.

109 Pringle 1993:1, 225–227.

110 "The Liturgy of the Coptic Jacobites, Including the Anaphora of S. Mark or S. Cyril," in Brightman 1896, 170.

111 Coquin and Rutschowskaya 1994, 116–117. Byzantine sources on this subject are numerous. For some of them, see Maraval 1971, 222–223, n. 2.

112 It can also be seen in the narrative scenes in the upper zone of the khurus (Bolman and Lyster, chapter 8).

113 The conservators observe that the later team did this, and also covered the interiors of the domes and the borders around other early thirteenth-century paintings. Luzi and De Cesaris, chapter 9.

114 See Pearson, chapter 14.

115 Lk 16:19–31. To my knowledge, Tim Vivian was the first person to identify this figure as Nineve, on a visit to the Monastery of St. Antony shortly after this vignette was uncovered.

116 George is also depicted at N25, figs. 4.5, 7.22.

117 Budge 1888, 207–208.

118 Budge 1888, 215.

119 Budge 1888, 234.

120 Budge 1888, 269.

121 "The Martyrdom of St. Mercurius the General," BMO6801, fol.4a–b; Budge 1915, 811. The source of the appellation is unclear. Karl-Heinz Brune hypothesizes a textual source based on an iconographic shift which he notes, comparing the drawing of the saint from Vatican Coptic Codex 66, fol. 287, and the painting in the Church of St. Antony. Brune 1995, 18.

122 Cited in Lucchesi-Palli 1978, 162.

123 See the discussion of the paintings in the chapel, in this chapter, for more information on the source of the fabric.

124 "Martyrdom," BMO6801, fol. 10b; Budge 1915, 817.

125 "Martyrdom," BMO6801, fols. 21a–21b; Budge 1915, 826.

126 Al-Mu'taman abu Ishaq al-'Assal, "Somme des aspects de la religion," part 2; Zanetti 1991, 81.

127 C-L 303; Piankoff 1946–1947, 57–61; Father Maximous El-Anthony, n.d., and Piankoff 1942, 17–18.

128 This summary is abstracted from passages in "The Liturgy of the Coptic Jacobites, Including The Anaphora of S. Mark or S. Cyril" in Brightman 1896, 1:144–188. It is also amplified by Taft 1987, 417.

129 See van Loon 1999b.

130 Van Loon 1993, 498–499.

131 Van Loon 1993, 498.

132 The first study to consider Coptic art in the context of a vision, which serves as a point of inspiration for this section, is van Moorsel's short work: van Moorsel 1982, 337–340. Many of the sources on visions used in this section were collected by Meinardus 1987, 155–170.

133 Quoted in Meinardus 1987, 165.

134 Quoted in Meinardus 1987, 167.

135 Committee Formed by His Holiness Pope Shenouda III 1993, 307.

136 Abu al-Barakat ibn Kabar, *La lampe des ténèbres*, chapter 24; Zanetti 1991, 84.

137 Van Loon 1992, 120–121. A visual parallel in a monastic setting is the much earlier encaustic painting of the subject from the Monastery of St. Catherine on Mount Sinai.

138 Robinson 1987, 31–32.

139 A famous early example is a mosaic in Sta. Maria Maggiore (Rome). The ninth-century Khludov Psalter, in Moscow, includes Melchizedek in the Communion of the Apostles. Melchizedek is dressed as a king in this scene: in Schiller 1972:2, fig.60. Another Byzantine Psalter, Bibliotheca Vaticana Barb., Gr. 372, also includes a kingly Melchizedek in the Communion of the Apostles, f. 188.

140 See Bolman, chapter 6.

141 Van Moorsel 1998, 329–342.

142 Van Moorsel 1998, 332.

143 "The Life and Journey of Daniel, Abbot of the Russian Land," in Wilkinson with Hill and Ryan 1988, 161–162.

144 Robinson 1987, 28.

145 Robinson 1987, 28–31.

146 Van Moorsel 1998, 332.

147 "The Rite of Initiation into Monasticism," in KHS-Burmester 1967, 192–193. This passage is from a fourteenth-century manuscript, MS Lit. 4, Coptic Museum, Cairo. Given the general conservatism of the Coptic Church, it seems legitimate to use a textual source that is about a century later than the paintings in question, although of course we cannot be sure that it reflects thirteenth-century practices.

148 Brightman 1896, 181–182. Additional symbolic parallels between the event in Isaiah and the Eucharist are made by Theodore of Mopsuestia. Mingana 1933, 118–120.

149 See Geymonat 1999, for a discussion of this iconographic subject in the Parma Baptistery and elsewhere.

150 Jerome, "Letters to Rusticus" 125-7, Oden and Hall 1998, 7.

151 Derda 1995, 16–17, 27–31; van Moorsel 1990, 21.

152 Bell 1983, 69.

153 John Chrysostom, attr. to, "Encomium on the Four Bodiless Living Creatures," New York, Pierpont Morgan Library M612, fols. 8va, 14va–15vb; Craig S. Wansink, trans. in Depuydt 1991, 33, 38–39.

154 The earliest evidence for this monogram on Eucharistic loaves is a bread stamp dated ca. sixth–seventh century and found on Cyprus. Galavaris refers to the text as the "eucharistic formula of John Chrysostom." A variation of it can be seen on a sixth–seventh century stamp from Achmim-Panopolis, now in Geneva. Texts from this period describe angels escorting the eucharistic elements to the altar. Galavaris 1970, 65, 73–76, 173, 175, fig. 37. The modern Greek Orthodox loaf includes the formula of John Chrysostom, and this monogram with the cross is also on the discs held by the archangels in the khurus archway. See Bolman and Lyster, chapter 8, figs. 8.14–8.15.

155 See Vivian, chapter 1, for Athanasius's *Life of Antony*.

156 See Vivian, chapter 1, for the Council of Chalcedon.

157 Note the pearl border directly across the sanctuary, on the southern wall (s5–s7; fig. 4.43), and the triangular motif, reversed and used as a footstool, under the feet of the three patriarchs (κ5; fig. 4.25).

158 Bolman, chapters 3 and 6.

159 "The Liturgy of the Coptic Jacobites," in Brightman 1896, 1:187–188.

160 Kasser, Khater and KHS-Burmester 1974, 14:48–49.

161 "The Liturgy of the Coptic Jacobites," in Brightman 1896, 1:187–188.

162 Jones, chapter 2.

163 Bolman, chapter 3.

164 Martin Werner has united disparate evidence and has made a compelling case for the origin in early Coptic art of this type; see especially Werner's lengthy discussion of the complex possibilities inherent in the St. Antony *zoa* as they are shown in the Deesis Chapel, Werner 1989–1990, 12–19, and Werner 1984–1986. Van Moorsel 1978 has also analyzed the four creatures at length. He has pointed out the closest parallel to the unusual depiction of the four creatures here, in a painting from the Nubian site of Sonqui Tino. Van Moorsel 1983.

165 Van Moorsel and Werner have identified the Deesis here. Van Moorsel 1995b, 174; Werner 1989–1990, 12.

166 "The Liturgy of the Coptic Jacobites," in Brightman 1896, 152.

167 Schick 1995, 163–166; Griffith 1985, 63–65.

168 Reinink 1992, 171–174.

169 For the decline of the cult of the cross in Byzantium, see Thierry 1981, 227–228. For other examples of painted crosses in Coptic churches, see Bolman, chapter 6.

170 Constantine the Great, St. Sylvester Chapel, SS. Quattro Coronati, Rome. My thanks to Jones, Luzi, and De Cesaris for this information. Daniel: Chapel of Daniel, Göreme. Bier of the Virgin Mary, Church of the Panagia Phorbiotissa, Asinou, Cyprus, illustrated in Evans and Wixom 1997, 112.

171 The León reliquary is lined with two pieces of different fabric, and the one in question is in the body of the box. Williams and Walker 1993, 239–244. I am grateful to John Williams and Charles Little for their help in furnishing me with a photograph of the textile.

172 For the cult of the cross see Viaud 1966 and Viaud 1967–1968. My thanks to Father Isaac for explaining current practice to me, and for permitting me to photograph the processional cross. Van Moorsel has studied the cult of the cross, and depictions of it, but the examples he has examined do not include draped cloth. Van Moorsel 1979, 409–415. See my remarks in chapter 6.

173 Werner interprets the program of this chapel as referring to the Second Coming of Christ, which also fits the intercessory character of the Deesis. Werner 1989–1990, 12–15.

5. THEODORE'S STYLE, THE ART OF CHRISTIAN EGYPT, AND BEYOND

1 Bolman, introduction and conclusion.

2 The two Coptic monasteries that have yielded the most paintings, the Monastery of Apa Apollo at Bawit and the Monastery of Apa Jeremiah at Saqqara, were excavated about a century ago, using what are now considered to be inadequate methods. On the excavation at Bawit, Hans-Georg Severin wrote: "There are for the moment no datings assured by excavation data (stratigraphy, ceramics, coins). Since building phases and even rebuildings, which we can identify in many sections on the basis of old excavation photographs, were almost without exception not observed or even documented at the time, we have no clues as to the relative chronology of the complex." Severin 1991, 364. Grossmann's work has increased our understanding of Saqqara considerably. Grossmann 1991e, 773–776. However, the fact remains that Quibell excavated most of the wall paintings. Quibell 1908, 1909, 1912. Even though he recorded more in the way of material evidence than did the excavators of Bawit, we still lack evidence to do more than very generally date the paintings. Rassart-Deberg

257

and Van Loon note the difficulty of dating Coptic art. Van Loon 1999b, 193–195; Rassart-Deberg 1981, 268.

3 For example, the newly discovered Annunciation in the Syrian Monastery has been dated variously to a period spanning four hundred years. Hunt 1995, 212; Innemée 1998b, 145.

4 Van Moorsel 1983, 28.

5 Leroy 1982, 19.

6 See Lyster, chapter 7, for a discussion of the martyrs' weaponry, and the inscription bordering the shield.

7 The paintings in the Syrian Monastery may one day be found to cover more wall space, after all of the overlying plaster has been removed, but large painted areas are in poor condition, and they were not all part of the same artistic program.

8 Van Moorsel went a long way toward resolving questions about the extent of the program that could be attributed to Theodore, but he explains that the density of over-painting in some areas makes an evaluation of them for links with Theodore's paintings impossible. Van Moorsel 1995b, 179–186. Hunt summarizes some of the earlier confusion about dating. Hunt 1985, 148, n. 37.

9 Hunt has linked the treatment of Christ's knee in the Deesis chapel (C2) with the rendering of the same anatomical part in the painting of the Ascension at the Syrian Monastery. Hunt 1985, 118. I find the St. Antony circles to be much more abstract than the examples that Hunt suggests and so do not assert a similar tie.

10 For example, the two angels flanking Christ in Majesty (S1), and several of the twenty-four elders (S33–36).

11 The level of the floor is higher now than it was in 1232/1233. See Jones, chapter 2.

12 On the small buildings, see Lyster, chapter 7, and Meinardus 1972.

13 One flaw in this reasoning is the oval ear type used in the painting of the sacrifice of Isaac (S38) and nearby scenes. Theodore's name is located within this painting, under the ram. Certainly Theodore could have had two modes for depicting ears. I find it more likely to imagine him painting the two major images of Christ and not the scenes of sacrifice around the inscription with his name, but of course this is conjectural. Van Loon assigns the sacrifice scene and others in the sanctuary to Theodore. Van Loon 1999b, 107.

14 My thanks to William Lyster for the frieze suggestion.

15 In conjunction with these words, it is interesting to consider instructions to a manuscript illuminator from the very beginnings of Christian art. The notations were written within the borders of each miniature, and later painted over. They are partially visible under flaking pigment. One example will show the iconographic specificity of these instructions: "Make a city, and outside the city make where the prophet kills the foreign king with a spear and Saul standing on the other side with two servants." *Quedlinburg Itala*, ca. A.D. 350–410. Davis-Weyer 1986, 23–24.

16 Meinardus is vague about the dating of the paintings in this chapel, but he places most of the paintings in the church to between the fourteenth and the mid-seventeenth centuries. Meinardus 1969–1970, 133. Rassart-Debergh implies, but does not directly state, that the paintings date between the tenth and twelfth centuries. Rassart-Debergh 1981, 246. Hunt has located the central apse painting from this chapel between ca. 1225–1250, which coincides with the dates I propose. She accepts 1175–1176 as a terminus post quem for the church itself, due to fire and a rebuilding, but because the entire building was not destroyed at that time, I find the basis for this premise uncertain. Hunt does not explain her reasons for dating the paintings in the Monastery of St. Mercurius to such a precise quarter-century. Hunt 1985, 118. Van Loon's important consideration of the paintings in the Monastery of St. Mercurius appeared just in time for brief consideration. Van Loon 1999b, 17–30. Zibawi 1995, 176.

17 Van Loon 1999b, 27–30.

18 For the north gallery painting: van Loon 1999b, figs. 30–31. For the Chapel of St. George archangel: van Loon 1999b, 288, fig. 10.

19 Van Loon 1999b, fig. 24.

20 Van Loon 1999b, 28. Of course, earlier Coptic paintings show a gray line below the eyelid, witness the face of Christ from Bawit, now in the Coptic Museum. Zibawi 1995, color plate 49. Nevertheless, the loose, calligraphic gray line below the eye in the Bawit painting is very different in character from the thick, more densely applied lines noted by van Loon, and it is this type of rendering that is also visible in the Church of St. Antony.

21 Zibawi 1995, color plate 53.

22 Leroy 1982, 112–113; van Loon 1999b, 55–60.

23 Leroy 1982, pls. 67 and 75.

24 Van Loon notes the similarities between this type of eye at the Church of St. Antony and those found in the Sanctuary of St. Mark (Wadi al-Natrun) and the Church of St. Mercurius (Old Cairo). She nevertheless dates these two latter monuments significantly earlier than the Church of St. Antony. Van Loon 1999b, 59–60 and nn. 261–262.

25 Walters 1974, fig. 6.

26 Leroy 1982, pls. 77–78.

27 A clear instance of this can be seen along the inner line of John the Baptist's cuff and left arm. Abraham's cloak is similarly articulated. Leroy 1982, pls. 60, 38.

28 See, for example, the hems of the clothing worn by Moses and Aaron. Leroy 1982, pls. 55–56.

29 Leroy 1982, pl. 42.

30 This decorative ribbon is an ancient motif that is also found with very similar details in Byzantine art—for example, at Kurbinovo, dated to 1191.

31 An example of drapery rendered in swirling patterns of gold wire is the so-called Holy Crown of Hungary, which includes late–eleventh century Byzantine enamels. A twelfth-century icon with gold lines is the Annunciation in the Monastery of St. Catherine on Mount Sinai. A manuscript illumination with gold-outlined drapery that looks as if it could actually be enamel is the depiction of Luke (fol. 87v) in the Ostromir Lectionary, made in Kievan Rus', 1056–1057. This image is "executed in a cloisonné-enamel-like style employing bright colors with heavy gold lines to indicate drapery folds." Olena Z. Pevny, in Evans and Wixom 1997, 294–296, fig. 198.

32 The drawing of the child is from one of the small vignettes framing a drawing of the Crucifixion. Auxerre, Cathedral of St. Étienne, Treasury. Considerable additional research would need to be done to prove stylistic use of Romanesque and Crusader art by Theodore and his team. My thanks to Jaroslav Folda for his consideration of this problem.

33 I do not see the parallels that van Loon does between the paintings in the Monastery of St. Mercurius and those in the Monastery of St. Bishoi (Chapel of Benjamin). I have not had time to consider her assertion more than briefly, and so my remarks are tentative. Van Loon 1999b, 81–82. I am not, however, including at this time the Bishoi Monastery paintings in the school of painting that includes Theodore and his team.

34 See chapter 7.

35 Hunt associates the paintings in the Deesis chapel with the workshop she has identified, partially on the basis of two Armenian inscriptions, and partially on stylistic grounds. Hunt 1985, 118, 141–144, and n. 37. Postcleaning, it is apparent that the writing in question is graffiti and not part of the painted program. I do not see close stylistic ties between the paintings by Theodore in the Church of St. Antony and any of the paintings Hunt includes in her workshop. Hunt's observations about the Deesis chapel are only a very small part of her extra-

ordinarily fine article. Her work carries further the groundbreaking formulations of Nelson 1983, 201–218.

6. Theodore's Program in Context

1 Mathews 1998, 55–59.

2 Several Coptic sources, including the ca. 1300 *Lampe des ténèbres* defend the use of images. Zanetti 1991, 77–92, esp. 83–86.

3 Hunt's work is a notable exception to this trend of neglect, including specific examples of the use of middle Byzantine iconography by Coptic artists. Hunt 1985, 129.

4 Hunt includes examples of Coptic artists drawing on Crusader art. Hunt 1985, 136.

5 Although some paintings from early monastic sites in Cappadocia have survived, most there date between ca. 900–1050. Wharton 1991, 379.

6 Rassart-Debergh 1989, 59; Rassart-Debergh 1986, 363–366.

7 Grossmann 1991e, 773–774; Severin 1991, 364; Krause and Wessel 1966, 1:570–573.

8 Some of the earliest paintings in Egypt come from mortuary chapels. Van Moorsel 1990, 19. I have chosen to describe the small monastic spaces with prominent eastern niches, painted with devotional subjects, as oratories. They can also be called cells, or simply rooms. Darlene Brooks-Hedstrom is currently studying these spaces in an attempt to clarify and analyze their functions. Brooks-Hedstrom, 2001.

9 Bolman 1998, 65–77; Bolman 1997, 215–271.

10 Rassart-Debergh 1981, 250–251, 273.

11 Saqqara cells 709, 733, and B.

12 Coptic Museum, Cairo, Inv. no. 7118.

13 In a White Monastery painting of this subject, the Virgin's hands are positioned at the bottom of the shield, and only the bust of the Christ Child is shown. This painting postdates that of Theodore.

14 Rassart-Debergh 1988; Rassart-Debergh 1989, 64, 67, 68, 74–76; Rassart-Debergh, 1986, 363–366; van Moorsel 1979, 409–415.

15 Saqqara, cell F. Coquin and Martin, 1991c, 2312. Rassart-Debergh 1987.

16 Saqqara, cell 1772. Another early example is a painted marble sanctuary pier, in the Monastery of St. Catherine, Mount Sinai.

17 Walters 1989, 205. The entire group of paintings may not have been done at one time, and their placement is unclear. Some of them seem to have belonged to a monastic church. Walters 1989, 191–192.

18 Leroy 1975b, 32. Exceptionally close stylistic parallels between the figures of Athanasius and Gregory in the South Church and the two monastic saints from Tebtunis suggest to me a more precise date of ca. 950. The parallels are so close that they may even have been painted by the same workshop. Compare plates 6–7, Leroy 1975b, with plate 21 from Walters 1989.

19 Godlewski 1997, 129. I tend to see the paintings in what is now the narthex at Naqlun as belonging to a somewhat different time period or painting campaign than those in the nave and sanctuary. Until I have been able to consult the forthcoming publication by Godlewski, my comments are of course preliminary. My thanks to Godlewski for a site tour and an extensive introduction to the paintings.

20 Another example of this subject is most likely shown on the northern church wall at Naqlun. Godlewski 1997, 131; Godlewski 1999.

21 Godlewski 1997, 131.

22 Walters 1989, pl. XVII.

23 See Vivian, chapter 1, for the development of monasticism, and Bolman, chapter 4, for more on Pachomius in the painted program of 1232/1233.

24 Godlewski 1997, 130.

25 My thanks to Godlewski for this information.

26 Leroy 1975b, pls. 5–7.

27 See Bolman, chapter 4.

28 Innemée 1998b, 147–148. Van Moorsel 2000, 29. A possible eleventh-century Nubian parallel may exist in fragmentary form, from the Faras Cathedral. It shows an olive tree, below which is a human face in flames. Michalowski 1974, 219–221. It seems to me that the tree could belong to a scene of paradise, with the patriarchs, and could include also a vignette of Hell underneath it.

29 Innemée suggests a possible date of ca. 1000. Lecture at ARCE, Cairo, October 18, 2000, "Dayr al-Surian: Wall Paintings in a Syrian-Coptic Community."

30 This can be seen in Mar Musa al Habashi and the Crusader church of Abu Gosh. Dodd 1992, figs. 40, 47; Folda 1995, 386, fig. 9.35-g.

31 Last Judgment mosaic, Sta. Maria Assunta, Torcello.

32 Epiphanius of Salamis, Letter to the Emperor Theodosius. Mango 1972, 41–42.

33 Walters 1989, pl. 17.

34 A.M. 846 or 896. Leroy 1975b, 33, pls. 39–48; Coquin 1975, 253–254.

35 See Bolman, chapter 5.

36 The parallels in the Monastery of St. Antony are located at N1, N2, N33, N12, N11, N30, and N32. In the Monasteries of the Romans and of St. Macarius the paintings are within the sanctuary. For the paintings in the Monastery of the Romans: van Moorsel 1992, 173.

37 For the Monastery of the Romans: van Moorsel 1992, figs. 5–7, 175. For the Monastery of St. Macarius: Leroy 1982, pls. 69–70. Geymonat discusses a rare Italian example of this iconography. Geymonat 1999, 431–450, figs. 2–8.

38 Badawy 1978, 272; Rassart-Debergh 1981, 250; Hunt 1985, 115; Laferrière 1993, 310; van Moorsel 1995b, 174–175; Werner 1989–1990, 7.

39 For photographs of Deir Abu Fana: Attalla n.d., 1:101–108; Capuani 1999, fig. 59c. For Sohag: Laferrière 1993, figs. 4–7, 10–11b. To my knowledge, these fabric-draped crosses have not been analyzed in conjunction with other depictions of the cross.

40 Military martyrs are also shown standing in early Coptic art, not only on horseback. For an image of Menas at Bawit, room 27: Maspero 1931, pl.41. Standing military saints are shown at Kellia, Qouçour el-Izelia, kom 14, room 15, east niche. Rassart-Debergh 1989, 61–62, fig.45. This standing tradition seems to have become very popular in later Byzantine art, but was much less so in later Coptic art.

41 Vivian, chapter 1; Bolman, chapter 4.

42 See Bolman, chapter 4, for a discussion of this incomplete northern wall.

43 Demus 1948, 26.

44 Gerstel 2000.

45 Grossmann 1982, 65; Grossmann 1991b, 554. Lyster, in conversation, 2000.

46 Demus 1948, 11.

47 The implications of this placement are explored by Mathews 1990, 191–214.

48 Bolman, chapter 4.

49 Walter 1968, 317, 327.

50 Two twelfth-century examples are in chapels 19 and 22, Göreme, Cappadocia. An upper-level chapel at the western end of the church of St. Sabas in Trebizond includes this scene, dated to ca. 1250–1300. Restle 1968, 3: pl. 68, figs. 529–530.

51 For the icon: Papageorghiou 1992, pl. 3. For the mosaic: Kitzinger 1990, 15, cat. no. 72, fig. 119. For the illumination: Mount Athos, Dionysiou Monastery MS 61, fol. 1v, in Rodley 1994, fig. 215, p. 256.

52 *Histoire Universelle,* Dijon, Bibliothèque Municipale 562 (323), fol. 3v, Acre, ca. 1250–1275; Buchthal 1957, 148, pl. 82, fig. b.

53 Belting 1994, 249–257, figs. 160, 227.

54 Bolman, chapter 4.

55 An unpublished fifteenth-century example from Crete is now in the Byzantine Museum, Athens. A delightful seventeenth-century example from the P. Kanellopoulos Collection, Athens, is illustrated in Ministry of Culture 1985, 158–159, 162, 164.

56 The pointing figure of Christ could have been transmitted via Byzantine or Crusader art.

57 The iconography is not identical but is similar enough to warrant this assertion of the Coptic source as a model. It is much closer to that at the Monastery of St. Antony than is the painting of Macarius on a nave column in the Church of the Nativity, Bethlehem, or in the Menologion of Basil II. In the column painting, the saint stands alone, without the cherub, is shown bareheaded, and wears a very different ascetic garb from the kind we see in the Church of St. Antony and the Sinai icon. The cherub is not included in either image. Illustrations: Folda 1995, 283–284; Anon. 1907, v.2, pl.334. My thanks to Anthony Cutler for the reference to the Menologion illumination.

58 A sixteenth-century source reports the existence of a hermitage dedicated to St. Antony located outside of the Monastery of St. Catherine. Labib 1961, 78. The early–twelfth century "Work on Geography" describes the following: the monks from the Monastery of St. Catherine on Mount Sinai "freely and quietly possess monasteries in Egypt and Persia, around the Red Sea and in Arabia, from which their livelihood is abundant." Wilkinson with Hill and Ryan 1988, 12, 186.

7. REFLECTIONS OF THE
TEMPORAL WORLD

My thanks to Renata Holod for some very useful suggestions on an earlier version of this chapter.

1 The visual evidence in Theodore's work does not enable us to make many observations about Jews, however the Cairo Geniza documents demonstrate this point emphatically. Goitein 1967–1994. There is one image of a Jew in Theodore's program (N25). He is shown wearing a turban, as are some of the Christians.

2 Lapidus 1972; Lev 1991, 185–189; Little 1976.

3 Atiya 1986, 92; Sanders 1998, 169–170.

4 Wilfong 1998, 184–186.

5 Little 1976, 556.

6 Lev 1991, 60.

7 Atiya 1986, 91–92; Cohen 1985, 75; Farré 1991, 1097–1098; Lev 1991, 190–191, 194–196.

8 For church revenues under the Fatimids, see Evetts 1895, 15.

9 Because many Coptic churches have not survived from the medieval period, this statement cannot be conclusively demonstrated.

10 Coptic textile roundel with an image of a mounted hunter, ca. 600–800: Moscow, State Museum of the Fine Arts, 1a 5175; in Institut du Monde Arabe 2000, 172, fig. 176.

11 Menas: Manchester, Ryland's Library, Coptic S. 33; in Leroy 1974, pl. 106, 2. Theodore: New York, Pierpont Morgan Library, M. 613; in Leroy 1974, pl. 107, 2.

12 Godlewski 1997, 130.

13 Lewis 1973, figs. 1–16.

14 Humphreys 1977, 23, n.16.

15 Goitein 1967–1994, v. 4, 158–159.

16 Creswell 1978, 1: al-Aqmar, 243; al-Azhar, 254; Salih Tala'i', 283.

17 See Pearson, chapter 14.

18 I would like to thank Alice Bouilliez for her numerous insights into Theodore's horses.

19 Despite the absence of an inscription, the identification of this figure as Athanasius seems certain. Godlewski 1997, 129–130; 1999, 160–161.

20 N1–N3, N7–N13, N15, N16, N28–N30, N32–N36, K7 (Palace of Nebuchadnezzar), s1 (Virgin Mary), s8, s9.

21 The earliest surviving examples of the pointed arch in Egypt are at the Nilometer on Roda Island (861–862) and the Mosque of Ahmad ibn Tulun (879), both in Cairo. Creswell and Allen 1989, 383–385, 392–406.

22 N7–N10, N12, N28, K7 (Palace of Nebuchadnezzar), s1 (Virgin Mary).

23 Fatimid examples in Cairo are found at the Mosque of al-Hakim (1013), the Mashhad of al-Juyushi (1085), and the Mausoleum of Yahya ash-Shabihi (ca. 1150). The same style of capital is also used in Coptic churches of Old Cairo, such as the Mu'allaqa and Abu Sarga. Butler described this form as a "Saracen capital"; see Butler 1884, 1:188.

24 Bierman 1998a, 357.

25 Bierman 1998a, 360–363; Hunt 1998, 325–326.

26 N7–N10, N12, N14–N16, N28, N32–N35.

27 Coptic frontispiece of St. Luke (1173): Bodleian Library, Oxford (Hunt. 17), fol. 197v; in Leroy 1974, fig. 40, 1. Wall painting of the Galaktotrophousa (thirteenth century): Church of SS. Sergius and Bacchus, Qarra, Syria; Leroy 1975a and Zibawi 1995, color pl. 18. Miniature of the "39th Session," *Maqamat* of al-Hariri, Baghdad, 1237, Bibliothèque Nationale, Paris

(ms. Arabe 5847) fol. 120r; Okhasah 1992, 126. Coptic illuminated Gospel (1249–1250): Institut Catholique, Paris (Copte-Arabe 1), fols. 57r (Suicide of Judas) and 109v (Christ in the synagogue of Nazareth); in Leroy 1974, figs. 82 and 87, and Boud'hors 1996, 238–239.

28 Atiya 1991c, 1462–1464.

29 See Pearson, chapter 14.

30 Contadini 1998, 52–53.

31 Philon 1980, 186.

32 Alpha and Omega: also see Rv 1:8. Al-Fadi: I would like to thank Samir Morcos for deciphering this inscription.

33 Contadini 1998, 43–48; Stillman 1986, 736–737.

34 Rosenthal 1967, 2:65–66.

35 Baker 1995, 57–60.

36 N3, N29, K3.8, s3, s4, s5, s6 (a vegetal tiraz), s7–s9, s11.

37 Cohen 1985, 69.

38 Thackston 1986, 48.

39 N25, N26, K3.

40 Van Moorsel, drawing on the work of Underwood at the Kariye Jami in Istanbul. Van Moorsel 1995b, 88–89.

41 Heath 1979, 6–7.

42 Barberini Ivory, sixth century, Musée du Louvre, Paris (OA 9063); in Mathews 1998, 16, fig. 6.

43 Luzi and De Cesaris discovered that there was originally some kind of round appliqué attached to these medallions, perhaps gold-painted parchment roundels.

44 Other examples include his flat crown and red boots. The process of assimilation could also work in the opposite direction. Basil II is depicted as a soldier saint in the miniature from his psalter. His head is surrounded by a nimbus and he receives two heavenly crowns. This identification is further emphasized by the six iconlike images of military martyrs flanking the emperor.

45 Maguire, Maguire, and Duncan-Flowers 1989, 3.

46 Nero: Sebasteion, north portico, Aphrodisias, Turkey; in Erim 1993, 64, and Barrett 1996, pl. 19. Honorius: Ivory consular diptych of Probus (406), Aosta Cathedral Treasury; in Volbach 1976, pl. 1.

47 Nicolle 1994, 31, 58.

48 Hitti 1987, 130.

49 Nicolle 1996, 166.

50 Stillman 1986, 739 (kalawta); Majda 1986, 751 (küläh).

51 Al-Hassan and Hill 1986, 99; Hillenbrand 1999, 457. Although the composite bow was used in the Roman army, it entered Christian painting late, and from the East.

52 Knotted horsetails and large saddlecloths: Minai-ware bowl, Rayy, Iran, ca. 1200, Brooklyn Museum, inv. 86.227.60; in Nicolle 1994, 22. Steel mirror with gold inlay, Anatolia, ca. 1200–1250, Topkapi Sarayi Muzesi, Istanbul, inv. 2/1792; in Evans and Wixom 1997, 424, fig. 282. Brass candlestick with silver inlaid, Mosul or Damascus, c. 1250, Museum of Islamic Art, Cairo, inv. 15121; in Ward 1993, 23, fig. 11.

53 See Leroy 1975b, plates 39–48.

54 Illustrated in Walters 1989, pl. 19.

55 Esna: Coquin says that the painting of Theodore Stratelates at Deir al-Shohada has a date which can be read either as A.M. 846 (1129–1130) or as A.M. 896 (1179–1180). Coquin 1975, 253–254 and 260–261. Tebtunis: An inscription at the site recorded in 1899 mentions the date A.M. 669 (953). Walters suggests that the paintings of Theodore Stratelates and the anonymous equestrian were produced ca. 950–1050, based on the Arabic kufic script found on both saints. Walters 1989, 205–206, pls. 18 and 19.

56 Claudius (N19) is less easy to interpret. He wears the crown, cuirass, cloak, and knotted sash found on most of the equestrian saints in the church. Due to damage, it is impossible to tell whether he is dressed in a tunic or quilted coat. Alone among the equestrians, Claudius wears leather leggings, similar to those worn by the three Hebrews (K6). His horse has cloven hoofs and is speckled with clove-shaped markings, reminiscent of the Hathor cow of ancient Egypt. His is one of the few horses in the program without a knotted tail. It also wears the most elaborate equipment, including a full body caparison and a large saddlecloth. I would like to thank Salima Ikhram for pointing out the similarities between this horse and the Hathor cow.

57 Nicolle 1996, 165.

58 N22, N25, K8. Cefalù Cathedral, Sicily: mosaic, ca. 1150, south presbytery; in Lowden 1997, 328, fig. 195.

59 The two saints wear mailed hauberks instead of the lamellar armor found in the Church of St. Antony.

60 Marshall 1992, 58–59.

61 Hunt 1991, 122.

62 See Bolman, chapter 4, and Pearson, chapter 14.

63 Evetts 1895, 182.

64 Gold medal of Constantius II (ca. 350). Paris, Cabinet des Médailles: Lewis 1973, 54–55, fig. 31.

65 Hartner 1968.

66 Knotted dragons: two bronze door knockers in the shape of winged dragons (ca. 1200) from the Ulu Cami, Cisre (Jazirat ibn ʿUmar), Turkey, David Collection, Copenhagen (38/1973) and Museum fur Islamische Kunst, Berlin; in Hayward Gallery 1976, 178, fig. 194, and Hillenbrand 1999, 41, fig. 2.6. Lost Talisman Gate of Baghdad (1221); in Gierlichs 1996, pl. 66. Stone relief from the city walls of Konya (thirteenth century), Ince Minare Müzesi, Konya; in Gierlichs 1996, pl. 38.1. An interesting and related, if not parallel, example can be seen in the pavement mosaic in the Capella Palatina, Palermo. Two twisted serpents flank the altar, and Tronzo has interpreted them as eastern in origin and apotropaic in function. Tronzo 1997, 34.

67 The astrological theories of pseudoplanetary nodes may have determined Theodore's use of knotted snakes in his program, but he does not seem to have been the first Coptic painter to employ this detail. A Coptic icon of Theodore Stratelates at the Monastery of St. Catherine, dated by Weitzmann to the ninth or tenth century, shows the saint spearing a knotted serpent. The image is part of a triptych in which two equestrians flank an icon of the Ascension. The soldier saints protect the central image in much the same way as Theodore Stratelates and Sisinnius guard the nave entrance at the Church of St. Antony. See Weitzmann 1976, 71.

68 Drescher 1946, 102.

69 Nicolle 1994, 56–57.

70 Mayer 1952, 21.

71 Maqrizi quoted in Mayer 1952, 27.

72 Mayer 1952, 28.

73 Nicolle 1994, 5.

74 See Pearson, chapter 14.

75 Freer Canteen (inv. 41.10), Washington, D.C.; in Atil 1975, 69–70.

76 Baer 1989.

77 *Estoire de la Guerre Sainte*, quoted in Leaf and Purcell 1986, 56–57.

78 Husselman 1965, 80–81.

79 For Armenia, Georgia, and Russia see Anderson 1997, 83. For the Crusader states see Folda 1995, 155. For the Arab world see Ettinghausen 1977, 67–80.

80 Grabar 1984.

81 Ettinghausen and Grabar 1987, 375–376.

82 Bibliothèque Nationale, Paris (Ms. Arabe 5847). See Grabar 1984 and Okhasah 1992.

83 Leroy 1974, 226–228.

84 Bibliothèque Nationale, Paris (Ms. Copte 13). See Leroy 1974, 113–148, pls. 41–74.

85 This New Testament is written in Bohairic Coptic with a parallel Arabic translation. The manuscript is now divided between the Institut Catholique, Paris (Copte-Arabe 1) and the Coptic Museum, Cairo (MS Bibl. 94). See Leroy 1974, 157–174, pls. 75–92, and 174–177, pls. 93–95.

86 For miniature painters of the thirteenth-century Arab world sharing the same artistic milieu, see Ettinghausen and Grabar 1987, 375. On the problem of identifying illustrated secular manuscripts from thirteenth-century Egypt, see Ettinghausen 1977, 60. For a discussion of a Christian workshop of painters active in Egypt at this time see Hunt 1985, 136–144.

87 Cotton Genesis, British Library, London (cod. Cotton Otho B. VI), Bristol IVv (Lot's House); Rossano Gospels, Rossano, fol. 8v (Christ before Pilate); Ashburnham Pentateuch, Bibliothèque Nationale, Paris (cod. n. acq. lat. 2334) fol. 76r (Moses Receiving the Law); in Weitzmann 1977, color plates 22, 31, and 47. Byzantine Gospel Book, ca. 1050–1075, Paris, Bibl. Nat. Gr. 74, fol. 51v (Last Judgment); in Lowden 1997, 302. Madrid Chronicle of John Skylites, South Italian (Palermo), ca. 1150–1175, Biblioteca Nacional, Madrid (Vitr. 26-2), fols. 43r (a), 102r (a), 103v (a), 112r (b), 145r (b), and 210v; in Evans and Wixom 1997, 6, 7, 9, 11, 14, 19.

88 Nelson notes that the Cairo New Testament (1249–1250) and an undated *Fables of Bidpai* in Paris (arabe 3465) share a common vocabulary of gesture, which has its ultimate origins in Byzantium. He remarks that by 1250, "these formerly Byzantine elements have been absorbed and fused with contemporary references to form a syncretistic style that renders labels like Muslim or Christian useless in this context." Nelson 1983, 208. Nebuchadnezzar's gesture is probably an example of such a "contemporary reference," in this case deriving from an Islamic, rather than Byzantine, source.

89 Bibliothèque Nationale, Paris (Ms. Arabe 5847), fols. 8r, 10v, 14r, 18r, 21v, 25v, 42v, 43r, 110v, 118v, 125v, 130v, 146v, 148r.

90 For fifteenth-century examples of this gesture in paintings from Shiraz and Herat, see Gray 1979, pls. 40, 44, 45, figs. 86, 90, 95, 118, 125, 127, 139.

91 Mathews 1993, 104–106.

92 Sadan 1976, 127–133.

93 Madrid Chronicle of John Skylites, Biblioteca Nacional, Madrid (Vitr. 26-2), fol. 47r.; in Evans and Wixom 1997, 7.

94 Frontispieces of Kitab al-Aghani: vol. 4, Dar al-

Kutub, Cairo (B.N. adab 579), fol. 1r; in Farès 1961, pl. 8; vol. 17, Millet Kutuphanesi, Istanbul (Feyzullzh Efendi 1566), fol. 1r; in Ettinghausen 1977, 65.

95 Detached miniature from the Materia Medica of Dioskorides, copied by Abdallah ibn al-Fadl, Iraq, 1224, Freer Gallery of Art, Smithsonian Institute, Washington, D.C. (32.20v); in Atil 1975, 20, fig. 25.

96 Hunt 1985.

97 Bibliothèque Nationale, Paris (Ms. Arabe 6094).

98 Gabra remarks that by the Bahri Mamluk period (1250–1382), "Coptic ornament had assumed an Islamic flavour." He sites a manuscript of the four Gospels (A.D. 1340) in the Coptic Museum with a frontispiece in the style of contemporary Mamluk Qurʾans; Gabra 1993, 74. Another Coptic gospel book dated to 1331, in the Monastery of St. Paul, has a similar frontispiece; Lyster 1999, 70. Also see Hunt 1998, 336.

99 Bibliothèque Nationale, Paris, Ms. Copte 13, fol. 2v.; in Evans and Wixom 1997, 381, cat. 251, and Leroy 1974, pl. 42.

100 Walters 1989, 205–206, pls. 18-19.

101 Coquin 1975, 253–254, 260–261.

102 Nicolle notes that padded kazaghand armor was known in the Crusader states only in the second half of the twelfth century. Nicolle 1996, 165.

8. The Khurus Vault

1 Luzi and De Cesaris, chapter 9.

2 The conservators were able to ascertain that the rows of round windows at the base of the vault predate the painted ceiling, because these windows are recessed, and plaster overlaps their edges. However, they could not say whether the irregular profile of the current vault and the hexagonal windows at its apex were new additions by the anonymous masters.

3 Van Moorsel considers them to be contemporary with those in the khurus ceiling zone and dates all of these paintings to the fourteenth century. Van Moorsel 1995b, 109, 114–115.

4 Luzi and De Cesaris, in conversation, May 1999. See also chapter 9. Precedents exist for embedding painted wooden panels into plastered walls. The heads only of the elders of the apocalypse in the Haykal of Benjamin, in the Monastery of St. Macarius, are painted wood. Leroy 1982, 23–25, pl. 10.

5 See the long-sleeved tunics of the two angels at the top of Christ's mandorla (C2), and Mary's clothing (C10).

6 See the traces of bright green in the throne of Abraham, Isaac, and Jacob in paradise (K5).

7 Carr and Morocco 1991, 35–36.

8 Carr and Morocco 1991, 100–101; Mouriki 1984, 200.

9 Carr and Morocco 1991, 89–92.

10 This icon was significantly repainted ca. 1200. Papageorghiou 1992, 22.

11 We are grateful to Annemarie Weyl Carr for this observation.

12 Our thanks to Carr for the dating of this icon.

13 Weitzmann 1966, 61–69.

14 For the icon in Istanbul, see Mathews 1998, fig. 45. See also another mosaic icon of the Virgin and Child (ca. 1150–1200). Karakatsanis 1997, 59, fig. 2.3.

15 Note three Cypriot examples: the mandylion (Kato Lefkara); Christ Pantocrator (Lagoudera); and an icon of Christ (Church of the Panagia, Moutoullas). In the Monastery of St. Catherine, see the Christ of the Anastasis, and also the Crucifixion, both dated to ca. 1275–1300. See also Cutler 1983, 35–45.

16 Kato Lefkara, Lagoudera, and the Sinai Anastasis.

17 See the entry into Jerusalem and the Crucifixion, among others, in Mouriki 1984, 200–212, pls. LXXIX–LXXX.

18 Thanks to Robert Nelson and Slobodan Ćurčić for directing our attention to the red backgrounds in Cypriot paintings. Two examples are the Church of the Holy Cross, Pelendri, of 1178, and the Panagia tou Moutoullas of 1280.

19 This icon may have been painted for a Crusader patron, according to Weitzmann. For a reproduction and list of the extensive bibliography on the subject, see Derbes 1989, 191–192, nn. 11–12, fig. 4.

20 We are very grateful to Carr and Christina Spanou for this observation, and for their careful consideration of the Figural Master's training.

21 Our thanks to Papageorghiou, who described this interpretive model to us in conversation, September 1999.

22 Maguire 1998, 64–65.

23 For earlier examples of this practice, see Weitzmann 1964, 346–347.

24 See Bolman, chapter 4, n. 106.

25 Bolman, chapter 4.

26 An example in the Monastery of St. Catherine is part of a series of festal scenes on an iconostasis beam. Other examples exist from Cyprus, Church of Hosios Loukas, Nicosia, early thir-

teenth century, and also from Cappadocia, Karanlik Kilise, Göreme Valley. The inspiration for my observation came from a fascinating article, Neff 1998, 254–273.

27 Maguire 1988, 89.

28 Monastery of St. Macarius, late twelfth century, reproduced in Leroy 1982, pl. 33A; and the Chapel of St. George, Church of St. Mercurius, Old Cairo.

29 Paris, Institut Catholique, MS Copte-Arabe 1, fol. 179r. Leroy 1974, 157.

30 Two examples exist. Paris, Institut Catholique, MS Copte-Arabe 1, fol. 57r.

31 Paris, Institut Catholique, MS Copte-Arabe 1, fols. 175r, 178v.

32 Paris, Institut Catholique, MS Copte-Arabe 1, fols. 66r, 109v. For a discussion of this motif and its Near Eastern ancestry, see Gelfer-Jørgensen 1986, 63–68.

33 Van Moorsel considered all four archangels to be by the same hand. Van Moorsel 1995b, 109, 114.

34 Our thanks to the conservator Gianluca Tancioni, who observed this point and the details supporting it.

35 Kühnel 1988, 190, pls. 68–70; Ševčenko 1991, 438.

36 Grabar 1957, 252–254.

37 To our knowledge, this subject does not appear anywhere in Coptic art.

38 Cypriot icons: Church of Panagia Angeloktistos, Kiti, fourteenth century, Papageorghiou 1992, pl. 50; Church of the Archangelos Pedoulas, ca. 1474, Papageorghiou 1992, 105, pl. 66. Wall painting: Church of Hagia Triada, Kranidi, 1244.

39 See Pearson, chapter 14.

40 Thirteenth-century Islamic coins and architecture decorated with figurative images: Hillenbrand 1999, figs 1.5, 1.18, 1.21, 1.23, 1.24, 2.7, 2.27, 3.2, 3.22, 4.1, 4.15, 7.8, 8.5, and pls. 1.6, 4.1, 4.24.

41 Sanders 1998, 162.

42 Atil 1975, 68.

43 Grabar 1987, 129; Lings 1976, 15; Schimmel 1970, 1–4.

44 Cenotaph of Imam Shafiʿi, 1211, Museum of Islamic Art, Cairo (408); in Baer 1998, 84, fig. 103.

45 Brass astrolabes: History of Science Museum, Oxford (CCA 103); in Irwin 1997, 205, fig. 166. British Museum (BM, OA 1855.7–9.1); in Brand 1991, 107, fig. 69.

46 Maqamat of al-Hariri (twenty-first session), Baghdad, 1237, Bibliothèque Nationale, Paris

(Ms. Arabe 5847), fol. 58v; in Okhasah 1992, 89.

47 Muʿallaqa panels: Hunt 1989, figs 3–9.

48 Syriac Gospel Book, Mosul, 1220, Vatican, Bibliotheque Apstolique (Ms. Siriaco 559), fol. 105r; in Ettinghausen 1977, 94. Other Syriac examples of this arabesque network: Syriac Lectionary, Syria (Mar Mattei?), 1216–1220, British Library, Oriental and Indian Office Collection (Add. Ms. 7170) 156v (Anastasis); in Evans and Wixom 1997, 384, cat. 254. Syriac Gospel book, Church of Mar Giwargis, Qaraqus (near Mosul), thirteenth or fourteenth century; in Leroy 1964, 1. 390-396; 2. pl. 16.1.

49 Brass candlestick inlaid with silver, gold, and copper, Egypt, ca. 1290, Walters Art Gallery, Baltimore (54.459); ceramic bowl with inscription containing the napkin (buqja) blazon of a jamdar (master-of-the-robes) (ca. 1350). Cairo, Museum of Islamic Art 5974; in Atil 1981, 65–67, cat. 16 and 183–185, cat. 93. Our thanks to Nasser O. Rabbat for pointing out the similarity between the khurus cross medallions and Mamluk rank blazons.

50 El-Said and Parman 1976, 50–51, 73, fig.51.

51 Frontispiece of prince and attendants with hexagonal architectural decoration, Kitab al-Diryaq, Mosul, ca. 1225–1250, Österreichische Nationalbibliothek, Vienna (Cod. AF 10) fol. 1; in Ettinghausen 1977, 91, and Brand 1991, 115, fig. 76. Canteen, Syria, c. 1240, Freer Gallery of Art, Smithsonian Institution, Washington, D.C. (41.10); in Atil 1981, 69–73. Brass tray inlaid with silver and gold made by Mosul craftsmen in the court of the Mongol Ilkhans, Tabriz (?), ca. 1280, British Museum (OA1878.12-30.706); in Ward 1993, 87.

52 Prisse d'Avennes 1877, pl. 58.

53 Censer, Damascus, ca. 1200, Aron Collection; in Irwin 1997, 28–29, fig. 16.

54 Sircali Medrese, 1242–1243, and Karatay Medrese, 1251–1253; in Baer 1998, 77, fig. 95.

55 Mathews and Sanjian have asserted that this floral motif began to appear in the 1280s, but the Walters' example is earlier: Baltimore, Walters Art Gallery, Armenian MS W539, Four Gospels, fol. 318r. Numerous examples can be seen in the canon tables of the Glajor Gospels. Mathews and Sanjian 1991, 4 (Eusebian Prologue: frame of arch), 16 (tables 6, 7: columns), 17 (tables 8, 9: columns), 20 (table 10: border).

56 Mathews and Sanjian 1991, 167.

57 See Pearson, chapter 14.

58 See Lyster, chapter 7.

59 Our thanks to Samir Morcos for his help in identifying Psalm 122.

60 Bierman 1998b.

61 Foundation inscription of the Citadel of Cairo;

in Rabbat 1995, pls. 11, 12.

62 Inscriptions of the funerary complex of Qalawun, Creswell 1978, v. 2, pls. 65a–b (façade), 70a (mausoleum).

63 See Blair 1998, 32, fig. 3.13.

64 See Pearson, chapter 14.

65 This inscription is so similar in style to the archway inscription between the nave and the annex (N17) that they were probably painted at the same time.

66 See Bolman, chapter 4.

67 Maqamat of al-Hariri, Baghdad, ca. 1225–1235, State Hermitage Museum, St. Petersburg (Ms. S. 23), 250 (thirty-seventh session), 256 (thirty-eighth session); in Ettinghausen 1977, 107, 106.

68 Institute Catholique, Paris (Copte-Arabe 1), fols. 1v (Matthew), 65v (Mark), 105v (Luke), 174v (John); in Leroy 1974, pls. 75, 83, 85, 89. Coptic Museum, Cairo (Bibl. 94 Copte-Arabe), fol. 129v (James, Peter, John, and Jude); in Leroy 1974, pl. 94.

69 Glajor Gospels (UCLA Armenian MS 1), Canon Tables, pp. 4, 5, 13, 16, 20; in Mathews and Sanjian 1991.

70 Ibn Fadl-Allah al-ʿUmari, quoted in Rabbat 1995, 202.

71 The dates of these ceilings are often uncertain; see Lézine 1972, 131. The dates used here are from the "Index to Mohammedan Monuments" appearing on the Special 1:5000 scale maps of Cairo in Creswell 1978.

72 Qaʿa of Muhib ad-Din al-Muwaqqiʿ; in Revault and Maury 1977, pls. 19–22.

73 Lézine 1972, 132.

74 Qaʿa of the Palace of Amir Bashtak; in Revault and Maury 1977, pls. 9–14, and Lézine 1972, pls. 14–15.

75 Qaʿa of the Palace of Amir Taz; in Revault and Maury 1977, pls. 45, 47, 48, and Lézine 1972, pl. 18.

76 Maqʿad in the Palace of Amir Taz; in Revault and Maury 1977, pl. 43.

77 These buildings are among the earliest surviving examples of qaʿas in Cairo. Most of them were probably constructed more than fifty years after the Ornamental Master was active in the Church of St. Antony. The tradition of painted wooden ceilings in Cairo, however, predates the fourteenth century. The Qaʿa of the Deir al-Banat (ca. eleventh century), the Mausoleum of Imam Shafiʿi (1211), the Madrasa of Sultan as-Salih Ayyub (1243), and the funerary complex of Sultan Qalawun (1285) all feature ornamented wooden ceilings with either coffers or projecting beams. Qaʿa of the Deir al-Banat, Lézine 1972, 78–79, 132. pl. 2.

For thirteenth-century wooden ceilings, see Creswell 1978, v. 2, pl. 26a (Imam Shafiʿi), pl. 37c (Sultan as-Salih Ayyub), pls. 67b, 73a–b (Sultan Qalawun).

78 Recent Spanish conservation of the painted tie-beams at St. Sergius in Old Cairo reveals many similarities with the khurus and quʿa motifs.

79 See Pearson, chapter 14.

80 See den Heijer, in Pearson, chapter 14.

81 See the painted wooden ceiling of the entrance of the Palace of Amir Beshtak; in Revault and Maury 1977, pl. 15.

82 For example, the Qaʿa of the Deir al-Banat probably originally belonged to a Coptic notable of the Fatimid period. Certainly, at some later time it became part of the Coptic convent of St. George in Old Cairo. Lézine 1972, 72–79.

83 Vatican Library, Copto 9, folios 22r, 146v, 236v, 338v, (but not fol. 20v) in Leroy 1974, plates H, 101–104.

84 She notes an Armenian connection, indicated by inscriptional evidence, in the White Monastery near Sohag. The Armenian artist worked there in 1124 and cannot therefore be the same artist who worked at the Monastery of St. Antony.

85 Hunt, 1985, 115, 121–122, 141.

86 Hunt, 1985, 125.

87 Nelson 1983, 218.

88 Cutler 1999, 635–648, pls. III.98, III.102.

9. CONSERVATION OF THE WALL PAINTINGS

We express our gratitude to our friend and fellow conservator, Lucia Morganti, for her help and friendly criticism in producing this technical report.

1 The project was divided into six missions: 7 November–22 December 1996; 20 January–17 April 1997; 20 September–21 December 1997; 16 March–29 May 1998; 8 October–19 December 1998; and 14 April–3 June 1999.

2 Cf. ANNEX A, pages I–VI, report by Luzi and De Cesaris 1995.

3 Luzi and De Cesaris 1995.

4 The photographic documentation was executed between 1974 and 1975. Van Moorsel 1995b.

5 Cf. Kraack 1997, 258–267.

6 Note the similarities between the windows under the cupola of the sanctuary in the Church of St. Antony and those of the refectory

at the so-called Syrian Monastery. Badawy 1978, 52.

7 The addition of organic fibers served to keep the mixture humid for a longer time, so as to improve the malleability of the plaster during application of the paint.

8 Bolman, chapter 3.

9 For example, it appears on the west wall and beneath the paintings of Pachomius (N12), Shenoute (N28), Arsenius (N10), and Barsuma (N11).

10 As far as the opening of this arch is concerned, the presence of a red line traced directly on the Coptic pictorial layer can be identified in a number of points and is still clearly visible at the edge of the Byzantine plaster. This line was evidently traced as a temporary indication of the area beyond which no changes were to be made to the Coptic paintings. Between this line and the actual archway there is a distance of approximately 40 cm, which corresponds to the inner walls of the arch.

11 In some cases, Byzantine intervention can be observed where there was a marked state of decay in the Coptic paintings. On the north wall of the upper khurus, at the feet of the three women at the tomb (K12), we identified painted plaster in a large gap, over which the Byzantine layer was applied.

12 The figures of the two saints situated on the pillars at the entrance to the sanctuary (S8, S9; fig. 4.30), however, had a thick layer of dirt made up of deposits of organic and carbon particles under a thin layer of gesso. These paintings must have been covered only at a later date, when the wooden beam, now removed, was inserted at the height of the two faces.

13 The use of a binding agent similar to the one used by artists in the subsequent Coptic phase can be assumed.

14 This yellow, which is also used for the haloes, does not appear to contain iron oxide, which, however, is found in the pigment coloring the crosses between the four roundels of the apostles.

15 All the elements framing the roundels are laid on in thin irregular strips approximately 1.5 cm wide.

16 One must bear in mind that the lettering described here falls coherently into the context of coeval Western painting, where similar technical lettering can be found throughout the Mediterranean basin: cf. Winfield 1968, 61–139; Mora, Mora, and Philippot 1984. This is true both in iconographic layouts and in the use of common tools and painting methods—the same ones used in Byzantine late-Romanesque

koiné for both monumental and panel paintings—variations of which are in many cases determined merely by the use of materials available and sometimes conditioned by climatic factors. On this subject, cf. also Rosa 1957, 58–77, who describes the single stages in Byzantine painting methods during the seventh to ninth centuries, with reference to the palimpsest wall in Santa Maria Antiqua, Rome. In this sense it may be interesting to compare technical data common to this Coptic phase in the Church of St. Antony with that found, for example, in the hermit chapels in Puglia—also dating from the late-Romanesque period, between the twelfth and thirteenth centuries— which have similarities in style and probably also in application method. Cf. Pina Belli d'Elia et al. 1980, 45–116; Mango 1978; Carità 1959; Medea 1938; Medea 1937, 3–18. Byzantine sources are also useful, especially the so-called Mount Athos manuscript, the *Hermeneia* by Dionysius of Fourna (cod. gr. 708 in the St. Petersburg Public Library), in Hetherington 1978, 12–15, which contains information about composition and application of plaster, the methods used to transpose drawing, the colors used in the backgrounds, faces, etc. Cf. Rassart-Debergh 1994, 300–306.

17 Exceptions: the roundel to the left of Claudius (N19) and near the pages to the left of Mercurius (K3).

18 The earlier paintings are from the second identified program in the church, dated sometime between the seventh century and 1232.

19 See Pearson, chapter 14.

20 The highlighting on the rocks in the Easter cycle of the khurus (K12, K18) combines fine parallel and crossed lines.

21 This method of execution is paralleled technically and visually to the execution of icons and monumental paintings, consistent with sophisticated Byzantine pictorial processes. Technical similarities can be clearly seen in the various cultural areas found around the Mediterranean, consisting of a common "Byzantine" pictorial language during the late-Romanesque period. Cf. also Mora, Mora, and Philippot 1984.

22 The oldest source to deal systematically with pictorial use of rigid cardboard templates is Valentin Boltz von Rufach's *Illuminierbuch,* printed in Basle in 1549, where this means is described as "patronenpapyr": cf. Rufach 1913. A number of other documents attest to the existence of this practice, however—that is to say, the use of *patroni,* for tracing. During the Byzantine period it is also possible to find systematic descriptions of how to obtain true copies from originals, known as *antybola.* Cf. Theophilus 1843; Brunello, 1971, LXVII; Nimmo

and Olivetti 1985–1986, 399–411.

23 For the pictorial palimpsest and the various layers of wax present at K15–K16, cf. stratigraphical sections in R & C Scientifica s.r.l. 1995, 7–14, analysis no. 1.

24 For the architectural structure of the wall, see the study made in 1994 by Michael J. Kujawski. Photographic documentation by Godeau was used to chart the various types of phenomena referred to here. Observations obtained from direct analysis of the surfaces were then transferred onto this photographic documentation by superimposing a number of transparent acetate sheets with symbols, indicating the various types of deterioration and the points where they are found. Subsequently, scale drawings were prepared for the various walls, with titles and topographical references, documenting the problems found in the complex and the method of conservation required. This work will remain useful instrument for future stability tests carried out on the treated areas.

25 To identify the areas of the church in which detachments have occurred at different levels, compare the graphic documentation for each drawing (available at ARCE).

26 During winter this area is subject, albeit rarely, to periods of copious rainfall.

27 In the paintings showing George and Mercurius the presence of these extensive areas of detachment may actually also be related to static settling due to compression of the master wall.

28 For a detailed map of the gaps in the plaster, see the tables in the graphic documentation.

29 The alteration of ceruse and of the pale colors manifest themselves in punctiform or more extensive browning.

30 Basic lead carbonate is changed into platnerite, dark brown in color, according to the following formula: $2PbCO_3 \cdot Pb(OH)_2 \rightarrow PbO_2$. The presence of only a very small amount of binding agent may also have contributed to this transformation into platnerite. The area in the Coptic lettering in the khurus that has remained unaltered, as well as coinciding with an area of the wall that was protected from the sun's rays, was also painted over a second time to correct the text, thus doubling the amount of binding agent present.

31 On this subject, cf. Matteini and Moles 1989.

32 Yellow ochre changes to hematite of a red color when heated, due to a loss of H_2O.

33 The figures used to express the ratio between the various solvents in the mixture indicate the number of parts by volume.

10. PERSPECTIVES ON THE MONASTERY OF ST. ANTONY

I would like to thank Dr. Marriane Eaton-Krauss for revising my English, and Elizabeth S. Bolman for her editorial work.

1 Evetts 1895, 160 (54b).

2 See a forthcoming long article by Gabra on the history and library of the Monastery of St. Antony, planned for the second book on the site, which is mentioned by Bolman in the introduction.

3 Bonnardot and Longnon 1878, 69–70; Meinardus 1992, 11 n. 31; Coquin and Martin 1991a, 722.

4 Hoffman 1942, 11–24; Bilanuik 1991, 1118–1119.

5 Horner 1898, LXIV–LXV; Hebbelynck and van Lantschoot 1937, 32.

6 Those arguing for 1484 are Rufailah 1898, 244; Simaika 1932, 109; Naḥla 1954, 68; Farag 1964, 46; Coquin and Martin, 1991a, 722; van Moorsel 1995b, vii. In favor of 1493 are Fedden 1937, 42; Doresse 1952, 7; Meinardus 1961, 44; and Meinardus 1992, 12–13.

7 Cf. Piankoff 1956a, 24, n. 22; Timm 1984–1992, 3: 1309 n. 119.

8 Meinardus 1992, 12; van Moorsel 1995b, vii n. 14. For Gabriel VI, see Samir 1991a, 1133.

9 Monastery of St. Antony, Library, Manuscript: Liturgy 391, fol. 180; see also C-L 275–278.

10 Anonymous 1951, 53.

11 Horner 1898, lxiv; Hebbelynck and Lantschoot 1937, 32–33; Samir 1991a, 1133–1134.

12 C-L 300–301, 317.

13 Van Moorsel 1995b, viii n. 15.

14 Atiya 1991b, 1919.

15 Evelyn-White 1973, 417–430.

16 Monastery of St. Antony, Library, Ms. biblical no. 164, fol. 132v; Simaika 1932, 114, no. 104, no. 164; see also, Fedden 1937, 48; Timm 1984–1992, 3: 1314; Meinardus 1992, 19; Coquin and Martin 1991a, 723.

17 El-Masri 1982, 508–513.

18 Behrens-Abouseif 1972, 98–99; el-Masri 1982, 515–516.

19 Atiya 1968, 106; Tedeschi 1991, 1035.

20 Atiya 1968, 105.

21 Fedden 1937, 49.

22 See Vivian, chapter 1, for a discussion of the monophysite doctrine.

23 Fiey 1972–1973, 297–326.

24 Scribal note in a Syriac manuscript: Evelyn-White 1973, 317 n. 4, 389–390.

25 Samir 1995, 133; Evetts 1895, 10a, 24.

26 Khater and KHS-Burmester 1970, 3.2: 114, 191–192.

27 Budge 1928, 1106–1110.

28 Hebbelnyck and van Lantschoot 1937, 32, n. 9. Khater and KHS-Burmester 1970, 3.3: 133, 228, "Gabriel . . . a nephew of the father Peter (Butrus) aš-Šâmi" (that is, the Syrian). Patriarch Damian (569–605) also originated from Syria: Hardy 1991, 688.

29 See Griffith, chapter 11.

30 It is now preserved in the Bibliothèque Nationale, Paris, Syrian 191. See Coquin and Martin 1991a, 722.

31 Martin 1996, 88 n. 240, 502–505.

32 Kamil 1950–1957, 9–10.

33 Khater and KHS-Burmester 1970, 3.2: 114, 192.

34 Khater and KHS-Burmester 1970, 3.2: 114, 192.

35 Timm 1984–1992, 3: 1299.

36 Budge 1928, 1106–1110.

37 Colin 1988, 300, 305, 315. Sem'on also translated the life of St. Basilides. Peeters 1922, 248.

38 See Timm 1984–1992, 3: 1310; Meinardus 1992, 13, 30.

39 Wansleben (Vansleb) 1678, 181.

40 Meinardus 1962, 57; Tedeschi 1991, 1033–1036.

41 Meinardus 1992, 20–21.

42 Atiya 1968, 156–157; Tedeschi 1991, 1034–1036.

43 El-Masri 1982, 514–515.

44 Aitya 1968, 106; Tedeschi 1991, 1035.

45 Evelyn-White 1973, 366.

46 Coquin and Martin 1991b, 764. For the influence of the Armenian viziers in Egypt, see Dadoyan 1996, 193–213.

47 Hunt 1985, 113 n. 29.

48 C-L 296 n. 36, 317; van Moorsel 1991b, 726; van Moorsel 1995b, 173, 184–185; Timm 1984–1992, 3: 1311.

49 See Griffith, chapter 11.

50 Farmer 1980, 158.

51 Van Zeelst 1991, 1122.

52 Meinardus 1966, 525–526.

53 See Griffith, chapter 11. As noted in the introduction, Piccirillo will contribute a short study of Father Bernardus to an additional volume on the Monastery of St. Antony.

54 Golubovich 1919, 217.

55 Van Zeelst 1991, 1122.

56 Sauneron 1971, 309, 316, 318.

57 Meinardus 1992, 14.

58 Tedeschi 1991, 1023.

59 Libois 1977, 5, 482.

60 Meinardus 1966, 526–527.

61 For references to the recorded travelers to the monastery, see Meinardus 1992, 10–26; Timm 1984–1992, 3: 1305–1330; and Coquin and Martin 1991a, 721–723.

62 Fedden 1937, 40. See also Vivian, chapter 1, and Bolman, chapter 4.

63 For example, Félix Fabri, who visited Egypt in 1483. See Masson 1975, fol. 49b [212].

64 Meinardus 1992, 10–11; Timm 1984–1992, 3: 1305–1309.

65 Bonnardot and Longnon 1878, 70–71.

66 Potvin and Houzeau 1878, 69–70.

67 Evelyn-White 1973, 393–407.

68 Sauneron 1971, 299–313.

69 Sauneron 1971, 310–311..

70 Sauneron 1971, 309.

71 Wansleben (Vansleb) 1678, 177–200.

72 Paris, Bibliothèque National, Section cartes et plans, Rés. Ge. C.5380. Sicard 1982, 17–18 n. 1, 132.

73 Lyster 1999, 32.

74 Sicard 1982, 24. The short descriptions of Le Sieur Tourtechot de Granger, who visited the monastery in 1730, do not provide any new information about the monastery in comparison with the detailed report of Sicard 1982. Fedden 1937, 47; Meinardus 1966, 18 n. 65; Timm 1984–1992, 3: 1314; Piankoff, unpublished manuscript, 93.

75 Timm 1984–1992, 3: 1315 and nn. 160–168.

76 Wilkinson 1843, 2: 381.

77 Uspensky 1856.

78 Piankoff, unpublished manuscript, 109–111.

79 Jullien 1884, 41–42.

80 Schweinfurth 1922, 157–200, esp. 173, 179.

81 See Jones, chapter 2, for the relevance of Schweinfurth's drawing of the nave, and Lyster, chapter 7, for a discussion of Christians wearing turbans.

82 For the monastery during the twentieth century see Timm 1984–1992, 3: 1314–1317; Meinardus 1992, 22–27; Meinardus 1983, 24–51.

83 Strzygowski 1902–1903, 51–52, 56–57, pl. II (2, 3).

84 Habachi and Tawudros 1929; Piankoff 1956a, 17 n. 2.

85 Simaika 1932, 109. In 1901 George Cordan, the minister of France in Egypt, found forty-one monks there. Cordan 1903, 72.

86 Johann Georg 1930, 32–43, 95–117.

87 Johann Georg 1930, 43.

88 Johann Georg 1930, 51, fig. 150. For other artifacts, which were preserved in the keep, see Meinardus 1964, 251–263.

89 Piankoff 1954, 19–20.; Leroy 1976, 347 n. 4.

90 Piankoff 1954, 20, 22; Piankoff 1950–1957, 151–163; Piankoff 1956a, 17–25.

91 Leroy 1976, 347–379. C-L 267–321.

92 Fedden 1937, 7.

93 Fedden 1937, 51–52.

94 Fedden 1937, 54.

95 Meinardus 1972, 315.

96 Fedden 1937, 48, 53–60; Simaika 1932, 113 n. 370.

97 Grossmann 1991d, 724.

98 Meinardus 1992, 5–32.

99 Timm 1984–1992, 3: 1287–1331.

100 Comment made to Meinardus by Qummus Murqus al-Antuni, hegumenos of the Monastery of St. Antony. Meinardus 1972, 315.

101 Van Moorsel 1983, 16–29; van Moorsel 1991b, 726–728; van Moorsel 1995b.

102 Sauneron 1971, fol. 128a.

11. THE HANDWRITING ON THE WALL

1 Crone and Moreh, 2000, 21–22.

2 For the premodern periods, pens would in all probability have been the reed pens of the sort used by the professional scribes, and ink would have been the popular, carbon based concoction, ideally black in color, that sometimes turned brown on wall or papyrus. Pedersen 1984, 67–71. People either carried writing implements with them or they made use of what they could find on the spot. According to the medieval literary account of an inscriber of a poetic graffito on a rock, "he pulled an inkstand and a pen out of his sleeve and wrote on a rock next to him." Crone and Moreh 2000, 86–87. Other accounts in the same collection speak of people who dipped pieces of cloth into ink and wrote with them, or who wrote with a piece of charcoal (Crone and Moreh 2000, 22, 27); one man "took a small knife he found in front of him and wrote . . . on the wall" (Crone and Moreh 2000, 24).

3 See C-L, 267–321.

4 See C-L, 24–30, where the labels under N19, N20, N22, and N23 are recorded.

5 After the cleaning of the wall, the label under N23 is only faintly legible; it is perfectly clear on a precleaning photograph and is correctly recorded by C-L, 24. However, there is a problem with the identification, as the disparity of names indicates. It is difficult to know how the inscriber differentiated between the significance of the ك in the name as written under N19, and the ق as it is written in the seemingly same name, Claudius, under N23, where Sisinnius is in fact portrayed.

6 See Samir 1991a, 1133–1135.

7 See C-L, 278.

8 26 October 1568.

9 25 November 1568.

10 The patriarch's father had been the parish priest of the church of St. Mercurius in Old Cairo. See Samir 1991a, 1133.

11 C-L 276 unaccountably translate 185, when their own transcription, and the text on the wall, read: مايتا, *mi'atā*. Samir 1991a, 1134 says, "in the presence of eighty-five bishops."

12 At this point the transcript in C-L, 276 there appears the untranslated phrase: وكسر فلا, which means "someone has made a break." I cannot now see this in the text on the wall.

13 For the Arabic text, French translation and commentary: C-L 275–279. The English translation furnished here is based on a fresh reading of the text on the wall, which is now fainter than it was when Coquin and Laferrière read it.

14 All of them are published in C-L nos., 27, 29, 49, pp. 289–290, 291–292, 300–302.

15 See C-L no. 27, pp. 289–290.

16 See C-L no. 29, pp. 291–292.

17 See C-L no. 49, pp. 300–302.

18 C-L 300 could not read the word ايدى, indicating its place with three dots in the text.

19 In fact, C-L 301 voiced just such a doubt, suggesting that the three introductory lines, which they say "appear not to be by the same hand," could be the end of another graffito, now disappeared. I see no real reason to suppose a different hand was at work.

20 See C-L 301. These lines are now scarcely visible on the wall.

21 See the remarks of the priest Monk Martyrius El Suriany, in an unpublished paper written in Arabic for Innemée, on the graffiti in the Monastery of the Syrians. Also, Father Martyrius presented some of this material at the Seventh International Congress of Coptic Studies, held in Leiden, August 27–September 2, 2000: "The Youngest Layer of Plaster in the Church of the Holy Virgin Mary in El-Sourian Monastery." It should appear in the Acts of that congress.

22 On Garshūnī/Gershūnī writing see Hatch 1946, 42–44. There is a record of a Syrian monk copying a manuscript at the Monastery of St. Antony in Garshūnī in the year 1393. See Coquin and Martin 1991a, 722.

23 East Syrian priests: presumably this description means that the visitors were "Nestorians," members of the "Church of the East." On the significance of these designations see Brock 1996, 23–35. Methed: the reading is very uncertain.

24 The Ethiopic graffiti as they are presented here have been transcribed, translated into English, and studied by Getatchew Haile of the Hill Monastic Manuscript Library at Saint John's University, Collegeville, Minn., 56321-7300.

25 The first part of the author's name is not legible.

26 *Nəəburanä əd* (sing. *nəburä əd*) are heads of religiously and politically important monasteries.

27 The "Year 202" is obviously the year this graffito was written: A.D. 1542.

28 Täklä Haymanot (d. ca. 1313) was the founder of the Monastery of Däbrä Asbo in Shoa, renamed Däbrä Libanos after his death. Däbrä Libanos, where his relics are still preserved, has been the leading Ethiopian monastery since the thirteenth century. The native head of the church, the *etchege* (*əcäge*), was the head of this monastery. Täklä Haymanot and his followers were responsible for the spread of Christianity in Shoa and further south. See Haile 1982–83, 7–38. Abba Samu'el is probably Samu'el of the monastery of Wali/Waldəbba in the province of Begemdir. See Turaiev 1902.

29 The Armenian graffiti are being studied by Monica J. Blanchard of The Catholic University of America, Washington, D.C., 20064.

30 See the text published by C-L 296.

31 The heraldic graffiti of later medieval noble travelers from western Europe have been studied by Detlev Kraack of the Technical University, Berlin. See Kraack 1997, 249–267.

32 See Kraack 1997, 259. For descriptions and locations of these graffiti, see Meinardus 1966, 525–527.

33 See Kraack 1997, 260; Meinardus 1966, 522.

34 See Kraack 1997, 261; Meinardus 1966, 521.

35 See Fedalto 1988, 586.

36 See Strothmann 1932, 30–31.

37 See Piankoff 1943, 61–66. Archimandrite Porphyrius later wrote an account of his visit to the monastery. See Gabra, chapter 10.

38 See Volkoff 1978, 12–15.

13. IN THE FOOTSTEPS OF THE SAINTS

1 Fasting is an important religious practice among Copts. For a complete list of Coptic fasts see "Fasts," *CE.* For an anthropological study of the practice of fasting: Wissa Wasef 1971.

2 The tamgīd is usually sung in front of the tomb of the saint, but because the remains of St. Antony are not displayed, this informal ritual may take place anywhere in the church.

3 The tamgīd is written in Arabic, but the Coptic word meaning "our father" is retained.

4 Pilgrims told me that this is the cloth helmet, embellished with crosses and worn by Coptic monks, that is said to have been given first to St. Antony as an aid in his struggle with temptation. The scholar Pieternella van Doorn-Harder explains this term alternatively as either the small skema or "mintaqa (belt) that the monk receives during his initiation" or the great skema, which "consists of a four-meter-long belt of plaited leather" and is the mark of a deep spirituality and unquestionable spiritual authority. Van Doorn-Harder 1995, 68.

5 The author of this popular tamgīd is Pope Shenouda III, who before his ascension was called Abuna Antonious. Pope Shenouda III has composed other tamgīd and spiritual poetry as well. For a copy of the Arabic text see Anon 1982.

6 Traditionally these saints' festivals are called mūlids, the same word used to describe the Muslim saint festivals with which they have much in common. There has been an effort by the church to have people use the word ʿaid (pl. ʿaiyād) instead, placing the emphasis on the spiritual significance of the event and downplaying the popular religious practices associated with them. Many rural Egyptians continue to use the word *mūlid.*

7 Today the most important yearly saint festivals include Saint George (Mitt Damsis), Mari Girgis Al-Hadidi (Luxor), Anba Shenouda (Sohag), and the many festivals for the Virgin Mary, including those held at Dronka, Gebel Tair, Musturud, and Zeitoun. The most complete discussion of these festivals can be found in Viaud 1979.

8 Nadr is a common practice among both Muslims and Copts in Egypt. It entails the promise of making some sort of personal sacrifice in return for a prayer's being answered.

9 In his dissertation on the Coptic monasteries, Mark Gruber notes that "Upper Egyptian mūlids, as those in [the monastery of] el Muharraq, are . . . closely associated with seasonal and agricultural cycles. . . . The mūlid at el Muharraq is profoundly agrarian. First fruits are brought to the deir [monastery] as offerings to the monks. The monks take from the sacrifices whatever they need for themselves and later redistribute the rest among the local poor. Animals are slaughtered by leading village laymen who parade past the deir with their blood-stained swords at the head of great ritual processions." Gruber 1990.

10 On the social function of saint festivals in the Arab world see Gellner 1969 and Marx 1977.

11 For a general overview of this period, see Haykal 1983 and Farah 1986.

12 On the growth of Islamicist movements in Egypt, see Kepel 1984.

13 On Pope Kyrollious's contributions to the beginnings of the Coptic Renaissance movement, see Wakin 1963.

14 For a list of Pope Shenouda's accomplishments, see Zaki 1996. For a detailed analysis of the effects of the bureaucratic reforms within the church under Pope Shenouda, see El-Khawaga 1993.

15 Tischendorf, *Travels in the East,* quoted in Meinardus 1992, 62.

16 El-Khawaga 1993, 16.

17 Augustinous 1993, 12. Trans. by Oram.

18 Meinardus 1992, ix–x.

19 One such figure is the abbot of the Monastery of St. Macarius, Mata Al-Miskīn.

20 For a detailed ethnographic description of this monastic naming ceremony, see Gruber 1990, 98–102.

21 The metaphoric link between prayer and incense as a sweet offering to God is made several times during the course of the liturgy.

22 Pilgrimage is sometimes referred to as *ziyara,* the same word used for a visit to a friend or family member.

23 Zayt is not to be confused with the magrūn or holy chrism that is ordinarily made only once during the reign of a pope and is used strictly by priests during certain sacraments and when anointing icons.

24 Classic studies of the rich variety of ways in which baraka manifests itself include Westermarck 1968 and Dermenghem 1954.

25 The only other pilgrimage activity that I know of that is equally tiring is the ritual climb to the cave above the White Monastery, which takes place at the mūlid of Anba Shenouda in July.

26 Self-mortification or physical exhaustion en route to a holy site is a critical part of many Christian pilgrimage traditions. See, for example, Eade and Sallnow 1990.

14. THE COPTIC INSCRIPTIONS IN THE OLD CHURCH OF ST. ANTONY

1 Piankoff 1954; 1956a; 1956b; 1958.

2 C-L.

3 Van Moorsel 1995b.

4 The Coptic Psalms are translated from the Greek Septuagint version (LXX). In that version Psalms 9 and 10 are treated as one, so after that the numbering differs from that of the Hebrew text that underlies our English versions, up to Psalm 147. LXX 146–147 are treated as one in the Hebrew, so the numbering of Pss 148–150 is the same in both versions.

5 Horner 1902, 14.

6 KHS-Burmester 1967, 102.

7 KHS-Burmester 1967, 338; *Liturgy* 1974, 223; part of the Anaphora of St. Basil the Great. The phrase also occurs in the Anaphora of St. Mark; see Brightman 1965, 1: 185.

8 *Liturgy* 1974, 39, 101, 325.

9 For Magnificat see *Liturgy* 1974, 290. For Theotokia see O'Leary 1923.

10 KHS-Burmester 1967, 51–53.

11 E.g., *Liturgy* 1974, 259, 281.

12 Coquin 1975, inscriptions F, G, J, M, and Q (pp. 267, 268, 272, 274, 279); F and G lack item 4; the prayer for blessing (1) is repeated in J and M. The Esna inscriptions are in Sahidic Coptic and date from around the same time as those of St. Antony (the dated inscriptions range from 1148/1149–1315/1316. Cf. also the donor inscription (dated A.D. 953) found at Tebtunis, on which see Walters 1989, 205.

13 See N31.2, commentary. The same term appears in a dedicatory inscription in the Sanctuary of St. Mark in the Monastery of St. Macarius (Wadi al-Natrun). The inscription runs around the sanctuary, now partially visible on all four walls, beneath the octagon. See Evelyn-White, 1973, 3: 106. The beginning of it (ⲀϤϢⲰⲠⲒ ⲚⲀ ⲠⲀⲒϢⲈⲚⲈⲢⲪⲘ[ⲈⲦ]Ⲓ ⲈⲐⲚⲀⲚⲈϤ Ⲉ[. . .]) is partially shown on plate 28.A. For a better view: Leroy 1982, pl. 41. The same term is also inscribed on part of a wooden door in the Sanctuary of Benjamin at St. Macarius: Evelyn-White 1973, 92 and note. The fragmen-

tary inscription L from the Monastery of the Martyrs has at the beginning of line 8 ⲚⲒⲈⲢⲘⲈⲨⲈ[. . . , which may have a similar function, assuming that the inscriber intended to write ⲚⲒⲈⲢⲠⲘⲈⲨⲈ, "the remembrance, memorial." See Coquin 1975, 254.

14 Kalopissi-Verti 1994.

15 For numerous examples, see Kalopissi-Verti 1994.

16 One of the two painters at Esna who are known by name is Theodore of Armant, who is also a priest and a monk (the other is called Mercurius). See Coquin 1975, 248–252. Two of the named painters discussed by Kalopissi-Verti are called Theodore. One painter, whose name is John, credits his work to God with the phrase θεοῦ τὸ δῶρον ("the Gift of God"), which is the etymology of the name Theodore (Kalopissi-Verti 1994, 179). In both of his signature inscriptions our Theodore humbly expresses his unworthiness to bear the name.

17 Cf. also the confusion in the rendering of the name of the martyr Noua, N15 ("Thouan"); the possible confusion in the rendering of Heraclea, N24; and the spelling of Sisoes' name, N9.

18 Examples: genitive particle Ⲛ- for ⲚⲦⲈ-: N19.2, N22.1, N26.1, N38.3, K3.1; definite article (masc.) ⲠⲒ- for ⲠⲒ-: N24.3, K4.1, S1.7, S38:3, C2.5, C10.2; definite article (fem.) Ⲧ- for ⲧ-: N31.2, N35.3, S1.7, C2.5, C10.2; ⲚⲞⲂⲈ for ⲚⲞⲂⲒ: N35.3; ⲠⲚⲞⲨⲦⲈ for ⲫⲚⲞⲨⲦ: C3.2, C10.2.

19 The Coptic language is the latest form of the ancient Egyptian language, given written expression with the use of the Greek alphabet (supplemented by letters rendering sounds that do not occur in Greek), and with the incorporation of numerous Greek words into the Coptic vocabulary. For a good general discussion: Emmel 1992, 180–188. The most egregious example of a case-ending quirk is ⲆⲞⲚ (=τόν, accusative of the definite article) for ⲟ (=ὁ, nominative): N13.1 et passim. The Greek definite article is correctly rendered, when it is used, in the Coptic inscriptions at Esna. See Coquin, 1975, 241 et passim.

20 In the thirteenth century a few (Arabic-speaking) Coptic scholars also developed Coptic philology. See Sidarus 1978.

21 On the nomina sacra see Roberts 1979, 26–48. For recent arguments for their first-century Christian origin, see Hurtado 1998.

22 On the possible causes for such loss, see Luzi and De Cesaris, chapter 9.

23 My thanks to the following colleagues for helpful comments on earlier versions of this chapter: Elizabeth S. Bolman, Tim Vivian, David Johnson, S.J., and Janet Timbie; and to Victor

Gold and Michael Guinan for their help with the Syriac at N11.2.

24 Van Moorsel 1995b, 141. On Antony see O'Leary 1937, 76–79, and sources cited; Guillaumont 1991a, 149–151.

25 Van Moorsel 1995b, 139. On Paul see O'Leary 1937, 222–223; Guillaumont and Kuhn 1991, 1925–1926.

26 See Polotsky 1987, 219.

27 *Life of Paul of Thebes*, ch. 10; translation in White 1998.

28 On Sarapion see O'Leary 1937, 245; Griggs 1991, 2095–2096.

29 C-L, inscrip. 11.

30 The conjectured reading *wrestler* (or *athlete, contender*) is based on Isaac's designation as a *luctator* (wrestler) in the Latin translation of the Arabic text of the Coptic Synaxary (Forget 1905, 2: 127). The motif, rather widespread in monastic contexts, is ultimately based on the story of Jacob's wrestling in Genesis 32:22–32. On Isaac the Presbyter see O'Leary 1937, 159; Regnault 1991b, 1304. On the Coptic Synaxary, its various editions, and its calendar of saints, see Atiya, 1991f, 2171–2190.

31 C-L, inscrip. 10. On Paul the Simple see Vivian, chapter 1; Guillaumont 1991d, 1923.

32 C-L, inscrip. 9. On Samuel see O'Leary 1937, 242; Alcock 1991, 2092–2093. Coquin and Laferrière were able to see more of the word *archimandrite* than is now visible.

33 C-L, inscrip. 8.

34 See O'Leary 1937, 106–107; Coquin 1991c, 2029; Evelyn-White 1973, 2: 111–115.

35 On John the Little see O'Leary 1937, 170–172; Regnault 1991c, 1359–1361; Evelyn-White 1973, 2: 106–111.

36 C-L, inscrip. 7. The Coptic version of this saint's name is ⲌⲒⲌⲰⲒ (Jijoi, see Chaine 1960, 27, 68, 80); the spelling given here (Shishoi) probably reflects Arabic influence. Sisoes (Greek Σισόης) is not included in the Synaxary, but he is prominent in the Apophthegmata Patrum. On him see Regnault 1991e, 2141. C-L, 274, restore the name of this saint as [Ⲡ?]ⲒϢⲰⲒ—that is, one of the others in the Synaxary named Pishoi (cf. N7).

37 C-L, inscrip. 6. On Arsenius see O'Leary 1937, 87; Regnault 1991a, 240–241.

38 Wietheger 1992, 105–106, and literature cited there.

39 C-L, inscrip. 5. On Barsuma see O'Leary 1937, 99.

40 On the pig and serpent see C-L, 272; van

Moorsel 1995b, 130–131, pls. 67–68.

41 C-L, inscrip. 4. On Pachomius see O'Leary 1937, 211–215; Veilleux 1991, 1859–1864. Coquin and Laferrière were able to see more of the word *koinonia* than is now visible.

42 C-L, inscrip. 3. On Pakaou (Kaou) see O'Leary 1937, 176–177. Pomme is probably Bamuyah, a village north of Medinat al-Fayoum, ancient Arsinoe.

43 See C-L, 271.

44 C-L, inscrip. 2.

45 So C-L, 270. Aba Noua is associated with Piroou and Athom. See O'Leary 1937, 233.

46 C-L, inscrip. 1.

47 See C-L, 270.

48 On Piroou and Athom see O'Leary 1937, 233–234.

49 C-L, inscrip. 32.

50 C-L, inscrip. 31.

51 On the identification of this saint (not Anatolius the Persian) see van Moorsel 1995b, 1: 164–165.

52 Balestri and Hyvernat 1907–1950, 1: 34.

53 On Theodore the Oriental see O'Leary 1937, 265–266; Orlandi 1991b, 2237–2238.

54 See Winstedt 1979, 97–100.

55 C-L, inscrip. 30. On Claudius Stratelates see O'Leary 1937, 111; Atiya 1991e, 1550–1559, esp. 1553.

56 See C-L, 292, note.

57 C-L, 293.

58 C-L, inscrip. 28. On Victor see O'Leary 1937, 278–281; Samir 1991b, 2303–2308.

59 C-L, inscrip. 26. On Menas see O'Leary 1937, 194–197; Krause 1991, 1589–1590.

60 C-L, inscrip. 25. On Theodore the General see O'Leary 1937, 262–265; Orlandi 1991b, 2237–2238.

61 Winstedt 1979, 161–163.

62 Winstedt 1979, 123–130.

63 C-L, inscrip. 24. On Sisinnius (Sousenyous) see O'Leary 1937, 258–259.

64 C-L, inscrip. 23.

65 C-L, 287; O'Leary 1937, 166.

66 C-L, inscrip. 27.

67 See Budge 1928, 963–965 (fourth of Sane).

68 O'Leary 1937, 280.

69 C-L, inscrip. 22. On George of Cappadocia see O'Leary 1937, 140–145; Megally 1991, 1139–1140.

For his martyrdom and miracles see Budge 1888.

70 Budge 1888, 248–252.

71 Cf. Balestri and Hyvernat 1907–1950, 2: 232.

72 C-L, inscrip. 21, where the saint is not identified.

73 On the two Phoebammons see O'Leary 1937, 229–231; Spanel 1991a, 1963–1965.

74 C-L, inscrip. 20. Cf. N6 and note. On Shenoute of Atripe see O'Leary 1937, 251–255; Kuhn 1991, 2131–2133.

75 C-L, inscrip. 19. On Pisentius see O'Leary 1937, 234–236; Müller and Gabra 1991, 1978–1980. Qift, Coptic Kebt, is the ancient town of Koptos.

76 C-L, inscrip. 18. On Moses the Black see O'Leary 1937, 206–207; Regnault 1991d, 1681.

77 C-L, inscrip. 17.

78 See Evelyn-White 1973, 3: 92 n. 7.

79 *Liturgy* 1974, 15.

80 See *Liturgy* 1974, 197; cf. also Brightman 1965, 1: 190.

81 C-L, inscrip. 16.

82 On Maximus and Domitius, the "Roman" sons of Valentinian, see O'Leary 1937, 192–194; van Esbroeck 1991a, 1576–1578; Evelyn-White 1973, 2: 96–104.

83 C-L, inscrip. 15. On Macarius the Great see O'Leary 1937, 182–184; Guillaumont 1991c, 1491–1492; Evelyn-White 1973, 2: 60–72, 104–106.

84 Presumably this is Macarius the Alexandrian, on whom see O'Leary 1937, 184–185; Guillaumont 1991b, 1489–1490; Evelyn-White 1973, 2: 55–59, 90–91. Another possibility is Macarius of Pispir, a disciple of Antony. On him see Evelyn-White 1973, 2: 12, 15, 67.

85 C-L, inscrip. 14, but only the signature inscription is given. The saint is not identified.

86 O'Leary 1937, 185.

87 See ten Hacken 1999; Coquin 1991a, 1679–1681. On the martyr Macrobius see Orlandi 1991a, 1494.

88 See Stewart 1991, 1313.

89 C-L, inscrip. 45.

90 C-L, inscrip. 51. On Mercurius see O'Leary 1937, 201–202; van Esbroeck 1991b, 1592–1594.

91 On the names of the cannibals, unattested in Coptic literature, see C-L, 303; Piankoff 1946–47, 58.

92 Piankoff 1954, 23.

93 C-L, inscrip. 51.8.

94 C-L, inscrip. 50.

95 For an extensive homiletical treatment of the story see *On Riches*, attributed to St. Peter of Alexandria (cf. s6), in Pearson and Vivian 1993, 104–108.

96 C-L, inscrips. 63.3–4.

97 See Budge 1888, 237. Cf. C-L, 310; van Moorsel 1995b, 93, 98–102.

98 C-L, inscrips. 63.1–2.

99 Budge 1888, 269–274.

100 Budge 1888, 325.

101 C-L, inscrips. 63.5–7.

102 E.g., *Acta Martyrum*, Balestri and Hyvernat 1907–1950, 2: 310.

103 C-L, inscrip. 64.

104 Cf. van Moorsel 1995b, 103.

105 C-L, inscrip. 46; cf. van Moorsel 1995b, 102–103.

106 C-L, inscrip. 48.

107 C-L, inscrip. 47.

108 Cf. van Moorsel 1995b, 103.

109 Cf. K13 and 14. ΘЄ at the end is superfluous.

110 C-L, inscrip. 64.

111 Giannelli 1953.

112 Thanks to Johannes Den Heijer for this translation and commentary.

113 This is also the work of Den Heijer.

114 C-L, inscrip. 58–61.

115 On the living creatures see van Moorsel 1991a, 525–526. Their names are given in a recently published homily attributed to St. John Chrysostom: Kheroubiel, Zaraphiel, Baroukhael, and Dothiel. See the Encomium on the Four Living Creatures, chapter 31, in Brakke 1991, 35.

116 C-L, inscrip. 56. On Athanasius see O'Leary 1937, 90–93; Atiya 1991a, 298–302.

117 C-L, inscrip. 57. On Severus see O'Leary 1937, 249–250; Knezevich 1991, 2123–2125.

118 C-L, inscrip. 55. On Dioscorus see O'Leary 1937, 125; Roncaglia 1991, 912–915.

119 C-L, inscrip. 54. On Theophilus see O'Leary 1937, 269–272; Spanel 1991b, 2247–2253.

120 C-L, inscrip. 53. On Peter I see O'Leary 1937, 224–225; Spanel and Vivian 1991, 1943–1947.

121 C-L, inscrip. 52.

122 C-L, 305.

123 Van Moorsel 1995b, 80 n. 17.

124 On Benjamin see O'Leary 1937, 104–105; Müller 1991, 375–377.

125 C-L, inscrip. 62. On Mark see O'Leary 1937, 188; Atiya 1991d, 1528–1533.

126 C-L, inscrip. 66.

127 C-L, inscrip. 66.

128 For the other names and discussion see Leroy 1982, 83–86.

129 C-L, inscrip. 68.

130 C-L, inscrip. 69.

131 C-L, inscrips. 70.1–3.

132 C-L, inscrips. 70.4–6.

133 C-L, inscrip. 65.1.

134 C-L, inscrip. 65.2.

135 C-L, inscrip. 65.3.

136 C-L, inscrip. 65.4.

137 C-L, inscrip. 65.5.

138 C-L, inscrip. 65.6.

139 C-L, inscrip. 44.

140 C-L, inscrips. 37, 38, 39.

141 C-L, inscrips. 33, 34, 35.

142 See, e.g., Horner 1902, 17.

143 See Bolman, chapter 3.

144 C-L, inscrips. 40–43.

CONCLUSION

1 I thank Tim Vivian, who pointed this out to me.

2 The graphic documentation of the conservators is at ARCE. Three copies of the photographic record are available, at ARCE (Cairo), the Monastery of St. Antony (Red Sea), and Dumbarton Oaks (Washington, D.C.).

3 See Luzi and De Cesaris, chapter 9.

4 Layers of paint are here distinguished from layers of plaster. See Luzi and De Cesaris, chapter 9.

5 The traditional method of coping with dirt on icons is to paint over it. This practice, called refreshment, has been practiced both within and outside of Egypt. I thank Zuzanna Skalova for this information.

6 Most noteworthy are s8–10, c4–9, K1, and parts of K3, K5, and K7.

7 "Coptic art is the most primitive phase of the early Christian; its inspiration, when one can penetrate its context, is more superstition than faith. The obsession with sex which transpires

from the detailed account of temptation in the lives of Egyptian monastic saints is apparently present also in the treatment of the mythological motifs which are much used in Coptic stone carving; a favorite theme is Leda and the swan, rendered with a sensual fatness in the nudes and an obvious interest in the implications of the story." Morey 1942, 50, critically noted by Vikan 1986, 15–16. A groundbreaking historiographic critique and reshaping of late antique art in Egypt has recently been written by Thelma Thomas. Thomas 2000, xvii–xxv.

8 See Bolman, introduction, note 7.

9 Leroy 1974, 1.

10 Tronzo suggests a parallel between court society and the art of the Cappella Palatina, which can be loosely described as "separate but equal." Tronzo 1997, 134–135.

11 For an interdisciplinary analysis of this monument, see Tronzo 1997.

12 This characteristic can be seen in icons painted in a Byzantine style with obviously Latin patrons and text, or apparently purely Byzantine icons with Christian patrons wearing turbans, and with half-Greek and half-Arabic inscriptions. Several are in the Monastery of St. Catherine, Mount Sinai.

13 After observing the connections between paintings in the Monastery of the Romans and the Chapel of the Martyrs at the Syrian Monastery, I was gratified to have them confirmed by the careful work of van Loon. Van Loon 1999b, 73. The paintings to which I am referring in the White Monastery are of an archangel and of the Virgin Mary and Child, on either side of the central sanctuary. Atalla n.d., 112. Although Hunt has presented a plausible account of the Syrian Monastery Annunciation as a product of the late twelfth century, I am not confident that it was made later than the tenth century. Hunt 1995. For a summary of dating hypotheses see van Moorsel 1995a, 520–521. I have therefore not included it in this discussion of twelfth- to fourteenth-century Coptic art.

14 It may well have been used for Jewish art and architecture as well, in the eastern Mediterranean region, witness the fourteenth-century synagogue in Toledo.

15 Paris, Institut Catholique MS Copte-Arabe 1; and Cairo, Coptic Museum, MS. Bib. 94. A Gospel manuscript made in Damietta in 1179–1180 (Paris, B.N. Copte-Arabe 13, in Leroy 1974, plates 41–74) is related to this avant-garde style in many respects (principally ornamental), but its figural style has few apparent ties to other work in Egypt.

16 Vatican Library, Copto 9, folios 22r, 146v, 236v, 338v (but not fol. 20v) in Leroy 1974, plates H, 101–104. Another manuscript in this mode is Cairo, Patriarchate MS 196, fols. 111v, 186v, 307v, dated 1291, in Leroy 1974, plates 96–97.

17 Dayr al-Qusayr, Turah. The church is pre-1125. Grossmann, 1991c, 854–855. Thanks to Grossmann for bringing this to my attention.

18 Hunt 1985, 117–125, 142; Hunt 1995, 186 n.13.

19 My thanks to Innemée for expressing his reservations about the "Syrian" character of the paintings, and for information about the state of knowledge about artistic production of Christians living under Muslim rule.

20 Rassart-Debergh makes a similar observation about early Coptic art, and Hunt about medieval Coptic art. Rassart-Debergh 1981, 269; Hunt 1985, 115, 121–122, 141; Hunt 1989. I disagree here with van Loon's conclusions. Van Loon 1999b, 194–195. Another important analysis of this subject, with respect to Syrian paintings, has appeared too late to be included as more than a note. See Dodd 2000, 124–126.

21 Van Moorsel charts many of the discoveries of recent years. Van Moorsel 2000, essay 20, 265–274.

GLOSSARY

Abba (from Aramaic *Apa*): "Father," a title of respect given to senior monks.

Abun: The Metropolitan of the Ethiopian church; until 1948 the abunate was usually occupied by a Coptic monk.

Abuna (Arabic): "Our Father," a title of respect given to monks.

A.M. (anno martyrorum): The beginning of the Coptic calendar corresponds to the year A.D. 284. This first "Year of the Martyrs" commemorates the extraordinary number of Christians killed under the Roman Emperor Diocletian's rule.

Amir (Arabic, "commander" or "prince"): Muslim military rank beneath that of sultan.

Anachorêsis (Greek): Withdrawal from society, usually to the desert.

Anchoretic: Type of monasticism in which monks live alone.

Apophthegmata: See *Sayings of the Desert Fathers.*

Arianism: Christological view, declared heretical by the Council of Nicea (325), which held that the Son was inferior to the Father.

Ascesis (Greek, "practice" or "training"): Discipline by which monks seek spiritual perfection; the root of *ascetic.*

Ayyubid: Muslim dynasty that ruled Egypt from 1171 to 1250.

Baraka (Arabic): The grace or holiness of a saint, which can be transmitted through contact with places or objects close to the saint.

Baramous, Deir al-: Monastery of the Romans, Wadi al-Natrun.

Caliph (Arabic): Successor (*kalifa*) of the Prophet Mohammed as leader of the Muslim community.

Cenobitic: Type of monasticism formed around cloistered, communal life.

Chalcedon: Site of the fourth ecumenical council, held in 451. The council formulated the "two nature" Christology, which resulted in the schism between the Coptic Church of Egypt and the Church of Constantinople.

Colzim, Mount: Antony's "inner mountain," where he moved in 313, and the site of the present day Monastery of Saint Antony.

Copt ("Egyptian," from Greek *aigyptios,* via Arabic *qibt*): Member of the Orthodox Church of Egypt.

Coptic Orthodox: Designation used by Copts for their church and doctrinal beliefs.

Cuirass: Body armor reaching to the waist.

Deir or dayr (Arabic): Monastery.

Difnar: Book comprising the liturgical commemoration of saints and feasts.

Al-Fadi (Arabic): "The Redeemer."

Fatimid: Muslim dynasty that ruled Egypt from 969 to 1171.

Garshuni: Arabic written in Syriac characters.

Gebel al-Galala: The two mountain ranges along the Red Sea coast that lie north and south of the Monastery of St. Antony.

Geʿez: An Ethiopian language.

Ḥanūṭ (Arabic): Fragrant spices wrapped around the remains of saints. They are changed each year and distributed to the faithful.

Haykal (Arabic): Sanctuary of a Coptic church.

Hêgoumenos: Superior or head of a monastery.

Himation: Mantle.

Horologion (horologia): Book with prayers listed according to the seven canonical hours of the day and night.

Keep (Arabic *qasr,* fortress): Fortified tower containing supplies, where the monks could retreat during an attack.

Khedive: Royal title adopted by successors of Mohammed ʿAli between 1867 and 1914.

Khidma (Arabic): Charitable service for the church.

Khurus: A transitional room in Coptic churches, located between the nave and the sanctuary and reserved for priests.

Lamellar: Consisting of thin plates or scales.

Laura or lavra: Semianchoretic community.

Loros (Greek): Long scarf, usually worn by emperors, empresses, and archangels.

Mamluk (Arabic, "possessed"): Literally, a military slave; more commonly, two Muslim dynasties of such slave soldiers that ruled Egypt from 1250 to 1517.

Mandorla: A large almond-shaped halo that surrounds the entire body.

Mandylion: The holy towel on which Christ's facial features were miraculously imprinted.

Maphorion: Shawl worn over the head and upper body.

Mazaar (Arabic, "visiting room"): Place where the remains of saints are displayed for pilgrims.

Melkites: Supporters of the Council of Chalcedon.

Metanoia: Praying mindfully, with repentance.

Minbar (Arabic): Pulpit in a mosque from which the Friday sermon is delivered.

Monophysites (Greek, "single nature"): Term used by Western scholars to describe the doctrinal position of the Coptic Church and that of other opponents of the Council of Chalcedon (451).

Pantocrator (Greek, "ruler of all"): Visual depiction of Christ in majesty.

Qaʿa: Central architectural unit of a medieval Egyptian palace, consisting of a series of raised rooms *(iwans)* opening on a central court *(durqaʿa).*

Qasr: See *Keep.*

Riḥla (pl. riḥlāt): Modern form of pilgrimage entailing short trips to working monasteries.

Riwaq (Arabic): Arcade of a mosque.

Sayings of the Desert Fathers (Apophthegmata Patrum): Sayings by, and stories about, the early desert monks of Egypt.

Scetis (from Coptic *shi hêt,* "to weigh the heart"): Ancient name for the Wadi al-Natrun.

Secco: Painting on dry plaster; cf. *fresco,* painting on wet plaster.

Shafiʿ: One's personal patron saint.

Spandrel: Triangular area between the springing of two arches.

Stratelates (Greek): General.

Sultan: Muslim monarch, theoretically appointed to rule on behalf of the caliph.

Synaxarion: Book containing texts about saints, arranged according to the feast days of the calendar.

Tamgīd: Ancient form of chant to a saint or holy figure.

Tarnīm: Modern hymns or spiritual songs.

Tasbiḥa: The first part of the monastic day, the morning service of praise, lasting from 3 to 6 a.m.

Tiraz: Honorific, embroidered textile denoting rank and favor at medieval Muslim courts. The term was expanded to include the workshops that produced such textiles.

Turāth: Collective heritage of a people, including their history, language, literature, customs, and folklore.

Wadi (Arabic): Valley; more precisely, a rocky water-course in the desert, dry except after occasional rain-storms.

Wadi al-Arabah: Arid wadi linking the Monastery of Saint Antony to the Nile Valley.

Wadi al-Natrun: Desert depression between Cairo and Alexandria, known as Scetis in late antiquity. It remains an important monastic center.

Waqf (pl. awqaf): Religious endowment.

Wazir or vizier: High official in a medieval Muslim government.

Zayt (Arabic): Oil.

BIBLIOGRAPHY

Alcock, A. 1991. "Samu'il of Qalamun, Saint." *CE.* 2092–2093.

Amélineau, Emile. 1893. *La Géographie de l'Égypte à l'époque copte.* Paris: Imprimerie Nationale.

———. 1894. *Monuments pour servir à l'histoire de l'Égypte chrétienne.* Paris: Leroux.

Anderson, Jeffrey C. 1997. "Manuscripts." In Evans and Wixom 1997. 83–87.

Anonymous. 1907. *Il Menologio di Basilio II.* 2 vols. Turin: Fratelli Bocca.

———. 1951. *Sirat al-Anba Yehnes Kama wa tarikh Dayr al-Suryan.* Wadi al-Natrun.

———. 1982. *Sabḥū Lil-Rabb Tasbīḥan Jadīdan al-Guz al-Awal* (Sing to the Lord a New Song, vol. 1). Cairo.

Atalla, Nabil Selim.

———. n.d. *Coptic Art: Wall-Paintings.* Cairo: Lehnert and Landrock.

Athanasius. 1980. *The Life of Antony and the Letter to Marcellinus.* Trans. Robert C. Gregg. Mahwah, N.J.: Paulist Press.

———. 1994a. "The Coptic Life of Antony." Trans. Tim Vivian. *Coptic Church Review* 15, no. 1–2: 3–58.

———. 1994b. *Vie d'Antoine.* Trans. and ed. G. J. M. Bartelink. Sources chrétiennes 400. Paris: Éditions du Cerf.

———. 2001. *The Life of Antony.* Trans. Tim Vivian and Apostolos N. Athanassakis. Kalamazoo, Mich.: Cistercian.

Atil, Esin. 1975. *Art of the Arab World.* Washington, D.C.: Freer Gallery of Art, Smithsonian Institution.

———. 1981. *Renaissance Of Islam: Art of the Mamluks.* Washington, D.C.: Smithsonian Institution Press.

Atiya, Aziz S. 1968. *A History of Eastern Christianity.* London: Methuen.

———. 1986. "Kibt." *EI2*, vol. 5. 90–95.

———. 1991a. "Athanasius I." *CE.* 298–302.

———. 1991b. "Dates and Successions of the Patriarchs." *CE.* 1913–1920.

———. 1991c. "Literature Copto-Arabic." *CE.* 1460–1467.

———. 1991d. "Mark, Saint." *CE.* 1528–1533.

———. 1991e. "Martyrs, Coptic." *CE.* 1550–1559.

———. 1991f. "Synaxarion, Copto-Arabic." *CE.* 2171–2190.

Augustinous Al-Baramousi, Bishop. 1993. *Dayr Al-Baramūs Bayn Al-Mauḍīt wa Al-Ḥāḍr* (The Monastery of Al-Baramous between the past and the present). Dar Nūbār Lil Ṭabāʿ.

Badawy, Alexander. 1978. *Coptic Art and Archaeology: The Art of the Christian Egyptians from the Late Antique to the Middle Ages.* Cambridge: M.I.T. Press.

Baer, Eva. 1989. *Ayyubid Metalwork with Christian Images.* Leiden: E. J. Brill.

———. 1998. *Islamic Ornament.* New York: New York University Press.

Baker, Patricia L. 1995. *Islamic Textiles.* London: British Museum Press.

Balestri, I., and H. Hyvernat, eds. 1907–1950. *Acta Martyrum. CSCO* vols. 43, 44, 86, 125. Scriptores Coptici vol. 3, nos. 1 and 2. Paris: Typographeo Reipublicae.

Baraz, Daniel. 1994. "Bartolomeo da Trento's Book of Marian Miracles: A New Insight into the Arabic Collections of Marian Legends." *OCP* 60: 69–85.

Barrett, Antony A. 1996. *Agrippina: Sex, Power, and Poli-*

tics in the Early Empire. New Haven: Yale University Press.

Bassett, René., ed. 1904. *Le Synaxaire arabe-jacobite, rédaction Copte.* Patrologia Orientalis vol. 1, no. 3. Paris: Firmin-Didot.

Behrens-Abouseif, Doris. 1972. *Die Kopten in der ägyptischen Gesellschaft, von der Mitte des 19. Jahrhunderts bis 1923.* Islamkundliche Untersuchungen vol. 18. Freiburg im Breisgau: K. Schwarz.

Bell, David N., intro. and trans. 1983. *The Life of Shenoute by Besa.* Kalamazoo, Mich.: Cistercian.

Belli d'Elia, Pina. 1980. *La Puglia fra Bisanzio e l'Occidente.* Milan: Electa.

Belting, Hans. 1994. *Likeness and Presence: A History of the Image Before the Era of Art.* Trans. Edmund Jephcott. Chicago: University of Chicago Press.

Bierman, Irene A. 1998a. "Art and architecture in the medieval period." In Petry 1998. 339–374.

———. 1998b. *Writing Signs: The Fatimid Public Texts.* Berkeley: University of California Press.

Bilanuik, Petro B. T. 1991. "The Copts and the Council of Florence." *CE.* 1118–1119.

Blair, Sheila S. 1998. *Islamic Inscriptions.* Edinburgh: Edinburgh University Press.

Bolman, Elizabeth S. 1997. "The Coptic *Galaktotrophousa* as the Medicine of Immortality." Ph.D. dissertation, Bryn Mawr College.

———. 1998. "*Mimesis, Metamorphosis,* and Representation in Coptic Monastic Cells." *Bulletin of the American Society of Papyrologists* 35: 65–77.

Bonnardot, F., and A. Longnon. 1878. *Le Saint Voyage de Jerusalem de Seigneur d'Anglure.* Paris: Société des anciens textes français.

Boud'hors, Anne. 1996. "Koptish-arabisches Evangeliar." In *Ägypten. Schätze aus dem Wüstensand: Kunst und Kultur der Christen am Nil.* Catalog. Gustav-Lübcke-Museum der Stadt Hamm. Wiesbaden: Ludwig Reichert Verlag. 236–239.

Bourguet, Pierre M. du. 1951. "Saint-Antoine et Saint-Paul du Désert." *Bulletin de la Société Française d'Égyptologie* 7: 37–46.

Brakke, David, et al., trans. 1991. *Homiletica from the Pierpont Morgan Library. CSCO* vol. 525. Scriptores Coptici 44. Louvain: Peeters.

Brand, Barbara. 1991. *Islamic Art.* London: British Museum Press.

Brightman, F. E., trans. and ed. 1896. *Liturgies Eastern and Western.* Vol. 1, *Eastern Liturgies.* Oxford: Oxford University Press. Rpt. 1965.

Brock, S. P. 1996. "The 'Nestorian' Church: A lamentable misnomer." *Bulletin of the John Rylands University Library of Manchester* 78, no. 3: 23–35.

Brooks-Hedstrom, Darlene. 2001. "'Your Cell Will Teach You All Things': The Relationship Between Monastic Practice and the Architectural Design of Monasteries in Egypt." Ph.D. dissertation, Miami University, Oxford, Ohio.

Brune, Karl-Heinz. 1995. "Vom St. Merkurios zum Abu Saifain: Zur Ikonographischen Wandlung eines Heiligen." *BSAC* 34: 15–20.

Brunello, F., ed. 1971. *Il Libro dell'Arte* (by Cennino Cennini). Padua: Neri Pozza.

Buchthal, Hugo. 1957. *Miniature Painting in the Latin Kingdom of Jerusalem.* Oxford: Clarendon.

Buckton, David, ed. 1994. *Byzantium: Treasures of Byzantine Art and Culture from British Collections.* London: British Museum Press.

Budge, Ernest A. Wallis, trans. and ed. 1888. *Martyrdom and Miracles of Saint George of Cappadocia.* London: D. Nutt.

———. 1907. *The Paradise, or Garden of the Holy Fathers.* 2 vols. London: Chatto and Windus.

———. 1909. *Texts Relating to Saint Mêna of Egypt and Canons of Nicea in a Nubian Dialect.* London: British Museum Press.

———. 1914. *Coptic Martyrdoms in the Dialect of Upper Egypt.* London: British Museum.

———. 1915. *Miscellaneous Coptic Texts in the Dialect of Upper Egypt.* London: British Museum.

———. 1923. *One Hundred Ten Miracles of Our Lady Mary.* London: Medici Society.

———. 1928. *The Book of the Saints of the Ethiopian Church.* 4 vols. Cambridge: Cambridge University Press. Rpt., Hildesheim, Germany: Georg Olms, 1976.

Bunge, Gabriel, and Adalbert de Vogüé. 1994. *Quatre ermites égyptiens: D'après les fragments coptes de l'Histoire Lausiaque.* Spiritualité Orientale vol. 60. Bégrolles-en-Mauges, France: Abbaye de Bellefontaine.

Butler, Alfred J. 1884. *Ancient Coptic Churches of Egypt.* 2 vols. Oxford: Clarendon.

———. 1902. *The Arab Conquest of Egypt and the Last Thirty Years of the Roman Dominion.* Oxford: Clarendon.

Butler, Cuthbert, ed. 1967. *The Historia Lausiaca of Palladius.* Cambridge: The University Press, 1898–1904. Rpt. Hildesheim, Germany: Olms.

Capuani, Massimo, with contributions by Otto F. A. Meinardus and Marie-Hélène Rutschowscaya. 1999. *L'Égypte Copte*. Paris: Citadelles and Mazenod.

Carità, R. 1959. "Cripte eremitiche pugliesi." *Il Veltro* 3: 25–30.

Carr, Annemarie Weyl, and Lawrence J. Morocco. 1991. *A Byzantine Masterpiece Recovered: The Thirteenth-Century Murals of Lysi, Cyprus*. Austin: University of Texas Press.

Cauwenbergh, Paul Van. 1914. *Étude sur les moines d'Égypte depuis le Concile de Chalcédoine (451) jusqu'à l'invasion Arabe (640)*. Paris: Imprimerie Nationale.

Chaîne, M. 1960. *Le Manuscrit de la version copte en dialecte sahidique des "Apophthegmata Patrum."* Cairo: IFAO.

Chester, Greville J. 1873. "Notes on the Coptic Dayrs of the Wady Natrun and on Dayr Antonios in the Eastern Desert." *Archaeological Journal* 30, no. 118: 105–116.

Clédat, Jean. 1904. Le Monastère et la nécropole de Baouît. MIFAO 12. Cairo: IFAO.

———. 1999. Le Monastère et la nécropole de Baouît. Edited by Dominique Bénazeth and Marie-Hélène Rutschowskaya. MIFAO 111. Cairo: IFAO.

Cody, Aeldred. 1991. "Scetis." *CE*. 2102–2106.

Cohen, Mark R. 1985. *Jewish Self-Government in Medieval Egypt*. Princeton: Princeton University Press.

Colin, G. 1988. "Le Synaxaire éthiopien. État actuel de la question." *Analecta Bollandiana* 106: 273–317.

Committee Formed by His Holiness Pope Shenouda III. 1993. *The Coptic Liturgy of St. Basil*. Cairo: J.B.P.H.

Contadini, Anna. 1998. *Fatimid Art at the Victoria and Albert Museum. London*: V&A Publications.

Coquin, R.-G. 1975. "Les Inscriptions pariétales des monastères d'Esna: Dayr al-Suhada'-Dayr al-Fahuri." *BIFAO* 75: 241–284, plates 40–50.

———. 1978. "Le Synaxaire des coptes. Un nouveau témoin de la recension de Haute Égypte," *Analecta Bollandia* 96: 351–365.

———. 1991a. "Moses of Abydos." *CE*. 1679–1681.

———. 1991b. "Paul the Simple, Saint." *CE*. 1923–1925.

———. 1991c. "Pishoi of Scetis." *CE*. 2029–2030.

Coquin, R.-G., and Maurice Martin. 1991a. "Dayr Anba Antyniys: Chronology." *CE*. 721–723.

———. 1991b. "Dayr Anba Shinudah: History." *CE*. 761–766.

———. 1991c. "Wadi Sarjah." *CE*. 2312.

Coquin, R.-G., and Marie-Hélène Rutschowskaya. 1994. "Les Stèles coptes du département des antiquités égyptiennes du Louvre." *BIFAO* 94: 107–131.

Cordan, George. 1903. *Relations du voyage fait au convent de Saint-Antoine dans le désert de la Basse Thébaïde*. Paris.

Creswell, K. A. C. 1978. *The Muslim Architecture of Egypt*. 2 vols. Oxford: Clarendon, 1952. Rpt. New York: Hacker Art Books.

Creswell, K. A. C., and James W. Allan. 1989. *A Short Account of Early Muslim Architecture*. Aldershot, England: Scolar, Gower; and Cairo: American University in Cairo Press.

Crone, Patricia, and Shmuel Moreh, trans. 2000. *The Book of Strangers: Mediaeval Arabic Graffiti on the Theme of Nostalgia, attributed to Abu'l-Faraj al-Isfahan*. Princeton: Markus Wiener.

Cutler, Anthony. 1983. "The Dumbarton Oaks Psalter and New Testament: The Iconography of the Moscow Leaf." *DOP* 37: 35–45.

———. 1999. "The Parallel Universes of Arab and Byzantine Art (with Special Reference to the Fatimid Era)." *L'Egypte Fatimide: Son art et son histoire*. Paris: Presses de l'Université de Paris-Sorbonne. 635–648.

Dadoyan, Seta B. 1996. "The Phenomenon of the Fatimid Armenians." *Medieval Encounters* 2, no. 3: 193–213.

Davis-Weyer, Caecilia. 1986. *Early Medieval Art 300–1150*. Toronto: University of Toronto Press, with the Medieval Academy of America.

Dawes, Elizabeth, and Norman H. Baynes, trans. 1977. *Three Byzantine Saints*. Crestwood, N.Y.: St. Vladimir's.

Delehaye, Hippolytus, ed. 1927. "Une vie inédite de Saint Jean l'Aumonier." *Analecta Bollandiana* 45: 5–74.

Demus, Otto. 1948. *Byzantine Mosaic Decoration*. London: Kegan Paul, Trench Trubner.

Depuydt, Leo. 1991. *Homiletica from the Pierpont Morgan Library*. Louvain: Peeters.

Derbes, Anne. 1989. "Siena and the Levant in the Later Dugento." *Gesta* 28: 190–204.

Derda, Thomasz. 1995. "The Naqlun Papyri and the *Codex Alexandrinus*." *The Spirituality of Ancient Monasticism*. Acts of the International Congress. Cracow-Tyniec, 16–19 November 1994. Edited by Marek Starowieyski. Cracow: Tyniec. 13–34.

Dermenghem, Émile. 1954. *Le Culte des saints dans l'Islam maghrébin*. Paris: Gallimard.

Descoeudres, Georges. 1989. "L'Architecture des ermitages et des sanctuaires." *Les Kellia: Ermitages coptes en Basse-Égypte*. Edited by Yvette Mottier and Nathalie Bosson. Geneva: Éditons du Tricorne. 33–55.

Devos, Paul. 1959. "Un Récit des miracles de S. Ménas en Copte et en Éthiopien." *Analecta Bollandiana* 77: 451–463.

Dodd, Erica Cruikshank. 1992. "The Monastery of Mar Musa al-Habashi, near Nebek, Syria." *Arte Medievale* ser. II, vol. 6, no. 1: 61–131.

———. 2000. "The Three Patriarchs of Mar Musa al-Habashi: Syrian Painting and Its Relationship with the West." *Al-Massaq* 12: 99–139.

Doresse, Jean. 1951. "Nouvelles études sur l'art copte; les monastères de Saint Antoine et Saint Paul." *CRAIB* 268–274.

———. 1952. "Deux monastères coptes oubliés: Saint Antoine et Saint Paul dans le désert de la mer Rouge." *La Revue des Arts* 2: 3–14.

Draguet, René. 1951. "Une lettre de Sérapion de Thmuis aux disciples d'Antoine (A.D. 356): En version syriaque et arménienne." *Le Muséon* 64: 1–25.

Drescher, James, ed. and trans. 1946. *Apa Mena: A Selection of Coptic Texts Relating to St. Menas.* Textes et Documents. Cairo: Société d'Archéologie Copte.

Dunn, Michael C. 1975. "The Struggle for Abbasid Egypt." Ph.D. dissertation, University of Michigan.

Eade, John, and Michael Sallnow, eds. 1990. *Contesting the Sacred: The Anthropology of Christian Pilgrimage.* London: Routledge.

Emmel, Stephen. 1991. "Languages (Coptic)." *ABD* 4: 180–188.

Erim, Kenan T. 1993. *Aphrodisias.* Istanbul: Net Turistik Yayinlar.

Ettinghausen, Richard. 1977. *Arab Painting.* Geneva: Skira.

Ettinghausen, Richard, and Oleg Grabar. 1987. *The Art and Architecture of Islam, 650–1250.* Harmondsworth: Peguin.

Evans, Helen C., and William D. Wixom, eds. 1997. *The Glory of Byzantium: Art and Culture of the Middle Byzantine Era, A.D. 843–1261.* New York: Metropolitan Museum of Art.

Evelyn-White, Hugh G. 1973. *The Monasteries of the Wadi 'n Natrun.* 3 vols. New York: Metropolitan Museum of Art, 1932–1933. Rpt. New York: Arno.

Evetts, B. T. A., ed. and trans. 1895. *The Churches and Monasteries of Egypt and Some Neighbouring Countries, Attributed to Abû Sâlih, the Armenian.* Oxford: Clarendon.

———. 1904–1914. *History of the Patriarchs of the Coptic Church of Alexandria.* By Sawirus ibn al-Muqaffa. Patrologia Orientalis 1.2, 4, 5.5, 10.5.

Farag, F. R. 1964. *Sociological and Moral Studies in the Field of Coptic Monasticism.* Leiden: E. J. Brill.

Farah, Nadia Ramsis. 1986. *Religious Strife in Egypt: Crisis and Ideological Conflict in the Seventies.* New York: Gordon Breach Science.

Farès, Bishr. 1961. *Vision chrétienne et signes musulmans: Autour d'un manuscrit arabe illustré au XIIIe siècle.* Cairo: IFAO.

Farmer, David H. 1980. *The Oxford Dictionary of Saints.* Oxford: Oxford University Press.

Farré, André. 1991. "Fatimids and the Copts." *CE.* 1097–1100.

Fedalto, Giorgio. 1988. *Hierarchia Ecclesiastica Orientalis.* Patriarchatus Alexandrinus, Antiochenus, Hierosolymitanus, vol. 2. Padova: Edizioni Messaggero.

Fedden, H. Romilly. 1937. "A Study of the Monastery of Saint Antony in the Eastern Desert." *Bulletin of the Faculty of Arts of the University of Egypt* 5, no. 1: 4–60.

Ferrari, G. 1956. "Sources for the Early Iconography of Saint Antony." *Antonius Magnus.* 248–253.

Festugière, André-Jean. 1971. *Historia Monachorum in Aegypto: Edition critique du texte grec et traduction annotée. Subsidia Hagiographica.* Vol. 53. Brussels: Société des Bollandistes.

Fiey, J. M. 1972–1973. "Coptes et Syriaques, contactes et échanges." *Studia Orientalia Christiana. Collectanea* 15. 297–326.

Folda, Jaroslav. 1995. *Art of the Crusaders in the Holy Land, 1098–1187.* Cambridge: Cambridge University Press.

Forget, J., trans. 1905–1926. *Synaxarium Alexandrinum. CSCO.* Vols. 47–49, 67, 78, 90. Scriptores Arabici vols. 2–5, 11–13. Louvain: Marcellus Istas.

Frend, W. H. C. 1972. *The Rise of the Monophysite Movement.* Cambridge: Cambridge University Press.

Gabra, Gawdat, with Antony Alcock. 1993. *Cairo: The Coptic Museum and Old Churches.* Cairo: Longman.

Galavaris, George. 1970. *Bread and the Liturgy: The Symbolism of Early Christian and Byzantine Bread Stamps.* Madison: University of Wisconsin Press.

Garitte, Gérard. 1943. "Panégyrique de Saint Antoine par Jean, évêque d'Hermopolis." *OCP* 9, no. 3: 100–134, 330–365.

Gelfer-Jørgensen, Mirjam. 1986. *Medieval Islamic Symbolism and the Paintings in the Cefalù Cathedral.* Leiden: E. J. Brill.

Gellner, E. 1969. *Saints of the Atlas.* London: Weidenfeld and Nicholson.

Gerstel, Sharon E. J. 2000. "Art and Identity in the Medieval Morea." *The Crusades from the Perspective of Byzantium and the Muslim World*. Edited by Angeliki E. Laiou and Roy P. Mottahedeh. Washington, D.C.: Dumbarton Oaks. 263–285.

Geymonat, Ludovico V. 1999. "Un apocrifio bizantino nei dipinti duecenteschi del Battistero di Parma." *Archivo storico per le Province Parmensi*. 4 ser., vol. 51. 429–456, figs. 1–23.

Gianelli, C. 1953. "Témoignages patristiques grecs en faveur d'une apparition du Christ ressuscité à la Vièrge Marie." *Revue des études byzantines* 11. *Mélanges Martin Jugie*. 106–119.

Gierlichs, Joachim. 1996. *Mittelalterliche Tierreliefs in Anatolien und Nordmesopotamien*. Deutsches Archäologisches Institut Abteilung Istanbul. Istanbul Forschungen. vol. 42. Tübingen: Ernst Wasmuth Verlag.

Godlewski, Wlodzimierz. 1986. *Le Monastère de Saint-Phoibammon*. Deir el-Bahari. vol. 5. Warsaw: PWN—Éditions Scientifiques de Pologne.

———. 1997. "Deir el Naqlun. Topography and tentative history." *Archeologia e papiri nel Fayyum: Storia della ricerca, problemi e prospettive*. Atti del convegno internazionale, Syracuse, Italy, May 24–25, 1996. Syracuse: Istituto Internazionale del Papiro. 123–145.

———. 1999. "Naqlun 1993–1996." *Acts 6*, 157–161.

Goehring, James E. 1999. *Ascetics, Society, and the Desert: Studies in Early Egyptian Monasticism*. Harrisburg, Pa.: Trinity.

Goitein, S. D. 1967–1994. *A Mediterranean Society: The Jewish Communities of the Arab World as Portrayed in the Documents of the Cairo Geniza*. 6 vols. Berkeley: University of California Press.

Golubovich, Girolamo. 1919. *Biblioteca Bio-bibliografica della Terra Santa e dell'Oriente Francescano III: Etiopia francescana*. vol. 1. Florence: Quaracchi Presso.

Grabar, André. 1957. *L'iconoclasme Byzantin*. Paris: Collège de France.

Grabar, Oleg. 1984. *The Illustrations of the Maqamat*. Chicago: University of Chicago Press.

———. 1987. *The Formation of Islamic Art*. Revised and enlarged. New Haven: Yale University Press.

Gray, Basil, ed. 1979. *The Art of the Book in Central Asia*. London: Serindia; Paris: Unesco.

Griffith, Sidney H. 1985. "Theodore Abu Qurrah's Arabic Tract on the Christian Practice of Venerating Images." *Journal of the American Oriental Society* 105.1: 53–73.

Griggs, C. W. 1991. "Sarapion of Tmuis, Saint." *CE*. 2095–2096.

Grossmann, Peter. 1982. *Mittelalterliche Langhauskuppelkirchen und verwandte Typen in Oberägypten*. Abhandlungen des Deutschen Archäologischen Instituts Kairo. Koptische Reihe 3. Glückstadt: Augustin.

———. 1990. "Early Christian Architecture in the Nile Valley." *Coptic Art and Culture*. Edited by H. Hondelink. Cairo: Shouhdy. 3–18.

———. 1991a. "Apa Mena." *CE*. 24–29.

———. 1991b. "Church Architecture." *CE*. 552–555.

———. 1991c. "Dayr Al-Qusayr." *CE*. 854–855.

———. 1991d. "Dayr Anba Antuniyus." *CE*. 723–726.

———. 1991e. "Dayr Apa Jeremiah: Archaeology." *CE*. 773–776.

———. 1995. "L'architecture de l'Église de Saint-Antoine." In van Moorsel 1995b. 1–19.

Gruber, M. 1990. "Sacrifice in the Desert: An Ethnography of the Coptic Monastery." Ph.D. dissertation. State University of New York, Stony Brook.

Guillaumont, Antoine. 1977. "Histoire des moines aux Kellia." *Orientalia Lovaniensia Periodica* 8: 187–203.

———. 1988. "Les moines des Kellia aux 4è et 5è siècles." Saint Antoine et les moines du désert. *Dossiers Histoire et Archéologie* 133: 6–13.

———. 1991a. "Antony of Egypt, Saint." *CE*. 149–151.

———. 1991b. "Macarius Alexandrinus, Saint." *CE*. 1489–1490.

———. 1991c. "Macarius the Egyptian, Saint." *CE*. 1491–1492.

———. 1991d. "Paul the Simple, Saint." *CE*. 1923.

Guillaumont, Antoine, and K. H. Kuhn. 1991. "Paul of Thebes, Saint." *CE*. 1925–1926.

Guy, Jean-Claude, trans. 1993. *Les Apophtegmes des pères: Collection systématique, chapitres I–IX*. Sources chrétiennes. vol. 387. Paris: Éditions du Cerf.

Habachi, Labib, and Zaki Tawudros. 1929. *Fi sahra al-ʿArab wa al-adyira al-sharqia*. Cairo.

Hacken, Clara ten. 1999. "Coptic and Arabic Texts on Macrobius, an Egyptian Monk of the Sixth Century." *Acts 6.2*, 117–126.

Haile, Getatchew. 1982–1983. "The Monastic Genealogy of the Line of Täklä Haymanot of Shoa," *Rassegna di Studi Etiopici* 29: 7–38.

Harbison, Peter. 1992. *The High Crosses of Ireland: An Iconographical and Photographic Survey*. 2 vols. Bonn: Rudolph Habelt *GMBH*.

Hardy, E. R. 1991. "Damian." *CE*. 688–689.

Harmless, William, S.J. Forthcoming. *The Desert Fathers: An Introduction.*

Hartner, Willy. 1968. "The Pseudoplanetary Nodes of the Moon's Orbit in Hindu and Islamic Iconographies." *Ars Islamica* 5: 113–154.

Harvey, Paul B., Jr. 1990. "The Life of Paul, the First Hermit, by Jerome." *Ascetic Behavior in Greco-Roman Antiquity: A Sourcebook.* Edited by Vincent Wimbush. Minneapolis: Fortress. 357–369.

Hassan, Ahmad Y. al-, and Donald R. Hill. 1986. *Islamic Technology, an Illustrated History.* Cambridge: Cambridge University Press.

Hatch, William H. P. 1946. *An Album of Dated Syriac Manuscripts.* Boston: American Academy of Arts and Sciences.

Haykal, Muhammad H. 1983. *Autumn of Fury.* New York: Random House.

Hayward Gallery. 1976. *The Arts of Islam.* London: Arts Council of Great Britain.

Heath, Ian. 1979. *Byzantine Armies, 886–1118.* London: Osprey.

Hebbelynck, Adolphe, and A. van Lantschoot. 1937. *Codices Coptici Vaticani.* Vol. 1. Vatican City: Biblioteca Apostolica Vaticana.

Hetherington, Paul, ed. 1978. *The "Painter's Manual" of Dionysius of Fourna.* London: Sagittarius.

Hillenbrand, Carole. 1999. *The Crusades: Islamic Perspectives.* Edinburgh: Edinburgh University Press.

Hitti, Philip K. 1987. *Memoirs of an Arab-Syrian Gentleman and Warrior in the Period of the Crusades.* Princeton: Princeton University Press, 1929. Rpt. London: I. B. Taurus

Hoffmann, G. 1942. "Kopten und Aethioper auf dem Konzil von Florenz." *OCP* 8: 11–24.

Horner, G. 1898. *The Coptic Version of the New Testament in the Northern Dialect.* Oxford: Clarendon. Rpt. Osnabruck: O. Zeller, 1969.

———. 1902. *The Service for the Consecration of a Church and Altar According to the Coptic Rite.* London: Harrison and Sons.

Horste, K. 1992. *Cloister Design and Monastic Reform in Toulouse.* Oxford: Clarendon.

Humphreys, R. Stephen. 1977. *From Saladin to the Mongols: The Ayyubids of Damascus, 1193–1260.* Albany: State University of New York Press.

Hunt, Lucy-Ann. 1985. "Christian-Muslim Relations in Painting in Egypt of the Twelfth to Mid-Thirteenth Centuries: Sources of Wallpainting at Deir es-Suriani and the Illustration of the New Testament MS Paris, Copte-Arabe 1/Cairo, Bibl. 94." *Cahiers Archéologiques* 33: 111–155.

———. 1989. "The al-Muʿallaqa Doors Reconstructed: An Early Fourteenth-Century Sanctuary Screen from Old Cairo." *Gesta* 28, no.1: 61–77.

———. 1991. "A Woman's Prayer to St. Sergios in Latin Syria: Interpreting a Thirteenth-Century Icon at Mount Sinai." *BMGS* 15: 96–145.

———. 1995. "The Fine Incense of Virginity: A Late-Twelfth-Century Wallpainting of the Annunciation at the Monastery of the Syrians." *BMGS* 19: 182–232.

———. 1998. "Churches of Old Cairo and the Mosques of al-Qahira: A Case of Christian-Muslim Interchange." *Byzantium, Eastern Christendom, and Islam: Art at the Crossroads of the Medieval Mediterranean.* vol. 1. London: Pindar. 319–342.

Hurtado, L. W. 1998. "The Origin of the *Nomina Sacra*: A Proposal." *Journal of Biblical Literature* 117: 655–673.

Husselman, Elinor M. 1965. "The Martyrdom of Cyriacus and Julitta in Coptic." *JARCE* 4: 79–86.

Hyvernat, Henri. 1886. *Les Actes des martyrs de l'Égypte.* Tirés des manuscrits coptes de la Bibliothèque Vaticane et du Musée Borgia. Texte copte et traduction français. vol. 1. Paris: Ernest Leroux.

Innemée, Karel C. 1990. "The Relationship Between Episcopal and Monastic Vestments in Nubian Wall-Painting." *Acts 3*, 161–163.

———. 1992. *Ecclesiastical Dress in the Medieval Near East.* Leiden: E. J. Brill.

———. 1998a. "Coptic Monastic Vestments and Their Relationship with Liturgical Vestments," *Acts 4*, 446–449.

———. 1998b. "The Iconographical Program of Paintings in the Church of al-ʿAdrah in Deir al-Sourian: Some Preliminary Observations." *Themelia.* 143–153.

———. 1999a. "The Wall-Paintings of Deir al-Sourian: New Discoveries and Conservation." Lecture at the Nederlands-Vlaams Institute in Cairo, 11 November 1999.

———. 1999b. "New Discoveries at Deir al-Sourian, Wadi al-Natrun." *Acts 6*, 213–222.

Institut du Monde Arabe. 2000. *L'Art copte en Égypte: 2000 ans de christianisme.* Exhibition catalog. May 15–September 3, 2000. Paris: Institut du Monde Arabe and Éditions Gallimard.

Irwin, Robert. 1997. *Islamic Art.* London: Laurence King.

Johann Georg, Duke of Saxony. 1930. *Neue Streifzüge*

durch die Kirchen und Klöster Ägyptens. Leipzig and Berlin.

Johnson, David W. 1986. "Anti-Chalcedonian Polemics in Coptic Texts, 451–641." In Pearson and Goehring 1986. 216–234.

Jones, Michael. 1995. "El-Deir El-Nahya." *BSAC* 34: 33–51.

Jullien, Michel. 1884. "Voyage dans le désert de la Basse-Thébaïde: Aux couvents de Saint-Antoine et de Saint-Paul." *Les Missions Catholiques* 16. Lyon. 211–214.

Kabès, Jean. 1952. "La Dévotion à la sainte Vièrge dans l'Église copte." *Les Cahiers coptes* 2: 4–7.

Kalopissi-Verti, S. 1994. "Painters in Late Byzantine Society: The Evidence of Church Inscriptions." *Cahiers Archéologiques* 42: 139–158.

Kamil, M. 1950–1957. "La dernière phase des relation historiques entre l'Église Copte d'Égypte et celle d'Éthiopie (jusqu' en 1952)," *BSAC* 14: 1–22.

Karakatsanis, Athanasios, et al. 1997. *Treasures of Mount Athos.* Trans. Andrew Hendry. Thessaloniki: B' Edition.

Kasser, Rodolphe. 1989. "Le Monachisme copte." *Les Kellia: Ermitages coptes en Basse-Egypte.* Musée d'art et d'histoire. Edited by Yvette Mottier and Nathalie Bosson. Geneva, October 12, 1989–January 7, 1990. Geneva: Tricorne.

Kasser, Rodolphe, Antoine Khater, and O. H. E. KHS-Burmester. 1974. *History of the Patriarchs of the Egyptian Church.* Textes et documents, vol. 14. Cairo: Société d'Archéologie Copte.

Kepel, Giles. 1984. *Muslim Extremism in Egypt: The Prophet and the Pharaoh.* Berkeley: University of California Press.

Khater, A., and O. H. E. KHS-Burmester, trans. 1970. *The History of the Patriarchs of the Egyptian Church.* vol. 3, no. 2. Cairo: Société d'Archéologie Copte.

Khawaga, Dina el-. 1993. "Le Renouveau Copte: La Communauté comme acteur politique." Ph.D. thesis, Institut d'Études Politiques de Paris.

KHS-Burmester, O. H. E. 1941. "The Copts in Cyprus." *BSAC* 7: 9–13.

———. 1967. *The Egyptian or Coptic Church.* Cairo: Société d'Archéologie Copte.

Kitzinger, Ernst. 1990. *The Mosaics of St. Mary's of the Admiral in Palermo.* Washington, D.C.: Dumbarton Oaks.

Knezevich, L. 1991. "Severus of Antioch." *CE.* 2123–2125.

Kraack, Detlev von. 1997. *Monumentale Zeugnisse der spättmittelalterlichen Adelsreise. Inschriften und Graffiti des 14.–16. Jahrhunderts.* Abhandlungen der Akademie der Wissenschaften in Göttingen No. 224. Göttingen: Vandenhoeck and Ruprecht.

Krause, Martin. 1971. "Zur Lokalisierung und Datierung koptischer Denkmäler. Das Tafelbild des Bischofs Abraham." *Zeitschrift für Ägyptische Sprache und Altertumskunde* 97: 106–111.

———. 1991. "Menas the Miracle Worker, Saint." *CE.* 1589–1590.

Krause, Martin, and Klaus Wessel. 1966. "Bawit." *Reallexikon zur byzantinischen Kunst.* vol. 1. Stuttgart: Anton Hiersemann. 570–573.

Krueger, Derek. 1997. "Typological Figuration in Theodoret of Cyrrhus's Religious History and the Art of Postbiblical Narrative." *Journal of Early Christian Studies* 5, no. 3: 393–419.

Kuhn, K. H. 1991. "Shenute, Saint." *CE.* 2131–2133.

Kühnel, Gustav. 1988. *Wall Painting in the Latin Kingdom of Jerusalem* ser. Frankfurter Forschungen zur Kunst 14. Berlin: Gebr. Mann Verlag.

Labib, Mafouz. 1961. *Pèlerins et voyageurs au Mont Sinaï.* Cairo: IFAO.

Ladner, Gerhart. 1958. "Anthropology of Gregory of Nyssa." *DOP* 12: 59–94.

Laferrière. Pierre, 1993. "Les croix murales du Monastère rouge à Sohag." *BIFAO* 93: 299–311.

Lane-Pool, Stanley. 1914. *A History of Egypt in the Middle Ages.* 2d ed. London: Methuen. Rpt. New York: Haskell, 1969.

Lapidus, Ira M. 1972. "The Conversion of Egypt to Islam." *Israel Oriental Studies* 2: 248–262.

Leaf, William, and Sally Purcell. 1986. *Heraldic Symbols: Islamic Insignia and Western Heraldry.* London: Victoria and Albert Museum.

Leipoldt, Johannes. 1903. *Schenute von Atripe.* Leipzig: Hinrichs.

Leroy, Jules. 1964. *Les Manuscrits syriaques à peintures conservés dans les bibliothèques d'europe et d'orient.* 2 vols. Paris: Librairie Orientaliste Paul Geuthner.

———. 1974. *Les Manuscrits coptes et coptes-arabes illustrés.* Paris: Librairie Orientaliste Paul Geuthner.

———. 1975a. "Découvertes de peintures chretiennes en Syrie." *Les Annales archéologiques Arabes Syriennes* 25, nos. 1–2: 95–113.

———. 1975b. *Les Peintures des couvents du désert d'Esna.* La peinture murale chez les coptes, vol. 1. Cairo: IFAO.

———. 1976. "Le Programme décoratif de l'église de

Saint Antoine du désert de la mer Rouge." *BIFAO* 76: 347–379.

———. 1982. *Les Peintures des couvents du Ouadi Natroun.* La peinture murale chez les coptes, vol. 2. Cairo: IFAO.

Lev, Yaacov. 1991. *State and Society in Fatimid Egypt.* Leiden: E. J. Brill.

Lewis, Suzanne. 1973. "The Iconography of the Coptic Horseman in Byzantine Egypt." *JARCE* 10: 27–63, figs. 1–38.

Lézine, Alexandre. 1972. "Les Salles Nobles des Palais Mamelouks." *Annales Islamologiques* 10: 62–148, pls. 1–33.

Libois, Charles, ed. and trans. 1977. *Voyage en Égypt du père Antonius Gonzales, 1665–1666.* Collection de voyageurs occidentaux en Egypt, vol. 19. Cairo: IFAO.

Lings, Martin. 1976. *The Quranic Art of Calligraphy and Illumination.* London: World of Islam Festival Trust Publishing.

Little, Donald P. 1976. "Coptic Conversion to Islam Under the Bahri Mamluks, 692–755 / 1293–1354." *Bulletin of the School of Oriental and African Studies* 39.3, 552–569.

Littmann, Enno. 1953. "Nabatean Inscriptions from Egypt." *Bulletin of the School of Oriental and African Studies* 15: 1–28.

Lowden, John. 1997. *Early Christian and Byzantine Art.* London: Phaidon.

Lucchesi-Palli, E. 1978. "Some Parallels to the Figure of St. Mercurius at Faras." *Nubian Studies.* Edited by J. M. Plumley. Warminster: Aris and Phillips. 162–169.

Luzi, Adriano, and Luigi De Cesaris. 1995. "Old Church of St. Antony, Interventions for Structural and Architectural Restoration and Restoration of Wall Paintings." Unpublished report. Egyptian Antiquities Project, American Research Center in Egypt.

Lyster, William. 1999. *Monastery of St. Paul.* Cairo: American Research Center in Egypt.

MacCoull, Leslie S. B. 1998. "Chant in Coptic Pilgrimage." *Pilgrimage and Holy Space in Late Antique Egypt.* Edited by David Frankfurter. Leiden: E. J. Brill. 403–413.

Maguire, Eunice Dauterman, Henry P. Maguire, and Maggie J. Duncan-Flowers. 1989. *Art and Holy Powers in the Early Christian House.* Urbana: University of Illinois Press.

Maguire, Henry. 1988. "The Art of Comparing in Byzantium." *AB* 70: 88–103.

———. 1993. "Disembodiment and Corporeality in Byzantine Images of the Saints." *Iconography at the Crossroads.* Edited by Brendan Cassidy. Index of Christian Art Occasional Papers 2. Princeton: Department of Art and Archaeology. 75–90.

———. 1998. "A Murderer Among the Angels." *Rhetoric, Nature, and Magic in Byzantine Art.* Aldershot: Ashgate, Variorum. 63–71.

Majda, T. 1986. "Libas. iv.—Turkey." *EI2*, vol. 5, 750–753.

Malan, Solomon C. 1873. *A Short History of the Copts and Their Church.* London: Nutt.

Malek, Nabil A. 1993. "The Copts: From an Ethnic Majority to a Religious Minority." *Acts 5*, vol. 2, pt. 2. 291–311.

Malone, Edward E. 1950. *The Monk and the Martyr: The Monk as Successor to the Martyr.* Studies in Christian Antiquity, vol. 12. Washington, D.C.: Catholic University of America Press.

———. 1956. "The Monk and the Martyr." *Antonius Magnus.* 201–228.

Maloney, George A., ed. and trans. 1992. *Pseudo-Macarius: The Fifty Spiritual Homilies and the Great Letter.* New York: Paulist.

Mango, Cyril, ed. and trans. 1972. *The Art of the Byzantine Empire, 312–1453.* Sources and Documents in the History of Art. Englewood Cliffs, N.J.: Prentice-Hall.

———. 1978. "Lo stile cosiddetto 'monastico' della pittura bizantina." *Habitat, strutture, territorio: Atti del terzo convegno internazionale di studio sulla Civiltà Rupestre medioevale nel mezzogiorno d'Italia.* Taranto-Grottaglie, September 1975. Galatina: Congelo.

Maraval, Pierre, ed. and trans. 1971. *Grégoire de Nysse, Vie de Sainte Macrine.* Paris: Éditions du Cerf.

Marshall, Christopher. 1992. *Warfare in the Latin East, 1192–1291.* Cambridge: Cambridge University Press.

Martin, Annick. 1996. *Athanase d'Alexandrie et l'église d'Égypte au IVe siècle (328–373).* Collection de l'École Française de Rome, vol. 216. Rome: École Française de Rome.

Marx, Emmanuel. 1977. "Communal and Individual Pilgrimage: The Region of Saints' Tombs in South Sinai." *Regional Cults.* Edited by R. Werbner. London: Academic Press. 29–51.

Maspero, Jean, and Étienne Drioton. 1931. *Fouilles exécutées à Baouît. MIFAO* 59.

Masri, Iris Habib el-. 1982. *The Story of the Copts.* Newberry Springs, Calif.: St. Antony Coptic Orthodox Monastery.

Masson, Jacques, trans. 1975. *Voyage en Égypte de Félix*

Farbi, 1483. 3 vols. Collection des voyageurs occidenteaux en Égypte, vol. 14. Cairo: IFAO.

Mathews, Thomas. 1990. "The Transformation Symbolism in Byzantine Architecture and the Meaning of the Pantokrator in the Dome." *Church and People in Byzantium: 20th Spring Symposium of Byzantine Studies 1990.* Edited by R. Morris. Birmingham, England: Center for Byzantine Studies. 191–214.

———. 1993. *The Clash of Gods: A Reinterpretation of Early Christian Art.* Princeton: Princeton University Press.

———. 1998. *Byzantium from Antiquity to the Renaissance.* New York: Harry N. Abrams.

Mathews, Thomas, and Avedis K. Sanjian. 1991. *Armenian Gospel Iconography: The Tradition of the Glajor Gospel.* Washington, D.C.: Dumbarton Oaks Research Library and Collection.

Matteini, Mauro, and A. Moles. 1989. *La chimica nel restauro: I materiale dell'arte pittorico.* Florence: Nardini.

Maximous El-Anthony, Father. n.d.. *Bahūth fi ayqunāt al-qadīsīn Khristufurs wa Harifis wa Arghana* (Research on icons of Saints Christopher, Herifis, and Arghana). Private printing.

Mayer, Leo A. 1952. *Mamluk Costume, a Survey.* Geneva: Albert Kundig.

Medea, Alba. 1937. "Osservazioni sugli affreschi delle cripte eremitiche di Puglia," *Japigia* 8, no. 1: 3–18.

———. 1938. "Mural Paintings in Some Cave Chapels of Southern Italy," *Americal Journal of Archaeology* 42: 17–29.

Megally, F. 1991. "George, Saint." *CE.* 1139–1140.

Meinardus, Otto F. A. 1961. *Monks and Monasteries of the Egyptian Desert.* Cairo: American University Press.

———. 1962. "A Brief History of the Abunate of Ethiopia." *Wiener Zeitschrift für die Kunde des Morgenlandes* 58: 39–65.

———. 1964. "The Collection of Coptica in the Qasr of the Monastery of St. Antony." *BSAC* 18: 251–263.

———. 1965. *Christian Egypt Ancient and Modern.* Cairo: IFAO.

———. 1966. "The Mediaeval Graffiti in the Monasteries of SS. Antony and Paul." *Studia Orientalia Christiana Collectanea* no. 11: 513–527.

———. 1969–1970. "The Medieval Wall Paintings in the Coptic Churches of Old Cairo." *BSAC* 20: 119–147.

———. 1972. "The Martyria of the Saints: The Wall-Paintings of the Church of St. Antony in the Eastern Desert." *Medieval and Middle Eastern Studies in*

Honor of Aziz Suryal Atiya. Edited by Sami A. Hanna. Leiden: E. J. Brill. 311–343.

———. 1983. *Die Wüstenväter des 20. Jahrhunderts.* Würzburg: Augustinus.

———. 1987. "The Eucharist in the Historical Experience of the Copts." *Texts and Studies,* vols. 5–6. London: Thyateira House. 155–170.

———. 1992. *Monks and Monasteries of the Egyptian Desert.* 1961. Rev. ed. Cairo: American University Press.

Meyer, Robert T., trans. 1964. *Palladius: The Lausiac History.* New York: Newman.

Michalowski, Kazimierz. 1974. *Faras: Wall Painting in the National Museum in Warsaw.* Warsaw: Wydawniztwo Artystyzzno Graficzne.

Mikhail, Maged S. n.d. "Late Antiquity in Egypt: Toward a Positive Definition." Unpublished paper.

Mikhail, Maged S., and Tim Vivian, trans. 1997. "Zacharias of Sakhâ: An Encomium on the Life of John the Little." *Coptic Church Review* 18, nos. 1–2: 3–64.

Mingana, A., ed. 1933. *Theodore on Eucharist and Liturgy.* Woodbrooke Studies, vol. 6. Cambridge: W. Heffer and Sons.

Ministry of Culture, Byzantine and Christian Museum. 1986. *Byzantine and Post-Byzantine Art.* Catalog of an exhibition held in Athens. Old University. July 26, 1985–January 6, 1986. Athens: T.A.P. Service.

Mora, Paolo, Laura Mora, and Paul Philippot. 1984. *Conservation of Wall Paintings.* London: Butterworths.

Morey, Charles Rufus. 1942. *Medieval Art.* New York: W. W. Norton.

Mouriki, Doula. 1984. "The Wall Paintings of the Church of the Panagia at Moutoullas, Cyprus." *Byzanz und der Westen: Studien zur Kunst des Europäischen Mittelalters.* Edited by Irmgard Hutter. Vienna: Verlag der Österreichischen Akademie der Wissenschaften. 171–203.

Müller, C. Detlef G. 1964. "Die koptische Kirche zwischen Chalkedon und dem Arabereinmarsch." *Zeitschrift für Kirchengeschichte* 75: 271–308.

———. 1991. "Benjamin I." *CE.* 375–377.

Müller, C. Detlef G., and Gawdat Gabra. 1991. "Pisentius, Saint." *CE.* 1978–1980.

Museum Bochum and the Stiftung für Armenische Studien, Bochum, eds. 1995. *Armenien: 5000 Jahre Kunst und Kultur.* Tübingen: Ernst Wasmuth Verlag.

Naḥla, Kamil Salih. 1954. *Silsilat tā'rīkh al-babawat batarikat al-kursi al-iskandari,* vol. 4. Wadi al-Natrun.

283

Neff, Amy. 1998. "The Pain of *Compassio:* Mary's Labor at the Foot of the Cross." *AB* 80, no. 2: 254–273.

Nelson, Robert. 1983. "An Icon at Mt. Sinai and Christian Painting in Muslim Egypt During the Thirteenth and Fourteenth Centuries." *AB* 65, no. 2: 200–218.

Nicolle, David C. 1988. *Arms and Armour of the Crusading Era, 1050–1350.* 2 vols. White Plains, N.Y.: Kraus International Publications.

———. 1994. *Saracen Faris, 1050–1250 A.D.* London: Osprey.

———. 1996. *Medieval Warfare Source Book.* vol. 2, *Christian Europe and Its Neighbours.* London: Arms and Armour Press.

Nimmo, M., and C. Olivetti. 1985–1986. "Sulle tecniche di trasposizione dell'immagine in epoca medievale." *Rivista dell'Istituto nazionale d'archeologia e storia dell'arte,* series 3, 8–9: 399–411.

Oden, Thomas C., and Christopher A. Hall, eds. 1998. *Mark: Ancient Christian Commentary on Scripture.* vol. 2, *New Testament.* Downers Grove, Ill.: InterVarsity.

Okhasah, Sarwat. 1992. *Fan al-Wasiti min khlaal Maqamat al-Hariri.* Cairo: Dar al-Sharuq.

O'Leary, De Lacy. 1923. *The Coptic Theotokia.* London: Luzak.

———. 1937. *The Saints of Egypt in the Coptic Calendar.* New York: Macmillan.

———. 1950. "The Coptic Theotokia." *Coptic Studies in Honor of Walter Ewing Crum.* Boston: Byzantine Institute. 417–420.

Orlandi, Tito, ed. and trans. 1988. *Paolo di Tamma: Opere.* Rome: C.I.M.

———. 1991a. "Macrobius, Saint." *CE.* 1494.

———. 1991b. "Theodorus, Saint." *CE.* 2237–2238.

Papageorghiou, Athanasias. 1992. *Icons of Cyprus.* Nicosia: Holy Archbishopric of Cyprus.

Partrick, Theodore Hall. 1996. *Traditional Egyptian Christianity: A History of the Coptic Orthodox Church.* Greensboro, N.C.: Fisher Park.

Patrich, Joseph. 1995. *Sabas, Leader of Palestinian Monasticism: A Comparative Study in Eastern Monasticism, Fourth to Seventh Centuries.* Washington, D.C.: Dumbarton Oaks.

Pearson, Birger A., and James E. Goehring. *The Roots of Egyptian Christianity.* Philadelphia: Fortress.

Pearson, Birger A., and Tim Vivian. 1993. *Two Coptic Homilies Attributed to Saint Peter of Alexandria: On Riches, On the Epiphany.* Rome: C. I. M.

Pedersen, Johannes. 1984. *The Arabic Book.* Trans. G. French. Princeton: Princeton University Press.

Peebles, Bernard M., trans. 1949. "Sulpicius Severus; Writings." *Writings: Nicetas of Remesiana.* Trans. Gerald A. Walsh et al. Fathers of the Church, vol. 7. New York: Fathers of the Church.

Peeters, Paul. 1922. "Traductions et traducteurs dans l'hagiographie orientale à l'époque byzantine," *Analecta Bollandiana* 40: 241–364.

Petry, Carl F., ed. 1998. *The Cambridge History of Egypt.* Vol. 1, *Islamic Egypt, 640–1517.* Cambridge: Cambridge University Press.

Philon, Helen. 1980. *Early Islamic Ceramics: Ninth to Late Twelfth Centuries.* Benaki Museum, Athens. *Catalogue of Islamic Art,* vol. 1. London: Islamic Art Publications.

Piankoff, Alexander. 1942. "Saint Mercure Abou Seifein et les Cynocéphales." *BSAC* 8: 17–24.

———. 1943. "Two Descriptions by Russian Travellers of the Monasteries of St. Antony and St. Paul in the Eastern Desert." *Bulletin de la Société Royale de Géographie d'Égypte* 21: 61–66.

———. 1946–1947. "Deux saints à tête de chien." *BSAC* 12: 57–61.

———. 1950–1957. "Peintures au Monastère de Saint Antoine." *BSAC* 14: 151–163.

———. 1954. "Thomas Whittemore: Une Peinture datée au Monastère de Saint-Antoine." *Les Cahiers coptes* 7–8: 19–24.

———. 1956a. "Deux peintures de saints militaires coptes au Monastère de Saint Antoine." *Les Cahiers coptes* 10: 17–25.

———. 1956b. "Les Peintures de la petite chapelle au Monastère de Saint Antoine." *Les Cahiers coptes* 12: 6–16.

———. 1958. "Peintures au Monastère de Saint Antoine." *BSAC* 14: 151–163.

Polotsky, Hans J. 1987. *Grundlagen des koptischen Satzbaus.* American Studies in Papyrology, vols. 27–28. Atlanta: Scholars Press.

Potvin, Charles, and J.-C. Houzeau, trans. 1878. *Œuvres de Ghillebert de Lannoy.* Louvain: Lefever.

Pringle, Denys. 1993. *The Churches of the Crusader Kingdom of Jerusalem: A Corpus.* Cambridge: Cambridge University Press.

Prisse d'Avennes, Émile. 1877. *L'Art arabe d'après les monuments du Kaire depuis le VIIe siècle jusqu'à la fin du XVIIIe.* Paris: A. Morel et CIE.

Quibell, Jean. 1908. *Excavations at Saqqara*. Vol. 2, 1906–1907. Cairo: IFAO.

———. 1909. *Excavations at Saqqara*. Vol. 3, 1907–1908. Cairo: IFAO.

———. 1912. *Excavations at Saqqara*. Vol. 4, 1908–1909, 1909–1910. Cairo: IFAO.

R. and C. Scientifica s.r.l. 1995. *Multi-method Analyses of Samples from Wall Paintings of the Monastery of St. Antony, Egypt*. Unpublished report.

Rabbat, Nasser O. 1995. *The Citadel of Cairo*. Leiden: E. J. Brill.

Ramsey, Boniface, trans. 1997. *John Cassian: The Conferences*. New York: Paulist.

Rassart-Debergh, Marguerite. 1981. "La Peinture copte avant le XIIè siècle: Une Approche." *Acta*. 221–285.

———. 1986. "Le Thème de la croix sur les peintures murales des Kellia, entre l'Égypte et la Nubie chretiennes." *Nubische Studien: Tagungsakten der 5. Internationalen Konferenz der International Society for Nubian Studies*. Heidelberg, September 22–25, 1982. Edited by Martin Krause. Mainz am Rhein: Philip von Zabern: 363–366.

———. 1987. "Les Trois Hébreux dans la fournaise: En Égypte et en Nubie chrétienne." *Rivista degli Studi Orientali* 58: 141–151.

———. 1988. "Quelques croix kelliotes." *Nubia et Oriens Christian: Festrschrift fur C. Detlef G. Müller zum 60 Geburtstag*. Bibliotheca Nubica 1. Cologne: 373–385.

———. 1989. "Les peintures." *Les Kellia: Ermitages coptes en Bassse-Égypte*. Musée d'Art et d'Histoire, Geneva, October 12, 1989–January 7, 1990. Geneva: Éditions du Tricorne. 57–77.

———. 1990. "De l'icône païenne à l'icône chrétienne." *Le Monde copte* 18: 39–70.

———. 1994. "Copti. Pittura." *Enciclopedia dell'Arte Medievale*, vol. 5. Rome: Instituto della Enciclopedia Italiana. 300–306.

Reeves, John C. 1996. *Heralds of that Good Realm: Syro-Mesopotamian Gnosis and Jewish Traditions*. Nag Hammadi and Manichaean Studies, vol. 41. Leiden: E. J. Brill.

Regnault, Lucien. 1990. *La Vie quotidienne des pères du désert en Égypte au IVè siècle*. Paris: Hachette.

———. 1991a. "Arsenius of Scetis and Turah, Saint." *CE*. 240–241.

———. 1991b. "Isaac, Saint." *CE*. 1304.

———. 1991c. "John Colobos, Saint." *CE*. 1359–1361.

———. 1991d. "Moses the Black, Saint." *CE*. 1681.

———. 1991e. "Sisoes." *CE* .2141.

Reinink, G. J. 1992. "Ps.-Methodius: A Concept of History in Response to the Rise of Islam." *The Byzantine and Early Islamic Near East*. Vol. 1, *Problems in the Literary Source Material*. Edited by Averil Cameron and Lawrence I. Conrad. Studies in Late Antiquity and Early Islam, vol. 1. Princeton: Darwin. 149–187.

Restle, Marcell. 1968. *Byzantine Wall Painting in Asia Minor*. Trans. Irene R. Gibbons. Rpt. Greenwich, Conn.: New York Graphic Society.

Revault, Jacques, and Bernard Maury. 1977. *Palais et maisons du Caire du XIVe au XVIIIe siècle*. Vol. 2. Cairo: IFAO.

Roberts, Colin H. 1979. *Manuscript, Society, and Belief in Early Christian Egypt: The Schweich Lectures 1977*. London: Oxford University Press.

Robinson, S. E. 1987. "The Apocryphal Story of Melchizedek." *Journal for the Study of Judaism* 18: 26–39.

Rodley, Lynn. 1994. *Byzantine Art and Architecture*. Cambridge: Cambridge University Press.

Roncaglia, M. 1991. "Dioscorus I." *CE*. 912–915.

Rosa, Leone A. 1957. *La tecnica della pittura dai tempi preistorici ad oggi*. Milan: Società Editrice Libraria.

Rosenthal, Franz, trans. 1967. *Ibn Khaldun, The Muqaddimah: An Introduction to History*. Vol. 3. Princeton: Princeton University Press.

Rubenson, Samuel. 1995. *The Letters of Antony: Monasticism and the Making of a Saint*. Studies in Antiquity and Christianity. Minneapolis: Fortress.

Rufailah, Y. N. 1898. *Tarih al-Umma al-Qibtiah*. Cairo.

Ruffach, Valentinum Boltz von. 1913. *Illuminierbuch, wie man allerlei Farben bereiten, mischen, und auftragen soll. Allen jungen angehenden Malern und Illuministen nutzlich und furdelich*. 1549. Edited by C. J. Benzinger. Munich: Callway.

Russell, Norman, trans. 1981. *The Lives of the Desert Fathers*. Kalamazoo, Mich.: Cistercian.

Rutschowskaya, Marie-Hélène. 1992. *La Peinture copte*. Paris: Réunion des Musées Nationaux.

Sadan, J. 1976. *Le Mobilier au proche Orient medieval*. Leiden: E. J. Brill.

Said, Issam el-, and Ayse Parman. 1976. *Geometric Concepts in Islamic Art*. London: World of Islam Festival Trust Publishing.

Samir, Samir Khalil. 1978. "Le Codex Kacmarcik et sa version arabe de la liturgie alexandrine." *OCP* 44: 74–106.

———. 1981. "Athanase evêque d'Aboutig († 1819), restaurateur de manuscrits." *OCP* 47: 213–222.

———. 1982. "Un Nouvel Acte de donation d'Athanase d'Abutig daté de 1791–1792." *OCP* 48: 177–185.

———. 1991a. "Gabriel VI." *CE.* 1133–1135.

———. 1991b. "Victor Stratelates, Saint," *CE.* 2303–2308.

———. 1995. "Vie et œuvre de Marc ibn al-Qunbar." *Christianisme d'Égypte: Homages à René-Georges Coquin.* Cahier de la bibliothèque copte 9. Louvain: Peeters. 123–158.

Sanders, Paula. 1998. "The Fatimid State, 969–1171." In Petry 1998. 151–174.

Sauneron, Serge, ed. 1971. *Voyage en Égypte de Jean Coppin, 1638–1639, 1643–1646.* Collection des voyageurs occident aux en Égypte. Vol. 4. Cairo: IFAO.

Schick, Robert. 1995. *The Christian Communities of Palestine from Byzantine to Islamic Rule: A Historical and Archaeological Study.* Studies in Late Antiquity and Early Islam, vol. 2. Princeton: The Darwin Press.

Schiller, Gertrud. 1972. *Iconography of Christian Art.* Trans. Janet Seligman. 2 vols. Greenwich, Conn.: New York Graphic Society.

Schimmel, Annemarie. 1970. *Islamic Calligraphy.* Leiden: E. J. Brill.

Schweinfurth, Georg August. 1922. *Auf unbetretenen Wegen in Aegypten.* Hamburg: Hoffmann und Campe Verlag.

Ševčenko, Nancy Patterson. 1991. "Christ: Types of Christ." *ODB* 437–439.

Severin, Hans-Georg. 1991. "Bawit: Archaeology, Architecture, and Sculpture." *CE.* 363–367.

Shepherd, Dorothy. 1969. "An Icon of the Virgin: A Sixth-Century Tapestry Panel from Egypt." *Bulletin of the Cleveland Museum of Art* 56, no. 3: 101–105.

Sicard, Claude. 1982. *Oeuvres: Lettres et relations inédites,* vol. 1. Edited by M. Martin. Bibliothèque d'Étude 83. Cairo: IFAO.

Sidarus, Adel Y. 1978. "Coptic Lexicography in the Middle Ages: The Coptic Arabic Scalae." *The Future of Coptic Studies.* Edited by R. McL. Wilson. Leiden: E. J. Brill. 125–142.

Simaika, Marcus. 1932. *Dalil al-muthaf al-qibti wa aham al-kanaʿis wa al-adyira al-ataryia: Guide to the Coptic Museum,* vol. 2. Cairo: Coptic Museum.

Sozomenus. 1979. "The Ecumenical History of Sozomen." Trans. Chester D. Hartranft. *A Select Library of Nicene and Post-Nicene Fathers.* 2d ser., vol. 2. Grand Rapids, Mich.: Eerdmans. 179–427.

Spanel, D. B. 1991a. "Phoibammon of Preht, Martyr." *CE.* 1963–1965.

———. 1991b. "Theophilus." *CE.* 2247–2253.

Spanel, D. B., and Tim Vivian. 1991. "Peter I." *CE.* 1943–1947.

Stewart, R. 1991. "Itfih." *CE.* 1313.

Stillman, Y. K. 1986. "Libas. i. In the Central and Eastern Arab Lands." *EI2,* vol. 5, 732–742.

Strothmann, Rudolph. 1932. *Die koptische Kirche in der Neuzeit.* Tübingen: J. C. B. Mohr, Paul Siebeck.

Strzygowski, Josef. 1902–1903. "Der koptische Reiterheilige und der hl. Georg," *Zeitschrift für ägyptische Sprache und Altertumskunde,* vol. 40: 49–60.

Stylianou, Andreas, and Judith A. Stylianou. 1997. *The Painted Churches of Cyprus: Treasures of Byzantine Art.* 2d ed. Nicosia: A. G. Leventis Foundation.

Taft, Robert F. 1987. "Liturgy and Eucharist: East." *Christian Spirituality.* Ed. J. Raitt et al. New York: Crossroad. 415–426.

Tedeschi, Salvatore. 1991. "Ethiopian Prelates." *CE.* 999–1044.

Teteriatnikov, Natalia. 1992. "The Frescoes of the Chapel of St. Basil in Cappadocia: Their Date and Context Reconsidered." *Cahiers archéologiques* 40: 99–114.

Thackston, Wheeler M., Jr., trans. 1986. *Naser-e Khosraw's Book of Travels (Safarnama).* New York: Bibliotheca Persica.

Theophilus. 1843. *Diversarum Artium Schedula.* Trans. Charles de L'Escalopier. Paris: J.-A. Toulouse.

Thierry, Nicole. 1981. "Le Culte de la croix dans l'empire byzantin du VIIè siècle au Xè dans ses rapports avec la guerre contre l'infidèle. Nouveaux témoignages archéologiques." *Rivista di studi bizantini e slavi* 1: 205–228.

Thomas, Thelma K. 2000. *Late Antique Funerary Sculpture: Images for This World and the Next.* Princeton: Princeton University Press.

Timm, Stefan. 1984–1992. *Das christlich-koptische Ägypten in arabischer Zeit.* 6 vols. Beihefte zum Tübinger Atlas des vorderen Orients, Reihe B (Geisteswissenschaften), nos. 41.1–6. Wiesbaden: Ludwig Reichert Verlag.

Trebbin, Heinrich. 1994. *Sankt Antonius: Geschichte, Kult und Kunst.* Frankfurt: Haag and Herchen.

Tronzo, William. 1997. *The Cultures of His Kingdom: Roger II and the Cappella Palatina in Palermo.* Princeton: Princeton University Press.

Turaiev, B. 1902. *Vita Samuelis Valdebani.* Monumenta Aethiopiae Hagiologica 2. St. Petersburg: St. Petersburg University.

Uspensky, Porphyrius. 1856. *Pute estvije po Egiptu I v monastyri Svjatgo Antonija Velikago I Prepodobnago Pavla Fivejskago v 1850 godu.* St. Petersburg.

Van Doorn-Harder, Pieternella. 1995. *Contemporary Coptic Nuns.* Columbia, S.C.: University of South Carolina Press.

Van Esbroeck, Michel. 1991a. "Maximus and Dometius, Saints." *CE.* 1576–1578.

———. 1991b. "Mercurius of Caesarea, Saint." *CE.* 1592–1594.

———. 1991c. "Three Hebrews in the Furnace." *CE.* 2257–2259.

Van Loon, Gertrud J. M. 1992. "The Iconography of Jephthah: A Wallpainting in the Sanctuary of the Old Church of St. Antony's Monastery Near the Red Sea." *Acts 4,* vol. 1. 115–123.

———. 1993. "The Symbolic Meaning of the Haykal." *Acts 5,* vol. 2, pt. 2. 497–508.

———. 1999a. "Church of Abu Sayfayn: Wall Paintings in the Chapel of Mar Girgis." *Acts 6,* 249–261.

———. 1999b. *The Gate of Heaven: Wall Paintings with Old Testament Scenes in the Altar Room and the Hurus of Coptic Churches.* Istanbul: Nederlands Historisch-Archaeologisch Instituut te Istanbul.

Van Moorsel, Paul P. 1978. "The Coptic Apse-Composition and Its Living Creatures." *Études Nubiennes.* Colloquium in Chantilly, July 2–6, 1975. Bibliothèque d'Étude, vol. 77. Cairo: IFAO. 325–333.

———. 1979. "The Worship of the Holy Cross in Saqqara: Archaeological Evidence." *Theologia Crucis—Signum Crucis. Festschrift für Erich Dinkler zum 70. Geburtstag.* Edited by C. Andresen and G. Klein. Tübingen. 409–415. Reprinted in van Moorsel 2000, 81–90.

———. 1982. "The Vision of Philotheus (On Apse Decorations)." *Nubische Studien.* Edited by Martin Krause. Mainz am Rhein: Philipp von Zabern. 337–340.

———. 1983. "Les Travaux de la mission de peintures coptes à Saint-Antoine." *Bulletin de la Société française d'Égyptologie* 97: 15–29.

———. 1990. "Forerunners of the Lord." *Coptic Art and Culture.* Edited by H. Hondelink. Cairo: Shouhdy. 19–42.

———. 1991a. "Christ, Triumph of." *CE.* 525–526.

———. 1991b. "Dayr Anba Antuniyus: Wall Paintings." *CE.* 726–728.

———. 1992. "Treasures from Baramous, with Some Remarks on a Melchizedek Scene." *Acts 4,* vol. 1. 171–177.

———. 1995a. "La Grande Annonciation de Deir es-Sourian." *BIFAO* 95: 517–531.

———. 1995b. *Les Peintures du Monastère de Saint-Antoine près de la Mer Rouge.* 2 vols. La peinture murale chez les Coptes, vol. 3. *MIFAO* vol. 112. Cairo: IFAO. All text references are vol. 1; all plates are vol. 2.

———. 1998. "A Different Melchizedek? Some Iconographical Remarks." *Themelia.* 329–342.

———. 2000. *Called to Egypt: Collected Studies on Painting in Christian Egypt.* Edited by Claudine Chavannes-Mazel et al. Leiden: Nederlands Instituut voor het Nabije Oosten.

Van Zeelst, Ladislaus. 1991. "Franciscans in Egypt." *CE.* 1121–1124.

Veilleux, Armand. 1980. *Pachomian Koinonia.* Cistercian Studies Series no. 45. 3 vols. Kalamazoo, Mich.: Cistercian.

———. 1986. "Monasticism and Gnosis in Egypt." Edited by Pearson and Goehring 1986. 271–306.

———. 1991. "Pachomius, Saint." *CE.* 1859–1864.

Viaud, Gérard. 1966. Note sur les processions de la Croix dans l'Église Copte." *Orient Syrien* 11, fasc. 2: 231–235.

———. 1967–1968. "La Procession des deux fêtes de la croix et du Dimanche des Rameaux dans l'Église Copte." *BSAC* 19: 211–226.

———. 1979. *Les Pélérinages coptes en Égypte (d'après les notes du Qommos Jacob Muyser).* Cairo: IFAO.

Vikan, Gary. 1982. *Byzantine Pilgrimage Art.* Washington, D.C.: Dumbarton Oaks.

———. 1984. "Art, Medicine, and Magic in Early Byzantium." *DOP* 38: 65–86.

———. 1986. "Meaning in Coptic Funerary Sculpture." *Göttinger Orientforschungen* 8. Studien zur frühchristlichen Kunst 2. Wiesbaden: Otto Harrassowitz. 15–24.

———. 1998. "Byzantine Pilgrims' Art." *Heaven on Earth: Art and the Church in Byzantium.* Edited by Linda Safran. University Park: Pennsylvania State University Press. 229–266.

Vivian, Tim. 1996. *Journeying into God: Seven Early Monastic Lives.* Minneapolis: Fortress.

———. 1997a. "The Life of Saint John the Little: An

Encomium by Zacharias of Sakha." *Coptic Church Review* 18: 1–2.

———. 1997b. "Saint Paul of Tamma: Four Works Concerning Monastic Spirituality." *Coptic Church Review* 18, no. 4: 105–116.

———. 1999. "A Journey to the Interior: The Monasteries of Saint Antony and Saint Paul by the Red Sea." *American Benedictine Review* 50, no. 3: 277–310.

———. Forthcoming (ed. and trans.). "Virtues of St. Macarius." *Disciples of the Soul's Beloved.* Vol. 2, *St. Macarius the Spirit Bearer.* Louvain: Peeters.

Vivian, Tim, and Birger A. Pearson. 1998. "Saint Paul of Tamma: On the Monastic Cell (*De Cella*)." Hallel 23, no. 2: 86–107.

Vivian, Tim, Kim Vivian, and Jeffrey Burton Russell, trans. 1999. *The Life of the Jura Fathers.* Kalamazoo, Mich.: Cistercian.

Vogüé, Adalbert de. 1991. *Le Monachisme latin.* Part 1, *Histoire littéraire du mouvement monastique dans l'antiquité.* Paris: Éditions du Cerf.

Volbach, Wolfgang Fritz. 1976. *Elfenbeinarbeiten der spätantike und des frühen Mittelalters.* Katalog vor- und Frügeschichtlicher Altertumer, vol. 7. Mainz am Rhein: Philipp von Zabern.

Volkoff, Oleg V. 1978. "Une Tentative d'union entre l'Église Copte et l'Église Orthodoxe Russe." *Le Monde copte* 5: 12–15.

Wakin, E. 1963. *A Lonely Minority.* New York: W. Morrow.

Walter, Christopher. 1968. "Two Notes on the Deesis," *Revue des études byzantines* 26: 322–336.

Walters, C. C. 1974. *Monastic Archaeology in Egypt.* Warminster: Aris and Phillips.

———. 1989. "Christian Paintings from Tebtunis." *Journal of Egyptian Archaeology* 75: 191–208.

Wansleben (Vansleb), Johann M. 1678. *Nouvelle relation en forme de journal d'un voyage fait en Égypte en 1672 et 1673.* 1677. English trans. *The Present State of Egypt.* London: Printed by R. E. for John Starkey.

Ward, Benedicta, trans. 1975. *The Desert Christian: Sayings of the Desert Fathers, the Alphabetical Collection.* New York: Macmillan.

———. 1984. *The Sayings of the Desert Fathers.* Rev. ed. Kalamazoo: Cistercian.

Ward, Rachel. 1993. *Islamic Metalwork.* London: British Museum Press.

Weitzmann, Kurt. 1964. "The Jephthah Panel in the Bema of the Church of St. Catherine's Monastery on Mount Sinai." *DOP* 18: 341–352.

———. 1966. "Icon Painting in the Crusader Kingdom." *DOP* 20: 49–83.

———. 1976. *The Monastery of St. Catherine on Mount Sinai.* Vol. 1, *The Icons.* Princeton: Princeton University Press.

———. 1977. *Late Antique and Early Christian Book Illumination.* New York: George Braziller.

———. 1979 (ed.). *The Age of Spirituality: Late Antique and Early Christian Art, Third to Seventh Century.* New York: Metropolitan Museum of Art and Princeton University Press.

Werner, Martin. 1984–1986. "On the Origin of Zoanthropomorphic Evangelist Symbols: The Early Christian Background." *Studies in Iconography* 10: 1–35.

———. 1989–1990. "On the Origin of Zoanthropomorphic Evangelist Symbols: The Early Medieval and Later Coptic, Nubian, Ethiopian, and Latin Evidence." *Studies in Iconography* 13: 1–47.

Westermarck, Edward. 1968. *Ritual and Belief in Morocco.* 2 vols. New York: University Press.

Wharton, Annabel Jane. 1991. "Cappadocia: Monuments of Cappadocia." *ODB.* 379.

White, Carolinne. 1998. *Early Christian Lives.* London: Penguin.

Wietheger, C. 1992. *Das Jeremias-Kloster zu Saqqara unter besonderer Berücksichtigung der Inschriften.* Arbeiten zum spätantiken und koptischen Ägypten 1. Altenberge: Oros Verlag.

Wilfong, Terry G. 1998. "The Non-Muslim Communities: Christian Communities." In Petry 1998. 175–197.

Wilkinson, Gardner. 1843. *Modern Egypt and Thebes: A Description of Egypt.* 2 vols. London: Murray. Rpt. Wiesbaden: Oros Verlag, 1981.

Wilkinson, John. 1977. *Jerusalem Pilgrims Before the Crusades.* Warminster: Aris and Phillips.

Wilkinson, John, with Joyce Hill and W. F. Ryan. 1988. *Jerusalem Pilgrimage, 1099–1185.* London: Hakluyt Society.

Williams, John, and Daniel Walker. 1993. "Catalog 110." *The Art of Medieval Spain, A.D. 500–1200.* New York: Metropolitan Museum of Art. 239–244.

Winfield, D. C. 1968. "Middle and Later Byzantine Wall Painting Methods: A Comparative Study." *DOP* 22: 61–139.

Winstedt, Eric Otto. 1979. *Coptic Texts on St. Theodore the General, St. Theodore the Eastern, Chamoul, and Justus.* London: Williams and Norgate, 1910. Rpt. Amsterdam: APA.

Wissa Wasef, Cerès. 1971. *Pratiques Rituelles et Alimentaires des Coptes.* Cairo: IFAO.

Woolley, Reginald. 1913. *Bread of the Eucharist.* London: A. R. Mowbray.

Wortley, John. 1992. "The Spirit of Rivalry in Early Christian Monachism." *Greek, Roman, and Byzantine Studies* 33: 383–404.

Wright, F. A., trans. 1980. *Select Letters of St. Jerome.* Cambridge: Harvard University Press.

Wright, W. 1870–1872. *Catalogue of the Syriac Manuscripts in the British Museum Acquired Since 1838.* London: British Museum Press.

Wüstenfeld, Ferdinand, ed. and trans. 1979. *Macrizi's Geschichte der Copten.* Göttingen, 1845. Rpt. Hildesheim: Olms.

Zaki, ʿAzzat. 1996. *Khamsa wa ʿIshrūn ʿĀmmān wa La Yazāl AlʿAtaʾ Mustamirn: Qadāsat Al-Bābā Shenouda Al-Thālith* (Twenty-five years and the giving continues: Pope Shenouda the Third). Cairo: Sons of Anba Ruweis.

Zanetti, Ugo. 1991. "Les Icônes chez les théologiens de l'église Copte." *Le Monde copte* 19: 77–91.

———. 1995. "Abul-Makarim et Abu Salih," *BSAC* 34: 85–138.

Zibawi, Mahmoud. 1995. *Orienti cristiani: Senso e storia di un'arte tra Bisanzio e l'Islam.* Milan: Jaca.

CONTRIBUTORS

Elizabeth S. Bolman is assistant professor of medieval art at the Tyler School of Art, Temple University, Philadelphia. She has published on Coptic monastic paintings and on color in Spanish manuscript illuminations.

Luigi De Cesaris teaches at the Istituto Centrale del Restauro in Rome. With Adriano Luzi he has undertaken conservation and restoration of such works of art as Bernini's *Ecstasy of St. Teresa* in Rome and the wall paintings in the tomb of Nefertari in the Valley of the Queens.

Mark Easton is a retired Foreign Service officer with an M.A. in Egyptology from Johns Hopkins University. He has completed his coursework toward a doctoral degree in Egyptology at the University of Pennsylvania. He served as Cairo director of the American Research Center in Egypt, 1992–2000. It was during his tenure that ARCE was awarded more than $50 million in USAID grants and endowments to pursue a program of conservation and restoration of Egyptian antiquities.

Gawdat Gabra is director of the Coptic Museum in Cairo. He is a Coptologist who has published many books and numerous articles on the Coptic heritage.

Patrick Godeau was born in France and has been living in Egypt since 1981. He has studied philosophy and Arabic and has worked as a journalist. He began his career as a professional photographer in 1986 and has been documenting monuments and conservation projects for ARCE since 1994.

Sidney H. Griffith is professor of Syriac patristics and Christian Arabic, and director of the graduate program in early Christian studies, at the Catholic University of America. He has published widely on Christians living under Islamic rule, and has translated Christian texts written in Arabic.

Michael Jones is an archaeologist and project manager for the Egyptian Antiquities Project of the American Research Center in Egypt. He has published numerous articles on his archaeological work.

Adriano Luzi is a master conservator who trained at the Istituto Centrale del Restauro in Rome. Luzi worked with Laura and Paulo Mora on the wall paintings in the tomb of Nefertari in the Valley of the Queens. He and Luigi De Cesaris are currently directing a team of conservators at several monuments in Rome and in Egypt.

William Lyster is an independent scholar who specializes in Islamic art and architecture and resides in Cairo. He has written books on the Citadel of Cairo and the Monastery of St. Paul, as well as articles on various topics in Islamic and Coptic art and history.

Father Maximous El-Anthony is a monk at the Monastery of St. Antony who has been actively involved in many aspects of conservation work, both in the Church of St. Antony and elsewhere in Egypt.

Elizabeth E. Oram is an anthropologist who is completing her doctoral work at Princeton University. The subject of her dissertation is the construction of modern Coptic identity through such practices as pilgrimage.

Birger A. Pearson is professor emeritus of religious studies at the University of California, Santa Barbara. He has written extensively on Coptic language and literature and was one of a group of scholars who translated the Nag Hammadi codices.

Robert K. Vincent, Jr., has been the project director for conservation work undertaken by ARCE since 1994. He first began his involvement in major conservation and archaeological projects in the Middle and Near East in 1968. He is a former president of the Institute of Nautical Archaeology at Texas A&M University and is a graduate of Yale University and the University of Pennsylvania Law School.

Tim Vivian is an independent scholar and an Episcopal priest. He has published numerous translations from Greek and Coptic of saints' lives, including one of the Life of St. Antony (with Apostolos N. Athanassakis), as well as important essays on the historical contexts of these saints.

Indexes to the Coptic Inscriptions

Persons Cited in the Inscriptions

Note: References to Jesus Christ and the Mother of God are omitted, except where Mary's name is given (N36.2).

Abraham *(biblical patriarch)*	K5.1, 2; S43.3
Abū...	N35.2
Abū l-Fakhry *(donor)*	S1.14
Abū l-Faraj *(donor)*	N31.2
Abū l-Maʿani *(donor)*	N31.2
Abū l-Uz *(donor)*	N31.2
Abū Ghalib *(donor)*	N31.2; K4.1
Abū Said *(donor)*	N35.2
Antony *(monastic founder)*	N1.1; N31.2
Arsenius *(monk)*	N10.1, 2
Athanasius *(patriarch)*	S2.1
Barsuma *(monk)*	N11.1, 2
Bartholomew *(apostle)*	C5.1

Basil *(saint)*	K3.8
Benjamin (?) *(patriarch)*	S7.1, 2
Claudius *(martyr)*	N19.1
Daniel *(prophet)*	S50.1, 2
David *(prophet)*	S49.1, 2
Diocletian *(emperor)*	N19.5
Dioscorus *(patriarch)*	S4.1
Domitius *(martyr)*	N32.4, 6
Elijah *(prophet)*	S46.1, 2
Euchius *(soldier)*	K8.2
Eutychius *(duke)*	N24.2, 3
Fadlel *(donor)*	S35.2
Feiro *(Mercurius' grandfather?)*	K3.5
Fmon (?) *(donor)*	N31.2
Gabriel *(archangel)*	K16.1; S1.4, 12; A9.1

PLACES CITED IN THE INSCRIPTIONS

INDEX

Page numbers in boldface refer to illustrations, while page numbers followed by "n." or "nn." refer to information in notes.

PHOTO CREDITS

Unless otherwise noted, all photographs are by Patrick Godeau.

All icons and objects shown without a note of location belong to the collection of the Monastery of St. Antony.

All interior and exterior shots described without the name of the building are of the Church of St. Antony, Monastery of St. Antony.

ADP/SA = Antiquities Development Project, St. Antony (photography by Godeau).

EAP/ARCE = Egyptian Antiquities Project, American Research Center in Egypt (photography by Godeau).

The plans were drawn by Peter Sheehan from a survey conducted by Mallinson Architects. The copyright for all plans is held by ARCE.

Archivi Alinari/Art Resource (figs. 6.14, 8.16); Elizabeth S. Bolman (figs. 1, 6, 20, 29, 1.3, 1.4, 1.10, 2.8, 3.2, 3.6, 3.8, 4.34, 4.35, 4.42, 5.1, 5.8, 5.14, 5.15, 5.18, 5.19, 5.20, 6.9, 6.10, 6.12, 6.13, 6.16, 6.19, 7.28, 7.34, 8.5, 8.8, 8.11, 8.14, 8.27, 8.29, 8.34, 8.36, 8.40, 9.8, 9.9, 11.2, 11.3, 11.5, 13.5); Clédat 1904 (figs. 6.2 [pl. 53]; 6.3 [pl. 55], 6.5 [pl. 96]); Johann Georg 1930 (figs. 10.8 [pl. 102], 12.4 [pl. 112]); Giraudon/Art Resource (fig. 3.10); Cynthia Hall (fig. 5.21 [Horste 1992, pl. 147]); Michael Jones (fig. 11.4); Adriano Luzi and Luigi De Cesaris (figs. 9.2, 9.3, 9.4, 9.5, 9.6, 9.7, 9.10, 9.11); William Lyster (figs. 7.26, 8.33, 8.35); Maspero 1931 (fig. 6.4 [pl. 21]); Elizabeth E. Oram (figs. 13.3, 13.6); Prisse d'Avennes 1877 (fig. 8.33 [pl. 58]); Robert Vincent (figs. 17, 23, 1.8); Evelyn White 1933, pt. 3 (fig. 6.11 [pl. 28]); Scala/Art Resource (figs. 6.23, 7.16); Schweinfurth 1922 (figs. 2.10 [facing p. 178], 10.4 [plate facing 163], 10.7 [plate facing p. 179]); Peter Sheehan (figs. 21, 2.3, 13.1); Woolley 1913 (fig. 8.15 [facing p. 44].